MARKET-DRIVEN MANAGEMENT

MARKET-LED STRATEGIC MANAGEMENT

MARKET-DRIVEN MANAGEMENT

Strategic and Operational Marketing

Third Edition

Jean-Jacques Lambin

Professor Emeritus, Université catholique de Louvain, Louvain-la-Neuve, Belgium
Professore Emerito, Università degli studi di Milano-Bicocca, Italy

with

Isabelle Schuiling

Professor, Louvain School of Management
Université catholique de Louvain, Louvain-la-Neuve, Belgium

© Jean-Jacques Lambin 2000, Jean-Jacques Lambin, Isabelle Schuiling and Ruben Chumpitaz 2007, Jean-Jacques Lambin and Isabelle Schuiling 2012

First edition published 2000
Second edition published 2007
Third edition published 2012 by
PALGRAVE MACMILLAN

Palgrave Macmillan in the UK is an imprint of Macmillan Publishers Limited, registered in England, company number 785998, of Houndmills, Basingstoke, Hampshire RG21 6XS.

Palgrave Macmillan in the US is a division of St Martin's Press LLC, 175 Fifth Avenue, New York, NY 10010.

Palgrave Macmillan is the global academic imprint of the above companies and has companies and representatives throughout the world.

Palgrave® and Macmillan® are registered trademarks in the United States, the United Kingdom, Europe and other countries.

ISBN: 978–0–230–27602–4

This book is printed on paper suitable for recycling and made from fully managed and sustained forest sources. Logging, pulping and manufacturing processes are expected to conform to the environmental regulations of the country of origin.

A catalogue record for this book is available from the British Library.

Library of Congress Cataloging-in-Publication Data
Lambin, Jean-Jacques, 1933–
    Market-driven management: strategic and operational marketing/ Jean-Jacques Lambin, Isabelle Schuiling.
        p. cm.
      Includes index.
     ISBN: 978–0–230–27602–4
       1. Marketing – Europe. 2. Marketing – Europe – Management. I. Schuiling, Isabelle, 1962– II. Title.
HF5415.12.E8L36 2012
658.8′02—dc23   2012008999

10 9 8 7 6 5 4 3 2 1
21 20 19 18 17 16 15 14 13 12
Printed in China

Contents

List of Figures

List of Tables

List of Boxes

List of Exhibits

Preface

Based on positive feedbacks from students, professors and marketing practitioners, and in view of the success of other editions of the book in French, Italian, Spanish, Portuguese, Polish, and Russian, we are encouraged to update the 2007 text and to propose a new edition of *Market-Driven Management.*

MAIN FEATURES OF THIS NEW EDITION

The distinctive feature of this new edition book remains its focus on the concept of *market orientation* as a substitute to the traditional *marketing concept* of the 4Ps popularized by US business schools. This is more than just a semantic issue. The traditional marketing orientation concept tends to be more short-term oriented and mainly concerned with the functional role of marketing in co-ordinating and managing the four Ps to promote the firm's offerings. The market orientation concept by contrast (a) de-emphasizes the functional roles of marketing departments, (b) enlarges the market definition to the key market actors (distributors, competitors, influencers, and other market stakeholders, (c) states that developing market relations and enhancing customer value is the responsibility of everyone in the organization; (d) claims that creating customer value is the only way for a firm to achieve its objective of profit and growth, thereby creating shareholder value. These changes of emphasis are motivated by the increased complexity of the world macro-economic environment which becomes global, deregulated, and deeply modified by the information technology revolution and by the constraints generated by the adoption of the sustainable development objective.

A second objective of this book is to introduce upfront the strategic dimension of the market orientation concept, while the most popular introductory marketing textbooks tend to treat marketing management as a stand-alone business function and to overlook the hidden part of the marketing iceberg, i.e. the strategic choices on which market-driven management decisions must be based. Similarly, most strategic management texts examine strategic decisions that are made at the corporate level but devote only scant attention to how these decisions are implemented at the operational level for individual brands or products. Our objective in this new edition is to propose a broader treatment of the marketing process integrating its strategic and operational dimensions. Marketing is both a business philosophy and an action-oriented process. Too often, the tendency among practitioners and the general public is to reduce marketing to its active dimension and to overlook the underlying business philosophy without which marketing is simply a set of short-term selling tools.

A third objective of this new edition is to integrate the development of the Internet technology. Markets are shifting towards two specialized yet collaborative global markets: Global Electronic Markets (GEM) and Global Traditional Markets (GTM). The GEM globally produces and distributes digital products and services, while GTM collaborates with GEM to consume or continue the physical part of production and distribution. The firms in traditional markets extend their demand and supply to GEM, while firms of electronic markets create new demand and supply of both GTM and GEM. New market actors coming from GEM and are playing an increasingly important role. Special efforts are made in this new edition to integrate the impact of the information technology revolution on the decision-making process for each marketing instruments, particularly for marketing communication.

STRUCTURE OF THE BOOK

The overall structure of the book is summarized in Figure I. It comprises five parts and twenty-one chapters in all.

Part 1 is devoted to the analysis of *the changing role of marketing* in the world market. In Chapters 1 and 2, we introduce and we contrast the traditional marketing concept and the market orientation concept. A distinction is made between operational marketing (the action dimension) and strategic marketing (the analytic and philosophy dimension) and the roles of new market actors are analysed. In the new world macro-economic environment (Chapter 3), firms are confronted with the issue of globalization – the customization-standardization dilemma – and with the challenge of poverty alleviation in the world economy. Chapter 4 is devoted to a review of the emerging values and issues in the world economy, and in particular of the objective of sustainable development and of the internet technology revolution.

The objective of *Part 2* is to analyse *the customer's purchase and response behaviour*, be it an individual (B2C) or an organization (B2B). Strategic marketing is, to begin with, the analysis of customers' needs (Chapter 5) and purchase behaviour (Chapter 6). A consumer is not after a product as such, but after the solution-to-a-problem that the product may provide. The role of marketing research (Chapter 7) is essential to gain certified knowledge to understand and predict customers behaviour and response.

Part 3 analyses in five steps the specific tasks to be performed by *strategic marketing*. The role of strategic marketing is to follow the evolution of the firm's *reference market* and to identify various potential product-markets or segments on the basis of an analysis of the needs which must be met (Chapter 8). Once the potential product-markets are identified, the *attractiveness* of the economic opportunities must be evaluated. The appeal of a product-market is quantitatively measured by the notion of market potential and dynamically measured by its economic life or its life cycle (Chapter 9). For any given firm, the appeal of a product-market depends on its *competitiveness*, in other words, on its capacity to meet buyers' needs better than its rivals can. This competitiveness will exist as long as the firm holds a competitive advantage, either because it can differentiate itself from its rivals due to sustainable distinctive qualities, or because of higher productivity putting it at a cost advantage (Chapter 10). On the basis of this strategic audit, the market-driven firm can formulate an appropriate *marketing strategy* for each business unit included in its product portfolio (Chapter 11) The strategic *marketing plan* describes objectives, positioning, tactics and budgets for each business unit of the company's portfolio in a given period and geographical zone (Chapter 12).

In *Part 4*, we examine the *implementation issues of strategic marketing* decisions. In order to be profitable, operational marketing must be founded upon a strategic design, which is itself based on the needs of the market and its expected evolution. The two roles of marketing are therefore closely complementary and cannot be dissociated. It is the classical commercial process of achieving a targeted market share through the use of tactical means related to new product development (Chapter 13) and to brand management (Chapter 14), distribution (Chapters 15 and 16), pricing (Chapter 17) and communication (Chapters 18 and 19) decisions. For each operational marketing decision, a special section is devoted on the impact of the internet technology.

In Part 5, we have two concluding chapters. In Chapter 20, we examine the issue of marketing accountability. A central problem in business today is that marketing lacks the kind of accountability and metrics common to the rest of the corporation. For a very long time, this imprecision has been tolerated and has been excused because marketing was supposed to be inherently "creative". Yet, as marketing consumes a larger and larger portion of the firm budget, the imperative grows to quantify marketing's direct contribution to the bottom line. Finally, Chapter 21 describes the structure and the content of the strategic and operational marketing plan and provides a detailed list of the questions to be addressed in a comprehensive marketing programme.

Acknowledgements

This book is a revision of the eighth edition of the French book *Marketing stratégique et opérationnel* (Paris, Dunod, 2012). This third English edition is the outgrowth of several years of research, teaching and consulting in Europe. This experience, the exchange of ideas and discussions with business professionals within various executive seminars or during consulting assignments have done much to further my knowledge of the marketing process.

Several people have directly or indirectly contributed at various stages to the development of this new edition, and in particular my colleagues from the marketing unit at my former university, the Louvain School of Management and from Chantal de Moerloose and Isabelle Schuiling and from Silvio Brondoni of the Università degli Studi di Milano-Bicocca. Last but not least, I am grateful to my students who – captive but challenging customers – have helped me to improve this text over the years.

The authors and publishers would like to thank the following for permission to reproduce copyright material:

American Marketing Association for Figure 12.2 from Day, G. S.(1977) 'Diagnosing the Product Portfolio', *Journal of Marketing*, 41 (2): 29–38.

Professor Noriaki Kano for Figure 14.1 from Kano, N., Seraku,N., Takahashi, F., Tshuji, S. (1996) *Attractive Quality and Must-Be Quality* **Kogan Page** for Figure 14.2 from Kapferer, J. N. (2004/2008), *The New Strategic Brand Management*, London, UK: Kogan Page.

Penguin for Table 14.5 from Davidson, H. (1997) *Even More Offensive Marketing*, London, UK: Penguin Books.

MIT Sloan Management Review for Figure 16.4 from Hoch, S. J. (1996) 'How Should National Brands Think About Private Labels?', *Sloan Management Review*, 37 (2): 89–102.

Philippe Ingold for Table 18.5 and Figure 18.5 from Ingold, P. (1995) *Promotion des ventes et action commerciale*, Paris, France: Vuibert.

Warc for Table 18.8 from des Thwaites, D., Anguilar-Manjarrez, R. and Kidd, C. (1998) 'Sports Sponsorship Development in Leading Canadian Companies: Issues and Trends', *International Journal of Advertising*, 17 (1): 29–49.

Elsevier for Table 21.1 from David, F. R. (1989) 'How Companies Define Their Mission?', *Long Range Planning*, 22 (1): 90–7.

Emerald Group Publishing Ltd. For Figure 21.6 from Day, G. S. (1986) 'Tough Questions for Developing Strategies', *The Journal of Business Strategy*, 6(3): 67–75.

Every effort has been made to contact all copyright-holders, but if any have been inadvertently omitted the publishers will be pleased to make the necessary arrangements at the earliest opporutunity.

Market–Driven Management

Strategic and Operational Marketing –Third Edition

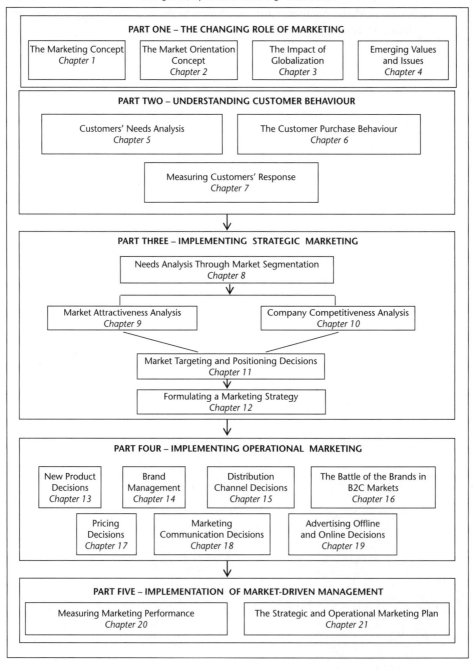

PART ONE – THE CHANGING ROLE OF MARKETING

| The Marketing Concept *Chapter 1* | The Market Orientation Concept *Chapter 2* | The Impact of Globalization *Chapter 3* | Emerging Values and Issues *Chapter 4* |

PART TWO – UNDERSTANDING CUSTOMER BEHAVIOUR

Customers' Needs Analysis
Chapter 5

The Customer Purchase Behaviour
Chapter 6

Measuring Customers' Response
Chapter 7

PART THREE – IMPLEMENTING STRATEGIC MARKETING

Needs Analysis Through Market Segmentation
Chapter 8

Market Attractiveness Analysis
Chapter 9

Company Competitiveness Analysis
Chapter 10

Market Targeting and Positioning Decisions
Chapter 11

Formulating a Marketing Strategy
Chapter 12

PART FOUR – IMPLEMENTING OPERATIONAL MARKETING

New Product Decisions
Chapter 13

Brand Management
Chapter 14

Distribution Channel Decisions
Chapter 15

The Battle of the Brands in B2C Markets
Chapter 16

Pricing Decisions
Chapter 17

Marketing Communication Decisions
Chapter 18

Advertising Offline and Online Decisions
Chapter 19

PART FIVE – IMPLEMENTATION OF MARKET-DRIVEN MANAGEMENT

Measuring Marketing Performance
Chapter 20

The Strategic and Operational Marketing Plan
Chapter 21

About the Authors

Jean-Jacques Lambin is Professor of Market-Driven Management at the Universita degli Studi di Milano, Bicocca, Italy. He is also Professor Emeritus at the Universite Catholique de Louvain, Belgium, and is jointeditor in chief of the European Business Forum (EBF). A specialist in strategic marketing, Lambin works as an analyst and consultant on problems of redeployment and restructuring of enterprises facing challenges due to the internationalisation of markets and market-driven management.

Isabelle Schuiling is Professor at the Louvain School of Management at the Universite Catholique de Louvain, Belgium. She specialises in Strategic Marketing, Brand Management and Global Marketing Strategies. Prior to her academic career she was Marketing Director at Procter & Gamble Europe and member of the management committee at Procter & Gamble, Belgium.

PART ONE

THE CHANGING ROLE OF MARKETING

CHAPTER ONE

THE MARKETING CONCEPT

Marketing is both a business philosophy and an action-oriented process. This first chapter aims to describe the system of thought, to clarify the ideological foundations of the marketing concept and its main implications regarding the firm's operations and organization. A distinction is made between strategic and operational marketing, that is, between the strategic brain and the commercial arm of the firm, respectively. The tasks of strategic and operational marketing are briefly described and will be analysed in more detail in the following chapters.

Chapter Learning Objectives

When you have read this chapter, you should be able to understand:

- The theoretical and ideological foundations of the marketing concept
- The difference between "strategic" and "operational" marketing
- The differences between "response" and "creative" strategic marketing
- The difference between transactional and relationship operational marketing
- The limitations of the marketing concept
- The marketing mix paradigm

1.1   THE MARKETING CONCEPT DEFINED

Since more than 50 years now, the marketing concept has been heralded by marketing academics and practitioners and its acceptance is still viewed as the optimal marketing management philosophy. In the management literature, the marketing concept has been described in various ways by different authors, but the term has become synonymous with having a customer orientation. The shortest definition of marketing is "meeting needs profitably". The traditional marketing concept is based on three pillars:

- A *customer orientation*: Implying that an intimate understanding of his or her needs and wants should be the focal point of all managerial actions.
- *Integration of efforts*: Implying coordination with the other functions (R&D, production, accounting and financial activities) within the firm to disseminate the customer orientation.
- A *profit objective*: The marketing concept is intended to make money for the firm, as a reward for its focus on customer satisfaction.

Developed in the management literature in the 1950s, the paternity of the concept is generally attributed to Drucker (1954) and to McKitterick (1957), a leading marketing executive from GE. Keith's article (1960) is one of the earliest presentations of the concept in the academic literature. For the layperson, the basic idea at the root of the marketing concept is by no means perceived as very original, if not simply a platitude. Any street vendor organizes its business to ensure that its clients get what they want, where and when they want it, and expects reward in return. Since the beginning of times, people have been engaging, through barter or trade, in mutually satisfactory exchange relationships and the customer focus clearly existed "when the king ordered boots from the boot maker". Under conditions of general scarcity, demand tends to be basic and the identification of attractive markets is easy. But in highly competitive markets, under conditions of oversupply, a business philosophy is required which states that supply should be market-driven and that the process of manufacturing should start with a clear statement of customers' needs.

The marketing concept suggests that the pursuit of customers' interests, in the end, serves the selfish interest of the firm: a *win–win* situation. The same idea was expressed by the Roman Emperor Marcus Aurelius in his Meditations on Stoic Philosophy (160 A.D.): "If you serve others, you serve yourself." In the economic literature, this principle was formalized by Smith (1776) and, till today, forms the basis of the market economy system and can be summarized as follows:

> Society' well being is the outcome, not so much of altruistic behaviour, but rather of the matching, through voluntary and competitive exchange, of buyer's and seller's self interest.

Although in modern economics this basic principle has been amended with regard to social (solidarity) and societal issues (externalities, collective goods, Government regulations), it,

Figure 1.1   The two faces of marketing
Source: Lambin (2000/2007).

nevertheless, remains the main principle driving the economic activity of a successful firm operating in a free – but regulated – market economy. Those ideas have been developed and implemented in management by authors such as Chamberlin (1933), Drucker (1954), Abbott (1955), Alderson (1957), McKitterick (1957), Howard and Sheth (1969), the main founding fathers of today's marketing discipline.

The implementation of the marketing concept assumes a twofold approach on the part of the firm, as shown in Figure 1.1. The term "marketing" – literally the process of delivering to the market – does not express the inherent duality of this process very well and emphasizes the "active" side of marketing more than the "analytic" side. As an aside, we may point out that to avoid the ambiguity – and the use of an English word in the common vocabulary – the French Academy (*l'Académie Française*) coined the terms *la mercatique* and *le marchéage* to illustrate these two facets of marketing. In practice, however, the French business community does not use these terms.

Strategic versus operational marketing

Today, most marketing textbooks have introduced the strategic marketing perspective in their content. See, for example, Baker (2007), Best (2004), Kerin, Hartely, Berkowitz and Rudelius (2007), Lendrevie, Lévy and Lindon (2007), Wind (2008). The differences between operational and strategic marketing are summarized in Table 1.1.

Strategic marketing is an *analysis-oriented* process focused on the analysis of the needs of individuals and organizations. The role of strategic marketing is to follow the evolution of the reference market (Levitt, 1975; Abell, 1980) and to identify various existing or potential product markets or segments on the basis of an analysis of the diversity of needs to be met. Once the product markets are identified, they represent economic opportunities whose quantitative and qualitative attractiveness needs to be evaluated. For a given firm, the appeal of a product market depends on its own competitiveness, in other words, on its capacity to meet customers' needs better than its rivals (Henderson, 1983). This competitiveness will exist as long as the firm holds a competitive advantage, either because it can differentiate itself from its rivals due to sustainable distinctive qualities or because of higher productivity, putting it at a cost advantage. The process of strategic marketing has a medium- to long-term horizon; its task is to specify the firm's mission, define objectives, elaborate a development strategy and ensure a balanced structure of the firm's product portfolio (Day, 1977).

Operational marketing is an *action-oriented* process that is extended over a short- to medium-term planning horizon and targets existing markets or segments. It is the classical commercial process of achieving a target market share through the use of tactical means related to the product, distribution, price and communication decisions. The operational marketing plan describes objectives, positioning, tactics and budgets for each brand of the company's portfolio in a given period and geographical zone. When restricted to operational marketing, marketing tends, however, to degenerate into a sales orientation and an exclusive concern for marketing communication. Operational marketing will be efficient only if it is based on well-defined and solid strategic options.

Table 1.1 Contrasting operational and strategic marketing

Operational marketing	Strategic marketing
Action-oriented	Analysis-oriented
Existing opportunities	New opportunities
Non-product variables	Product-market variables
Stable environment	Dynamic environment
Reactive behaviour	Proactive behaviour
Day-to-day management	Longer-range management
Marketing function	Cross-functional organization

Source: Lambin (2000/2007).

The tasks of strategic marketing

Strategic marketing is, to begin with, the analysis of the needs of individuals and organizations. From the marketing viewpoint, the buyer is not seeking a product as such, but is after the solution to a problem which the product or the service might provide. This solution may be obtained via different technologies, which are themselves continually changing. The role of strategic marketing is to follow the evolution of the reference market and to identify various existing or potential product markets or segments on the basis of an analysis of the diversity of needs to be met.

Once the product markets are identified, they represent economic opportunities whose attractiveness needs to be evaluated. The appeal of a product market is quantitatively measured by the notion of the potential market, and dynamically measured by its economic life, or its life cycle. For a given firm, the appeal of a product market depends on its own competitiveness, in other words, on its capacity to meet buyers' needs better than its rivals. This competitiveness will exist as long as the firm holds a competitive advantage, either because it can differentiate itself from its rivals due to sustainable distinctive qualities or because of higher productivity, putting it at a cost advantage.

Figure 1.2 shows the various stages of strategic marketing in relation to the firm's other major functions. Irrespective of whether a product is market-pull or company-push (or technology-push), it has to undergo the process of strategic marketing to evaluate its economic and financial viability. The interface between R&D, operations and strategic marketing plays a decisive role in this respect. The choice of the product market that results from this confrontation is of crucial importance in determining production capacity and investment decisions, and hence is vital to the equilibrium of the firm's overall financial structure.

Figure 1.2 The two roles of strategic marketing
Source: Lambin (2000/2007).

The role of strategic marketing is therefore (a) to lead the firm towards existing opportunities or (b) to create attractive opportunities, that is, opportunities which are adapted to its resources and know-how and which offer a potential for growth and profitability. The tasks of strategic marketing are summarized in the left column of Table 1.2.

Response versus proactive strategic marketing

As illustrated in Figure 1.2, innovations or new product ideas can have two very distinct origins: the market or the firm. If the new product idea comes from the market as a result, for example, of a market research study having identified unfilled (or poorly filled) needs or wants, the market observation is communicated to R&D people who will try to find an appropriate response to this unfilled need. The question is, "Is it feasible?" The innovation is *market-pull*. The role of operational marketing will then be to promote the new solution proposed to the identified target segment.

Another origin of an innovation may be the laboratory or R&D people who, as a result of fundamental or applied research, discover or develop a new product, a new process or a new organizational system to meet better existing or latent needs. Many companies gain competitive advantage and roar past rivals by creating breakthrough innovations. These companies are *technology-driven* rather than customer-oriented. Such innovations come from the creativity and insight of scientists and engineers who make

Table 1.2 The complementary roles of strategic and operational marketing

Tasks of strategic marketing	Tasks of operational marketing
To design a value proposition,	To make the value proposition,
…for a well-identified group of potential customers,	…known by and conveniently accessible to,
…sufficiently differentiated from competition,	…the well-identified group of potential customers,
…taking into account the roles of the other market actors,	…at a price acceptable by them and profitable for the firm,
…and sustainable by the firm.	…with the support of an appropriate personal and impersonal communication programme.

Source: Authors.

Box 1.1   Implementation problem: is a technology-driven strategy a real alternative to a market-driven strategy?

Some marketing scholars (Hayes and Abernathy, 1980; Bennett and Cooper, 1981) have argued that the market orientation concept hurts rather than helps the competitive performance of firms because of its over-reliance on market-pull innovations (i.e., response strategic marketing). Many companies, indeed, gain competitive advantage by being primarily technology-driven and not customer-driven. Imagine – say these scholars – consumers trying to tell a market researcher about their need for a mobile phone or a digital camera before those products were introduced.

This criticism is based on a truncated view of the market orientation concept by ignoring the proactive approach of strategic marketing. Scientists and engineers, rather than consumers, may well be the source of new product ideas in technology-driven companies, but the products that arise from those ideas must satisfy customers needs, even if latent or unarticulated, or they will end up serving no market at all. Thus, technology-driven companies must ultimately apply the market orientation concept if they are to be successful. There are enough examples, in industrial history, of technological monsters developed in ivory towers by engineers that have never found a market.

technological discoveries and then work them into radically new products. The innovation *is technology-push*.

In this case, the role of strategic marketing is more complex. The question is, "Is there a need and a potentially profitable market segment?" Strategic marketing will have then to assess the size of the target segment and the success factors of the innovation. The role of operational marketing may be more complex and challenging because its role is to create the market for a product or service which is not explicitly demanded or expected by the market and which may require from potential customers a change in their consuming or using habits.

Innovation is at the core of strategic marketing. New product ideas can have two very distinct origins: the market or the firm. Thus, in strategic marketing, a distinction must be made between two distinct but complementary approaches: response strategic marketing and creative (or technology-driven) strategic marketing.

- In *response strategic marketing*, the objective is to meet expressed needs or wants and to fulfil them. The goal of operational marketing is to develop an existing demand or potential market. Innovations are market-pull. The key question is, Is it feasible?
- In *supply-driven or proactive strategic marketing*, the objective is to identify latent or unarticulated needs or to find new ways to fill existing needs or wants. The objective is to create new markets through technology and/or organizational creativity. Innovations are technology-push. The key question is, Is there a need?

In affluent economies, where most needs and wants are well met and where the majority of existing markets are stagnant, proactive strategic marketing has an important role to play to create new market opportunities in the future. The Internet technology provides these new opportunities. As Akio Morita, Sony's leader puts it:

> Our plan is to lead the public with new products rather than ask them what kind of products they want. The public does not know what is possible, but we do. So instead of doing a lot of market research, we refine our thinking on a product and its use and try to create a market for it by educating and communicating with the public. (Schendler, 1992)

Kotler and Keller (2006, p. 724), in their apology of an excellent "holistic marketing" practice make a distinction between "market-driven" and "market-driving" management.

Box 1.2   How to promote a proactive strategic marketing?

- Helping customers anticipate developments in their markets.
- Continuously trying to discover additional needs of customers of which they are unaware.
- Incorporating solutions to unarticulated customer needs in new products or services.
- Brainstorming on how customers use our products and services.
- Innovating even at the risk of making our own products obsolete.

- Searching for opportunities in areas where customers have a difficult time expressing their needs.
- Working closely with lead users who try to recognize customer needs months or even years before the majority of the market recognize them.
- Extrapolating key trends to gain insight into what users in a current market will need in the future.

Source: Adapted from Narver, Slater and MacLachlan (2004).

We agree with Day (1999, p.37), who says that "this is a distinction without a difference". Market-driven firms are not only reactive through response strategic marketing, but they are also driving changes by breaking the rules of the game through proactive strategic marketing. Good examples of proactive strategic marketing are given by firms like Ice-watch, Dell Computers or Ikea.

In short, the objective of strategic marketing is not only (a) to listen to customers and then to respond to their articulated needs, but also (b) to lead customers where they want to go, even if they do not know it yet. This underlines the importance of the distinction between expressed (or *articulated*) and latent (or *unarticulated*) needs. What a customer wants is an appropriate solution to his or her problem. Merely satisfying expressed needs may be insufficient for a firm to attract or to retain customers.

The tasks of operational marketing

The economic role that marketing plays in the operation of the firm is shown in Figure 1.2. The main relationships between the four major managerial functions (R&D, operations, marketing and finance) are illustrated. The main task of operational marketing is to generate sales revenues that are the target turnover. This means to "sell" and to obtain purchase orders by using the most efficient sales methods while at the same time minimizing costs. The objective of realizing a particular sales volume translates into a manufacturing programme as far as the operations department is concerned, and a programme of storage and physical distribution for the sales department. Operational marketing is therefore a determining factor that directly influences the short-term profitability of the firm.

The vigour of operational marketing is a decisive factor in the performance of the firm, especially in those markets where competition is fierce. Every product, even those of superior quality, must have a price acceptable to the market, be available in the network of distribution adapted to the purchasing habits of the targeted customers and be supported by some form of communication which promotes the product and enhances its distinctive qualities. It is rare to find market situations where demand exceeds supply or where the firm is well known by potential users or where competition is non-existent.

There are many examples of promising products that have failed to prevail in the market due to insufficient commercial support. This is particularly the case in firms where the "engineering" spirit predominates, whereby it is believed that a good-quality product can gain recognition by itself, and the firm lacks the humility to adapt to the needs of customers.

Operational marketing is the most spectacular and the most visible aspect of the marketing discipline, particularly because of the important role played by advertising and promotional activities. Some firms have embarked on marketing through advertising. In contrast, some other firms – like many producers of industrial goods – have for a long time tended to believe that marketing does not apply to their business, thus implicitly linking marketing to advertising. Operational marketing is therefore *the firm's commercial arm* without which even the best strategic plan cannot lead to satisfactory results. However, it is also clear that without solid strategic options, there can be no ultimately profitable operational marketing. Dynamism without thought is merely unnecessary risk. No matter how powerful an operational marketing plan, it cannot create demand where there is no need, just as it cannot keep alive activities doomed to disappear. Hence, in order to be profitable, operational marketing must be founded upon a strategic design, which is itself based on the needs of the market and its expected evolution. The tasks of operational marketing are summarized in the right column of Table 1.2.

Transactional versus relationship operational marketing

Operational marketing is the commercial arm of the firm and its key function is to generate sales. Commercial negotiation and selling techniques are often thought to be the same. These are, however, two completely different procedures that will be discussed in more details in Chapter 18 (see Table 18.4). Transactional selling techniques are indubitably efficient *to close the sale* and are often associated with various aggressive selling methods: hard sell or manipulative marketing. These techniques were popular in the 1960s in operational marketing when the *sales orientation* was predominant. They have been challenged over the past ten years, under the influence of all the changes in customer behaviour and in the competitive environment. The differences between transaction and relationship marketing are many.

- Transaction marketing focuses on a discrete, individual sale. The relationships end once the sale is consummated.
- Relationship marketing is oriented towards a strong and lasting relationship. Maintaining and cultivating the customer base is the key objective, in order to create a mutually profitable relationship.
- Relationship marketing presupposes the opportunity for shared benefits, while transaction marketing works on a model of contradictory needs: the buyer wants a good price; the seller wants a high profit.
- Relationship marketing differs from transaction marketing in other respects as well. While the latter focuses almost solely on price, the former shifts the emphasis to non-economic benefits, such as services, delivery time and the certainty of continued supply.

The practice of relationship or counselling selling – as opposed to the "impose–convince–suggest–please" system – is characterized by the importance accorded (a) to true and nonmanipulative exploration of the customer's motivations and motives and (b) to the search of a long-lasting mutually satisfactory relationship between buyers and sellers. Relationship selling has shifted attention from "closing" the singular sale to creating the necessary conditions for a long-term relationship between the firm and its customers that in the long run breeds successful sales encounters. In market-oriented firms, there is a tendency to change the vocabulary from sales force to *sales counsellors*, *professional representatives* or *sales consultants*.

The marketing programme

This job of reflection and strategic planning is very different from operational marketing and requires different talents in the individuals who exercise it. Nevertheless, the two roles are closely complementary, as illustrated by Table 1.2, in the sense that the design of a strategic plan must be carried out in close relation to operational marketing. Operational marketing emphasizes nonproduct variables (distribution, pricing, advertising and promotion), while strategic marketing tends to emphasize on the ability to provide a product with superior value at a competitive cost. Strategic marketing leads to the choice of product markets to be exploited in order of priority and the forecast of primary demand in each of these product markets. Operational marketing, on the other hand, sets out market share objectives to reach in the target product market, as well as the marketing budgets necessary for their realization.

As shown in Figure 1.3, the comparison of the market share objective and primary demand forecast in each product market makes it possible to develop a sales objective first in volume and then in terms of turnover, given the chosen pricing policy. The expected gross profit is obtained after deducting direct manufacturing costs, possible fixed costs for

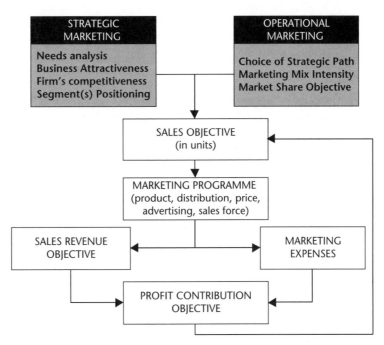

Figure 1.3 The integrated marketing programme
Source: Lambin (2000/2007).

specific structures, marketing expenditure attributed to the sales force and advertising and promotion as allowed for in the marketing budget. This gross profit is the contribution of the product market to the firm: It must cover overhead and leave a gross profit. The content and structure of the marketing plan are described in detail in Chapter 21.

The marketing mix paradigm

The operational counterpart or support of the marketing concept is commonly referred as to the *marketing mix or to 4Ps paradigm* – product, place (or distribution), price, promotion (or communication) – proposed by McCarthy (1960), that is, the specific techniques by which the firm seeks to meet consumers needs (the firm's commercial arm). The marketing mix paradigm includes the marketing tools that the manager combines in a specific way to deal with a specific marketing situation.

Borden (1964) groups these techniques in the following areas: product planning, pricing, branding, channels of distribution, personal selling, advertising, sales promotion, service, physical distribution and market research. Recognizing the special character of services as products, Booms and Bitner (1981) add, in addition to the standard 4Ps, an extra three Ps, totalling seven: *people*, any person coming into contact with customers, *process*, the "servuction" process involved in providing the service and the *physical evidence* provided to make the service tangible for the potential customer.

Several criticisms have been formulated against the marketing mix in the academic literature. For an extensive review, see Constantinides (2006) and Möller (2006). The most significant criticism of the 4Ps or 7Ps paradigm is its lack of strategic content, making it unfit as a planning instrument, in particular in turbulent environments. It is implicitly assumed in the marketing mix paradigm that the business to cover, the customers to serve, the competitors to outperform and the distributors to partner with are known and well identified. These strategic tasks are the most difficult to assume and will determine the long-term future of the firm. It is only once these strategic options are taken that the marketing mix paradigm becomes relevant.

A second important criticism is that, unconsciously, the marketing mix paradigm emphasizes an "inside-out" view of the market, whereas the marketing concept pretends to be an "outside-in" approach giving the primacy to customers. In the market orientation concept described in the following chapter, the 4Ps or 7Ps paradigm is analysed in a more customer-centric perspective in the framework of the "solution to a problem" approach.

Finally, a third criticism formulated in particular by Grönroos (1991, 1994) is that the marketing mix paradigm's focus is more on short-term market transactions than on building relationship with customers, an approach more appropriate for fast moving consumer goods (FMCG) markets but less relevant for services and B2B markets. Grönroos and his colleagues from the Nordic School (Gummesson, 1987, 1997) view marketing as an interactive process where relationship building and management are the priority objectives. Marion (2001) challenges this distinction between transaction and relationship marketing made by Grönroos. As soon as we have exchange, there is a relationship. A distinction between "limited" and "extensive" relationship would probably be more appropriate.

Still, today many firms are inclined to assimilate marketing with the marketing mix paradigm, which in fact is a *supply-driven* approach of the market. The objective is to use the understanding of consumers' needs to mould demand to the requirements of supply, thereby focusing on the needs of the seller. The true customer orientation concept is concerned with what can be done for customers by adapting supply to the expectations of demand, in a *win–win* perspective. To clarify the real role of marketing, the distinction made above (see Table 1.1) between strategic and operational marketing is essential.

1.2   STEPS IN IMPLEMENTING STRATEGIC MARKETING

The role of strategic marketing is (a) to lead the firm towards existing opportunities or (b) to create attractive opportunities, that is, opportunities which are adapted to its resources and know-how and which offer a potential for growth and profitability. The process of strategic marketing has a medium- to long-term horizon; its task is to specify the firm's mission, define objectives, elaborate a development strategy and ensure a balanced structure of the product portfolio. This process can be implemented in seven steps summarized here, but is discussed in more detail in Part 3 of this book.

Step 1: Reference market definition (see Chapter 8)

As put by Levitt (1960) and Abell (1980), the first question to address in a strategic thinking exercise is, *"What business are we in?"* The objective is to define the reference market in terms of generic needs in order to anchor the firm's business on stable ground and in a market-oriented perspective. The business definition is the starting point for strategy development. It helps identify the customers to be served, the competitors to surpass, the key success factors to master and the alternative technologies available for producing the service or the function sought by customers. The reference market definition does not imply that the firm should pursue all the options identified, but is helpful to delineate the battle field and to identify the opportunities and threats likely to come from substitute and/or complementary activities. Ideally, the business definition should be stated in terms narrow enough to provide practical guidance, yet broad enough to stimulate imaginative thinking, such as openings for product line extensions or for diversification into adjacent product areas.

Step 2: What is the diversity of needs in the reference market? (see Chapter 8)

In the majority of reference markets, there is a large diversity of needs and it is impossible to satisfy all customers with a single product or service. The "one size fits all" concept is obsolete in most advanced economies. Different consumers have varying desires and interests. This variety stems from basic variations of customers' expectations and benefits they seek from products. Increasingly, companies have found it essential to move away from mass marketing towards a target marketing strategy, where the focus is on one (or several) well-identified group(s) of customers. The objective is to sub-divide the market in more homogeneous sub-groups in order to adapt the firm's offering on the basis of a better understanding of their needs. Knowing how to creatively segment the market is one of the most important strategic skills a firm should have. Segmentation is generally done in two steps: macro- and micro-segmentation. Different methods of micro-segmentation exist: socio-demographic, benefit, behavioural and life style. The expected output is a segmentation grid describing the profile of the three or five (maximum) most important segments in qualitative (needs, buying habits, sensitivities to marketing variables, strength of competition, etc.) and quantitative terms (size, growth, profitability, etc.).

Step 3: How attractive is the business opportunity of the identified segments? (see Chapter 9)

Before deciding which segment(s) to target, the firm has to evaluate the intrinsic attractiveness of each segment, that is, its current size, absolute market potential, growth rate, accessibility, logistic support, competition intensity and so on. All those indicators are objective and out of the control of the firm. They describe the economic and competitive environment of each segment within which each competing firm operates. These market indicators can be evaluated through standard market research. Attractiveness indicators, and in particular sales potential estimates and projections, are used by general management to calibrate future investments and production capacity, should the firm decide to target one of these segments.

Step 4: Do we have a sustainable value proposition to propose to each segment? (see Chapter 10)

A market segment can be very attractive in itself, but not for a particular firm, given the skills and resources required to be a successful player. A firm should concentrate on those areas where its creative abilities lie. The objective here is to identify the kind of competitive advantage that the firm can enjoy in each segment and to assess its sustainability. Competitive advantage refers to those characteristics or attributes of a product or a brand that give the firm some superiority over its direct competitors while generating value to customers. A company can outperform rivals only if it can establish a difference that it can preserve. A strategic competitive advantage is more sustainable than an operational competitive advantage in the long term.

Step 5: Which segment(s) to target by priority? (see Chapter 11)

Having completed the market segmentation and the "attractiveness/competitiveness" analyses of the different product markets and segments, the next task is to decide what type of market coverage to adopt. Several market coverage strategies can be considered. In a *focused strategy,* market boundaries are defined narrowly. In a *full market coverage strategy,* two options exist: (a) a "mass marketing" strategy, where the firm focuses on what is common in the needs of customers rather than on what is different; (b) a "mass customization" strategy, where the firm approaches the market with a tailor-made programme for each segment. In a *mixed strategy,* the firm diversifies its activities to ensure that its portfolio of activities is well balanced in terms of profit and growth potentials and well diversified in terms of risks.

Step 6: How do we want to compete in the target segment(s)? (see Chapters 11 and 12)

Once the market coverage decisions are made, the next step is to decide on the positioning strategy to adopt within each targeted segment(s). Selection of the positioning strategy provides the unifying concept for the development of the marketing mix programme. This is one of the most critical steps in the implementation of strategic marketing, because the firm has to decide how to best differentiate its brand from competing brands. Positioning is defined as the decision made by the firm to choose the benefit(s) that the brand has to put forward to gain a distinctive place in the market. In a price-sensitive market, product positioning generally requires a lower price, because other sources of differentiation are not valued by target customers. For markets in which differentiation is possible and valued by target customers, three types of differentiation strategies are possible: product differentiation, price differentiation and image differentiation. The objective of the company will then be to communicate clearly the chosen positioning to potential customers so that it is clearly recorded in their minds.

Step 7: How to get a well-balanced product portfolio? (see Chapter 12)

The purpose of a product portfolio analysis is to help a multi-business firm decide how to allocate scarce resources among the target segments it competes in, called the *Strategic Business Units* (SBUs). Product portfolio analysis relates attractiveness and competitiveness indicators to help guide strategic thinking by suggesting specific marketing strategies to achieve a balanced mix of SBUs that will ensure growth and profit performance in the long run, given their differentiated positions along the attractiveness–competitiveness dimensions.

Portfolio analysis is obviously not a panacea, but it has the merit of emphasizing some important aspects of strategic management.

- It moderates excessively short-term vision by insisting on keeping a balance between immediately profitable activities and those that prepare the future.
- It encourages the firm to keep both market attractiveness and competitive potentials in mind.
- It establishes priorities in allocation of human as well as financial resources.
- It suggests differentiated development strategies per type of activity on a more data-oriented basis.
- It creates a common language throughout the organization and fixes clear objectives to reinforce motivation and facilitate control.

The output of these seven steps of the strategic marketing process constitutes the backbone of the operational marketing plan. Once the answers to these questions are obtained, the task remains to define the positioning options to be taken, to define the means required to achieve the stated objectives and, last but not least, to prepare a projected profit and loss statements for each activity and for the company as a whole.

1.3 MORE QUESTIONS ABOUT THE MARKETING CONCEPT

The term "marketing" itself generates ambiguity. In plain English it refers to the process of going to the market and the term implicitly places the emphasis on the "downstream" activities of the marketing process, that is, the marketing mix in action, and does not refer to the "upstream" activities that necessarily precede the market entry, that is, the confrontation of customers needs with the firm's creative abilities and skills.

Ambiguity of the term "marketing"

Many authors and managers do not make a careful distinction among *customer-oriented*, *marketing-oriented* and *market-driven*. They lean towards the traditional marketing concept to describe the orientation of a firm that stay close to its customers.

The linguistic definition of polysemy refers to "a word that has multiple but related meanings". Unlike finance people, marketing people are still divided in their understanding about the meaning of the word "marketing". The lack of consensus on language among managers – and in particular among chief executive officers (CEOs) – is evidenced by the answer received to the first interview question posed to a sample of CEOs: "How has marketing been changing in your company in the past three years?" The reply is along the lines of "that depends upon what you mean by marketing" (Webster, Malter and Ganesan, 2005, p. 36).

This level of confusion remains high among marketing practitioners and scholars as well. For example, while we will call "market-driven management" what the whole firm is doing to secure customer preference and thereby to achieve higher returns, Ambler (2000, p. 61) uses the term "pan-company marketing" and Kotler and Keller (2006, p. 17) the term "holistic marketing". In many sectors, companies tend to equate marketing with sales; others with brand management and sales; others with advertising, merchandising and sales and others with sales and communication, and so on. As stated by Kotler, Rackham and Krishnaswamy (2006, p.74), "All too often, organisations find that they have marketing function inside Sales and a sales function inside Marketing." This conceptual looseness and lack of semantic rigour are unworthy of a discipline having, since more than 60 years now, scientific and academic ambitions.

This definitional confusion about the labelling and the scope of the marketing concept creates problems, not only for the teaching of marketing, but more importantly for its implementation. We have seen many examples of poor marketing practices adopted in the name of the marketing concept. As stated by Christensen, Cook and Hall (2005), "Thirty thousand new consumer products are launched each year. But over 90% of them fail – and that's after marketing professionals have spent massive amounts of money trying to understand what their customers want. What's wrong with this picture? We believe that some of the fundamental paradigms of marketing are broken. We are not alone in that judgment." Even Procter & Gamble's (P&G) CEO A.G. Lafley (2005), cited in Christenson, Cook, and Hall (2005), arguably the best-positioned person in the world to make this call, says, "We need to reinvent the way we market to consumers. We need a new model." Rust, Moorman and Bhalla (2010) consider, for example, that the traditional marketing department must be reconfigured as a customer department that puts building customer relationships ahead of pushing specific products.

Performance of the marketing concept

The success of the marketing concept, born in the 1950s and adopted during the Golden 1960s, can be explained by the fact that both American and European companies were operating at that time in fast-growing seller markets, with demand larger than supply and well-known needs and wants.

Marketing has played an important role in the American and European market economies, not only by improving the productivity of the distributive system of goods and services but also because, by doing so, it has triggered a virtuous circle of economic development. The steps of this development process are the following:

- The marketing concept helps identify poorly satisfied or unmet market needs and stimulates the development of new or improved products.
- The tools of operational marketing (the *7Ps*) create and/or develop market demand for these new products or services.
- This increased demand generates cost decreases that make possible price reductions, thereby opening the market to new groups of customers.
- The resulting enlargement of the market requires new investments in production capacity that generates economies of scale and stimulates further efforts in R&D to create new generations of products.

These developments were so dramatic in the past 50 years that the period was characterized as the golden years of progress to the *Good Life*, as evidenced by the wide variety of modern discretionary purchase categories that were not even imaginable 100 years earlier: cars, televisions, videos, DVDs, computers, vacation homes, boats, recreational vehicles, pension funds, health clubs and widespread travel opportunities, and so on, with market penetration rates of well above 60 per cent observed in most industrialized countries.

The marketing concept has contributed to the development of a business democracy because:

- it starts with the analysis of the citizen-consumers' needs,
- it guides investment and production decisions on the basis of these expressed or anticipated market needs,
- it is respectful of the diversity of tastes and preferences by developing adapted products,
- it stimulates innovation and entrepreneurship.

In the 1970s, the development of strategic planning (Ansoff, 1965), with its emphasis on short-term financially oriented measures of management performance, contributed to the decline of management interest in the marketing concept. The major criticism (Webster, 1981, p. 11) was that marketing managers are generally unsophisticated in their understanding of the financial dimensions of marketing decisions and lack a bottom line orientation. They tend to focus more on sales volume and market share changes than on profit contribution and returns on assets. The challenge of measuring marketing performance is addressed in Chapter 21 of this book.

The changes in the business environment in the 1990s – saturation of core markets, technology-push innovations, globalization – have contributed to increase the complexity of markets and to reduce the effectiveness of traditional marketing practice. A resurgence of management interest for marketing has been observed in the 1990s (Webster, 1988 and Wind, 2008), with the development of the market orientation concept presented in the next chapter.

The risk of manipulative marketing

Despite the undisputable achievements of the marketing concept, several criticisms have been formulated about the marketing practice (Kaldor, 1971; Bell and Emory, 1971). The most severe criticism is the charge of *manipulative marketing*, through hard selling and misleading advertising, with the objective to mould demand to the requirements of supply instead of adapting supply to the expectations of the market (Table 1.3). In the 1960s, leading corporations have been accused of:

■ misleading and manipulating children through TV advertising;
■ producing merchandise with miracle ingredients which in fact are of little value;
■ advertising ordinary or inferior features in a way to suggest that they are actually superior features;
■ offering warranties for the consumer protection that are not understood by the consumer and, in fact, protecting the seller more than the buyer;
■ using advertising in a way that exploits the agonies and anxieties of individuals.

The excesses of manipulative or "wild marketing" have led to the birth of countervailing powers (a) in the form of consumers' organizations (the consumerist movement) initiated by consumers in particular by Nader (1965) and (b) in the form of legislation which increasingly reinforces the protection of consumers' legal rights prompted by public authorities and (c) by self-discipline by companies and the adoption of rules of ethics that have contributed to the development of a more ethical behaviour. It is clear today that manipulative marketing is self-destructive for a company or for a brand and goes against its best long-term interest.

Marketing: a frightening word

In the popular language, the word marketing has become the synonym – in the best case – of selling but also of misleading, deceptive, untruthful, manipulating, boosting, superficial, window dressing. Why such contempt and how to explain the discrepancy between what the marketing concept pretends to be and its public perception?

This insidious fear of marketing is in everybody's mind. A preliminary explanation of this mistrust is clearly due to the too numerous cases of manipulative marketing still observed from time to time in industrialized markets. A more paradoxical explanation can be suggested, however (Lambin and Herman, 2001). If marketing, viewed as a process of market conquest, is guided by the rules of science – a belief generally held by public opinion – this would imply the existence of forms of determinism in the functioning of the market. In other words, cause and effects relationships or laws (even probabilistic laws), observable and measurable, that the firm can exploit to influence and even to manipulate consumers' behaviour in order to achieve its own growth and profit objectives would exist. This idea is worrying and is in contradiction with the free market ideology of the consumer-king, viewed as an independent economic decider. The marketing concept would disturb and

Table 1.3 Examples of manipulative marketing

– Sales of dangerous or defective products.
– Exaggeration of the product content through the use of flashy packaging design.
– Resorting to fraudulent practices with regard to price and delivery policies.
– Resorting to promotional techniques which exploit impulsive buyer behaviour.
– Advertisements which exploit the agonies or anxieties of individuals.
– Enticing people to over-consume using hard selling techniques.

Source: Lambin (2000/2007).

parasitize the natural spontaneity of the "invisible hand". The claimed individual freedom and the postulated autonomy – "I choose therefore I am"– seem to be incompatible with a deterministic marketing process.

We have to recognize, however, that the axiom of complete individual freedom is unrealistic because any individual in his or her role of decision-maker is a human being socially and culturally formed. This implies that the motives of his or her choice are more influenced by imitation and social conditioning than by rational deliberation and by psychic spontaneity – a reality sometimes difficult to accept – and this state of affairs can also explain the instinctive mistrust vis-à-vis marketing. Moreover, marketing professionals know perfectly well that the scientific nature of marketing is very relative and that few companies today are able to measure the profitability of their marketing efforts, even more modestly, to evaluate the effectiveness of their marketing and advertising investments. As discussed in Chapter 21, substantial progress is made today in linking marketing action and financial performance.

Is the marketing concept of universal application?

The marketing concept holds that products or services should be created in response to the expressed needs and wants of their consuming publics because that would be the way to meet the organization's own needs, whether these needs are financial profits or some other non-financial goals. Is this normative framework applicable for any organization insofar as they have customers and products? As argued by Kotler and Levy (1969), marketing constitutes an applied behavioural techno-science consisting of a set of functions, the core of which is the exchange transaction (Bagozzi, 1979). Such reasoning expanded the marketing concept from the realm of economically based exchange to resources-based exchange in a broad range of social organizations. Topics range from public transportation, to political campaigns, hospitals, universities and the arts.

In contradiction with this view, Hirschman (1983, p. 46) argued that the marketing concept – as a normative framework – is not applicable to two broad classes of producers, artists and ideologists, because their personal goals are not satisfied by commercial success. Typically, the artist is motivated by the need to achieve self-fulfilment via his or her creativity, that is, the creative process itself is intrinsically satisfying. Artists achieve success in their own eyes. Similarly, ideologists formulate beliefs about the nature of reality and values regarding desirable states of reality. These creators, like artists, formulate ideology largely out of a need for self-expression. This includes religious leaders who seek to have their own religion tenets accepted, but would not be willing to modify them to achieve greater market acceptance. These producers are characterized by "self-oriented creativity" and practice "product-centred marketing". For this category of creators, Hirschman (1983) states, "There are three potential audiences: (1) the self, the creator's own feelings of self fulfilment and satisfaction; (2) peers and industry professionals, such as other artists or ideologists or professional critics; and (3) the public at large, which may consist of one or several market segments." To the extent that personal and peer values conflict with those of the public at large, then the customer orientation advocated by the marketing concept is irrelevant.

Two other categories of producers do not rely on the marketing concept. The producer who has fixed established inventories or production facilities (sunk costs) and does not have the opportunity to tailor offerings to suit the needs of customers. Also, when product offerings are highly desirable but available in limited supply, there is little incentive for the marketer to seek out his or her customer. In these situations, the "production-oriented" or the "sales-oriented" concepts are more appropriate business philosophies (Lambin, 2000/2007).

Needed clarifications of the marketing concept

The marketing concept has meant little more than looking to the customer for guidance as to what can be sold at a profit, but several ambiguities remain in the interpretation of the concept. Also, key issues are left out and this reduces substantially the operational value of the concept for guidance of the firm. Several important questions remain unresolved.

- Does the marketing concept imply creating needs?
- Does the concept refer only to "expressed" needs or also latent or unarticulated needs?
- Does the concept assume that consumers know what is needed and are able to express their needs?
- Are consumers able to conceptualize and evaluate highly innovative product ideas and concepts proposed by R&D and laboratories?
- Is the objective short-term or long-term satisfaction? How to define and measure customer satisfaction?
- Who is the real customer? No distinction is made between the different customer roles: buyer, payer and user.
- Does the concept imply protection of customer's well-being and safety in the use of the product?
- How far should the firm go in promoting its products and in stimulating needs?
- Are individual needs' satisfaction always compatible with the common good and public interest?
- What about other buying influences? The concept refers to customers only: wholesalers, retailers and others actors in the distribution channels. What about influencers like doctors, architects or consultants who do not buy, do not use and do not pay, but recommend products or brands? What about other stakeholders like consumerists, ecologists?
- Profit for whom? For the shareholder only or for other stakeholders as well?
- Does integration of the marketing function implies that marketing should take over the other functions or simply direct these activities? How to organize the required cross-functional coordination?
- Should marketing be held accountable for the environmental side effects of its activities?

Particularly restrictive in the marketing concept is the exclusive focus on customers, completely ignoring the influence of other key market actors. Knowing what customers want is not too helpful (a) if competitors are already providing the same product or service; similarly, (b) if powerful distributors refuse to list the brand, preventing the firm to reach the targeted customers; or (c) if powerful influencers do not certify or shortlist the product, or, (d) last but not least, if powerful stakeholders decide to boycott the brand. The dominant orientation towards customers in the marketing concept has deflected attention from the pursuit of competitive advantage over other stakeholders.

These questions will be reviewed in more detail in the following chapters, but it is already clear that the marketing concept does not address these issues. The operational statement and labelling of a revised concept that more clearly shows what it is and what it is not, while taking into account the challenges of the new market environment, is necessary.

> ## Chapter Summary
>
> Marketing is both a business philosophy and an action-oriented process. Within the firm, marketing's function is twofold: (a) to create opportunities or to lead the firm towards market opportunities adapted to its resources and know-how and which offer a potential for profit and growth (strategic marketing); (b) to be the firm's commercial arm for achieving a targeted market share through the use of tactical means related to product, distribution, price and communication decisions (operational marketing). Strategic marketing has two roles: to be responsive and to be proactive in needs analysis. Strategic marketing can be implemented in seven steps that will re-examined one by one in the following chapters. Operational marketing can be transactional or relationship. Several aspects of the marketing concept have to be clarified and these questions will be examined in the following chapters.

BIBLIOGRAPHY

Abbott, L. (1955), *Quality and Competition*, New York, John Wiley & Sons.

Abell, D.F. (1980), *Defining the Business: The Starting Point of Strategic Planning*, Englewood Cliffs, NJ, Prentice-Hall.

Alderson, W. (1957), *Marketing Behaviour and Executive Action*, Homewood, IL, R.D. Irwin, Inc.

Ambler, T. (2000), Marketing Metrics, *Business Strategy Review*, 11, 2, pp. 59–66.

Ansoff, H.I. (1965), *Corporate Strategy*, New York, McGraw Hill.

Bagozzi, R.P. (1979), *Toward a Formal Theory of Marketing Exchanges*, in *Conceptual and Theoretical Developments, in Marketing*, O.C. Ferrell, S.W. Brown, and C.W. Lamb, Jr. (eds.), Chicago, IL, American Marketing Association.

Baker, M.J. (2007), *Marketing Strategy & Management*, London, Palgrave Macmillan, 4th edition.

Bell, M.L. and Emory, C.W. (1971), The Faltering Marketing Concept, *Journal of Marketing*, 35, 4, pp. 37–42.

Bennett, R. and Cooper, R. (1981), The Misuse of the Marketing Concept: An American Tragedy, *Business Horizons*, 24, 6, pp. 51–60.

Best, R.J. (2004), *Market-Based Management*, Upper Saddle River, NJ, Prentice-Hall, 3rd edition.

Booms, B.H. and Bitner, M.J. (1981), *Marketing Strategies and Organisation Structures for Service firms*, in *Marketing of Services*, J.H. Donnelly and W.R. George (eds.), Chicago, IL, American Marketing Association.

Borden, N.H. (1964), The Concept of the Marketing Mix, *Journal of Advertising Research*, 4, June, pp. 2–7.

Chamberlin, E.H. (1933), *The Theory of Monopolistic Competition*, Cambridge, MA, Harvard University Press.

Christensen, C.M., Cook, S. and Hall, T. (2005), Marketing Malpractice: The Cause and the Cure, *Harvard Business Review*, December, pp. 76–83.

Constantinides, E. (2006), The Marketing Mix Revisited: Toward the 21st Century Marketing, *Journal of Marketing Management*, 22, pp. 407–38.

Day, G.S. (1977), Diagnosing the Product Portfolio, *Journal of Marketing*, 41, 2, pp. 29–38.

Day, G.S. (1999), Misconceptions about Market Orientation, *Journal of Market-Focused Management*, 4, 1, pp. 5–16.

Drucker, P. (1954), *The Practice of Management*, New York, Harper & Row.

Grönroos, C. (1991), The Marketing Strategy Continuum: Towards a Marketing Concept for the 1990s, *Management Decision*, 29, 1, pp. 7–13.

Grönroos, C. (1994), From Marketing Mix to Relationship Marketing: Towards a Paradigm Shift in Marketing, *Management Decision*, 32, 2, pp. 4–20.

Gummesson, E. (1987), The New Marketing – Developing Long-Term Interactive Relationships, *Long Range Planning*, 20, 4, pp. 10–20.

Gummesson, E. (1997), Relationship Marketing as a Paradigm Shift: Some Conclusions from the 30R Approach, *Management Decision*, 35, 4, pp. 267–72.

Hayes, R. and Abernathy, W. (1980), Managing Our Way to Economic Decline, *Harvard Business Review*, 58, 4, pp. 67–78.

Henderson, B. (1983), The Anatomy of Competition, *Journal of Marketing*, 47, 2, pp. 7–11.

Hirschman, E.C. (1983), Aesthetics, Ideologies and the Limits of the Marketing Concept, *Journal of Marketing*, 47, 3, pp. 45–55.

Howard, J. and Sheth, J.N. (1969), *The Theory of Buyer Behaviour*, New York, John Wiley & Sons.

Kaldor, A.G. (1971), Imbricative Marketing, *Journal of Marketing*, 35, 2, pp. 19–25.

Keith, R.J. (1960), The Marketing Revolution, *Journal of Marketing*, 24, 3, pp. 35–8.

Kerin, R.A., Hartley, S.W., Berkowitz, E.N. and Rudelius, W. (2007), *Marketing*, Milano, McGraw-Hill, 8th edition.

Kotler, P. and Keller, K.L. (2006), *Marketing Management*, Upper Saddle River, NJ, Pearson Prentice Hall, 12th edition.

Kotler, P. and Levy, S.J. (1969), Broadening the Concept of Marketing, *Journal of Marketing*, 33, 1, pp. 10–15.

Kotler, P., Rackham, N. and Krishnaswamy, S. (2006), Ending the War between Sales and Marketing, *Harvard Business Review*, 84, 7/8, pp. 68–78.

Lambin, J.J. (2000/2007*), Market-Driven Management: Strategic and Operational Marketing*, London, Palgrave Macmillan.

Lambin, J.J. and Herman, J. (2001), Faut-il tenir le marketing en respect?, Unpublished working paper, IAG, School of Management, Louvain-la-Neuve.

Lendrevie, J., Lévy, J. and Lindon, D. (2007), *Mercator*, Paris, Dunod, 8th edition.

Levitt, T. (1960), Marketing Myopia, *Harvard Business Review*, 38, 4, pp. 45–56.

Levitt, T. (1975), Marketing Myopia, *Harvard Business Review*, 53, 5, pp. 26–183.

Marion, G. (2001), Le marketing relationnel existe-t-il ?, *Décisions marketing*, 22, Janvier–Avril, pp. 7–16.

McCarthy, J. (1960*), Basic Marketing: A Managerial Approach*, Homewood, IL, R.D. Irwin, 1st edition.

McKitterick, J.B. (1957), What is the Marketing Management Concept?, in *The Frontiers of Marketing Thought and Science*, F. Bass (ed.), Chicago, IL, American Marketing Association.

Möller, K. (2006), Comment on: The Marketing Mix Revisited: Toward the 21st Century Marketing, *Journal of Marketing Management*, 22, pp. 439–50.

Nader, R. (1965), Unsafe at Any Speed, New York, Brossman Publisher, Inc.

Narver, J.C., Slater, S.F. and MacLachlan, D.L. (2004), Responsive and Proactive Market Orientation and New-Product Success, *Journal of Product Innovation Management*, 21, pp. 334–47.

Rust R.T., Moorman C. and Bhalla G., (2010), Rethinking Marketing, *Harvard Business Review*, January–February.

Schendler, B.R. (1992), How Sony Keeps the Magic Going, *Fortune*, February.

Smith, A. (1776), *The Wealth of Nations*, London, Methuen.

Webster, F.E. (1981), Top Management's Concerns about Marketing: Issues for the 1980's, *Journal of Marketing*, 45, 3, pp. 9–16.

Webster, F.E. (1988), The Rediscovery of the Marketing Concept, *Business Horizons*, 31, 3, pp. 29–39.

Webster, F.E., Malter, A.J. and Ganesan, S. (2005), The Decline and Dispersion of Marketing Competence, *MIT Sloan Management Review*, 46, 4, pp. 35–43.

Wind, Y. (2008), A Plan to Invent the Marketing We Need Today, *MIT Sloan Management Review*, 49, 4, pp. 21–8.

CHAPTER TWO

THE MARKET ORIENTATION CONCEPT

The objective of this chapter is to introduce the market orientation (MO) concept presented as an alternative to the marketing concept. Internet technology is creating a dual-trading arena where traditional market actors have changing roles and new actors are emerging. To cope with this increased market complexity, a distinction is made between a cultural and an instrumental definition of the MO concept. MO as an organizational culture is a corporate business philosophy that puts the customer's satisfaction first, taking into account the role played by the other market actors. The MO, as an instrumental function, can be defined as a set of capabilities, activities and behaviours. A distinction is made between two types of capabilities in the instrumental function: the strategic marketing and the operational marketing capabilities.

Learning Objectives

When you have read this chapter, you should be able to understand:

- The MO concept
- The role performed by the different market actors
- The misconception in customer orientations
- The costs of a weak MO
- Shortcomings of the traditional marketing organization
- Characteristics of a market-driven organization

2.1 AN ALTERNATIVE: THE MARKET ORIENTATION CONCEPT

To deal with the complexity of the global market, in the 1990s, there was increasing focus in the academic literature on a reorientation of the traditional marketing concept. This new MO concept is the outgrowth of a double dissatisfaction: the weak implementation of the traditional marketing concept discussed in the previous chapter and, more important, its conceptual shortcomings which does not provide appropriate normative guidance for the firm in today's context. As pointed out in 1980 by the editors of the *Journal of Marketing, Day and Wind* (1980, p. 7), "There is a growing belief that a solely consumer-oriented search for differential advantages is an unbalanced approach to strategy formulation and that greater weight must be given to competitive factors and other stakeholders." The objective of this section is to propose a revised and updated definition of the marketing concept that we shall call the extended MO concept, called for short, the EMO concept.

Different conceptualizations of the MO concept have been proposed in the academic and professional literature. The main contributions are those of Day (1990, 1999b), Kohli and Jaworski (1990), Narver and Slater (1990), Lambin (1986, 2000) and Deshpandé and Farley (1998). For reviews of this literature, see Langerak (2003), Gotteland (2005), Gonzalez-Benito and Gonzalez-Benito (2005) and Kirca, Jayachandran and Bearden (2005). For a review of the relationship between MO and new product success, see Baker and Sinkula (2005). Kumar, Jones, Venkatesan and Leone (2011) have recently confirmed the impact of MO on the performance of the firm by analysing companies over a nine-year period from 1997 to 2005. Interestingly, they show that the sustained advantage in business performance is greater for the firms that very early on developed a MO. In what follows, we shall refer mainly to the early seminal contributions on the subject.

The Kohli and Jaworksi (K&J) model of market orientation

Kohli and Jaworski (1990) use the term "market orientation" to mean the implementation of the marketing concept, which is viewed retrospectively as an idealistic business philosophy short of practical value. These authors have proposed an operational definition of MO where two of the three pillars of the traditional marketing concept (customer focus and integration) are operationally defined. Kohli and Jaworski (1990) offer the following formal definition:

> Market orientation is organisational wide generation of market intelligence pertaining to current and future customers needs, dissemination of the intelligence across departments and organisational wide responsiveness to it. (Kohli and Jaworski, 1990, p. 69)

Thus, for these authors, the three key elements of MO are market intelligence generation, market intelligence dissemination and responsiveness.

- *Market intelligence generation* is a broader concept than customer intelligence. It includes monitoring factors like competition, government regulations, technology and other environmental forces. It pertains not just to customers' current needs but also to future needs as well.
- *Market intelligence dissemination* implies that responding to a market need requires the participation of virtually all departments in an organization. This means that market intelligence must be communicated to all the departments, through formal and/or informal formal dissemination procedures or through what is called horizontal communication (Zeithaml, Berry and Parasuraman, 1988).
- *Responsiveness* is the action taken in response to market intelligence that is generated and disseminated. Responsiveness takes the form of selecting target segments, designing the products or services that cater to current and future needs and promoting them.

Thus, the K&J model gives a more operational view of the first two pillars of the traditional marketing concept: customer focus and integration. It is interesting to note that, in the K&J model, the profit objective is not part of MO but rather a consequence, an opinion shared by Levitt (1969, p. 236), who considers that viewing profit as a component of MO is "like saying that the goal of human life is eating".

From an operational viewpoint, the K&J model remains very general, however. For instance, neither does it specify the type of market intelligence to collect nor the type of response to be taken by the firm. No direct link is made with the marketing function (Kohli, Jaworski and Kumar, 1993).

The Narver and Slater (N&S) model of market orientation

Narver and Slater (1990) are concerned by the problem of developing a valid measure of MO and of analysing its effect on business profitability. In the N&S model, MO is defined by reference to three behavioural components – customer orientation, competitor orientation and inter-functional co-ordination – with two decision criteria, that is, long-term focus and profitability. Customer and competitor orientation include all the activities involved in acquiring information about customers and competitors in the target market and disseminating it throughout the organization. Inter-functional co-ordination refers to the business-co-ordinated efforts involving business functions other than the marketing department.

If the similarity with the K&J model is substantial, the N&S model is not only more specific but also conceptually more restrictive, since it is limited to two market actors: customers and competitors. A strong point of the N&S model is its explicit insistence on competitors' orientation. As stated by Dickson (1992, p. 78), "The marketing concept can be linked to the invisible hand by recognizing that it is competition that forces a customer or market orientation. The greater the rivalry between sellers, the greater will be the customer focus and service." Thus, a competitive focus is not an alternative to a customer focus, as suggested by Ries and Trout (1986). On the contrary, a balance of the two orientations is needed (see Day and Wensley, 1988).

Using a sample of 140 business units consisting of commodity product businesses and non-commodity businesses, N&S have found a substantial positive effect of MO on the profitability of both types of businesses. As stated by N&S, this study gives marketing scholars and practitioners a basis beyond mere intuition for recommending the superiority of the MO concept over the traditional marketing concept (Deshpandé, Farley and Webster, 1993).

Pitfalls in implementing market orientation

The majority of studies linking the level of MO with the firm's business performance have found supportive evidence. Despite the credibility of the MO concept, contemporary research (Mason and Harris, 2005) finds that many companies have difficulties in evaluating the extent of MO of their company (Day, 1999a) and in implementing a high level of MO. For a review of eight common misinterpretations of MO among a sample of 101 practitioners, see Mason and Harris (2005). Several factors can explain this state of affairs.

First, there are a range of differing definitions of the MO concept itself. For the majority of MO theorists, MO is limited to two market players – customer and competitors – neglecting the other key market actors like distributors in B2C markets, influencers in B2B markets and other key market stakeholders like consumerist, ecologists. Thus the dominant definition of MO gives an incomplete view of the real complexity of today's markets. It is not surprising therefore that practitioners in B2C markets, for example, confronted with powerful mass merchandisers have difficulties in developing a genuine MO strategy.

Second, in those early studies, MO is viewed as an *organizational culture* and no formal links are established with the *marketing function* and no normative implications are proposed to implement effectively this MO culture. What role should the marketing function play and what capabilities should the marketing function have in an organization that has a strong MO? Thus, there is a missing link with the marketing function.

MO is more than simply a culture. A distinction should be made between a cultural and an instrumental definition of MO (Moorman and Rust, 1999; Gonzalez-Benito and

Gonzalez-Benito, 2005). MO as an *organizational culture* is a corporate business philosophy that puts the customer's satisfaction first, taking into account the role played by the other market actors. The MO as an *instrumental function* (the marketing function) can be defined as a set of capabilities, activities and behaviour needed to implement a strong MO. The majority of the MO studies published so far have not simultaneously used cultural and instrumental measures of MO. The merit of the EMO model presented hereafter is to provide an integrative framework analysing MO in its different dimensions, cultural and instrumental, thereby establishing a link with the marketing function.

Finally, as a result of these shortcomings in the definition of the MO concept, the scales proposed in the literature for measuring MO do not properly reflect the complexity of the market and provide incomplete measures of MO.

2.2   THE EXTENDED MODEL OF MARKET ORIENTATION

Building on these previous works and on their shortcomings in the MO concept, we adopt the following definition:
Several features have to be noted in this definition.

> Market orientation is a business corporate culture, disseminated in the organization through inter-functional co-ordination, having the objective to design and promote, at a profit for the firm, superior value solutions to the firm's direct and indirect customers and to the other involved market stakeholders. (Lambin, 2008)

- The term "design" refers to the analysis function performed by strategic marketing and the term "promote" refers to the firm's commercial arm articulated by operational marketing.
- By "superior value solutions", we mean bundles of products and services satisfying customers' articulated or latent needs which are better than competitors' offerings. Whereas products are about functionality, solutions are about outcomes or results that make life easier or better for customers.
- This definition recognizes the existence of different types of customers, "direct and indirect", and of other stakeholders.
- Inter-functional co-ordination is the vehicle used to disseminate the EMO culture in the organization.

Following Lambin (1986) and Webster (1992), this definition of MO makes a distinction between the cultural dimension of the MO concept and two dimensions of the instrumental function: analysis and action (see Table 2.1).

- *Culture* refers to the corporate business philosophy at the core of the social market economy, which places the emphasis (a) on the process of value creation for the market participants, (b) in a way compatible with the objective of sustainable development, (c) as the best means for the firm to achieve its profitability objective.

Table 2.1 The MO concept in theory

Components	Activity	Organizational position
Analysis	The strategic brain	The business units
Action	The commercial arm	The marketing function
Culture	A business philosophy	The corporation

Source: Lambin (2000/2007).

- *Analysis* refers to the firm's strategic brain or to its strategic capabilities (a) to develop market sensing tools to understand the market structure and to anticipate current and future customer's needs, (b) to design sustainable value solutions to customers' problems and (c) to differentiate these solutions from competition.
- *Action* refers to the commercial arm of the firm and to its operational marketing instruments (the 4Ps or 7Ps) used to make the value proposition (a) known, (b) conveniently accessible and (c) at a price affordable by the target customer group.

Thus a distinction is made between two types of capabilities in the instrumental function: the *strategic marketing* capabilities (analysis) to identify market opportunities and the positioning options for the firm and the *operational marketing* capabilities (action through the 4Ps or 7Ps) required to implement the options taken. This distinction is important to avoid falling into the trap of the short-term perspective of the 4Ps or 7Ps paradigm which refers only to the "action" dimension. The effectiveness of the operational marketing programme will be determined by the solidity of the strategic options taken by the firm. The weakness of the strategic thinking is one of the main causes of the high failure rate of new products launching (Christensen, Cook and Hall, 2005).

Figure 2.1 summarizes the concept of the EMO model. Strategic marketing can be "responsive" or "proactive" depending on the types of needs addressed (expressed or latent) and operational marketing can be "transactional" or "relationship" depending on the type of market served and the intensity of the trade relationship between the buyer and the seller.

Central in this EMO model is the view of the market as a complex grouping of market stakeholders – suppliers, customers (direct and indirect), competitors, distributors, influencers and other stakeholders – representing the civil society voices that gain mutual benefit from one another. Thus, the existence of sub-orientations in the EMO concept is recognized. The MO configuration of each specific market can, of course, be different but this presentation has the merit of greater generality.

The proposed model assigns responsibilities for the three dimensions of the EMO concept: "culture" or the business philosophy is a transversal corporate responsibility assumed

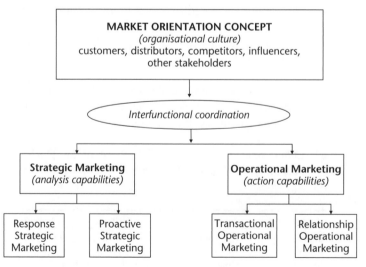

Figure 2.1   The EMO
Source: Lambin (2000/2007).

by the CEO of the firm through inter-functional co-ordination; "analysis" is the transversal responsibility of strategic marketing assumed by the head of each business unit or, in a small business company, by a cross-functional group of managers; "action" is typically the responsibility of operational marketing assumed by the marketing function. Thus a link is established here with the marketing function which defines the content of market-driven management.

Is the EMO model really different from the marketing concept?

To reply to this question, one can identify four elements of differentiation between the marketing concept and the EMO concept.

- The marketing concept is basically customer-oriented, while the EMO concept is oriented towards customers, and also towards the other key market actors: competitors, distributors, influencers and other stakeholders, be they offline or online.
- The marketing concept is based on the commonsensical market-pull model (response strategic marketing), while the EMO concept is based, of course, on the market-pull and also on the technology-push (proactive strategic marketing) innovation models.
- The marketing concept in practice is basically "action-oriented" using the 4Ps (or the 7Ps) paradigm, while the MO concept is based on the solution approach, a more customer-centric view.
- The marketing concept is generally confined to the marketing function, while the EMO concept is viewed as an organizational culture disseminated at all levels and in every function of the firm.

One could add that marketing has been developed by reference to physical markets while today, with the development of the Internet technology, most firms operate in a dual-trading arena, physical and electronic markets. In this new and more complex environment, the roles of strategic and of operational marketing are deeply modified.

The need for a new terminology

For consistency and clarity, the adoption of the EMO model would imply some change in the vocabulary commonly used in the marketing discipline. The term *market-driven or market-focused management* appears to be preferable to the popular term *marketing management* and this is for four reasons.

- First, as mentioned above, the term "marketing" has lost credibility among the general public (in particular among management students) and is heavily loaded. It suggests more selling and advertising than customers' and stakeholders' needs satisfaction.
- Second, the label market-driven management suggests that the concept is not exclusively the concern of the marketing function. Rather, all the departments should participate in the analysis of the market needs and configuration and in the design of the appropriate response.
- Third, the label market-driven management is less politically charged in that it does not inflate the importance of the marketing function and is therefore more likely to be accepted by the other departments.
- Fourth, the term focuses on the market and not only on customers and designates other market actors and environmental forces. The term *marketing management* should be used only to describe the tasks of operational marketing.

In what follows, we shall analyse in more depth the managerial and organizational implications of this business philosophy both in the global traditional market (GTM) and in the global electronic market (GEM).

2.3   ACTORS IN THE GLOBAL MARKET

In a market economy, an ecosystem is a complex grouping of market actors, companies and customers, suppliers, competitors, distributors, influencers and partners that gain mutual benefit from one another. In physical markets, we identify five market actors: suppliers, direct and end-customers, distributors, competitors, influencers and other market stakeholders. As suggested by Guo and Sun (2004), with the development of the Internet technology, markets are shifting towards two specialized yet collaborative global markets: GEMs and GTMs. The GEM globally produces and distributes digital products and services, while the GTM collaborates with GEM to consume or continue the physical part of production and distribution

The firms in traditional markets extend their demand and supply to GEM, while firms of electronic markets create new demand and supply of both GTM and GEM. New market actors coming from GEM are playing an increasingly important role. In what follows, we shall describe the role and motivation of the key actors in the global market as presented in Figure 2.2.

Direct and end-customers

Customer satisfaction is at the core of the MO concept. It implies the commitment to understand customer needs, to create value for the customer and to anticipate new customers' problems. Customers may be close to or remote from the firm depending on the type of

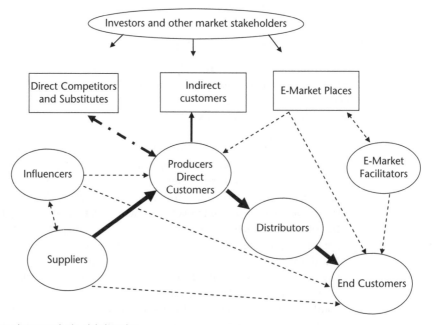

Figure 2.2   Key market actors in the global market
Source: Lambin (2008).

organization: B2C or B2B markets. The B2B firms generally operate within an industrial chain and are confronted with several customers: its direct customer and the customers of its customer, the end-customer being situated at the end of the chain. Being customer-oriented involves taking actions based on market intelligence, not only on direct customers, but on end-customers as well. Increasingly B2C and B2B customers have access to the GEM and are ordering across country borders. They expect broader selections, cheaper prices and customized services.

Partners and indirect demand

Direct and end-customers belong to the traditional or core market of the firm and express a "direct demand" for the goods or services and the firm knows who these customers are and how to satisfy them. In many sectors, however, there are additional customers groups representing a potential demand often ignored because firms are not able to reach these customers directly. This "indirect demand" exists because the value of certain products is realized when they are used with other products. At first sight, for instance, there is no reason why *Nestlé*, a manufacturer of chocolate confections, should have any dealing with *Baxter International*, a medical device conglomerate and distribution company. In fact, the two companies have formed an alliance for jointly offering liquid nutritional supplements to be used intravenously with hospital patients who therefore are indirect customers of *Nestlé*.

To become fully demand-driven by satisfying indirect demand as well, many companies have adopted a "solution-selling" approach. For the company aiming at becoming a solution provider, it is unlikely that it will have the resources to supply all the required solutions components (e.g., products, service, financing). Therefore the challenge is to find the right partners to take advantage of indirect demand. To target direct demand, wholesalers and retailers are the traditional business partners. For targeting indirect demand, many more functions than simply location and assortment must be provided. The types of partners found in various customer ecosystems are aggregators, integrators, syndicators, educators, and underwriters (Manning and Thorne, 2003). In B2B markets, for example, catalogue aggregators are important indirect customers based in e-marketplaces.

Distributors and resellers in GTM

The struggle for the control of the end-market has always been a major issue both for manufacturers and for distributors. In the food sector, for many years, manufacturers have succeeded in restricting the role of distributors to the physical tasks of distribution. Their relationship was more that of partners having common interests, even if conflicting interests were inevitably also present.

The retailer looks for maximum return on space and contribution to overall retailer image. The supplier seeks maximum shelf space, trial for new (unproved) products and preference over competitors. It is easy to see where the potential for conflicts lie.

The shift of power from suppliers to mass retailers in the FMCG sector requires the adoption of a much more proactive strategy vis-à-vis distributors. Today, as underlined above, key changes in the environment include increasing retailer concentration, the growth of internationally based retail buying groups and the growing use of information technology by European food retailers. While suppliers would like to see retailers as partners, it is clear that retailers tend to see their relationships with manufacturers more in terms of competition than co-operation.

The level of competition or co-operation is influenced by the market structure that determines the power of prospective partners in a market. With the exception of the situation where both levels of concentration are weak, manufacturers have to explicitly define appropriate relationship marketing strategy vis-à-vis distributors. Internet technology is changing the balance of power between producers and distributors, thereby creating new market opportunities.

Direct and substitute competitors

The traditional marketing concept focuses solely on customers' needs and ignores the effects of competition, thereby providing an incomplete view of a market. Competitors, be they direct or substitute competitors, are key market participants and the attitude to be adopted towards competition is central in any strategy formulation, since it will serve as the basis for defining competitive advantage. As noted by Trout (1985), "Knowing what the customer wants isn't too helpful if a dozen other companies are already serving the customers wants."

The objective is to set out a strategy based on a realistic assessment of the forces at work and to determine the most appropriate means of achieving defined objectives. Competitors' orientation includes all the activities involved in acquiring and disseminating information about competitors in the target market.

The firm's autonomy is influenced by two kinds of factors: the sector's competitive structure and the importance of the product's perceived value for customers. With the exception of the situation of perfect competition, an explicit account of competitors' position and behaviour is required in the most frequently observed common market situations.

In saturated or stagnant markets, the aggressiveness of the competitive struggle tends to increase and a key objective is to counter rivals' actions. In this competitive climate, the destruction of the adversary often becomes the primary preoccupation. The risk of a strategy based only on warfare marketing however, is that too much energy is devoted to driving rivals away at the risk of losing sight of the objective of satisfying customers' needs. A proper balance between customers' and competitors' orientations is therefore essential and a MO, as described in this chapter, tends to facilitate the implementation of this objective.

Influencers

In many markets, in addition to the traditional market actors – customers, distributors and competitors – other individuals or organizations can play important roles in advising, recommending or prescribing brands, companies, products or services to customers or to distributors. The most obvious example is the pharmaceutical market where doctors exert a key influence on the success of a drug and are viewed by pharmaceutical companies as the most important market player or intermediate customer, even if they are not actually users, buyers or payers. A similar role is assumed in the home building market by architects, who are important influencers for many construction pieces of equipment, like window frames, glass, heating systems and so on. Independent designers in the furniture market or in the "haute couture" or fashion markets are also playing an important role as influencers. The development of consumer generated media on the Web has contributed to increasing the role of opinion leaders.

E-tailers and e-marketplaces

The market forces of a GEM come from the demand and supply of global services generated by global market participants in both traditional and electronic markets. A GEM can be defined as a virtual online market, that is, a network of company interactions and relation-ships, where consumers, suppliers, distributors and sellers find and exchange information, conduct trade and collaborate with each other via an aggregation of content from multiple suppliers.

In GEM, electronic retailers, or e-tailers, use the Internet as their communication means of retailing. Pure play e-tailers use Internet exclusively, while brick-and-click e-tailers use the Internet to promote their goods or services and also have the traditional physical store accessible to consumers. Pure play e-tailers, like Amazon.com and Dell Computers, are gen-erating higher profit margins by eliminating the expenses associated with a physical retail space (rent, labour, inventory, etc.). Moreover, they can reach customers worldwide 24 hours a day, 7 days a week. For customers, and for goods like books, DVD, electronic equipment, e-tailing can be a fast and convenient way to shop. But problems can sometimes occur for securing payments, goods delivery and exposure of privacy.

In B2B markets, a growing number of firms are experimenting with buying and sell-ing goods through e-marketplaces, which become increasingly important for the organization of procurement and sales activities. An e-marketplace may be defined as an inter-organizational information system, which allows the participating buyers and suppliers to exchange information about prices and product offerings, thereby eliminating inefficien-cies of traditional supply chain.

E-entrepreneurs have launched marketplaces, like www.netbuy.com, with a virtual inven-tory four times larger than the biggest distributor in the electronic components market. As a result, product searches that took a week of catalogue sifting and phone calls now take seconds. Companies such as Chemdex, (www.chemdex.com), PlasticsNet (www.plasticsnet.com), Alibaba (www.alibaba.com) for international trade among many others are doing the same thing. These agents are called catalogue aggregators. Their challenge is to gather the information from hundreds of catalogues of product offerings into a database for presenta-tion on a single website easily accessible. These catalogues must be constantly maintained as products availability and prices change.

As observed by Rask and Kragh (2004), the main motivational factor for buyers to partici-pate in e-marketplaces is efficiency, that is, obtaining price, process time and cost reductions through paperless transactions. For sellers, following existing buyers and suppliers and fear of falling behind technological development are the main motives.

Online marketplaces provide an efficient platform connecting buyers and sellers from around the world. By making it easier to compare products attributes and prices, e-market-places put a downward pressure on prices. In a survey conducted by the Boston Consulting Group (www.bcg.com), 24 per cent of sellers using e-marketplaces said they have felt price pressure as existing customers move online, and 79 per cent said they expected to feel it in the near future. Thus, with the development of e-marketplaces, sellers must prepare to compete more aggressively on prices.

Online market facilitators

Market facilitators are a special group of service providers in both GTM and GEM. They are motivated to provide infrastructure of markets and secure the operations of markets. In GTM, banks, warehouse, shipping companies, customs and taxation offices are market facilitators. In GEM, providers of Internet services, online financial services, logistics, secu-rity and legal services are the new market facilitators. Where disintermediation takes place, the absence of physical contact between the seller and the buyer creates a new need among consumers, the need for assistance in collecting and processing information. In traditional markets, and in particular in B2C markets, the seller has more information than the buyer:

information on costs, levels of quality, product availability and prices of competing or substitute products. Different levels of middlemen (wholesalers, retailers, agents) were there to disseminate this information along the distribution chain. The elimination of these filters transfers the responsibility of the search and of the selection costs directly to the consumer who is confronted with a problem of information overload.

Towards an integrated dual-trading arena

The development of Internet technologies in the global economy is shaping a dual-trading arena with two types of market: GTMs and GEMs. The motives and expected benefits for participating in this dual-trading arena are different for each participant.

- *Consumers* expect broader selections, lower prices, higher quality and more personalized services. They have the ability to easily compare prices between multiple vendors and to search larger catalogues. They can interact with people thousands of miles away.
- *Retailers* have an unprecedented opportunity to increase their trading area, using the services of e-market facilitators. Pure e-tailers can reduce overhead costs and transaction costs, both order-taking and customer service costs, by automating processes.
- *Digital producers* supply GEM with digital products such as software, MP songs and digital books. To their customers, they propose "versioning" (Shapiro and Varian, 1998), that is, the strategy of offering information goods in different versions, at zero or very low cost for them, to appeal to different types of customers.
- *Physical producers*, the traditional producers of physical products and onsite services, can enlarge their market size and decrease production costs by using the services provided by e-market facilitators.
- In markets driven by electronic commerce, a new breed of intermediaries – the "infomediaries" – is emerging and assumes the management of information on behalf of the customer. The success factor for an infomediary is customer trust. This new type of middleman can solve four problems for the consumer: (a) to reduce the costs of collecting information, (b) to provide relevant and unbiased information, (c) to certify the reliability and quality of the suppliers and (d) to facilitate transactions.

In contrast with traditional intermediaries who typically relay the manufacturer's message and share its profit margin, these new networks of middlemen reverse the communication flow through systematic use of tenders. The GEMs typically offer a wide variety of ancillary services required by members of the trading community. They perform three particular functions:

- They act as an exchange for business transactions – not only for purchasing but also for checking prices and stock availability, invoicing and order chasing.
- They manage catalogue content, converting product information into a common format understood by all parties.
- They provide additional services to support the trading process, from shipping, payment and tax to online auction, tendering and vetting a company financial status.

In the Internet age, the global market can be viewed as dual-trading arena (see Figure 2.3) where all market participants can take advantage over GTM and GEM. Collaboration in and between GTM and GEM would reduce costs of production, distribution and procurement (Guo and Sun, 2004).

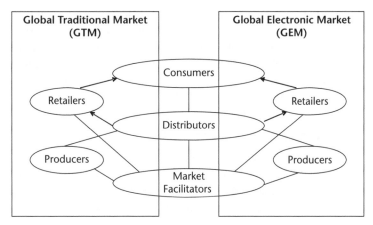

Figure 2.3 The global market: a dual-trading arena prescribers
Source: Adapted from Guo and Sun (2004).

Other market stakeholders

In a social market economy, many other actors can have a powerful influence in the market. Who are these other stakeholders? A popular definition is that "stakeholders" are any group or individual who can affect or are affected by the firm's objectives. Thus in addition to the above key market players, other stakeholders could be employees, unions, non-governmental organizations (NGOs), local community, consumerists, investors and, last but not least, the environment. The *stakeholder approach* asserts that the firm is responsible to and should be run for the benefit of number of constituencies, that is, its stakeholders. The stakeholder approach does not specify, however, which stakeholder group has priority over another (Mitchell, Agle and Wood, 1997). At the heart of the stakeholders model – a somewhat slippery concept – is the principle that all persons must be respected and that the firm exists to equally satisfy all stakeholders, a complex objective. Multiple stakeholders only compound the complexities.

2.4   THREE MISCONCEPTIONS IN CUSTOMER ORIENTATION

Customer orientation is at the core of the MO concept. In implementing the customer orientation concept, Day (1999b) draws our attention to three common misconceptions or misinterpretations of the customer orientation concept: (a) being compelled by customers, (b) feeling superior to customers, (c) becoming oblivious to customers. Being customer-driven implies maintaining a difficult balance between a customer focus and the concern for superior profitability.

Becoming compelled by customers

Some firms, overreacting to a myopic product orientation, are inclined to do whatever customers want through unrestricted line extensions and promotions, believing that every customer is worth pursuing. As a result, one observes a proliferation of weakly differentiated brands, too many line extensions and variants with minor differences, clogging supermarket shelves and confusing consumers. For example, the toothpaste brand *Colgate* has 33 variants and *Crest* 23. Understanding customers – not necessarily following them blindly – is the key point.

What is missing in consumer-compelled companies is the discipline needed to set priorities for which market to serve with which benefits and features, instead of trying to be all things to everyone. Remember, the objective is not to meet customers' needs at any cost, but at a profit for the firm. The profit objective will always have priority over the objective customers' needs satisfaction. Meeting unprofitable consumers' needs is the task of the State or of not-for-profit or relationship organizations.

Feeling superior to customers

Other firms make the opposite mistake and consider that customers are unable to envision breakthrough products or services, because customers tend to respond most positively to what is familiar and comfortable (a rear mirror view) and research methods are incapable of sorting out customers contradictory requirements, in particular because customers in a survey aren't choosing with their own money.

As put by Day (1999b, p. 34), this criticism of traditional market research fails to recognize the difference between asking customers to identify a problem (a realistic objective) and expecting them to develop solutions (an unrealistic objective). Thus what matters is an "intimate understanding" of customers' behaviour and problems. For instance, the accountant might state that a rapid numerical manipulation of data is a need but, before the invention of the computer, he could not have stated that he wanted a computer. Thus, to be customer-driven means seeing past the short-sighted and superficial inputs of customers, to gain a deep understanding of customers problems, latent needs and changing requirements. As underlined above, a large variety of approaches exist to identify unarticulated needs, from observation to disciplines like anthropology and psychology.

Becoming oblivious to the customer

Some successful firms are so impressed by their success that they no longer view that the market is changing. This was the case of *IBM* in the 1980s and of *Levi Strauss* in the 1990s. These firms achieved prosperity because at one time they had a clear and widely shared concept of how to deliver superior customer value. In retrospect, the *Levi Strauss Company* in the 1990s exhibited the typical symptoms of a self-centred organization. Having created the market, *Levi Strauss* management felt that it was benefiting from such brand awareness and brand leadership position that nothing could happen to itself.

2.5   THE COSTS OF A WEAK MARKET ORIENTATION

The absence of a strong MO culture may have significant impact on the competitiveness of the firm. Several potential problems may arise:

- *Environment monitoring.* If the marketing function is the only one in charge of managing the interface between the firm and its environment, is there not a risk to see the announced changes underestimated by the other functions within the organization? Have the marketing staff enough credibility and enough weight to induce major changes within the firm? For example, it is surprising to see how the chemical industry was caught unprepared when new legislation suddenly imposed severe restrictions on non-recyclable plastic bottles, while this environmentalist issue had been a much-debated question for more than 20 years.

- *The links between R&D and innovations.* If the MO is confined within the marketing department, the dialogue between R&D and strategic marketing will be more difficult and the link between inventions and innovations weaker. As a consequence, R&D activities will give rise to fewer successful implementations of inventions. According to a recent European study, it seems that fundamental research in Western Europe is indeed less productive than in the United States and in Japan.

- *New product development process.* Developing a new product is typically a cross-functional effort which involves not only the marketing department, but all other functions as well. In companies where the dominant culture is not MO, new product development processes are generally sequential and the project is passed from one specialist to another. This process ends up with a desirable "target price" reflecting the successive internal costs and which becomes the market price suggested to (or imposed upon) sales personnel. In a market-driven company, on the other hand, it is the "acceptable market price" which is identified upfront and which becomes the constraint to be met by R&D and production people. The success rate of new products is much higher in this second case.

- *Competitive advantage and the value chain.* The definition of a sustainable competitive advantage is a major responsibility of strategic marketing. As shown by Porter (1980), the value chain is a basic tool for diagnosing competitive advantage and finding ways to create and sustain it. Thus, a firm must define its competitive advantage by reference to the different value activities – primary and support – that are performed. Each of these value activities, and not only the marketing activities, can contribute to a firm's relative cost position and create a basis for differentiation. If the firm is not market-oriented, it is not easy to induce the non-marketing activities to participate in the search for a sustainable competitive advantage. The risk is then to base competitive positioning on minor points of differentiation of low added value to the customer.

- *Financial implication of sales promotions.* A good indicator of performance for the marketing department is an increase in sales revenue that, in non-expandable markets, implies a market share increase. In B2C markets, an easy but short-sighted way to achieve this objective is to embark on trade promotions and coupon offers which is in fact a disguised form of price cutting. These promotional actions, because of their effectiveness, generate strong retaliatory actions from competition who respond by more promotions or coupon offers. This escalation leads to a situation of almost permanent promotions that eventually undermine brand loyalty and profitability. As a result of this "marketing myopia", marketing activities are under increasing challenge and control from the finance department that questions the wisdom of this type of action.

Exhibit 2.1   The top priority of innovations

More than two-thirds of the 100 global companies surveyed in 2004 by the Conference Board indicated that innovation is a top priority (Conference Board, 30 June 2004). Separate research on the manufacturing sector confirms the expected pace: By 2007, noted Deloitte, sales of new products introduced in the three preceding years are expected to generate 34 per cent of total revenue – up from 21 per cent only seven years ago (Deloitte Research, March 2004). Yet CEOs are often disappointed by the level of innovation in their businesses, a situation for which they hold marketing at least partially accountable.

Source: Webster, Malter and Ganesan (2005, p. 41).

- *Transactional versus relationship selling.* Finding new customers is traditionally an important objective of transactional marketing that is mostly interested in immediate sales results. In mature markets, this objective loses relevance and cultivating the existing customer base becomes the priority goal. In B2B marketing, the repeat purchase rate of satisfied customers is around 90 to 95 per cent (Goderis, 1998) and, therefore, attracting new customers is viewed as an intermediate objective. Relationship selling tries to create and maintain a long-term mutually profitable relationship with customers. This customer satisfaction objective, however, is not just the responsibility of the marketing function, but again of all other functions participating in the process of value creation for the customer. Thus, everyone within the organization must share the customer satisfaction objective.

Thus, it appears that the lack of MO of a given firm may seriously undermine its capacity to meet the challenges of the new macro-marketing environment.

2.6   THE CHANGING MARKETING ORGANIZATION

The analysis of today's markets reveals an explosion of customers segments, products, media vehicles and distribution channels that has made market-driven management more complex, more costly and less effective. With the growing fragmentation of markets, products and services options available have doubled or even tripled. As sub-brands and line extensions multiply, so do the messages and the media required to sell them. An increasing number of distribution channels such as the Internet, product resellers, large retailers and online marketplaces have become important players that sell to consumers and businesses alike. All these factors taken together have dramatically pushed up the complexity and the cost of designing

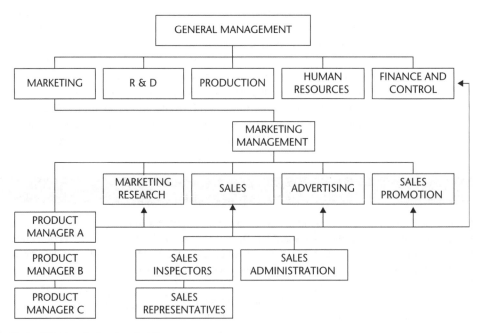

Figure 2.4   The traditional marketing department
Source: Lambin (2000/2007).

and managing a marketing programme, just when boards and CEOs have been pushing their chief marketing officers (CMOs) to improve the return on marketing expenditures. To meet this new challenge, a new model of marketing management must be developed.

Traditional organization of the marketing function

From an organizational viewpoint, the implementation of the traditional marketing concept has been achieved by the creation of powerful marketing departments in charge of both strategic and operational marketing. Brand and product management play a key role (see Figure 2.4) in these organizational structures. A brand manager is concerned with the strategic issues such as R&D and product innovation, branding policies and communication, business analysis and forecasting. His or her task is also to organize a dialogue with the other functions within the firm and to co-ordinate and control all the operations or activities related to the brand. A separate sales department is responsible for the sales tasks and for getting products on to retailers' shelves. This system, adopted by most consumer goods companies and also by many industrial firms, contributed to establishing manufacturers' brand dominance in the market. To review the latest work on the influence of the marketing department within the firm, see Comstock, Gulati and Liguori (2010) and Verhoef and Leeflang (2009).

The brand management system

According to a survey conducted in France (Kueviakoe, 1996), the responsibilities of a typical brand or product manager would be the ones presented in Table 2.2, in their order of importance. An analysis of Table 2.2 suggests that most of these responsibilities pertain more to operational than to strategic marketing. In principle, the product manager is supposed to be responsible for the medium- to long-term development of the product, while sales people are responsible for the implementation of the marketing plan in the short term, under the leadership of the marketing manager.

The brand management organization introduces several *advantages*:

- The presence of a brand manager creates dynamism and emulation in the organization by designating individuals in charge of the development of the different brands. He or she behaves more like an entrepreneur responsible for his or her own product development (a mini president).
- Smaller brands are less neglected, because they have a product advocate.
- The brand manager is well placed to harmonize and co-ordinate all the activities related to his or her own brand or product, thereby increasing efficiency.
- The product manager can react more quickly to problems in the marketplace than a committee of functional specialists.

Table 2.2 Main responsibilities of brand managers: a survey

To co-ordinate all activities related to the product	To order marketing research studies
To prepare the marketing plan	To brief market research companies
To fix the sales price	To design and decide on packaging
To estimate the unit cost	To choose the advertising platform
To prepare the marketing budget	To monitor laws and regulations
To compare actual and expected sales	To train the sales force
To propose promotional actions	To prepare the contracts and agreements
To assist the sales force	

Source: Adapted from Kueviakoe (1996, p. 81).

- The brand manager is a single point of contact for all the other functions and therefore internal communication is greatly facilitated.
- Being responsible for the preparation of the annual marketing plan, the product manager can concentrate on developing a cost-effective marketing mix for the product to ensure its profitability.
- In charge of the medium- to long-term development of the product, the brand manager can initiate product improvements in co-operation with R&D people to take advantage of new market opportunities.

But a price has to be paid for these advantages. Among the *problems and difficulties* generated by a brand management organization, let us consider the following points:

- The brand management system is based on the principle of decentralization and delegation, and this implies a clear political accord between the managing director and the marketing manager.
- The brand manager has a staff position and as such does not necessarily have enough authority to carry out his or her responsibilities effectively. He or she has to rely on persuasion to get the co-operation of advertising, sales, manufacturing and other departments. The function is demanding and requires diplomatic skills.
- The brand management system is costly and implies a duplication of contacts between the sales force, the functional specialists and the product managers.
- Brand managers are generally junior people who normally manage their brand for only a short time. This short-term involvement induces them to give priority to short-term operational marketing activities, at the expense of longer-term strategic thinking.

In this structure, it is up to the marketing manager to deal with these potential conflicts between the product managers, the sales force and the other functional departments and to delineate clearly the limits of the product managers' role and responsibility. Brand managers report directly to the marketing manager who can therefore devote time and effort to strategic issues in close liaison with the managing director.

Rust, Moorman and Bhalla (2010) have recently indicated that, in view of the changes generated by Internet that facilitate direct interaction with customers, companies must radically review their organization in a way that puts the objective of cultivating relationships ahead of the objective of building brands. The pros and cons of relationship marketing will be examined in more details in Chapter 18.

Strategic marketing in small business firms

The product or brand management organization is a costly structure unaffordable by a small- or medium-sized business firm. An alternative which works well is the cross-functional team in charge of strategic marketing issues. It consists of the key functional managers (operations, finances, human resources, operational marketing) and is chaired by the firm's CEO. Two different structures can be considered:

- The *temporary ad hoc team* – or task force – in charge of a specific problem during a limited period of time, typically the launching of new product.
- The *permanent cross-functional team* reviewing regularly (twice a month) strategic marketing problems, typically the management of the firm's product portfolio, a task which does not necessarily require a full-time job.

One of the benefits of this organization structure, in addition to its low cost, is the dissemination of the MO culture in the entire organization.

A credibility gap for marketers

As put in a McKinsey report (Cassidy, Freeling and Kiewell, 2005), "Marketers have a credibility problem because the creativity that is their lifeblood often runs counter to the discipline required to excel in other parts of the organisation." Today's marketers must tailor and integrate their strategies with a more complex set of approaches to product development, supply chains, manufacturing and relationship selling and so on. These approaches imply close co-operation with the other functions. In the McKinsey survey most CEOs expressed some variation on the concern: "Marketers in spite of their creative strengths don't think like businessmen." Many CEOs, for instance, expressed frustration at being asked for funds in absence of – or even in contradiction to – data regarding the proposed initiatives

In recent years, several studies published in the United States (Rust et al., 2004; Cassidy, Freeling and Kiewell, 2005; Webster, Malter and Ganesan, 2005) and in Europe have evidenced a growing dissatisfaction from CEOs and from board directors with the performance of marketing and in particular with its lack of financial accountability and with the low productivity of traditional functional organizations. The main reproaches or criticisms about traditional marketing's performance are the following:

- To have confined MO to the marketing department, thereby preventing the development of a market culture within the organization.
- To be a big spender and to have failed to put in place metrics and processes to track the impact of marketing initiatives.
- To have privileged tactical marketing instruments over strategic ones, by giving precedence to advertising and promotions over product innovations.
- To be risk-adverse by placing more emphasis on minor market-pull innovations over more revolutionary (but more risky) technology-push innovations.
- To have responded to environmentalism by green advertising unsupported by prior product redesign, thereby undermining the credibility of green marketing.
- To have neglected in B2C markets the "fewer frills, low price" segments, thereby opening the door to private labels development.
- To have created confrontational rather than collaborative relationships with large retailers and to lose the battle of the brand in several product categories.
- To lose contact with the new consumer and to have failed to develop a long-term relationship with the customer base.

Marketers need a more rigorous approach, one that jettisons mentalities and behaviour from advertising's golden age and treats operational marketing not as "spend" but as the investment is really is (Court, 2004).

Today, an increasing number of firms believe that the marketing function must reinvent itself in a way that reinforces the overall MO of the firm. Thus the problem is not with marketing, but rather with the marketing function (see Webster, Malter and Ganesan, 2005; Christensen, Cook and Hall, 2005; Wind, 2008). In the new competitive environment, market-driven management has become too important to be left to the marketing function alone. In the new world economy, the marketing directors' jobs have never been so difficult but also so potentially rewarding: Today's marketers need to be skilled and well trained to

Table 2.3 Evolution of the priority role of marketing

Product orientation	The firm is product-oriented and has an *inside-in* perspective
Sales orientation	The firm is sales-oriented and has an *inside-out* perspective
Customer orientation	The firm is customer-oriented and has an *outside-in* perspective
Market orientation	The firm is market-oriented and has a *global* perspective

Source: Lambin (2000/2007).

analyse international markets, understand the cultural differences and get insights from consumers from all over the world (Table 2.3).

One major issue faced by many companies is where and how to position Internet-based channels in the marketing organization. Early organization systems isolated Internet channels from the rest of the business, thereby creating conflicts between GTM and GEM. The real challenge is to integrate the Internet in the core business by adopting brick-and-click marketing systems.

The evolution of the changing priority role of marketing is summarized in Table 2.3. The environmental changes mentioned above all imply a reinforcement of the MO for companies operating in highly industrialized markets. Companies need to review their strategic options in order to face the new challenges presented by the economic, competitive and socio-cultural environment and by the internationalization of the world economy.

2.7   CHARACTERISTICS OF A MARKET-DRIVEN ORGANIZATION

The developments in the macro-marketing environment and the wide adoption of a MO at all levels of the firm have had several implications for the marketing function.

First, the brand management system so successfully adopted by many companies during the past 40 years seems, today, unable to face the complex challenges of the new environment. As put by George, Freeling and Court (1994) and Webster, Malter and Ganesan (2005), brand managers today are:

- too junior, too inexperienced, and too narrowly centred on operational marketing,
- too removed from the source of value added (which is not just advertising),
- too overwhelmed with day-to-day tasks (like developing trade promotions),
- too focused on implementing quick fix solutions that will get them promoted in 18 months.

They are not the "mini general managers" they were supposed to be and are not able to provide the cross-functional leadership required in complex markets.

Second, as the MO concept becomes more and more accepted and increasingly implemented across all functions within the firm – in particular as a result of the adoption of the solution-to-a-problem strategy – the specific role of marketing as a separate function is coming under questioning and has to be reassessed.

Main characteristics of an MO organization

As suggested by Day (1999b), the main characteristics of a market-driven company can be summarized as follows:

- An externally oriented *culture* with dominant beliefs, values and behaviours emphasizing superior customer value and the continual quest for new sources of advantages.

- Distinctive *capabilities in market sensing*, market relating, and anticipatory strategic thinking. This means market-driven firms are better educated about their markets and better able to form close relationships with valued customers.
- A *configuration* that enables the entire organization continually to anticipate and respond to customer requirements and market conditions.

Supporting these three elements is a shared knowledge base in which the organization collects and disseminates its market insights. This knowledge builds relationships with customers, forms the company strategy and increases the focus of employees on the needs of the market.

The challenge for a market-driven organization is to devise a structure that combines the depth of knowledge found in a vertical hierarchy with responsiveness of horizontal process teams as illustrated in the matrix organization form presented in Figure 2.5.

Towards cross-functional forms of organizations

The matrix form is a grid-like organizational structure that allows a company to address multiple business dimensions using a multiple command structure (Sy and D'Annunzio, 2000). As illustrated in Figure 2.5, basic matrix structures have two dimensions: a functional responsibility and a specific project, such as a new product launch, category management or customer relationship management assumed by a cross-functional team, also called *Venture Marketing Organization* (VMO). The matrix allows companies to leverage resources while staying small and task-oriented and to focus employees on MO. This matrix structure also facilitates the dissemination of the market culture throughout the entire organization and encourages innovation and fast action.

This cross-functional team approach extends the idea of venture teams as a way of responding to high-priority opportunities faster than conventional organizational approaches allow. The VMO adopts the principles of venture capitalism. They have a number of defining characteristics (Aufreiter, Lawver and Lum, 2000).

- Fluidity to keep pace with the market; the VMO continually reconfigures, with little formal structure or fixed membership in opportunity teams.

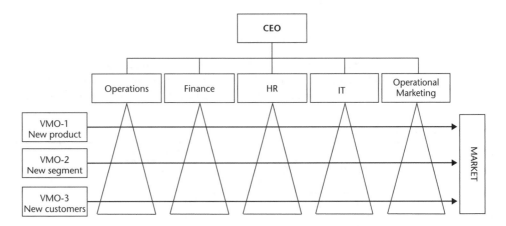

Figure 2.5 Typical organization of a market-oriented company
Source: Lambin (2000/2007).
VMO: Venture Marketing Organisation.

- People have allocated roles, not jobs: the issue is managing talent within the organization.
- Fast decision-making is made from the top. Opportunity identification is everyone's job.
- Resources are focused on the highest payback opportunity and losers are quickly pruned.

According to McKinsey, today's marketing organizations are organized around two roles, integrators and specialists, linked together through teams and processes rather than functional or business unit structures.

Integrators (or process managers) are marketers with broad skills who will play the critical role of guiding activities across the firm's entire value chain, identifying which market segments to compete in and which levers to pull to maximize long-term profitability. They will be charged with tearing down the walls that divide function from function and with leading cross-functional teams to execute these strategies. Typically, they will be responsible for marketing strategy development. Integrators can be responsible for a distinct end-user segment (consumer integrators) or specific group of business customers like giant retailers (customer integrator) or be responsible for a process, like new product development (process integrators).

Specialists will provide the technical and specialized skills required to successfully implement the marketing strategy in the different disciplines such as marketing research, business intelligence, pricing strategy, advertising, promotion, online communication, direct marketing and so on. The trend will also be towards sub-contracting to outside specialists marketing activities such as market research and analysis, database management and even the execution of some operational marketing tasks.

In this new organizational context, inter-functional co-ordination is particularly important because it implies the involvement of all levels in the firm's organization. The key idea here is to consider that MO is the business of everyone and not only of the marketing people. But marketers have a key role to play in disseminating the MO culture within the organization. They have to take the lead in turning the organization in this direction. For a review on the impact of the diffusion of MO as a social learning process, see Lam, Kraus and Ahearne (2010).

Levels of market orientation

In the general case, that is when the four key market participants are active, the firm must be fully market-oriented and should integrate the four orientations in its business practice. Thus, in the general case, the firm must be fully market-oriented and should integrate the

Table 2.4 The different levels of MO

Company examples	Degree of MO			
	Customers (K)	Competitors (C)	Distributors (D)	Prescribers (P)
Pfizer/SKG/...	Yes	Yes	Yes	Yes
P&G/Unilever/...	Yes	Yes	Yes	–
Ryan Air/Dell/...	Yes	Yes	–	–
Recticel/Intel/...	Yes	Yes	–	Yes
BR/ Eurostar /...	Yes	–	Yes	–
RATP/EDF/GDF	Yes	–	–	–

Source: Lambin (2000/2007).

four orientations in its business practice. In several markets, less complex market configurations can exist, however.

As shown in Table 2.4, in some markets manufacturers are dealing directly with end-customers by bypassing distributors or are creating their own exclusive distribution network. Also, prescribers are not always significant market players. Still in other markets – such as public services – there is no competition, a situation that becomes exceptional. (Agreement–disagreement: scale 1 to 7)

Chapter Summary

MO is a business corporate culture, disseminated in the organization through inter-functional co-ordination, having the objective to design and promote, at a profit for the firm, superior value solutions to the firm's direct and indirect customers and to the other involved market stakeholders. In a market economy, an ecosystem is a complex grouping of market actors, companies and customers, suppliers, competitors, distributors, influencers and partners that gain mutual benefit from one another. In physical markets, we identify five market actors – suppliers, direct and end-customers, distributors, competitors, influencers – and other market stakeholders. As suggested by Guo and Sun (2004), with the development of Internet technology, markets are shifting towards two specialized yet collaborative global markets: GEMs and GTMs. From an organizational viewpoint, the implementation of the traditional marketing concept has been achieved by the creation of powerful marketing departments in charge of both strategic and operational marketing. Brand and product management play a key role in these organizational structures. The main characteristics of a market-driven organization are discussed in this chapter.

MARKET ORIENTATION QUESTIONNAIRE

(Agreement–disagreement: scale 1 to 7)

In the scale designed by Lambin & Chumpitaz to measure the extended market orientation model, each sub-orientation is described by four propositions, two for "analysis" (AL) and two for "action" (AT). In addition, four propositions are used for the interfunctional co-ordination variable and one proposition to measure the intensity of each of five environmental turbulences: technology, economy, distribution, competition and ecology.

Thus, in the most general case, we have six sub-orientations, and a total of 33 (24+4+5) propositions to be evaluated by the respondent. The performance indicators (maximum five) can be expressed in quantitative terms or in subjective evaluation terms. Respondents are required to comment on the degree to which each indicator of MO is present in their company, using a Likert-type scale.

The L&C model has been implemented in several empirical studies in Europe, using either subjective or objective measures of performance: in the private insurance sector (Lambin, 1996), in the metallic sector (Lambin and de Moreau, 1996) and in the European manufacturing sector (Lambin and Chumpitaz, 2000, 2006). In each study, the results have evidenced a positive effect of MO on business performance, thereby confirming the results of Narver and Slater (1990).

In addition to inter-functional co-ordination, there are several similarities between the K&J and N&S models. "Analysis" and "action" in the EMO model correspond to "market intelligence generation" and to the "firm's responsiveness", respectively, in the K&J model. In the N&S model, two sub-orientations (customer and competitor) are included. In the three models, business performance is viewed as a consequence of the intensity of the MO. The results also demonstrate that environmental turbulences affect the MO–performance relationship.

1 Inter-functional co-ordination (IC)

1-IC-2. Market information (on customers, competitors, distributors ...) is diffused systematically to all departments 1-IC-1. We encourage direct contact with customers at all company levels and functions within the firm.

2-IC-3. Marketing staff in our SBU spend time discussing customers' future needs with other functional departments.

3-IC-4. We have interdepartmental meetings at least once a quarter to discuss market trends and developments.

2   Competitors' orientation (CO)

4-CO-1. We systematically analyse the strengths and weaknesses of our direct competitors.

5-CO-2. We systematically analyse the threats coming from substitute products.

6-CO-3. We analyse the best practice of competition to improve the quality of our own offers.

7-CO-4. We are fast to respond to competitors' actions directed at our customers.

3   Distributors' orientation (DO)

8-DO-1. We help our distributors to achieve their performance objectives by providing training and technical assistance.

9-O-2. We regularly measure the level of satisfaction/dissatisfaction of our distributors and their image of our company.

10-DO-3. We regularly analyse the compatibility of our strategy with the objectives of our distributors.

11-DO-4. Our managers are personally committed in the firm's contacts with our distributors.

4   Response customers' orientation (RKO)

12-RKO-1. Individuals from our SBU interact directly with direct (and/or indirect) customers to learn how to serve them better.

13-RKO-2. In B2B markets, we also analyse the needs of the customers of our direct customers.

14-RKO-3. At least once a year, we measure the level of our customers' satisfaction/dissatisfaction.

15-RKO-4. Principles of market segmentation guide our strategy to best meet the diversity of our customers' needs.

16-RKO-5. We periodically measure our customers' perceived image of our brand(s) or company.

17-RKO-6. We are fast to respond to new emerging needs of our customers.

5   Proactive customers' orientation (PKO)

18-PKO-1. We meet with customers at least once a year to find out what products or services they will need in the future.

19-PKO-2. We search for opportunities in areas where customers have a difficult time expressing their needs.

20-PKO-3. We continuously try to discover additional needs of our customers of which they are unaware.

21-PKO-4. We help our customers anticipate developments in their markets.

22-PKO-5. We work closely with lead users to identify customer needs months or even years before the majority of the market may recognize them.

6   External influencers' or prescribers' orientation (PRO)

23-PRO-1. We have identified the key external influencers who do not buy, pay or use our products but who certify or recommend them to our customers.

24-PRO-2. We regularly examine the influence and the role played by these external influencers vis-à-vis our customers.

25-PRO-3. We regularly organize information and/or training sessions for external influencers about the characteristics of our products.

26-PRO-4. We periodically measure the perceived image of our brand(s) or company among key influencers.

7   Other civil society stakeholders' orientation (STO) *(consumerists, ecologists, NGOs, etc.)*

27-STO-1. We know well the socio-economic changes that could have a substantial impact on our industrial activity.

28-STO-2. We are aware of the socio-ecological side effects of our industrial activities.

29-STO-3. We are maintaining contacts and a dialogue with the main civil society' stakeholders operating in our reference market.

30-STO-4. We take actions to minimize the negative ecological impact of our products and of our industrial activity.

BIBLIOGRAPHY

Aufreiter, N.A., Lawver, T.L. and Lum, C.D. (2000), A New Way to Market, *McKinsey Quarterly*, 2, pp. 43–61.

Baker, W.E. and Sinkula, J.M. (2005), Market Orientation and the New Product Paradox, *Journal of Product Innovation Management*, 22, 6, pp. 483–502.

Cassidy, F., Freeling, A. and Kiewell, D. (2005), A Credibility Gap for Marketers, *McKinsey Quarterly*, 2, pp. 9–10.

Christensen, C.M., Cook, S. and Hall, T. (2005), Marketing Malpractice: The Cause and the Cure, *Harvard Business Review*, December, pp. 76–83.

Comstock, B., Gulati, R. and Liguori, S. (2010), Unleashing the Power of Marketing, *Harvard Business Review*, October, pp. 90–8.

Court, D.C. (2004), A New Model for Marketing, *McKinsey Quarterly*, 4, pp. 4–5.

Day, G.S. (1990), *Market-Driven Strategy*, New York, The Free Press.

Day, G.S. (1999a), Misconceptions about Market Orientation, *Journal of Market-Focused Management*, 4, 1, pp. 5–16.

Day, G.S. (1999b), *The Market-Driven Organisation*, New York, The Free Press.

Day, G.S. and Wensley, R. (1988), Assessing Advantage: A Framework for Diagnosing Competitive Superiority, *Journal of Marketing*, 52, 2, pp. 1–20.

Day, G.S. and Wind, J. (1980), Strategic Planning and Marketing: Time for a Constructive Partnership, *Journal of Marketing*, 44, 2, pp. 7–8.

Deshpandé, R. and Farley, J.U. (1998), Measuring Market Orientation: Generalization and Synthesis, *Journal of Market-Focused Management*, 2, 3, pp. 213–32.

Deshpandé, R., Farley, J.U. and Webster, F.E. (1993), Corporate Culture, Customer Orientation, and Innovativeness in Japanese Firms: A Quadrad analysis, *Journal of Marketing*, 57, 1, pp. 23–37.

Dickson, P.R. (1992), Toward a General Theory of Competitive Rationality, *Journal of Marketing*, 56, 1, pp. 69–83.

George, M., Freeling, A. and Court, D. (1994), Reinventing the Marketing Organisation, *McKinsey Quarterly*, 4, pp. 43–62.

Goderis, J.P. (1998), Barrier Marketing: From Customer Satisfaction to Customer Loyalty, *CEMS Business Review*, 2, 4, pp. 285–94.

Gonzalez-Benito, O. and Gonzalez-Benito, J. (2005), Cultural vs. Operational Market Orientation and Objective vs. Subjective Performance: Perspective of Production and Operations, *Industrial Marketing Management*, 34, 8, pp. 797–829.

Gotteland, D. (2005), *L'orientation-marché: nouvelles méthodes, nouveaux outils*, Paris, Editions d'Organisation.

Guo, J. and Sun, C. (2004), Global Electronic Markets and Global Traditional Markets, *Electronic Markets*, 14, 1, pp. 4–12.

Kirca, A.H., Jayachandran, S. and Bearden, W.O. (2005), Market Orientation: A Meta-Analytic Review and Assessment of Its Antecedents and Impact on Performance, *Journal of Marketing*, 69, 2, pp. 24–41.

Kohli, A.K. and Jaworski, B.J. (1990), Market Orientation: The Construct, Research Propositions, and Managerial Implications, *Journal of Marketing*, 54, 2, pp. 1–18.

Kohli, A.K., Jaworski, B.J. and Kumar, A. (1993), MARKOR: A Measure of Market Orientation, *Journal of Marketing Research*, 30, 4, pp. 467–77.

Kueviakoe, D. (1996), Entre grande stabilité et faible autorité: la position du chef de produit dans les entreprises, *Revue Française du Marketing*, 156, 1, pp. 79–91.

Kumar, V., Jones E., Venkatesan, R. and Leone, R.P. (2011), Is Market Orientation a Source of Sustainable Competitive Advantage or Simply the Cost of Competing?, *Journal of Marketing*, 75, pp. 16–30.

Lam, S.K., Kraus, F. and Ahearne, M. (2010), The Diffusion of Market Orientation Throughout the Organization: A Social Learning Theory Perspective, *Journal of Marketing*, 74, pp. 61–79.

Lambin, J.J. (1986), *Le marketing stratégique*, Paris, McGraw-Hill, 1st edition.

Lambin, J.J. (1996), The Misunderstanding about Marketing, *CEMS Business Review*, 1, pp. 37–56.

Lambin, J.J. (2000), *Market-driven Management*, London, Palgrave Macmillan, First edition.

Lambin, J.J. (2000/2007*), Market-Driven Management: Strategic and Operational Marketing*, London, Palgrave Macmillan.

Lambin, J.J. (2008), *Changing Market Relationships in the Internet Age*, Presses Universitaires de Louvain.

Lambin, J.J. and Chumpitaz, R. (2000), Being Customer-Driven Is Not Enough, *European Business Forum*, 2, pp. 2–8.

Lambin, J.J. and Chumpitaz, R. (2006), L'orientation-marché est-elle une stratégie rentable pour l'entreprise?, *Recherche et Applications en Marketing*, 21, 2, pp. 1–29.

Lambin, J.J. and de Moreau, J.P. (1996), *Orientation-marché et performance commerciale et financière dans le secteur Fabrimetal*, Unpublished Working Paper, IAG, Louvain School of Management.

Langerak, F. (2003), An Appraisal of Research on the Predictive Power of Market Orientation, *European Management Journal*, 21, 4, pp. 447–64.

Levitt, T. (1969), *The Marketing Mode*, New York, McGraw-Hill Company.

Manning, B. and Thorne, C. (2003), *Demand Driven*, New York, McGraw-Hill.

Mason, K. and Harris, L.C. (2005), Pitfalls in Evaluating Market Orientation: An Exploration of Executives' Interpretations, *Long Range Planning*, 38, 4, pp. 373–91.

Mitchell, R.K., Agle, R.R. and Wood, D.J. (1997), Toward a Theory of Stakeholder Identification and Salience: Defining the Principle of Who and What Really Count, *Academy of Management Review*, 22, 4, pp. 853–86.

Moorman, C. and Rust, R.T. (1999), The Role of Marketing, *Journal of Marketing*, 63, 4, pp. 180–97.

Narver, J.C. and Slater, S.F. (1990), The Effect of a Market Orientation on Business Profitability, *Journal of Marketing*, 54, 4, pp. 20–35.

Porter, M.E. (1980), *Competitive Strategy*, New York, The Free Press.

Rask, M. and Kragh, H. (2004), Motives for e-market Participation: Differences and Similarities between Buyers and Suppliers, *Electronic Markets*, 14, 4, pp. 270–83.

Ries, A. and Trout, J. (1986), *Warfare Marketing*, New York, McGraw-Hill..

Rust, R.T., Ambler, T., Carpenter, G.S., Kumar, V. and Srivastava, R.K. (2004), Measuring Marketing Productivity, Current Knowledge and Future Directions, *Journal of Marketing*, 68, 4, pp. 76–89.

Rust, R.T., Moorman, C. and Bhalla, G. (2010), Rethinking Marketing, *Harvard Business Review,* January–February, pp. 94–101.

Shapiro, C. and Varian, H.R. (1998), Versioning: The Smart Way to Sell Information, *Harvard Business Review,* 76, 6, pp. 106–14.

Sy, T. and D'Annunzio, L.S. (2000), Challenges and Strategies of Matrix Organizations, *Human Resources Planning,* 28, 1, pp. 39–48.

Trout, J. (1985), Forget Satisfying the Consumer – Just Outfox the Competition, *Business Week,* October 7.

Verhoef, P.C. and Leeflang, P.S.H. (2009), Understanding the Marketing Department's Influence Within the Firm, *Journal of Marketing,* 73, pp. 14–37.

Webster, F.E. (1992), The Changing Role of Marketing in the Corporation, *Journal of Marketing,* 56, 4, pp. 1–17.

Webster, F.E., Malter, A.J. and Ganesan, S. (2005), The Decline and Dispersion of Marketing Competence, *MIT Sloan Management Review,* 46, 4, pp. 35–43.

Wind Yoram. (2008), A Plan to Invent the Marketing We Need Today, *MIT Sloan Management Review,* Summer.

Zeithaml, V.A., Berry, L.L. and Parasuraman, A. (1988), Communication and Control Processes in the Delivery of Service Quality, *Journal of Marketing,* 52, 2, pp. 35–48.

CHAPTER THREE

THE IMPACT OF GLOBALIZATION

In the last two decades, global marketing was adopted by a majority of international companies. Globalization was the name of the game and all business sectors were concerned. By virtually any measure – development of free trade, growing border mergers and acquisitions, strength of the alter-globalization debate – globalization is becoming increasingly pervasive. The objective of this chapter is to describe the development of free trade in a globalized economy, to analyse the opportunities and threats created by globalization and to examine the role likely to be played by marketing management to alleviate poverty in the world.

Learning Objectives

When you have read this chapter, you should be able to understand:

- the benefits and pitfalls of free trade
- the industry globalization drivers
- the different international environments
- the difference between and customization and standardization
- the benefits and drawbacks of globalization
- the benefits of localism
- the challenges of marketing to the poor

3.1 THE DEVELOPMENT OF FREE TRADE

Globalization refers to a historical process by which regional economies, societies and cultures become integrated through a global network of communication, transportation and trade. The term is used here to refer specifically to economic globalization: the integration of national economies into the international economy through trade, foreign direct investments, capital flows, migration and the spread of technology (Bhagwati, 2010). Free trade has played a key role in the process of the world market internationalization.

The postulates of free trade

Free trade is a system of trade policy that allows traders to act and transact without restrictions imposed by governments and without governments resorting to subsidies, taxes, tariffs and tariff barriers. The postulates of free trade can be summarized as follows:

- Competition spurs innovation, raises productivity and lowers prices.

- The division of labour allows specialization, which raises productivity and lowers prices.
- The larger the production unit, the greater the division of labour and specialization and thus the greater the benefits.

In addition to competition, the two pillars of free trade are specialization and the scale effect. Sp*ecialization* is based on the law of comparative advantage formulated by Ricardo (1817) and which states that it is in the interest of each country to specialize only in those items it produces most efficiently. Each community or each nation should specialize in what it does best. This implies that communities and nations should abandon self-reliance and embrace dependence: that we abandon our capacity to produce many items and concentrate only on a few; that we import what we need and export what we produce (Morris, 1996). The second pillar of free trade is the *scale of the production* unit, which leads logically to the need of global markets. Bigger is better. Anything that sets up barriers to ever-wider markets reduces the possibility of specialization and thus raises the costs, making us less competitive. Thus, market deregulation is a necessity. It is typically the language of ultraliberalism, as described above. The Ricardo law of comparative advantage rests on the assumption that capital would rest immobile between nations, an assumption which is not met in today's world where billions of dollars can be transferred every day between nations at the speed of light.

Most nation-states conduct trade policies that are to a lesser or greater degree protectionist. More generally, producers often favour domestic subsidies and tariffs on imports in their home countries, while objecting to subsidies and tariffs in their export markets. The General Agreement on Tariffs and Trade (GATT) and the World Trade Organization (WTO) were created to open markets and promote international trade based on the free trade paradigm. While free trade is still hotly debated among economists, trade liberalization is ranked high on the list of development priorities for fighting poverty in the world. Even if the picture of free trade is not always rosy, the academic debate is currently settled in favour of free trade because the benefits of specialization coupled with economies of scale increase the global production and because the reduction of subsidies and of tariffs levels – in particular in the field of agriculture – improve the well-being of the poorest. In what follows, we will review the benefits and the drawbacks of free trade.

The benefits of free trade

Free trade is supposed to a *win–win* policy for rich and poor countries. For the rich countries the first advantage is to have broader access to foreign products for consumers and companies at prices lower than the ones obtained under local production. A second advantage is obtained by investing in emerging economies, thus gaining access to enlarged markets and generating economies of scale.

Thanks to free trade, industrialized countries are induced to invest in developing economies, contributing to the building of a modern economy by investing in the field of education and thereby reducing poverty. The overall result of globalization is illustrated by the examples of successful countries like Taiwan, South Korea, China and selected countries of South-East Asia.

Qualitative analysis suggests that free trade stimulates cross-cultural contacts and the dissemination of values like the democratic ideal, contributes to the creation of the "global village" effect and makes war less likely. The *World Bank* also mentions the following socio-economic arguments in favour of free trade:

- Reduction of poverty in the world
- Improvement of economic and social status of the women

- Progress in the domain of public health policies
- Decrease of exploitation of child labour
- Emergence of a middle class
- Growth of cross cultural contacts
- Development of tourism
- Export of local products
- Emergence of a world culture
- Enhancing of national security, etc.

At the economic level, too often poor countries are not fully participating in the process of globalization. It is, nevertheless, a required step for joining the club of industrialized countries and for being not simply an exporter of raw materials. Participation in the process of globalization implies stable public institutions, well-established rules of law, absence of corruption and a good level of development in the fields of health and education.

The drawbacks of free trade

Opponents to globalization are there to remind us that free trade and deregulation of international commerce can also introduce the following inefficiencies:

- Half of all international trade involves the simultaneous import and export of essentially the same goods from country to country across the globe and back again.
- The costs of transportation internationally, which are energy intensive, should be internalized into prices, which is not always the case since the cost of energy is often subsidized by governments. Should prices reflect environmental costs, products will become more expensive, forcing people to think long and hard about what they should make locally or trade internationally and why.
- Free trade allows companies the possibility of outsourcing the production of goods for domestic sales and in that way it hurts developed nations because it takes jobs from those nations to move to other countries.
- Free trade creates conditions that allow companies to circumvent domestic regulations by producing elsewhere and encourages industries to shift their production activities to the countries that have the lowest standards of cost internalization (social dumping).
- If specialization develops, it contributes to reduce the range of occupational choices by creating economies too dependent on narrow specialties.
- Free trade undermines national security of nations becoming dependent on key commodities or on food imports.

Governments can intervene to reduce the impact of some of these inefficiencies, for example, by levy, compensating tariffs on trade with nations that do not internalize environmental or social costs.

The temptation of outsourcing

Relocation of economic activities is a major preoccupation for rich countries. Relocation is the transfer of one industrial activity from one country to another one. In a narrow sense, a plant is closed in France and a new one is built in China to produce the same products that will be re-imported in France. In a broader sense, it is the transfer of some or of all production activities in a low-wages emerging economy, via the creation of a subsidiary or by using the services of a sub-contractor or of a foreign supplier. In each case, outsourcing reinforces the profitability of the firm since the main objective is to push production costs down. Most European companies relocate to penetrate emerging markets, but their main objectives is also to decrease labour costs.

The temptation is strong when one compares hourly labour costs in the manufacturing industries among countries: 24 dollars in Germany (world record), 21 in the United States, 19 in Japan and about 17 in France. But it is only 5 dollars in Poland and in the Czech Republic and 0.6 dollars in China, that is approximately 30 times less expensive than in France and 40 times less than in Germany.

A negative side effect of globalization underlined by the anti-globalization movement is the "race to the bottom", that is, the transfer of foreign investments to countries having the lowest wages and where the environmental and social regulations are lax or non-existent. Between 2003 and 2005, several companies from the electronic, mechanical and tools manufacturing sectors moved to Asia, causing loss of several hundreds of jobs in France. In the automobile sector, car manufacturing companies moved to Eastern European countries (Artus and Virard, 2009, p.22). Moreover, the delocalization movement is now gaining momentum in the service sector with software development, call platforms, financial analyses and information.

3.2   THE CUSTOMIZATION–STANDARDIZATION DILEMMA

Confronted with the emergence of a dynamic global common market based on the freedom of exchange of goods and characterized by increased competition, companies active in international marketing have to decide which strategy to adopt in their approach to foreign markets. The option is between a multi-domestic approach where the strategy is adapted to each market's characteristics or a global approach which looks for standardization, emphasizing similarities among markets. The customization or adaptation strategy is more market-driven while the standardization or global approach is more supply-driven. In the real world, the frontier between these two strategies is often blurred.

Globalization is no longer confined to few industries such as electronics, pharmaceuticals, automobiles or branded consumer goods. In the last decade, globalization has become a reality even for companies that used to own and manage local service firms, like supermarkets (Carrefour, Ahold, Ikea), neighbourhood cafés (Starbucks cafés), banks (Citybank, Amro, etc.), corner photography shops (Fnac , Kodak kiosks, etc.), fast food restaurants (McDonald's, Quick, Haagen Daz, etc.). For empirical evidence, see the A.T. Kearney Globalisation Index (A.T. Kearney Inc., 2002) and Mizik and Jacobson (2009).

In this context, firms concentrated their efforts on the development of global brands that could ideally attract a maximum number of people on a global basis with the same standardized marketing approach. These global brands became powerful tools to penetrate international markets: They are real assets for companies and, by way of consequence, are highly valued by financial markets. For example, according to Interbrand (2010), the top five brands in the world in terms of financial valuation (in billion dollars) are Coca-Cola ($70), IBM ($65), Microsoft ($61), Google ($44) and GE ($43). These are all American brands.

Typology of international environments

The necessity for the firm to adopt a global approach in international marketing is dependent upon the characteristics of its market environment. Goshal and Nohria (1993) suggest analysing the international environment by reference to two dimensions.

1. *Local forces* like local customers, tastes, purchasing habits, governments and regulatory agencies, which create strong needs for *local responsiveness and adaptation*.

2. *Global forces* like economies of scale, uniform customer demands, worldwide competi-
    tion, product uniformity that are powerful incentives for *global integration and standard-
    ization*.

For each of these two dimensions, one can identify two levels (weak and strong) and broadly
distinguish among four environmental conditions faced by multinational companies
(MNCs), as illustrated in Figure 3.1.

■   The environment is *global* when forces for global integration are strong and local
    responsiveness is weak. In such markets, structural uniformity in the organization is
    best suited to these conditions. It is the situation observed in many high-technology
    markets where local forces are non-existent and inoperative. The trend is towards stand-
    ardization and centralization of responsibilities.
■   In the *multinational (or multi-domestic)* environment, on the contrary, the forces for
    national responsiveness are strong and the forces for global integration weak. In this
    type of market, adaptation to local conditions is a key success factor and companies
    tend to adopt different governance modes to fit to each local context. Many food com-
    panies fall into this category, where taste and culinary habits are important determi-
    nants of preferences and of purchase behaviour.
■   In the *placid international environment* both forces are weak. The business of producing
    cement is an example.

    Cement products are highly standardised and distribution systems are similar across
    countries. Thus demands for local responsiveness are weak. However, the trade-offs
    between the economics of cement production and transport costs are such that global
    integration is not attractive. (Goshal and Nohria, 1993, p. 26)

■   In the *transnational* environment both forces, local and global, are strong. It is the
    most complex situation where some degree of standardization and centralization
    is necessary, while maintaining the capacity to respond to local situations is also
    required.

    It is the case, for example, of a brand like Carlsberg, which has all the characteristics of
    a global brand. Distributed in 130 countries throughout the world, its taste, logo and
    bottle design are identical. Nevertheless, the "beer culture" is very different from one
    country to the other, even within Europe. Thus a transnational organisation combining
    centralisation and local (or regional) adaptation is better suited to this brand.

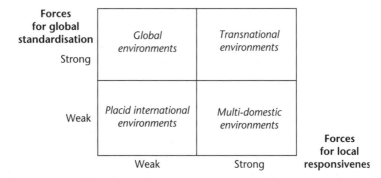

Figure 3.1 Typology of international environments
Source: Adapted from Goshal and Nohria (1993).

Another example is the case of Volvo Truck (Lambin and Hiller, 1990). Trucks are designed upfront for the world market and are identical with few minor adaptations. But a key success factor in any market remains the role played by the local dealer who is in charge of after-sales service and of the warranty. A highly centralized organization would not suite this market environment.

The drivers of globalization

To achieve the benefits of globalization, managers have to recognize when industry conditions are favourable. As suggested by Yip (1989), four industrialization drivers should be analysed, knowing that each industry globalization driver changes over time.

Market drivers

- Customers in different countries want essentially the same type of product or service.
- Global customers buy on a centralized or co-ordinated basis for decentralized use.
- Channels of distribution may buy on a global or at least on a regional basis.
- Operational marketing elements, such as brand names and advertising, require little local adaptation.

Cost drivers

- A single country market may not be large enough for the local business to achieve all economies of scale or scope.
- Expanded market participation and activity concentration can accelerate the accumulation of learning and experience.
- Centralized purchasing of new materials can significantly contribute to lower costs. A favourable ratio of sales value to transportation cost enhances the company's ability to concentrate.
- Costs generally vary across countries as well as the availability of particular skills.
- Developing few global or regional products rather several national products can reduce these costs.

Governmental drivers

- Import tariffs and quotas, non-tariff barriers, export subsidies, local content requirements, currency and capital flow restrictions and requirements on technology transfer directly affect the globalization potential.
- Differences in technical standards limit the extent to which products can be standardized.
- Marketing regulations, that is, the marketing and advertising environment of individual countries affect the extent to which uniform global operational marketing approaches can be used.

Competitive drivers

- When activities such as production are shared among countries, a competitor's market share in one country affects its scale and overall cost position in the shared activity.
- Matching or pre-empting individual competitor moves may be necessary.

The relative importance of theses drives must be evaluated country by country. A global strategy is mainly *supply-driven* and developed at the expense of a more market- or customer-driven strategy in order to achieve the benefits of globalization described below. Management has to recognize when industry conditions are favourable.

Benefits of marketing globalization

The benefits generated by a globalization strategy are well known and several authors (Buzzell, 1968; Levitt, 1983; Quelch and Hoff, 1986; Boddewyn, Soehl and Picard, 1986; Jain, 1989; Lambin, 2001; Bhagwati, 2010) have highlighted the potential advantages that marketing globalization can bring.

The most important benefit is certainly the possibility of generating important *economies of scale*. Having a scale superiority effect reduces costs and this is a key competitive advantage that all companies want to achieve. Economies of scale can be found in many areas of the business system; in R&D by concentrating research in a few geographic locations and on a limited number of product ranges; in manufacturing by concentrating production on a limited number of plants in a few countries worldwide; in logistics by the development of standardized products to be marketed all over the world; in selling and distribution by standardizing operational marketing and in particular packaging and communication. Most international companies have already restructured their operations to benefit from these economies of scale.

The second major benefit is the *speed to market*. Globalized firms are much more centralized. This enables them to centrally plan and organize new product introductions worldwide within less than one year. This is not possible with a multi-domestic international organization, where every local subsidiary has a decision power in product or branding policies. The centralization of all R&D efforts on a limited number of innovations has also an impact on quality and costs.

A third key benefit is the advantage of creating a *unique worldwide brand name* and brand identity for the global company. This leads to substantial savings in communication by targeting the same segments of customers worldwide with the same product concept. This

---

Exhibit 3.1   McDonald's: a successful globalization?

The folks at McDonald's like to tell the story about a young Japanese girl who arrived in Los Angeles, looked around and said to her mother: "Look, mom, they have McDonald's here too." You could excuse her for being surprised that this was an American company. With 2,000 restaurants in Japan, McDonald's Japan is the biggest McDonald's franchise outside the United States. "You don't have 2,000 stores in Japan by being seen as an American company," said James Cantalupo, head of McDonald's International.

The way McDonald has packaged itself is to be a "multi-local" company. By insisting on a high degree of local ownership, and by tailoring its products just enough for local cultures, it has avoided the worst cultural backlashes that some other US companies have encountered. Not only the localities now feel a stake in McDonald's success but also, more important, countries do. Poland, for instance, has emerged as one of the largest regional suppliers of meat, potatoes and bread for McDonald's in Central Europe. That is real power. McDonald is gradually moving from local sourcing of its raw materials to regional sourcing and to global sourcing. One day soon, all McDonald's meat in Asia will come from Australia, all its potatoes from China. Already, every sesame seed on every McDonald's bun in the world comes from Mexico. That's as good as a country discovering oil.

Source: Friedman (1996).

is particularly important for luxury and fashion goods, for global food products but also for hi-tech products (computers, phones hi-fi, etc.) targeting transnational segments of customers.

Drawbacks of marketing globalization

It is clear that the benefits of standardization are mostly supply-driven and not market-driven. Several drawbacks also exist and cannot be underestimated.

The first possible drawback is the negative effect of centralization. Centralization can accelerate the speed of major product launches on a worldwide basis but it can also *slow down other marketing decisions*. Too slow reactions to local competitor's actions or to specific local consumer problems can be dangerous. The reason is that too many layers often exist in a centralized organization between the local brand managers and the marketing directors based in the company headquarters.

The second potential drawback is the insensitivity to local markets conditions and a resulting *lower responsiveness*. Since most marketing initiatives and strategies are developed in the company headquarters, marketing managers have fewer contacts with local markets. They do not perceive local consumer problems or insights well. Their objective is to build

---

Exhibit 3.2   A global marketplace means global vulnerability

Coca-Cola Co., one of the world's most powerful corporations, discovered some time back (14–19 June 1999) what it feels like to be on the losing end of globalization. The soft-drink giant was rocked by a health scare in Europe that spread faster than a computer virus. Regulators in Belgium, France, Luxembourg and the Netherlands pulled the company's soft drinks from shelves after reports of contaminated Coke. And Coca-Cola spokesmen, after curtly insisting there wasn't any danger, began scrambling to offer assurance and apologies.

The Coca-Cola flap shows that just as capital and technology move instantaneously in the global economy, so does bad news. Consumer problems that start in Belgium can race around the globe – tarnishing the world's most powerful brand name and even affecting its stock price on Wall Street. For America's hard-charging corporate executives, this is the flip side of globalization. For even as the technology revolution is empowering corporations, it is also giving new leverage to regulators and consumer groups. There are no such things as a "local problem" anymore, as Coca-Cola's experience shows. "Global brand name recognition has an Achilles heel of vulnerability," says the consumer advocate Ralph Nader. The vents show that the value of Coca-Cola's brand, built up over more than a century, can be shaken as suddenly and capriciously as the Thai baht or the Indonesian ringgit.

Source: International Herald Tribune (22 June 1999).

Exhibit 3.3   The Vioxx case

An example of global brand vulnerability is given by the Vioxx case in the pharmaceutical industry. In September 2004, the company Merck announced that they would immediately withdraw from the world market their "blockbuster" Vioxx brand. They had discovered that the brand – launched in 1999 – was causing cardiovascular problems. The brand is estimated to have caused 150,000 heart attacks and 27,785 deaths since its launch. This is a major scandal from the patients' point of view. It also represents not only a financial loss of an estimated $50 billions for the stockholders but a substantial damage to the firm's corporate image as a result of the extensive media coverage.

Source: Industry.

on similarities among markets and not on what differentiate them. At the end, there is a loss of knowledge of local consumers.

The third potential drawback is the danger of developing products that are not in line with consumer needs. The objective of product standardization is to develop products that meet the needs of a majority of people on a global basis. Products are therefore developed on the *lowest common denominator*. There is the risk that in the end consumers are not satisfied with the standardized product.

A last pitfall that is not often underlined is related to *risk management*. A portfolio of brands constituted of a majority of global brands is *more vulnerable*. As the world becomes more linked and interconnected by global media such CNN and the Internet, a problem arising in a local country on a global brand is rapidly made public and can be communicated to the whole world within a few hours or even minutes. It is therefore much more financially risky for the bottom line of the firm. If we take the example of a large multinational firm in the food or the pharmaceutical industries, a quality problem arising on one of its global brands might have a devastating impact on the results of the total company.

3.3   QUESTIONING THE BENEFITS OF GLOBALIZATION

In the last years, several signals suggest that globalization has reached a critical turning point. The first signal came from several global firms, among the most prestigious, which realized that going too far on the globalization track was detrimental to their success. Companies such as Coca-Cola and P&G, for example, have changed dramatically their international strategy in the last two years. A second signal comes directly from the market. Socio-economic and cultural changes are modifying the balance of power between international firms and their customer base. These two evolutionary changes will have a fundamental impact on the level of globalization companies will adopt in the future.

The main changes coming from the market are linked to social and political factors. They are summarized in Table 3.1.

The first change is the anti-globalization movement and the popular success of the *alter-globalization* movement. Consumers are looking for more diversity in their brand choices. Also, they are less attracted by low prices but are rather looking for better value for money. They are not satisfied anymore with a limited number of global brands present in every

---

Exhibit 3.4   Even little companies are now going global

Philip Chigos and Mary Domenico are busy building a children's pyjama business. They are refining patterns, picking fabrics and turning the basement of their two-bedroom apartment into office. Then there is a critical step of finding the seamstresses in China: A growing number of tiny mom-and-pop operations, industry experts say, are turning to places like Sri Lanka, China, Mexico and Eastern Europe to make clothes, jewellery, trinkets and even software programmes. The ability of Chigos, 26, and Domenico, 25, to reach across borders has as much to do with technology as it does with globalization. Computers, the Internet and modern telecommunications, of course, make it possible for start-ups to market their goods to customers anywhere.

Infrastructure also enables even the smallest employers to find workers far away in countries they will never visit and in factories they will never inspect. They can communicate with those workers cheaply via e-mail messages and telephone, transmit images and design specifications and track inventory. Offshoring for small entrepreneurs can be rough, however.

Source: Ritchell (2005).

Table 3.1 The emerging globalization market drivers

Traditional market drivers	Emerging market drivers
Isolated individual consumers	Powerful consumerist movements
Passive and docile consumers	Educated and smart shoppers
Interest for low price	Search for more value for money
Homogeneous customer needs	Multiplicity of supranational segments
Attractiveness of global culture	Search for local identity
Prestige of global brands	Nostalgia for local brands
Undisputed power of global brands	Development of private labels
Politically uncommitted consumption	"Politically correct" consumption
Low sensitivity for ethical issues	Growing sensitivity to ethical issues
Low interest for product greenness	Eco-conscious consumers
No concern for product origin	International traceability

Source: Schuiling and Lambin (2003).

store they visit and in different countries when they travel. Consumers are not necessarily attracted by the same global names in every product category. As a consequence, a multiplicity of supranational segments have emerged reflecting this diversity of needs and behaviours.

A growing number of consumers feel that they have lost their identity in the current globalized world and develop *nostalgia* vis-à-vis traditional brand names in several markets. People are happy to find traditional brand names that they are familiar with since so many years. Old brand names are even re-launched to capitalize on this trend. Interestingly, in Eastern European countries, there is also a return to old brand names. The US brands do not necessarily attract consumers as strongly as before.

> In Hungary, for example, consumers are attracted by names from the old soviet time. They prefer "Tizsa" shoes instead of Nike and they drink "Traubisoda" drink instead of Coca-Cola.

A study (Schuiling and Kapferer, 2004) has indicated that local brands generate more trust than their global counterparts.

Negative reactions against the economic and political power of the United States and against the power of global brands (mostly American) are voiced, as illustrated by the successful plea of Naomi Klein (1999) in her book *No-Logo*.

The benefits of localization

In the era of globalization it is easy to forget that local businesses have been the economic norm for most of human history and still have a great potential in promoting sustainable development. As a social movement, localization highlights the importance for every community to maximize its level of self-reliance in a sustainable way, that is, by meeting its present and future needs without compromising the needs of future generations living in other communities, present or future. Viewed in this perspective, localization can contribute to avoid sustainability problems (Shuman 2010):

- An economy highly dependent on non-local businesses must continually make sustainability compromises to prevent its most important firms from exiting.
- The absence of local ownership means that non-local corporations can dictate the terms of sustainability in the communities in which they operate.
- The ability of non-local firms to exit means that they can easily leave environmental problems behind.

Localization also has several positive and direct impacts on sustainability:

■ The presence of local business owners in a community can lead to greater environmental responsibility through accountability to their own neighbourhoods.

■ Local businesses tend to use local materials and sell to local markets, their inputs and outputs requiring less shipping, less energy and resulting in less pollution.

■ The immobility of local businesses means that economic development efforts focused on them are more likely to produce enduring results.

■ A local business tends to generate a higher economic multiplier than a comparable non-local business, because local businesses spend more of their money locally.

■ Food localization reduces the need for and expense of many components of distribution, such as refrigeration, packaging, advertising and third parties.

Perhaps the biggest obstacle to localization is the unavailability of capital. The biggest public policy change sought by localization advocates is to overhaul the priorities of economic development. Public monies should be focused by priority on nurturing local business. Bhattacharya and Michael (2008) have observed that local companies can win over multinationals. Other authors, such as Alexander and Korine (2008), analyse situations where companies should not go global.

A return to localization seems to be emerging among multinational firms, as suggested by the changes observed in the branding strategies of firms like P&G and the Coca-Cola Company. These companies are now acknowledging that they have gone too far on the standardization track and are coming back to customization strategies. To review more recent work on the consumer's attitude towards global and local products, see Steenkamp and de Jong (2010). This study covering 13,000 respondents from 28 countries provides strategic direction on how to market products in a globalized world.

3.4 CAN MARKETING ALLEVIATE POVERTY IN THE WORLD

One of the big challenges of the twenty-first century will be to deal with the world poverty issue. Some 4 billion people – approximately two-thirds of the world population – live on less than 1,000 dollars a year. They outnumber the rich – or at least those earning $10,000 or more a year – by a factor of 8 to 1. It is today a well-established fact that economic growth of a country is closely correlated to the creation of new enterprises of the country. Thus, entrepreneurship can be a powerful means to reduce poverty (Rahul, 2002; Ponson, 2003).

Exhibit 3.5   Netchising: the next global wave

Companies have long taken "going global" to mean having a physical presence at locations everywhere. It has meant executives in transit and brick-and-mortar facilities on the ground. Today an increasing number of companies are succeeding overseas without massive foreign investments by adopting the global business model called "netchising" (Morrison, Bouquet and Beck, 2004). This new business model relies on the Internet for procurement, sales and maintaining customer relationships, and non-equity partnership arrangements to provide direct customer interfaces and local adaptation and delivery of products and services. *Netchising* offers potentially huge benefits over traditional exporting or foreign direct investment approaches to globalization.

Source: Adapted from Morrison, Bouquet and Beck (2004).

Marketing and poverty in the world

For many decades, various institutions have tried to address this challenge: developed country governments, international organizations like the World Bank and the United Nations (UN), numerous consulting firms (Little, 2003), private foundations and NGOs. Shouldn't we – marketing scholars and marketing professionals – also develop forms of low-cost or low-frills marketing – both in strategic and in operational marketing to give poor countries' entrepreneurs appropriate marketing instruments?

More recently, management experts and business schools have entered the field. In particular Prahalad (2004), from the University of Michigan Business School, has argued in his book – *Fortune at the Bottom of the Pyramid* – that selling to the poor can simultaneously be profitable and eradicate poverty. Prahalad's propositions can be summarized as follows:

- There is a much untapped purchasing power at the bottom of the pyramid. Private companies can make significant profits by selling to the poor.
- By selling to the poor, private companies can bring prosperity to the poor and thus can help eradicate poverty.
- Large MNCs should play the leading role in this process of selling.

Prahalad (2004, p. 18) argues that the priority objective should be to *create the capacity to consume* in developing countries. To achieve this, three simple principles should guide management:

- *Affordability* – Make unit packages that are small and therefore affordable. The *single serve* revolution.
- *Access* – Stores must be easy to reach, often within a short walk. The *geographical intensity* of distribution.
- *Availability* – Consumers in developing markets cannot defer buying decisions. The *distribution efficiency.*

Prahalad's vision has drawn much attention from senior managers and from economists. Yet limited research supports Prahalad's recommendations and many marketing scholars question the objective that selling to the poor at a profit is an appropriate way to alleviate poverty. Can marketing really contribute to eradicate poverty or is it a mirage, as suggested by Karnani (2007)?

A fortune at the bottom of the pyramid?

A key assumption of Prahalad's book is the existence of a substantial untapped market potential among poor people, at the bottom of the pyramid. Researchers disagree on the size of this target market. The level of poverty is usually defined at $2 per day at purchasing power parity (PPP) rates in 1990 prices (equivalent to $3.10 in 2006 prices). At this level of poverty the basic needs of survival are met, but just barely. Prahalad states that there are more than 4 billion people with per capita income below $2 per day, while the World Bank estimated the number at 2.7 billion in 2001. The average consumption of poor people is $1.25 per day. With 2.7 billion poor people, this implies a market potential of $1.2 trillion, at PPP in 2002. For several economists (Karnani, 2007; Landrum, 2007), this figure is grossly overestimated and the global market potential would be less than a $0.3 trillion, a small market compared to the $11 trillion economy in the United States alone.

Some companies are now deliberately targeting the poor by adapting their marketing strategy. Several options can be considered by the firm having the objective of selling to the poor.

Smaller packaging strategy

A frequently adopted strategy is to reformulate consumer goods being sold in much smaller packages, thus making them affordable for the poor. This single serve strategy has been adopted for various products like shampoos, ketchup, tea, biscuits, cigarettes, skin cream. The effectiveness of this strategy is doubtful as illustrated by the following examples.

> In India, Coca-Cola has launched a carbonated soft drink in smaller packages size of 200 ml and Amul, a large diary Indian cooperative, has introduced a 50 ml serving of ice cream (a luxury in tropical India). Both products were sold at Rs.5, a so called "affordable" price, but which is nevertheless the equivalent to $0.57 (at PPP). Not too many people living on less than $2 per day will find that a bargain. (Karnani, 2007)

Even though small packages create value by increasing convenience and helping manage cash flow, they neither increase "affordability" nor solve the problem of hunger and malnutrition.

- The only way the poor can purchase a newly available product is to divert expenditure from some other product, with the risk of neglecting higher-priority needs such as education or health.
- Many products sold in a smaller package size are marketed exactly at the same price per kilogram as larger packages.
- The proliferation of single serve plastic packaging has a negative impact on the environment; a serious problem in poor villages and slums, where trash collection is inadequate.

It is clear that simply selling to the poor does not necessarily improve their welfare or reduce poverty.

Lower price strategy

The only way to help the poor and alleviate poverty is to raise the real income of the poor. There are only two ways to do this: lower the price of the goods (which will in effect raise the income) or raise the income that the poor gain. The only way to increase real affordability is to reduce the price per use. There are only three ways to reduce prices: reduce profits, reduce costs without reducing quality and reduce costs by reducing quality.

The potential for profit reduction is in general very limited because markets for selling to the poor are costly to serve. The poor are generally geographically dispersed and the markets have weak infrastructure in transportation, cold chain, communication, media, and limited potential for economies of scale. This contributes to increase costs of doing business. Also, charging lower prices for brands of the same quality generate risks of parallel imports from low-price countries to high-price countries, a risk particularly high for pharmaceutical products.

Some companies have taken that risk. A good example is the *Groupe Danone* which has launched a dairy product at a highly affordable price that is specially developed to meet specific nutritional needs of Bangladeshi children. The project was developed in 2006 in partnership with GAIN (Global Alliance for Improved Nutrition) (www.gainhealth.org) and with the Grameen Group (www.grameen-info.org). The plan was to use local supplies and to design simple equipment to facilitate the appropriation by local workers. The long-term objective is to gradually deploy this model within the whole country with around 50 small plants (www.csreurope.org/solutions).

Some companies provide credit even for low- or unpredictable-income consumers, charging a low interest rate. These financing schemes provide value to the poor (instant gratification), but do not change the affordability of the product, which is a function of its price.

Reduced product quality

To really reduce costs, without undermining the global strategy of the firm, it is often necessary to reduce quality in such way that the cost–quality trade-off is acceptable to poor consumers. Karnani (2007, p. 101) gives the example of an Indian firm, *Nirma*, having launched a very low-price detergent of clearly inferior quality to that of Surf, the brand marketed by Hindustan Lever. To reduce cost, the brand *Nirma* does not contain whitener, perfume or softener. Nevertheless, in ten years, this brand has increased its market share from 12 per cent to 62 per cent.

Selling inexpensive, low-quality products does not hurt the poor as long as they understand any trade-offs related to safety. In rich countries, the success of private labels sold by distributors at a lower price than national brands but for reduced quality products supports this observation. Other realistic ways to make products more affordable are:

- the *shared-access* model, where products like cell phones, washing machines, bicycles are rented or shared;
- adopting technologies like solar cells to generate electricity in low-income communities;
- trying to cut transaction costs by introducing more appropriate distribution systems that link old and new technologies (bicycles and mobile phones).

Thus, developing a marketing strategy for selling to the poor implies a redesign of the product concept itself where the emphasis is placed on the core service or function, neglecting the frills and the secondary benefits. Similarly, distribution and communication policies must be customized to meet the specific needs and characteristics of these markets.

The role of microcredit

In awarding the Nobel Prize to the pioneer of microcredit, Muhammad Yunus, the Nobel committee affirmed that microcredit plays a major part in eliminating poverty. In reality, most studies suggest that microcredit is beneficial, but only to a limited extent. Several reasons have been identified by Khawari (2004):

- Microcredit does not alleviate poverty, but rather reduces vulnerability by smoothing consumption.
- The majority of microcredit clients are caught in subsistence activities with no prospect for competitive advantage.
- Microcredit businesses operate at too small a scale, with no paid staff, very few assets, low productivity and modest earnings.
- Only a small fraction has used credit for entrepreneurial purposes. They are "own account workers", and they do little to create jobs for others.

In China where the incidence of poverty has declined significantly, a large and growing fraction of the population is employed for wages, as opposed to self-employed or farmers. Economists agree today that creating decent employment opportunities is the best way to take people out of poverty.

Ethical issues

If making profits from poverty may make good financial sense, is it ethically acceptable? The argument goes like this: if those who are currently excluded from consumer society are not brought into the economy, the divide between rich and poor will widen further, creating more social tension and undermining future development.

A word of caution. The poor are vulnerable by virtue of lack of education, lack of information and economic, cultural and social deprivation. Aggressive operational marketing could induce the poor to spend money on products such as television, shampoos, tobacco and alcohol that would have been better spent on higher-priority needs such as nutrition, education and health. Consumer protection, restrictions on advertising and "sin taxes" for alcohol and tobacco that exist in rich countries are inadequate or non-existent in the developing countries.

In conclusion, it seems that marketing, and in particular strategic marketing, has indeed a role to play in reducing poverty, but this role is modest and should be carefully calibrated to meet the needs of the poor. The best opportunities exist when the firm develops affordable products by innovatively changing the price–quality trade-off in a way acceptable to consumers in developing countries.

In contradiction with the recommendation of Prahalad (2004), rather than focusing on the poor as *a consumer*, the best way to eradicate poverty is to develop the poor as *a producer* and as an entrepreneur, in order to raise his or her income by creating more employment opportunities.

Searching for the appropriate business model

In view of the problems and limitations of a pure play for-profit business model, the question regarding which business model should be adopted by social and environmental entrepreneurs to successfully contribute to alleviate poverty is raised. Social and environmental entrepreneurs operate across a spectrum of enterprises, from the purely charitable to the purely commercial. On the purely charitable side, customers pay little or nothing; capital comes in the form of donations and grants, the workforce is largely made up of volunteers and suppliers make in-kind donations. At the purely commercial end of the spectrum, by contrast, most transactions are at market rates. Elkington and Hartigan (2008, p. 3) observed that the most interesting experiments take place in the middle ground, where *hybrid organizations* pursue new forms of *blended value*, where better-off customers sometimes subsidize less well-off customers. Blended value is what results when businesses – whether for-profit or non-profit – create value in multiple dimensions, economic, social and environmental. This blended value concept is at the base of the Triple Bottom Line (TBL) reporting system (Elkington, 1997) promoted by social and environmental entrepreneurs.

In the past, there has been a real separation in the notion of value. Corporations sought to maximize economic value, while public interest groups have sought to maximize social and environmental value. However, a growing group of practitioners, investors, philanthropists are advancing strategies that intentionally blend social environmental and economic value. These activities have resulted in a wave of new practices across the for-profit and non-profit sectors. Corporations are realizing that the positive social and environmental impacts of their work can increase (or at least not compromise) shareholder value while simultaneously addressing the concerns of wider stakeholder groups. Many non-profits are seeing that by incorporating business practices that create economic value into their management strategies, they can better deliver on their social and environmental missions (www.blendedvalue.org). Several interesting short case histories illustrating this hybrid approach are represented in Elkington and Hartigan's book (2008).

The prevailing business models adopted by social entrepreneurs tend to fall into three categories: the non-profit business model (model 1), the hybrid non-profit (model 2) and the social business (model 3).

- In the *non-profit model* (model 1*)*, social entrepreneurs aim to meet needs that are ignored by current market mechanisms. They want to act where governments are not able or willing to provide a public good or a service and where the private sector cannot justify the risk in relation with a realistic prospect for profit. A public good is delivered to the most economically vulnerable who are unable to afford the service rendered. The key success factor is the ability to leverage available resources. Non-profit enterprises are totally dependent on philanthropic donations and this dependence runs counter to the possibility of expansion, as the supply of donors' monies is limited. The sustainability of such a business model is fragile.
- In the *hybrid non-profit model* (model 2), as in the previous model, the objective is to deliver products and services to populations that have been excluded by mainstream markets, but the notion of making profit and of reinvesting a profit is not excluded. To avoid being 100 per cent donor dependent, the social enterprise will try to recover a portion of its costs through the sales of goods and services. For instance, the enterprise will charge wealthy patients more and poorer patients less. While keeping its specific social objective, the organization will have to evolve progressively towards a social business model to ensure access to capital market and achieve sustainability,
- The *social business model* (model 3), in contrast with models 1 and 2, is set up from the outset as for-profit but it differs from mainstream business model about what to do with any profits. The specific mission is to drive transformational social and/or environmental changes. Profits are generated but the main objective is not to maximize financial returns for the shareholders but instead to financially benefit low-income groups and to grow the social venture. The social entrepreneur seeks investors interested in combining financial and social returns. To leverage resources, social business models are significantly easier to understand for business people and to develop partnerships. Their opportunities for growth and sustainability are also greater because they can take on debt and equity.

By way of conclusion, one has to realize that to eradicate poverty in the world is big business. Without downplaying the importance of philanthropy, neither non-profit social entrepreneurs alone nor governments alone have the capacity to leverage the required financial, human and organizational resources to eradicate poverty. To give an example, there are an estimated 37 million people worldwide who are blind and an additional 124 million who are visually impaired. The global economic burden of blindness is estimated to be around $25 billion per year. In India alone, an estimated 12 million are blind, yet 60 per cent of blindness there is a result of cataracts which are almost always curable. To resolve a problem of this magnitude, the market mechanisms and the management know-how have clearly a role to play.

In India, the social entrepreneur Aravind Eye Care System (www.aravind.org) has pioneered a sustainable business model that follows the principle that large-volume, high-quality, and community-centric services can result in low cost and long-term viability. By charging wealthier patients more and poorer customers less, it has developed a sustainable social business model. Treating over 2 million patients a year, with less than 1 per cent of country's ophthalmic workforce, Aravind performs about 5 per cent of all cataracts surgeries in India. Since its inception, Aravind has performed more than 2.8 million surgeries and handled over 22 million outpatients and is still managing to make a profit that is reinvested in growing the enterprise and continuously upgrading its services. This success has been achieved without diluting poor patient's quality of care. As a result of the fee system, and effective management, Aravind is able to provide free eye care to two-thirds of the patients and still maintain profit margins of 40 per cent

---

Chapter Summary

Free trade has played a key role in the process of world market internationalization. Free trade is a system of trade policy that allows traders to act and transact without restrictions imposed by governments. Free trade is supposed to be a win–win policy for rich and poor countries, but drawbacks exist, in particular the temptation of outsourcing to low-wages emerging economies. In designing their strategy, international firms are confronted with two approaches: a multi-domestic approach where the strategy is adapted to each market's characteristics or a global approach which looks for standardization, emphasizing similarities among markets. Each strategy has its merits and its drawbacks. A key assumption made by several marketing scholars is the existence of a substantial untapped market potential among poor people, at the bottom of the pyramid. Some companies are now deliberately targeting the poor by adapting their marketing strategy. Several options can be considered by the firm having the objective of selling to the poor.

BIBLIOGRAPHY

A.T. Kearney Inc. (2002), *Globalization's Last Hurrah?* A.T. Kearney/Foreign Policy Magazine Globalization Index, January–February.

Alexander, M. and Korine, H. (2008), When You Shouldn't Go Global, *Harvard Business Review,* December, pp. 70–7.

Artus, P. and Virard, M.P. (2009), *Le capitalisme est en train de s'auto-détruire*, Paris, la Découverte.

Bhagwati J., (2010), *Plaidoyer pour la mondialisation*, Paris, Odile Jacobs.

Bhattacharya, A. and Michael, D.C., How Local Companies Keep Multinationals at Bay, *Harvard Business Review*, March, pp. 85–94.

Boddewyn, J.J., Soehl, R. and Picard, J. (1986), Standardisation in International Marketing: Is Ted Levitt in fact Right?, *Business Horizons*, 29, 6, pp. 68–75.

Buzzell, R.D. (1968), Can you Standardize Multinational Marketing?, *Harvard Business Review*, 46, 6, pp. 106–13.

Elkington, J. (1997), *Cannibals with Forks: The Triple Bottom Line of 21st Century*, Oxford, Capstone/John Wiley.

Elkington, J. and Hartigan, P. (2008), *The Power of Unreasonable People*, Boston, MA, Harvard Business Press.

Friedman, T.L. (1996), McDonald: A successful Globalization?, *International Herald Tribune, December 12*.

Goshal, S. and Nohria, N. (1993), Horses for Courses: Organizational Forms for Multinational Corporations, *Sloan Management Review*, 34, 2, pp. 23–35.

Interbrand (2010), *Best Global Brands 2010*, www.interbrand.com.

Jain, S.C. (1989), Standardisation of International Marketing Strategy: Some Research Hypotheses, *Journal of Marketing*, 53, 1, pp. 70–9.

Karnani, A. (2007), The Mirage of Marketing to the Bottom of the Pyramid: How the Private Sector Can Help Alleviate Poverty, *California Management Review*, 49, 4, pp. 90–111.

Khawari, A. (2004), *Microfinance: Does It Hold Its Promises? A Survey of Recent Literature, Discussion Paper 276*, Hamburg Institute of International Economics.

Klein, N. (1999), *No Logo,* Knopf Canada.

Lambin, J.J. (2001), The Benefits of Globalisation, *European Business Forum*, 6, pp. 67–70.

Lambin, J.J. and Hiller, T.B. (1990), Volvo Trucks Europe, in J.J. Lambin (ed.), *Problèmes de marketing,* Paris, Ediscience International.

Landrum, N.E. (2007), Advancing the Base of the Pyramid Debate, *Strategic Management Review*, 1, 1, pp. 1–12.

Levitt, T. (1983), The Globalization of Markets, *Harvard Business Review*, 61, 3, pp. 92–102.

Little, A.D. (2003), *The Ethics of Making Money from the Poor*, Boston, MA, ADL Environment and Risk Discussion Forum.

Mizik, N. and Jacobson, R. (2009), Valuing Branded businesses, *Journal of Marketing*, 73, 6, pp. 137–53.

Morris, D. (1996), *Free Trade – The Great Destroyer,* in J. Mader and E. Goldsmith (ed.), *The Case against the Global Economy*, San Francisco, Sierra Club Books.

Morrison, A., Bouquet, C. and Beck, J. (2004), Netchising: The Next Global Wave?, *Long Range Planning*, 37, 1, p. 7.

Ponson, B. (2003), Fighting Poverty through Entrepreneurship, *European Business Forum*, 15, Autumn.

Prahalad, C.K. (2004), *Fortune at the Bottom of the Pyramid: Eradicating Poverty through Profits*, Saddle River, New Jersey, Wharton School Publishing.

Quelch, J.A. and Hoff, E.J. (1986), Customizing Global Marketing, *Harvard Business Review*, 64, 3, pp. 59–68.

Rahul, J. (2002), A No-frills Chain Sells to the Poor, *The Financial Times*, 25 March.

Ricardo, D. (1817*), On the Principles of Political Economy and Taxation*, London, Murray.

Ritchell, M. (2005), Even Little Companies Are Now Going Global, *International Herald Tribune*, 19 June.

Schuiling, I. and Kapferer, J.N. (2004), Real differences between Local and International Brands: Strategic Implications for International Marketers, *Journal of International Marketing*, 12, 4, pp. 97–112.

Schuiling, I. and Lambin, J.J. (2003), Do Global Brands Benefit from a Unique Worldwide Image? *Symphonya: Emerging Issues in Management*, 2.

Shuman, M.H. (2010), *Relocalizing Business, 2010 State of the World*, The World Watch Institute, New York, W.W. Norton & Company, pp. 110–5.

Steenkamp, J.-B. E.M. and de Jong, M.G. (2010), A Global Investigation into the Constellation of Consumer Attitudes toward Global and Local Products, *Journal of Marketing*, 74, pp. 18–40.

Yip, G.S. (1989), Global Strategy in a World of Nations, *MIT Sloan Management Review*, Fall, pp. 29–41.

CHAPTER FOUR

EMERGING VALUES
AND ISSUES

The ongoing planetary financial and economic crisis has generated a flurry of comments from various social observers announcing the end of the capitalist system and calling for a drastic change of the world economic organization. The crisis has shattered confidence in the public opinion on the capacity of the capitalist system to regulate itself to avoid catastrophic situations as presently observed in the world. The objective of *sustainable development* is today a matter of great urgency as dramatically evidenced by the financial and economic crisis, the globalization of the world economy, the acceleration of climatic change and the exhaustion of natural resources. In this chapter we shall also review new emerging issues on corporate social responsibility (CSR) and governance.

Learning Objectives

When you have read this chapter, you should be able to understand:

- The objective of sustainable development
- The life-cycle inventory (LCI) mode
- The functional service and the loop economy models
- The emerging power of civil society
- The implications of the shareholder versus stakeholder debate
- The issues of CSR
- The impact of Internet on marketing management
- The solution approach in virtual markets

4.1   THE OBJECTIVE OF SUSTAINABLE DEVELOPMENT

The question is to know whether the capitalist system will be able to evolve towards a business model compatible with the objective of sustainable development, a central preoccupation for the world economy. To the firm, and in particular for marketing, the challenge is formidable: how to reconcile the profitability imperative with green marketing and the necessity to reduce waste, pollution and carbon emissions?

Sustainable development defined

The objective of sustainable development is well known and was used by the Brundtland commission (1989) and is defined as "a development that meets the needs of present without compromising the ability of future generations to meet their own needs". D'Humières (2010, p.63) gives a more explicit definition as "a method of economic decision making based on the democratic participation of all stakeholders – shareholders, workers, customers and citizens – across generations, /.../ while maintaining the collective, natural and cultural patrimony." This vision modifies the management of the market and public policies in three aspects:

- The decision-making process extended to *all stakeholders* and integrating the *precautionary principle* in order to create the largest social utility.
- The regulation of market mechanisms to give access to public goods and to integrate negative externalities in market prices, implying the application of the "polluter pays" principle.
- The allocation of results adopting a logic of fairness and a long-term perspective in line with the nonrenewal of scarce physical resources to be preserved.

One of the main weaknesses of shareholder capitalism was to underestimate the importance of human capital and of natural capital in the final production.

The adoption of the socio-ecological view of consumption

The adoption of the sustainable development objective changes the traditional view of consumption. The socio-ecological view of consumption reflects a new awareness of the scarcity of natural resources, the uncontrolled growth of waste and the social cost of consumption (see Figure 4.1). Between 1890 and 1990, the world population has multiplied by 4, while consumption in industrial products has multiplied by 40, energy use by 16, water consumption by 9, fish consumption by 35 and the total world production by 14. This discrepancy between population and consumption growth is even higher in highly industrialized countries.

This new awareness regarding the scarcity of resources reflects a changed attitude to consumption as something, which is no longer, viewed as an end in itself but which must take

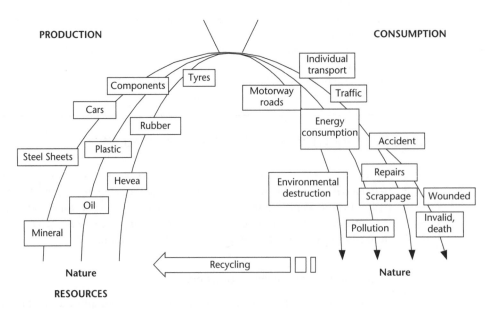

Figure 4.1   The socio-ecological view of consumption
Source: Lambin (2000/2007).

into account its upstream (opportunity cost) and downstream (repair and prevention cost) implications. Globalization is positively disseminating this new culture as markets become more interdependent and as procurement and production activities spread across the planet.

The basic argument of the ecologist is to set a price on the use of the environment which was until recently regarded as a "free good". The economic instruments used to set a price to the use of the environment generally take the form of a direct tax on the polluting activities, either in prevention (eco-taxes) or in a repairing perspective (eco-fees).

The LCI model is the basic tool used by the ecologist and through which a product's total environmental impact is evaluated from "cradle to grave". LCI is a process that quantifies the use of energy, resources and emission to the environment associated with a product throughout its life cycle. It accounts for the environmental impact of raw materials procurement, manufacturing and production, packaging, distribution and in-use characteristics straight through to after-use and disposal.

Faced with this thinking, firms are being forced to review their underlying product concepts in the light of everything from raw material procurement to after-use and disposal. In future, the certification ISO-14001, which measures and certifies the degree of greenness, will probably become a pre-condition for being short-listed in international tenders, as it is already the case for the ISO-9000 norm.

A European Union (EU) directive adopted by the European parliament is a good example of the practical implications of ecology. Under its terms, vehicle makers will have to bear the expense of recycling their cars, buses and trucks. The directive encourages the use of recycled material. It requires 85 per cent of the weight of all vehicles sold in the EU after 2007 to be made from reclaimed substances. This directive will be in application retroactively as soon as 2006, which means that the European automobile industry will have to recycle 170 million cars currently in use in Europe.

The environmental concern behind this directive comes from the market and is the expression of new needs within society. It is not a fad or a protest trend. It is a way of life which has and will spread rapidly throughout all levels of society and throughout the world. This preponderance of collective over individual needs is a new economic phenomenon and represents a check to the wilder forms of capitalism.

Until recently, such environmental consciousness could be viewed as a preoccupation of industrialized economies, but the interdependence of markets that comes with globalization has changed this. It also explains why new environmental norms are at the core of the ongoing international trade negotiations, although the EU's attempts to impose higher standards are often seen by the United States as an obstacle to free trade and by developing countries as a form of disguised protectionism.

The objective of eco-efficiency

The socio-ecological view of consumption induces firms to improve their *eco-efficiency*, that is to increase the volume of production per unit of natural resource. This objective will be reached by applying to the use of natural resources the principle adopted by Henri Ford during in the years 1920 in the use of human resources: "to do more with less".

> Historically, labour productivity has increased by a factor 200 in industry and by a factor 20 in agriculture. This means that, in industry, one worker do the job where 200 workers were required three centuries ago. By comparison the productivity in the use of natural resources and energy per production unit has increased by a factor 10 only since the eighteen century. Nevertheless, this productivity gain makes possible today to produce one ton of steel with 10 times less energy than before. (Lambin, 2004)

Exhibit 4.1   Economic analysis of environmentalism

- In 1972, the Meadow report of the Club de Rome called the attention of the economic and social world to the limits of economic growth, the risk of exhausting non-renewable resources, the destruction of the environment and the uncontrolled growth of waste. This new awareness led public authorities and political movements to listen to the recommendations made by economists.

- To the economist, the environment is part of the economy and the best way to protect the environment is to assign a price to its use instead of considering it as a free public good, in contrast with the other goods found in a market economy.

- If there is no market price, consumers and manufacturers are motivated to use the environment as a *free reservoir* even if the social costs generated by their polluting behaviour are high, since the market does not assess these costs. Thus, the ones generating these social costs do not pay them and are not held responsible for the costs involved by their elimination.

- The solution proposed by the economists is to set a price to the use of the environment. This price should be equal to the sum of the total social costs generated by pollution as the polluted parties evaluate them. Given this price, polluters would use the environment only to the extent the expected benefits of this use are higher than the price they would have to pay. This way, the polluters would assume the social cost of pollution. This is the idea behind the principle *who pollutes pays.*

- The economic instruments used to set a price to the use of the environment generally take the form of a direct tax on the polluting activities, either in prevention (eco-taxes) or in a repairing perspective (eco-fees).

All specialists agree: the potential for improving the eco-efficiency of most products is enormous (through de-carbonization, de-materialization, reduction of waste and pollution, etc.). Beneficial for the environment, improving the eco-efficiency also improves the firms' profitability thereby creating a *win-win situation*, where gains are achieved on both the environmental and economic sides.

Last but not least, the image of the firm having a good ecological reputation is becoming a stronger argument for creating loyalty among customers, employees and shareholders. Today, more investors are expressing their preferences for ethical funds regrouping firms having good social and ecological credentials, as illustrated by the growth of sustainable investments funds. For more details about the development of sustainable products, see the new emerging trends analysed by McKinsey (Beinhocker, Davis and Mendonca, 2009).

Sustainability is now the key driver of innovation. Nidumolu, Prahalad and Ranfgaswami (2009) have studied the sustainability initiatives of 30 large companies and have found that smart companies now treat sustainability as innovation's new frontier. The authors have observed that these firms go through five different stages of change implying different challenges and capabilities.

4.2   NEW ECO-SENSITIVE BUSINESS MODELS

To implement the sustainable development objective, firms have to adopt new business models which are more eco-sensitive. The traditional business model follows a linear process – raw material extraction, manufacturing, distribution, consumption and accumulation of waste, what can be described as a "cradle to grave" process. The globalization of this industrial model is not feasible. For the entire world to live as an American or European, we would need 2 more planets earth to satisfy everyone, 3 more still, if population should double, and 12 earths altogether if worldwide standards of living should double over the next 40 years. The performance economy model developed by Stahel (2006) makes a distinction between three types of economies:

■ The industrial economy, also called a *River Economy*, which is characterized by high annual resource consumption and fast replacement of goods, a model which is unsustainable in the long term (a "cradle to grave" approach).
■ The *Functional Service Economy*, where the focus is placed on assets management and on utilization and use capabilities, rather than on physical goods delivery, thereby creating in-sourcing jobs (a "cradle to cradle" approach).
■ The *Loop Economy* which starts at the end of a good utilization period, when used products become consumer waste (a "grave to cradle" approach).

The models of a loop economy and of a functional service economy are complementary and propose promising solutions for developing an eco-responsible capitalism. These two new business models can contribute to amend the capitalist system and to support the objective of sustainable development by decoupling economic growth and environmental destruction.

The functional service economy

A functional service economy is possible when the firm is selling a performance, a result, and not simply a product. The sale of a service, that is, the product's function or solution provided, is substituted with the sale of a physical product. Underlying the concept of solution is the idea that a customer is looking for a solution to his or her problem and for not the product itself. The physical product is simply a means used to obtain the desired outcome?

■ *Carrier*, the world's leading maker of air-conditioning equipment, reasoned that customers don't want what an air-conditioning system is; they only want what it does. *Carrier* is offering "cool services" and contracts to keep a client's house or apartment within a certain temperature range in hot weather during certain hours at a certain cost, taking advantage of the very efficient and reliable equipment's operating benefits.
■ Similarly, *Schindler*, the leading Swiss maker of elevators, makes 70 per cent of its earnings by leasing "vertical transportation services" rather than by selling elevators. *Schindler*'s lifts are more efficient and reliable than many competing brands, so by leasing their services, the company can capture the operational savings. Its lease provides the service, not the equipment.

Can this view be extended to the whole economy? In a functional service economy, consumers buy individual mobility instead of buying a car, a climatic comfort instead of an air-conditioning system, a gardening maintenance service instead of a set of gardening machines and tools and so on. Functional sales then take the form of short- or long-term leasing contracts or of mutual ownership of goods. For the manufacturer, the economic objective is to create the highest possible usage value, during the longest period possible while using the smallest possible quantity of resources. Instead of being motivated to sell products having a short life time to stimulate replacement demand, the manufacturer is induced (by an invisible hand) to optimize the long-term usage of the products that the customers do not need to own. The products owned by the manufacturer become capital goods providing sustainable revenues. It is the manufacturer's best interest to design reliable products that lend themselves to re-manufacturing, repairing and recycling without an externalization of the costs, risks and wastes.

The model of a performance economy has been promoted in France by Nicolas Hulot (2007) in his book on an ecological pact. There is already a long list of firms having adopted this strategy (Rank Xerox, Michelin, Electrolux, DuPont, Dow Chemicals), which is a difficult option because industrial firms have to reinvent their business.

Benefits of the functional economy

This economic system has the virtuous effect to reduce industrial production and the wastes generated by consumption, while maintaining long-lasting relationships with customers. Firms do not have to increase their production and their sales levels to increase revenues. The profitability of the product is assured over time: the longer it is used, the larger its amortization. When the product reaches the end of its life time with the customer, the manufacturer is induced to recycle or to repair as many components as possible and to reintroduce them in its production process without rejecting in the environment the costs and wastes. A strategy of service-life extension for durable goods – such as infrastructure, building, ships, aircraft, equipment and cars – is thus equivalent to a substitution of manpower for energy and materials. This strategy creates jobs at home, while at the same time reducing resources throughput in the economy (Stahel, 2006, p. 62).

Difficulties of implementation

In the field of consumer goods, the service functional economy implies a drastic change in consumers' behaviour, since consumers have to accept to substitute the ownership of a good by its mere usage, a renunciation difficult to tolerate when the emotional value associated to the ownership of the good is central. The needs of ownership, fashion, innovation and differentiation (conspicuous consumption) are social phenomenon observable in all market economies. In any case, the functional economy model is applicable only to products where separating physical possession and usage is meaningful, thereby excluding products and services for which consumption means destruction. Thus, the functional economy model has a more limited scope in B2C markets, where goods are "toys" designed for amusement, not to earn money, than in B2B markets where production and investments goods are "tools" used by economic actors to make money (Stahel, 2006, p. 177).

A second difficulty, hard to measure, is the complexity of the contractual relationship generated by the leasing agreement between the firm and its customers, regarding the liability of the leaseholder, including the "moral hazard" of customers who would not manage properly the rented equipment or would waste the rented energy (leaving windows open).

The loop or circular economy

In a traditional economy, the product life cycle is linear "from cradle to grave". In a loop economy by contrast, this linear life cycle is replaced by a loop "from cradle to a new cradle", by adopting reusing, re-manufacturing and technology-updating strategies and by recycling used products and the wastes generated by a particular production process for other productions or for other industries. Repair, reuse, upgrading, remanufacturing, recycling and downcycling are the six main closed-loop principles to keep the gift of good materials and good work moving on to other users and other uses. The small the loop the more profitable it is. Do not repair what is not broken, do not remanufacture something that can be repaired, do not recycle a product that can be remanufactured, do not incinerate or land-fill a product that can be downcycled.

When *Caterpillar*, the US heavy equipment company, started to take back diesel engines for remanufacturing, it sold the remanufactured engines at a large discount. When *Caterpillar* changes its strategy to buy the used engines back for a price that depended on its condition and completeness, the quality of the used engines significantly improved. The remanufac-tured engines are now sold with the same guarantee and for the same price as new ones (Stahel, 2006).

Eco-designed products

Repair works better if the product was designed to facilitate it. Obviously, it is much easier to disassemble product for re-manufacturing or reuse of its parts if it was designed with that end in mind. Unfortunately, in many cases, repairing is more expensive than buying a new product.

Renovating a building or re-manufacturing a train needs nearly as much manpower as building a new one, yet conserves 80 per cent of the original investment in materials and energy. What if an item's options for repair, reuse and re-manufacturing are exhausted? Then it can be recycled to reconstitute it into another similar product. As a last resort, it can be downcycled – ground, melted or dissolved so its basic materials can be reincarnated for a lower purpose, such as a filler material. When those closed-loop principles are applied to everything from packaging to the 3 billion tons of construction materials used each year, a substantial amount of reclaiming is at stake – and every ton not extracted, treated and moved means less harm to natural capital (Hawken and others, 1999, p. 80).

Very frequently, only a limited fraction of the raw material or of the energy used is inte-grated into an end-product. It has been estimated (Ayres, 1989) that in the US economy, only 6 per cent of its vast flows of materials actually end up in products. The leftover is either lost or transformed into a sub-product of low value or in waste. These sub-products, however, can have value for another industry or for another consumer group. A common observation is that the costs of re-manufacturing or of reusing high added value compo-nents are more than offset by the savings generated by the reduction of raw materials.

The Chinese government is very active in implementing this concept of a loop economy by promoting the creation of industrial eco-parks regrouping enterprises involved in an exchange system based on the recycling and on the reusing of wastes, the waste of one industry being used as raw materials of the other. The concept of a loop economy can be adopted by any eco-sensitive firm, but its adoption generally implies a form of intersectoral coordination and a substantial reorganization of the production processes. An emblematic example of this strategy is given by Rank Xerox and its successful strategy entirely focused on re-manufacturing and reusing its used products.

Importance of the recycling industry

The recycling industry in the EU, in 2008, had a turnover of €24 billion and employed about 500,000 persons. It was made up of over 60,000 companies. Waste generation in the EU is estimated at more than 1.3 billion tons per year at rates comparable to economic growth. For example, both gross domestic product (GDP) and municipal waste grew by 19 per cent between 1995 and 2003. One consequence of this growth is that despite large increases in recycling, landfill – the most problematic way to get rid of waste – is only reducing slowly. High standards exist for landfills and incinerators. Industry now seeks to make a profit from waste instead of dumping it.

The loop economy model can be adopted by any firm even if it implies deep changes in the organization of production systems. These changes have to be initiated by the eco-sensitive management and supported by public authorities.

4.3   AFFIRMATION OF CIVIL SOCIETY'S POWER

The growing power of citizens generates new expectations which directly contribute to improving the functioning and transparency of the market: liberty of choice, better information, pressure on prices, product safety, after-sales responsibility of the manufacturers and ecologically friendly products. It also constitutes a *strong countervailing power* to the

---

Exhibit 4.2   Recycling around the world

Most countries in the world today have developed incentives programmes to encourage people and enterprises to recycle their waste, but current practices vary largely.

- In the United States, efforts to improve recycling rates and to reduce household and commercial waste are led by the US Environmental Protection Agency (EPA), which has 180,000 full-time employees. Today, the United States recycles about 28 per cent of its waste, a rate that has almost doubled during the past ten years. Recycling of specific materials has grown even more drastically; 42 per cent of all paper, 40 per cent of plastic soft drink bottles, 55 per cent of all aluminium beer and soft drink cans, 57 per cent of all steel packaging, and 52 per cent of all major appliances are now recycled.

- In Denmark, one of Europe's greenest countries, the environment policy has been to regard waste as a resource. Tough standards have been set by governments, but it is up to local authorities to collect waste that households produce. In 2003, that averaged 559 kg of waste per Dane. Nearly 10,000 Danes are in the business of collecting waste, more that 1 per cent of the entire population. Data for 2003 suggest that 31 per cent of all household waste was recycled, while 62 per cent was incinerated. The remaining 6 per cent was landfill waste.

- The Germans like to think of themselves as the world champions of the environment. When it comes to separating your household rubbish, this can be a complicated business. There are at least five types of rubbish bins in the courtyards of apartment buildings and inside people's houses. Luckily, the bins are colour-coded to avoid any confusion – a yellow bin for packaging (old milk cartons, etc.), a blue bin for

paper and cardboard, bins for glass (separated into ones for clear, brown and green glass), a bio bin designed for leftover food and plant waste. Finally, there is a black bin for the rest of the rubbish. People are obliged under German law to take any "special rubbish", such as batteries or chemicals, to a recycling centre.

- In Greece, every year 1 billion plastic drinking water bottles are thrown away, along with 1 billion of soft drinks bottles and yet another billion plastic containers for cleaning fluids. One-fifth of the entire waste produced by this country is plastic and yet just 1 per cent is recycled. Greece is at least 15 years behind the rest of the EU in almost all areas of recycling and is unlikely to meet the EU target in the near future.

- In Italy, waste disposal regulations vary from district to district. In Rome, people who do not separate their rubbish can be fined up to €619 if they have a recycling bin within 500 metres of their front door. Romans often claim that it is hard to find one that is not full. They are colour-coded, green for household waste, white for paper and blue for plastic. In southern Italy, local politicians claim that the waste management industry is controlled by organized crime.

- In Senegal, recycling is not done on an industrial scale, but it is part of daily life for many resourceful Senegalese. Everything is recycled, from plastic bags to school exercise books, food cans, bottles of mineral water and even fruit peel. The peel is said to be collected for use in cheap perfume. Tomato tins become drinking cups, old newspapers and administrative documents are used to wrap bread, fruit or peanuts. Plastic bags are used to make shoes.

Source: Adapted from BBC News (2005).

power of companies and even to the power of public authorities. New and more responsible relationships between consumers and the industrial world are developing.

New consumer behaviour

In the industrialized world, being better educated and exposed to the consumerist culture, consumers represent a force of responsible citizen-consumers that firms and public authorities can no longer ignore. Seven attitudes characterize the new consumer:

- *A feeling of power.* consumers behave in markets where supply is plentiful, brands proliferate, competition for consumer's loyalty is intense and independent information sources are numerous.
- *A professional purchasing behaviour.* well-educated and experienced, consumers are smart shoppers, able to make a trade-off between brands, stores, advertising and the recommendations of salespeople. They become increasingly discriminating in their demand for customized services and want complete information about their purchases. From passive consumers, they have become more active "consum'actors".
- *The satisfaction–delight–loyalty relationship.* The new consumer holds the firm responsible in case of dissatisfaction. Thus a dissatisfied customer is a lost customer, a damaging effect in zero-growth markets, where replacing a lost customer by a new one is particularly difficult and costly. Moreover, research results show that simply giving what is expected is not enough to keep a customer loyal. The objective should be to give more than expected, to have *delighted customers*. An interesting article from Dixon, Freeman and Toman (2010) reviews the objective delighting customers.
- *A search for new values.* In industrialized countries, economic prosperity and mass consumption have lifted the aspirations of consumers from materialistic needs to the search for new values. Initially looking mainly for comfort and safety, they are more and more looking for stimulation, pleasure, change, innovation, surprise.
- *A need for a dialogue.* Consumers are represented by powerful and vocal consumerist organizations and by NGOs. Just as significant is the growing influence of environmental groups, human rights activists, labour and religious groups and a host of other organizations that collectively make up "civil society".
- *A search for rewarding experiences.* Many consumers are moving from "conspicuous consumption" to "calculated consumption", a "back to basics" movement where consumers are more interested in experiences than in possessions of goods.
- In addition, consumers want an *ethical consumption* and do not want to have guilty feelings from their purchases or from the advertising associated with their brands. Shopping with attitude. Buying and using products and brands having acceptable price and quality ratios, but also brands meeting ethical criteria such as the product greenness, the social and human practice of the firm, its political and strategic commitments and so on.

This emerging trend toward ethical consumption is confirmed in the United Kingdom by the survey results conducted in 1994 and in 2004 by Co-op UK (see Table 4.1). The key conclusion is that consumers today are more concerned with ethical issues (up 23 per cent compared to in 1994) as shown by three key measurements:

- 64 per cent (up 12 per cent) say that they are more concerned about ethical issues.
- 84 per cent (up 35 per cent) say they are ready to pay a little extra for products that meet ethical standards, provided that quality is as good.
- 80 per cent (steady) say that they are prepared to boycott a product on ethical grounds.

Table 4.1 Who cares about ethics? A Co-op UK consumer survey

Ethical issues	1994 n=31,000	2004 n=29,500	Change
General concern about issues – Are you more concerned now than in the past?	57%	64%	+12%
Support for Third World – Should retailers help growers in developing countries?	55%	80%	+45%
Willingness to pay more – Are you willing to pay a little extra for ethical alternatives?	62%	84%	+35%
Active boycotting – Have you boycotted a product on ethical grounds?	33%	29%	–12%
Preparedness to boycott – Are you likely to boycott in the future?	60%	60%	Steady
Informative labelling – Do food labels give full information?	62%	96%	+54%
Honest labelling – Should misleading labels be banned?	62%	90%	+56%
Farm animal welfare – Very important that retailers buy humanely reared meat	66%	71%	+7%
Wildlife welfare – Very important to support products not harmful to wildlife	59%	70%	+18%
Conserve natural resources – Very important to stop products from non-sustainable sources	55%	64%	+16%
Pollution of environment – Very important that business minimize pollution	52%	67%	+29%
Packaging – Very important that retailers minimize packaging	52%	58%	+11%
Average increase across all areas of study	**Up 23%**		

Source: Croft (2004).

A more recent evolution is the so-called "politically correct consumption" (or the committed consumption), which designates a purchasing behaviour in which the consumer is more involved by considering that a brand purchase is similar to a political act. To select a brand or a company is comparable to a political vote: one selects a candidate in whom we trust. Similarly, in the marketplace one can make politically correct purchase decisions.

> A case in point is the Mecca-Cola brand launched in the French market and targeting the Muslim community. Its slogan is: "Do not drink stupid, drink committed." The brand also promises to give 10% of its net profit to Palestinian charities. (http://mecca-cola.com/)

These observed changes in consumer behaviour challenge the stereotype of a manipulated and defenceless consumer. This growing power of citizens generates new expectations which directly contribute to improving the functioning and transparency of the market: liberty of choice, better information, pressure on prices, product safety, after-sales responsibility of the manufacturers and ecologically friendly products. It also constitutes a *strong countervailing power* to the power of companies and even to the power of public authorities. New and more responsible relationships between consumers and the industrial world are developing.

4.4 THE EMERGENCE OF NEW VALUES

Our era is characterized by a number of paradoxes. As stated by de Woot (2005), "Our capacity to produce wealth has never been greater while the inequalities in the world have never been larger. The extraordinary dynamism of the market economy exists alongside the near total poverty of half of humanity. The economic tendency is towards globalisation while politics have remained mainly national in character. It's as if the technical and economic system had been left to its own devices. The environment is deteriorating while scientific knowledge, technical know-how and accumulated wealth could safeguard the planet."

This situation, which is the result of an extremely complex accumulation of factors, affects companies and obliges them to rethink their responsibilities toward society and to consider the market economy in its environment together with its strengths but also its weaknesses and malfunctions. Today an increasing number of voices (European Commission, business leaders, NGOs, etc.) supporting the idea of sustainable development and what is called the stakeholders' approach in management are being raised.

The "shareholders" versus "stakeholders" debate

Since the mid-1980s we have witnessed an increasing focus on shareholder value in particular in US and UK companies. The traditional *shareholder approach*, following the views of Nobel Prize' Milton Friedman (1970), holds that the purpose of business is to increase profits or shareholder value. The main argument for supporting shareholder value is quite straightforward: failure by managers to recognize the primacy of the shareholder value group will result in poorer returns to shareholder, reduced motivation for potential investors and eventually reduced activity and unemployment. An example of the mission statement of a shareholder-focused business is that of the Coca-Cola Company, which states:

> We exist to create value for our share owners on a long-term basis by building a business that enhances the Coca-Cola trademarks. This is also our ultimate commitment.

On the other hand, the *stakeholder approach* asserts that the firm is responsible to and should be run for the benefit of number constituencies, that is, its stakeholders. Who are these stakeholders (see Figure 4.2)?

A popular definition is that stakeholders are any groups or individuals who can affect or are affected by the organization's objectives: employees, customers, suppliers, local community and the environment. The stakeholder approach does not specify, however, which

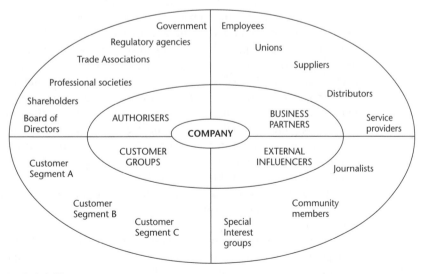

Figure 4.2 Corporate Stakeholders
Source: Dowling (2001).

stakeholder group has priority over another. An example of a mission statement of a stake-holder business is that of Cadbury Schweppes, which states:

> Our task is to build our tradition of quality and value and to provide brands, products, finan-cial results and management performance that meet the interest of our shareholders, consum-ers, suppliers and the communities in which we operate.

At the heart of the stakeholders model – a somewhat slippery concept – is the principle that all persons must be respected and that the firm exists to equally satisfy all stakeholders, a complex objective. Multiple stakeholders only compound the complexities.

This is not highlighted when executives bestow upon themselves huge pay increases, with paltry rises to employees, when returns to shareholders have been modest, and prices to consumers have not dropped, nor service enhanced. A notorious case is Barclay Bank in 1998, which awarded its CEO massive pay rises while reducing its workforce by 7500 and closing down 172 branches.

At first sight, it seems that it is difficult for both approaches to co-exist in harmony within a particular economy. The argument for supporting the stakeholders approach has its own merit, however. Unless the needs of stakeholders are properly addressed there will be an adverse effect on company performance and therefore on shareholders' returns.

The idea that satisfying the needs of all those with a stake in the business can go hand in hand with superior returns to shareholders has obvious appeal. The emergence of new values described in this section suggests that substantial progress is made in that direction. To review how to reinvent capitalism and unleash a wave of innovation and growth, see Porter and Kramer (2011) and Lambin (2011).

Towards global governance

The globalization of the world economy raises the issue of the role of the nation-state and of global governance. It is an established fact that nation states are deprived from their national prerogatives to the extent that they do not control transnational activities. The contrast between the means that the nations have at their disposal for national govern-ance (between 30 per cent and 50 per cent of the gross national product (GNP)) and the weakness of resources at the global level is striking. It is recognized that a market economy needs a strong governance to define and enforce the rules of the competitive game. It is up to the state, for example, to balance the main macro-economic issues (such as price stabil-ity) and to ensure a minimum social cohesiveness and solidarity. A market economy, be it national of global, needs a strong governance to function smoothly. In a market that is hardly regulated or not regulated at all, the risk of wild capitalism prevailing is high. If the market economy system in Russia did not work well during the first years of its adoption it was largely due not to the market, but to a too weak government and to the absence of the market and economic regulations that are necessary to ensure a smooth functioning of a market economy. In this type of unregulated market, "might is right" and the mafia or a bunch of corrupted individuals run the show.

But in an under-regulated global market, which international organization will assume this global governance? In other words, if there is a *global village* which municipal board will be in charge?

In today's world, the urge to maintain and to claim one's own cultural identity is stronger than ever and, in the years to come, it will be the *subsidiarity principle* that will guide decision-making. *What can be best dealt with at a local level should be addressed locally.*

For transnational issues, like ecology, privacy on the Web, safety, terrorism, health, on the other hand, forms of world governance are necessary. A world government is hardly on the agenda but new forms of concerted global effort – similar to the Kyoto, Montreal and the Hague conferences in the field of ecology, and to the Davos and Porto Alegre forums in the socio-economic field – can contribute to solutions.

Global capitalism needs strong countervailing powers, which go beyond the power of national governments. Contrary to the demands of the anti-globalization supporters, the powers of supranational organizations like the WTO, the International Monetary Fund (IMF) and the World Bank should be reinforced and new supranational organizations created to deal with these transnational issues. Without them the risk is increased that we end up with a much wilder form of capitalism than we have at the moment operating in a completely deregulated market.

Corporate social responsibility

Firms everywhere are embracing the concept of corporate social responsibility (CSR), and the financial corporate scandals in the United States (Enron, Worldcom) have contributed to reinforce this evolution. The reasons for the adoption of this business philosophy at the corporate level can be summarized as follows:

- Any firm needs a healthy and prosperous environment to reach its own development objectives. Economic progress cannot be built on a social disaster.
- A global economic system in which half of humanity finds itself excluded is obviously not viable politically nor acceptable morally.
- The welfare state and the social and fiscal solutions it implies have clearly reached their limits, both on qualitative and on financial grounds.
- Rather than paying more taxes, civil society should wake up and commit itself, where it has the appropriate skills and resources.

The responsible corporation acknowledges that it has a responsibility towards society and not only to its shareholders. It is an organization, large or small, which wishes to establish a long-term and sustainable relationship with the community where it lives and from which it gains its prosperity. Participating in social life, the responsible corporation commits its resources and competence to help combat social problems, often in co-operation with public authorities. The domains where the responsible corporation can contribute are several and varied: to develop the economic fabric of a region, to maintain or develop employment, to participate in education programmes, to protect the environment, to dialogue with stakeholders, to promote urban development, to fight against social exclusion.

A key part of the vision is that corporations are the most powerful force for change in the modern world: state, church and university should not shy away but their actions, slower by nature, merely complement the more important role of companies.

In the new global economy, ethical behaviour which consists of "of doing well (financially) by doing good (socially)" is not only compatible with the objective of modern capitalism – as evidenced by the success of ethical funds – it represents a competitive advantage by meeting the market's demand. Again, the interdependence of markets created by globalization helps ensure that these new standards of behaviour become an imperative for any firm with the ambition to become a player in the global market.

The CSR process is important but it has a credibility gap problem to the extent that the concept is used intensively in the firm's communication platform. It is imperative that governments themselves define the ethical objectives and the laws required to implement them. One has to move away from the field of "morality" to establish clear rules legally defined. As now stated in international norms, the CSR ISO-2600,[1] the objective of CSR is to contribute to the implementation of the sustainable development objective and to people's health and well-being. In total the field of the new CSR covers seven responsibilities: respect for human rights, rules of corporate governance, social obligations, protection of the environment, business practices, consumer relationships and societal commitment. It is very likely that in 2020, CSR will be a common practice and not an exception in corporate governance.

This philosophy of responsible management is rapidly gaining acceptance in Europe in the business community, as evidenced by the proliferation of charters and codes of conduct, the growing adoption of the TBL reporting systems, the charter of Human Responsibility suggested by the Alliance for a responsible world, the efforts of Transparency International, the anti-bribery convention of the Organization for Economic Cooperation and Development (OECD) and so on. TBL is particularly important and represents the idea that businesses should account for their performance on economic, environmental and social criteria and attempt to satisfy their stakeholders on all three sets of criteria.

Luo and Bhattacharya (2009) have questioned whether firms excellent in CSR are financially rewarded or punished by Wall Street? Their empirical results show that superior CSR relative to competitors is capable of boosting shareholder wealth by lowering the undesirable volatility of firms' stocks prices. The results also empower marketers to communicate more effectively with investors. However, firms need to guard against being perceived as "cause over-exploitive" by being authentic and sincere in the way they approach and implement CSR programmes.

The potential impact of social accountability certification

As the world becomes more linked and interconnected by global media, alleged and actual corporate social misbehaviour is rapidly made public.

> For example Nike's labour and environmental practices in Vietnam during the 1990s quickly became a public scandal and a significant marketing problem for Nike, resulting in boycotts, loss of revenue and, most significantly, tremendous damage to Nike's corporate reputation.

Exhibit 4.3   How to improve ethical reasoning?

1. *The legal test:* Does the contemplated action violate the law?
2. *The duties test:* Is this action contrary to widely accepted moral obligations such as fidelity, gratitude, justice, non-malfeasance and beneficence?
3. *The special obligation test:* Does the proposed action violate any other special obligation that stems from the type of marketing organization at focus (pharmaceutical firms, toy manufacturers, etc.)?
4. *The motive test:* Is the intent of the contemplated action harmful?
5. *The utilitarian test:* Is there a satisfactory alternative action that produces equal or greater benefits to the parties affected than the proposed action?
6. *The rights test:* Does the contemplated action infringe upon property rights, privacy rights or the inalienable rights of the consumer (such as the right to information, the right to be heard, the right to choice and the right to remedy)?
7. *The justice test:* Does the proposed action leave another person or group less well off?

Source: Adapted from Laczniak and Murphy (1993, p. 49).

A major social responsibility issue that corporations must address is the contextual nature of what constitutes a "social good". In Europe and in the United States, children are protected by society and are not considered a household economic asset. But this is simply not true in some cultures where the economic value of children is a significant contribution to household income.

These differences in what is considered the proper and responsible use of resources by business are motivation factors that are driving initiatives such as the UN's nine principles and the adoption of ISO14000 (environment) and SA8000 (CSR) certification by global corporations.

> SA8000 is a set of international workplace and human rights standards developed by Social Accountability International, with inputs from the United Nations and numerous NGOs. SA8000 is enjoying widespread adoption similar to that of ISO9000 ISO 14000 as multinational corporations are encouraged by their stakeholders to become more socially accountable.

This global and comprehensive set of CSR guidelines can be applied throughout a marketer's supply chain, and it is possible that SA8000 certification may eventually become an "international passport" for registered firms or a barrier to entry for unregistered firms in international and domestic markets. The standards are also expected to eventually trickle down to the suppliers of the larger firms, that is, the small- and medium-sized enterprises.

What is the link, if any, between social responsibility and financial performance? In other words, does it pay to be good? The two stakeholder areas that seem to dominate the relationship are those of employees and customers. The data linking customer orientation and corporate financial performance are compelling. Companies that are more responsive to customers tend to generate greater profits. For a review of these studies see Gotteland (2005). Several studies (Kotter and Heskett, 1992) have also found that a variety of HR practices are positively correlated with financial performance. Beyond employees and customers, the evidence linking other stakeholder areas to financial performance is very weak. There is little evidence that a company's commitment to social activity in its various forms such as traditional philanthropy, cause-related marketing or events involving local communities will increase profits, at least directly, even if many firms believe that such activity may improve their corporate image (Johnson, 2003).

Exhibit 4.4   Is self-regulation effective?

To promote CSR the importance of self-regulation and codes of conduct as main instruments of voluntary rule-setting has long been embraced (Arrow, 1973). Thirty years later, questions about effectiveness of self-regulation continue to be raised, in view of the growing number of companies spontaneously adopting corporate codes of conduct. The question is particularly relevant knowing that the American company Enron, one year before the financial scandal was made public, was congratulated for the quality of its corporate code of conduct. Kolk and van Tulder (2002) have closely examined the nature of child labour codes of six pioneering international garment companies (Levi Strauss, Nike, Gap, C&A, Hennes & Mauritz, and WE) active in the textile and footwear sectors where child labour is a very sensitive issue. The authors clearly conclude that self-regulation, with codes of conduct as most common instruments, is considered effective in promoting CSR, in particular when monitored systems exist such as the SA8000 international certification.

Source: Kolk and van Tulder (2002).

Box 4.1   Implementation problem: how to apply social accountability standards: the SA8000 standards

1. Child labour

Prohibits the use of child labour (less than 15 years of age, unless local regulations are higher), requires corporate support for the education of school-age workers; time spent daily on work and school cannot be more than ten hours; that the corporation does not expose children inside or outside the work place to hazardous or healthy situations.

2. Forced labour

Prohibits the use of forced labour.

3. Health and safety

Requires safe and healthy working conditions, health and safety training for all workers, clean and sanitary working and living conditions (if company provided).

4. Freedom of association and the right to collective bargaining

Requires that the corporation allow, without discrimination, workers to form trade unions and engage in collective bargaining.

5. Discrimination

Prohibits discrimination based on gender, race, caste, and so on, in hiring, compensation, training, promotion, or retirement.

6. Disciplinary practices

Prohibits use of coercion or corporal punishment.

7. Working hours

Prohibits required work in excess of 48 hours/week, and requires at least one day in seven off. Allows up to 12 hours/week overtime at a wage premium.

8. Compensation

Requires that the corporation pay workers a legal minimum and locally derived "living wage".

9. Management systems

Requires a company policy for social accountability that includes social accountability audits for the corporation itself and its suppliers and sub-contractors.

Source: SA8000 (2001).

In short, the emerging values in the corporate world place the shareholder versus stakeholder debate in a new perspective and suggest that there is an increasing convergence between the shareholder and the stakeholder models. Our views can be summarized as follows:

- The shareholder approach is the foundation stone of a market economy system and should be clearly reaffirmed: *the role of the firm is to create shareholder value*. To challenge this view is like shooting on one's own foot and it undermines the credibility of the capitalist system and the trust of investors, keeping in mind that those investors are increasingly institutional investors.
- In a competitive market economy, there is no other way for creating shareholder value than *by creating first customer value*. Compelling empirical evidence (Anderson, Fornell and Mazvanceryl, 2004) supports the proposition that customer satisfaction generates shareholder value. Thus, the objective of customer satisfaction by adopting the market-driven business philosophy described in this book should be the central preoccupation of the firm.
- Today's customers are more demanding in their recognition of value. They do not want to have guilty feelings about their consumption. They expect good behaviour criteria such as product greenness, social and human practice of the firm, its political and strategic commitments, ethical conduct and so on from the firms or the brands they are dealing with.

It is therefore the objective of customer satisfaction that will eventually induce (force) firms to adopt the stakeholder approach. The market-oriented firm will joyfully adopt this approach because it contributes to increasing shareholder value.

4.5   IMPLICATIONS FOR MARKET-DRIVEN MANAGEMENT

Within the globalized economy, strategic marketing has a more important social role than it ever had. It remains the best mechanism to adjust demand to supply, but it also triggers a virtuous circle of economic and social development, reinforced today by the social, cultural and technological changes observed in the market. These evolutions in the interconnected global economy create grounds for optimism in that they are contributing to a more democratic and transparent market economy, based on new values. In this new environment, national and supranational authorities have a key role to play: to monitor and to control the initiatives taken to meet emerging needs in order to reconcile market efficiency with the imperatives of a social vision.

What are the managerial implications of the three evolutionary changes reviewed in this chapter? As discussed in Chapter 2, the market orientation paradigm is complex and can be defined by reference to three dimensions: culture, analysis and action. To what extent the market evolutionary changes described above impinge on these three dimensions?

- *Culture.* The corporate philosophy is the one of a social market economy system. It is by creating value for the customer that the firm will achieve its own objectives of profit and growth, thereby creating shareholder value. More relevant than ever, this objective is also more challenging in a globalized and interconnected competitive economy. Moreover, to meet the expectations of the new consumers, companies will have to integrate the objectives of sustainable development and of social solidarity that differentiate a social market economy system, a model largely accepted within the EU.
- *Analysis.* The objective of strategic marketing is to propose to a well-defined market segment a value proposition both differentiated from competition and sustainable by the firm. In the new economy, this objective is more difficult given the complexity of world markets with the emergence of new powerful players such as the civil society voice, consumer power, vocal NGOs, mass merchandisers. This new complexity of markets requires a reinforcement of the strategic brain of the firm.
- *Action.* Stimulated and empowered by the development of the NICT, the firm's commercial arm has until today unthinkable capabilities: one-to-one segmentation, personalized communication, access to the world market any where, any time, low barriers to entry, customized pricing, relationship selling. In short, the capacity to move away from a "strategy of product" toward a "strategy of solution".

4.6   THE IMPACT OF INTERNET TECHNOLOGY

The development of the new technologies of information and communication gives a new impetus to the MO concept by breaking down the traditional barriers of the physical market and allowing the identification of individual consumers and of their demographic and preferences profiles. Thus, the ultimate objective of the MO concept, that is, to provide customized solutions and services according to individual preferences, becomes a more realistic objective thanks to the development of the Internet technology.

From e-commerce to e-business

Despite the early setbacks of e-commerce in late 1999, expansion of Internet use has proceeded without interruption. Consumer and public confidence in the Internet has been restored, fostering renewed growth and expansion. The Internet is increasingly integrated into the daily routines of households and businesses throughout the world. By all measures, a majority of adults are now online and increasing numbers have access to broadband connections.

Initially, Internet was assimilated to e-commerce and perceived as a narrow selling instrument deployed through a website – little more than a banner presenting the company and a catalogue of products from which customers can order directly online. E-business is the application of information and telecommunication technologies to conducting business. Compared to e-commerce, e-business is a more generic term because it refers not only to information exchange related to buying and selling, but also to servicing customers and collaborating with business partners, distributors, and suppliers (Papazoglou and Ribbers, 2006).

It has been widely assumed that the Internet is cannibalistic, that it will replace all conventional ways of doing business and overturn all traditional advantages. "It is now clear that it was a vast exaggeration" (Porter, 2001, p. 73). In many cases, Internet complements, rather than cannibalizes, companies' traditional activities and ways of competing. Virtual activities do not eliminate the need for physical activities but, on the contrary, often amplify their importance. In addition, Internet creates new opportunities for meeting customers' needs in a more efficient way.

Impact of Internet

The main characteristics of Internet are well known: virtual ubiquity of demand and supply, easy access to quality information by a large public any where, any time, worldwide comparison of offerings and prices, absence of entry barriers, separation between production and selling, equal opportunities for each seller.

The explosive growth of Internet has often confused companies, provoking widespread questioning and reassessment of the way markets are likely to be organized and marketing strategy developed in the future. Analysing the impact of the Internet, Porter (2001) and Papazoglou and Ribbers (2006) have identified several trends from the perspective of producers and of customers.

- The Internet tends to weaken the bargaining powers of channels by providing companies with new, more direct avenues to customers.
- The Internet can augment an industry's efficiency by expanding the size of the market and by improving its position relative to traditional substitutes.
- Internet technology provides consumers with easier access to information about products and suppliers, thus bolstering their bargaining and countervailing power.
- The Internet mitigates the need for an established sales force or access to existing channels, reducing barriers to entry.
- By enabling new approaches to meeting needs and performing functions, the Internet creates new substitutes.
- Because the Internet is an open system, companies have more difficulty maintaining proprietary offerings, thus intensifying the rivalry among competitors.
- The use of Internet also tends to expand the geographic market, bringing many more companies into competition with one another.

Thus, Internet technology not only modifies the functioning of the market, but more importantly facilitates the implementation of the MO concept by reinforcing the power of the market players over the firms' market power. In this context, the objective of value creation for the client becomes more difficult to achieve given the limited potential for differentiation and the absence of protection of new ideas

Most firms today have created their own website, but a growing number of companies have so far been able to sell to their end-customers through the Web. By contrast, however, many have adopted Electronic Data Interchange (EDI) systems, which hook together computers of commercial partners via telephone lines. Once established, this connection facilitates and accelerates communication within the supply chain for ordering between suppliers, distributors, and customers, for disseminating information and thereby generating substantial cost savings. In addition to selling online and to EDI, other electronic applications include an extranet to reinforce links with traditional commercial partners (wholesalers, importers, retailers), multimedia kiosks at the points of sale to present a catalogue, or a system of personalized electronic messages to maintain continuous relationships.

The Internet has two unique characteristics: the ability to distribute digital products at close to zero costs to a large number of customers and the ability to network, that is, to connect large numbers of people. Many products and services are either totally or largely non-digital: cars, steel, chemicals, food, hair care and hospital services. On the other hand, some are almost completely digital: music, data, stock prices, software, schedules, banking and insurance. There is a composite alternative that is physical but can be made digital. These "digitizable" products include newspapers, books, entertainment, films, financial services, images. Simon (2003) considers that the highest gains from Internet will be achieved for digital/digitizable products that are sold to many customers through versioning.

Penetration of Internet in Europe

According to *eMarketer* (2008), more than 50 per cent of Europeans were Internet users in 2008. *eMarketer* (www.emarketer.com) defines an Internet user as any person who uses the Internet from any location at least once per month. Internet penetration varies largely across the continent, the highest penetrations being observed in Nordic countries, the United Kingdom and Germany.

While Western European online users primarily value the non-commercial side of Internet – information search and e-mail – the proportion of users involved in online commerce is less than 50 per cent but is expected to increase steadily over time. A *Jupiter Research* Consumer Survey (2005) has observed that online tenure is a major factor in online purchasing. More than half of all Internet users with tenure of five or more years make purchases online. Online buyers represent more than one-half of all Internet users in long tenured markets such as the United Kingdom and the Nordic countries, while online buyers represent only one-third of all Internet users in short tenured markets such as Italy and Spain. Thus, as people gain confidence and experience online, they become more serious in the things they do online (Rainie, 2006).

The share of European online retail spending used to be very small, ranging in 2007 from 3 to 4 per cent of total retail sales and is expected to reach 7 per cent in 2011. This share of the online channel varies widely, however, between countries and between product categories like apparel, books, consumer electronics, DVD and videos, travel, leisure.

The information role of Internet

As already underlined above, a minority of firms have been able to sell to their end-customers through the Web. The major role played by Internet is information providing. In a survey conducted by Pew (www.pewInternet.org) (Rainie, 2006, p. 12), to the question, "what role did the Internet play in the event like buying a car, making a major investment, getting additional career training, choosing a school for self or child or helping someone with a major illness or health condition", the replies were:

Help you find advice and support from other people	34 per cent
Help you find information or compare options	30 per cent
Help you find professional or expert services	28 per cent

Thus, Internet facilitates word-of-mouth communication which has always been among the top and most reliable information sources. As observed in the 15 barometers published by the Interactive Advertising Bureau (IAB, 2008), not surprisingly, the information most expected online are product prices, practical information, contact information and vendor location. In the IAB travel barometer, websites are the number 1 information source followed by word-of-mouth and travel agencies.

In short, Internet has changed consumer behaviour in the following ways.

- Potential customers are more connected, informed, and discerning.
- They prefer to use the Internet and user-generated media to research products.
- They tend to ignore the advice of the sales staff and push marketing efforts.
- Websites are mainly used to search information before and after the purchase.
- Traffic to websites is mainly conducted through search engines.
- Communication devices are no longer place-bound: 45 per cent of Internet users go online from some place other than work or home (Rainie, 2006, p. 3).
- As people gain experience online, they become more sophisticated in the things they do online.
- The rise of interactive Web 2.0 technologies has enabled people to tell their own stories that have the capacity to reach considerable audiences.

Surveys conducted all over the world agree: getting information is the most highly valued and most popular type of everyday activity done online. For confirmation see the McKinsey Global Survey (2007) on how companies are marketing online (www.mckinseyquartely.com).

4.7   DIFFERENTIAL ADVANTAGES OF INTERNET TECHNOLOGY

Internet technology has a major impact on the way in which markets function. Several trends are emerging that distinguish electronic markets from traditional physical markets.

- *Personalization and customization.* Consumer tracking technology allows the identification of individual buyers and of their demographic and preference profiles. Increasing sales effectiveness comes from being able to design the appropriate products to address the needs of individual consumers and from being able to identify the moment when a customer's purchasing decision is likely to occur.

- *Product bundling*. The seller must decide which components or features will be included to the "solution" proposed to the customer and whether they will be marketed and priced individually or as a package. The costs of bundling (production, distribution, binding and menu pricing costs) impose fewer constraints in electronic than in traditional markets. New types of intermediaries arise who create value by bundling products and services that used to be offered by separate industries.

- *Information goods*. The Internet allows the almost costless creation and distribution of perfect copies of digital information goods, such as books, articles, digital images, software and music. This creates new opportunities for meeting indirect demand by versioning, repackaging content, bundling, site licensing, subscriptions, rentals, differential pricing, per use fee.

- *Search*. Electronic markets lower the costs consumers face for obtaining information about prices and product features as well as the costs sellers face for advertising such information. E-markets also enable buyers to identify and purchase a better solution to their problem and stimulate the emergence of new markets.

- *Price discrimination*. Charging of different prices to end-consumers is facilitated by Internet technology as data generated by customer relationship management (CRM) help measure customers' willingness to pay and price sensitivity. The implementation of this pricing strategy is difficult.

- *Facilitation*. Electronic markets improve information between consumers and sellers, which helps lowering logistic costs and promotes quick just-in-time delivery, which in turn leads to lower inventories.

Sellers in the electronic market increasingly contract with third-party providers for direct delivery from the manufacturers to the final consumer, reducing cost and time delivery. Delivery providers such as FedEx and DHL emerged as major Internet intermediaries because of their logistics expertise and their economies of scale in distribution. The growing accessibility of information technologies makes the tools required to develop networks, to cooperate with competitors and to co-create value with customers within everyone's reach.

4.8   THE SOLUTION APPROACH AND THE VIRTUAL MARKET

As the market-driven business philosophy is gaining acceptance in industry, many product companies have tried to partner with their customers and other market players to become a "solution provider" by selling solutions, that is, "a unique combination of products and services components" – rather than mere products – that could solve a customer's problem. On the "solution to a problem approach", see Roegner, Seifert and Swinford (2001), Foote, Galbraith, Hope and Miller (2001), Sheridan and Bullinger (2001), Johansson, Krisnamurthy and Schlissberg (2003). The decision to sell solutions is usually based on two objectives: to obtain higher profit margins than sales of products and to generate longer customer contracts. Solutions are proving lucrative for many companies, even as the profitability and growth of their products have come under pressure.

The concept of a customer solution

Before adopting the solution approach firms must have a good understanding of what a solution is and how it differs from products or bundles of products and services.

In the broadest sense, a solution is a combination of products and services that *create value beyond the sum of its parts*. Many companies are failing for one of the three following reasons.

1. Some companies believe that they are selling solutions by merely bundling products and/or services that create little value when offered together and then have difficulty of obtaining a premium price.
2. They underestimate the difficulty of selling solutions which costs more to develop and have longer sales cycle and demand a deep understanding of the customer problems.
3. Many companies sell solutions (intangible services) much as they sell products and do not adopt a relationship selling strategy instead of the traditional transactional selling.

Thus, a solution is not simply the bundling together of related components. It is the level of customization and of integration that sets solutions above products or services or bundles of products and services and that justifies a price premium.

> Take the fast food example. Customers can buy a hamburger, fries and a soft drink separately, or they can get a "meal deal" that groups all three together. In both cases, the solution "assuage the hunger" is achieved. But the extra value they get from the deal is a discount the restaurant grants. The meal deal is simply a bundling achieving commercial integration but not the customization needed to justify a premium price. On the contrary the restaurant must provide a discount.

What makes a solution valuable and distinctive is that it focuses on results by applying some level of expertise and at times a proprietary method that justifies a premium price. By contrast, look at the following case of paint manufacturer (Johansson, Krisnamurthy and Schlissberg, 2003).

> A manufacturer that had long supplied paints to carmakers used its knowledge of them and of its industry, as well as proprietary knowledge, to become a solutions provider. Recognizing that customers would place a higher value on a delivered service – painted cars – than on paint alone, it offered to take over their paint shop operations and very quickly helped a carmaker use 20 percent less paint per automobile. This distinctive offering enabled the paint manufacturer to become the leading provider of paint solutions to automakers around the world, with 70 percent of the market. In so doing, the company created value for its customers and changed its value metric from the product-oriented dollars per gallon of paint to the customer-oriented dollars per painted car.

Roegner, Seifert and Swinford (2001) have made a distinction between four types of actors in the design of a solution, by referring to two dimensions at two levels each (high and low): the degree of integration and the degree of packaging or bundling. Thus, four profiles can be identified.

1. The *"component specialist"* provide discrete products, services or both to specific customers and provide a low degree of integration and of bundling.
2. The *"bundlers"* assemble groups of components for specific customers and has a low degree of integration and high degree of bundling.
3. The *"integrators"* glue together components to fulfill a customer specific need and has a high degree of integration but a low degree of bundling.

4. The *"solution providers"* package and integrate components, bundles of both to deliver a complex turnkey solution meeting a specific customer need. They have a high degree of integration and of bundling.

The predominant view in the literature is that a solution is a customized and integrated combination of goods and services for meeting a customer's business need. A study conducted by Tuli, Kohli and Bharadwaj (2007) with 49 managers in customer firms and 55 managers in supplier firms showed that customers and suppliers have different views of the solution concept. Suppliers view a solution as a customized and integrated combination of goods and services, while in contrast customers view a solution as a set of customer–supplier relational process comprising (1) customer requirements definition, (2) customization and integration of goods and services, (3) their deployment, and (4) post-deployment customer support, all of which are aimed at meeting customer's business needs. In a market-oriented company, it is useful to define a solution consistently with the views of customers, a much more demanding concept.

Strategic marketing defines the market by reference to generic needs, or by reference to "problems" experienced by potential customers. What operational marketing is proposing is not products but *"solutions"* to these problems. As the market-driven business philosophy is gaining acceptance in industry, many product companies have tried to partner with their customers and other market players to become a "solution provider" by selling solutions, that is, "a unique combination of products and services components" that could solve a customer's problem.

The solution approach and the marketing mix

In the solution approach, understanding customer's problems is the priority objective. Potential customers raise questions like, How can I organize a nice birthday party? How can I insure the access control of my plant? How can I make a good espresso? How can I organize my personal and independent mobility problem? How can I decorate my home interior? In their cognitive space and in raising these questions, customers do not necessarily look after specific products but rather to a comprehensive solution, which can imply the use of a bundle of products and services. This is an "outside-in" view of

---

Box 4.2   Implementation problem

How to become a successful solution provider?

Five success factors can be identified:

- Solution design must reflect a *deep understanding of customers' needs* and of the pattern of their business issues. The firm must move closer to its customers.
- The firm must augment its internal capabilities by *finding partners* who can help provide a complete solution by providing all the required components.
- Effective solutions demand the company's best thinking and the establishing of a *cross-functional solution team* comprising people from multiple product units

and having the authority to define the value proposition.

- The sales approach is *relationship selling* and should reflect the differences between selling products and selling solutions where the solution provider is a business partner that helps the customer at every stage.
- The firm must create a *solution-based organization* that requires a new more flexible set of competencies, because the sales process is less predictable than the sales of a product.

Source: Sheridan and Bullinger (2001).

the market which is fully customer-centric, in contrast with the traditional marketing concept which is more supply-oriented. The solution approach provides a different way to look at the elements of the marketing mix (For a similar approach, see Chekitan and Schultz (2005)).

- *Product:* a solution to a problem and the package of benefits that the product represents.
- *Place:* a convenient access to the solution sought by the buyer.
- *Price:* all the monetary and non-monetary costs (including price) supported by the customer to acquire the solution sought.
- *Communication:* the information, messages, and signals communicated about the solutions available and about their distinctive qualities.
- *Selling:* the negotiation process or the dialogue organized with the potential customer in his or her search for the appropriate solution to his or her problem.

To achieve the solution sought, customers engage in different activities directly or indirectly related to the desired outcome. These related activities form what is called a virtual market.

What is a virtual market?

While in general markets are organized around the supply of products and services, the customer purchasing process is structured by reference to activities that are linked in his or her cognitive space. Virtual markets lead to an offering or to an assortment of offerings defined by reference to all the activities undertaken and all the services sought by the customer to achieve a specific generic result. Thus, a virtual market represents an end-to-end temporal sequence of activities logically related in the cognitive space of customers who search for a solution to a generic need.

For example, as illustrated in Figure 4.3, to achieve the "home ownership" generic need, customers might engage with contractors, realtors, insurance companies, mortgage firms, removal companies, telecom, interior designers and so on. Similarly, in the personal mobility virtual market, in addition to car purchasing, related activities cover car maintenance, car insurance, roadside assistance, emergency services dispatch, route support, stolen vehicle location and so on.

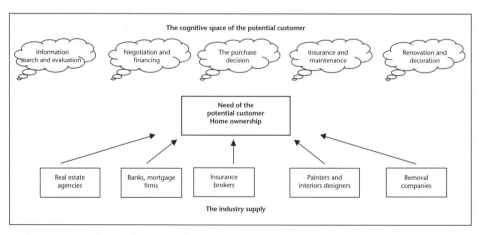

Figure 4.3   The home ownership virtual and meta-markets
Source: Lambin (2008).

In a virtual market, the activities undertaken by potential customers generally cut across traditional industry and product-market boundaries and are not necessarily in the traditional core business of the firm. As a result, virtual markets absorb a much higher proportion of customer spending than a specific product market and represent a higher market potential. Thus to confine the market to the product market may be misleading.

The challenge for the firm is to move from the rather abstract concept of virtual market to the "meta-market" (Sawhney, 1999; Sawhney, Balasubramian and Krishnan, 2004) that consists in an offering or in an assortment of offerings defined by reference to all the elements (activities and services) which comprise the cognitive space of the client. In other words, a meta-market is created when the cognitive association between different logically related activities is reproduced in the physical marketplace, thereby streamlining customer activities and providing them with seamless experience.

An agent that represents the different partners participating in the solution provided in the meta-market is called a *metamediary*. The Knot (www.theknot.com) and Ceremonie (www.ceremonie.com) are metamediaries for the bridal market (all you need for organizing a wedding ceremony). Edmunds in the United States (www.edmunds.com) is a metamediary for the car buying market (all you need about cars). Metamediaries solve four major consumer problems: search time, quality assurance, facilitated transactions for related purchases and unbiased content information. Metamediary partners benefit by having traffic directed to their sites as well as by co-branding with the metamediary. They pay commission for referrals. The key to a metamediary's success is consumer trust.

How to define a virtual market?

In defining a virtual market, the following procedure should be adopted:

- Do not define your reference market in terms of product categories (cars, metallic grids, construction toys, etc.).
- Refer to the result or the generic outcome customers want to achieve (personal mobility, access control, edutainment, etc.).
- Identify all the activities which, from the customer's point of view, are part of the virtual market.
- Create the reference meta-market by reproducing in the physical marketplace the mental associations made by the customers.
- If necessary, augment the internal capabilities of the firm by finding the right partners to provide the solution sought by customers.
- Present to customers the total solution they seek.

Internet technology makes this solution to a problem approach more achievable.

The customer activity chain concept

Another example of virtual market is given by the customer activity cycle. In seeking a particular outcome, customers engage in temporal activities. These activities can be mapped along a customer activity chain (Vandermerwee, 1993, 2000), which describes a sequence of directly or indirectly related activities undertaken by customers before, during or after the purchasing decision.

- Before, when customers are deciding what to do.
- During, when customers are doing what they decided upon.

■   After, when customers are maintaining the results obtained (reviewing, renewing, extending, upgrading, updating, etc.)

This methodology can help managers to assess the opportunities for providing new kind of services in filling gaps in the activity chain that could give access to competitors.

The case of *IBM* is interesting in this respect. In late 1980, *IBM* was so fixated on PCs and mainframes (viewing itself as hardware provider) that it allowed consultants, software houses, procurements specialists and third-party maintenance providers to leap into IBM's value gaps and siphon off both customers and potential wealth from the "global-networking capability" market space (Vandermerwee, 2000, p. 32). Having redefined its business, in a first step, as providing "computerized solutions of managerial problems" and, in a second step, as providing "global-networking capabilities", today IBM earns more money from value-add-on services than from its hardware, software and middleware.

Expected benefits of the solution approach

The decision of a firm to sell solutions is usually based on two objectives: (a) to obtain higher profit margins than the one obtained by the sales of products and (b) to generate longer customer contacts. Solutions are proving lucrative for many companies, even as the profitability and growth of their products have come under pressure. In the case of IBM, $38 billion of its revenue – 43 per cent of the total – comes from the solution-related businesses it has developed since the early 1990s (Foote, Galbraith, Hope and Miller, 2001, p. 84).

Before adopting the solution approach firms must have a good understanding of what a solution is and how it differs from products or bundles of products and services. In the broadest sense, a solution is a combination of products and services that *create value beyond the sum of its parts*. As explained above (see p. 88), many companies are failing to become a successful solution provider.

What makes a solution valuable and distinctive is that it *focuses on results* by applying some level of expertise and a proprietary method that justifies a premium price. The main benefits of the virtual market concept can be summarized as follows.

■   The concept is perfectly aligned with the customer's views and thereby fully customer-oriented.
■   The concept facilitates the communication to potential customers.
■   The revenue potential of a virtual market is always larger than the discrete product market.
■   It enables the firm to offer a total solution to customers, thereby building exclusivity, loyalty and trust.
■   It helps in identifying growth opportunities in activities directly or indirectly related to the core service.
■   It helps in identifying who are the indirect or potential competitors.

The firm must create a *solution-based organization* that requires a new more flexible set of competencies, because the sales process is less predictable than the sales of a product (Sheridan and Bullinger, 2001).

Engaging online communities to design innovative solutions

Internet technology offers new possibilities to acquire a deep understanding of customers' problems. As shown by the seminal work of Von Hippel (1978), it is often the role of the "would-be customer" to develop the idea for a new product and to select a supplier capable of making the product. In B2C markets, examples of breakthrough innovations initiated by innovative users include the mountain bike, the snowboards and also open-source software developments like Linux. Many customers are not only knowledgeable, but also able to develop solutions for themselves, and the Internet has greatly facilitated forms of collaboration to design and create new products.

Innovative consumer behaviour can be seen in online communities. Online groups of enthusiastic consumers can be found for almost every product or service. Community-based innovation is a method of identifying and accessing consumers in online communities and then interacting with them to get valuable input for new product development (Fuller and Hienerth, 2004). Consumers as members of online communities can add value to innovation at all stages, from the idea generation stage to the concept and design and test stages.

A popular example of active online community is the community formed around the Lego high-tech toys. With Lego *Mindstorm* (http://mindstorms.lego.com), users build real robots out of programmable bricks that can be turned into two-legged walking machines or into just about anything a teenage mind can envision. Today Lego offers in its website a downloadable software development kit that consumer enthusiasts can use to post descriptions of their *Mindstorm* creations, and of the software code, programming instructions and Lego parts that the device require. The company benefits hugely from the work of these volunteer customers. Each time a customer posts a new application for *Mindstorm*, the toy becomes more valuable.

In a McKinsey Global Survey (McKinsey, 2007) on how companies are marketing online, the observation was that some two-thirds of all survey respondents use online tools to involve their customers in product development; about a quarter do so frequently. The reasons vary notably by industry; respondents in both financial services and manufacturing, for example, focus on testing concepts and screening ideas, while those in high tech focus on generating new ideas.

From customer orientation to customer co-creation

The *customer-active paradigm* is gaining increased popularity in the professional and academic literature with the publication of the bestseller book by Tapscott and Williams (2006), entitled *Wikinomics*. The book supports the view that the new communication technologies are democratizing the creation of value through mass collaboration, that is, through mass outsourcing. Mass collaboration relies on free individual agents to come together and cooperate to improve a given operation or solve a problem.[2] The *Wikinomics* business model is based on four basic principles: openness, peering, sharing and acting globally. This is a business model very different from the hierarchical, closed, secretive and insular multinational business model that dominates today's markets, even if forms of coopetition (as discussed above) are a well-known topic in strategic management.

An interesting aspect of the business model promoted by *Wikinomics* is its emphasis on the potential development of a system of peer production where people join forces in self-organized communities to innovate and to produce new goods and services that rival those of the world's largest and best financed enterprises. The concept of "prosumer" or of "prosumption" was introduced by Toffler (1980) to describe how the gap between producers and consumers is blurring, a concept which is different from "customer centricity" where companies decide what the basics are and collaborate with customers to create or customize goods and services. Such is the current view of the customer orientation concept described earlier in this book and which is viewed here as "company-centric".

The "prosumer-centric" paradigm is different and refers to a model where customers participate in the creation of products in an active and ongoing way. The consumers actually co-innovate and co-produce the product they consume. They will do it on their own terms, in their own networks and for their own ends.

In the words of the authors, "co-creating with consumers is like tapping the most uniquely qualified pool of intellectual capital ever assembled /..:/ Products that don't enable and invite customer participation will be anathema – said old-fashioned remnants of a less customer friendly era." Customer co-creation is the ultimate level in the application of the consumer orientation concept. On this topic, read Prahalad and Ramaswamy (2004).

This impending prosumer revolution is already taking shape as illustrated by the success of online market places like *InnoCentive* (www.innocentive.com) or yet2.com (www.yet2.com) where "seekers", posting anonymously R&D problems, are meeting "solvers" who submit their solutions in a bid to capture cash prizes.

In the late 1990s, P&G launched an internal survey and discovered it was spending $1.5 billion in R&D, generating a lot of patents, but using less than 10 per cent of them in its own products. The company, once renowned for its insularity, now makes every patent in its portfolio available for licence through online marketplaces to any outsiders having previous contacts with P&G (Tapscott and Williams, 2006, p. 103).

Chapter Summary

The adoption of the sustainable development objective changes the traditional view of consumption. The socio-ecological view of consumption reflects a new awareness of the scarcity of natural resources, the uncontrolled growth of waste and the social cost of consumption. The socio-ecologic view of consumption induces firms to improve their "eco-efficiency", that is, to increase the volume of production per unit of natural resource. To implement the sustainable development objective, firms have to adopt new business models which are more eco-sensitive. As the market-driven business philosophy is gaining acceptance in industry, many product companies have tried to partner with their customers and other market players to become a "solution provider" by selling solutions, that is, "a unique combination of products and services components" – rather than mere products – that could solve a customer's problem. A virtual market represents an end-to-end temporal sequence of activities logically related in the cognitive space of customers who search for a solution to a generic need.

NOTES

1.   ISO 26000. To know more, go to http://www.iso.org.
2.   As frequently observed in so-called "new" management theory, many old ideas are hidden behind new words. Co-opetition, partnerships, joint ventures, co-branding, co-creation and so on are concepts and strategies in the management vocabulary and practice since many years and very close to the concepts of "sharing" and "peering".

BIBLIOGRAPHY

Prahalad, C.K. and Ramaswamy, V. (2004), Co-creation Experiences: The Next Practice in Value Creation, *Journal of Interactive Marketing*, 18, 3, pp. 5–14.

Anderson, E.W., Fornell, C. and Mazvancheryl, S.K. (2004), Customer Satisfaction and Shareholder Value, *Journal of Marketing*, 68, October, pp. 172–85.

Arrow, K.J. (1973), Social Responsibility and Economic Efficiency, *Public Policy*, 21, pp. 303–17.

Ayres, R.U. (1989), *Technology and Environment*, National Academy of Sciences, Washington DC.

BBC News, *Recycling around the World*, June 25, 2005.

Beinhocker, E., Davis I. and Mendonca, L. (2009), The 10 Trends You Have to Watch, *Harvard Business Review*, July–August, pp. 55–60.

Chekitan, S.D. and Schultz, D.E. (2005), A Customer-focused Approach Can Bring the Current Marketing Mix into the 21st Century, *Marketing Management*, 14, 2, pp. 18–24.

Croft, D. (2004), Shopping with Attitude: How citizen-consumers are Behind a Radical Overhaul of the Co-op Brand, *European Retail Digest*, 42, pp. 38–41.

D'Humières P. (2010), *Le développement durable va-t-il tuer le capitalisme?* Paris, Maxima

de Woot, P. (2005), *Responsabilité sociale de l'entreprise*, Paris, Economica.

Dixon, M., Freeman K. and Toman, N. (2010), Stop Trying to Delight Your Customers, *Harvard Business Review*, July–August, pp. 116–122.

Dowling, G.R. (2001), *Creating Corporate Reputation. Identity, Image performance*, Oxford, Oxford University Press.

eMarketer (2008), *The New European Internet Hot Spots*, February 13.

Eurostat Report (2002), *E-Commerce in Europe. Results of the Pilot Surveys carried out in 2001*, Eurostat, July.

Foote, N.W., Galbraith, J., Hope, Q. and Miller, D. (2001), Making Solutions the Answer, *McKinsey Quarterly*, 2.

Friedman, M. (1970), The Social Responsibility of Business Is to Increase Its Profits, *New York Time Magazine*, September 13.

Fuller, J. and Hienerth, C. (2004), Engaging the Creative Consumer, *European Business Forum*, 19, Autumn, pp. 54–7.

Gotteland, D. (2005), *L'orientation-marché: nouvelles méthodes, nouveaux outils*, Paris, Editions d'Organisation.

Hawken P. Lovins A. and Lovin L.H., (1999), *Natural Capitalism*, New York, Little, Brown and Company.

Hulot, N. (2007), *Pour un pacte écologique*, Paris, Calman-Lévy.

Interactive Advertising Bureau (2008), *15 Barometers*, February 19.

Johansson, J.E., Krishnamurthy, C. and Schlissberg, H.E. (2003), Solving the Solutions Problem, *McKinsey Quarterly*, 2.

Johnson, H.H. (2003), Does It Pay to Be Good? Social Responsibility and Financial Performance, *Business Horizons*, 46, 6, pp. 34–40.

Jupiter Research (2005), *European Online Retail Forecast 2005 to 2010*.

Kolk, A. and van Tulder, R. (2002), The Effectiveness of Self-regulation: Corporate Codes of Conduct and Child Labour, *European Management Journal*, 20, 3, pp. 260–71.

Kotter, J.P. and Heskett, J.L. (1992), *Corporate Culture and performance*, New York, The Free Press.

Laczniak, G.R. and Murphy, P.E. (1993), *Ethical Marketing Decisions*, Boston, MA, Allyn and Bacon.

Lambin, J.J. (2000–2007), *Market-driven Management*, London, Palgrave Macmillan, First and second edition.

Lambin J.J. (2011), *Quel avenir pour le capitalisme?*, Paris Dunod Editeur.

Lambin, E. (2004), *La terre sur un fil*, Paris, Edition Le Pommier.

Lambin, J.J. (2007), *Market-driven Management: Strategic and Operational marketing*, London, Palgrave Macmillan, 2nd edition.

Lambin, J.J. (2008), *Changing Market Relationships in the Internet Age*, Louvain, Presses universitaires de Louvain.

Luo, X. and Bhattacharya, C.B. (2009), The Debate over Doing Good: Corporate Social Performance, Strategic Marketing Levers, and Firm-Idiosyncratic Risk, *Journal of Marketing*, 73, pp. 198–213

McKinsey Global Survey (2007), *How Companies Are Marketing Online.*

Nidumolu R., Prahalad C.K. and Rangaswami M.R. (2009), Why Sustainability Is Now the Key Driver of Innovation, *Harvard Business Review*, September.

Papazoglou, M.P. and Ribbers, P.M.A. (2006), *e-Business*, The Atrium Southern Gate, Chichester, John Wiley and Sons.

Porter, M. (2001), Strategy and the Internet, *Harvard Business Review*, March, pp. 63–78.

Porter, M.E. and Kramer, M.R. (2011), Creating Shared Value, *Harvard Business Review,* January–February, pp. 62–77.

Rainie, L. (2006), *How the Internet is Changing Consumer Behavior and Expectations*, Speech to SOCAP Symposium, Washington DC.

Roegner, E.V., Seifert, T. and Swinford, D.D. (2001), Putting a Price on Solutions, *McKinsey Quarterly*, 2.

Sawhney, M. (1999), Making New Markets, *Business 2.0.*, May, pp. 116–21.

Sawhney, M., Balasubramian, S., and Krishnan, V.V. (2004), Creating Growth with Services, *MIT Sloan Management Review*, 45, 2, pp. 34–43.

Sheridan, S. and Bullinger, N. (2001), Building a Solution-Based Organisation, *Journal of Business Strategy*, January–February.

Simon, H. (2003), Seven e-Commerce Lessons, *European Business Forum*, pp. 58–63.

Stahel, W.R. (2006), *The Performance Economy*, London, Palgrave Macmillan.

Tapscott, D. and Williams, D.W. (2006), *Wikinomics, How Mass Collaboration Changes Everything*, New York, Penguin Books.

Toffler, A. (1980), *The Third Wave*, New York, Bantam Books.

Tuli, K.R., Kohli, A.K. and Bharadwaj, S.G. (2007), Rethinking Customer Solutions: From Product Bundles to Relational Processes, *Journal of Marketing*, 71, July, pp. 1–17.

Vandermerwee, S. (1993), Jumping into the Customer Activity Cycle, *Columbia Journal of World Business*, 28, 2, pp. 46–64.

Vandermerwee, S. (2000), How Increasing Value to Customers Improve Business Results, *MIT Sloan Management Review*, 42, 1, pp. 27–37.

Von Hippel, E. (1978), Successful Industrial Products from Customer Ideas, *Journal of Marketing*, 41, 1, pp. 39–49.

PART TWO

UNDERSTANDING CUSTOMER
BEHAVIOUR

CHAPTER FIVE

CUSTOMERS' NEEDS ANALYSIS

The objective of this chapter is to present a general conceptual framework describing the way market-driven management decodes customer purchasing motivation in consumer (B2C) and organizational (B2B) markets. The satisfaction of customers' needs is at the heart of a market economy and of market-driven management. This chapter aims to make clear such basic conceptions of the needs theory as generic absolute versus relative needs, generic versus derived needs and needs hierarchy. In the first step, we shall examine the main positions of economics and marketing theoreticians concerning the role strategic marketing plays in adapting firms to the constant development in needs satisfaction. Then we shall turn to psychology and in particular to the contributions experimental psychology has made in the study of human motivation. In B2B markets, we introduce the concept of the customer as a decision centre and we analyse the motivation of the B2B customer.

Learning Objectives

When you have read this chapter, you should be able to understand:

- The difference between generic and derived needs
- The importance of unarticulated or latent needs
- The determinants of well-being
- The multi-dimensional structure of customers' needs
- The motivation of the B2B customer
- The concept of industrial decision centre

5.1 THE NOTION OF GENERIC NEED

The notion of need is a term that creates endless polemic because it contains elements of subjective judgement based sometimes on morality or ideology. Beyond the vital minimum that everyone accepts – but which no one tries to define – is it really necessary to vary one's food to satisfy taste, to travel out of curiosity or to have different hobbies? We must admit that, at least as far as consumer markets are concerned, these questions are not irrelevant, especially in view of the following facts: (a) the uninterrupted arrival of new products and brands on the market; (b) the continuous and spectacular presence of advertising in increasingly varied forms; and (c) the relative stability of the level of consumer satisfaction, despite the undisputed improvement in standard of living. These facts then raise the following questions:

- Do all these new products and brands really correspond to pre-existing needs?
- Would producers accept such high advertising expenditures if consumers were not allowing themselves to be influenced?
- Is the growth and economic development that marketing claims to encourage useful in the long term?

Economic theory does not help to answer these questions. Economists believe it is not part of their discipline to worry about what motivates an action, or to enter into an introspection, which is always difficult, or especially to formulate a value judgement. It is useless to say that man strives for pleasure and avoids pain; it suffices to see that this indeed is the essence of the "want to use"' to justify its utility. The driving force, economic or otherwise, that makes an individual take an economic action is outside the scope of economics; only the results are important. The wish to be satisfied is the only acknowledged cause of behaviour.

A need must be felt before a choice is made, which means that the scale of preferences logically precedes effective choices. If an individual is intellectually adult and reasonable, it should be possible to predict the person's behaviour, which results from rational calculation.

The economic theory of consumer behaviour is therefore limited to the analysis of the logical implications of the hypothesis of man's rationality. The problem of motivation is totally avoided since economists believe that the real behaviour of the consumer reflects his or her preferences and inversely that the consumer's preferences are revealed by his or her behaviour.

The weakness of the basic assumptions in economics has been underlined on many occasions. In economic theory, the concept of rationality is defined as equivalent to the concept of coherence. However, the predictive value of coherence conditions depends mainly on the existence of well-known and stable preferences in the mind of the decider. But this is far from being satisfied if the original motivations are ignored, poorly known or simplified to the extreme, as is the case in economic models. How can we then be surprised by the observed difference between the "economic person" and the "real person"? We should, nevertheless, mention that, over the last 50 years, many serious efforts have been made to enrich the abstract psychology of the economic person and to come closer to the real person. Some examples of this approach are given by the works of Katona (1951), Abbott (1955), Becker (1965), Lancaster (1966), Ratchford (1975) and Sheth, Newman and Gross (1991).

The stability of generic needs

According to the dictionary, a generic need is a *requirement of nature or of social life*. This definition distinguishes two kinds of needs: innate or *absolute needs*, which are natural, inherent in nature or in the human organism, and *relative needs* which are cultural and social and depend on experience, environmental conditions and the evolution of society.

In the frame of market-driven management analysis, it is practical to view *generic needs* – both absolute and relative – as *problems* of potential customers who try to solve them by acquiring different products or services. If we take this view, then, following Abbott (1955) we can define a *derived need* as a particular technological response (the product or the service) to the generic need, as well as being the object of desire.

> For example, the car is a derived need with respect to the absolute generic need of individual mobility. Similarly, the ownership of a costly and prestigious car can be a response to the relative generic need of social recognition.

Thus, the popular view that it is the firm's marketing activity that creates needs has to be revised. Marketing cannot create generic needs that pre-exist and are inherent to human nature, but it can only create demand for the derived need, that is, the demand addressed to a specific technological response.

Generic needs are stable and cannot become obsolete. Obsolescence relates only to derived needs, in other words, to the dominant technological response at the time. At a given point, one may detect a tendency towards the saturation of the derived need, because of increased consumption of the good at a particular stage in its life cycle. The marginal utility of the derived need tends to diminish. But the generic problems (personal mobility, social recognition, protection and so on) do not disappear, which means that generic needs remain unaffected. Thanks to the impulse given by technological progress, the generic need simply evolves towards higher levels due to the arrival of improved products and therefore new derived needs.

The production of goods for the satisfaction of generic needs will therefore be incessantly subject to the stimulus of its own evolution. The latter will encourage the arrival of new products on the market, which are more suitable to satisfying the new level of needs. These derived needs will become obsolete in their turn and be replaced by new, more developed products.

The phenomenon of relative obsolescence (decline) brought about by technological progress, which is the basis of the product life cycle (PLC) model discussed later on in this book, is observed for most goods and at two levels: first, in the improvement of technological performance of products themselves (more economical cars, more powerful computers and so on); and, second, in the pure and simple substitution of a particular technological answer by another with higher performance (compact disc replacing vinyl records, fax replacing telex and so on). The latter form of innovation, or destructive innovation, is becoming ever more important due to the generalization of technological progress in all sectors, as mentioned before.

Furthermore, it seems that the move to a product that is hierarchically superior tends to increase the marginal utility yet again. The decline of the marginal utility is thus interspersed with sudden peaks. Goods are often desired for their novelty features and the privilege of owning them, even if little is added to their performance.

Therefore, the distinction between generic and derived needs makes it clear that, although there can be no general satiation, it is perfectly possible to detect sectoral technological decline. An important role for strategic marketing is thus to encourage the firm to adapt to this observed development in needs satisfaction. In this framework, it is better for the firm to define its mission by reference to generic rather than derived needs, given that the latter are changing and continually influenced by technology while the former are not. These are the basics of the market orientation concept described in the previous chapter.

The satiation impossibility of relative generic needs

Going further in the analysis of generic needs, Keynes (1936) underlined the fact that satiation is possible only for a certain part of them, for the absolute needs.

> Needs which are absolute in the sense that we feel them whatever the situation of our fellow human beings may be, and those which are relative in the sense that we feel them only if their satisfaction lifts us above, make us feel superior to our fellows. (Keynes 1936, p. 365)

Absolute needs are satiable, while relative needs are not. Relative needs are insatiable, because the higher the general level, the more these needs tend to surpass that level. This is how individuals, even when they have in absolute terms enjoyed net improvements in their standard of living, often tend to think that their situation has deteriorated if those who normally serve as the yardstick have improved more relative to them. Cotta (1980, p. 17) writes, "others' luxury becomes one's own necessity." The distance between reality and the level of aspiration tends to move continuously with growing dissatisfaction.

In these conditions, producing to satisfy relative needs is tantamount to developing them, that is, to trigger a process of escalation and of higher bids in the process of relative needs satisfaction. As pointed out by Rochefort (1995, p. 13), the relative disenchantment of consumers in affluent societies can be explained by three factors.

- First of all, affluent consumers are becoming less aware of the improvements in their living conditions as these become less spectacular in view of the progress already achieved in their standard of living.
- Second, well-being and comfort induce people to forget what a choice implies in demanding at the same time the butter and the money of the butter, more free time and more money, more social protection and higher salaries and so on.
- Finally, the loss of the time perspective and of the resulting patience: consumers today want everything and everything right now.
- The distinction between absolute and relative needs is not always clear-cut as one might at first think. One could say, for example, that anything essential to survival is infinitely more important that any other consumption. This idea is inexact.

> To live is certainly an important objective for each of us, but suicide exists. Heroic acts too. More generally, every consumer, in his day-to-day search for satisfaction of various needs, takes risks that put his life in danger either immediately or in the long run. Smoking, overeating, driving, working too hard or not looking after one's health properly, travelling: these are all activities that one should avoid if survival is placed above all else. (Rosa, 1977, p. 161)

Needs of a psycho-sociological origin may be felt just as strongly as the most elementary needs. For example, being deprived of intimacy and attention may provoke death or serious deficiencies in psychic and social functioning in the more extreme cases.

Despite this lack of clear-cut clarity, the distinction between absolute and relative needs remains interesting in two respects. On the one hand, it shows that relative needs can be just as demanding as absolute needs. On the other hand, it brings to the fore the existence of a dialectic of relative needs which leads to the observation of the general impossibility of satiation. Even the tendency towards material comfort cannot objectively define a state of satisfaction. When an individual reaches a predefined level, he or she can then catch a glimpse of a new stage of possible improvement.

Latent versus expressed needs

Understanding customer needs and wants is not always a simple task and it is useful to establish a distinction between latent and expressed needs. Latent needs or latent solutions are defined as needs and solutions of which the potential customer is unaware. Latent needs are no less "real" than expressed needs. But they are not in the consciousness of the customer:

> For example, at the outset of the development of personal computers, mobile or digital photography, the need for the benefits of these new products categories was a latent need.

Latent needs are universal. They exist in every customer and the role of proactive strategic marketing is to discover them and to analyse their profit potential though an interfunctional dialogue between R&D, market analysts and operations people. The following distinction is useful.

Articulated needs

■ Stated needs (what the customer says)
■ Unstated needs (what the customer expects)
■ Imaginary needs (what the customer dreams of)

Unarticulated needs

■ Real needs (the well-being of the customer)
■ Unconscious needs (what unconsciously motivates the customer)

Responding only to the customer's articulated needs may be misleading, leaving interesting opportunities unexploited. The objective of strategic marketing is to provide customers with an appropriate solution based on a good understanding of their real needs, be they articulated or not. The success story of Geox (see Exhibit 5.1) is interesting in this respect.

False versus true needs

The criticism frequently levelled at modern marketing is that it has changed the market into a mechanism that creates needs rather than satisfies them. We have seen above that this argument can have some validity for derived needs but not for generic needs.

One of the extreme views was put forward by Attali and Guillaume (1974). They believe that producers exploit the dynamics of wants to find markets allowing them to preserve

---

Exhibit 5.1   Example of latent need: the sweaty feet problem

■ **The problem**

Our feet produce up to 100 litres of sweat a year. Rubber sole cause condensation on the sole of the foot giving you that classic feeling of wet feet. Rubber soles create a plastic-bag effect around the foot.

■ **The solution**

Geox's CEO Mario Moretti Polegato has developed a revolutionary technology consisting of covering a perforated rubber sole with a special membrane lining (the same material used by NASA for astronauts' suits) that lets perspiration through but not water, achieving the first rubber sole in the world that keeps water out and the feet dry. The benefit of this technology is that the feet are always dry, eliminating once and for all the problems of perspiration, overheating and unpleasant odours.

■ **Interview of the Geox's Chairman**

The footwear market is saturated today and everyone is competing according to an overworked common denominator: design. Geox stands out from the crowd with this new technology /.../. Today's consumers are much more attentive to health. It is important to know how to interpret consumers' needs when they are clear and *to foresee them when latent and unexpressed*. We have to anticipate rather than follow, innovate rather than copy, ride the wave of change immediately and not when it is so high that we risk being overpowered by its explosive force.

Source: Interview of Mario Moretti Polegato, Chairman of Geox.

their economic power. Rosa (1977) notes that this analysis makes the implicit assumption that there are *real* needs and *false* needs and that the false needs are created by society and by the producer.

> In this school of thought, there is a fundamentally unequal exchange relationship between a dominated consumer and a dominant producer; society corrupts the individual by creating artificial wants in order to better subjugate and alienate him. The conclusion that follows is simple; it suffices to make the "good" political choice to get "good" structures which will necessarily develop the flourishing and expression of "real' needs". (Rosa 1977, p. 176)

This analysis, which is still widespread among so-called *left intellectuals* in Europe at one stage (see, for example, Henochsberg, 2001), has one important weakness, in that it never indicates how to distinguish true needs from false needs. Given that the vast majority of our present wants are indeed of a cultural origin, where should we draw the line, and especially who will be the enlightened dictator of consumption? Clearly, it is very difficult to answer these questions objectively.

> To substitute the disputed sovereignty of the consumer for the questionable sovereignty of a bureaucrat or of an intellectual can only create more problems that it can ever hope to resolve. (Rosa 1977, p. 159)

It should also be added that the hypothesis of individual consumer impotence is daily rejected by facts such as the figures available on the rates of failure of new products; more than one in two products fails to enter the market successfully. The discretionary power of the consumer is a reality and firms know it well. We must therefore recognize that the debate of *true* versus *false* needs is in the first place an ideological debate.

Solvent versus insolvent needs

In a market economy, production relies on customers' needs supported by money and not on the needs per se, that is, on the most urgent needs of those who are cannot afford to pay. The rich, who are confronted with secondary needs, can order everything and the poor nothing, despite the fact that their needs are essentials. It is the purchasing power of the customer which triggers the economic system.

As suggested by Ruyer (1969), the satisfaction of the solvent needs is simply the expression of the principle: "To everyone according to his work." The unemployed person who cannot purchase because he or she cannot work and gain the purchasing money is not the victim of the purchasing law but rather the victim of the poor functioning of the economic system. The cure is then in the recourse to fixing processes and in the revitalization of the economy. The economic system is able to meet consumers' needs only by asking to potential purchasers the money they have earned before. Exchanges take place only if there is something to exchange and charity is not an exchange. The same rule prevails for a public service. A state cannot start from scratch to meet insolvent needs, even if they are priority needs. The state can engage in charity only in a secondary phase, once it has created an efficient economic system according to economic laws, that is, by first generating wealth. Free education, social housing, free food imply the existence of a rich economy. Free distribution must be preceded by free production. Demand must be supported by money; if it is not the complainant's money, it is the money of someone else who, from an economic viewpoint, is the true complainant.

The expression "solvent need", as a term for profit or profitability, has a negative connotation for the humanist. To make profit through the exploitation of people's needs, instead of providing direct solutions to their problems, is perceived as a sordid mercantile action. How can one make money through the exploitation of people's state of needs? Engaging in charity is of course a morally superior action than an economic action, but to give is possible only within the limits of what is owned. To engage in charity within the economic system cannot become a universal law and no economic system could survive under such a principle. Those who give are those who have first won through economic means. If the state is a welfare state it is only for a minority group and it is necessarily a spoliatory state for others. By definition an economic system cannot be based on charity only. As reminded by Ruyer (1969), the term "donation economy" is inappropriate. If a donation has an economic intent, it can only be a very long-term credit. The producer's profit should not be opposed to the consumer's need. It is a signal guiding the market and indicating that the consumer's demand has been effectively met.

5.2 MOTIVATION OF THE INDIVIDUAL CUSTOMER

Economists, as we saw, make no distinction between what consumers choose and what suits them, and never consider the process of needs formation. What do individuals seek in their quest for well-being and how does this state of well-being come about? These two questions are never tackled by economic theory. Yet it is clear that a more thorough analysis of consumer behaviour and the structure of their motivation would make it easier to understand the links that both economists and marketing try to establish between supply and demand. Experimental psychology has made enlightening contributions in this field and helps us discover a whole range of general motivational orientations that determine various individual behaviours. This section is based on the seminal works of Hebb (1955), Duffy (1957), Berlyne (1960), Scitovsky (1976) and Nuttin (1980).

The "stimulus–response" theory

A central preoccupation of the theory of motivation has been to study why the organism moves into a state of activity. Motivation here becomes energy mobilization. Originally, experimental psychology was mostly interested in needs and drives of a purely physiological nature, such as hunger, thirst, sex and so on. In this scheme, called the "stimulus–response theory" (or S–R theory), the stimulus is considered as the active starting point of the organism's reaction. One then speaks of *homeostasis*, which is a mechanism whereby a disorder creates an urge, giving rise to activity that restores equilibrium and thus removes the urge. In this framework, the organism is basically assumed to be reactive: in other words, it responds in specific ways to stimuli. This more or less repudiates the problem of motivation. Inactivity is supposedly the natural state of the individual.

We observe, however, that the human organism does not always react to the stimulus presented by its surroundings. Furthermore, it is a common occurrence to find individuals embarking on activities that disrupt equilibrium and setting up states of tension which would be hard to explain if one believed S–R theory. This theory reduces the mechanism of motivation to a process of reducing tension and practically ignores the ascending phase of motivation, that is, the process by which new tensions or conflicts are worked out. However, this type of behaviour is frequently observed, especially in affluent societies, where basic needs are mostly met. A need, seen as a homeostatic need, cannot totally explain individual behaviour.

> More mysterious than the process of discharge is the process that can be called recharging; and more central than the reduction of tension is the act by which man seeks increased responsibilities, takes bigger risks and finds himself new challenges. (Nuttin, 1980, p. 201)

Today, experimental psychology emphasizes more and more the spontaneous activity of the nervous system and considers behavioural activity to be tied to the organism's being, just as much as physiological activity is.

The concept of arousal

Motivation theorists nowadays tend to explain behaviour in a new way, particularly because of the fact that neuro-physiologists have considerably improved their knowledge of the way the brain functions and now have a completely different viewpoint. Hebb (1955, p. 246), for instance, formulates a hypothesis that is based not on reactivity but on the natural activity of the nervous system. Contrary to the beliefs held until then, the brain does not have to be excited from outside in order to be active and to discharge. It is not physiologically inert and its natural activity constitutes a system of self-motivation. Hebb (1955) and also Duffy (1957, p. 267) put forth the idea that the general state of motivation can be equated with arousal, or the activity emanating from the reticular formation of the brainstem. Activity level depends on the degree of organic energy mobilized, which is on the variation in the level of arousal and vigilance. The level of arousal is measured by the variations in electric current controlled with an electroencephalogram (EEG); these variations show up as waves in the EEG; the faster the electric discharge of neurones, the higher the level of arousal and the higher the frequency of oscillations in the EEG, measured in periods per second.

Scitovsky (1976) underlines the importance of the concept of arousal in understanding the reasons for a given behaviour.

> A high arousal is associated with vigilance and quick response; it makes the senses more sensitive to stimuli, increases the brain's capacity to process information, readies the muscles for action, and so shortens the total reaction time that elapses between an incoming sensation and the response through action. It makes you feel excited, emotional, anxious and tense. On the other hand, when you feel slow, less than vigilant, lax and drowsy, you are in a state of low arousal. (Scitovsky, 1976, p. 19)

The increased level of arousal increases the organism's state of vigilance, thus providing favourable ground for the cerebral mechanism of stimulus–response to function rapidly and directly. The psychological measures of the level of arousal therefore provide a direct measure of the motivational and emotional (drive) force of a given situation for the individual (Duffy, 1957, p. 267). Also, this description of the concept of arousal suggests the existence of a continuum in the individual's level of activation.

Well-being and the optimal level of arousal

It is clear that the level of arousal has a great influence on the feeling of well-being or discomfort felt in general by people, and consequently bears on the determination of their behaviour. Excessive stimulation provokes tension, anxiety, nervousness, worry, frenzy, even panic; on the other hand, stimulation which is too weak, or non-existent, brings about boredom, or a certain degree of displeasure, and creates the desire for a bigger stimulation. A job which is too simple or too monotonous can become painful if one is forced to pursue it without interruption over a long time. In fact, psychologists (Hebb, 1955, p. 250) accept that there is an optimal level of arousal and stimulation, optimal in the sense that it creates a feeling of comfort and well-being. Deviations below the optimum provoke a feeling of weariness, and deviations above the optimum provoke a sensation of fatigue and anxiety. Experimental observations show that, on the whole, individuals try to maintain an intermediary level of activation (Berlyne, 1960, p. 194).

Here we can identify the initial motivation in individuals: ensure comfort and prevent discomfort. This motivation implies, on the one hand, the reduction of tensions, which satisfies various corporal and mental needs and reduces the level of arousal, which may be too high; on the other hand, it implies a battle against boredom, a behaviour which looks for stimulation and thus increases the level of arousal, which might be too low. These two types of behaviour have one thing in common; both try to fill up a gap and to ensure a "negative good", that is to stop pain, inconvenience and discomfort (Scitovsky, 1976, p. 69).

For economists, the reduction of arousal and tension is particularly important because as far as they are concerned almost all human activity, including consumption, is based on this process. We find here the notion of need defined by economists as simply a state of deficiency. However, economists ignore the other type of behaviour, that is, the raising of a level of arousal that is too low. This is commonly observed in more affluent economies, where prosperity has largely eliminated discomfort due to tension, but where the search for stimulation, novelty and change is becoming ever more important.

> The consumer is also a dreamer. She (or he) buys a product, certainly to use it, but even more for the magic it offers him as premium. (Séguéla, 1982, p. 50)

In some situations, finding sufficient stimulation to combat boredom can be a matter of life or death. This is true for old people, for example. It is also well known that longevity is strongly related to having been able to keep a satisfying job late in life.

The need for stimulation

Berlyne's work in this area is interesting, especially because it is based on solid experimental ground. Berlyne (1960) shows that novelty (meaning anything surprising, different from past events and from what one expected) attracts attention and has a stimulating effect.

> Novelty stimulates and pleases especially when it creates surprisingness, change, ambiguity, incongruity, blurredness and power to induce uncertainty. (Berlyne, 1960, p. 290)

It is as if the incongruence of the new event produces a dynamic effect which sets in motion exploratory actions. It must, however, be made clear that the new and surprising is attractive only up to a limited degree, beyond which it becomes disturbing and frightening. Attractiveness first increases, then diminishes with the degree of newness and surprisingness.

This relationship takes the shape of an inverted U-curve, known as the Wundt curve (Berlyne, 1960). What is not new or surprising enough is boring, and what is too new is bewildering? An intermediate degree of newness seems to be the most pleasing.

The stimulation provoked by the collative properties of goods forms an important source of satisfaction for individuals. Much of the activity of marketers, such as new product policies, segmentation and positioning, communication and promotion, focuses on meeting this expectation. For better or for worse, goods act as stimuli over the nervous system, a little bit like toys for children. The intelligence of a child can become stagnant with lack of adequate toys. In the same manner, an adult deprived of all the stimuli, provided notably by the consumer society, can be overcome with boredom, depression and alienation.

> Many people feel younger when they purchase a brand new car and associate the age of their car with that of their own body. Thus buying a new car takes on symbolic proportions by representing physical rejuvenation. (Valaskakis, Sindell and Smith, 1978, p. 167)

Therefore, the organism needs a continuous stream of stimuli and different experiences, just as it needs air and food. Human beings need to need. This basic motivation, as well as the more obvious motivation of reducing tensions, explains a large variety of individual behaviour that can only elude the deductions made by economists. The theory of "novelty seeking" provides an explanation for consumers' actions, which introduce change, variety and novelty into their life style.

The need for pleasure

The sensation of comfort or discomfort is related to the level of arousal and depends on the latter's situation with respect to the optimum. Experimental psychologists have now proven that pleasure exists as a phenomenon different from absence of suffering or presence of comfort. The sensation of pleasure begins with variations in the level of arousal, in particular when a level of arousal, which is too low or too high, is approaching its optimum (Berlyne, 1960, p. 187).

Two sources of pleasure can be identified: one results from the satisfaction of a need and the resulting reduction in tension; the other comes from the stimulation itself. Satisfaction of a need is pleasant in itself and drives the organism to pursue its activity to the point of satiation and even beyond.

> In very poor communities, families often plunge into debt for the sake of a funeral feast or a wedding celebration. Such behaviour horrifies economists of the not-so-poor countries... Yet the very universality of the custom of feasting among the poor people of so many different cultures is evidence that the pleasures of a good meal for those who seldom taste one are very great and weigh heavily against the biological needs of survival. (Scitovsky, 1976, p. 66)

The economic theory of the rational behaviour of consumers implies a judicious balance between different needs and does not take into account pleasure, which can lead the individual to an allocation different from that predicted by economic theory. It is in fact frequently observed that people behave so as to have full satisfaction from time to time, and they properly space out the moments or periods during which they completely fulfil their wants. This type of behaviour is frequently observed in industrialized countries, in the leisure sector, for example, and in particular in holiday expenditure.

Note that the pleasure inherent in the satisfaction of a need implies that discomfort must precede pleasure. This common-sense rule is a very old one; the ancient Greeks debated it. Psychiatrists call it the *law of hedonic contrast*. It follows from the rule that too much comfort may preclude pleasure (a child who is nibbling all day long cannot appreciate a good meal). This fact can explain the malaise observed at times in affluent societies, when satisfaction of needs does not bring about any pleasure. By eliminating simple joys, excessive comfort forces us to seek strong sensations.

At this stage the second source of pleasure, the one resulting from the stimulation itself, comes into its own. Here the object of the need is not to make up for a shortage, but to contribute to the development of the individual. To quote Nuttin (1980), this is the ascending phase of motivation, a phase in which new tensions and discordance are established, giving individuals the will to progress and surpass themselves. This is Maslow's self-actualization need. People take pleasure in excitement. They get more satisfaction out of the struggle of reaching an objective than they get when they actually reach it. Once individuals have passed the moment of triumph, they almost regret having reached their goal. Most people then give themselves an even more distant objective, probably because they prefer to act and fight rather than passively observe their success (Nuttin, 1980, p. 201). In this way, individuals force their environment to stimulate them or to continue to stimulate them.

The pleasure of this type of stimulation results from the temporary tension it creates. Such pleasure is more constant than the pleasure of comfort and outlasts it, because this stimulation leaves more room for imagination and creativity to the individual.

> The object of this stimulation is almost unlimited. By meeting them, tension goes up rather than down. Thus the tendency persists beyond the point where the objective is reached. (Nuttin, 1980, p. 202)

Here, we are now talking about insatiable needs. It is in the nature of self-development needs to know neither the saturation nor the periodicity of homeostatic needs.

> We see here what pleasure is and its relation to comfort: the former is the variation of the latter. If happiness is simply comfort, then it depends on the intensity of satisfied wants. Pleasure is complete when the want is a little or much more satisfied than it was. If happiness is not comfort but pleasure, then it is condemned to only live some privileged moments, prolonged with the help of memory. (Cotta, 1980, pp. 11–12)

From the psychologist's point of view, seeking pleasure is an important factor in human behaviour, and it is a fundamental motivational force that must be taken into account in any analysis of individual buying behaviour.

Determinants of the individual's well-being

An overview of the major contributions of experimental psychology to the study of human motivation finally arrives at a much wider understanding of the notion of need. We started from the point of view of economists, for whom need is essentially a "state of shortage" revealed by the buying behaviour, without any explanation of the origin or the nature of motivations at the root of this state of deficiency. The absence of theory about motivations leads economists to make normative recommendations which have as much value as their starting assumptions, but which have little to do with actual observed behaviour. An interesting analysis of the notion of well-being in relation with marketing is made by Gibbs (2004).

Research by psychologists makes it possible to retain three general motivational directions, which can explain a large variety of behaviours and which appear to be factors that explain the individual's general well-being. These determinants can be regrouped as comfort, pleasure and stimulation. Figure 5.1 explains diagrammatically the relations between

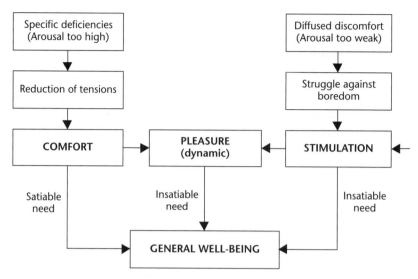

Figure 5.1   The determinants of well-being
Source: Lambin (2000/2007).

these three determinants on the one hand and their relation to individual well-being on the other.

The *three motivational forces* determining individual well-being can be briefly described as follows:

- The search for *comfort*, which results from two kinds of behaviour: one that reduces tensions by satisfying homeostatic needs; and one that struggles against boredom with the help of stimuli such as novelty, change, incongruity, uncertainty, risk and so on.
- The search for *pleasure*, which also results from two sources: pleasure inherent in the reduction of tensions and pleasure obtained from stimuli.
- The search for *stimulation*, not only as a means to combat boredom, but as a goal in itself, without any other objective in mind but the tension it arouses, by generating pleasure and creating the opportunity of development and actualization for the individual.

The search for comfort aims to make up for a deficiency and thus to ensure a defensive good; pleasure and stimulation aim to ensure a creative good.

By relying on this description of the major motivational forces we are in a better position to answer the questions facing marketing mentioned at the beginning of this chapter. The increased use of marketing – which takes the form of products being continually renewed, more and more subtle differentiation, sophisticated perceptual positioning, advertising suggesting elaborate life styles and so on – in reality only responds to the rise in needs of pleasure and stimulation observed in richer societies, where basic needs are well met, but where, on the other hand, needs such as novelty, surprise, complexity and risk have become vital necessities.

The need to try varied experiences, to live different life styles and the possibility to try new products and to have new sources of satisfaction form an important subject matter in this type of society. This search is endless, because there is no possible saturation in this type of need.

Some philosophers advocate rising above all wants in order to escape this endless escalation, which, far from bringing internal peace, causes worry and creates an infernal cycle. The wise Hindu Sarna Lakshman writes:

> Desire tells us: get this and then you will be happy. We believe it and we try to acquire the relevant object. If we don't get it, or if we don't get enough, we suffer. If we get it, then desire immediately suggests another objective, and we don't even see that we have been fooled. (Quoted by Boirel, 1977)

These philosophers are advocating the ideal of ataraxy that is the absence of turmoil as a result of the extinction of desire. The alternative to this extreme solution is *creative consumption*, that is, consumption that encourages ascending motivations of progress, self-actualization and excellence. If it is true that "man prefers hunting to the catch", as Pascal said, then want, as being the driving force of activity, can be the first cause of satisfaction brought about by creative consumption.

5.3 STRUCTURE OF THE INDIVIDUAL CUSTOMER'S NEEDS

The contributions of motivation theory help us to identify more general motivational orientations in human beings. These orientations govern a large variety of individual behaviours. These disciplinary contributions, however, provide only a general description of the needs structure, with little attempt at operationalization and no explicit reference to buying behaviour. Moreover, they tend to focus on one dimension of behaviour (economic, social, psychological and so on) and do not propose a comprehensive framework that integrates the concepts used in each contributing discipline. The question is to know what are the values sought by the buyer and how to translate these values in products and services adapted to the buyers' expectations. Several attempts have been made to develop a comprehensive list of the needs sought.

Well-being means having a product or service to satisfy each need, so a natural approach is to develop a list of needs and to compare it with available goods. The word "goods" here has a special meaning. They are not only physical entities or services, but may be abstract, social or psychological entities, such as love, prestige and so on. The seminal works of Murray (1938), Maslow (1943), Rokeach (1973) and Sheth, Newman and Gross (1991) are representative of this approach.

Murray's inventory of human needs

Murray calls a need a hypothetical construct because it is of a physiochemical nature that is unknown. It resides in the brain and is thus in a position to control all significant behaviour. In Murray's words:

> A need is a hypothetical construct that stands for a force in the brain region that organises and directs mind and body behaviour so as to maintain the organism in its most desirable state. (Murray, 1938, p. 123)

Murray gives a rather systematic inventory, classifying individuals' needs into four dimensions: *primary (viscerogenic) and secondary (psychogenic)* needs, according to whether they are of physiological origin or not; *positive and negative needs*, depending on whether the individual is attracted by the object or not; *manifest or latent needs*, according to whether the

---

Exhibit 5.2   Maslow's hierarchy of needs

Primary needs

- Physiological needs

These are fundamental; once satisfied, they cease to be determinant factors of motivation and no longer influence behaviour.

- Safety needs

Physical safety, preservation of the physical structure of the organism, psychological safety, conservation of the psychic structure of personality. Need for own identity, to feel in charge of one's destiny.

Secondary needs

- Social needs

People are social animals and feel the need to fit into a group, to associate with their fellows, they feel the need to love and be loved. Mutual help, belonging and sense of community are also social needs.

- Self-esteem needs

Self-esteem, personal dignity, confidence in oneself and one's own competence. The feel that one's objectives are valid. The esteem that others feel for us. The need for recognition, to be respected, to have a social status.

Tertiary needs

- Self-actualization needs

Those needs are at the top of the scale of human needs, and include self-realization and development; the need of people to surpass themselves; to use all their capacities and push their limits and to give a meaning to things and find their "raison d'être".

Source: Adapted from Maslow (1943).

---

need drives to a real or imaginary behaviour; and *conscious or unconscious needs*, according to whether or not they drive the individual to take introspective steps. Murray lists 37 needs covering these categories.

Murray believes that all people possess the same needs, but he recognizes that the expression of them will differ from one person to another because of differences in personality and in environmental factors. Needs could be provoked by either internal or external stimuli, and they could be weak or strong at any particular time. Needs exist in three different states: (1) refractory, in which no incentive will arouse it; (2) inducible, in which a need is inactive but susceptible to excitation; and (3) active, in which the need is determining the behaviour of the organism (Murray, 1938, pp. 85–6). Thus, marketing activities could have a direct impact on inducible needs.

Maslow's needs hierarchy

Maslow (1943) adopts a similar approach, grouping fundamental needs into five categories: physiological, safety, social, esteem and self-actualization needs. Exhibit 5.2 describes these needs. Maslow's analysis, however, goes further and is not limited to a simple classification. Maslow postulates the existence of a hierarchy of needs, which depends on the individual's state of development (see Table 5.1).

According to Maslow, there is an order of priorities in needs, in the sense that we begin to try to satisfy dominant needs before going on to the next category. Once the needs of a lower order have been satisfied, they allow needs of the higher order to become motivators and influence our behaviour. There is a progressive abatement in the intensity of needs already met and an increasing intensity of needs of a higher order not yet satisfied. As illustrated in Figure 5.2, we observe an evolution of the structure of needs depending on the individual's development as he or she goes from an overall objective of survival or living standard towards more qualitative objectives regarding life style or quality of life.

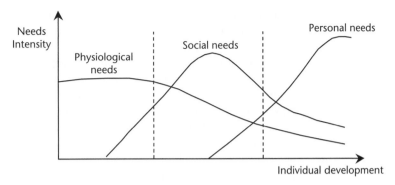

Figure 5.2 Maslow's hierarchy of needs
Source: Adapted from Maslow (1943).

Table 5.1 Organic food interpreted by Maslow's hierarchy

Needs hierarchy	Interpretation
Self-actualization needs	It helps save the planet
	It's better for the environment
Esteem needs	It's trendy
	It's healthier
Social needs	I support local farmers
	I'm doing the right thing
Safety needs	It's better for my children
	It's safer
Physiological needs	It tastes better

Maslow's analysis is interesting because it puts forth not only the multi-dimensional structure of needs, but also the fact that needs have different degrees of intensity in different individuals. In reality, there is always some coexistence of these categories of needs, with one category or another becoming more important according to the individual, or according to the circumstances of one particular individual.

Products to be developed for satisfying needs must therefore be planned accordingly. A good or product may have more than one role or function beyond just the basic one. Individuals use goods not only for practical reasons, but also to communicate with their environment, to show who they are, to demonstrate their feelings and so on.

> For example, the food products available on the market today provide at the same time (a) physiological solutions to consumers due to their nutritional structure, (b) safety guaranteed through the certified quality control and labelling, (c) belonging and sense of community through the signals as local or regional products, and (d) self-esteem created by the prestige or reputation of the brand.

It is important for marketing to be aware of the role played by goods and brands, not simply for their functional value, but also for their emotional or symbolic values. We shall see later in this chapter that the multi-dimensional structure of needs also exists with the organizational customer.

Rokeach's list of values

Human values research stresses the important goals that most people seek. Values are closely linked to human needs, but exist at a more realistic level. They are the mental representations of underlying needs, not only of individual needs but also of societal and institutional needs. In other words, values are our ideas about what is desirable.

> A value is an enduring belief that a specific mode of conduct or end-state of existence is personally or socially preferable to an opposite or converse mode of conduct or end-state of existence.

A value-system is an enduring organisation of beliefs concerning preferable modes of conduct or end-states of existence along a continuum of relative importance. (Rokeach, 1973, p. 5)

There are two types of values: (1) terminal and (2) instrumental. Terminal (or end-state) values are beliefs we have about the goals or end-states for which we strive (e.g., happiness, wisdom). Instrumental (or means) values refer to beliefs about desirable ways of behaving to help us attain the terminal values (e.g., behaving honestly or accepting responsibility).

Since values are transmitted through cultures, most people in a given society will possess the same values, but to different degrees. The relative importance of each value will therefore be different from one individual to another and these differences can be used as market segmentation criteria, as shown in Chapter 8. The prominence of different values can also change over time. Rokeach postulates that the total number of values that a person possesses is relatively small. In his empirical work, Rokeach identifies 18 terminal and instrumental values (Rokeach, 1973, p. 28).

In recent years, researchers have been working to develop a shortlist of values that can be measured in a reliable manner. Kahle (1983) has identified eight summary terminal values:

■ Self-respect
■ Security–Warm relationships
■ Sense of accomplishment
■ Self-fulfilment
■ Being well-respected
■ Sense of belonging
■ Fun/enjoyment/excitement

Several researchers have found that these values relate well to various aspects of consumer behaviour or to social change.

For example, people who value fun and enjoyment may desire a cup of coffee for its rich taste, whereas people who value a sense of accomplishment may wish to use coffee as a mild stimulant to increase productivity; and people who value warm relationships with others may want to share a cup of coffee as an aspect of a social ritual. (Kahle, Poulos and Sukhdial, 1988)

The logic of this methodology can be summarized as follows: to understand individuals' motivation, one place to start is to try to understand their values, particularly with products that involve consumer value. Also, an understanding of the way values are changing in a given society will facilitate the development of effective strategies for dealing with the dynamics of societal change.

The means–end chain model

The works of Maslow (1943) and Rokeach (1973) have shown values to be a powerful force in governing the behaviour of individuals in all aspects of their lives. Their use in marketing research is interesting, both from an analytical and from a predictive point of view, to relate consumers' behaviour to their values. Such is the objective of the means–end chain (MEC) concept developed by Gutman (1982) and by Reynolds and Gutman (1988).

For example, knowing that consumers want to look well dressed doesn't tell us much about their values level consideration, unless we know why they want to look that way, that is their "desired end-state". Is it a purely functional objective, a desire to seduce a partner, the search for novelty and stimulation, a concern for integration in a social or professional group, or simply a personal accomplishment objective?

The MEC model attempts to explain how consumers select products that will be instrumental in helping them achieve their desired consequences, which in turn move consumers towards their valued end-states. The means are the purchased products or services, while the ends are the desired terminal values proposed by Rokeach and viewed as desirable end-states of existence sought by individuals through their consumption behaviour. As illustrated by Figure 5.3, a conceptual representation of the chain is divided into three parts: (a) the product attributes (tangibles and intangibles); (b) the consequences (physiological or psycho-sociological) resulting from the consumption behaviour accruing directly or indirectly to the consumer, and (c) the terminal or instrumental values.

For uncovering means and ends hierarchies as described above, Reynolds and Gutman (1988) have developed an in-depth interviewing and analysis methodology, called the laddering technique, which involves a tailored individual interviewing format with the goal of determining the links between the key perceptual elements across the range of attributes, consequences and values. Interpretation of this type of information permits an understanding of consumers' underlying personal motivation with respect to a given product class. This is more the field of qualitative or in-depth research. To go further on this topic, see Reynolds and Gutman (1988), Valette-Florence (1994) and Pellemans (1998).

The Sheth–Newman–Gross theory of consumption values

Applying the concept of "value" to buying behaviour, Sheth, Newman and Gross (1991, pp. 18–25) describe market choice as a multi-dimensional phenomenon involving multiples values: functional, social, emotional, epistemic and conditional. They define these values as follows:

- *Functional Value.* The perceived utility acquired by an alternative as the result of its ability to perform its functional, utilitarian or physical purposes. Alternatives acquire functional value through the possession of salient functional, utilitarian or physical attributes.

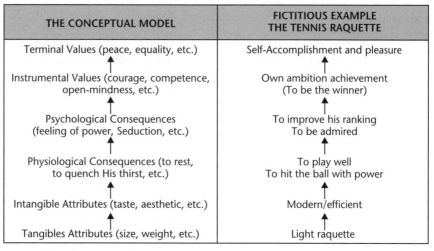

Figure 5.3 The means–end chain model
Source: Adapted from an example proposed by Derbaix (1997).

- *Social Value.* The perceived utility acquired by an alternative as a result of its association with one or more social groups. Alternatives acquire social value through association with positively or negatively stereotyped demographic, socio-economic and cultural ethnic groups.
- *Emotional Value.* The perceived utility acquired by an alternative as a result of its ability to arouse feelings or affective states. Alternatives acquire emotional value when associated with specific feelings or when they facilitate or perpetuate feelings.
- *Epistemic Value.* The perceived utility acquired by an alternative as a result of its ability to arouse curiosity, provide novelty and/or satisfy a desire for knowledge. Alternatives acquire epistemic value through the capacity to provide something new or different.
- *Conditional Value.* The perceived utility acquired by an alternative as a result of the specific situation or the context faced by the choice maker. Alternatives acquire conditional value in the presence of antecedent physical or social contingencies that enhance their functional or social value, but do not otherwise possess this value.

These five values make differential contributions to specific market choices in the sense that some values can contribute more than others. Those values are also independent. They relate additively and contribute incrementally to choice. Although it is desirable to maximize all five values, users are often willing to accept less of one value to obtain more of another. That is why buyers are willing to trade off less salient values in order to maximize those that are most salient (Sheth, Newman and Gross, 1991, p. 12).

Considerable overlaps are observed, when comparing these summary values with the different need categories proposed by diverse disciplines. The functional value corresponds to the general motivation for comfort in Murray's viscerogenic needs and in Maslow's safety and physiological needs. The social and emotional functions correspond with Maslow's social needs of belongingness and love, with Rokeach's values of "social recognition" and "true friendship" and with the more general motivation for stimulation. The epistemic value is similar to Maslow's need for "self-actualization", to Rokeach's values of "exciting life" and "pleasure" and also to the general need for stimulation and pleasure. Previous contributions did not include the conditional value construct, which is particularly well adapted to the situation of buying behaviour. In addition, Sheth, Newman and Gross (1991) have operationalized their theory by developing a generic questionnaire and a standardized procedure for adapting the analysis to any specific market situation.

The "value" approach provides the market analyst with a simple but comprehensive framework for analysing the need structure of the individual buyer and for segmenting markets. The five summary values proposed by Sheth–Newman–Gross theory will be used in the following section to define the concept of the multi-attribute product.

5.4   MOTIVATION OF THE B2B CUSTOMER

So far, our analysis has concerned only the needs and motivations of the individual as a customer. But a large part of commercial activity, in any economy, is made up of transactions between organizations, or B2B. This includes firms selling equipment, goods, intermediary products, raw materials and so on to other firms using these products in their own manufacturing process. Although the principles governing marketing are just as pertinent for firms selling industrial goods as for firms selling consumer goods, the concrete manner in which these principles are implemented may appear very different.

Specificities of B2B markets

The main differences between consumer and B2B marketing can be regrouped into three categories according to whether they relate to demand, to the profile of the organizational customer and to the characteristics of the industrial products or services (Bingham and Gomes, 2001).

The demand for industrial goods

The industrial or organizational demand is a derived demand, that is, a demand expressed by an organization which uses the products purchased in its own manufacturing process, in order to meet either the demand of other organizations or the demand of the end-user. Thus, industrial demand is part of a chain – a supply chain – which depends on a down-stream demand and is ultimately "derived" from the demand of consumer goods. Industrial demand, and particularly capital equipment demand, is highly fluctuating and reacts strongly to small variations in final demand (the acceleration principle). Industrial demand is often price inelastic, in so far as the product represents a small fraction of its costs or con-stitutes a key component, perhaps made to exact specifications, which has no substitute.

The organizational customer

The industrial firm faces several customers: its direct customers and the customers of its direct customers also participating in the supply chain. At each level of the supply chain, the organizational customer has a collegiate structure: a group of individuals, the buying centre, who exercise different functions and roles and have distinct competencies and moti-vations. The organizational customer is a professional buyer, technically competent; the purchase decision involves a degree of normalization not found in consumer purchasing. Thus, the problem-solving approach in B2B markets is in general extensive.

Industrial product characteristics

The products sought are generally well defined by the customer who knows what is wanted; specifications are clearly defined and the supplier has little room for manoeuvring. Industrial products enter into the manufacturing process of the industrial customer and thus have a strategic, if not vital, importance. Industrial products often have a very large number of dif-ferent uses, unlike consumer goods that are almost inevitably for a specific use.

The B2B customer as a decision centre

In an industrial firm, buying decisions, and especially the more important ones, are mostly taken by a group of people called the buying group or the buying centre.

> The buying centre is defined as consisting of those individuals who interact for the specific purpose of accomplishing the buying task. These persons interact on the basis of their par-ticular roles in the buying process. The buying group is characterised by both a pattern of communication (interaction) and a set of shared values (norms) that direct and constrain the behaviour of the individual within it. (Webster and Wind, 1972, p. 35)

There are several distinct roles in the buying centre: users, influencers, purchasers, deciders and gatekeepers. These individuals are either involved in the purchase itself or concerned about its possible consequences on the firm's activity, and thus participate in the purchase

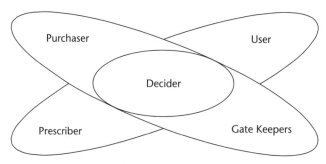

Figure 5.4 Typical composition of the B2B customer's decision centre
Source: Adapted from Webster and Wind (1972).

decision-making process one way or another. Understanding those roles will help one understand the nature of interpersonal influence in the buying decision process. The buying centre comprises individuals with different functions and therefore with different goals, motivations and behaviours. Hence many purchase decisions are conflicting, and they follow a complex process of internal negotiation. The composition of the buying centre varies with the importance of the decisions to be made. In general, the buying decision centre includes the following five roles, which can be occupied by one or several individuals (see Figure 5.4):

- *Purchasers* have formal authority and responsibility for selecting alternative brands and suppliers and for determining the terms of purchase and negotiating contracts. The purchasing manager usually does this.
- *Users* are the persons who use the product: the production engineer or the workers. The users can formulate specific purchase requirements or refuse to work with some materials. Generally speaking, users are better placed for evaluating the performance of purchased goods and services.
- *Influencers* do not necessarily have buying authority but can influence the outcome of a decision by defining criteria that constrain the choices that can be considered. R&D personnel, designers, engineering and consultants and so on typically belong to this category.
- *Deciders* have formal authority and responsibility to determine the final selection of brands or vendors. There is generally an upper limit on the financial commitment that they can make, reserving larger decisions for other members of the organization, for instance, the board of directors.
- *Gatekeepers* are group members who control the flow of information into the group and who can exercise indirect influence on the buying process.

The composition of the buying centre will vary with the complexity and the degree of uncertainty of decisions in the firm. One can distinguish three kinds of situation:

1. *New task*: the purchase of a new product in a new class of products for the client organization.
2. *Modified rebuy*: problem and product are known, but some elements of the buyers' specifications are modified.
3. *Straight rebuy*: purchase of a known product, not modified and with which the firm has extensive experience.

In the first two cases the buying centre intervenes totally. One can see that it is vital for the supplier to identify all those involved in the purchasing process, because it must identify the targets of its communication policy. It is equally important to understand how these participants interact among themselves and what their dominant motivation is.

Generic needs of the B2B customer

The industrial customer is therefore identified with the 'buying centre' that comprises persons from different functions in the organization, who thus have distinct personal and organizational motivations. The notion of need in industry goes beyond the conventional idea of rational choice based only on the quality–price criterion. Choices are rational, as in the case of the individual consumer, in so far as all motivations and constraints with a bearing on purchase decisions are taken into account: personal motivations, interpersonal relations, economic and organizational constraints, environmental pressures and so on. As in the case of the individual consumer, need therefore has a multi-dimensional structure. The generic needs of an industrial customer can be described with reference to at least five values:

- *Technology*: product specifications, state-of-the-art technology, up-to-date and constant quality, just-in-time delivery and so on.
- *Finance*: price competitiveness, transfer costs, installation and maintenance costs, payment terms, delivery reliability and so on.
- *Assistance*: after-sales service help with installation and operation, technical assistance and servicing and so on.
- *Information*: communication, qualified sales personnel, priority access to new products, training, business intelligence and so on.
- *Strategy*: reciprocal relations, compatibility of organizational forms, brand or company reputation and so on.

The examples presented in Exhibit 5.3 illustrate the multi-dimensional nature of the industrial customer's need.

We note that the determinants of well-being for the industrial client are of a very different nature from those governing the well-being of the individual consumer. The structure of motivations of the industrial customer is both more complex and simpler. It is more complex because it involves an organization and different individuals operating in the organization; it is simpler because the main motivations are more objective and thus easier to identify. However, despite the real differences that exist between the two areas, the basic ideas of the market orientation concept have the same relevance in the industrial market as they have in the consumer market: to adjust supply to the overall need of the customer.

If this principle is not implemented, the penalty in the industrial market is probably paid more rapidly because of the buyer's professionalism and the fact that needs are more clearly defined.

Exhibit 5.3   The needs of an industrial customer: an example

The statement from the purchase manager – "No, we won't work with this supplier any more, they are not reliable" – may have different meanings:

- The quality of their products is not constant (technical value).
- Their prices are whimsical (financial value).
- They were supposed to have repaired a machine two months ago (assistance value).

- They have promised to send one of their engineers to tell us about new products being developed; we have called many times and they still haven't done it (information value).
- They treat us as insignificant (psycho-sociological value).

Source: Valla (1980, p. 25).

Chapter Summary

The satisfaction of customers' needs is at the heart of a market economy, yet it is popular in some quarters to claim that marketing creates needs. The notion of need generates controversy because it contains value judgement based on morality or ideology. Apart from the ethical or social rules imposed by society, marketing is pluralist and respects the diversity of tastes and preferences. The distinction between absolute and relative generic needs brings to the fore the existence of a dialectic of relative needs, which leads to the general impossibility of saturation. Similarly, the distinction between generic and derived needs shows that saturation does not relate to generic needs but only to derived needs, that is, the dominant technological response at the time. Experimental psychology has proposed a range of motivational orientations. Particularly useful are the conceptual frameworks proposed by the stimulus–response theory, Maslow's needs hierarchy and the Sheth–Gross–Newman theory of consumption values. If the principles governing organizational or B2B marketing are the same as for consumer marketing, a major difference exists. The industrial customer is represented by a group of individuals, called the buying centre, who exercise different functions and have distinct motivations.

BIBLIOGRAPHY

Abbott, L. (1955), *Quality and Competition*, New York, John Wiley & Sons.

Attali, J. and Guillaume, M. (1974), *L'anti-èconomique*, Paris, Presses Universitaires de France.

Becker, G.S. (1965), A Theory of the Allocation of Time, *The Economic Journal*, September, pp. 494–517.

Berlyne, D.E. (1960), *Conflict, Arousal and Curiosity*, New York, McGraw-Hill.

Bingham, F.G. and Gomes, R. (2001), *Business Marketing*, Chicago, IL, NTC Contemporary Publishing Inc., 2nd edition.

Boirel, M. (1977*), Comment vivre sans tension?* Brussels, Marabout.

Cotta, A. (1980*), La société ludique*, Paris, Grasset.

Derbaix, C. (1997), *Analyse du comportement du consommateur*, Notes de cours, FUCAM.

Duffy, E. (1957), The Psychological Significance of the Concept of Arousal and Activation, *The Psychological Review*, 64, September, pp. 265–75.

Gibbs, P. (2004), Marketing and the Notion of Well-Being, *Business Ethics: A European Review,* 13, 1, pp. 5–14.

Gutman, J. (1982), A Mean–End Chain Model on Consumer Categorization Processes, *Journal of Marketing*, 46, Spring, pp. 60–72.

Hebb, D.O. (1955), Drives and the C.N.S. (Conceptual Nervous System), *The Psychological Review*, 62, July, pp. 243–54.

Henochsberg, M. (2001), *La place du marché*, Paris Denoel.

Kahle, L.R. (1983), *Social Values and Social Change, Adaptation to Life in America*, New York, Praeger.

Kahle, L.R., Poulos, B. and Sukhdial, A. (1988), Changes in Social Values in the United States During the Past Decade, *Journal of Advertising Research*, February–March, pp. 35–41.

Katona, G. (1951), *Psychological Analysis of Economic Behavior*, New York, McGraw-Hill.

Keynes, J.M. (1936), *Essays in Persuasion – Economic Possibilities for our Grandchildren (*The Collected Writings of J.M. Keynes), 9, London, Macmillan.

Lambin, J.J. (2000–2007), *Market-Driven Management*, London, Palgrave Macmillan, First and second edition.

Lancaster, K.J. (1966), A New Approach to Consumer Theory, *The Journal of Political Economy*, 74, April, pp. 132–57.

Maslow, H. (1943), A Theory of Human Motivation, *The Psychological Review*, 50, pp. 370–96.

Murray, H.A. (1938), *Explorations in Personality*, New York, Oxford University Press.

Nuttin, J.(1980), *Théorie de la motivation humaine*, Paris, Presses Universitaires de France.

Pellemans, P. (1998), *Le marketing qualitatif*, Brussels, De Boeck Université.

Ratchford, B.T. (1975), The New Economic Theory of Consumer Behaviour. An Interpretive Essay, *Journal of Consumer Research*, 2, September, pp. 65–78.

Reynolds, T.J. and Gutman, J.(1988), Laddering Theory, Method, Analysis and Interpretation, *Journal of Advertising Research*, February–March, pp. 11–31.

Rochefort, R. (1995), *La société des consommateurs*, Paris, Odile Jacobs.

Rokeach, M.O. (1973), *The Nature of Human Values*, New York, The Free Press.

Rosa, J.J. (1977), Vrais et faux besoins, in J.J. Rosa et F. Aftalion (eds), *L'économique retrouvé*, Paris, Economica.

Ruyer R., (1969), *Eloge de la société de consommation*, Pais, Calman-Lévy.

Scitovsky, T. (1976), *The Joyless Economy*, Oxford, Oxford University Press.

Séguéla, J. (1982*), Hollywood lave plus blanc*, Paris, Flammarion.

Sheth, J.N., Newman, B.I. and Gross, B.L. (1991), *Consumption Values and Market Choices: Theory and Applications*, Cincinnati, OH, South Western Publishing Company.

Valaskakis, K., Sindell, P. and Smith, J.G. (1978), *La société de conservation*, Montreal, Les éditions Quinze.

Valette-Florence, P. (1994), Introduction à l'analyse des chaînages cognitifs, *Recherche et Applications en Marketing*, 9, 1, pp. 93–117.

Valla, J.P. (1980), Le comportement des groupes d'achat, in *L'action marketing des entreprises industrielles*, Paris, Collection Adetem, pp. 22–38.

Webster, F.E. and Wind, Y. (1972), *Organizational Buying Behavior*, Englewood Cliffs, NJ, Prentice Hall.

CHAPTER SIX

THE CUSTOMER PURCHASE BEHAVIOUR

The objective of this chapter is to describe the way customers make purchasing decisions. We shall first describe the different customer roles in B2C markets and then the customer purchasing behaviour successively in the B2C and in the B2B environments. In the B2B section, we will introduce the concept of the industrial supply chain, a key notion in B2B market-driven management. We will also present the concept of a product viewed by the customer as a bundle of values. Finally, after a brief discussion of the customer response behaviour, we shall analyse the customer after-usage behaviour.

Learning Objectives

When you have read this chapter, you should be able to understand:

- The different customer roles in B2C markets
- The customer problem-solving approach in B2C and B2B markets
- The concept of industrial supply chain
- The product viewed as a bundle of attributes
- The concept of CRM
- The customer behaviour after usage or consumption
- The measures of satisfaction/dissatisfaction

6.1 THE DIFFERENT CUSTOMER ROLES

Any marketplace transaction requires at least three customer roles: (1) buying that is selecting a product or service; (2) paying for it and (3) using or consuming it. Thus, a customer can be a buyer, a payer or a user/consumer (Sheth, Mittal and Newman, 1999) see Figure 6.1:

- The user is the person who actually consumes or uses the product or receives the benefits of the service.
- The payer is the person who finances the purchase.
- Finally, the buyer is the person who participates in the procurement of the product from the marketplace.

Each of these roles may be carried out by the same person (e.g., the housewife) or by an organizational unit (e.g., the purchase department) or by different persons or departments.

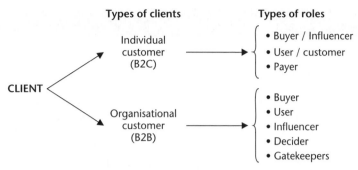

Figure 6.1   The different customer roles in B2C and B2B markets
Source: Lambin (2000/2007).

The person who pays for the product or service is not always the one who is going to use it. Nor is the person who uses it always the person who purchases it. Any of the three customer roles (user, payer or buyer) makes a person a customer (Table 6.1).

Table 6.1   Cross classification of customer roles and values

Values	Buyer	Payer	User
Universal	Service value	Price value	Performance value
Group-specific	Convenience value	Credit value	Social value
Individual-specific	Personalization value	Financing value	Emotional value

Source: Sheth, Mittal and Newman (1999, p. 61). Reproduced with permission.

It is therefore important in any market situation to know the possible ways in which customers divide their roles among themselves in order to adapt the marketing efforts to the type of role specialization. Four types of role specialization can be identified:

User is buyer and payer

Most consumer products purchased for personal use fall into this category, like clothing, watches, sporting goods, haircuts. A single person combines all three roles. This is the traditional domain of consumer analysis, even if the same concentration of roles can also be observed in business markets for small business owners.

User is neither payer nor buyer

Here the user is different from both the payer and the buyer, a situation met in consumer markets for a whole range of products purchased by the housewife for her household or children's use. Similarly, in B2B markets, the purchasing department buys and pays for many products like office furniture and equipment, consumable products for employees who are using the goods, while not associated in the buying decision. As we shall see in the next section, in B2B markets, for high perceived risks buying decisions, the purchasing process is more complex and the role of specialization less clearly defined.

User is buyer but not payer

In some situations, the user may be the buyer but not the payer for the product or service. All purchasing decisions made on expense accounts fall into this category. Also, the user,

Exhibit 6.1 Family as a purchase decision centre

As discussed in more details below, the question of the *buying centre* and its structure is fundamental in B2B markets. It is also important in B2C markets, since buying decisions are hardly ever made by isolated individuals and mostly made within the family, which, in fact, constitutes a buying centre comparable to the one observed in an organization.

Knowledge of purchasing habits implies identification of the respective roles (buyer, user, payer) of the mother, the father and the children, and this by product category and at different stages of the buying process. These questions are important to marketers, who must adapt their product, price and communication policies to their real client, especially since the distribution of the roles and influence of spouses tends to change, due in particular to the rapidly changing role of women in society. One of the first proposed typologies suggests four allocations of roles (Herbst, 1952):

■ Autonomous decision by the husband or the wife
■ Dominant influence of husband
■ Dominant influence of wife
■ Synchretic decision, that is, taken together

The role of children is still to be taken into account. Comparison of the results of studies on the allocation of roles for various product categories shows that the influence of spouses varies greatly according to the type of product (Davis and Rigaux, 1974).

Pras and Tarondeau (1981, p. 214) emphasize that the aim of this kind of research is to define the strategies to be adopted due to a better understanding of the behaviour of the target group. Their relevance can be summarized as follows:

■ Properly choose the persons to be questioned
■ Determine the content of advertising messages
■ Choose the best adapted support material
■ Adapt product conception to the needs of the person with greatest influence
■ Choose the most appropriate distribution network.

Mastering this set of information about buying habits will contribute to a significant improvement in the firm's marketing practice and thus increase the impact of behavioural response.

who is, nevertheless, the buyer, does not pay the services offered within the framework of insurance coverage or social security programmes. For example, in many companies, a large variety of health plans are offered from which employees choose. Although the employee is the buyer and the user, he or she is not paying. The risk of over-consumption is often observed in this type of situations.

User is payer but not buyer

In some cases, the user is payer but not the buyer. For example, in B2B markets, an external agent may be retained to purchase equipment, raw materials or supplies for a company which uses and pays for them. In the financial markets, stockbrokers act as agents for clients.

When a single customer embodies all the roles, the firm will use a different strategy than when different people are user, payer and buyer.

6.2 THE PURCHASING PROCESS IN B2C MARKETS

From the marketing point of view, buying behaviour covers all activity preceding, accompanying and following the purchase decisions. The individual actively takes part in this process in order to make choices in a systematic way, as opposed to random or stochastic selections. The purchasing behaviour can be seen as a process of problem solving.

Steps in the purchasing process

All possible steps that may have something to do with the resolution of the problem are therefore part of the buying process. They can be grouped into five stages:

1. Problem recognition
2. Information search
3. Evaluation of alternatives
4. Purchase decision
5. Post-purchase behaviour

This view of an active buyer is in total contrast with that of the passive buyer who is dominated by the unconscious and is defenceless against the selling activities of the firm and advertisers. The complexity of the decision process varies, however, with the type of buying decisions and with the risk implied by the choice.

The principle of limited rationality

In this framework, purchasing behaviour is neither erratic nor conditioned by the environment. It is rational in the sense of the principle of limited rationality, which means within the bounds of individuals' cognitive and learning capacities. The implicit assumptions are as follows:

- Consumers make choices after deliberation, the extent of which depends on the importance of the perceived risk.
- Choices are based on anticipation of future data and not only on short-term observations.
- Choices are also guided by the principle of generalized scarcity according to which any human acts. Any decision has an opportunity cost.

We live in an environment where everything is scarce: not only money and goods, but also information and especially time, our scarcest resource because it is perfectly inextensible (Becker, 1965).

This approach is called a "rational approach to problem solving". The use of the term "rational" is not in contrast with the term "emotional", which implies a value judgement on the quality of the choice. The steps undertaken are considered to be rational as long as they are "consistent" with the set objectives, whatever these objectives may be.

> For example, an individual, for whom the social value or status effect is important, is prepared to pay more for a product with the same quality. Such action is considered to be rational because the behaviour is consistent.

In other words, as long as information about the objective is sought, critically analysed and processed, behaviour is rational within the limits of the gathered information and the cognitive capability of the individual. This, however, does not exclude the existence of another "better" choice.

We are using here the notion of "consistency" that is so dear to economists, with a fundamental difference. The consumer is consistent with respect to his or her own set of axioms, and not with respect to a set of axioms defined with no reference to a specific situational context or preferences structure. Rational behaviour does not exclude impulsive behaviour. As long as the latter is adopted deliberately, either for the simple pleasure of acting impulsively or for the excitement of being confronted with unexpected consequences, the behaviour is said to be rational.

Rationality here implies no more than the adoption of a kind of systematic choice procedure. This could be defined as the coherent use of a set of principles forming the basis of choice. When choice is made at random, behaviour is unpredictable and erratic and analysis is impossible. Marketing accepts the existence of the latter type of behaviour, but believes that it is not representative of actual behaviour observed in most real-life situations.

This concept of consistency of behaviour makes it possible to reconcile different disciplinary approaches (economic, psychological and sociological) in the study of buying behaviour. Market-driven management is interested in the real person, the individual with all his or her diversity, as illustrated by the list of values described in the previous chapter. Actual choices are influenced by several values, but the individual or the organization may very well accept a sub-optimal level of functional value, for example, in order to maximize social or epistemic value. This type of choice will be termed "rational" because it is consistent with the personal set of values prevailing in the specific choice situation (conditional value).

The different problem-solving approaches

Three types of approach to problem solving can be distinguished, extensive problem solving, limited problem solving and routine response behaviour (Howard and Sheth, 1969):

- *Extensive problem solving* is adopted when the value of information and/or the perceived risk are high. For example, this happens in situations where the buyer is confronted with an unfamiliar brand in an unfamiliar product class. The choice criteria by which alternatives are assessed will be weak or non-existent and an intensive information search will be necessary to identify the relevant criteria.
- *Limited problem solving* applies to the situation of a buyer confronted with a new, unfamiliar brand in a familiar product class, usually where existing brands do not provide an adequate level of satisfaction. Choice criteria already exist, but there will still be a certain amount of search and evaluation prior to purchase.
- Finally, *routine response behaviour* is observed in the case where the consumer has accumulated enough experience and knowledge and has definite preferences about one or more familiar brands within a familiar product category. Here the process of choice is simplified and repetitive, with little or no prior information search. Under this situation of low involvement, considerable consumer inertia and/or brand loyalty would be expected.

Importance of the perceived risk

Not every purchase decision requires a systematic information search. The complexity of the approach to problem solving depends on the importance of the perceived risk associated with the purchase, in other words, on the uncertainty about the scope of the consequences of a particular choice. There are six kinds of risk or unfavourable consequences normally perceived by the buyer (Jacoby and Kaplan, 1972):

- A *functional risk*, if the product characteristics or attributes are not in conformance with prior expectations.
- A *financial loss*, when the product is faulty and needs replacement or repair at one's own expense.

- A *loss of time*, due to hours of making complaints, returning to distributors, repairs and so on.
- A *physical risk*, due to the consumption or use of products potentially harmful to one's health or the environment.
- A *social risk*, if the brand purchased conveys a social image which does not correspond to the true personality of the customer.
- A *psychological risk*, when a bad purchase leads to loss of self-esteem or creates general dissatisfaction.

Market research shows that buyers develop strategies and ways of reducing risk that enable them to act with relative confidence and ease in situations where their information is inadequate and the consequences of their actions are incalculable (Bauer, 1960, p. 120).

To reduce the perceived risk before the purchase decision, the buyer can use various forms of information, such as personal sources (family, neighbours, friends), commercial sources (advertising, salespersons, catalogues), public sources (comparative tests, official publications) and experimental sources (product trials, inspection). The higher the perceived risk, the more extensive the information search will be.

The concept of *consumer involvement* has received considerable attention in the marketing literature. Involvement can be defined as "a state of energy (arousal) that a person experiences in regard to a consumption-related activity" (Wilkie, 1994, p. 164).

Thus involvement implies attention to something because it is somehow relevant or perceived as risky. High involvement requires high levels of prior deliberation and strong feelings, while low involvement will occur when consumers invest less energy in their thoughts

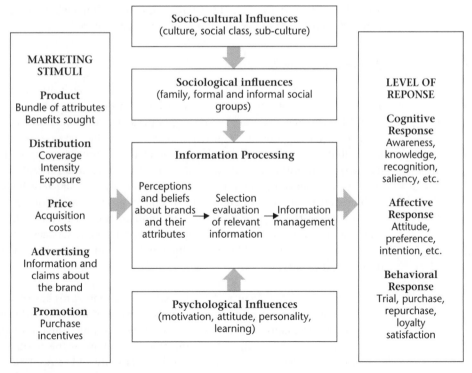

Figure 6.2   The fields of customer behaviour analysis
Source: Lambin (2000/2007).

and feelings. The concept of involvement, which overlaps somewhat with Howard and Sheth's classification of problem-solving situations above, is useful for analysing consumer behaviour at different levels of involvement and for deciding on the type of communication strategy to adopt in each situation.

The costs of information

An individual facing a problem of choice undertakes the search for information mainly to reduce uncertainty about available alternatives, their relative values and the terms and conditions of purchase. We can classify the various costs incurred by this information search into three categories:

- *Inspection costs*, implied by studying different markets and defining the range of possibilities (including substitutes) that the buyer could include in the set being contemplated.
- *Perception costs*, borne in view of identifying the relevant characteristics of goods included in the choice set, as well as the terms of exchange (places of purchase, price, guarantee and so on).
- *Evaluation costs*, resulting from the evaluation of how much the sought attributes are present and how authentic the market signals are about the quality of goods.

These costs are mainly in the form of time spent. But the cost of time – measured by its opportunity cost – varies from individual to individual; it also varies with factors of circumstance. For example, the cost of time is not the same during holidays as it is during a period of work. Therefore, it is not always in the consumer's interest to prolong the information search beyond a certain level. The extent of searching efforts will also vary with the degree of perceived risk in the buying decision under consideration.

The sources of information

The cost of perceiving attributes varies with the observable nature of product attributes and benefits. Nelson (1970, p. 214) establishes a distinction between *search goods* (having observable external qualities), *experience goods* (having verifiable internal qualities) and *credence goods* (having unverifiable internal qualities). For the first category of goods, the product attributes can easily be checked before purchase by simple inspection; these are products like clothing, furniture and toys for which the choice criteria can easily be verified with little cost. For experience goods, however, the most important characteristics are only revealed with use, after purchase. Examples of this type of products are books, medicines, cars and computers. For this type of product, perception costs can be very high for a single individual, and even higher for credence goods (like professional services). But the efficiency of surveying can be improved by using different sources of information, which have various degrees of reliability:

- *Information sources dominated by the producer*, in other words advertising, opinions and advice given by sellers and distributors, displays and brochures. The advantage of this kind of information is that it is free and easily accessible. The information is, however, incomplete and biased, in the sense that it emphasizes the positive qualities of the product and tends to overshadow others (Abernathy and Frank, 1996).
- *Personal information sources*, dominated by consumers; this is information communicated by friends, neighbours, opinion leaders or what is better known as "word of

mouth". This kind of information is often well adapted to the needs of the future buyer. Its reliability obviously depends on that of the person transmitting the information.

■ *Information sources which are neutral*, such as articles published in newspapers and reviews specializing in housing, furnishing, hunting, audio-visual products and automobiles. Such publications often provide a lot of information at a relatively low cost. This category also includes publications such as official reports or reports of specialized agencies, laboratory tests and comparative tests initiated by consumer associations. The advantage of this source of information is its objectivity, its factual nature and the competence of the opinions reported.

It is worth underlining here the specific role played by consumer associations. In a situation where the perception of the attributes of a product is particularly costly, it is in the interest of the individual consumer to regroup with other consumers in order to proceed with a thorough analysis that would be impossible for an individual alone. This is a form of unionization of consumers, which constitutes a countervailing force vis-à-vis the firm, and has the reduction of the cost of information to the consumer as its main objective.

6.3   THE PURCHASING PROCESS IN B2B MARKETS

The analysis of the buying process basically consists of identifying the specific roles played by each member of the buying centre at different stages of the decision-making process, their choice criteria, their perceptions of the performance of products or firms in the market and the weight given to each point of view and so on.

Steps in the buying process

As in the case of the buying decision of the individual consumer, the industrial buying process can be divided into several stages. As illustrated in Table 6.2, Webster and Wind (1972, p. 80) suggest six phases in the process:

1. Anticipation and identification of need.
2. Determination of specifications and scheduling the purchase.
3. Search for buying alternatives.
4. Evaluation of alternative buying actions.
5. Selection of suppliers.
6. Performance control and appraisal.

Table 6.2 Decision stages and roles of the buying decision centre: an example

Stages in the buying process	Composition of the buying centre				
	User	Influencer	Buyer	Decider	Gatekeeper
Identification of needs	*				*
Establishing specifications	*	*			*
Identifying alternatives			*		*
Evaluating alternatives	*	*	*	*	*
Selecting the supplier			*	*	*
Evaluation of performances	*				

Source: Adapted from Webster and Wind (1972).

This is typically the same sequence as that observed in the case of an *extensive problem-solving approach*.

Clearly, the decision of an industrial client does not always follow this process. The complexity of the decision and its degree of risk or novelty determine how formal the buying process will be. Furthermore, the decision-making and organizational processes can also vary according to the firm, in terms of both its size and its fields of activity. One can imagine that the roles of the members of the buying centre are different at each stage of the decision-making process.

The type of information required to understand the decision process in a B2B company is summarized in Box 6.1. This information is usually collected by survey. It helps to clarify the issue, particularly when it comes to training salespeople by helping them to understand the mechanism of the industrial buying process better.

Valla (1980, p. 27) underlines the fact that training salespeople to understand this type of analysis particularly helps them to:

- understand better the buyer's role as well as the system of motivations and constraints within which the buyer operates;
- go beyond mere contact with the purchaser by identifying other possible communication targets within the industrial client's organization;
- determine better when is the best moment to directly intervene vis-à-vis appropriate targets in order to increase efficiency of contacts;
- be in a better position to take advantage of opportunities when they present themselves, due to broader relations with all members of the buying centre.

We shall see in the following chapter that the way the buying centre functions is an important segmentation criterion in industrial markets.

The industrial supply chain

A central concept in B2B markets is the industrial supply chain. The notion of an industrial chain goes beyond a list of names by branch or by sector and makes the conventional division of the economy into primary, secondary and tertiary sectors out of date. An industrial chain consists of

> all the stages of production, from raw materials to satisfying the final need of the consumer, irrespective of whether this final need concerns a product or a service.

There is a hierarchy of industries that are either clients or suppliers of a given firm according to whether they are upstream or downstream. The strategic force of an industrial client

---

Box 6.1   Implementation problem: how to analyse the decision process in a B2B market?

The analysis of the purchasing process must answer the following questions:

- Who is a major participant in the decision-making process of buying a given industrial product?
- Who are the key influencers intervening in the process?

- What is the level of their influence?
- What evaluation criteria does each decision participant use?
- What is the weight given to each criterion?

depends, among other things, on its ability to anticipate and control the end-market of the chain in which it participates.

Typical structure of an industrial chain

The following list describes the structure of a typical industrial demand (see Figure 6.3). Clearly, the chain of demands may be much longer and more complex in some cases. Though this is not an exhaustive list, the following distinctions can be established:

■ *First transformation.* Demand is for processed materials that are transformed into semi-finished goods, for instance, steel bars, sheets, chemicals, leather and so on.
■ *Final transformation.* Demand is for primary products that will be transformed into more elaborate processed products. For example, transformation of raw sheet metal into

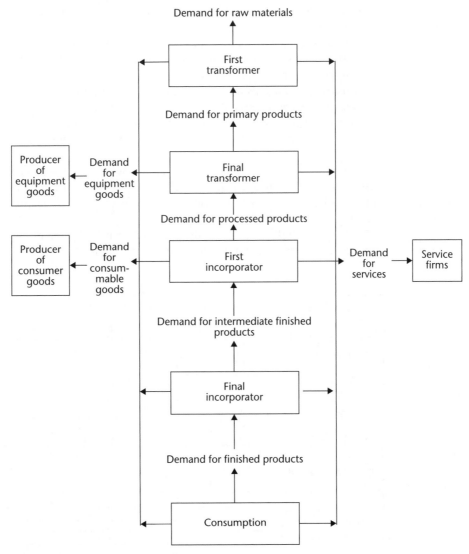

Figure 6.3 Typical structure of an industrial supply chain
Source: Lambin (2000/2007).

rustproof sheet metal either plated or pre-painted. Bekaert transforms raw steel into wires of different diameters.

■ *First incorporation*. Demand is for finished goods used to manufacture more complex products which are themselves components of other products. For example, pre-painted sheet metal is used to manufacture radiators; wires are used to manufacture radial tyres.

■ *First transformation*. Demand is for processed materials that are transformed into semi-finished goods, for instance, steel bars, sheets, chemicals, leather, and so on.

■ *Final transformation*. Demand is for primary products that will be transformed into more elaborate processed products. For example, transformation of raw sheet metal into rust-proof sheet metal either plated or pre-painted. Bekaert transforms raw steel into wires of different diameters.

■ *First incorporation*. Demand is for finished goods used to manufacture more complex products which are themselves components of other products. For example, pre-painted sheet metal is used to manufacture radiators; wires are used to manufacture radial tyres.

■ *Final incorporation*. Demand is for finished products incorporated in manufacturing finished products for final demand, for example, tyres and batteries, spark plugs, TV tubes, automobile windscreens, and so on.

■ *Assemblers*. Demand is for a large variety of products that will be put together to form systems or large compounds. For example, radiators are placed with other products to form a heating system. Similarly, a system of public transport, such as an underground rail system, brings together a tremendous variety of different products.

In addition to these successive demands that follow one another in a chain, there are also lateral demands of capital equipment goods, consumable items (fuel, wrapping materials, office supplies and so on) and services (maintenance and repair, manufacturing and business services, professional services).

Therefore the industrial firm in the position of the beginning of the production chain is faced with a sequence of independent demands that finally determine its own demand.

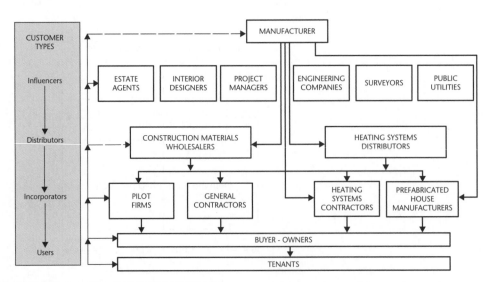

Figure 6.4 Vertical structure of the domestic heat pump market
Source: Lambin (2000/2007).

It faces two categories of clients: its direct customers and the customers of its customers. In order to apply active marketing, the firm must take into account the specific demands of its direct customers, of the intermediary customers and of those who express final demand at the end of the chain. Figure 6.4 gives an example of the successive customers, direct and indirect, facing a manufacturer of heat pumps.

6.4   THE PRODUCT AS A BUNDLE OF BENEFITS

We have seen that, from a customer's point of view, a product can be defined as a "bundle of attributes" which provides the customer with the functional value or "core service" specific to that class of product, as well as a set of secondary values or utilities (called benefits or services) which may be necessary or added (see Figure 6.5). These additional services differentiate the brands and may have a determining influence on customers' preferences.

The core service or benefit

The core service provided by a brand corresponds to the functional value of its class of product; it is the basic and generic benefit provided by each of the brands in a given product category.

For an air compressor, the core service is the production of compressed air; for a toothpaste, dental hygiene; for a watch, it will be time measurement; for an airline company, the transportation from Paris to New York; for wallpaper, home decoration, and so on.

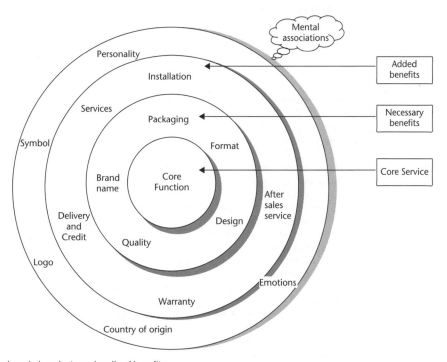

Figure 6.5   The branded product as a bundle of benefits
Source: Lambin (2000/2007).

As underlined earlier, the core service defines the reference market in generic terms by providing an answer to the question: "What business are we in?" The rationale is the following:

- The customer is not looking for a product as such, but for the core service it provides.
- The customer can get the same core service from technologically different products.
- Technologies are moving and changing rapidly and profoundly, whereas the needs, to which the core service responds, remain stable.

Levitt (1980) states that in order to avoid the risk of myopia, it is in the firm's best interest to define its *reference market* with respect to the core service provided, rather than to a particular technology. This allows potential customers to identify the alternative solutions likely to be considered when they are confronted with a choice problem.

All brands in the same reference market provide the customer with the same core service in a way that tends to become uniform, given that competition and the diffusion of technological progress balance out technological performance. Consequently, in a significant number of markets, the core service by itself is no longer a determining factor in the customer's decisions. The way in which the core service is provided or delivered becomes more of a deciding factor.

The peripheral services

In addition to the basic functional utility, a brand provides a series of other utilities or peripheral services which are secondary compared to the core service, but which may prove to be decisive when competing brands tend to have even performances. These peripheral services may be of two kinds: "necessary" services and "added" services.

Necessary peripheral services identify with the mode of production of the core service (fuel efficiency, roominess, noise and so on) and all that normally accompanies the core service (packaging, delivery, payment terms, after-sales service and so on).

For example, Atlas-Copco "oil-free" compressors produce compressed air which is totally free of oil particles; Epson printers are particularly quiet; Japanese cars are well-known for their

Table 6.3   The bundle of attributes: the brand Häagen-Dazs

Objective characteristics	Brand attributes	Values
Patronymic brand name from the Polish founder based in the United States	A suggestive Danish name, a country known for the quality of its dairy products	Healthy product
Per cent of air in the cream: 10 per cent against 50 per cent in competing brands.	Full mouth, high density of the cream, unctuousness	Gourmet pleasure
Four noble ingredients: milk cream instead of butter, sugar cane, egg yolk instead of sweetening, farm milk instead of powder milk	Good and powerful taste, fully natural product	Reassurance
Vanilla from Madagascar Pecan nuts, strawberries from Oregon	Large variety of flavours	Diversity
Box of 500 ml designed by HD and easy to store.	Exclusive package stored and refrigerated	Convenience
Price twice that of competing brands but affordable by everybody	Image of craft product, mass deluxe concept	A treat
Identical concept, brand name, packaging and communication worldwide	A global brand	Guarantee

Source: Lambin (2007).

reliability; Apple microcomputers are very user-friendly; Bang and Olufsen products have an outstanding design; Swatch has a large variety of designs, and so on.

Added peripheral services are utilities unrelated to the core service, which the brand provides as extras. Hence they constitute an important source of differentiation.

For instance, Singapore Airlines offers a frequent flyers programme "Privileged Passenger Service" (PPS) that is especially attractive; some makes of cars include radio equipment in their basic price; some credit cards give the right to preferential conditions in five star hotels; and so on.

These peripheral services themselves, whether necessary or added, form attributes which generate satisfaction for the customer. These attributes may differ greatly according to the brand and can thus be used as choice criteria. Furthermore, one can imagine that different buyers attach different degrees of importance to the presence of some attributes. Thus, a brand can be defined as a bundle of attributes that produces the core service plus the peripheral services, necessary or added, whose importance and performance potential customers can differently perceive.

Note that any brand has at least one unique feature (generally more than one), which is simply its brand name and also mental associations (emotion, symbolic value, personality and so on) which form the brand identity. The customer's global perception of a brand is commonly referred to as the brand image (for example, see Table 6.4).

6.5 CUSTOMER RELATIONSHIP MANAGEMENT

The customer's satisfaction is at the heart of the marketing process and yet it is only in the 1980s (Berry, 1983) that companies began to systematically measure the degree of satisfaction felt by customers and to follow up their attitude and satisfaction after use or consumption.

Exhibit 6.2   Contrasting product characteristics, benefits and values

- **Characteristic**
  The physical or technical features of the product
  (A fry pan coated with Teflon)

- **Benefit**
  The advantage brought to the customer by the characteristic
  (A nonsticky cooking)

- **Value**
  The mental representation of the need met thanks to the benefit
  (The pleasure of a trouble-free culinary experience)

Exhibit 6.3   Examples of package of benefits

- **Small electrical motors**: power, reliability, consumption, resistance, response speed, safety, size, weight.
- **Industrial equipment**: performance, reliability, ease of use, versatility, installation, maintenance, repair parts, delivery time, information, resell value.
- **Automobiles**: power, consumption, comfort safety, design, maintenance, resell value, prestige.
- **Toothpaste**: whitens teeth, fresh breath, cavity protection, gums protection, taste, pleasant texture.

Table 6.4 Evaluation of a supplier in an industrial market viewed as a bundle of attributes

Macro-attributes (and weight)		Key sub-attributes	Internal metrics
Equipment	30	Reliability	% Repair call
		Easy to use	% Calls for help
		Features/functions	Function performance test
Sales	30	Knowledge	Supervisor observations
		Response	% Proposals made on time
		Follow-up	% Follow-up made
Installation	10	Delivery interval	Average order interval
		Does not break	% Repair reports
		Installed when promised	% Installed on due date
Repair	15	No repeat trouble	% Repeat reports
		Fixed fast	Average speed of repair
		Kept informed	% Customers informed
Billing	15	Accuracy: no surprises	% Billings inquiries
		Resolve on first call	% Resolved on first call
		Easy to understand	% Billings inquiries
Total	100	–	–

Source: Adapted from Kordupleski, Rust and Zahorik (1993).

Previously, analysis was restricted to internal measures of quality such as ISO-9000. The most obvious level of satisfaction would seem to be the level of sales or market share, just as the number of complaints would be the sign of dissatisfaction.

In fact, things are much more complicated. There can be a big difference between what the company thinks customers want and what the customer is really looking for. In other words, the gap between the designed and the expected quality may be very large, even if the customer never formally expresses his or her dissatisfaction. This is why it is necessary to directly interview customers to assess scientifically their level of satisfaction/dissatisfaction. The value of this type of study is also to permit international comparisons for the same brand from country to country and to allow longitudinal analyses to keep track of the changes in satisfaction over a certain period.

Customer relationship management defining

Although the term Customer Relationship Management, or CRM, is relatively new, the principles behind it are not: Firms have long practised some form of CRM generally assumed by the Sales Administration service. As explained by Payne and Frow (2006), what sets present-day CRM apart is that organizations now have an increased potential to utilize technology and manage *one-to-one relationships* (Pepper and Rogers, 1993) with potentially huge number of customers in a context of the global market. The purpose of CRM is

> to efficiently and effectively increase the acquisition and retention of profitable customers by selectively initiating, building and maintaining appropriate relationships with them. (Payne and Frow, 2006, p. 136)

The objective of *relationship marketing* is to develop long-term and mutually profitable relationships not only with valued customers but with multiple stakeholders, while the focus of CRM should be primarily on the customer.

The starting point is to identify in the target segment the *suspects*, that is, those potential customers who could have a strong potential interest in the product or service, *prospects* are those potential customers having a strong interest in the product and the ability to pay for it and *disqualified prospects* are those whom the company rejects because they have poor credit or would be unprofitable to serve. The firm will then try to convert qualified prospects to *first-time customers*, and if satisfied to *repeat customers or clients. The next challenge is to turn clients to advocates*, that is, customers who praise the company and encourage others to buy from it (Griffin, 1995) (see Figure 6.6).

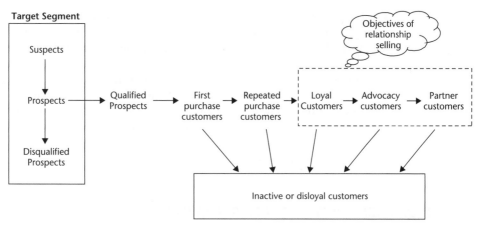

Figure 6.6 Typology of customers in a CRM perspective
Source: Adapted from Griffin (1995). Reproduced with permission.

Advances in information technology can help in building these selective relationships. Companies have at their disposal a range of database, data mart, and data warehouse technologies as well a growing number of CRM software. Such developments make it possible to gather vast amount of customer data and to analyse, interpret and utilize it constructively. Furthermore, the advantages presented by increasingly powerful hardware, software and e-services are augmented by decreasing costs of running them. By using a wide range of CRM tools, companies can potentially target their most promising client opportunities more effectively (Payne and Frow, 2006).

This does not mean that such benefits will automatically be achieved by the purchase of CRM software solutions, as illustrated by many examples of CRM failure (Fournier, Dobscha and Mick, 1998). Research has shown that successful CRM demands that members of different functions such as operational marketing, information technology and human resources management work to gather in cross-functional teams. It also implies that the market or the customer orientation culture is well disseminated at all levels within the firm. CRM is *customer-centric* and this business philosophy is a prerequisite for successful application of CRM. In the 8th Bain & Company Annual Management Tools Survey, of the 25 tools rated by respondents, CRM ranked fourth from last for use satisfaction, with a 35 per cent global usage rate (Siddle and Rigby, 2001).

The B2B customer–supplier relationship management

In B2B markets, customers are more or less willing and able to control the customer–supplier relationship or to be actively involved in their relationship with their suppliers, as implied by CRM. In B2B markets, one can identify three major categories of customers, each varying in their degree of control and willingness to co-operate over their customer experience (Manning and Throne, 2003).

■ *The collaborative customer*. These customers are able and willing to share in the control of the relationship with their suppliers. Shared control involves an exchange of information on the wants and desires of the customer along with the basic offerings by the supplier. This is the ideal type of customer orientation for one-to-one marketing to work. In the automotive sector, for example, parts suppliers are increasingly expected to provide expertise in the development and engineering of products.

- *The activist customer.* In some circumstances, customers seek a high level of control of the business customer experience. In many industrial markets, this is the most common relationship. Manufacturers that act as customers set the specifications, delivery requirements and costs parameters, and their suppliers meet these terms.
- *The passive customer.* A passive customer is primarily one who has a low level of involvement with his customer experience. Passive customers do not tend to be particularly loyal and they show low willingness to become more knowledgeable or to participate in the development of new products or solutions.

This typology of customers is important to adapt CRM.

6.6   CUSTOMER POSTPURCHASE BEHAVIOUR

The objective of CRM is to build long-term and mutually profitable relationships with valued customers. To achieve this objective, (a) monitoring customer satisfaction, (b) handling properly complaints of dissatisfied customers, (c) designing appropriate solutions to their problems and (c) rewarding loyal customers are the key ingredients for success.

The behaviour of dissatisfied customers

In a meta-analysis of customer satisfaction studies based on 500 surveys conducted in Europe in B2B business sectors, with an average of 300 interviews per survey, Goderis (1998, p. 285) obtained the following data:

- only 2.9 per cent of sales transactions result in complaints made directly to the company,
- on average, 28.6 per cent of transactions result in indirect complaints to the sales representatives, neighbours, friends and so on,
- in addition, 9.2 per cent of the complaints are never communicated.

There are two different explanations for this last group. Buyers have minimized the problem or they were pessimistic about the outcome of a complaint, given the dominant position of the supplier or because, in previous instances, a complaint has remained unanswered.

Thus, in total, 40.7 per cent of the transactions of an average firm may cause problems to customers, a level of dissatisfaction that is not well reflected by the tip of the iceberg, which is the 3 per cent of formal complaints.

Exhibit 6.4   Airline delight: an example

If you dropped your cash-filled wallet in an airline seat, your natural expectation is that it is gone forever. You would be *satisfied* if the ground staff handled your report promptly with a promise, even without guarantees, that they would try their best to recover your wallet. You would be *annoyed* if you encounter red tape and indifference when you filed the report. You would be *delighted* if the airline found your wallet in no time and notified you that you may get your wallet with all the cash intact at the airline counter in your next destination. You would be *surprised* if an airline staff hand carries your wallet to your home. As a delighted and surprised customer, you would write an unsolicited letter of compliment to the airline management; you would also become a loyal frequent flyer and tell the whole world about your wonderful experience with the airline.

Source: Domingo (1997, p. 282).

In so far as a complaint is efficiently handled by after-sales service, the negative consequences for the firm can be limited. On the other hand, a real problem remains with the 30 per cent group of dissatisfied customers who do not communicate with the supplier but who could really affect market share in the long run. This is why the adoption of a proactive attitude by measuring regularly the level of satisfaction/dissatisfaction of different customer groups and identifying their causes is important. Remember that in sectors where primary demand is non-expansible, 80 to 90 per cent of the turnover is due to existing customers. It is easy to understand why it is important to maintain satisfaction for this portfolio of existing customers.

An additional argument is provided by analysis of the behaviour of dissatisfied customers whose complaints were well handled by the firm. The findings reported in the Goderis study (1998, p. 286) have shown the following results:

■ For satisfied customers, the average repeat purchase rate is 91 per cent.
■ Among customers who had made a complaint but had received a poor response from the firm, the repeat purchase rate drops to 54 per cent.
■ Of dissatisfied customers who had complained and had received an appropriate response from the firm, the repeat purchase rate was 96 per cent, a rate higher than that observed for satisfied customers.

Problem customers are (a) those dissatisfied but who do not complain and (b) those that complain but are not happy with the way their complaint has been treated by the company. The loss of customers comes from these two groups which constitute a form of negative advertising by word of mouth, costly for the firm and very difficult to control. Research findings (Rhoades, 1988) show that "dissatisfied customers will tell ten other people about their bad experience with a company or a brand".

Three important conclusions can be drawn from these various studies on dissatisfied customers' behaviours.

■ The level of satisfaction/dissatisfaction is key input data in the market information system of any company.

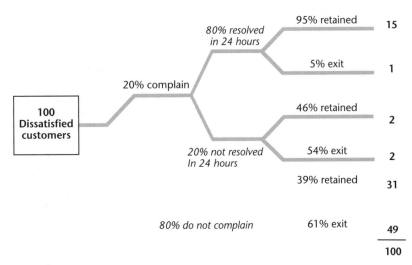

Figure 6.7 Customer base analysis
Source: Adapted from Best (2004).

- A complaint is not necessarily negative because the customer will accept a problem to the extent the company finds a good solution to the problem.
- Complaints are important sources of information, allowing a company to better understand customer needs and their perception of the product quality.

Current complaint management is only one aspect, necessary but insufficient, of a total quality programme aiming at complete customer satisfaction (see Figure 6.7).

Methods of measuring satisfaction/dissatisfaction

The conceptual model underlying satisfaction/dissatisfaction research is simply the attitude multi-attribute model discussed earlier in this chapter. The questions concern the importance of each attribute and the degree of perceived presence of the attribute (performance) in the evaluated product or service.

The interviewing procedure is in three steps. First, the overall level of satisfaction is obtained from the respondent; then importance and performance scores are requested for each attribute on a ten-point rating scale. Finally, repeat purchase intentions are measured.

Analysis of customer satisfaction

The first step is to calculate the average performance score for each attribute as well as its standard deviation. These scores are then compared to the average scores observed in the sector or to the scores obtained by priority competitors. This comparison will result in a good picture of how the market perceives the quality of the product, viewed as a package of benefits.

The performance scores obtained on the attributes are situated along two axes: on the horizontal axis are placed the average performance scores and on the vertical axis the standard deviations for these scores. A high standard deviation means that few respondents have the same opinion, and a low standard deviation will, on the contrary, show that most customers share the same opinion.

The choice of a cut-off point for these two axes is always a sensitive problem. It is common practice to use the average score observed in the sector or the score of the priority competitor. We then have a two-by-two matrix defining four quadrants as shown in Figure 6.8.

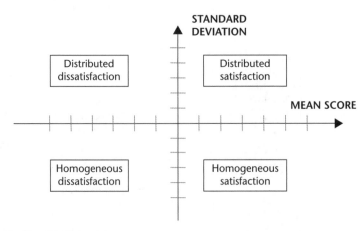

Figure 6.8   The satisfaction/dissatisfaction matrix
Source: Adapted from Goderis (1998).

In the lower right-hand quadrant, the attributes of brand or company X have an average score superior to the sector's average and also a lower than average standard deviation. This means that customers are generally satisfied and agree to say so. We have here a case of *homogeneous satisfaction*.

In the top right-hand quadrant, the brand's attributes also have an above average score, but the standard deviation this time is high which means that customers have varying opinions. We thus have a situation of *distributed satisfaction*, which can be caused, for example, by a lack of consistency in the quality of the services provided. Identification of the dissatisfied customers and of the causes of their dissatisfaction is a priority objective to adopt the individualized remedial actions before customers switch to competition.

In the upper-left quadrant, the average is below the sectoral average and the standard deviation is high. This is case of *distributed dissatisfaction*; most of the customers are dissatisfied, but some are less dissatisfied than others are. This state of affairs can be explained by a product or service ill adapted to some customer group(s).

In the last quadrant, the lower left-hand one, customers are dissatisfied and agree to say so. This is the most unfavourable situation of *homogeneous dissatisfaction*.

Satisfaction–dissatisfaction response styles

Customers can and do engage in multiple responses to satisfaction or dissatisfaction. The typology proposed by Jones and Sasser (1995) is particularly useful. Six types of loyalty behaviour are proposed.

- The *apostle*: A very satisfied customer who tells it to other prospects.
- The *loyalist*: A satisfied customer but who does not tell it to other people.
- The *defector*: A dissatisfied customer who keeps quiet.
- The *terrorist*: A very dissatisfied customer who talks too much.
- The *mercenary*: A customer who is mostly satisfied but who would do anything for obtaining a better deal.
- The *hostage*: A customer, satisfied or not, who has no option or no other choice.

Each company should analyse its customer base using this typology in order to adapt its response behaviour. An example of such an analysis is presented in Exhibit 6.5.

6.7 THE SATISFACTION–LOYALTY RELATIONSHIP

As already underlined, a high level of satisfaction leads to increased customer loyalty and increased customer loyalty is the single most important driver of long-term financial performance. The relationship between satisfaction and loyalty has been empirically established, namely, by Jones and Sasser (1995), as shown in Figure 6.9.

The brand loyalty concept

There are several approaches for operationally defining brand loyalty and for long the most popular one was based on the observation of purchase sequence. For example, a 12-trial purchase sequence of AABAACAADAAE would qualify a consumer as being loyal to Brand A according to a per cent-of-purchase definition, but not according to most sequence definitions which require three or four consecutive purchases of the same brand as the criterion

---

Exhibit 6.5   Complaint behaviour in the professional service sector: an example

Dart and Freeman (1994) have developed a typology of response styles among professional service clients. Three factors or types of complaint behaviour were identified:

Voice: responses directed towards the firm.
Private: word-of-mouth communication and/or discontinuance of the relationship with the firm.
Third party: complaining to external agencies.
In a cluster analysis conducted on a sample of 224 respondents among business users of professional services (accounting), four segments were identified.
Passives (42 per cent): customers whose intentions to complain are below average on the three factors, especially for voicing complaints directly to the firm.

Voicers (34 per cent): dissatisfied customers who are more likely to complain to the firm and to engage in negative word-of-mouth behaviour.
Irates (5 per cent): customer who demonstrate above-average private response such as negative word-of-mouth or switching firms.
Activist (19 per cent): customers who are likely to engage in above-average behaviour in all three types of complaint behaviour.

Source: Dart and Freeman (1994).

---

of loyalty. This purely behavioural view of loyalty has clear limitations, because attention is focused entirely on the *outcome of* rather than the *reasons for* the behaviour.

> For example, is the woman who always buy Brand A because it is the cheapest, "loyal" in the same sense as the woman who buys brand A because she prefers it? And what of the woman who buys brand A because it has the most favourable shelf space or because it is the only nationally advertised and distributed brand carried by the store in which she shops? (Day, 1969)

It is clear that, underlying the loyalty behaviour, there is an *evaluative process or an attitudinal component* linked to the purchaser's degree of satisfaction that must be identified. The repeat purchase behaviour is a necessary but not sufficient condition for defining brand loyalty. Jacoby and Kyner (1973) have presented six criteria considered necessary and collectively sufficient for defining brand loyalty.

> Brand loyalty is (1) the biased (i.e., non-random), (2) behavioural response (i.e., purchase), (3) expressed over time, (4) by some decision-making unit, (5) with respect to one or more alternative brands out of a set of such brands, and (6) is a function of psychological (decision-making, evaluative) processes. (Jacoby and Kyner, 1973)

The term "decision-making unit" implies that the decision-maker need not be (a) the user or even the purchaser of the product; but can also be the prescriber. Similarly, the decision-making unit can be an individual or a collection of individuals (family or organization). The fifth condition is important because it introduces the concept of *multibrand loyalty, or brand repertoire*: Individuals can be and frequently are multibrand loyal. A brand switch can occur within a set of brands to which the buyer remains loyal. This behaviour is revealing of a loyal behaviour to a reduced set of brands, a construct close to the consideration set concept (see Howard and Sheth, 1969).

The brand (or company) loyalty concept is important in several respects and in particular in view of the relationship existing between loyalty and satisfaction – as discussed in the next section – and also because of the impact of customer loyalty on corporate profitability, as illustrated in Figure 6.9.

PURCHASE LOYALTY

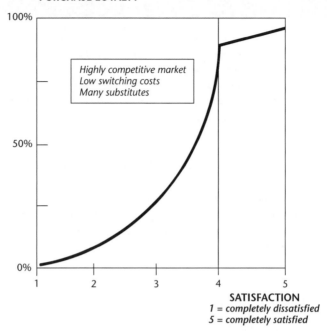

Figure 6.9   The satisfaction–loyalty relationship
Source: Adapted from Jones and Sasser (1995).

The satisfaction–loyalty relationship

According to conventional wisdom, the relationship between satisfaction and loyalty should be a simple linear relationship: as satisfaction increases, so does loyalty. A research conducted at Rank Xerox and replicated by Jones and Sasser (1995) showed a much more complex relationship. The two extreme curves of Figure 6.9 are representative of two different competitive situations:

- *In non-competitive markets* – the upper-left zone – satisfaction has little impact on loyalty. These markets are typically regulated monopolies like telecommunication, electrical or transportation utilities; or market situations where switching costs are very high. Customers in fact have no choice; they are captive customers. This situation can change rapidly, however, if the source of monopoly disappears, because of deregulation or the emergence of alternative technology.
- *In competitive markets* – the lower-right zone – where competition is intense with many substitutes and low switching costs, a very large difference is observed between the loyalty of "satisfied" (score of 4) and "completely satisfied" (score between 4 and 5) customers.

This was namely the discovery made at the Xerox Corporation: "these totally satisfied customers were six times more likely to repurchase Xerox products over the next 18 months than its satisfied customers (Jones and Sasser, 1995, p. 91).

The implications are profound. Merely satisfying customers who have the freedom to make choices is not enough to keep them loyal. The only truly loyal customers are totally satisfied customers.

Exhibit 6.6   Customer longevity is profitable

The more a customer is loyal, the more he or she contributes to the profitability, since the costs to find a new customer are supported only once. If every year, 5 per cent of the customer base quit and must be replaced, it means that a customer has an average life of 20 years.

If the loyalty rate can be increased from 95 to 96 per cent thanks to a higher customer satisfaction level, only 4 per cent of customers have to be replaced and the average customer life jumps to 25 per cent, with a resulting strong improvement of the firm's profitability.

6.8   POST-RECESSION CONSUMERS' BEHAVIOUR

In most developed countries, pre-recession consumer behaviour was the product of more than 30 years of uninterrupted growth and prosperity? The 2008–2009 recession has a long-term impact on buying behaviour and Flatters and Wilmott (2009) have identified eight trends that can be regrouped on the basis on their maturity or whether they are growing or declining.

Dominant trends

1. *A demand for simplicity*: Many consumers are feeling overwhelmed by the profusion of choices and are starting to simplify.
2. *A focus on corporate governance*: The financial crisis has put the spotlight on the malfeasance of some executives and the complicity of their companies' boards.

Advancing trends

3. *Discretionary thrift*: Some consumers have no choice but to be thrifty, but many affluent consumers are economizing as well.
4. *Mercurial consumption*: Consumers have bought increasingly erratic loyalty into recession.

Slowed trends

5. *Green consumerism*: Consumers have increasingly embraced green products, during the past decade, but green consumerism has slowed in this recession.
6. *Decline of deference*: There is mounting scepticism about the quality of information by traditional sources of authority.

Arrested trends

7. *Ethical consumerism*: Like most altruistic spending, ethical consumption will take a back seat in this recession.
8. *Extreme-experience seeking*: Exotic experiences that are frivolous, risky or environmentally destructive are suffering from a mood of seriousness and responsibility.

Some consumers may return to boom-time consumption patterns in the coming decades, but millions of people under age 35 entering this recession may well remain simplicity-seeking, thrifty, green yet mercurial consumers.

> ### Chapter Summary
>
> Customer purchasing behaviour is neither erratic nor conditioned by the environment. It is rational in the sense of the principle of limited rationality, which means within the bounds of individuals' cognitive and learning capacities. An industrial chain consists of all the stages of production, from raw materials to satisfying the final need of the consumer, irrespective of whether this final need concerns a product or a service. From a customer's point of view, a product can be defined as a "bundle of attributes" which provides the customer with the functional value or "core service" specific to that class of product, as well as a set of secondary values or utilities (called benefits or services) which may be necessary or added .These additional services differentiate the brands and may have a determining influence on customers' preferences. What sets present-day CRM apart is that organizations now have an increased potential to utilize technology and manage one-to-one relationships with customers. Postbehaviour is based mainly on the degree of satisfaction–dissatisfaction of customers. A good indicator of customer satisfaction is loyalty rate. Recession has modified consumers' behaviour and these new trends are likely to stay in the decades to come.

BIBLIOGRAPHY

Abernathy, A.M. and Frank, G.R. (1996), The Information Content of Advertising: A Meta-analysis, *Journal of Advertising*, 25, 2, pp. 1–17.

Bauer, R.A. (1960), *Consumer Behaviour as Risk Taking*, in *Proceedings, Fall Conference of the American Marketing Association*, Hancock A.S. (ed.), Chicago, IL, June, pp. 389–98.

Becker, G.S. (1965), A Theory of the Allocation of Time, *The Economic Journal*, September, pp.494–517.

Berry, L.L. (1983), *Relationship Marketing*, in *Emerging Perspectives on Services Marketing*, Berry, L.L., Shostack, G.L. and Upah, G. (eds.), Chicago, IL, American Marketing Association, pp. 25–8.

Best, R.J. (2004), *Market-Based Management*, Upper Saddle River, Prentice-Hall, 3rd edition.

Dart, J. and Freeman, K. (1994), Dissatisfaction Response Styles among Clients of Professional Accounting Firms, *Journal of Business Research*, 29, 1, pp. 75–81.

Davis, H.L. and Rigaux, B.P. (1974), Perceptions of Marital Roles in Decision Processes, *Journal of Consumer Research*, 1, 1, pp. 51–62.

Day, G.S. (1969), A Two-Dimensional Concept of Brand Loyalty, *Journal of Advertising Research*, 9, 3, pp. 29–35.

Domingo, R.T. (1997), *Quality Means Survival*, Singapore, Prentice-Hall.

Flatters, P. and Willmot, M. (2009), Understanding the Post Recession Consumer, *Harvard Business Review*, July–August, pp. 106–112.

Fournier, S., Dobscha, S. and Mick, D.G. (1998), Preventing the Premature Death of Relationship Marketing, *Harvard Business Review*, 76, 1, pp. 42–51.

Goderis, J.P. (1998), Barrier Marketing: From Customer Satisfaction to Customer Loyalty, *CEMS Business Review*, 2, 4.

Griffin, J. (1995), *Customer Loyalty: How to Earn It? How to Keep It?*, New York, Lexington Books.

Herbst, P.G. (1952), The Measurement of Family Relationships, *Human and Relations*, 5, pp. 3–34.

Howard, J.A. and Sheth, J.N. (1969), *The Theory of Buyer Behaviour*, New York, John Wiley & Sons.

Jacoby, J. and Kaplan, L.B. (1972), *The Components of Perceived Risk*, in *Proceedings, 3rd Annual Conference*, Venkatesan, V. (ed.), College Park, MD, Association for Consumer Research.

Jacoby, J. and Kyner, D.B. (1973), Brand Loyalty versus Repeat Purchasing Behavior, *Journal of Marketing Research*, 10, 1, pp. 1–19.

Jones, T.O. and Sasser, W.E. (1995), Why Satisfied Customers Defect?, *Harvard Business Review*, 73, 6, pp. 88–99.

Korupleski, R.E., Rust, R.T. and Zahorik, A.J. (1993), Why improving quality doesn't improve quality (or whatever happened to marketing?), *California Management Review*, 35, 3, pp. 82–95.

Lambin, J.J. (2000–2007), *Market-Driven Management*, London, Palgrave Macmillan, First and second edition.

Lambin, J.J. (2000/2007), *Market-Driven Management: Strategic and Operational Marketing*, London, Palgrave Macmillan.

Levitt, T. (1980), Marketing Success through Differentiation – Of Anything, *Harvard Business Review*, 58, 1, pp. 83–91.

Manning, B. and Throne, C. (2003), *Demand Driven,* New York, McGraw-Hill.

Nelson, D. (1970), Information and Consumer Behaviour, *Journal of Political Economy*, 78, March–April, pp. 311–29.

Payne, A. and Frow, P. (2006), Customer Relationship Management: From Strategy to Implementation, *Journal of Marketing Management*, 22, pp.135–68.

Pepper, D. and Rogers, M. (1993), *The One-to-One Future*, New York, Doubleday/Currency.

Pras, B. and Tarondeau, J.-C. (1981), *Comportement de l'acheteur*, Paris, Editions Sirey.

Rhoades, K. (1998), The Importance of Consumer Complaints, *Protect Yourself,* January, pp. 115–18.

Sheth, J., Mittal, B. and Newman, B.I. (1999), *Customer Behaviour, Consumer Behaviour and Beyond*, Fort Worth, TX, Dryden Press.

Siddle, R. and Rigby, D. (2001), What's the Matter with CRM?, *European Business Forum*, 7, Autumn, pp. 48–50.

Valla, J.D. (1980), Le comportement des groupes d'achat, in *L'action marketing des entreprises*, Paris, Collection Adetem, pp. 22–38.

Webster, F.E. and Wind, Y. (1972), *Organizational Buying Behaviour*, Englewood Cliffs, NJ, Prentice-Hall.

Wilkie, W.L. (1994), *Consumer Behaviour*, New York, John Wiley & Sons, 3rd edition.

 ## WEBSITE COMPANION FOR CHAPTER 6

Visit the Market-Driven Management accompanying website at www.palgrave.com/business/lambin3 to find:

Note on Measuring the Cognitive Response
Note on Measuring the Affective Response
Note on The Importance–Performance Matrix
Note on Brand Switching Analysis

CHAPTER SEVEN

MEASURING CUSTOMERS' RESPONSE

The central problem confronting a market-oriented organization is how to monitor the needs of customers and the evolution of the macro-marketing environment in order to anticipate the future. In response to this need for information, the concept of a formalized market information system (MIS) has emerged to acquire and to distribute market data within the organization, thereby facilitating market-oriented decisions. The objective of an MIS is to integrate market and customers' data into a continuous information flow for marketing decision-making. Within an MIS, marketing research has mainly an ad hoc data-gathering and analysis function to perform. Marketing research can supply information regarding many aspects of customers' behaviours. In this chapter, we shall review the main components of an MIS, in placing more emphasis on the tasks and methods of marketing research.

Learning Objectives

After reading this chapter, you should be able to understand:

- The importance of market information in a market-driven company
- The structure of an MIS
- Why marketing research must be scientifically conducted
- The differences between exploratory, descriptive and causal research
- The characteristics of the main primary data collection methods
- The potential of the new methods of causal research

7.1 STRUCTURE OF A MARKET INFORMATION SYSTEM

Few managers are happy with the type of market information they receive. The usual complaints are:

- Available information is very often not relevant to decision needs.
- There is too much information to be used effectively.
- Information is spread throughout the firm and difficult to locate.
- Key information arrives too late to be useful or is destroyed.
- Some managers may withhold information from other functions.
- The reliability and accuracy of information are difficult to verify.

The role of an MIS is to study information needs carefully, to design an information system to meet these needs, to centralize the information available and to organize its dissemination throughout the organization. An MIS has been defined as follows:

> A marketing information system is a continuing and interacting structure of people, equipment and procedures to gather, sort, analyse, evaluate and distribute pertinent, timely and accurate information for use by marketing decision-makers to improve their marketing planning, implementation and control. (Kotler 1991, 2006)

The best-performing companies have developed an "information orientation" comprising not only good IT practices but also information management practices and information behaviour and values (Marchand, 2002). The structure of an MIS is described in Figure 7.1. The figure shows the macro-marketing environment to be monitored by management. These flows of information are captured and analysed through three subsystems of data collection: the internal accounting system, the business intelligence system and the marketing research system. A fourth subsystem – the analytical market system, which is in charge of the data processing and transfer of information to management, as aids to understanding, decision and control – will be discussed in the five chapters regrouped in Part 3 of the book.

Thus, viewed in this perspective, marketing research appears as only one component of an MIS. Marketing research's role is clear and confined to a specific decision problem, while the role of an MIS is much broader and is organized on a permanent basis. Let us briefly examine the tasks and content of the three subsystems.

The internal accounting system

All organizations collect internal data as part of their normal operations. These data, which are collected for purposes other than research, are called internal secondary data. Sales data are recorded within the "order–shipping–billing" cycle. Cost data are recorded, sales representatives and dealers submit sales reports, advertising and promotion activities are recorded, R&D and manufacturing reports are made. These are but a few of the data sources available for research in a modern organization. Sales records should allow for

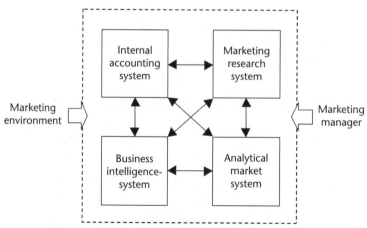

Figure 7.1 Structure of an MIS
Source: Adapted from Kotler (1991, 2006).

classification by type of customer, payment procedure, product line, sales territory, time period and so forth.

By way of illustration, a monthly sales statement classified by product, customer group, and sales territory will permit the following analyses:

- Comparison of year-to-date sales in volume and value.
- Analysis of the product mix structure of the total turnover.
- Analysis of the concentration rate of the turnover per customer.
- Evaluation of the sales efficiency by comparing territory sales, number of sales calls, average revenue per sales call and so forth.
- Analysis of the market penetration per territory by reference to buying power indices.

Many companies do not collect and maintain sales and cost data in sufficient detail to be used for research purposes. These data, stored and processed by the market analytical sub-system, should constitute a database of time series useful, namely, for forecasting purposes. The types of analyses to be conducted are, for example:

- Graphic analyses to identify trends, seasonality patterns and growth rates.
- Short-term sales forecasts based on endogenous sales forecasting techniques, such as exponential smoothing.
- Correlation analyses between sales and key explanatory factors such as distribution rates, advertising share of voice, relative price.
- Multi-variable or multi-equation econometric models.

The generalized use of computers has greatly facilitated the development of internal accounting systems. A certain number of attributes should be met in designing a reporting system:

- *Timeliness*: the information must be available when needed and not reported too late.
- *Flexibility*: the information must be available in varied formats and detail such that the specific information needs of alternative decision situations can be served.
- *Inclusiveness*: the reporting system must cover the entire range of information needs, while avoiding the risk of information overload.
- *Accuracy*: the level of accuracy should fit the needs of the decision situation, and the information should not be presented in too much detail.
- *Convenience*: the information must be easily accessible to the decision-maker and presented in a clear and usable manner.

Data from the internal accounting system originate within the organization and are available at minimal cost. They constitute the backbone of the MIS. The sources of information used by firms are multiple and varied. It is interesting to note that, frequently, the most important source of information is the customers themselves.

The business intelligence system

The data provided by the internal accounting system must be complemented by information about the macro-marketing environment and about competition. It is the role of the business intelligence subsystem to gather information about developments in the environment, to enable management to monitor the strengths and weaknesses of the firm's competitive position.

Several methods can be used to collect business intelligence information: the casual method, the use of the sales force, the establishment of information centres or the purchase of data from syndicated services:

1. The *casual method* is the informal search for information carried on by managers on their own through reading newspapers and trade publications, talking to suppliers, distributors, customers, or by participating in professional meetings, trade shows, and so on.
2. The *sales force* is often in good position to provide data regarding many aspects of the market situation and to spot new market developments or new competitive actions. Sales representatives should be trained and motivated to report market information.
3. Where the staff systematically scan and analyse major trade industrial or professional publications. For example, much can be learned about competition through reading competitors' published reports. Newsletters or bulletins are then published and disseminated within the company.
4. Most companies also purchase *syndicated data* from outside firms, which collect and sell standardized data about market shares, retail prices, advertising expenditures, promotions and so on.

Besides internal accounting information and market intelligence, marketing management also requires studies on specific problems or opportunities, such as a product concept test, a brand image study or a sales forecast for a particular country or region. It is the role of marketing research to conduct these types of focused studies.

The marketing research system

The role of marketing research is to provide market information data that will help management to adopt and implement a market orientation. Its role can be defined in the following terms:

> Marketing research involves the diagnosis of information needs and the selection of relevant interrelated variables about which valid and reliable information is gathered, recorded and analysed (Zaltman and Burger, 1975, p. 3).

According to this definition, marketing research has four distinctive functions to perform:

1. The *diagnosis of an information need,* which supposes a good interactive relationship between the decider and the market analyst.
2. The *selection of the variables* to be measured, which implies the capacity to translate a decision problem into empirically testable research questions.
3. The *responsibility of the internal and external validity* of the collected information, which implies a good command of the research methodology.
4. The *transfer of information* to management as an aid to understanding, decision and control.

The role of the market analyst is not confined, therefore, to the technical aspects linked to the execution of a research project. He or she has to participate actively in the research problem definition, the design of the research plan and the interpretation and exploitation of the research results.

Managerial usefulness of marketing research

Marketing research has its usefulness for strategic and operational marketing decisions. Three types of objectives can be identified:

- *Understanding aid*: to discover, describe, analyse, measure and forecast market factors and demand.
- *Decision aid*: to identify the most appropriate marketing instruments and strategies and determine their optimal level of intervention.
- *Control aid*: to assess the performance of the marketing programmes and evaluate results.

The first objective is more directly linked to strategic marketing decisions and has an important creative component: to discover new opportunities and/or untapped market potential. The other two objectives are felt more directly by operational marketing people.

Marketing research often has important implications for functions other than marketing. For example, research results on the changing mood of the market vis-à-vis ecology may induce R&D and production staff to develop environmentally sounds products. Similarly, sales forecasting is a key input for financial analysis and for distribution planning and logistics.

Timing of market research

A key question for a manager faced with a decision problem is to decide whether or not a specific marketing research study should be conducted. Several factors must be considered in examining this question:

1. *Time constraint.* Marketing research takes time, and in many instances decisions have to be taken rapidly even if the information is incomplete. The time factor is crucial and the urgency of the situation often precludes the use of research. This factor reinforces the importance of the MIS, which is a permanent information system.
2. *Availability of data.* In many instances, management already possesses enough information and a sound decision may be made without further research. This type of situation will occur when the firm has a well-managed permanent MIS. Sometimes, marketing research is, nevertheless, undertaken to prevent the criticism of ill-prepared decisions. Marketing research here takes the form of an insurance that will be useful if the decision taken happens to be the wrong one.
3. *Value to the firm.* The value of marketing research will depend on the nature of the managerial decision to be made. For many routine decisions, the cost of a wrong decision is minimal and substantial marketing research expenditures are difficult to justify. Thus, before conducting a research, managers should ask themselves: "Will the information gained by marketing research improve the quality of the marketing decision to an extent large enough to warrant the expenditure?" In many cases even a modest marketing research study may substantially improve the quality of managerial decisions (see Figure 7.2).

Frequently, marketing research projects are not directly linked to a particular decision but are purely exploratory. The objective is then to improve the understanding of a market or to search for opportunities in a new unknown market. This type of research is likely to improve the choice of strategic options by the firm.

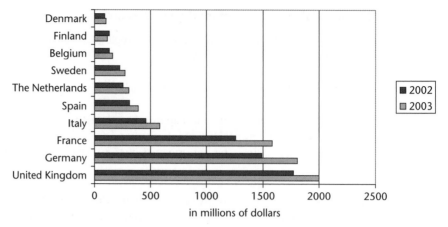

Figure 7.2 Top ten European markets by marketing research expenditures
Source: ESOMAR, Amsterdam, the Netherlands.

7.2   MARKETING RESEARCH AND THE SCIENTIFIC METHOD

If nobody questions today that management is much more of an art than a science, it is important to state clearly that marketing research must be scientific. It is important because marketing research has to deal with accredited (or certified) knowledge, and without accredited knowledge good management decisions cannot be made (Zaltman and Burger, 1975, p. 7). The implication of this statement is that the scientist attempts to uncover objective "truths". Because management is primarily interested in making decisions based on accurate and unbiased data, it is clear that the market researcher must follow a scientific procedure in order for data to be collected and analysed properly.

The rules of the scientific method are designed to provide, among others, two types of validity, internal and external:

■   *Internal validity* is concerned with the question of whether the observed effects of a marketing stimulus (price, advertising message, promotion and so on) could have been caused by variables other than the factor under study. Is the relationship established without ambiguity? Without internal validity the experiment is confounded and the causal structure is not established.
■   *External validity* is concerned with the generalizability of experimental results. To what populations, geographic areas and treatment variables can the measured effects be projected?

This problem of scientific reliability is fundamental because, on the basis of marketing research results, management will make highly risky decisions, such as the launch of a new product, modification of a price or adoption of a specific advertising theme.

Characteristics of scientific knowledge

The understanding of the main features of science is essential to performing marketing research scientifically, and therefore we shall now briefly review the main scientific knowledge is factual. Science starts by establishing facts and seeks to describe and explain them.

Established facts are empirical data obtained with the aid of theories and, in turn, help to clarify theories.

1. *Science goes beyond facts.* The market analyst should not confine his or her work to facts that are easily observed and already in existence. Thus qualitative research is an integrated part of the research process. The market analyst may want to find new facts, but new facts should be authentic and lend themselves to empirical verification or falsification.

2. *Scientific knowledge is verifiable (or falsifiable).* Scientific knowledge must be testable empirically through observational or experimental experiences. This is one of the basic rules of science. It must be possible to demonstrate that a given proposition or theory is false. The scientist can only say: "I have a theory which I have objectively tested with data and the data are consistent with my theory."

3. *Science is analytic.* The market researcher tries to decompose the buying decision process into its basic parts to determine the mechanisms that account for the way the process functions. After analysing the component parts separately and also their interrelationships, the market researcher is then able to determine how the whole decision process emerges. An illustration of this analytic process is given in the next chapter in the discussion of the concept of attitude.

4. *Scientific knowledge is clear and precise.* Scientific knowledge strives for precision, accuracy and reduction of error although it is almost impossible to achieve these completely. The researcher attempts to reach these objectives by stating questions with maximal clarity, giving unambiguous definitions to concepts and measures and recording observations as completely and in as much detail as possible.

5. *Scientific knowledge is communicable.* Research must be in principle communicable – that is, it must be sufficiently complete in its reporting of methodologies used and sufficiently precise in the presentation of its results to enable another researcher to duplicate the study for independent verification or to determine if replication is desirable.

6. *Scientific knowledge is general.* The market researcher should place individual facts into general patterns, which should be applicable to a wide variety of phenomena. This provides generalizations that can guide marketing decisions. The market analyst is concerned with learning not just what an individual buyer does, but rather what that buyer does that others are also likely to do in the same situation.

The manager–researcher interface

The managerial value of marketing research is largely determined by the quality of the interface between the market analyst responsible for the research project and the decision-maker who has to use the research results. In many instances, market researchers are not sufficiently management-oriented and many managers are not sufficiently research-oriented. To overcome this difficulty of communication, the manager's and the researcher's responsibilities should be clearly defined and accepted by both parties.

The user of the research should keep the market researcher informed on:

- the precise problem faced by the firm and the way that a decision is going to be made,
- the background of the problem and its environment,
- all limitations on costs and time for doing the study and on the courses of action that the company can realistically consider,

- what data will be provided by the firm and where to obtain it,
- any changes in the situation that arises as the study is under way.

Similarly, the *responsibilities of the researcher* are:

- being honest and clear regarding the meaning and any limitations of the expected findings,
- being of maximum help in presenting and explaining the conclusions and aiding the decision-maker's application,
- demanding that the decision-maker provide the information needed to plan and conduct the study,
- insisting that valid and full reporting be made of the findings,
- refusing to distort or abridge them on behalf of the user's biases and prejudices.

In reporting research findings some researchers fail to recognize that their role is *advisory*; they are not being asked to make the decision for management. Similarly, some managers operate as if the researcher is clairvoyant regarding the nature of the decision situation and the information needed to reduce the decision uncertainty. Consequently, many research projects are not decision-oriented because of the manager's poor communication skills.

Stages in the research process

Systematic inquiry requires careful planning in an orderly investigation. Marketing research, like other forms of scientific research, is a sequence of interrelated activities. The five stages of the research process are presented in Figure 7.3.

1. *Problem definition.* The first step in research calls for the manager (the user of the research result) and the market analyst (the researcher) to define the problem carefully and to agree on the research objective. In marketing research, the old adage "a problem well defined is a problem half solved" is worth remembering. Another way to express the same idea would be: "if you don't know what you are looking for, you won't find it." Thus, at this stage a working interface "decider–analyst" is essential and the research objective should state, in terms as precise as possible, the information needed to improve the decision to be made.

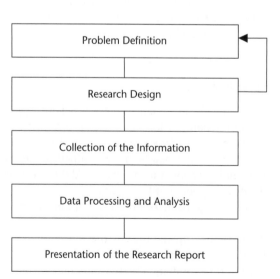

Figure 7.3   Stages in the research process

2. *Research design.* The research design is a master plan specifying the methods and procedures for collecting and analysing the needed information. It is a framework for the research plan of action. This is typically the responsibility of the market analyst. The research plan should be designed professionally and specify the hypotheses and the research questions, the sources of

information, the research instrument (focus groups, survey or experimentation), the sampling methodology, the schedule and the cost of the research. The decider should approve the research plan to ensure that the information collected is appropriate for solving his or her decision problem.

3. *Collection of the information.* Once the research design is approved, the process of gathering the information from respondents may begin. In many cases, the data collection phase is sub-contracted to a specialized market research company. Data collection methods are rapidly changing under the impact of telecommunications and computers. Telephone interviews combined with data-entry terminals, computer-assisted interviews, interactive terminals in shopping malls, fax interviews, electronic cash registers using the Universal Product Code (UPC) are new techniques which accelerate the data-gathering process and also eliminate the risks of errors. There are generally two phases in data collection: pre-testing and the main study. The pre-test phase, based on a small sub-sample, is used to determine whether the data-gathering plan for the main study is appropriate.

4. *Data processing and analysis.* Once the data have been collected, they must be converted into a format that will answer the manager's questions. This stage implies editing the data, coding, tabulating and developing one-way or two-way frequency distributions. These tasks are also generally sub-contracted to specialized agencies, and strict controls should be made on the rules and procedures adopted. Statistical analysis techniques will be used to summarize the data, to present them in a more meaningful way, to facilitate the interpretation or to help discover new findings or relationships. Advanced multivariate statistical analyses should be used only if they are relevant for the purpose of the study.

5. *Presentation of the research report.* The final stage in the research process is that of interpreting the information and making conclusions for managerial decisions. The research report should communicate the research findings effectively, that is in a way which is meaningful to a managerial audience. The risk here is to place too much emphasis on the study's technical aspects, even if any responsible manager will want to be convinced of the reliability of the results, otherwise he or she will not use them. Thus again a close interaction between the manager and the researcher is a key success factor.

This research process is of general application even if the stages of the process overlap continuously. The relative importance of each phase also varies with the nature of the market research.

Types of marketing research

Marketing research studies can be classified on the basis of techniques or of the nature of the research problem. Surveys, experimentation or observational studies are the most common techniques. The nature of the problem will determine whether the research is exploratory, descriptive or causal. Examples are provided in Table 7.1.

- *Exploratory research* is conducted to clarify the nature of a problem, to gain better understanding of a market situation, to discover ideas and insights and to provide directions for any further research needed. It is not intended to provide conclusive evidence from which to determine a particular course of action. The methods used are desk research and qualitative studies.

Table 7.1 Types of marketing research problems

Exploratory research	Descriptive research	Causal research
Sales of brand A are declining and we don't know why?	What kind of people buys our brand? Who buys the brand of our direct competitor?	Do buyers prefer our product in an "eco-design" package?
Would the market be interested by our new product idea?	What should be the target segment for our new product?	Which of the two advertising themes is more effective?

Source: Adapted from Churchill and Iacobucci (2005).

- *Descriptive research* seeks to determine answers to "who", "what", "when", "where" and "how" questions. Descriptive research is concerned with determining the frequency with which something occurs or the relationship between two variables. Unlike exploratory research, descriptive studies are based on some previous understanding of the nature of the research problem. Descriptive information is often all that is needed to solve a marketing problem. The methods used are typically secondary data, observation and communication. Most marketing research studies are of this type.
- *Causal research* is the most ambitious form of research and is concerned with determining cause-and-effect relationships. In causal studies, it is typical to have an expectation of the relationship, which is to be explained, such as predicting the influence of price, packaging and advertising. Causal studies usually take the form of controlled experiments.

In principle, exploratory and descriptive research precedes cause-and-effect relationship studies and is often seen as preliminary steps, as illustrated in Figure 7.4. But other sequences may also exist. For example, if a causal hypothesis is discovered, the analyst might need another exploratory or descriptive study. In the following sections, we shall analyse in more detail the objectives and the methods used in these three types of market research studies.

7.3 EXPLORATORY RESEARCH STUDIES

Marketing research is of an exploratory type when the emphasis is placed on gaining insights and ideas rather than on formally testing hypotheses derived from theory or

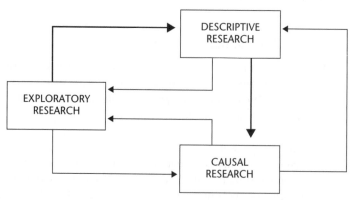

Figure 7.4 The different sequences of research
Source: Adapted from Kerlinger (1973) and Churchill and Iacobucci (2005).

from previous research studies. This type of study is very popular among firms, because of its low cost, speed, flexibility and emphasis on creativity and on the generation of ideas.

Objectives of exploratory research

The need for exploratory research typically arises when the firm is confronted with ill-defined problems such as "sales of brand X are declining and we do not know why" or "would people be interested in our idea for a new product?" In these two examples, the analyst could guess a large number of possible answers. Since it is impractical to test them all, exploratory research will be used to find the most likely explanation(s) that will then be tested empirically. Thus, the main objectives of exploratory research are the following:

- To quickly examine the threats of a problem or the potential of an opportunity.
- To formulate a poorly defined problem for more precise investigation.
- To generate hypotheses or conjectural statements about the problem.
- To collect and analyse readily available information.
- To establish priorities for further research.
- To increase the analyst's familiarity with a problem or with a market.
- To clarify a concept.

In general, exploratory research is appropriate to any problem about which little is known.

Hypothesis development

Exploratory research is particularly useful at the first stage of the research process, that is, at the problem formulation phase, to translate the research problem into specific research objectives. The objective is to develop testable hypotheses. Hypotheses state what we are looking for; they anticipate the possible answers to the research problem and add a considerable degree of specificity. Normally there will be several competing hypotheses, either specified or implied.

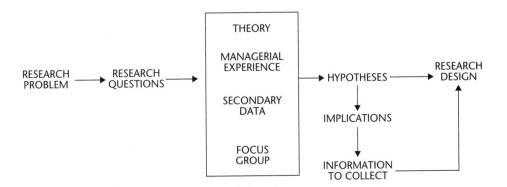

Figure 7.5   The process of hypothesis development
Source: Lambin (1990).

How does the analyst generate hypotheses? The process of hypothesis development is illustrated in Figure 7.5. Four main sources of information can be identified.

1. Theory from such disciplines as economics, psychology, sociology or marketing.
2. Management experience with related problems.
3. The use of secondary data (see below).
4. Exploratory research when both theory and experience are lacking.

After an exploratory research, the market analyst should know which type of data to collect in order to verify or falsify the competing explanations. An example is presented in Table 7.2, concerning the low level of market penetration of cable TV in some regions. The exploratory study has identified seven possible explanations (or hypotheses). The derived research objectives clearly indicate the type of data required to verify these tentative explanations.

Since the objective of exploratory studies is to find new ideas, no formal design is required. Flexibility and ingenuity characterize the investigation. The imagination of the researcher is the key factor. The techniques used are the study of secondary data, key informant survey, analysis of related cases and qualitative research through focus groups.

Use of secondary data

Secondary data are previously published data collected for purposes other than the specific research needs at hand. Primary data, on the other hand, are collected specifically for purposes of the investigation. The main sources of secondary data, internal and external, are presented in Figure 7.6.

Secondary data can be classified as coming from internal or external sources, the former being available within the organization and the latter originating from outside. Internal data are centralized in the internal accounting system described in the first section of this chapter. External data come from an array of sources such as government publications, trade association data, books, bulletins, reports and periodicals. Data from these sources are available at minimal cost or free in libraries. External sources not available in a library are usually standardized marketing data, which are expensive to acquire. These syndicated data sources are consumer panels, wholesale data, media and audience data and so on.

Table 7.2 From a research problem to research questions

Research problem: *Why is the penetration rate of TV cable in private homes far below average in several geographic areas?*

Hypotheses	Research questions
1. Good TV reception is available without cable.	• How is the quality of TV reception without cable?
2. Residents are illegally connecting their sets to the cable network.	• Is it technically possible to be illegally connected?
3. There is a very transient population in these regions.	• What is the mobility rate in these regions?
4. Residents have had poor experience with cable services.	• What is the corporate image of the cable company in the regions?
5. The price is too high given the level of income in the region.	• How different are income statistics among regions?
6. The sales force coverage has been inadequate.	• How active was the sales force in the regions?
7. A large part of the residents are in age or social class groups that watch little TV.	• Analyse demographic and social class statistics per region.

Source: Adapted from Kotler (1991, 2006).

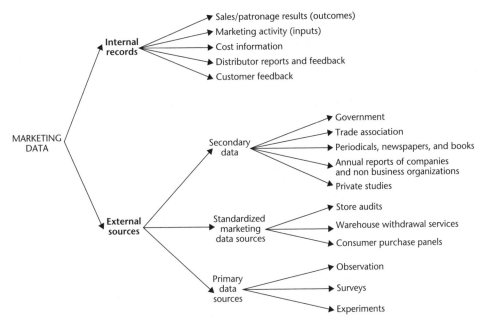

Figure 7.6 Sources of marketing data
Source: Adapted from Aaker and Day (1980).

To start with, secondary data are the most logical thing to work on and their useful-ness should not be underestimated. The primary advantage of secondary data is that it is always faster and less expensive to obtain them than to acquire primary data. Also, they may include information not otherwise available to the researcher. For example, truck and car registrations are secondary data published by the car registration administration. A com-petent market analyst should be familiar with the basic sources pertaining to the market studied (see Table 7.3).

Secondary data, however, present a certain number of disadvantages and the market analyst should examine their relevance thoroughly. The most common problems asso-ciated with secondary data are (1) outdated information, (2) variation in definition of terms, (3) different units of measurement. Another shortcoming is that the user has no control over the accuracy of secondary data. Research conducted by other persons may be biased to support the vested interest of the source. Also, the user of secondary data must critically assess the data and the research design to determine if the research methodology was correctly implemented. The following rules should be followed in the use of second-ary data:

- Always use the primary source of secondary data and not secondary sources that secured the data from the original source.
- Assess the accuracy of secondary data by carefully identifying the purpose of the publication.
- Examine the overall quality of the methodology; a primary source should provide a detailed description of how the data were collected, including definitions, collection forms, sampling and so forth.

The above is not to say that the analyst cannot use such data. Rather, it is simply to suggest that such data should be viewed more critically.

Key informants survey

After having explored secondary sources, additional insights and ideas can be gained by talking with individuals having special knowledge and experience regarding the problem under investigation. These knowledgeable persons may be "players" or "experts". By "players" we mean anyone participating in the market situation, such as the personnel within the firm, wholesalers, retailers, suppliers or consumers. By "experts" we mean anyone having privileged information due to their function, such as civil servants, economists, sociologists, R&D personnel, members of a professional organization and so forth.

> For example, a publisher of children's books [who is] investigating a sales decrease gained valuable insights by talking with librarians and schoolteachers. These discussions indicated that an increased use of library facilities, both public and school, coincided with the product's decline in sales. These increases were, in turn, attributed to a very sizeable increase in library holdings of children's books resulting from federal legislation that provided money for this purpose. (Churchill, and Iacobucci, 2005, p. 78)

No attempt should be made to have a probability sample in this type of survey, but it is important to include people with different points of view. The interviews are informal and do not use structured questions, such as those on a questionnaire. Rather, very flexible and free-flowing situations are created in order to stimulate the search for ideas and to uncover

Table 7.3 Selected government data sources

Source	Website	Type of information
European Union	www.europa.eu	Statistical information on members countries
Euromonitor International	www.euromonitor.com	Information on the EU and other countries and companies
University of Strathclyde, UK	www.strath.ac.uk	Company profiles, country information, economic export data and company directories
OECD	www.oecd.org	Statistics, economic indicators and other information on member countries
Eurostat	www.ec.europa.eu/eurostat	Statistics at European level that enable comparison between countries and regions
Europe Direct	*www.europa.eu/europedirect/ index_en.htm*	Information on the EU
Department of Trade and Industry	www.dti.gov.uk	Information on UK companies and trade
Financial Times	www.ft.com	Several data banks, e.g., on mergers and acquisitions
Business Week	www.businessweek.com	Information on companies, e.g., top 500 firms
World Bank	www.worldbank.org	Economic, social and national/regional information on more than 200 countries
International Trade Administration (ITA), USA	www.ita.doc.gov	ITA helps US firms to compete in foreign markets
Center for International Business Education and Research (MSU-CIBER). A centre at Michigan State University, USA	www.ciber.bus.msu.edu	A website presenting different market information in the world
Trade Compass	*www.tradecompass.eu*	Business related information on different markets and companies

Source: Lambin (2007).

the unexpected. Various hypotheses may be presented to these individuals to test their reaction and see whether reformulation is necessary.

Analysis of selected cases

A third method currently used in exploratory research is the detailed analysis of cases that are similar to the phenomenon under investigation in order to seek explanations or to gain ideas for actions. For example, in many situations the United States is ahead of Europe and it is interesting to analyse the US situation to understand the problems that might occur in the European market.

> For example, convenience stores in petrol stations have been in operation in the USA for many years. Petroleum companies in Western Europe have recently adopted the same concept. A detailed study of selected stores in the USA proved to be very useful when determining the types of assortment, the opening hours, and the layout of these convenience stores.

Some situations are particularly productive of hypotheses – namely, cases reflecting abrupt changes or cases reflecting extreme behaviour.

Focus group discussions

The focus group interview is a more elaborate exploratory study. A focus group interview is an unstructured, free-flowing interview with a small group of 8 to 12 people. It is not a rigidly constructed question-and-answer session but a flexible format discussion of a brand, an advertisement or a new product concept. A focus group functions as follows:

The group meets at a location at a pre-designated time; it consists of an interviewer or moderator and 8 to 12 participants; the moderator introduces the topic and encourages group members to discuss the subjects among themselves. Focus groups allow people to discuss their true feelings, anxieties and frustrations as well as the depth of their conviction.

The primary advantages of focus group interviews are that they are relatively rapid, easy to execute and inexpensive. In an emergency situation three or four group sessions can be conducted, organized and reported on in less than a week. From the first discussion the

---

Exhibit 7.1   The results of a group discussion: motivations for coffee consumption in Belgium

1. Time and space structure

Coffee gives a certain rhythm to your day; it is a ritual which punctuates the different parts of a day: morning, morning break, mealtime, after a meal, evening, weekend, afternoon break and so on. Each moment has its own identity, typical to its environment and conditions for the expected satisfaction for consumption.

2. Social function

Offering a cup of coffee is a typical sign of hospitality. A cup of coffee relaxes and welcomes, develops a feeling of harmony, a certain atmosphere. Coffee brings people together and is a pretext for bringing people together.

3. Sensorial function

Coffee is satisfying to the individual himself or herself, catering as much to the emotions as to the senses. The sense of smell, taste, the appearance and the warmth of coffee are all involved.

4. Function as a stimulant

Coffee supposedly acts as both a physical and a psychological stimulant. Even a restorative, curative function is attributed to coffee; it picks you up; it is an affective, emotional comforting tonic.

Source: Lambin(1990).

analyst invariably learns a great deal. The second interview produces more, but less is new. Usually, in the third and fourth sessions, much of what is said has been heard before and there is little to be gained from continuing. By way of illustration, the result of a group discussion about coffee consumption is presented in Exhibit 7.1.

In addition to the advantage of time, the following *advantages* for group interviews also exist.

- The group interview is a superb mechanism for generating hypotheses when little is known about the problem under study.
- The group method drastically reduces the distance between the respondent who produces research information and the client who uses it.
- Another advantage of the group interview technique is its flexibility, by contrast with survey interviewers who work from a rigid question schedule.
- The group interview has the ability to handle contingencies of consumer behaviour of the type: "if…otherwise", an answer unlikely to emerge in a survey.
- In a group discussion respondents stimulate one another and more information is spontaneously obtained than in individual interviews.
- Finally in a group interview study, the findings emerge in a form that most people fully understand.

The *limitations* of focus group interviews are important and should not be underestimated:

- The respondents are not representative of the target population given their number and the recruiting procedure. Thus, the external validity of the results is necessarily limited.
- The interpretation of the results is typically judgemental and highly dependent on the personality of the analyst. Given the absence of a structured questionnaire and the wealth of disparate comments usually obtained, the analyst can always find something which agrees with his or her view of the problem. The importance of this bias is difficult to measure, however.
- The risk always exists to see one participant dominating the session and to provoke negative reactions from the other members of the group.
- Evaluations by means of group interviews tend to be conservative. It favours ideas that are easy to explain and understand and, therefore, not very new.
- Very disturbing is the unethical practice of some market research firms specializing in focus groups to recruit "professional respondents" to make the session go well.

Despite these limitations, focus group interviews are very popular, particularly among advertising agencies. In the field of qualitative research, it is common practice to use interpretation models such as the Freudian or the Jungian models (Pellemans, 1995). The risk here is to privilege one scheme of interpretation. To avoid this trap, several interpretative models should be used simultaneously and their results confronted.

Projective techniques

Respondents are often reluctant or embarrassed to discuss their feelings but may be more likely to give a true answer (consciously or unconsciously) if the question is disguised. A projective technique is an indirect means of questioning that enables respondents to "project" their beliefs or feelings to a third person when exposed to an unstructured stimulus. Projective techniques are currently used in clinical and personality tests. The theory behind such a technique is that when a person is asked to structure or organize an essentially unstructured or ambiguous situation he or she can do so only by calling upon and revealing his or her own personality or attitudinal structure.

> The more unstructured and ambiguous a stimulus, the more a subject can and will project his emotions, needs, motives, attitudes and values. (Kerlinger, 1973, p. 515)

The most common projective techniques in marketing research are picture–story association, sentence completion, word association and role-playing.

Limitations of exploratory research

Exploratory research cannot take the place of quantitative, conclusive research. Nevertheless, there is great temptation among many managers to accept small sample exploratory results as sufficient for their purpose because they are so compelling in their reality. The dangers of uncritical acceptance of the unstructured output from a focus group or a brief series of informal interviews are twofold:

- First, the results are *not representative* of what would be found in the population and, hence, cannot be projected.
- Second, there is typically a great deal of *ambiguity* owing to the moderator's interpretation of the results.

In fact, the greatest danger of using exploratory research to evaluate an alternative advertising copy strategy, a new product concept and so on is not that a poor idea will be marketed, because successive steps of research will prevent that; the real danger is that a good idea with promise may be rejected because of findings at the exploratory stage. In other situations, where everything looks positive in the exploratory stage, there is the temptation to market the product without further research (Adler, 1979).

In view of these pitfalls, these methods should be used strictly for insights into the reality of the customer's perspective and to suggest hypotheses for further research.

7.4 DESCRIPTIVE RESEARCH STUDIES

Descriptive studies, as their name suggests, are designed to describe the characteristics of a given situation or of a given population. Descriptive studies differ from exploratory studies in the rigour with which they are designed. Exploratory studies are characterized by flexibility. Descriptive studies attempt to obtain a complete and accurate description of a situation. Formal design is required to ensure that the description covers all phases desired and that the information collected is reliable. The most popular technique used in descriptive research is the survey.

Objectives of descriptive studies

Descriptive research encompasses a vast array of research objectives. The purpose is to provide a graph of some aspect of the market at a point of time or to monitor an activity over time. The objectives of descriptive studies are the following.

- To describe the organization, the distribution channels or the competitive structure of a specific market or segment.

- To estimate the proportion and the socio-demographic profile of a specified population which behaves in a certain way.
- To predict the level of primary demand over the next five years in a given market using heuristic or extrapolating sales forecasting methods.
- To describe the buying behaviour of certain groups of consumers.
- To describe the way buyers perceive and evaluate the attributes of given brands against competing brands.
- To describe the evolution of lifestyles among specific segments of the population.

Descriptive research should be based on some previous understanding and knowledge of the problem in order to determine with precision the data collection procedure. As illustrated in the previous section, it should rest on one or more specific hypotheses. Three conditions must be met before beginning a descriptive research:

1. One or several hypotheses or conjectural statements derived from the research questions to guide the data collection.
2. A clear specification of the "who", "what", "when", "where", "why" and "how" of the research.
3. A specification of the method used to collect the information: communication or observation.

A specification of the information to collect is presented in Exhibit 7.2.

Two types of descriptive studies can be identified: cross-sectional and longitudinal.

1. *Cross-sectional studies* involve a sample from the population of interest and a number of characteristics of the sample members are measured once at a single point of time.
2. *Longitudinal studies* involve panels; they provide repeated measurement over time, either on the same variables (panels) or on different variables (omnibus panels).

The sample members in a panel are measured repeatedly, as contrasted to the one-time measurement in a cross-sectional study. The most common form of cross-sectional study is the sample survey.

Exhibit 7.2   Specification of the information to collect

A firm is considering the launching of new food product to be purchased by medium-high income family housewives. The questions which must be examined before the beginning of the field work are:

1. *Who?*   Who is the target person? The buyer, the user, the prescriber?
2. *What?*   Which characteristics to measure: the socio-demographic profile, the attitude, preferences, purchasing habits and so on?
3. *When?*   When to ask? Before or at the purchasing time, after the use of the product, how long after and so on?
4. *Where?*   At the purchasing place, at home, at the working place and so on?
5. *Why?*   What is the purpose of the study, what use will be made of the results?
6. *How?*   How to proceed? Face-to-face interview, telephones, mail and so on.

The answers to these questions are not obvious. The results of the exploratory study should be useful to reduce the sources of uncertainty.

Source: Lambin (1990).

Primary data collection methods

In Figure 7.6 a distinction was made between three methods of primary data collection: observation, communication and experimentation. Experimentation differs from the other methods in terms of degree of control over the research situation. Experimentation is the method typically used in causal research and its characteristics will be discussed in the next section. The observation and the communication methods are used for cross-sectional and longitudinal studies.

Observation methods

Scientific observation is the systematic process of recording the behavioural pattern of people, objects and occurrences without questioning or communicating with them. The market analyst using the observation method of data collection witnesses and records information as events occur or compiles evidence from records of past events. At least five kinds of phenomena can be observed:

1. Physical actions and evidence, such as purchases, store locations and layout, posted prices, shelf space and display, promotions.
2. Temporal patterns, such as shopping or driving time.
3. Spatial relations and locations, such as traffic counts or shopping patterns.
4. Expressive behaviour, such as eye movement or levels of emotional arousal.
5. Published records, such as analysis of advertisements or newspaper articles.

The most important advantage of the observational method is its unobtrusive nature since communication with the respondent is not necessary. The "observer" may be a person or the data may be gathered using some mechanical device such as a traffic counter, TV audiometers placed in homes to record and observe behaviour or optical scanners in supermarkets to record sales and purchase behaviour. Observational data are typically more objective and accurate than communication data.

Technological systems such as the UPC have had a major impact on mechanical observations, and UPC consumer panels now provide companies with quick, accurate and dynamic data about how their products are selling, who is buying them and the factors that affect purchase.

Despite their advantages, observation methods have one crucial limitation; they cannot observe motives, attitudes, preferences and intentions. Thus, they can be used only to secure primary behavioural data.

Communication methods

Communication involves questioning respondents to secure the desired information, using a data collection instrument called a questionnaire. The questions may be oral or in writing and the responses may also be given in either form. There are four methods of collecting survey data: personal interviewing, telephone interviewing, mail or self-administered questionnaires and online surveys.

1. *Personal interviewing*. This method is well suited for complex product concepts requiring extensive explanations or for new products. Information is sought in face-to-face question-and-answer sessions between an interviewer and a respondent. The interviewer

usually has a questionnaire as a guide, although it is possible to use visual aids. Answers are generally recorded during the interview. Personal interviews get a high response rate, but are also more costly to administer than the other forms. The presence of an interviewer may also influence the subjects' responses.

2. *Telephone interviewing*. This is best suited for well-defined basic product concepts or specific product features. Questioning is done over the telephone. The information sought is well defined, non-confidential in nature and limited in amount. The method has the advantage of speed in data collection and lower costs per interview. However, some telephone numbers are not listed in directories, and this causes problems in obtaining a representative sample. Absence of face-to-face contact and inability to use visual materials are other limitations.

3. *Mail questionnaires*. These are used to broaden the base of an investigation. They are most effective when well-defined concepts are involved and specific limited answers are required. They are generally less expensive than telephone and personal interviews, but they also have a much lower response rate. Several methods can be used to encourage a higher response rate. Questionnaires by mail must be more structured than others. The fourth method is on line survey as explained in Table 7.4.

A comparison of the advantages and disadvantages of these four methods is made in Table 7.4. Each method of data collection has its own merits. Often these methods can be used in combination; for example, the telephone can be used to introduce the topic and to secure co-operation from the respondent. If the attitude is positive, the questionnaire is then sent by mail with a covering letter. Through this procedure, reasons for refusal can be obtained and follow-up calls can be made to secure the needed response.

Questionnaire design

Good questionnaire design is the key to obtaining good survey results. A questionnaire is simply a set of questions selected to generate the data necessary for accomplishing a research project's objective. Developing questionnaires may appear to be simple, especially to those who have never designed one.

> A good questionnaire appears as easy to compose, as does a good poem. The end-product should look as if effortlessly written by an inspired child, but it is usually the result of long, painstaking work. (Erdos, 1970)

The function of the questionnaire is that of measurement. The questionnaire is the main channel through which data are obtained from respondents and transferred to research-ers, who in turn will transfer this certified knowledge to managers for decision-making. This channel has a dual communication role: (a) it must communicate to the respondent what the researcher is asking for and (b) it must communicate to the researcher what the respondent has to say. The accuracy of data gathered through questionnaires will be greatly influenced by the amount of distortion or "noise" that occurs in the two types of communi-cation. A sloppy questionnaire can lead to a great deal of distortion in the communication from researcher to respondents, and vice versa.

> To assume that people will understand the questions is a common error. People simply may not know what is being asked. They may be unaware of the product or topic of interest; they may con-fuse the subject with something else, or the question may not mean the same thing to everyone interviewed. Respondents may refuse to answer personal questions. Most of these problems may be minimised if a skilled researcher composes the questionnaire. (Zikmund, 1986, 1994, p. 371)

Table 7.4 Comparison of survey methods

Type	Advantages	Disadvantages
Personal interview	1. Allows interviewer to gain additional information from his or her own observation.	1. Can be costly when compared to other methods, especially when wide geographic areas must be covered.
	2. Better control over the sequence of questions.	2. Interviewer bias can seriously cause misleading responses and misrecording of answers.
	3. Allows more detailed information to be gathered.	3. Requires detailed supervision of data-collection process.
	4. Usually get a higher percentage of completed answers, since interviewer is there to explain exactly what is wanted.	4. Time-consuming to train interviewers and to obtain data.
	5. Can use visual aids (e.g., tables, charts, samples and prototypes) to demonstrate concepts.	5. May distract respondents if interviewer is talking and writing answers at the same time.
	6. Allows in-depth exploration of product attributes and how to solve problems.	6. Different approaches by different interviewers make it difficult to standardise conduct of survey.
	7. Is flexible to allow interviewer to adjust questions to respondent's greatest interests.	
	8. Personal contact often stimulates greater co-operation and interest by respondents.	
Telephone survey	1. Fast (e.g., quicker than personal or mail).	1. Limited to number published in telephone directory.
	2. Inexpensive (e.g., cost of an equal number of personal interviews would be substantially greater).	2. Can usually obtain only a small amount of information.
	3. Easier to call back again if respondent is busy at the time.	3. Can usually provide only limited classification data.
	4. Usually has only a small response bias because of closed-end questions.	4. Difficult to obtain motivational, and attitudinal information.
	5. Has wide geographical reach.	5. Difficult for highly technical products or capital goods.
		6. Can become expensive if long distance calls are involved.
Mail survey	1. Can get wide distribution at a relatively low cost per completed interview.	1. Accurate, up-to-date mailing lists are not always available to ensure successful distribution.
	2. Helps avoid possible interviewer bias; absence of interviewer may lead to a more candid reply.	2. As many as 80–90 per cent may not return questionnaires. Respondents generally have stronger feelings about the subject than non-respondents do.
	3. Can reach remote places (e.g., drilling engineer on site in Saudi Arabia).	3. Questionnaire length is limited.
	4. Unless his or her name is requested, the respondent remains anonymous and, therefore may give confidential information that otherwise would be withheld.	4. Inability to insure those questions is understood fully and answers are properly recorded.
	5. Respondent may be more inclined to answer since he or she can do so at their leisure.	5. It is difficult to lead respondents through questions one at the time since the respondent can read the entire questionnaire before answering.
		6. Time consuming.
		7. Troublesome with certain highly technical products.

Continued

Table 7.4 – Continued

Type	Advantages	Disadvantages
Online survey	1. The fastest and least expensive method.	1. Bad representation: limited to the population having Internet access and having good control.
	2. Possibility of world coverage.	
	3. Good control on the order of questions	2. Non-random sampling.
	4. Automatic control of material errors (recall of non-respondents, possibility of multiple answers)	3. Poor control and identification of the respondent.
	5. Immediate encoding	4. Impersonal contact
	6. Possibility to use visual aid	5. Fear of private life invasion (lack of confidentiality).
	7. No bias due to the interviewer	

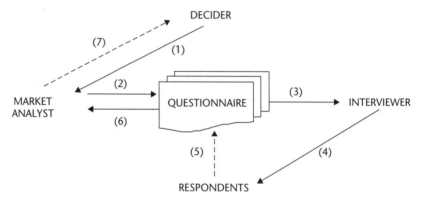

Figure 7.7   The key role of the questionnaire in a survey
Source: Lambin (1990).

Figure 7.7 shows that the questionnaire is at the interface of the four participants in any survey:

1. The decider, who needs specific information to solve a decision problem.
2. The market analyst, whose role is to translate the research problem into research questions.
3. The interviewer, who has to collect reliable information from respondents.
4. The respondents, who have to agree to communicate the information sought.

One important characteristic of a good questionnaire is its degree of standardization – a condition required ensuring that the answers obtained from different respondents and through different interviewers are indeed comparable and therefore lend themselves to statistical analysis.

Sampling methods

Once the market analyst has developed and tested the questionnaire, the next question is the selection of the respondents from whom the information will be collected. One way to do this would be to collect information from each member of the target population through a census. Another way would be to select a fraction of the population by taking a sample of respondents. The census approach is frequently adopted in industrial market research studies when the target population has a total size of 100 to 300 units. In most situations, however, the population sizes are large and the cost and time required to contact each member of the population would be prohibitively high. Thus, sampling can be defined as follows:

> Sampling is the selection of a fraction of the target population for the ultimate purpose of being able to draw general conclusions about the entire target population.

Sampling techniques can be divided into two broad categories of probability and non-probability samples:

> In a *probability sample*, an objective selection procedure is used and each member of the population has a known, non-zero chance of being included in the sample.
>
> In a *non-probability sample*, the selection procedure used is subjective and the probability of selection for each population unit is unknown.
>
> These two sample selection procedures have their own merits. The main superiority of probability sampling is that there are appropriate statistical techniques for measuring random sampling error, while in non-probability samples the tools of statistical inference cannot be legitimately employed. If, as a general rule, a probability sample should be preferred, there are situations where non-probability samples are useful, namely, because they are less costly and easier to organize.

Probability samples

The different types of probability samples are simple random samples, stratified samples (proportionate or disproportionate), cluster samples and multi-stage area samples:

- A *simple random sample* is a sampling procedure that assures that each element of the population will have not only a known but also an equal chance of being included in the sample. Different drawing procedures exist (random number, systematic sampling), which all presuppose the existence of a list of the population members.
- In a *stratified sample* the target population is sub-divided into mutually exclusive groups – based on criteria such as size, income or age – and random samples are drawn from each group, called a "stratum". In a proportionate stratified sample the total sample is allocated among the strata in proportion to the size of each stratum, while in a disproportionate stratified sample, the total sample is allocated on the basis of relative variability observed in each stratum.
- In a *cluster sample*, the target population is divided into mutually exclusive sub-groups called clusters instead of strata, and a random sample of the sub-groups is then selected. Thus, each sub-group must be a small-scale model (or a miniature population) of the total population.
- *Multi-stage area sampling* involves two or more steps that combine some of the probability techniques of cluster sampling. Instead of picking all the units from the randomly chosen clusters (or area), only a sample of units is randomly picked from each of them; the selected sub-clusters themselves can be sub-sampled. The main advantage of multi-stage area sampling is to permit probability samples to be drawn even when a current list of population is unavailable.

In general, probability sampling methods will be more time-consuming and expensive than non-probability sampling methods because (1) they require an accurate specification of the population and an enumeration of the units of the population and (2) the selection procedure of the sample units must be precisely followed.

Non-probability samples

Three types of non-probability sampling can be identified – convenience, judgemental and quota:

- *Convenience sampling* refers to a sampling procedure of obtaining the respondents who are most conveniently available for the market analyst.
- *Judgemental sampling* is a procedure in which the market analyst exerts some effort in selecting a sample of respondents that he or she feels most appropriate for the research objectives.
- *Quota sampling* resembles stratified random sampling and convenience sampling. The interviewer finds and interviews a prescribed number of people in each of several categories. The sample units are selected on a subjective rather than a probabilistic basis.

In general, the choice between probability and non-probability sampling involves a trade-off between the capability to generalize the sample results to the target population with a known degree of accuracy and lower time/cost requirements.

Errors in survey research

One of the main responsibilities of the market analyst in charge of a survey is to estimate the overall accuracy and reliability of the survey results. The total error associated with a survey can be sub-divided into two broad categories: sampling error and non-sampling error, also called systematic bias. The different sources of error, sampling and non-sampling, are described in Figure 7.8.

The size of the sampling error can be reduced by increasing the sample size or by improving the design of the sampling procedure. More difficult to control are the non-sampling errors, which arise from a multitude of factors, such as poor questionnaire construction, ill-trained interviewers, errors from respondents or errors in coding responses. The best way to minimize non-sampling errors is to have a strict control over the entire process of primary data gathering, coding and analysis. If the survey research is sub-contracted to a market research company, the market analyst should give precise instructions and closely supervise the fieldwork.

From data collection to knowledge

Once data have been collected, emphasis in the research process turns to analysis. The raw data collected in the field must be transformed into information that will help to answer the questions raised by the decider. The transformation of raw data into information and to knowledge is achieved in several steps – data conversion, descriptive analysis and inferential analysis:

- *Data conversion* implies data editing, coding, storing and tabulating, in order to obtain an organized collection of data records (called a data set or data bank) which lends itself to analysis.

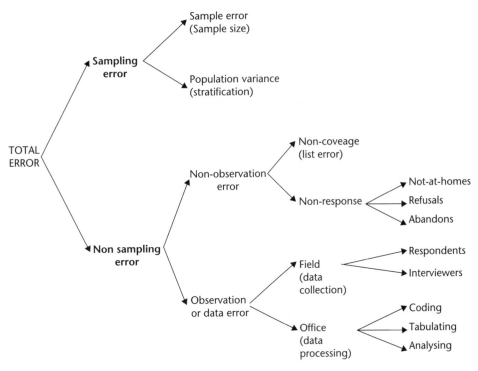

Figure 7.8 Total errors in survey research
Source: Adapted from Kerlinger (1973).

- *Descriptive analysis* gives an initial idea about the nature of the data; it involves obtaining appropriate measures of central tendency and of dispersion of the data for all variables, frequency distribution, cross-tabulations, graphic representations and so forth. Multivariate techniques like factorial analysis can also be used to summarize data.
- *Inferential analysis* aims at exploring the extent and nature of possible associations between pairs of variables, to test hypotheses about the target population or to examine the statistical significance of differences.

Attitude and brand (or corporate) image measurement is an important application of surveys. Several multivariate data analysis methods are based on survey data. These methods are used to extract meaningful information from primary data. The most popular ones are simple and regression analysis, discriminant analysis, factorial analysis, multi-dimensional scaling and cluster analysis. For an overview of applications and problems of these techniques, see Hair et al. (1992).

7.5   CAUSAL RESEARCH STUDIES

The use of a two-way table to uncover a relationship between two variables is common practice in descriptive research. A frequent temptation when a two-way table shows evidence of a statistically significant relationship, especially if one variable is presumed to influence the other (as in regression analysis), is to view this result as conclusive evidence of a causal relationship. This temptation should be resisted unless the empirical evidence stems from an experiment in which the other variables that may influence the response variable were controlled. A causal research design is required to establish the existence of a causal link. A descriptive study can only suggest the existence of a causal link. The basic tool used in causal studies is the controlled experiment.

Objectives of causal studies

In descriptive studies it is impossible to separate entirely the effect of a given variable from the effect of other variables. Causal studies overcome this difficulty by organizing the data-gathering procedure in such way as to permit unambiguous interpretation. Causal studies have three distinct, although very complementary, research objectives.

- To establish the direction and the intensity of a causal link between one or several action variables and one response variable.
- To measure in quantitative terms the rate of influence of an action variable on a response variable.
- To generate predictions of a response variable for different levels of the action variables.

These three objectives can be dissociated and several causal studies have the sole objective of establishing a cause-and-effect relationship in order to gain a better understanding of the phenomenon under study. In these cases, no quantitative estimates of the influence rate are sought.

Three rather intuitive types of evidence are relevant for evaluating causal relationships:

- Evidence that the action variable precedes the response variable.
- Evidence that a strong association exists between an action and an observed outcome.
- Evidence that the influence of other possible causal factors has been eliminated or controlled.

This last condition is particularly demanding and requires that all extraneous variables be controlled in order to ensure that the experiment has not been confused. The most important threats to internal validity in an experiment are briefly described here:

- *History*: event external to the experiment that affects the responses of the people involved in the experiment.
- *Maturation*: changes in the respondents that are a consequence of time, such as ageing, getting hungry or getting tired.
- *Testing effect*: awareness of being in a test, which can sensitize and bias respondents.
- *Before-measure effect*: the before-measure effect can also sensitize and bias respondents, therefore influencing both the after-observation and the respondent's reaction to the experiment treatment.
- *Instrumentation*: the measuring instrument may change, for example, when there are many observers or interviewers.
- *Mortality*: respondents may drop out of the experiment.
- *Selection bias*: an experimental group may be systematically different in some relevant way from the target population.

The market analyst to ensure that these extraneous factors are eliminated or controlled specifically constructs an experimental design.

Experimentation defined

Experimentation is a scientific investigation in which the researcher manipulates and controls one or more action variables and observes the response variable(s) for variation concomitant to the manipulation of the action variable. Treatments are the action variables that are manipulated and whose effects are measured. The test units are the entities, respondents or physical units to whom the treatments are presented and whose response is measured.

An experimental design involves the specification of (a) the treatments that are to be manipulated, (b) the test units to be used, (c) the response variable to be measured and (d) the procedure for dealing with extraneous variables.

Two types of experimentation can be distinguished:

- In a *laboratory experiment* in which the researcher creates a situation with the desired conditions (a trailer set up as a store or a survey situation) and then manipulates some variables while controlling others.
- A *field experiment* is organized in a realistic or natural situation (in-store test), although it too involves the manipulation of one or more action variables under carefully controlled conditions.

In general, field experiments are superior to laboratory experiments in terms of external validity.

Types of experimental design

In a typical experiment two groups of respondents (or stores) are selected in such a way that the groups have similar characteristics as far as the purpose of the study is concerned. The causal factor or the treatment (e.g., advertising A) is introduced into one of the two groups, called the experimental group. No such factor is introduced in the other group, called the control group. If sales increase within the experimental group but not in the control group, it is inferred that the hypothesis is tenable, that is, that advertising caused the sales increase. If no sales increase occurs in the experimental group, or if sales increase to the same extent in the control group, it is inferred that the hypothesis is not tenable (Boyd and Westfall, 1956, p. 82).

Within this general pattern, experimental designs vary in the manner in which experimental and control groups are selected and the degree of control that is exercised over the extraneous factors that affect the results. To illustrate this, two pre-experimental designs and two true experimental designs will be discussed briefly.

- The "one shot" case study. A single group of test units is exposed to treatment (X) and then an "after" measurement (O) is then taken on the response variable. Thus we have

$$X\ O$$

This is not a true experimental design and it is clearly impossible to draw any meaningful conclusions from it. The observed level of O may be the result of many uncontrollable factors and in the absence of pre-treatment observation, it is impossible to conclude.

- The one group "before–after" design. In this design a "before" measurement is made in addition to the "after" measurement. Thus, we have

$$O1\ X\ O2$$

The difference between the "after" and "before" measurements ($X2$–$X1$) would be assumed to be the effect of the treatment (X). This assumption is questionable, however, because the difference between the "after" and the "before" measurements could very well be a measure of the treatment plus the changes caused by all the uncontrolled factors, such as history, maturation, testing effect and so on.

- The "before–after" design with control group. A true experiment is one where the researcher is able to eliminate all extraneous factors as competitive hypotheses to the treatment. An experimental and a control group are selected in such way that they are interchangeable for purposes of the experiment. The control group is measured at the same time as the experimental group, but no treatment is introduced. Thus, we have

$$\text{Experimental group:} \quad O1 \; X \quad O2$$
$$\text{Control group:} \quad O3 \quad O4$$

Thus, the difference between the "after" and the "before" measurements of the control group ($O4$–$O3$) is the result of uncontrolled variables. The difference between the "after" and "before" measurements of the experimental group ($O2$–$O1$) is the result of the treatment plus the result of the same uncontrollable events affecting the control group. The effect of the treatment alone is obtained by subtracting the difference in the two measurements of the control group from the two measurements of the experimental group.

$$\text{True treatment effect} = [O1 - O2] - [O4 - O3]$$

All potential destroyers of internal validity are controlled by this design, except the testing effect in the experimental group, which is not eliminated.

Thus, when the "before" measurement is made in an undisguised way – for example, by interviewing respondents – the interactive testing effect is likely to be present and cannot be separated from the treatment effect. If the collection of the data is made without the knowledge of the individuals involved, this design is appropriate. In the other cases, a way to escape the problem of the testing effect is the "after-only with control group" design.

- "After-only with control group" design. In this design, the experimental and the control groups are selected in such a way as to be equivalent. No "before" measurement is made in both groups and the treatment is introduced in one of the groups selected as the experimental group.

$$X \quad O1$$
$$O2$$

The effect of the treatment is determined by computing the difference between the two "after" measurements ($O2$–$O1$). In this design, uncontrollable factors influence both the control and the experimental groups and there is no testing effect because no pre-measurements are made. The only weakness of this design is its static nature, which does not permit an analysis of the process of change as in the "before–after" design. A classic example of application of this design is the "Instant Nescafe study" summarized in Table 7.5.

The objective of the study was to determine the image of the housewife who uses instant coffee. Two comparable groups of housewives were shown similar shopping lists and asked to describe the housewife who prepared the list. On the list shown to the control group, one item was Maxwell House Coffee, a well-known drip grinds coffee brand. On the list shown the experimental group, Nescafé Instant Coffee, a relatively new concept at the time, replaced the item. The results measured were the percentages of the respondents who described the shopping list author as having various characteristics. The effect of the treatment (Nescafé Instant Coffee user) was the difference in the percentage ascribing each characteristic to the "instant coffee woman" from the percentage ascribing the same characteristics to the "drip grind" woman. (Boyd and Westfall, 1972, p. 96)

Table 7.5 Statistical tools used in a marketing decision system

Statistical tools Objectives	Marketing application
Multiple regression	
A statistical technique that can be used to analyse the relationship between a single dependent variable and several independents variables. The objective is to use the independents variable whose values are known to predict the single dependent value.	The marketing manager is interested in estimating how the company sales are influenced by changes in the level of advertising expenditures, sales force size, price and competition intensity.
Discriminant analysis	
The objective is to identify the variables that discriminate "best" between two or more groups. Using the identified variables for developing an index that will parsimoniously represent the differences between the groups and developing a rule to classify future observations into one of the groups.	The marketing manager is interested in determining the salient characteristics that successfully differentiate between brand-loyal and non-loyal customers, and in employing this information to predict purchase intentions of potential customers.
Logistic regression	
A statistical technique similar to discriminant analyses but logistic regression does not make any assumptions about the distribution of the independent variables.	The marketing manager is interested in determining the probability that a household would subscribe to a package of premium channels given the occupant's income, education, occupation, age, marital status and number of children
Canonical correlation	
The objective is to correlate simultaneously several metric-dependent variables and several metric-independent variables. The underlying principle is to develop a linear combination of each set of variables in a manner that maximizes the correlation between the two sets.	The marketing manager of a consumer goods firm is interested in determining if there is a relationship between type of products purchased and consumers' lifestyles and personality
Factor analysis	
The objective is to represent a set of observed variables in terms of a smaller number of hypothetical, underlying and unknown dimensions, which are called factors.	The marketing manager of an apparel firm wants to determine whether or not a relationship exists between patriotism and consumers' attitudes about domestic and foreign products
Cluster analysis	
The objective is to separate objects into groups such that each object is more like other objects in its group than like objects outside the group.	A marketing manager is interested in identifying groups of consumers who have similar behaviour and attitudes.
Multi-dimensional scaling	
The objective is to determine what dimensions respondents use when evaluating objects, how many dimensions they may use and the relative importance of each dimension.	A marketing manager wants to see where his or her brand is positioned in relation to the national and international competitive brands.

Source: Lambin (2007).

The results of this experiment are a replication of a study conducted by Mason Haire in 1950. A chi-square test shows that there are no significant differences between characteristics ascribed to the Maxwell shopper and those for the Nescafé shopper.

A fundamental principle is implicitly assumed to be applicable in experimental design: the market analyst does not care what extraneous factors are operative as long as they operate equally on all experimental and control groups. Thus random selection of the test units and of the groups and random allocation of the treatments among the groups are key conditions of validity.

With the development of scanner systems in supermarkets, the organization of marketing experiments is greatly facilitated today.

Conjoint analysis

Conjoint analysis is a multivariate technique used specifically to understand how consumers develop preferences for products or services and to formulate predictions about market attitude vis-à-vis new product concepts. The method is based on the multi-attribute product concept that is on the premise that consumers evaluate the value or utility of a product/service idea, by combining the separate amounts of utility provided by each attribute. The power of the method is to provide an explanatory model of consumers' preferences, which can then be used to define the product concept constituting the optimum combination of attribute levels. In a more precise way, a conjoint analysis brings answers to the following questions:

- For the respondent, what is the *partial utility* (or value) of each level of each attribute used to define the product/service?
- What is the *relative importance* (weight) of each attribute in the overall evaluation of the product concept?
- How to compare the *total utilities of several concepts* representing different bundles of attributes?
- What kind of *trade-off or arbitrage* are potential consumers willing to make between levels of attributes?
- What is the *share of preferences* of potential buyers for the different product concepts investigated?

A more detailed description of conjoint analysis is available at the website www.macmillanbusiness/lambin.

Structural equations modelling

Data analysis methods have made considerable progress during the last decade and these techniques, called second-generation data analysis methods, or structural equation modelling (SEM), have the capacity to examine a series of dependence relationships simultaneously, while standard multivariate techniques can examine only a single relationship at a time. In reality, the market analyst is often faced with a set of interrelated questions. For example, in a study aiming at measuring the performance of a store, the following interrelated questions have to be examined:

- What variables determine a store's image?
- How does that image combined with other variables (proximity, assortment) affect purchase decisions and satisfaction at the store?

- How does satisfaction with the store result in long-term loyalty to the store?
- How does loyalty to the store affect visit frequency and exclusivity?
- How does visit frequency and exclusivity determine store profitability?

We have here a series of dependence relationships where one dependent variable (store image) becomes an independent variable (among others) in subsequent dependence relationship (satisfaction), which in turn "explains" another dependent variable (loyalty), and so on. Until the 1980s, none of the multivariate techniques allowed us to address these questions with a single comprehensive method. For a review of these methods, see Hair et al. (1992) and Croutsche (1997).

The neural network technology

Neural network technology belongs to the field of artificial intelligence and gets its name because it performs many of the tasks that humans do.

These include making distinctions between items (classification), dividing similar things into groups (clustering), associating two or more things (associative memory), learning to predict outcomes based on examples (modelling), being able to predict the future (time series forecasting) and finally juggling multiple goals and coming up with a good-enough solution (constraint satisfaction) (Gibus, 1966, p. 41).

Neural network is a computing model grounded on the ability to recognize patterns in data. In contrast to SEM described in the preceding section, it is a model-building approach that *does not require prior definition of the causal structure*. Neural networks learn from examples. They take complex, noisy data and make educated guesses based on what they have learned from the past. It is a heuristic process. The user specifies a type of pattern and the so-called "intelligent agent" searches the data, looking for a particular pattern. Neural networks are said to be "intelligent", because they learn from examples, just like children learn to recognize dogs from examples of dogs, and because they exhibit some structural capability for generalizations and memorization.

The field of artificial intelligence is vast and clearly beyond the scope of this book, but its potential for market research is considerable. To go further on this topic and for a description of how neural networks can be applied to business problems, see the excellent book by Gibus (1996).

Marketing applications of the neural network technology

At present, the most commonly used applications of neural networks are the areas of micro-marketing, risk management and fraud detection. An example of micro-marketing is given by the US giant retail chain Wal-Mart, a frequent user of market basket analysis through this technology to find associations between products. This information is then used to determine product affinities and suggest promotion that can maximize profits.

> In trawling through some historical data and analysing it, the manager of a large US retailer noticed a distinct correlation between the sales of nappies and beer, just after work hours, which was particularly marked on a Friday. Further research confirmed the explanation: the man of the family was stopping off on his way home to pick up nappies for the baby – and a six-pack for himself. The retailer responded by merchandising nappies closer to the beer section and was rewarded by an increase in sales of both items. (Gooding, 1995, p. 25)

Other applications of the neural network technology are found in *micro-segmentation* and in *risk management*, particularly in the personal credit and the private insurance sectors.

> In insurance, for example, it has long been recognised that female drivers are a lower risk than their male counterparts and can be offered cheaper car insurance premiums. Data mining is used to find further sub-segments of female drivers with different price and risk profiles; instead of providing a standard premium to women in the same age category, insurers can now price differently in order to retain their most profitable customers or encourage customers who are likely to be unprofitable to go elsewhere.

A third popular domain of application is *fraud detection* as used by the credit card company Visa International. In concept neural networks are extremely simple. People tend to have patterns of buying. They tend to spend within certain limits, buy certain types of goods and acquire new things at a fairly predictable rate. Neural networks are designed to identify behaviours that do not fit these patterns. The expert system uses 30 to 35 different parameters and routinely analyses millions of transactions every day from around the world to detect patterns that appear fraudulent and send the scores to the card-issuing banks several times a day. It is then up to the local bank to decide whether or not to contact customers.

> An example of an established fraud pattern is as follows: a credit card is used to pay for petrol at a service station and that transaction is followed by the purchase in rapid succession of a series of large price-tag consumer electronics. The purchasing pattern would alert the neural network to possible fraud, immediately signalling the likelihood of a credit card theft by a criminal intent on using up all remaining credit as quickly as possible.

The field of information technology is changing fast with the increasing use of microcomputers, the proliferation of mobile phones and the explosion of the Internet. Information technology really does have the potential to make marketing management more effective because it enables organizations to build powerful personal relationships with their customers, to understand better their needs and to respond faster to their expectations. For an introduction to the subject, see O'Connor and Galvin (1997).

Chapter Summary

A market-oriented firm has to develop an MIS to monitor changes in the macro-marketing environment. The role of marketing research is to provide market information data that will help management implement a market-oriented strategy. Marketing research has to provide management with accredited (or certified) knowledge and, for this reason, has strictly to follow the rules of scientific method. The development of a research project implies a sequence of interrelated activities, which ensures a systematic and orderly investigation process. Three types of marketing research can be identified: exploratory, descriptive and causal studies. The objective of exploratory research is to generate hypotheses and to translate the research problem into research objectives. The techniques of exploratory research are use of secondary data, key informant surveys, analysis of selected cases and focus group discussions. Group discussions, also called qualitative research, are particularly useful, but they should be used strictly to suggest hypotheses for further research and not as conclusive

> ## Chapter Summary – Continued
>
> evidence. Descriptive studies attempt to obtain a complete, quantitative and accurate description of a situation and must follow a precise methodology. The techniques used are observation and communication. The most popular communication method is by far the survey method through personal, telephone or mail interviewing. Good questionnaire design is the key to obtaining good survey results and a seven-step procedure is proposed to help in designing a questionnaire. Sampling techniques can be divided into two categories: probability and non-probability samples. These two sampling techniques have their own merits. The two sources of error in survey research are sampling and non-sampling errors. To minimize non-sampling error the market analyst should have strict control over the entire data-gathering process. Causal research is used to establish the existence of a causal link between an action and a response variable. An experimentation is a scientific investigation in which the researcher manipulates and controls one or more action variables and observes the response variable for variation concomitant to the manipulation of the action variable. Different types of experimental designs exist which vary in the way the analyst controls extraneous factors.

BIBLIOGRAPHY

O'Connor, J. and Galvin, E. (1997), *Marketing and Information Technology*, London, Pitman Publishing.

Aaker, D. A. and Day, J.S. (1980), *Marketing Research*, New York, John Wiley & Sons, 2nd edition.

Adler, L. (1979), To Learn What's on the Consumers' Mind, Try Focus Group Interviews, *Sales and Marketing Management*, pp. 76–80.

Boyd, H.W. and Westfall, R. (1956/1972), *Marketing Research: Text and Cases*, Homewood, IL, R.D. Irwin Inc.

Churchill, G.A. and Iacobucci, D. (2005), *Marketing Research, Methodological Foundations*, Orlando, FL, Thompson, South Western, 9th edition.

Croutsche, J.J. (1997), *Pratique de l'analyse des données*, Paris, Editions ESKA.

Erdos, P.L. (1970), *Professional Mail Surveys*, New York, McGraw-Hill.

Gibus, J.J. (1996), Data Mining with Neural Networks: *Solving Business Problems from Application Development to Decision Support*, New York, McGraw-Hill Book Company.

Gooding, C. (1995), Boosting Sales with the Information Warehouse, *Financial Times*, 1 March.

Hair, J., Anderson, R.E., Tatham, R.L. and Black, W.C. (1992), *Multivariate Data Analysis*, New York, Macmillan Publishing Company, 3rd edition.

Kerlinger, F.N. (1973), *Foundations of Behavioural Research*, London, Holt Rinehart and Winston, Inc.

Kotler, P. (1991/2006), *Marketing Management*, Englewood Cliffs, NJ, Prentice-Hall, Inc., 10th edition with Keller.

Lambin, J.J. (1990), *La Recherche Marketing*, Paris, McGraw-Hill.

Lambin, J.J. (2000–2007), *Market-Driven Management: Strategic and Operational Marketing*, London, Palgrave Macmillan, Second edition.

Marchand, D. (2002), Is Your Company Effective at Using Information? *European Business Forum*, 8, Winter, pp. 54–7.

Pellemans, P. (1995), *Jungian Analysis as a Tool for New Qualitative Research Methods in Marketing*, Unpublished Working paper, IAG, Louvain-la-Neuve, Belgium.

Zaltman, G. and Burger, P.C. (1975), *Marketing Research: Fundamentals and Dynamics*, Hinsdale, IL, The Dryden Press.

Zikmund, W.G. (1986/1994*), Exploring Marketing Research*, Chicago, IL, The Dryden Press, 2nd and 5th editions.

WEBSITE COMPANION FOR CHAPTER 7

Visit the Market-driven Management accompanying website at www.palgrave.com/business/lambin3 to find:

Note on Questionnaire Design Procedure
Note on Conjoint Analysis
Examples of Questions in Survey Research
Selected Reviews and Journals Useful in Marketing Research

PART THREE

IMPLEMENTING STRATEGIC MARKETING

CHAPTER EIGHT

NEEDS ANALYSIS THROUGH MARKET SEGMENTATION

One of the first strategic decisions a firm has to make is to define its reference market and to choose the customer segment(s) to target (Smith, 1956). This choice implies the splitting of the total market into groups of customers with similar needs and behavioural or motivational characteristics, which constitute distinct market opportunities. A firm can elect to serve all possible customers or to focus on one or several specific segments within the reference market. The typical output of a segmentation analysis is a segmentation grid, describing the qualitative and quantitative profile of the most important segments (generally four or five). Using this mapping of the reference market, the firm will then evaluate the attractiveness of each segment (see Chapter 9) and assess its own competitiveness (see Chapter 10) before making decisions regarding which segment(s) to target and which positioning to adopt within each chosen segment (see Chapter 11).

Learning Objectives

When you have read this chapter, you should know and understand:

- The concept of reference market
- The objectives of market segmentation
- The advantages and disadvantages of different segmentation methods
- The requirements for effective segmentation

8.1 STEPS IN THE STRATEGIC SEGMENTATION PROCESS

The implementation of the segmentation strategic process consists of four basic steps (as shown in Figure 8.1):

- *Segmentation analysis,* or subdividing product markets into distinct groups of potential buyers having the same expectations or requirements (homogeneity condition), and being different from customers who are in other segments (heterogeneity condition).
- *Market targeting,* or selecting particular segment(s) to target, given the firm's strategic ambition and distinctive capabilities, a decision based on the results of the attractiveness and competitiveness analyses.
- *Market positioning,* or deciding how the firm wants to be perceived in the minds of potential customers, given the distinctive quality of the product and the positions already occupied by competitors.

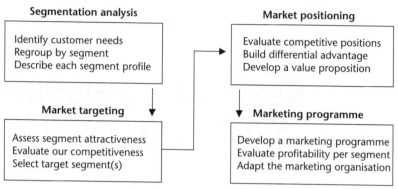

Figure 8.1 Steps in the strategic marketing process
Source: Lambin (2000/2007).

- *Marketing programming* aimed at target segments. This last step involves the development and deployment of specific marketing programme(s) specially designed to achieve the desired positioning in the target segment(s).

The first step, segmentation analysis of the reference market, is generally done in two steps, corresponding to different levels of total market desegregation. The first step, called *macro-segmentation*, has the objective of identifying "product markets", while in the second, called *micro-segmentation*, the goal is to uncover customers' "segments" within each product market previously identified. Micro-segmentation can be implemented in four different ways:

- *Descriptive segmentation*, which is based on socio-demographic characteristics of the customer irrespective of the product category.
- *Benefit segmentation*, which considers explicitly the product category and the person's system of values.
- *Lifestyle segmentation*, which is based on socio-cultural characteristics of the customer, irrespective of the product category.
- *Behavioural segmentation*, which classifies customers on the basis of their actual purchasing behaviour in the marketplace.

Each of these segmentation methods has its own merits and weaknesses, which will be discussed in the following sections.

8.2 MACRO-SEGMENTATION ANALYSIS

In the majority of markets, it is almost impossible to satisfy all customers with a single product or service. Different consumers have varying desires and interests. This variety stems from diverse buying practices and basic variations of customers' needs and the benefits they seek from products. Increasingly, therefore, companies have found it essential to move away from mass marketing towards target marketing strategy, where the focus is on a particular group of customers. This identification of target customer groups is market segmentation, where the total market is desegregated into sub-groups, with similar requirements and buying characteristics. Knowing how to segment a market is one of the most important skills a firm must possess, for an example, see Figure 8.2. Segmentation defines what business

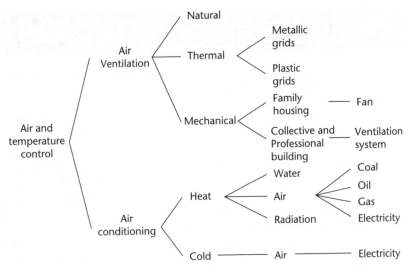

Figure 8.2 Example of a reference market definition
Source: Adapted from the Case Sedal, Ecole de Management, Lyon, 1976.

the firm is in, guides strategy development and determines the capabilities needed in the business unit.

Defining the reference market in terms of solution

Implementing a market segment strategy should begin with a business definition statement that reveals the true function or purpose of the firm in a customer-oriented perspective. Three fundamental questions should be addressed:

- What business(es) are we in?
- What business(es) should we be in?
- What business(es) should we not be in?

To answer these questions in a customer-oriented perspective, the business definition should be made in generic terms, which is in terms of the "solution" sought by the customer and not in technical terms, to avoid the risk of myopia.

The rationale behind the *solution approach* has been explained in Chapter 4. It can be summarized as follows:

- To the buyer, the product is what it does.
- No one buys a product *per se*. What is sought is a solution to a problem.
- Different technologies can produce the same function.
- Technologies are fast changing, while generic needs are stable.

It is therefore important for the market-oriented firm to define its reference market in terms of a generic need, rather than in terms of a product. Examples of market reference definitions are presented in Box 8.1.

Ideally, the business definition should be stated in terms narrow enough to provide practical guidance, yet broad enough to stimulate imaginative thinking, such as openings for product line extensions or for diversification into adjacent product areas.

> **Box 8.1 Implementation problem: examples of reference market definitions in terms of generic needs**
>
> - *Lego*, the Danish toy company, has a worldwide market share in the construction-toy market of 72 per cent. The company has redefined its market as the "edutainement" (education–entertainment) market, "having fun and exercising the mind".
> - *Colgate-Palmolive* defines its reference market as the *oral care* market and proposes a full range of toothpastes, mouthwash, toothbrushes and cleanup tools.
> - *Derbit Belgium* is operating in the European roofing market and manufactures membranes of APP-modified bitumen. The company defines its market as follows: "We are selling guaranteed waterproof solutions to flat roofing problems in partnership with exclusive distributors and highly qualified roofing applicators."
>
> - *Sedal*, a small French company manufacturing metallic ventilation grids, defined its business as the "air and temperature control" business and expanded its offerings to air ventilation and air-conditioning systems (see Figure 8.3).
> - *Automatic Systems* manufactures gates and doors, but defines its business as the sales of "access control solutions" and offers its customers the hardware and the software (security systems) as well.
> - *IBM* defines its mission in the following terms: "We are in the business of helping customers solve problems through the use of advanced information technology. We are creating value by offering the solutions, products and services that help customers succeed."
>
> Source: Lambin (2000/2007).

At the Grumman Corporation, the guidelines for the mission statement advise:

> We should be careful not to confine the market boundaries by our existing or traditional product participation. The market definition analysis is purposely meant to create an outward awareness of the total surrounding market, and of its needs and trends that may offer opportunity for, or on the other hand, challenges to, our current or contemplated position. (Hopkins, 1982, p. 119)

The business definition is the starting point for strategy development. It helps identify the customers to be served, the competitors to surpass, the key success factors to master and the alternative technologies available for producing the service or the function sought.

The adoption of the *solution approach* in defining the reference market changes substantially the nature of the firm's business, since the firm is transforming itself into a *service provider*.

Conceptualization of the reference market

The objective is to define the reference market from the buyer perspective and not from the producer's point of view, as is too often the case. As suggested by Abell (1980), a reference market can be defined in three dimensions:

- *Customer group or who is being satisfied.*
- *Customer functions or needs; what is being satisfied.*
- *Technologies used to meet the needs; how customer needs are being satisfied.*

We thus have a three-dimensional framework, as shown in Figure 8.3. To segment the market, the first step is to identify the relevant criteria for describing each of these three dimensions.

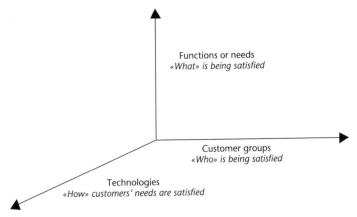

Figure 8.3 The three-dimensional framework of a reference market
Source: Adapted from Abell (1980).

Needs or functions

We refer here to the need to be fulfilled by the product or the service. Examples of functions would be:

Home interior decoration; international transportation of goods; waterproof roof protection; rust prevention; teeth cleaning; deep versus shallow drilling; diagnostic imaging; and so on.

Functions have to be conceptually separated from the way the function is performed (i.e., the technology). The dividing line between "functions" and "benefits" is not always clear, as functions are narrowly subdivided or are considered as assortments of functions, for example, teeth cleaning plus decay prevention, shampoo with anti-dandruff treatment. Thus, functions can also be defined as a package of benefits sought by different customer groups.

Customer groups

We describe the different customer groups that might buy the product. The most common criteria used are:

households versus industrial buyers, socio-economic class, geographic location, type of activity, company size, original equipment manufacturer versus user, decision-making unit, and so on.

At this level of macro-segmentation, only broad customer characteristics are retained. For consumer goods, more detailed criteria are often necessary, such as age group, benefits sought, lifestyle, purchase behaviour, and so on. This is the object of micro-segmentation.

Technologies

These describe the alternative ways in which a particular function can be performed for a customer.

For example, paint or wallpaper for the function of home interior decoration; road, air, rail or sea for international transportation of goods; bitumen or plastic for roof protection; toothpaste or mouthwash for teeth cleaning; X-ray, ultrasound or computerised tomography for diagnostic imaging, and so on.

As underlined above, the technology dimension is dynamic, in the sense that one technology can displace another over time. For example, ultrasound, nuclear medicine and computed tomography (CT) scanning as alternative imaging diagnostic techniques are displacing X-rays. Similarly, e-mail is tending to displace printed materials in the field of written communication.

Market boundary definitions

Using this framework, we may distinguish between a "product market", a "solution market" and an "industry" (see Figure 8.4):

- A specific customer group, seeking a specific function or assortment of functions based on a single technology defines *a product market*.
- A *solution market* is defined by the performance of given functions in given customer groups, but including all the substitute technologies to perform those functions. It corresponds to the concept of "category".
- An *industry* is based on a single technology, but covers several businesses, that is, several functions or assortments of functions and several customer groups.

These alternative boundary definitions correspond to different market coverage strategies, each having their own merits and weaknesses.

The *industry definition* is the most traditional one, but also the least satisfactory because it is supply-oriented and not market-oriented. From a marketing point of view, this definition of the reference market is much too general, since it includes a large variety of functions and customer groups.

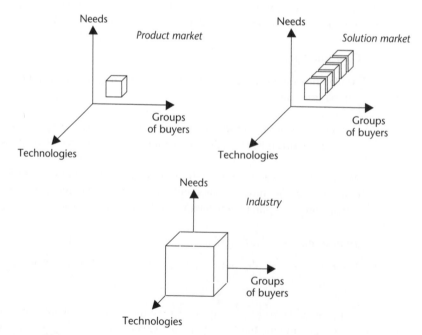

Figure 8.4 Reference market boundaries
Source: Adapted from Abell (1980).

In the household appliances industry, for example, this would include microwave ovens and laundry irons, two very different products in terms of growth potential and of customers' behaviour characteristics.

However, most industrial and foreign trade statistics are industry-based and it is therefore difficult to avoid industry definitions completely.

The *solution market definition* (see Chapter 4) is very close to the generic need concept and has the merit of emphasizing the existence of substitute products or technologies for performing the same function. A technological innovation can dramatically change existing market boundaries. The monitoring of substitute technologies is enhanced by this reference market definition. The major difficulty stems from the fact that the technology domains involved may be very different.

> Customers with a need for a 6 mm hole will normally use a metal twist drill, but some segments are finding lasers or high-pressure water jets to be a better solution. Also, companies that refine cane sugar wrestle with this question often. Their product is a sweetener, but the needs of soft drink and candy manufacturers for sweetening can be satisfied with sugar made from corn (fructose) or sugar beets. Depending on market conditions, these alternatives may be cheaper. Should they offer all sweetening materials? (Day, 1990, p. 27)

The *solution market* definition is very useful for giving directions to R&D and for suggesting diversification strategies and also for organizing markets. *Category management* is based on this concept, which also modifies substantially the marketing mix concept, as already explained above in chapter 4 (see p. 26).

The *product market definition* is the most market-oriented definition. It corresponds to the notion of SBU and is very close to the real world market. This market definition automatically dictates six key elements of the firm's strategic thrust:

- The customers to be served
- The package of benefits to be provided
- The direct competitors to surpass
- The substitute technologies and competitors to monitor
- The key capabilities to acquire
- The main market actors to deal with

This partitioning of the total reference market into product markets will guide market coverage decisions and will determine the type of organizational structure to adopt. One shortcoming of this market definition is the difficulty of finding appropriate market measurements, most government statistics being industry-based and not market-based.

8.3   DEVELOPMENT OF A MACRO-SEGMENTATION GRID

Once the relevant segmentation variables are identified, the next task is to combine them to develop a segmentation grid. To illustrate this process, let us consider the market of heavy-duty trucks. The identified segmentation variables are the following:

- *Needs*: regional, national and international transport of goods.
- *Technologies*: air, rail, water and road.
- *Customers*: types of activity, that is, own account, professional transporters and renting companies; size of fleet: small (1–5 trucks), medium (5–10 trucks) and large (>10 trucks).

Exhibit 8.1   The marketing mix and the *solution to a problem* approach

- *Product:* a solution to a problem and the package of benefits that the product represents.
- *Category:* the set of products giving a solution to the customers' problem.
- *Place:* a convenient access to the solution sought by the buyer,
- *Price:* all the costs, including price, supported by the buyer to acquire the solution sought.

- *Advertising:* the messages and signals communicated about the solutions available and about their distinctive qualities.
- *Selling:* the negotiation process or the dialogue organized with the potential buyer in his or her search for the appropriate solution to his or her problem.

Source: Lambin (2000/2007).

Exhibit 8.2   Implications of the solution approach: from selling widgets to providing services

From General Electric Co. to Wang Laboratories Inc., from Xerox Corp. to Hewlett-Packard Co., American companies that a few years ago got almost all their profits from selling widgets are rapidly transforming themselves into service providers. Computer companies like Unisys Corp. and IBM Corp. are designing, installing and running other companies' computer operations. Document processors like Xerox and Pitney Bowes Inc. now run mailrooms and copy centres and distribute documents electronically. Honeywell redesigns refineries. Hewlett-Packard not only designs and operates data systems, but also pays for the whole package and then leases it out. "Customers want to finance a solution, not a little piece of it," says Ann Livermore, vice-president of Hewlett-Packard's service operations. "The move to services is one of the hottest strategies in US business, and it is driven by changes at the very foundations of manufacturing. /.../ Services generate huge cash flows and today's business are run for cash flow", says Nicholas Heymann, an analyst with NatWest securities.

Source: Deutsch (1997).

If we consider all possible combinations, we have here a total of 108 (3×5×3×3) possible segments. To refine the analysis, let us adopt the following rules:

- Ignore transportation modes other than road transportation.
- Establish a distinction between trucks below and above 16 tonnes.
- Forget about truck renting companies.
- Subdivide regional transport into three categories: distribution, construction and others.

We now obtain 60 (5×2×2×3) segments as shown in Table 8.1, which is still much too high.

The size of these segments varies widely, however, as the figures of Table 8.2 show. Those numbers represent the percentage of registered licence plates for trucks within each segment. Each segment does not necessarily have to be considered, as the pertinence analysis should demonstrate.

Pertinence analysis

In developing a realistic segmentation grid, the following rules should be adopted:

- The analyst should start with the longest list of segmentation variables to avoid overlooking meaningful criteria.

Table 8.1 Macro-segmentation of the truck market (per cent total truck population)

Activity/functions	Fleet size and weight						Total
	Small (1–4)		Medium (4–10)		Large (>10)		
	<16t	>16t	<16t	>16t	<16t	>16t	
Own account transporters	Segment 1: 19.3%				Segment 2: 11.1%		
Distribution	7.3	4.5	1.1	1.8	0.4	2.1	16.2
Construction	0.1	1.1	0.9	1.4	1.7	1.6	6.8
National	4.7	1.6	1.4	3.8	1.7	3.6	16.8
International	1.3	0.9	0.2	1.3	–	1.4	5.1
Others	–	0.6	0.3	–	2.5	–	3.4
Professional transporters	Segment 3: 13.9%				Segment 4: 26.1%		
Distribution	1.1	0.8	0.9	1.6	–	1.6	6.0
Construction	0.2	1.6	–	0.4	–	1.2	3.4
National	1.4	1.5	1.4	3.0	2.5	8.5	18.3
International	0.2	0.7	0.5	6.1	0.4	14.7	22.6
Others	–	0.4	–	–	–	–	0.4
Total	16.3	13.7	6.7	19.4	9.2	34.7	100.0%

Source: Adapted from Lambin and Hiller (1993).

- Only those variables with a truly significant strategic impact should be isolated.
- Collapsing together variables that are correlated can reduce the number of variables.
- Some cells are generally unfeasible combinations of segmentation variables and therefore can be eliminated.
- Some segments can be regrouped if the differences among them are not really significant or their size is too small.
- The segmentation grid should include potential segments as well and not only segments that are currently occupied.

In the case of Volvo Trucks Company, re-examination of the segmentation grid suggested the regrouping of the most similar segments that must be served together, to retain eventually *four major segments*, which altogether represent 70.5 per cent of the total truck population in the Belgian market.

This phase is the most difficult one. The task is to reconcile realism and efficiency, two often-contradictory objectives. When eliminating segments, one must eliminate only the unfeasible combinations of segmentation variables but keep the empty cells, which, while currently unoccupied, could become potential segments in the future.

Testing the macro-segmentation grid

To verify the usefulness of the grid, the company's customers and direct competitors should be located in the different segments. The objective is to evaluate the potential of each segment in terms of size and growth, and to measure the market share held by the firm within each segment. The questions to examine are the following:

- Which segment(s) display the highest growth rate?
- What is our present market coverage?

- Where are our key customers located?
- Where are our direct competitors located?
- What are the requirements of each segment in terms of service, product quality, and so on?

The answers to these questions will also help the firm to define its market coverage strategy and to regroup segments having the same requirements and/or the same competitors.

Searching for new segments

Some segmentation variables are readily apparent as a result of industry convention or established norms for dividing buyers. Macro-segmentation analysis goes beyond conventional wisdom and accepted classification schemes and gives the opportunity for discovering new ways of segmenting the market.

Finding new ways to segment the market can give the firm a major competitive advantage over rivals.

In a given sector of activity, business definitions may differ from one competitor to another. A firm specializing in a particular function can be confronted by a rival specializing in a particular customer group interested in the same function. The first competitor will probably have a cost advantage over the second, who will be probably more efficient in terms of distribution or customer service. The competitor analysis system should help identify the distinctive qualities of direct competitors.

Box 8.2   Implementation problem: how to discover new potential segments

In searching for potential new segments, the following questions should be considered:

- Are there other technologies to perform the required functions?
- Could an enhanced product perform additional functions?
- Could the needs of some buyers be better served by reducing the number of functions and possibly by lowering the price?

- Are there other groups of buyers requiring the same service or function?
- Are there new channels of distribution that could be used?
- Are there different bundles of products and services that could possibly be sold as a package?

Box 8.3   Implementation problem: how to verify the heterogeneity condition between segments?

The following questions can also help decide whether or not two products belong to the same strategic segment:

- Are the main competitors the same?
- Are their customers or groups of customers the same?

- Are the key success factors the same?
- Does divesting in one affect the other?

Positive answers to these four questions would tend to show that both products belong to the same product market.

Changes in market boundaries

Under the pressure of technological progress and changing consumption habits, definitions of market boundaries keep on changing along any one of three dimensions – functions, technologies or customers:

- *Extension to new customer groups* through a process of adoption and diffusion, for example, adoption of microcomputers in the classroom.
- *Extension to new functions* through a process of systematization and through the creation of products to serve a combination of functions, for example, telephone sets combined with a fax and with an automatic answering device.
- *Extension to new technologies* through a process of technological substitution, for example, digital photography replacing chemical-based photography.

These changing forces explain the changing profiles of PLCs, a key criterion for assessing the attractiveness of product markets. The PLC model will be analysed in the next chapter.

8.4   MICRO-SEGMENTATION ANALYSIS IN B2C MARKETS

The objective of micro-segmentation is to analyse the diversity of customers' requirements in a more detailed way within each of the product markets (or macro-segments) identified at the stage of macro-segmentation analysis. Within a particular product market, customers seek the same core service, for instance, time measurement in the watch market. However, keeping in mind the multi-attribute product concept, the way the core service is provided and the secondary services that go with the core service can be very different. The goal of micro-segmentation analysis is to identify customer groups searching for the same package of benefits in the product. This can lead to a differentiation strategy to obtain a competitive advantage over rivals by doing a better job of satisfying customer requirements.

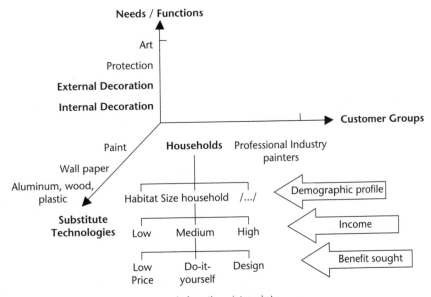

Figure 8.5   From macro- to micro-segmentation: an example from the paint market
Source: Lambin J.J., (2000–2007).

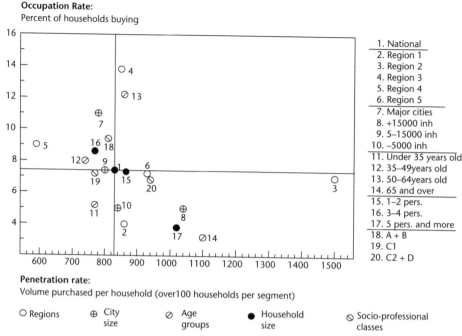

Figure 8.6   Socio-demographic segmentation: the case of new food product
Source: Industry.

Descriptive or socio-demographic segmentation

Socio-demographic segmentation is an indirect segmentation method. The basic assumption embedded in this buyer's classification is the following:

> People having different socio-demographic profiles also have different needs and expectations regarding products and services.

This is obvious in many fields. Women and men have different needs for products like clothes, hats, cosmetics, jewellery and so on, and similarly for teenagers or senior citizens, for low- and high-income households, for rural versus urban households and so on. Thus, socio-demographic variables are used as proxies for direct need analysis.

The most commonly used variables are sex, age, income, geographic location, education, occupation, family size and social class, all variables which reflect the easily measurable vital statistics of a society. Frequently, a socio-demographic segmentation combines several variables, as shown in Figure 8.6.

The case analysed here is that of a recently launched new brand in the food sector. The market response is described by reference to two dependent variables: the proportion of households having purchased the brand (market occupation rate) and the average quantity purchased per household (market penetration rate). The national average is at the intersection of the two dotted lines, the other points describing the behaviour of different socio-economic subgroups.

For instance, one observes that the highest occupation rates are within the subgroups denoted respectively 5/13/7/18: (region 3), (age group 50–65), (large cities), (classes A+B). Similarly, the market penetration rate is higher within the following subgroups: 3/15/8/17: (region 2), (age group 65 and higher), (middle size cities), (household composition: 5 persons and higher).

This information is essential to verify whether the target group has been reached and, if not, to adjust the marketing programme accordingly.

Usefulness of socio-demographic data

The *merits* of socio-demographic segmentation are its low cost and ease of application. In most markets, information on socio-demographic variables is readily available in published sources. In addition, consumer panels use these criteria in their monthly or bimonthly reports on a similar base across the main European countries.

Also, in recent years significant socio-demographic changes have been observed in industrialized countries. Among these changes are:

- declining birth rate,
- increase in life expectancy,
- increasing number of working women,
- postponement of the age of marriage,
- increasing divorce rate,
- increasing numbers of single-parent families.

These changes all have direct implications on the demand structure and on consumer purchase behaviour. They create new market segments and new requirements in existing segments. Examples are:

- the *senior citizen* (over 65) segment for banking services, recreational activities, medical care and so on;
- the segment of *single-adult households,* that is, the unmarried, divorced, widowed or single-parent families;
- the *dual-income households* having higher discretionary income, also called the "DINKS" (double income no kids);
- the segment of *working women* for all time-saving goods and services, like microwave ovens, catalogue shopping, easy-to-prepare foods, fast-food restaurants and so on.

Several uses are currently made of socio-demographic data, namely:

- to describe and better understand present customers,
- to have the ID profile of a target segment,
- to select media having a higher probability of reaching a target group,
- to identify prospective buyers of a new product.

The application problem presented in Table 8.2 provides an illustration of the usefulness of socio-demographic data.

Limitations of descriptive segmentation

Socio-demographic segmentation (as well as behavioural segmentation) is *ex-post analysis* of the kind of people who make up specific segments. The emphasis is on describing the characteristics of segments rather than on learning what causes these segments to develop. This is why it is called "descriptive segmentation."

Table 8.2 Changing society: implications for organic food

Changing features in society	Organic food implications
Smaller households; more singles	Desire for smaller portions and more eating out habits
Children at older age	Mature purchase decision-making
More women in the work force	Purchasing higher-quality food.
Rich getting richer	Less time available, guilt, convenience food
Healthy living	Non-price-sensitive food purchasing
Vegetarianism	Increased concern for diet (salt, fat, additives and so on)
Multiculturalism	Much greater awareness of food and food ingredients
Globalization	Increased variation in diet and new food types
	Expectation of consistent year-round supply
	Loss of seasonal food consumption

Source: Coriolis Research (2000).

Another major weakness is the *declining predictive value* of socio-demographic segmentation in industrialized countries as, increasingly, different persons adopt the same consumer behaviour with the growing standardization of consumption modes across social classes. In other words, the fact of belonging to the upper class no longer necessarily implies the existence of purchase behaviour different from that of a middle-class person. Today, two consumers of the same age, same family structure and same income may have extremely different behaviours and attitudes, reflected in different buying habits, product preferences and sometimes completely opposite reactions to advertising. Socio-demographic segmentation must be complemented by other methods to understand and predict a buyer's behaviour.

Benefit segmentation

In benefit segmentation, the emphasis is placed on differences in peoples' values and not on differences in socio-demographic profiles. Two persons identical in terms of socio-demographic profiles may have very *different value systems*. Moreover, the same person having different experiences with products can hold different values towards each product that is purchased.

> For example, a person who buys a refrigerator because it is the cheapest available may want to buy the most expensive TV set simply because of its superior design. Or, the individual who pays a high price for a bottle of wine may own a very cheap watch.

Thus, the value or the benefit sought in purchasing a particular product is the critical motivational factor to identify. The objective of benefit segmentation is to explain differences in preferences and not simply to give ex-post descriptions of purchase behaviour.

In the watch market, for instance, one can identify four distinct benefit segments, each representing different values attributed to watches by different groups of consumers:

- *Economy segment.* This group sees a watch mainly as time-measurement device and purchase mainly on the basis of price for any watch that works reasonably well. Brands like Seiko, Pulsar and Citizen are typically in this segment.
- *Prestige and quality segment.* This group wants a watch with a long life, good workmanship, good material and good styling. They are willing to pay for these product qualities. Omega and Rolex are in this segment.
- *Fashion segment.* This group wants useful product features but also meaningful emotional qualities. The watch is viewed as a fashion accessory and is issued in many different faces

and colours. It appeals as a fashion item to young, active and trendy people. The leading brand in this segment is clearly Swatch, who created the "fun wear" concept.

- *Symbolic segment.* Here, a well-known brand name, fine styling, a gold or diamond case and a jeweller's recommendation are important. The symbolic segment has become more sophisticated with new benefits like elegance and fashion (Gucci and Armani), sport (Tag Heuer, Breitling), luxury and refinement (Patek Philippe) emerging.

Without such an understanding, the demographic characteristics of customers were most confusing. It turns out, for example, that people with both the highest and the lowest incomes buy the most expensive watches. On the other hand, some upper-income consumers are no longer buying costly watches, but are buying cheap, well-styled watches to throw away when they require servicing. Other upper-income consumers, however, continue to buy fine, expensive watches for suitable occasions.

At one time, most watch companies were oriented almost exclusively towards the prestige and quality segment, thus leaving the major portion of the market open to attack and exploitation. The US Time Company, with the Timex brand, took advantage of this opening and established a very strong position among buyers in the economy segment and later Swatch in the fashion segment.

Required market data

Benefit segmentation requires obtaining detailed information on consumer value systems. Each segment is identified by the benefits it is seeking. It is the total package of benefits sought which differentiates one segment from another, rather than the fact that one segment is seeking one particular benefit and another a quite different benefit. Individual benefits are likely to have appeal for several segments. In fact, most people would like as many benefits as possible. However, the relative importance they attach to individual benefits when forced to make trade-offs can differ a great deal and, accordingly, can be used as an effective criterion in segmenting markets. Thus, opportunities for segmentation arise from *trade-offs* consumers are willing to make among the benefits possible and the prices paid to obtain them.

Thus, the *multi-attribute product concept* is the implied behavioural model in benefit segmentation. Its implementation requires the following information from a representative sample of target consumers:

- The list of attributes or benefits associated with a product category.
- An evaluation of the relative importance attached to each benefit.
- A regrouping procedure of consumers with similar rating patterns.
- An evaluation of the size and profile of each identified segment.

In the oral care market, for instance, the attributes identified through consumer research were the following: whiteness, freshness, good taste, product appearance, decay prevention, gum protection and economy. Four segments can be identified as shown in Table 8.3. Supplementary information should also be collected about the people's profile in each of these segments:

1. The *cosmetic segment*, which comprises people who mainly show concern for fresh breath and the brightness of their teeth. It includes a relatively large group of young married couples. They smoke more than average and their lifestyle is very active. New offerings have emerged in this group with the launching of the whitening and the

herbal toothpastes. The tooth-whitening sub-segment is fast growing in this toothpaste category.

2. The *therapeutic segment* contains a large number of families with children. They are seriously concerned about the possibilities of cavities and gum protection. They show a definite preference for paramedical brands sold mainly in pharmacies, at a price three times the price of regular cosmetic brand. A new offering in this segment is the brand *Sensodyne* designed for people having very sensitive teeth.

3. The *sensory segment* is particularly concerned with the flavour and the appearance of the product. In this segment, large portions of the brand users are children, the kids' sub-segment. Their use of spearmint toothpaste is well above average. Toothpaste manufacturers are licensing cartoon characters, like Colgate Barbie. A new arrival in this toothpaste category is the nighttime toothpaste to fight nighttime's breath, with the Arm& Hammer's P.M. brand.

4. The *economy segment* is price-oriented and shows a dominance of men. It tends to be above average in terms of toothpaste usage. People in this segment see very few meaningful differences between brands and are attracted by all-in-one brands like Aquafresh and by private labels.

Table 8.3 Benefit segmentation of the toothpaste market

Benefits sought	Benefit segments			
	Cosmetic	Therapeutic	Sensory	Economy
White and freshness Whitening Nighttime breath	Colgate, White Glo, Signal, Arm&Hammer P.M.			
Cavity, tartar and gum protection Sensitive teeth		Crest, Parogencyl, Parodontax, Sensodyne		
Taste, flavour, colour, fun			Colgate Barbie, Crest Kids	
Core function Low price All in one				Private labels

Source: Representative brands only. Toothpaste companies have a multi-segment strategy.

Exhibit 8.3   The Crest brand success story

Crest, a brand made by P&G, was first introduced in 1955 as the first toothpaste clinically proven to help prevent cavities and tooth decay. A new formula was released in 1981. Crest is endorsed by the American Dental Association (ADA) as an "effective decay-preventive dentifrice that can be of significant value". Crest became the leader in the US market. The Crest brand now covers over 20 brands of toothpaste, toothbrushes, mouthwash and dental floss. Crest also has a teeth-whitening product called *Crest Whitestrips*. In 1955, most toothpaste companies, and the market leader Colgate-Palmolive in particular, were mostly concentrated in the cosmetic segment. Crest was the first offering to the latent therapeutic segment. Since then Crest has lost its exclusive therapeutic positioning as most brands today offer a combination of the cosmetic and therapeutic benefits (see Table 8.3). Also, the strong therapeutic positioning of Crest has made its forays in cosmetic dentistry less credible. Same is the case with the foray of the cosmetic Colgate into the therapeutic segment.

Source: Industry.

Benefit segmentation has important implications for the product policy of the firm. Once marketing understands the expectations of a particular consumer group, new or modified products can be developed and aimed at people seeking a specific combination of benefits.

Limitations of benefit segmentation

The greatest difficulty in applying this approach lies in the selection of the benefits to emphasize, mainly in the consumer goods markets. When market analysts ask consumers what benefit they want in a product, they are not likely to provide very new information about product benefits, since they are not highly introspective. If direct market analysis is supplemented with information about consumers' problems, however, new insights can be obtained.

> For example, in the toothpaste market, protection of sensitive teeth is a new benefit promoted by brands having adopted a paramedical positioning. This is the outcome of dental hygiene analysis conducted with the dental profession.

Another difficulty of benefit segmentation stems from this fact: if we are gaining in understanding of consumer preferences, we are losing in terms of knowledge of the socio-demographic profiles of different customer groups. How do we reach, selectively, the "worriers"? Thus, additional information must be collected to be able to describe these segments in socio-demographic terms.

Benefit segmentation analysis requires the collection of primary data, always a costly exercise. In addition, sophisticated multivariate measurement techniques (cluster analysis) must be used to identify the different customer groups. In some cases, however, interesting insights on benefits sought can be obtained through qualitative research, as illustrated in Table 8.4 with an example from the hi-fi chains market.

Segmenting markets with conjoint analysis

The method of conjoint analysis has been described and illustrated in Chapter 7. As explained, the focus of conjoint analysis is on the measurement of buyer preferences for product attribute levels and of the buyer benefits generated by the product attributes. Since measurements are made at the individual level, if preference heterogeneity exists, the market analyst can detect it and regroup individuals displaying the same utilities.

An empirical example will clarify the methodology. The application involves a bimonthly book magazine that publishes new book reviews, book guidance and advice, book digests

Table 8.4 Hi-fi chain market benefit segments and principal benefits sought

- **The technicians**
  - Mean to enjoy high-fidelity sound in its technical aspects.
  - Look for the quality and purity of the sound.
  - Mostly interested by the technical features without being necessarily qualified.
- **The musicians**
  - Mean to enjoy music.
  - Look for the spirit of the music, its musical space and colour.
  - Mostly interested by the musical interpretation without having necessarily a great musical culture.
- **The snobs**
  - Mean to show their resources, taste and aesthetic sense.
  - Look for prestige, demonstration effects and social integration.
  - Often poorly informed, tend to buy what is known and safe.
- **The others**

and short articles. The editor is considering three alternative modifications of the editorial content:

1. Concentrating on book reviews and analyses and dropping all the other editorial sections *(book review)*.
2. Concentrating on guidance and advice on a larger number of books using standardized evaluation grids *(reader's guide)*.
3. Limiting the number of book reviews, but adding a section on literary news with interviews of authors and special topical sections *(literary news)*.

A *do nothing* alternative is also considered, that is, to keep the present editorial content unchanged. As to the selling price, three levels are considered: the present price of €3.8, an increased price of €5.0 and a decreased price of €2.5, the number of pages remaining unchanged (30 pages). A questionnaire was mailed to 500 respondents selected among a group of readers and 171 valid questionnaires were used to estimate the utility functions. A cluster analysis programme was then used to regroup the respondents having the same utilities. As shown in Table 8.5, four different segments were identified:

- In *segment 1*, the respondents seem to be happy with the present editorial content. They react very negatively to the first two alternatives, and positively, but without enthusiasm, to the "literary news" concept.
- In *segment 2*, there is a clear preference for the "book reviews" concept and a negative attitude towards the other two editorial concepts.
- In *segment 3*, it is the "reader's guide" concept which is preferred, the other two being clearly rejected.
- In *segment 4*, the present editorial content is the best alternative, but the range of utilities is also the smallest.

Thus in terms of benefits sought, the four segments are very different. As to the prices, the largest price sensitivity is observed in segment 5, as evidenced by the range, while segments 1 and 2 react in a very similar way, segment 3 being the least price sensitive. Analysis of the composition of these four segments showed that segment 5 was largely composed of librarians, while high-school teachers were an important group in segment 3.

For a comprehensive review of the contributions of conjoint analysis in market segmentation, see Green and Krieger (1991).

Table 8.5 Benefit segmentation through conjoint analysis: book review example

Attributes	Segment 1 (35.5%)	Segment 2 (21.0%)	Segment 3 (11.3%)	Segment 4 (32.2%)
Content	–6.1	1.2	–6.2	–1.8
Book review	–6.4	–6.9	2.9	–3.1
Book guide	0	0	0	0
Present content	*0.3*	*–2.1*	–6.8	*–3.3*
Literary news	6.7	9.1	9.7	3.3
Range				
Price	0.5	0.6	0.3	1.1
Bf100	0	0	0	0
Bf142	*–0.7*	*–0.6*	*–0.4*	*–1.0*
Bf200	1.2	1.2	0.7	2.1
Range				

Source: Adapted from Roisin (1988).

Behavioural segmentation

Usage segmentation attempts to classify consumers on the basis of their actual purchase behaviour in the marketplace. As such, it is also a descriptive and ex-post segmentation method. The criteria most commonly used are product usage, volume purchased and loyalty status:

1. *Product-user segmentation.* A distinction can be made between users, non-users, first users, ex-users, potential users and occasional versus regular users. A different selling and communication approach must be adopted for each of these user categories.
2. *Volume segmentation.* In many markets, a small proportion of customers represents a high percentage of total sales. Often, about 20 per cent of the users account for 80 per cent of total consumption. A distinction between heavy, light and non-users is often very useful. Heavy users, or key accounts, deserve special treatment.
3. *Loyalty segmentation.* Among existing customers a distinction can be made between hard-core loyal, soft-core loyal and switchers. Markets like cigarettes, beers and toothpaste are generally brand-loyal markets. Keeping loyal customers is the objective of relationship marketing. Appropriate marketing strategies can be developed to attract competitors' customers or to increase the loyalty of switchers.

Note that behavioural segmentation – like socio-demographic segmentation – is an ex-post segmentation method based on the internal information system of the firm and on the customer data banks. This method is extensively used in CRM, also called relationship selling.

Socio-cultural or lifestyle segmentation

As mentioned above, socio-demographic criteria are losing predictive value in affluent societies as consumption patterns become more and more personalized. Individuals from the

---

Box 8.4   Implementation problem: how to exploit different price sensitivities per segment?

- Consider a firm having the following target prices: $50 at 20K units and $35 at 50K units. The additional cost of producing a superior version of the same product is $10. Two segments of about the same size exist (20K each) but have different price sensitivity. The luxury segment is not price-sensitive and potential customers are ready to pay $50 for the superior version. The other segment is price-sensitive and will not pay more than $30. What market coverage strategy should be adopted? In what version and at what price should the firm sell the product?

- Costs and profit constraints seem to exceed prices if the firm decides to sell to only one segment at only one price. If the firm targets the low-price segment, the market potential is limited to 20K customers and the maximum acceptable price is $30, while the target price at this level of production is $50. Similarly,

if the firm targets the high price segment, the market potential is 20,000 customers willing to pay $50, but the target price is now $60 ($50+$10). This strategy is also unfeasible.

- A premium price strategy can solve the problem. The firm should produce 50K units and sell 20K units of the standard product for $30 and 20K units of the superior version for $50, for an average target price of $50. The target prices are, respectively, $35 and $55, but the market prices will be $30 and $50. Thus, the firm takes a premium on its higher-priced version and a loss on its lower-priced version, but can profitably produce and sell the product to both segments.

Source: Adapted from Tellis (1986).

same socio-demographic groups can have very different preferences and buying behaviour, and vice versa.

Socio-cultural segmentation, also called *lifestyle* or *psychographic segmentation*, seeks to supplement demographics by adding such elements as activities, attitudes, interests, opinions, perceptions and preferences to obtain a more complete consumer profile. It attempts to draw human portraits of consumers adding detail at the less obvious levels of motivation and personality. Wells and Tigert make the following point:

> Demographics have been and continue to be extremely useful, but they are unsatisfying. They lack colour. They lack texture. They lack dimensionality. They need to be supplemented by something that puts flesh on bare statistical backbone. (Wells and Tigert, 1971)

The basic objective is to relate personality-type variables to consumer behaviour. Lifestyle descriptors are used as proxies for personality traits. "Lifestyle" refers to the overall manner in which people live and spend time and money. A person's lifestyle (or psychographic profile) can be measured and described in a number of ways:

- At the most stable and persistent level is the person's *valuing system and personality traits*, which are, of course, more difficult to measure.
- At an intermediate level, a person's *activities, interests and opinions* reveal his or her value system.
- At a superficial level, but directly observable, consumers' lifestyles are reflected by the *products and services purchased* and by the way in which buyers are using or consuming them.

Valette-Florence (1986) suggests defining a person's lifestyle as the interaction of these three levels: the group of persons having a similar behaviour at each of these levels is homogeneous in terms of lifestyle. Thus a *lifestyle is the outgrowth of a person's value system, attitudes, interests and opinions (AIO) and of the individual's consumption mode*. It describes the sort of person he or she is and at the same time it differentiates him or her from other persons.

Lifestyle studies can be conducted at one of these three levels. The closer we are to actual purchase decisions, the easier the measurements, but also the more volatile the conclusions. The largest majority of empirical lifestyle studies have been conducted at the AIO level, where research measures:

- people's *activities* in terms of how they spend their time,
- their *interests*, what they place importance on in their immediate surroundings, and
- their *opinions* in terms of views of themselves and the world around them.

Table 8.6 lists the elements included in each major dimension of lifestyle. Lifestyle studies provide a broad everyday view of consumers, a living portrait that goes beyond flat socio-demographic descriptions and helps understand actual consumer behaviour.

Limitations of lifestyle segmentation

The results of lifestyle studies are stocked and regularly updated. Factorial analyses are used to uncover principal components or macro-characteristics and meaningful clusters of answers, which correspond to *stereotypes* or *socio-styles* observed in society or within the specific group under study. Two kinds of lifestyle studies can be made: general lifestyle or product-specific lifestyle studies.

General lifestyle studies classify the total population into groups based on general lifestyle characteristics, such as "receptivity to innovation", "family centred", "ecological sensitivity" and so on. Each subgroup represents a different pattern of values and motivations and the analyst can discern which types of consumers are strong prospects for their products, what other things appeal to these prospects and how to communicate with them in the most effective way.

The researchers of the International Research Institute on Social Change (RISC) have identified eight socio-cultural forces that shape our society and in particular European society. They are presented in Exhibit 8.4.

Table 8.6 Lifestyle dimensions

Activities	Interests	Opinions	Demographics
Work	Family	Themselves	Age
Hobbies	Home	Social issue	Education
Social events	Job	Politics	Income
Vacation	Community	Business	Occupation
Entertainment	Recreation	Economics	Family size
Club membership	Fashion	Education	Dwelling
Community	Food	Products	Geography
Shopping	Media	Future	City size
Sports	Achievements	Culture	Life cycle

Source: Adapted from Plummer (1974) and from Valette Florence (1986).

Exhibit 8.4   Forces of social change

- *Self-development.* Affirming oneself as an individual.
- *Hedonism.* Giving priority to pleasure.
- *Plasticity.* Adapting to circumstances.
- *Vitality.* Exploiting one's energy.
- *Connectivity.* Relating to others: clicking in and out, mixing cultures.
- *Ethics.* Searching for authenticity and meaning in life.
- *Belongings.* Defining social links and cultural identities.
- *Inertia.* Actively, or more often passively, resisting change.

Source: Hasson (1995).

Exhibit 8.5   Examples of general lifestyle statements

- I find myself checking the prices in the grocery stores even for small items (price-conscious).
- An important part of my life and activities is dressing smartly (fashion-conscious).
- I would rather spend a quiet evening at home than go out to a party (homebody).
- I like to work on community projects (community-minded).
- I try to arrange my home for my children's convenience (child oriented).
- /.../

The updating of lifestyle data keeps track of the changing emphasis of the different socio-styles and keeps up with the changes in motivation and behaviour of different social sub-groups. The usefulness of lifestyle analyses is twofold:

1. to identify emerging trends and sensitivities within society and to assess the opportunities and threats associated with these changes; it is the dynamic aspect;
2. to determine whether a particular subgroup is ahead of or lagging in a socio-cultural trend; it is the more static aspect of the analysis.

In *product-specific lifestyle* studies, the objective is to understand consumer behaviour related to a particular product or service. The AIO statements are then more product-specific.

To illustrate, here are examples of AIO statements adapted to the credit cards market:

- I like to pay cash for everything I buy.
- I buy many things with a credit card or a charge card.
- In the past year, we have borrowed money from a bank or finance company.
- To buy anything other than a house or a car on credit is unwise.

Lifestyle research methodology also has some important advantages over motivation research and depth interviews: (a) samples are large; (b) conclusions do not rely heavily on interviewer interpretation of relatively unstructured responses; (c) data are easily analysed by a variety of well-understood statistical methods and (d) less highly trained interviewers can be employed.

8.5   MICRO-SEGMENTATION ANALYSIS IN B2B MARKETS

Conceptually, there is no difference between B2B (or industrial) and consumer market segmentation, but the criteria used to segment the market vary greatly. The same distinction between macro- and micro-segmentation can be made. The method of macro-segmentation described earlier in this chapter is of direct application. The micro-segmentation criteria tend to be different, however.

Descriptive segmentation

The simplest way to segment industrial markets is to use broad firmographic characteristics describing the profile of the B2B customer, such as industrial sectors (NACE or Standard Industrial Classification (SIC) category), company size, geographic location, shareholder composition or end-market served. This information is easily accessible since this type of data is readily available through government agencies, which publish detailed industrial classifications. Many companies choose to have separate sales service for large and small customers. The company directly services large customers while distributors will deal with small customers.

In a segmentation analysis of the *Corporate Banking* market, one key finding of the research was to discover that a rather large number of NGOs (social and charity) had in fact substantial financial funds – therefore representing an attractive segment for banks – while the majority of banking services offered were designed for profit organizations and poorly adapted to the specific needs of NGOs.

A typical segmentation grid is presented in Table 8.7.

Table 8.7   Typical segmentation grid comparative analysis of the segments profiles

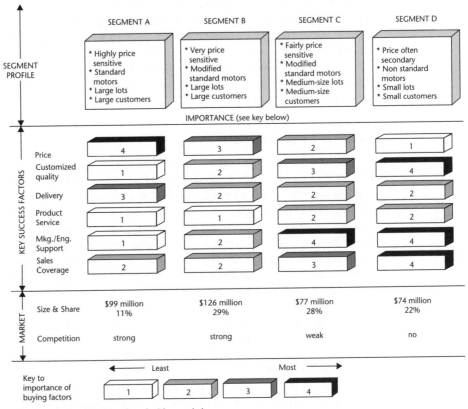

Source: Adapted from Day (1990). Reproduced with permission.

Benefit segmentation

As for consumer goods, *benefit segmentation* is the most natural method. It is based on the specific needs, in general well defined, of the B2B customer. In industrial markets, this means classifying the customers by type of industry or by end-use. End-users are generally looking for different benefits, performance or functions in a product. Industrial products often have a wide range of possible uses, for instance, in electric motors, ball bearings, steel sheets. The classification by industry type points out the priority needs and their relative importance.

By way of illustration, let us consider the case of a company specializing in the manufacture of small electric motors, a product that has a very large number of possible uses. For each end-use, beyond the core function, one or several product characteristics may be particularly important. This is the case for the following three industrial applications:

- Motors incorporated in petrol pumps: security norms (spark-free) are essential.
- Motors incorporated into computers or in medical instruments used in hospitals: the response time must be instantaneous.
- Motors incorporated in industrial sewing machines; resistance to frequent stopping and starting is important and fast reaction is secondary.

The functions of an industrial good and their importance in the customer's industrial process vary according to whether it is a major equipment good (turnkey factory, steel mill, alternator) or secondary equipment good (radiator, light trucks, typewriter); semi-finished intermediate products (coated steel sheets); parts to be incorporated (electric motors, gear shifts); finished goods (tools, oil); raw materials (coal, grease, polyurethane foam); services (engineering, industrial cleaning, maintenance) In each case, the perceived economic value of the product by the customer will be very different.

It is important to recall that in many B2B sectors, sales are based on orders with detailed specifications. In this type of market situation, the product is naturally adjusted to the particular needs of the customer.

Behavioural segmentation

Behavioural *segmentation* is important for industrial markets. Its purpose is to develop a strategy for approaching B2B customers according to their structures and the way their buying decision centre operates (see Figure 8.7). The buying process can be more or less formalized according to the complexity of decisions and organizational structures.

In some companies, buying is centralized and precise rules govern the purchase decisions. Other companies, in contrast, decentralize buying and the approach to such a company will be similar to that used for a smaller firm. Other characteristics of the buying centre are also important: motivations of different members of the buying team, the different forces at play between the representatives of different functions, the degree of formalism and the length of time necessary for a decision. These behavioural characteristics are not usually directly observable and thus are often hard to identify. However, as seen above, these are important things for salespeople to be aware of.

Because of the complexity and variety of possible bases for segmentation industrial markets, Shapiro and Bonona (1983) have expanded the use of macro- and micro-segmentation into what is called a *"nested approach"*. This method assumes a hierarchical structure of segmentation bases that move from very broad or general bases to very organization-specific bases. Rather than a two-step process, the nested approach allows three, four or five steps. The list of segmentation criteria is presented in Table 8.8.

Benefit segmentation is also easier in industrial markets than in consumer markets, because users are professional people who have less difficulty in expressing their needs and in qualifying the relative importance of different product attributes.

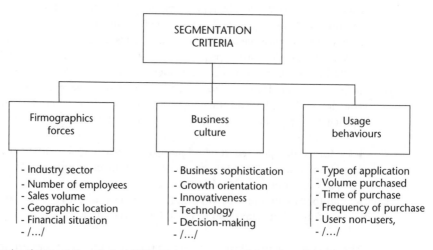

Figure 8.7   Examples of segmentation criteria in B2B markets

Table 8.8 Industrial segmentation: the nested approach

Organizational demographics	Situation factors
– Industry sectors	– Urgency
– Company size	– Application
– Geographic location	– Size of order
Operating variables	**Personal Characteristics**
– Technology	– Motivation
– User–non-user status	– Buyer and seller relationship
– Customer capabilities	– Risk perception
Purchasing approaches	
– Decision centre organization	
– Purchasing policies	
– Purchasing criteria	

Source: Adapted from Shapiro and Bonona (1983).

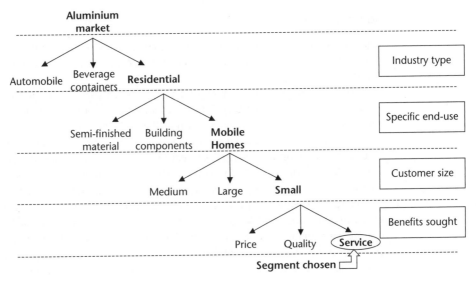

Figure 8.8 Segmentation of the aluminium market
Source: Industry.

In practice several segmentation methods are used simultaneously as illustrated in Figure 8.8 presenting a segmentation analysis of the aluminium market.

8.6   REQUIREMENTS FOR EFFECTIVE SEGMENTATION

Before examining the targeting and positioning decisions, a preliminary question must be raised, however: to verify to what extent the requirements for effective segmentation are met. To be effective and useful a segmentation analysis should identify segments that meet five criteria: differential response, adequate size, measurability, accessibility and actionability (Kotler, 1967/2006).

Differential response

This is the most important criterion to consider when choosing a segmentation strategy. The segments must be different in terms of their sensitivity to one or several marketing variables under the control of the firm. The segmentation variable should maximize the behavioural difference between segments (heterogeneity condition) while minimizing the differences among customers within a segment (homogeneity condition).

A key requirement is to avoid segment overlapping, the risk being the possibility of cannibalism among products of the same company but targeted to different segments. The more a product has distinctive and observable characteristics, the more homogeneous the segment will be.

We must, however, remember that segment homogeneity does not necessarily imply that all categories of buyers are mutually exclusive. An individual may of course belong to more than one segment. Products from different segments may be bought by the same person for different people within the household, for different types of use or just for the sake of variety. Observation of shopping trolleys outside a supermarket often shows that brands from both the high and the low end of the range have been purchased at the same time. One segment does not necessarily cover the buyers, but rather the products purchased by the buyers.

Adequate size

Segments should be defined so that they represent enough potential customers to provide sufficient sales revenue to justify the development of different products and marketing programmes.

Identified segments must represent a market potential large enough to justify developing a specific marketing strategy. This condition affects not only the size of the segment in volume and frequency of buying but also its life cycle. All markets are affected by fashion. It is essential to verify that the targeted niche is not temporary and that the product's lifespan is economically long. Finally, the size requirement also implies that the added value of the product, because of its specificity, will be financially worthwhile, in the sense that the market price acceptable by the target segment is sufficiently rewarding for the firm.

Meeting this requirement often implies a trade-off between two logics: the logic of marketing management, which tries to meet the needs of the market through a narrow definition of segments in order to adapt the firm's offering to the diversity of market needs as best as possible, and the logic of operations management, which emphasizes the benefits of economies of scale through standardization and long production runs.

Measurability

Before target segments can be selected, the size, purchasing power and major behaviour characteristics of the identified segments must be measured. If the segmentation criteria used are very abstract, such information is hard to find. For example, if the prospects were companies of a certain size, it would be easy to find information about their number, location, turnover and so on. But a segmentation criterion like "innovativeness of companies" does not lend itself to easy measurement and the firm would probably have to conduct its own market survey. Abstract criteria are often used in benefit and lifestyle segmentations, while descriptive segmentation is based on more concrete and observable criteria.

Accessibility

Accessibility refers to the degree to which a market segment can be reached through a unique marketing programme. There are two ways to reach prospects:

- *Customer self-selection* involves reaching a more general target while relying on the product and appeal of advertising to the intended target group. These consumers themselves select the product by paying attention to the advertisements.

- *Controlled coverage* is very efficient because the firm reaches target customers with little wasted coverage of individuals or firms who are not potential buyers.

Controlled coverage is more efficient from the firm's point of view. This communication strategy implies a good knowledge of the socio-demographic profile of the target group, which is not always the case when using benefit or lifestyle segmentation.

Actionability

Specific marketing programme(s) can be formulated and implemented to reach the target segment(s).

8.7   EMERGENCE OF TRANSNATIONAL MARKET SEGMENTS

In the Triad countries, one observes the existence of *transnational segments*, that is, groups of consumers present in each country and having the same needs and expectations. Thus globalization need not mean standardization of lifestyles across countries. In the world today, in parallel with the globalization of the economy, there has been an explosion of identity crises among nations, regions, religions, ethnic and linguistic groups having the desire to maintain and to claim their cultural difference. So globalization does not mean uniformity.

> The fact that one dominant country tends today, consciously or not, to impose its culture, its language, its life styles can create the illusion of uniformity. But behind a superficial layer of uniformity created by a few popular brands (always the same: Disney, Hollywood, McDonald, Coca-Cola, Marlboro, CNN ...) are hidden important cultural, religious, racial and linguistic differences.

We are confronted with a paradox. The interdependence of markets referred to above, combined with this cultural fragmentation, results in a cultural convergence, thereby creating transnational market segments, that is, groups of consumers present in each country and having the same needs and expectations. Thus globalization need not mean standardization of lifestyles across countries. It simply means that, across countries, there are groups of consumers with the same profiles that can be approached with the same brands and communication campaigns.

> It is still difficult today to refer to a European consumer, even if one observes a growing convergence in life styles and in consuming habits within the European Union. By contrast, there are numerous trans-national segments such as executives of international companies, students in management, sport professionals, high-fashion conscious women, etc.

The affirmation of the individual and the identity crisis forces companies to adopt a *mass-customization strategy* whereby goods and services are individually customized in high volumes but at relatively low cost. Flexible manufacturing and electronic commerce make possible today this mass-customization approach.

With the globalization of the world economy, opportunities are growing to create demand for universal products. International segmentation is a way in which a global approach can be adopted to sell a physically similar product worldwide. The objective is to discover in different countries and/or regions groups of buyers having the same expectations and requirements *vis-à-vis* products, despite cultural and national differences. Those segments, even if they are small in size within each country, may represent in total a very attractive opportunity for the international firm. To adjust to local differences, the physical product can be customized through services, accessories or inexpensive product modifications. The potential for globalization is not the same for each product category and different approaches can be adopted. For a review of the literature on this topic, see Gupta and Westney (2003).

Chapter Summary

In a market-oriented company, the target market is identified in the buyer's perspective, that is, by reference to the "solution" sought by the customer and not in technical terms. Given the diversity of buyers' expectations, the choice of a target market implies the partitioning of the total market into subgroups of potential customers with similar needs and behavioural characteristics. A first level of market segmentation, called macro-segmentation, splits the market by reference to three criteria: (a) solutions or functions performed, (b) groups of buyers and (c) technologies. A key output of this exercise is a segmentation grid, which can help to decide on the market coverage strategy, and which can also be used as an instrument to discover new potential segments. The objective of micro-segmentation is to analyse the diversity of potential customer profiles in a more detailed way within each previously identified macro-segment. Four micro-segmentation methods exist which each have their own merits and weaknesses: socio-demographic, benefit, lifestyle and behavioural segmentation. Different market coverage strategies can be considered: undifferentiated or standardized marketing, differentiated or focused marketing. To be effective, a segmentation strategy must meet four criteria: differential response, adequate size, measurability and accessibility. International segmentation is a key issue in global marketing. The objective is to identify supranational or universal segments that can be reached with a standardized marketing programme.

BIBLIOGRAPHY

Abell, D.F. (1980), *Defining the Business: The Starting Point of Strategic Planning,* Englewood Cliffs, NJ, Prentice-Hall.

Coriolis Research (2000), *Organics in the United Kingdom: A Market Overview,* Research Report, November.

Day, G.S. (1990), *Strategic Market Planning,* St Paul, MN, West Publishing.

Deutsch, C.H. (1997), A New High-Tech Code: From Widgets to Service, *International Herald Tribune.*

Green, P.E. and Krieger, A.M. (1991), Segmenting Markets with Conjoint Analysis, *Journal of Marketing,* 55, 4, pp. 20–31.

Gupta, A.K. and Westney, D.E. (eds) (2003), *Smart Globalization,* Boston, MA, Jossey-Bass, A Wiley Reprint.

Hasson, L. (1995), Monitoring Social Change, *Journal of the Market Research Society,* 37, pp. 69–80.

Hopkins, D.S. (1982), *The Marketing Plan,* New York, The Conference Board.

Kotler, P. (1967/2006), *Marketing Management,* Upper Saddle River, NJ, Prentice-Hall, 12th edition.

Lambin, J.J. (2000/2007*), Market-Driven Management: Strategic and Operational Marketing,* London, Palgrave Macmillan.

Lambin, J.J. and Hiller, T.B. (1993), *Volvo Trucks Europe,* in *Strategic Marketing Problems,* Kerin, R.A. and Peterson, R.A. (eds), Boston, MA, Allyn & Bacon.

Plummer, J.T. (1974), The Concept and Application of Life Style Segmentation, *Journal of Marketing,* 38, 1, pp. 33–7.

Roisin, J. (1988), *Etude du concept d'une revue littéraire: une application de l'analyse conjointe,* Louvain-la-Neuve, IAG.

Shapiro, B.P. and Bonona, T.V. (1983), *Segmenting Industrial Markets,* Lexington, MA, Lexington Books.

Smith, W. (1956), Product Differentiation and Market Segmentation as Alternative Marketing Strategies, *Journal of Marketing*, 21, 1, pp. 3–8

Tellis, G.C. (1986), Beyond the Many Faces of Price: An Integration of Pricing Strategies, *Journal of Marketing*, 50, 4, pp. 146–60.

Wells, W.D. and Tigert, D.J. (1971), Activities, Interests and Opinions, *Journal of Advertising Research*, 11, 4, pp. 27–35.

Yorke, D.A. (1982), The Definition of Market Segments for Banking Services, *European Journal of Marketing*, 16, 3, pp. 14–22.

CHAPTER NINE

MARKET ATTRACTIVENESS ANALYSIS

The output of a segmentation analysis takes the form of a segmentation grid displaying the different segments or product markets, which belong to the reference market. The next task is to assess the business opportunity of each of these segments in order to decide which segment(s) to target. Attractiveness analysis has the objective of measuring and forecasting the size, life cycle and profit potential of each segment or product market. Measuring the sales potential of a market is the responsibility of strategic marketing. These market projections will then be used by general management to calibrate investments and production capacity. Market potential forecasting and measurement is a key input for these decisions. The objective of this chapter is to review the major concepts of demand analysis and in particular the concept of virtual market.

Learning Objectives

When you have read this chapter, you should be able to:

- Describe the major concepts of demand analysis
- Understand the concepts of virtual and meta-markets
- Explain the structure of demand for consumer and industrial goods, for durable and non-durable goods and for services
- Explain how to detect growth opportunities in a given market through gap analysis
- Describe the PLC model and its strategic implications
- Understand the financial implications of the PLC

9.1 BASIC CONCEPTS IN DEMAND ANALYSIS

At its simplest level, the demand for a product or service is the quantity sold. At the outset it is important to distinguish clearly between two levels of demand: primary demand or total market demand and company demand (also called selective demand).

The primary demand for a particular product is the total sales volume bought by a defined customer group, in a defined geographic area, time period, economic and macro-marketing environment.

The term *"product category need"* or *"category need"* is also commonly used. Thus, primary demand measurement implies prior definition of the segment or product market. Also, it is a function of both environmental and total industry marketing efforts.

> Company demand is the company or brand's share of primary demand in the product category in a specific product market or segment.

Any diagnostic of a given firm or brand performance makes implicit reference to these two notions. Let us examine the following three fictitious cases.

1. Brand A's sales in volume have a yearly growth of 15 per cent, a result which seems very satisfactory. Given that primary demand in the reference market is also growing by 15 per cent the brand's performance is modest having simply succeeded to keep its market share unchanged.
2. With the same growth rate of 15 per cent for brand A, if primary demand has increased instead by 20 per cent, the performance is very mediocre since brand A has a decreasing market share in a fast-growing market. By contrast, if primary demand's growth is only 10 per cent, brand A's performance is excellent.
3. Finally, if brand A's sales are declining in volume by 5 per cent, while primary demand is declining by 10 per cent, brand A's performance is also very good with a growing market share in a declining market.

Thus, any interpretation of brand A's performance is dependent on the selected benchmark that will be determined by the segmentation of the reference market.

Expansible versus non-expansible primary demand

Two well-differentiated market situations can be observed: markets where primary demand is expansible and markets where demand is stagnant and non-expansible.

> Primary demand is said to be *expansible*, when it is influenced by the macro-marketing environment and by the size and intensity of total marketing efforts.

This situation will prevail in the introduction and growth phases of the PLC of a product new to the world (see below), when the market occupation rate (horizontal coverage) and the penetration rates (vertical coverage) are weak (say below 20 per cent).

> Primary demand is said to be non-expansible when the level of total sales is not affected by the macro-marketing environment and by the marketing efforts of the competing firms. Markets are stagnant.

This situation is observed in the markets that have reached maturity, where market occupation and penetration rates are very high and where replacement demand for durable goods is the largest part of market sales. In this type of market situation, the firm knows that any major increase of its sales will come only through an increase of its market share.

Primary demand as response function

Primary demand is not a fixed number but a function, which relates the level of sales to its causes, termed *"demand determinants"*. The causes of sales are twofold: external or uncontrollable factors linked to the macro-marketing environment and controllable factors represented by the total marketing efforts made by the competing firms in the market.

The impact of marketing factors

The relationship between primary demand and total industry marketing efforts is depicted in Figure 9.1. The response function is S-shaped with total demand on the vertical axis and total marketing intensity on the horizontal axis. The curve of Figure 9.1 is defined assuming a constant macro-marketing environment.

Typically, the relationship is not linear. Some minimum level of demand (Q_0) will occur at zero marketing intensity; as the total marketing pressure on the market increases, sales also increase, but at a decreasing rate. Beyond a certain level of marketing intensity, primary demand reaches an upper limit (Q_m) called the "saturation level" or the *"current market potential"*.

The impact of the macro-marketing environment

The level of primary demand is influenced not only by the total marketing efforts made by the firms operating in the segment, but also by environmental factors. A change in the socio-economic environment will move the response curve vertically, as illustrated in

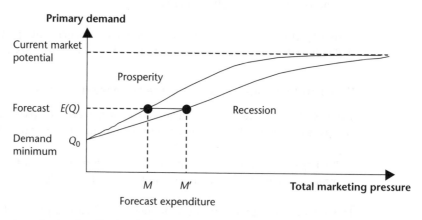

Figure 9.1 Primary demand as function of total marketing efforts

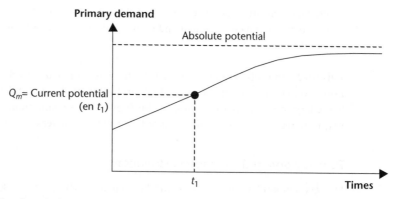

Figure 9.2 AMP is time-dependent

Figure 9.2. A distinction must be made, therefore, between a movement along the response curve and a shift of the response curve itself.

> Two scenarios are represented in Figure 9.1 a scenario of prosperity and a scenario of recession. Under the prosperity scenario, the forecast or expected level of total sales is E(Q), assuming the level M for total industry marketing effort. Now, if the recession scenario prevails, to achieve the same sales volume, total marketing effort should be at the level M′ and not M.

Firms cannot do much about the prevailing market scenario, except to try to anticipate future environmental conditions as best as possible. In the turbulent and disruptive environment of the 2000s this is a particularly difficult task and many firms are systematically developing alternative scenarios (such as a worst case scenario) to increase their capacity to react quickly to a disruptive change in the environment.

Absolute versus current market potential

One can establish a distinction between current market potential as defined above and absolute market potential (AMP). As illustrated in Figure 9.1, the *current market potential* is the limit approached by primary demand as total industry marketing efforts tend towards infinity, in a given environment and in a given time period.

The AMP defines the upper limit of the market size under the somewhat artificial assumption of optimum market coverage.

Thus, AMP corresponds to the total sales level (in volume or value) that would be observed under three assumptions:

- Everyone who could reasonably be expected to use the product is using it.
- Everyone who is using it is using it on every use occasion.
- Every time the product is used, it is used to the fullest extent possible (full dosage, full serving, and so on).

The concept is useful for assessing the size of a business opportunity and for estimating the growth opportunity in a particular market given the present level of primary demand.

The AMP is time-dependent, as illustrated in Figure 9.2. Its evolution over time under the influence of diffusion and contagion effects are caused by external factors such as change in level of prices, government regulations and so on. The firm has no direct control over these factors, yet they have a decisive influence on the development of the market. Occasionally, firms are indirectly able to influence these external causes (through lobbying, for instance), but their power is limited. Most of the firm's efforts, therefore, are directed towards the anticipation of changes in the environment.

9.2 BUSINESS OPPORTUNITY ANALYSIS IN A VIRTUAL MARKET

The development of Internet technology and of electronic commerce has enlarged considerably the size of the potential market by making virtual markets accessible by the firm. Virtual markets lead to an offering or to an assortment of offerings defined by reference to all the activities undertaken and all the services sought by the customer to achieve a specific generic result. While in general markets are organized around the supply of products and services, the customer purchasing process is structured by reference to activities that are linked in his (or her) cognitive space.

The cognitive space of the customer

To achieve the generic result sought, customers engage in different activities directly or indirectly related to the desired outcome. Thus, a virtual market represents an end-to-end temporal sequence of logically related activities in the cognitive space of customers.

> For example, as illustrated in Figure 4.4 below (see page 90) to achieve the "home ownership" generic need, customers might engage with contractors, realtors, insurance companies, mortgage firms, removal companies, telecom, interior designers, etc.

Similarly, in the personal mobility virtual market, in addition to car purchasing, related activities cover car maintenance, car insurance, roadside assistance, emergency services dispatch, route support, stolen vehicle location and so on.

In a virtual market, the activities undertaken by potential customers generally cut across traditional industry and product market boundaries and are not necessarily in the traditional core business of the firm. As a result, virtual markets absorb a much higher proportion of customer spending than a specific product market and represent a higher market potential. Thus to confine the market to the product market may be misleading, as illustrated by the case of Lego, the Danish toy company presented in Exhibit 9.1.

The challenge for the firm is to move from the rather abstract concept of virtual market to the "meta-market" (Sawhney, 1999; Sawhney, Balasubramanian and Krishnan, 2004) that consists in an offering or in an assortment of offerings defined by reference to all the elements (activities and services) which comprise the cognitive space of the client. In other words, a meta-market is created when the cognitive association between different logically related activities are reproduced in the physical marketplace, thereby streamlining customer activities and providing them with seamless experience.

How to build a meta-market?

The virtual market concept is at the foundation of the "solution-to-a-problem" approach. Increasingly, market-oriented companies aim to partnering with their customers and to becoming a "solution provider" by assembling a unique combination of products and services that could solve a customer's problem. The implications for a solution-based organization are summarized in Box 9.1.

Exhibit 9.1   The virtual market of the Lego Company

In 1995, the Lego Company has a worldwide market share of 72 per cent in the construction toy market. But children were spending more spare time with computers, video games and television than with traditional toys. So while Lego had been gaining market share in its traditional product market, toys in general and construction toys in particular had been losing their share of children's spare time activities. In fact, the generic need addressed by Lego is family "edutainement" (education-entertainment) and not simply construction toy. The generic need can be defined as "having fun and exercising the mind". The Lego virtual market is a convergence of toys, education, interactive technology, software, computers and consumer electronics.

Source: Example quoted by Sawhney, Balasubramanian and Krishnan (2004).

Internet technology makes this solution approach more achievable.

The *benefits* of the meta-market concept are important.

- The concept is perfectly aligned on the customer views and thereby facilitates communication.
- The revenue potential of a meta-market is always larger than the discrete product market.
- It enables the firm to offer a total solution to customers, thereby building exclusivity, loyalty and trust.
- It helps identification of growth opportunities in activities directly or indirectly related to the core service.
- It helps identifying who are the indirect or potential competitors.

An example of meta-market is presented in Figure 9.3. Kodak is the leader in helping people take, share, print and view images for information or for entertainment. Today, Kodak has created new services designed to provide to consumers a total solution to help consumers

---

Box 9.1   Implementation problem: how to build a meta-market?

- Do not define your reference market in terms of product categories (cars, metallic grids, construction toys, etc.).
- Refer to the result or the generic outcome customers want to achieve (personal mobility, access control, edutainment, etc.).
- Identify all the activities which, from the customer point of view, are part of the virtual market.

- Create the reference meta-market by reproducing in the physical marketplace the mental associations made by the customers.
- If necessary, augment the internal capabilities of the company by finding the right solution partners.
- Present to customers the total solution they seek.

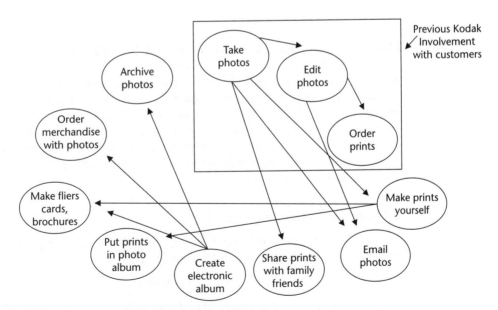

Figure 9.3   The meta-market of Kodak in the digital photography market
Source: Adapted from Sawhney, Balasubramanian and Krishnan (2004).

"manage and share memories" using digital photography. Until the advent of digital photography, Kodak's involvement with customers ended with when they ordered prints. The company has since found ways to add significantly to its interaction with consumers, namely, through the acquisition of a start-up called Ofoto (Sawhney, Balasubramanian and Krishnan, 2004).

The customer activity chain concept

In seeking a particular outcome, customers engage in activities. These activities can be mapped along a customer activity chain (Vandermerwe, 1993, 2000), which describes a sequence of directly or indirectly related activities undertaken by customers before, during or after the purchasing decision.

- Before, when customers are deciding what to do.
- During, when customers are doing what they decided upon.
- After, when customers are maintaining the results obtained (reviewing, renewing, extending, upgrading, updating and so on).

This methodology can help managers to assess the opportunities for providing new kinds of services in filling gaps in the activity chain that could give access to competitors. The case of IBM is interesting in this respect.

> In the late 1980, IBM was so fixated on PCs and mainframes (viewing itself as hardware provider) that it allowed consultants, software houses, procurements specialists and third-party maintenance providers to leap into IBM's value gaps and siphon off both customers and potential wealth from the "global-networking-capability" market space. (Vandermerwe, 2000, p. 32)

Having redefined its business in terms of a solution provider of global networking capabilities, today IBM earns more money from value-add-on services than from its hardware, software and middleware.

9.3   STRUCTURE OF PRIMARY DEMAND FOR CONSUMER GOODS

Demand analysis, measurement and forecast are the primary responsibility of market research. The goal is to estimate in quantitative terms the size of the market potential and the current level of demand, and to formulate forecasts of its future development over a number of years. Aggregate estimates of total demand are rarely available and the role of the market analyst is to identify and estimate the key components of market potential. The structure of demand is different for consumer products (durable or non-durable goods), for industrial goods and for services.

Demand for consumer goods

Demand estimates are usually based on two factors: the number of potential consuming units (n) and the quantity purchased per unit (q). Thus, we have

$$Q = n \times q$$

Where "Q" designates total demand in units. Similarly, total sales revenue will be given by

$$R = n \times Q \times P$$

Where *"R"* denotes total sales revenue and *"P"* the average price per unit. The empirical measurement of these basic concepts raises different issues depending on the type of product category. We will examine the demand structure for the main product categories.

Demand for non-durable consumer products

If the consumer good is *not linked to the use of a durable good*, total demand can be estimated in the following way:

- Number of potential consuming units.
- Proportion of customers using the product (market occupation rate).
- Size or frequency of purchases (market penetration rate).

The distinction between *occupation rate* and *penetration rate* is important to identify the priority objectives in a market development strategy: increase the number of users or increase the average quantity used per user.

Exhibit 9.2   The case of the Dutch Construction Group Heimans N.V.: interview with its CEO

Both individuals and organizations are now looking for construction companies that can provide a complete set of services: design, financing, construction maintenance and other services. This is why we have decided to increase our activity in the front end of the value chain – in particular activities giving us a greater grip on the development phases of a project – from its current level of 25 per cent to 35 per cent by 2008. We also want to increase our presence at the back end of the value chain – namely, more maintenance activities and take it from its current level of 5 per cent to 20 per cent in 2008.

We need to bolster our full-service offerings through partnership not only with our customers, but also with our suppliers and sub-contractors. This is the exciting part of a growing business like ours, because it marks a historical turn in the company's development: from a technologically driven entity to a market-driven service provider.

Source: Bain and Company News Letter (2004).

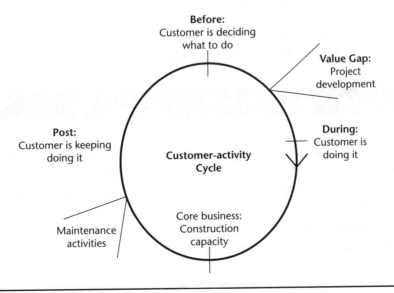

The AMP is determined by assuming a 100 per cent occupation rate and the optimum penetration per use occasion. The current level of primary demand implies data on current purchasing behaviour. These data can sometimes be obtained from trade associations, from government publications or through primary market research. A major problem in measuring current demand is the degree to which purchase rates vary among different customer groups. Only primary sources of market research, such as consumer panels, can provide this type of data.

If the consumer good is *linked to the use of a durable good* (soap and washing machines, for instance), the equipment rate of the consuming units must be considered, in addition to the utilization rate of the equipment. We thus have:

- Number of potential consuming units.
- Rate of equipment of these consuming units.
- Equipment utilization rate.
- Consumption rate per use occasion.

Here also, the AMP can be determined assuming a 100 per cent equipment rate, an average utilization rate and an average consumption rate that is technically defined in most cases. As for the estimation of the level of current market demand, primary market research data are necessary.

Demand for durable consumer goods

In this case, a distinction must be made between first equipment demand and replacement demand. The components of *first equipment demand* are:

- number of effective users and rate of increase of their equipment rate, and
- number of new users and equipment rate of these new using units.

The diffusion rate is an important factor in the growth of first equipment demand within the target population. The analysis of penetration curves for similar products is very useful in this respect.

Replacement demand is more complex to estimate. The following components of replacement demand must be identified and estimated:

- Size of the current population.
- Age distribution of the current population.

Exhibit 9.3   Estimation of primary demand for diapers

N = number of children below three years age

h = Per cent of children using disposable diapers (occupation rate or horizontal penetration)

q = number of diapers used per child and per year (penetration rate or vertical penetration)

Current level of primary demand

N = 330,000 children below three years of age (110,000 births per year)

h = 90 per cent of children using diapers

q = 6 diapers per day (7 per day up to 2.5 years old and 1 after) or 2,200 per year.

$Q = N \times h \times q$ = 653.4 million of diapers per year, or 90 per cent of the AMP.

Source: Authors.

- Service life of the equipment (technical, economic or fashion obsolescence).
- Scrappage rate.
- Substitution effect (new technologies).
- Mortality rate of users.

Replacement demand is directly dependent on the rate at which owners scrap a product because of wearing out or obsolescence. Market analysts can estimate *scrappage rates* by examining either the technical service life of a product or the historical long-term rate of voluntary scrappage.

If historical data on scrappage rates can be calculated from a sample of users, market analysts can use actuarial methods to estimate the replacement potential for products of different ages.

Replacement demand depends directly on the size of the current population and on the service life of the durable good. The replacement rate is not necessarily identical to the scrappage rate. Scrappage rate designates the fraction of the stock of existing durable goods which is sent to breakage, or, in other words, which disappears. A durable good can be obsolete because its economic performance has become inferior or simply because it is out of fashion in the eyes of the users.

> In general, one tends to consider that scrappage rates are proportional to the length of the physical life cycle of the products of a given product category. In other words, if the average duration is 12 years, the annual scrappage rate should in theory be equal to its reciprocal, that is, 8.3 per cent.

The predictions made about the technical service life of a durable good will have a direct impact on the expected level of primary demand in the years to come.

Some of the data required to estimate the size of primary demand can be derived from times series sales data, namely, the size of the population and its age distribution. The age distribution can also be estimated through sampling of car owners, for instance, when they decide to replace their old equipment. The estimated replacement rates do not permit us to identify, however, the type of obsolescence responsible for the replacement decision. A technically well-functioning product can be replaced for economic reasons; for instance, if

---

Exhibit 9.4   Primary demand for soap in dishwashing machines (Households segment)

Primary demand $= Q = N \times e \times f \times q$

N = number of potential consuming units (number of households)

e = equipment rate (per cent of households with dishwasher)

f = use frequency of the equipment (number of use per week $\times$ 52)

q = quantity used per use occasion (quantity of soap per usage)

Example: Estimation of primary demand for soap for dishwashing machines

N = 420,000 households

e = 37 per cent of households having the equipment

f = 4 uses in average per week, or 200 per year

q = 1 scoop of 20 g per use occasion

$Q = N \times e \times f \times q$ = 6,216 tons of diswasher soap per year

The AMP can be calculated by taking maximum values for e, f and q.

Source: Lambin (2007).

Exhibit 9.5   Estimation of primary demand for television sets

Q = First equipment demand + Replacement demand

$Q = [(n \times \Delta e) + (\Delta n \times e)] + [t \times (s + 1/v)]$

n = number of consuming units
(number of households)

Δe = Increase of the equipment rate
(Δ of average number of TV/household)

Δn = Net increase of new consuming units
(number of new households – death)

e = Equipment rate of households
(average number of TV/new household)

t = size of the TV population
(number of TV sets)

v = average life
(number of years of a TV set)

s = substitution rate
(per cent of TV replaced by new models)

Example: Estimation of primary demand for TV sets

N = 4,200,000 households

Δe = 2 per cent of households having a TV and buying another each year

Δn = 35,000 new households per year

e = 1.2 TV per new household

t = 5,000,000 TV (4,200,000 × 1,2)

s = 5 per cent of replacement by a new model

v = Life 10 years (or 10 per cent of replacement for technical deficiency)

$Q = [(n \times \Delta e) + (\Delta n \times e)] + [t \times (s + 1/v)]$

$Q = [(4,200,000 \times 0,02) + (35,000 \times 1.2)] + [5,000,000 \times (5\% + 10\%)]$

Q = 80,000 additional TV per household already equipped with a TV + 42,000 TV for new households + 25,000 TV of new models + 50,000 defective TV

Q = 197,000 TV per year

The AMP can be calculated by using maximum values for Δe, e, s and v.

Source: Lambin (2007).

---

the operating costs of newly developed products are sharply reduced. It can also be replaced for psychological reasons when the user is sensitive to the design of the new models. Finally, at the time of the replacement decision, the buyer can also decide to switch to another product category performing the same core function.

Significant technical progress has been made in the market of central heating systems, with low temperature boilers, which are much more economical in terms of fuel consumption. This innovation has accelerated the replacement rate of existing boilers. In parallel, other technologies have also improved their technical performance, like heat pumps that, for many applications, were substituted for traditional fuel heating systems.

In most Western economies' markets, household equipment rates are very high and close to the maximum and therefore the largest share of sales of durable goods correspond to a replacement decision.

9.4   THE DEMAND FOR CONSUMER SERVICES

The demand structure for services can be estimated as described above for consumer goods. It depends on the number of potential consumers and on the frequency rate of use of the service. Services have, however, a certain number of characteristics that greatly impact the marketing management of them. These characteristics are due to their intangible and perishable nature and to the fact that their production implies direct contact with the service person or organization. The managerial implications of these characteristics are significant (Shostack, 1977; Berry, 1980; Eiglier and Langeard, 1987).

Classification of services

There are a large variety of services and several attempts have been made to classify them in a meaningful way. One classification system is based on the evolution of services in five categories:

1. *Unskilled personal services.* This category includes housekeeping, janitorial work, street cleaning and so on, as observed in a traditional society.
2. *Skilled personal services.* These emerged as society became more industrialized as it passed out of the subsistence stage, as needs arose for government services, repair businesses and retail/wholesale specialists.
3. *Professional services.* As products became more plentiful, highly skilled specialists appeared, such as lawyers, accountants, consultants and marketing researchers.
4. *Mass consumer services.* Discretionary income gave rise to any number of consumer service industries that flourished because of scale effects. These include national and international transport, lodging, fast food, car rental and entertainment companies.
5. *High-tech business services.* The growth in the use of sophisticated technologies has created a need for new services as well as more efficient older ones. Thus, in recent years, we have seen a rapid growth in repair services relating to information processing, telecommunications and other electronic products.

Services can also be classified by whether they are *equipment or people-based*, by the *extent of customer contact*, by a *public or private* organization.

Unique service characteristics

Intangibility of services

Services are *immaterial*. They exist only once produced and consumed. They cannot be inspected before purchase and the selling activity must necessarily precede the production activity. As the consumer goods firm, the service firm is selling a *promise of satisfaction*. But, contrary to a consumer good, the service sold has no physical support, except the organizational system of the service firm when visible to the customer. The service cannot be seen, touched, smelled, heard or tasted prior to the purchase, except when service firms have tangible assets or physical structures (buildings, aircraft, hotel facilities and so on) that are used to perform the service.

Thus, from the buyer's point of view the uncertainty is much larger and the communication role of the firm is to reduce that uncertainty by providing physical evidence, signs, symbols or indicators of quality. On this topic, see Levitt (1965) and Zeithmal, Parasuraman and Berry (1990).

Perishability of services

Since services are intangible, they cannot be stored. The service firm has a service production capacity, which can be used only when demand is expressed. Demand peaks cannot be accommodated and the potential business is lost.

For example, if an airliner takes off with 20 empty seats, the revenue that these 20 seats could have produced is lost forever. In contrast, if a pair of jeans does not sell today, a retailer can store it and sell it at a later time.

Perishability can cause the reverse to occur. Demand can be greater than supply. In this situation, for example, the airline does not have enough seats for everyone. Customers are left at the gate and the sale is lost.

Thus, a key challenge for service firms is to better synchronize supply and demand, by adjusting production capacity, that is, by reshaping supply, but also by reshaping demand through pricing incentives and promotions.

Inseparability of services

Services are produced and consumed at the same time, and the customer participates in the process of service production. The implication is twofold here. First, the service provider necessarily has a direct contact with the customer and is part of the service. There is a large human component involved in performing services. Thus, standardization is difficult because of the personalized nature of services. Second, the client participates in the production process and the service provider–customer interaction can also affect the quality of the service.

An implication of these characteristics is the difficulty of maintaining a constant level of quality of the services. Total quality control of services is a major issue for the service firm.

Variability of service quality

A distinction is usually made between *search quality* goods or services that can be evaluated prior to purchase, *experience quality goods* that can be evaluated only after purchase and *credence quality goods* and services difficult to evaluate even after the purchase. Services tend to be high in experience and credence qualities. It is particularly the case for the services provided by consultant, lawyers, doctors, accountants, advertising agencies and so on.

In discussing service quality, four characteristics of services should be kept in mind:

- Service quality is more difficult for the consumer to evaluate than the quality of goods, because services tend to be high in *experience* and *credence* qualities.
- Service quality is based on consumers' perception, not only of the outcome of the service, but also on their evaluation of the process by which the service is performed.
- Service quality perception results from a comparison of what the consumer expected prior to the service and the perceived level of the service received. Different individuals can have different perceptions and different prior expectations.
- A *human factor* is heavily involved in the process of service delivery and therefore a stable and fully standardized level of quality is more difficult to achieve. Different individuals will perform differently in delivering the same service and the same service provider can have a different performance level from one time to another.

To go further on the issue of service quality measurement see Zeithmal, Parasuraman and Berry (1990) and Berry (1999). For a good text on services marketing, see Kurtz and Clow (1998).

Implications for services management

These characteristics of the demand for services have direct implications on the management of services and firms must try to reconcile (a) productivity constraints leading to standardization and to the maximum use of information technology, (b) quality control objectives, leading to the development of personal interaction with customers and finally

(c) differentiation objectives. As shown by Schemenner (1986), service delivery activities can be classified by reference to two main dimensions at two levels each: *labour intensity* of the service delivery activity and *degree of interaction and customization.*

Using these two dimensions, four types of service activities can be identified:

- *Service factories.* Service businesses that have a relatively low labour intensity and a low degree of customer interaction, like airlines, trucking, hotels and resorts.
- *Service shops.* Here the degree of customer interaction or customization increases. These service businesses still have a high degree of plant and equipment relative to labour, but they offer more interactions and customization; hospitals, car repair garages and restaurants are examples of service shops.
- *Mass service.* These businesses have a high degree of labour intensity but a rather low degree of interaction and customization, such as retailing, schools, laundry, cleaning and so on.
- *Professional services.* When the degree of interaction with the customer increases and/or customization of this service becomes the watchword, mass services give way to professional services: doctors, lawyers, accountants, architects are classic examples.

This classification of services is not necessarily fixed as service firms innovate or modify their service operations.

For example, with the advent of fast food, interaction and customization for the consumer have been lowered dramatically, as has labour intensity. Fast food restaurants are moving to the service factory quadrant.

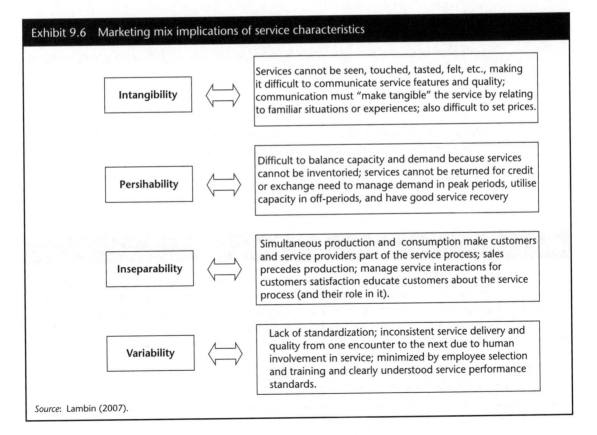

Exhibit 9.6   Marketing mix implications of service characteristics

Intangibility ⟺	Services cannot be seen, touched, tasted, felt, etc., making it difficult to communicate service features and quality; communication must "make tangible" the service by relating to familiar situations or experiences; also difficult to set prices.
Persihability ⟺	Difficult to balance capacity and demand because services cannot be inventoried; services cannot be returned for credit or exchange need to manage demand in peak periods, utilise capacity in off-periods, and have good service recovery
Inseparability ⟺	Simultaneous production and consumption make customers and service providers part of the service process; sales precedes production; manage service interactions for customers satisfaction educate customers about the service process (and their role in it).
Variability ⟺	Lack of standardization; inconsistent service delivery and quality from one encounter to the next due to human involvement in service; minimized by employee selection and training and clearly understood service performance standards.

Source: Lambin (2007).

Similarly, in the retailing sectors, the expansion of catalogue stores, electronic commerce and warehouse stores has shifted the emphasis of traditional retailing operations towards a lower degree of labour intensity. The opposite evolution is also observed in retailing with the proliferation of boutiques within stores, where interaction and customization are stressed. In this last example, the evolution is from the lower left quadrant to the lower right quadrant.

9.5   THE DEMAND FOR INDUSTRIAL GOODS

Industrial demand is actually *derived* from the consumer marketplace. Thus, industrial marketers must be cognisant of conditions in their own markets, but must also be aware of developments in the markets served by their customers and by their customers' customers. Of course, many industrial products are far removed from the consumer and the linkage is difficult to see. This separation becomes more apparent as the number of intermediate customers increases between a given manufacturer and the end-user. In other cases, the linkage is quite clear, such as the impact of car sales on the steel industry.

> Thus, if consumers are not buying homes, autos, clothing, stereos, educational or medical services, there will be less need for lumber, steel, cotton, plastics, computer components and hospital forms. Consequently, industry will require less energy, fewer trucking services and not as many tools or machines. (Morris, 1988, p. 390)

The planning task can become quite complex when a manufacturer's output is used in a wide variety of applications.

The demand for industrial goods is structured differently according to whether they are consumable goods, industrial components or industrial equipment. The data needed for the evaluation of demand are practically identical to the data for consumer goods, with only few exceptions.

The demand for industrial consumable goods

We have here products that are used by the industrial firm but not incorporated in the fabricated product. The components of demand are the following:

- Number of potential industrial users (by size).
- Proportion of effective users (by size).

Exhibit 9.7   Estimating the demand for a consumable industrial product

The Cleanchem Company has developed a water treatment chemical for paper manufacturers. Total paper shipments in the northeast region represent a value of $700 million. Data found in trade reports and information received from local water utility show that paper mills use 0.01 gallons of water per dollar of shipment value. Cleanchem engineers recommend a minimum of 0.25 ounces of the water treatment chemical per gallon of water and 0.30 ounces per gallon of water to be optimal. The AMP is estimated to range between 1,750,000 ounces ($700 million times 0.01 times 0.25) and 2,100,000 ounces. These estimates must be adjusted for the activity level of paper mills.)

Source: Morris (1988, p. 183).

- Level of activity per effective user.
- Usage rate per use occasion.

The usage rate is a technical norm easy to identify. The number of companies classified by number of employees, payroll, value of shipments and so on can be obtained in the Census of Manufacturers. An example is presented in Exhibit 9.7. The current proportion of effective users in this example is the major source of uncertainty.

The demand for industrial components

Industrial components are used in the product fabricated by the customer. Thus, their demand is directly related to the volume of production of the client company. The components of their demand are the following:

- Number of potential industrial users (by size).
- Proportion of effective users (by size).
- Quantity produced per effective user.
- Rate of usage per product.

Producers of car parts are a good example of a sector that responds to this type of demand. Fluctuation in consumer demand for cars will eventually result in a variation of the demand for their components. Thus a careful observation of the evolution of demand for the end-product is imperative for the producer of industrial components who wishes to predict his own demand.

The demand for industrial equipment

Here we have products such as industrial machines or computers that are necessary to the production activity. They are durable goods and thus the distinction between primary and replacement demand is important. *Primary equipment demand* is determined by the following factors:

- Number of companies equipped (by size)
- Increase of the production capacity
- Number of new-user companies (by size)
- Production capacity

Replacement demand is determined by the following factors:

- Size of the existing population
- Age distribution and technology level of the population

Exhibit 9.8   Estimating replacement demand: an example

By way of an example let's look at the car market. Let us assume that the average technical service life is around 10 to 11 years. If the expectation is to have a service life of 12.5 years, the yearly scrappage rate will be around 8 per cent, which represents a level of replacement demand of 1.7 million cars, given the current size of the car population. If, on the contrary, the expected service life were only 9 years, the scrappage rate would be 11.1 per cent with a level of replacement demand of 2.1 million.

- Distribution of the product life spans
- Rate of replacement
- Effect of product substitution
- Effect of reduction of production capacity

The acceleration effect

The demand for industrial equipment is directly related to the production capacity of the client companies, and thus even a small fluctuation in final demand can translate into a very large variation in the demand for industrial equipment. This phenomenon is known as the *acceleration effect*.

> For example, suppose that the life span of a population of machines is ten years. If the demand for the consumer goods produced by these machines increases by 10 per cent, 10 per cent of the existing population will need to be replaced, and an additional 10 per cent production capacity will be needed to meet the increased demand. Thus the demand for the machines will double. If the demand for the consumer goods decreases by 10 per cent, the required production capacity will only be 90 per cent, and thus the 10 per cent that fail will not need to be replaced. Thus the demand for the machines falls to 0.

The *volatility of the demand for industrial equipment* means that for accurate demand forecasting, companies must analyse both their own demand and the final demand of the companies they supply.

Marketing implications of industrial-derived demand

In addition to the difficulty of forecasting sales, derived demand also has implications for operational marketing. The dynamic industrial firm may decide to target its selling efforts not only on the immediate customer but also towards *indirect customers* further down the production chain, as shown in Figure 9.4 and also in Figure 9.5.

> Thus Recticel has advertised the benefits of its polyurethane foam to armchair and sofa distributors and to the general public as well. Its goals are twofold here: first to encourage end-users and distributors to place demands upon various furniture manufacturers to begin using the Recticel foam as a component in their production process; and second, to provide promotional efforts for furniture manufacturers currently using Recticel's product.

By focusing efforts further down the industrial chain, the industrial firm is adopting a *pull strategy* which complements more traditional selling efforts targeted at direct customers (*push strategy*). To limit their dependence on direct customers, dynamic industrial firms have to adopt a proactive marketing behaviour and to play an active role in demand stimulation at each level of the industrial chain.

9.6   GROWTH OPPORTUNITY ANALYSIS IN EXISTING MARKETS

> The gap between the current and the absolute level of primary demand is indicative of the rate of development or underdevelopment of a product market. The larger the gap, the greater the growth opportunity; conversely, the smaller the gap, the closer the market is to the saturation level.

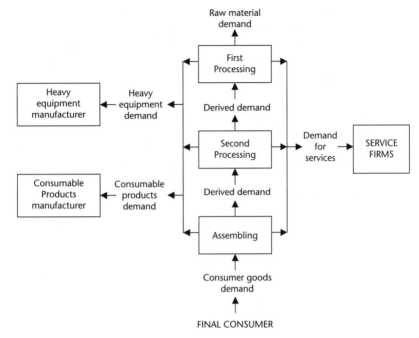

Figure 9.4   The supply chain for industrial equipment
Source: Lambin (2000/2007).

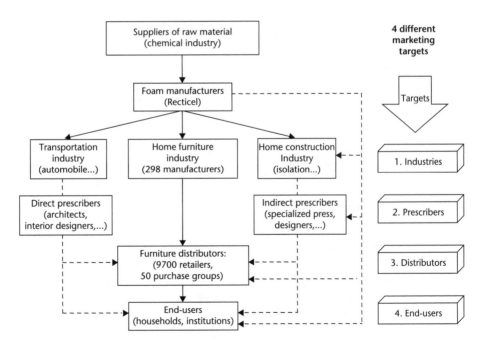

Figure 9.5   Example of derived demand: the market for polyurethane foam
Source: Lambin (2000/2007).

Weber (1976) has developed a framework, called gap analysis, to analyse the gaps between AMP and current company sales. Four growth opportunities are identified: the usage gap, the distribution gap, the product line gap and the competitive gap. The *competitive gap* is due to sales of directly competitive brands within the product market and also to substitute products. The other gaps present growth opportunities that will be briefly reviewed below.

Distribution gaps

The *distribution gap* is due to absence or inadequate distribution within the product market. Three types of distribution gap can be observed:

- The *coverage gap* exists when a firm does not distribute the relevant product line in all geographic regions desired.
- The *intensity gap* exists when a firm's product line is distributed in an inadequate number of outlets within a geographic region where the firm has distribution coverage.
- The *exposure gap* exists when a firm's product lines have poor or inadequate shelf space, location, displays and so on within outlets where the firm does have distribution for the product.

Sales of a particular product line can be adversely affected by any or all of these three different distribution gaps. Before adopting new product lines, the firm should try to close these distribution gaps.

Usage gaps

The *usage gap* is due to insufficient use of the product. Three types of usage gap can be identified:

- The *non-user gap*, that is, the customer who could potentially use the product but is not using it.
- The *light user gap*, that is, the customer who uses the product but does not use it on every use occasion.
- The *light usage gap*, that is, the customer who uses the product but by less than a full use on each use occasion.

A strategy aiming at closing these gaps will contribute to the development of primary demand and will therefore benefit all competing firms as well.

Product line gaps

The product line gap is caused by the lack of a full product line. Seven types of product line gaps could exist:

- *Size-related product line gaps*. Product "size" can be defined along three dimensions: "container size" for consumables like soft drinks or detergents, "capacity" for durables like refrigerators or computers and "power" for car engines or industrial machinery.
- *Options-related product line gaps*. A firm desiring to cater to specific demands of individual customers can offer optional features. Cars serve as one good example. By offering

a large number of options, car manufacturers can produce a large number of cars, each one in some way different from every other one.

- *Style, colour, flavour and fragrance-related product line gaps.* Style and colour can be important for clothing, shoes, appliances, cars and so on; flavours and fragrances can become important means of expanding product lines in food and drink products, tobaccos, toiletries and so on.
- *Form-related product line gaps.* One form of a product may be more attractive for customers than another. Possible dimensions of form include method or principle of operation (petrol versus electric mowers), product format (antacids: chewable, swallowable liquid, effervescent powder or tablets); product composition (corn oil, vegetable oil margarine) and product containers (resealable, returnable, throwaway bottles, easy-open cans).
- *Quality-related product line gaps.* Price lining is a popular practice used by marketers to provide consumers with a choice of products differentiated by overall quality and prices. Sporting goods manufacturers market tennis rackets and golf clubs in a range from beginners' models (low price) up to professional models (high price).
- *Distributor brand-related product line gaps.* Many manufacturers realize a significant proportion of their sales through selling to retailers who then put their own brand names on the products, like Saint Michael for Marks and Spencer in the United Kingdom. For manufacturers who recognize the private brand market as a separate segment, private brands can account for product line gaps.
- *Segment-related product line gaps.* A firm can adopt different market coverage strategies. A firm has a product line gap for any segment for which it does not have a product.

Each of these identified product line gaps constitutes a growth opportunity for the firm through innovation or product differentiation.

9.7   THE PLC MODEL

In attractiveness analysis, market potential analysis is a first, and essentially quantitative, step (see Figure 9.6). The analysis must be completed by a study of the PLC, or the evolution of the potential demand for a product or service over time. An essentially dynamic concept borrowed from biology, the PLC model takes the form of an S-shaped graph comprising five

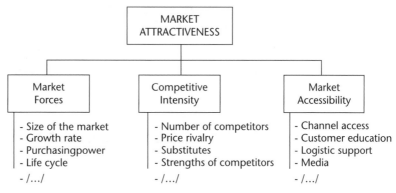

Figure 9.6   Selected indicators of market attractiveness

Table 9.1 Main indicators of market attractiveness: an example

Indicators of attractiveness	Weight (100)	Evaluation scale		
		Weak 1 2	Moderate 3 4	Strong 5
Market accessibility	_____	Outside Europe and USA	Europe and USA	Europe
Market growth rate	_____	≤5%	5–10%	≥10%
Length of the life cycle	_____	≤2 years	2–5 years	≥5 years
Gross profit potential	_____	≤15%	15–25%	≥25%
Strength of competition	_____	Structured oligopoly	Unstructured competition	Weak competition
Potential for differentiation	_____	Very weak	Moderate	Strong
Concentration of customers	_____	Very dispersed	Moderately dispersed	Concentrated

Source: Lambin (2000/2007).

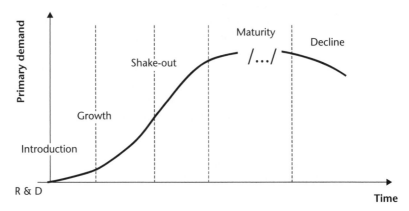

Figure 9.7 The idealized shape of the PLC model

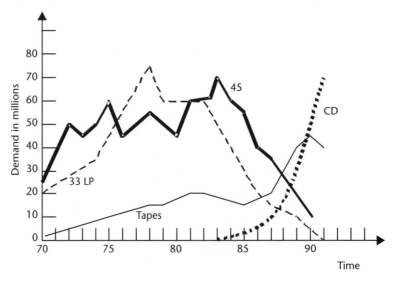

Figure 9.8 The PLC of the audio market
Source: Industry.

phases (Day, 1981). The first phase is a take-off, or introductory phase, followed by an expo-nential growth phase, a shakeout phase, a maturity phase and a decline phase. Figure 9.7 presents an idealized representation of the PLC, while Figure 9.8 portrays the life cycle of audio products in France, and in particular long-playing records and the compact disc.

Determinants of the PLC model

Before moving to an explanation of the PLC, its stages and its marketing implications, it is important to explain what type of products should be dealt with in a life-cycle analysis. Should it be a category of products (computers), a particular type of product within the category (microcomputers), a specific model (laptop computers or note books) or a specific brand (Compaq)?

While a life-cycle analysis at any level can have value if properly conducted, the most useful level of analysis is that of a *product market*. A product market lends itself best to a life-cycle analysis because it best describes buying behaviours within a particular product category and it most clearly defines the frame of reference: *a product seen as a specific package of benefits, targeted to a specific group of buyers*. The same product can very well have differ-ent life-cycle profiles in different geographic markets or different segments within the same market. Every product market has its own life cycle which reflects not only the evolution of the product, largely determined by technology, but also the evolution of primary demand and of its determinants.

Thus, a clear distinction should be made between the PLC and the brand life cycle (BLC).

The PLC model

For a product market, primary demand is the principal driving force and its determining factors are both non-controllable environmental factors and industry's totally controllable marketing variables. One of the most important non-controllable factors is the *evolution of technology*, which pushes towards newer, higher performance products, and makes older products obsolete. A second factor is the *evolution of production and consumption norms*, which makes certain products no longer suitable for the market and calls for others. Thus, the PLC model portrays the sales history of a particular product technology, which constitutes one specific solution (among many others) for a specific group of buyers to a market need.

These factors exist in all business sectors, which do not, however, exclude the possibility that certain better-protected product markets have a much longer life cycle than others. The life cycle also remains largely influenced by industry marketing efforts, particularly when the market is expanding. Dynamic companies are the driving force in a market, guiding its evolution, development and eventual relaunch sparked by modifications to the product. The PLC is thus not fixed, and research in the field has identified a great variety of life-cycle patterns (Cox, 1967; Swan and Rink, 1982).

Strategic implications of the PLC

As product markets grow, mature and decline over time, marketing strategy must evolve with the changing buyers' behaviour and competitive environment. To say that a product has a life cycle implies four things:

- The economic and competitive environment is different at each phase.
- The priority strategic objective must be redefined at each phase.
- Products' cost and profit structures are different at each phase.

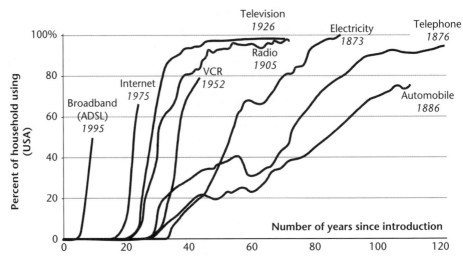

Figure 9.9 Examples of introductory phases of the PLC
Source: Industry.

- The marketing programme must be adapted in each stage of the PLC.

The shortening of the PLC is a major challenge for the innovative firm which has less and less time to achieve its objectives.

The introductory phase

In the introductory phase, the market is often (not always) characterized by a slow growth of sales because of various environmental factors:

- The first of these is the *technology uncertainty*, which is often not yet entirely mastered by the innovating company that has to exploit its first-mover advantage (see Table 9.2). In addition, the technology may still be developing or evolving in reaction to the first applications, and thus the producer cannot yet hope to produce at maximum efficiency.
- *Distributors* are a second environmental force, and can be very reluctant at this stage to distribute a product that has not yet proven itself on the larger market. In addition, an industrial distributor will need to familiarize himself or herself with the product, its technical characteristics and its principal functions, which will additionally slow the process.
- *The potential customer* makes up a third environmental factor. They can often be slow to change their consumption or production habits because of switching costs and caution towards the innovation. Only the most innovative of consumers will be the first to adopt the new product. This group constitutes a rather small initial segment for a product in the introduction phase, and is thus another contributing factor to slow sales.
- A final environmental force is the *competition*. Typically, the innovating company is without direct competition for a period of time, depending of the strength of the patent protection if any. Substitute product competition can still be very strong, however, except in the case of breakthrough innovation.

Table 9.2 First-mover advantage: myth or reality?

First-mover advantages	Free-rider advantages
Image and reputation	Risk reduction in time and money
Brand loyalty	Lower R&D costs
Opportunity for the best market position	Lower education costs
Technological leadership	Entry through heavy promotion
Opportunity to set product standards	Technological leapfrog
Access to distribution	Imposing a new standard
Experience effects	Learning from a changing market
Patents as barrier to entry	Shared experience
Switching costs as barrier to entry	

Source: Adapted from Schnaars (1998, pp. 160–5).

This phase is characterized by a high degree of uncertainty because, as technology is still developing, competitors are not yet identified, the reference market is blurred and there is little market information available. The more revolutionary the innovation, the larger is the uncertainty.

Internal company factors, which also characterize the introduction phase, include highly negative cash flows, large marketing expenses, high production costs, and often large R&D costs to be amortized. All of these factors put the new product in a very risky financial position. For this reason, the shorter the introduction phase of the product, the better for the company's profitability.

The *length of the introductory phase* of the PLC is a function of the speed of adoption of the less innovative potential buyers, which is influenced by various factors:

- Importance to the buyer of the new product's benefits.
- Presence or absence of adoption costs to be borne by the buyer.
- Compatibility of the product with current modes of consumption or production.
- Observable nature of the new product's benefits.
- Possibility of trying the new product.
- Competitive pressures inducing buyers to adopt the innovation.

Given these factors, the company's highest-priority strategic objective is *to create primary demand* as rapidly as possible and thus to keep the introduction phase as short as possible.

This priority objective includes:

- creating awareness of the product's existence,
- informing the market of the new product benefits,
- inducing potential customers to try the product, and
- securing channels for current and future distribution.

Thus the marketing strategy in the early phase of the PLC typically stresses market education objectives. To respond to these priorities, the *marketing programme* in the introduction phase will tend to have the following characteristics:

- A basic, core version of the product
- An exclusive or selective distribution system
- A low price sensitivity situation
- An informative communication programme

Several alternatives exist as to the types of launching strategies, particularly in terms of pricing: the dilemma of "skimming versus penetration" pricing will be discussed in more detail in Chapter 17.

The growth phase

If the product successfully passes the test of its introduction to the market, it enters into the *growth phase*. This phase is characterized by growth of sales at an accelerating rate (see Figures 9.9 and 9.10). The causes of this growth are the following:

- The first satisfied users become repeat customers and influence other potential users by word of mouth; thus the rate of occupation of the market increases.
- The availability of the product due to wider distribution gives the product more visibility, which then further increases the product's diffusion in the market.
- The entrance of new competitors increases the total marketing pressure on demand at a moment when it is expansible and strongly elastic.

An important characteristic of this phase is the regular decrease of production costs due to the increase in the volume produced. The effect of experience also begins to be felt. Prices have a tendency to decrease, which allows progressive coverage of the entire potential market. Marketing expenses are thus spread over a strongly expanding sales base, and cash flows become positive.

The characteristics of the *economic and competitive environment* change markedly:

- Sales are growing at an accelerating rate.
- The target group is now the segment of early adopters.
- New competitors enter the market.
- The technology is well diffused in the market.

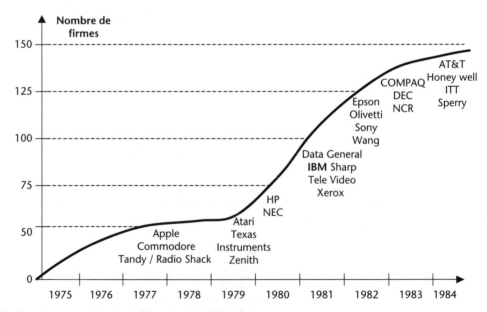

Figure 9.10 Entry of new competitors in the PC market in the United States
Source: Industry.

To meet these new market conditions, the *strategic marketing objectives* are changed as well. They now include:

- expanding the size of the total market,
- maximizing the occupation rate in the market,
- building a strong brand image, and
- creating brand loyalty.

To achieve these new objectives, *the marketing programme* will also be modified, as follows:

- Product improvements and features addition strategy.
- Intensive distribution and multiple channels strategy.
- Price reductions to penetrate the market.
- Image building communication strategy.

This primary demand development strategy requires large financial resources, and, if the cash flows are positive and profits rising, the equilibrium break-even point is not necessarily reached yet.

At this time, there is no intensive competitive rivalry in the product market, since the marketing efforts of any firm contribute to the expansion of the total market and are therefore beneficial for other firms.

The shakeout phase

This is a transitory phase where the rate of sales growth is decelerating, even though it remains above of the general economy. The target group is now the majority of the market. The weakest competitors start dropping out, as a result of successive decreases in the market price, and the market becomes more concentrated. The competitive and economic environments once again have changed:

- Demand is increasing at a slower rate.
- The target is the majority group in the market.
- The weakest competitors are dropping out of the race because of the reduced market prices.
- The industrial sector is more concentrated.

The key message of the shakeout phase is that things will be more difficult in the market because of the slowing down of total demand. Competing firms are led to redefine their priority objectives in two new directions:

- First, the strategic emphasis must shift from developing primary demand to building up or maximizing *market share*.
- Second, *market segmentation* must guide the product policy to differentiate the firm from the proliferation of "me too" products and to move away from the core market. The majority rule has become the majority fallacy.

The new *priority objectives* are:

- to segment the market and to identify priority target segments,
- to maximize market share in the target segments,

- to position the brand clearly in consumers' minds, and
- to create and maintain brand loyalty.

To achieve these objectives, the *marketing programme* will stress the following strategic orientations:

- Product differentiation guided by market segmentation.
- Expansion of distribution to obtain maximum market exposure.
- Pricing based on the distinctive characteristics of the brands.
- Advertising to communicate the claimed positioning to the market.

The shakeout period can be very short. The competitive climate becomes more aggressive and the key indicator of performance is market share.

The maturity phase

Eventually, the increase of primary demand slows down and stabilizes at the growth rate of the real GNP or the rhythm of demographic expansion. The product is in the *phase of maturity*. The majority of products can be found in this phase, which usually has the longest duration. The causes of this stabilization of global demand are the following:

- The rates of occupation and penetration of the product in the market are very high and very unlikely to increase further.
- The coverage of the market by distribution is intensive and cannot be increased further.
- The technology is stabilized and only minor modifications to the product can be expected.

At this stage, the market is very segmented as companies try to cover all the diversity of needs by offering a wide range of product variations. Over the course of this phase the probability of a technological innovation to relaunch the PLC is high, as everyone in the industry tries to extend the life of the product.

The emerging trends observed in the shakeout period have materialized and the characteristics of the *economic and competitive environment* are the following:

- Non-expansible primary demand growing at the rate of the economy.
- Durable goods demand is determined by replacement demand.
- Markets are highly segmented.
- A few powerful competitors dominate the market and the market structure is oligopolistic.
- The technology is standardized.

The firm's *priority objective* is to defend, and if possible to expand, market share and to gain a sustainable competitive advantage over direct competitors. The tools to be used for achieving this objective are basically of three types:

- To differentiate the products through quality, feature or style improvements.
- To enter new market segments or niches.
- To gain a competitive advantage through the non-product variables of the marketing mix.

The slowing of market growth certainly has an impact on the competitive climate. Production capacity surpluses appear and contribute to the intensification of the competitive situation. Price competition is more frequent, but has little or no impact on primary demand, which has become inelastic to price. It will only affect the market share of the existing competitors. In as much as the industry succeeds in avoiding price wars, this is the phase where profitability is highest, as shown in Figure 9.11. In theory, this profitability will be as strong as the market share retained is high. As observed by Sheth and Sisodia (2002), in this type of market situation, the "rule of three" applies in the sense that there is only room for three full-line generalists along with several product or market specialists.

The decline phase

The *decline phase* is characterized by a structural decrease in demand for one of the following reasons:

- *New, more technologically advanced products* make their appearance and replace existing products with the same function.
- Preferences, tastes or *consumption habits* change with time and render products outdated.
- Changes in the social, economic and political *environment*, such as modifications in environmental protection laws, make products obsolete or simply prohibited.

As sales and potential profits decrease, certain companies disinvest and leave the market, while others try to specialize in the residual market. This represents a valid option if the decline is progressive. Except in a turnaround of the market, which is sometimes observed, the abandonment of the technologically outdated product is inevitable. In Table 9.3 a summary of the marketing strategies over the PLC is presented and in Table 9.4 the reader will find a PLC evaluation grid.

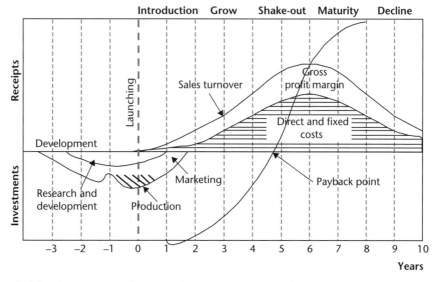

Figure 9.11   Financial flows and the PLC
Source: Lambin (2000/2007).

Exhibit 9.9 Is the minicassette eternal?

Philips was the first to introduce the minicassette for recorder in the market. After more than 30 years, and despite the CD competition (also invented by Philips), about 3 billion cassettes are sold every year worldwide. Philips has made the product universal by offering the licence at no cost to the other manufacturers, thereby imposing its standard. The minicassette is compatible not only with recorders but also with car radios and with baladeurs. In fact, it is compatible with any form of recording or listening. From the beginning, the cassette was launched with a massive marketing support at a low price. Since then several technical improvements have been made, which have opened more selective markets with higher added value. The life of this product seems eternal.

Source: Le Figaro-Economie, 6 January 1992.

Table 9.3 Marketing programme over the PLC: a summary

Phase of the PLC	Macro-marketing environment	Priority strategic objectives	Marketing Programme
Introduction	– Slow growth of primary demand – Target: segment of innovators – Monopoly, or few rivals – Fast technological evolution	– To create primary demand – To educate potential users – To induce trial purchase – To secure large distribution	– Core product – basic model – Selective or exclusive distribution – Skimming or penetration pricing – Generic and informative communication
Growth	– Growth at an accelerating pace – Target : segment of early adopters – Entry of new competitors – Diffused technology	– To expand primary demand – To increase market occupation rate – To build brand or corporate image – To create brand or corporate loyalty	– Improved product with new features – Intensive distribution and market coverage – Price reductions to enlarge the market – Image building communication
Shakeout	– Growth at a declining pace – Target : majority of the market – Weakest rivals start dropping out. – Second-generation technology emerges	– To target specific segments – To maximize market share – To position the brand clearly – To create and maintain brand loyalty	– Differentiation based on segmentation – Intensive distribution – High price and value pricing strategy – Brand positioning communication
Maturity	– Non-expandable primary demand – Highly fragmented market – Few powerful rivals dominate – Standardized technology	– To differentiate products – To enter new segments or niches – To refine the positioning strategy – To add new product features	– Differentiation based on segmentation – Return to selective distribution – Forms of non-price competition – Brand positioning communication
Decline	– Zero growth or declining market – Target: segment of laggards – Competitors leave the market – Outdated technology	– To divest quickly or selectively – To become the industry specialist – To slow down the decline of the market	– Limited product line and assortment – Highly selective distribution – High prices due to low price sensitivity – Communication to hard-core loyal

Source: Lambin (2000/2007).

Exhibit 9.10   Traditional chemical-based cameras wiped out by digital cameras

Never in the history of leisure electronics has such a fast downturn in demand been observed between two technologies. In France, digital cameras sales started growing in 1999 and have more than doubled every year since then to reach 2.2 millions units in 2003 and 3.5 millions the following year, according to the last estimates of GFK. Distribution has of course followed the trend: if in 2001, 75 per cent of the space was dedicated to traditional cameras in the photographic equipment department of Fnac and 25 per cent to digital cameras, the proportion is exactly the reverse today.

Source: Le Figaro Economie, 29 October 2003.

Table 9.4 PLC evaluation grid

Market characteristics	Phases of the PLC				
	Introduction	Growth	Shakeout	Maturity	Decline
PRIMARY DEMAND					
Slow growth	———	———	———	———	———
Fast growth	———	———	———	———	———
Slowing down	———	———	———	———	———
Decreasing	———	———	———	———	———
NEW COMPETITORS					
Some	———	———	———	———	———
Many	———	———	———	———	———
Few	———	———	———	———	———
Even fewer	———	———	———	———	———
REAL PRICES					
Stable	———	———	———	———	———
Decreasing	———	———	———	———	———
Erratic	———	———	———	———	———
RANGE OF PRODUCTS					
Increasing	———	———	———	———	———
Few changes	———	———	———	———	———
Decreasing	———	———	———	———	———
DISTRIBUTION					
Low growth	———	———	———	———	———
Fast growth	———	———	———	———	———
Few changes	———	———	———	———	———
Decreasing	———	———	———	———	———
PRODUCT MODIFICATIONS					
Few	———	———	———	———	———
Many	———	———	———	———	———
Very few	———	———	———	———	———
COMMUNICATION CONTENT					
Core service	———	———	———	———	———
Main attributes	———	———	———	———	———
New uses	———	———	———	———	———
Secondary attributes	———	———	———	———	———

Source: Adapted from Taylor (1986, p. 27).

9.8   THE PLC MODEL AS A CONCEPTUAL FRAMEWORK

More than a planning tool, the life-cycle model is a *conceptual framework* for analysing the forces which determine the attractiveness of a product market and which provoke its evolution. Markets evolve because certain forces change, provoking pressures or inciting changes. These changing forces are important to identify, and for that purpose the PLC model is useful (Levitt, 1965).

Diversity of actual PLC profiles

A difficulty in interpreting the PLC model comes from the fact that available experimental observations show that the PLC profile does not always follow an S-curve as suggested by the model. Rink and Swan (1979) identified as many as 12 different profiles. Sometimes products escape the introduction phase and enter directly into growth; others skip the maturity phase and pass directly from growth to decline; still others skip decline and find a new vigour after a brief slowdown, and so on (see Figure 9.12). Thus there is not only one type of evolution that will invariably intervene, and it is often difficult to determine in which phase a product is currently situated. This difficulty reduces the utility of the concept as a planning tool, and even more so as the duration of the phases varies from one product to another, not to mention from one country to another for the same product.

> In 1960, most of the European producers of TV sets had planned their production capacity for colour TV (at that time in the introductory phase) by reference to the PLC of colour TV in the USA, which had a very long introductory phase. In Europe, however, the market penetration was very rapid, the European market and environment being very different.

The different profiles observed can be explained by the evolution of the following explanatory factors: technology, consumption habits and company dynamism. The PLC model does not exempt the market analyst from a systematic analysis of the driving forces at the origin of these changes. The obvious difficulty is to determine, before the facts, the type of evolution that will prevail.

Product rejuvenation strategies

Another explanation of the observed differences in the profiles comes from the fact that companies can act upon the pattern of the PLC profile by innovating, repositioning the product, promoting its diffusion to other groups of consumers or modifying it in various manners. Throughout the life cycle, the dynamic firm will try to pursue the following objectives:

- Shortening the introduction phase
- Accelerating the growth process
- Prolonging the maturity phase
- Slowing the decline phase

The ideal profile of a PLC is one where the development phase is short, the introduction brief, the growth phase rapid, the maturity phase long and the decline long and progressive.

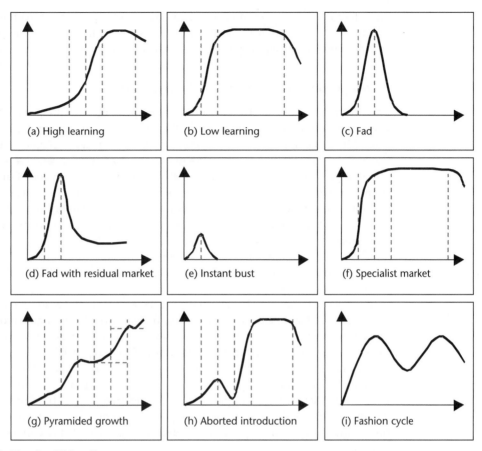

Figure 9.12   Diversity of PLC profiles
Source: Adapted from Wasson (1974).

The initiatives taken by an innovating firm can thus modify the life-cycle profile of a product market.

> A classic example of a life cycle with successive product relaunches is the nylon industry, where the growth phase was prolonged several times due to successive technological innovations. (Yale, 1964)

It is clear that if all the competitors in a product market consider maturity or decline inevitable, the phases risk being realized sooner than expected.

Some industrial sectors, once considered as declining or stagnant, have suddenly experienced a new lease of life resulting from a rejuvenating supply-led innovation adopted by a manufacturer or by a distributor.

> Ikea, in the home furniture distribution, Swatch in the watches market, Benetton in the garment market and Kinepolis in the movie distribution market are good examples of placid or stagnant markets rejuvenated.

The relevant question to examine is to know whether the product market is really in decline or whether it is the strategy adopted by the competing firms within the product market which is obsolete or delivers only limited value to customers?

How to reconcile growth and profit objectives?

The structure of the financial flows which accompany the (idealized) evolution of primary demand over time is described in Figure 9.12. One observes that, in the general case considered here, the financial flows are very unevenly allocated among the different phases of the PLC. In phases 1 and 2, past investments and marketing expenditures heavily undermine the profitability that can remain negative for a significant period of time, particularly in markets where the introductory phase is long. It is only in the shakeout or even in the maturity phase that the innovating firm reaches the profitability zone, having recouped previous losses and achieving higher gross profit margins and lower costs due to experience of economies of scale effects.

A golden managerial rule resulting from this cost and revenue allocation along the PLC is to maintain permanently a balanced structure of the firm's product portfolio in terms of profitability and growth.

It is clear, for example, that a firm having 85 per cent in its turnover achieved by products or activities situated in phases 1 or 2 of the PLC would have a high growth potential, but would certainly be confronted with severe liquidity or cash flow problems, being unable to generate enough cash to finance the firm's expansion. It is often the case for promising hi-tech companies having plenty of new product ideas, but not enough cash to finance them. Conversely, a firm achieving 85 per cent of its turnover through products or activities situated in phases 4 or 5 would have substantial financial means, but would be highly vulnerable in terms of growth potential, being completely dependent on a market turnaround or on a sudden decline of primary demand in its main reference markets.

A *balanced product portfolio* implies the presence of so-called *cash cow products* generating more cash than required for their development, and so-called *problem children products* or new products having a high growth potential but requiring substantial financial support to ensure their development. These objectives of balanced portfolio structure are at the basis of the portfolio analysis methods.

Chapter Summary

The key demand concepts are "primary" versus "company" demand, "absolute" versus "present" market potential, "end" versus "derived" demand, "first equipment" versus "replacement" demand for durable goods. The objective of demand analysis is to give an empirical content to these concepts through market research in order to objectively assess the attractiveness of each potential target segment and to identify the determinants of demand. These concepts are useful for detecting growth opportunities in the reference market through gap analysis. The PLC model is a conceptual framework which describes the evolution of primary demand in a dynamic perspective. A large variety of profiles exist for the PLC, which can be explained by the evolution of technology and consumption habits and by the size of industry marketing efforts. The competitive situation and the financial structure (turnover and profits) are different at each stage of the PLC and the priority strategic objective and the marketing programme must be adapted accordingly.

BIBLIOGRAPHY

Bain and Company News Letter (2004), *Interview of Guus Hoefloot, CEO of Heilmans*, September–October.

Berry, F.W. (1980), Services Marketing Is Different, *Business Magazine*, May–June.

Berry, L. (1999), *Discovering the Soul of Service*, New York, The Free Press.

Cox, W.E. (1967), Product Life Cycle: Marketing Models, *Journal of Business*, 40, 4, pp. 375–84.

Day, G.S. (1981), The Product Life Cycle: Analysis and Application Issues, *Journal of Marketing*, 45, 4, pp. 60–7.

Eiglier, P. and Langeard, E. (1987), *Servuction*, Paris, Ediscience International.

Kurtz, D.L. and Clow, K.E. (1998), *Services Marketing*, New York, John Wiley & Sons.

Lambin J.J. (2000–2007), *Market-Driven Management: Strategic and Operational Marketing*, London, Palgrave Macmillan, Second edition.

Levitt, T. (1965), *L'imagination au service du marketing*, Paris, Econmica.

Morris, M.H. (1988), *Industrial and Organizational Marketing*, Columbus, OH, Merrill.

Rink, D.R. and Swan, J.E. (1979), Product Life Cycle Research: A Literature Review, *Journal of Business Research*, 7, 3, pp. 219–42.

Sawhney, M. (1999), Making New Markets, Business 2.0, May, pp. 116–21.

Sawhney, M., Balasubramanian, S. and Krishnan, V.V. (2004), Creating Growth with Services, *MIT Sloan Management Review*, 45, 2, pp. 34–43.

Schemenner, R.W. (1986), How Can Service Business Survive and Prosper?, *Sloan Management Review*, Spring.

Schnaars, S.P. (1998), *Marketing Strategy*, New York, The Free Press.

Sheth, J. and Sisodia, R. (2002), The Rule of Three in Europe, *European Business Forum*, 10, Summer, pp. 53–7.

Shostack, G.L. (1977), Breaking Free from Product-Marketing, *Journal of Marketing*, 41, 2, pp. 73–80.

Swan, J.E. and Rink, D.R. (1982), Fitting Market Strategy to Varying Product Life Cycles, *Business Horizons*, 25, 1, pp. 72–6.

Taylor, J.W. (1986), *Competitive Marketing Strategies*, Radnor, PA, Chilton Book Company.

Vandermerwe, S. (1993), Jumping in to the Customer Activity Cycle, *Columbia Journal of World Business*, 28, 2, pp. 46–65.

Vandermerwe, S. (2000), How Increasing Value to Customers Improves Business Results?, *MIT Sloan Management Review*, 42, 1, pp. 27–37.

Wasson, C.R. (1974), *Dynamic Competitive Strategy and the Product Life Cycle*, St. Charles, IL, Challenge Books.

Weber, J.A. (1976), *Growth Opportunity Analysis*, Reston, VA, Reston Publishing.

Yale, J.P. (1964), The Strategy of Nylon's Growth: Create New Market, *Modern Textiles Magazine*, February.

Zeithmal, V.A., Parasuraman, A. and Berry, L.L. (1990), *Delivering Quality Service*, New York, The Free Press.

CHAPTER TEN

COMPANY COMPETITIVENESS ANALYSIS

Having evaluated the intrinsic appeal of the product markets and segments in the reference market, the next stage of strategic marketing is to analyse the climate or the competitive structure of each of the product markets, and then evaluate the nature and intensity of the competitive advantage held by the various competitors in each market. A product market may be very attractive in itself, but not so for a particular firm, given its strengths and weaknesses and compared to its most dangerous competitors. Therefore, the aim of measuring business competitiveness is to identify the kind of competitive advantage that a firm or a brand can enjoy and to evaluate to what extent this advantage is sustainable, given the competitive structure, the balance of existing forces and the positions held by the competitors.

Learning Objectives

When you have read this chapter, you should be able to:

- Define a competitive advantage that is sustainable in a target market
- Describe the nature and strengths of the competitive forces at play in an industry
- Assess the impact of the competitive situation on the strategic and operational marketing objectives
- Predict the type of competitive behaviour to expect given the competitive environment
- Explain the importance of differentiation as a source of competitive advantage
- Use the experience curve to measure the extent of a cost advantage or disadvantage over direct competitors
- Understand the concept of international competitive advantage

---

10.1 A GROWING COMPETITIVE INTERDEPENDENCE

One of the most important effects of globalization is the interdependence it creates between markets. National markets cannot be viewed as separate entities any more, but rather as belonging to a regional or world reference market. What happens in one market directly influences others. Here are two examples.

- The relatively minor pollution problems of Coca-Cola in Belgium and in France in 1999 triggered a health scare that spread rapidly to other European nations, which hit the Coca-Cola share price on the New York stock market. Many commentators cited the crisis at the time as one of the contributory factors to the Coca-Cola CEO's surprise early retirement.

- In few months, the severe acute respiratory syndrome (SARS) epidemic has contaminated 30 countries over the world and the bird flu is a global phenomenon.

An economy that is highly integrated in the world network becomes more vulnerable to external shocks such as devaluation, a sudden rise in the oil price, a financial crisis or a war threat. This evolution has several managerial implications.

- The traditional multi-domestic (or multinational) organization forms become obsolete and are replaced by transnational organizations covering a region or the entire world. The problem is to develop a *global mind set* (Begley and Boyd, 2003) consisting in maintaining a good balance between:

  - global formalization and local flexibility of behavioural rules,
  - global standardization or local customization of products and brands, and
  - global dictates versus local delegation of decisions.

- What is clear today is that many firms are revisiting the full standardization rule "one size fits all".
- Mergers and acquisitions are necessary to reach the critical size required to compete in an enlarged market (Daimler–Chrysler, AOL–Time Warner, Carrefour–Promodès, ING–BBL). A strategic move which is far from being complete in Europe, in particular in view of the recent enlargement of the EU to 25 countries.
- Standardization of brands and communication strategies are motivated by the necessity to achieve economies of scale to remain competitive in the enlarged market. This is the reason why, in 1999, the Unilever Company decided to concentrate its activities on 400 international brands and to eliminate 1,200 brands or 75 per cent of its brand portfolio.

For the international firm, it is always difficult to maintain a good balance between the two conflicting objectives, standardization which is *supply-driven* and adaptation which is *market-driven*. The problem is to know how far to go in the standardization track, the risk being to lose contact with the local market simply to reduce costs.

Exhibit 10.1   Examples of the dilemma "adaptation versus standardization"

- A recent study of 500 brands from the food sector covering four European countries (France, Italy, the United Kingdom and Germany) has shown that local brands enjoyed a level of awareness higher than international brands and a stronger brand image on several attributes and in particular on the criterion of trust (Schuiling, 2002).
- The CEO of the Coca-Cola company, the undisputed leader of brand globalization, has acknowledged that a too strong standardization strategy damages the brand image. The CEO has invited the local country marketing teams to adapt locally the Coca-Cola brand strategy and even to introduce new local brands.
- In Belgium, P&G, a strong supporter of global marketing, has unsuccessfully tried to weaken the local brand Dash, by stopping all advertising for more than 9 months, in order to push its international brand Ariel, only number 2 in the detergent market.

This issue is particularly typical in Europe since the launching of the euro, the new European currency, which by facilitating price comparisons between countries, reveals substantial price disparities, which stimulate parallel imports with an alignment to the lowest current level of price.

This new competitive interdependence affects every company in their domestic market and in the international market and obliges them to re-evaluate their competitive advantage, taking as benchmark the strongest competitor in the enlarged reference market. Thus, in this new competitive environment, it is not enough to be customer-oriented. The firm must also become *competitor-oriented*. A competitors' orientation includes all activities involved in acquiring and disseminating information about competitors in the target market and requires an explicit account of competitors' position and behaviour in strategy definition.

10.2 THE NOTION OF COMPETITIVE ADVANTAGE

Competitive advantage refers to those characteristics or attributes of a product or a brand that give the firm some *superiority over its direct competitors*. These characteristics or attributes may be of different types and may relate to the product itself (the core service), to the necessary or added services accompanying the core service, or to the modes of production, distribution or selling specific to the product or to the firm. When it exists, this superiority is relative and is defined with respect to the best-placed competitor in the product market or segment. We then speak of the most dangerous competitor, or the *priority competitor*. A competitor's relative superiority may result from various factors, and the value chain model is particularly useful to identify them. Generally speaking, these can be classified into three main categories, according to the nature of competitive advantage they provide.

The quality (or external) competitive advantage

A quality competitive advantage is based on some distinctive qualities of the product which give superior value to the customer, either by reducing its costs or by improving its performance, giving therefore firm the capacity to charge a price higher than the competition.

An external competitive advantage gives to the firm increased *market power*. It can force the market to accept a price above that of its priority competitor, which may not have the same distinctive quality. A strategy based on an external competitive advantage is a *differentiation strategy*, which calls into question the firm's marketing know-how, and its ability to better detect and meet those expectations of customers which are not yet satisfied by existing products.

To succeed with an external advantage strategy, the price premium the customer is willing to pay must exceed the cost of providing that extra value.

The cost (or internal) competitive advantage

A cost competitive advantage is based on the firm's superiority in matters of cost control, administration and product management, which bring value to the producer by enabling it to have a lower unit cost than its priority competitor.

Internal competitive advantage results from better productivity, thus making the firm more profitable and more resistant to price cuts imposed by the market or by the competition.

Box 10.1   Implementation problem: how to create value by reducing customer's costs?

- Lower required rate of usage of the product.
- Lower delivery, installation or financing costs.
- Lower direct costs of using the product such as labour, fuel, maintenance, required space.
- Lower indirect costs of using the product.

- Lower customer's costs in activities unconnected with the product.
- Lower risk of failure and lower expected cost of failure.

Source: Porter M. (1980).

A strategy based on internal competitive advantage is a *cost domination strategy*, which mainly calls into question the firm's organizational and technological know-how. To succeed, a cost strategy must offer acceptable value to customers, so that prices are close to the average of competitors. If too much quality is sacrificed to achieve a low-cost position, the price discount demanded by customers will more than offset the cost advantage.

The search for a sustainable competitive positioning

These two types of competitive advantage have distinct origins and natures, which are often incompatible because they imply different abilities and traditions. Figure 10.1 shows the two aspects of competitive advantage, which can be expressed as questions:

- *Market power:* to what extent are customers willing to pay a price higher than the price charged by our direct competitor?
- *Productivity:* is our unit cost higher or lower than the unit cost of our direct competitor?

The horizontal axis in Figure 10.1 refers to maximum acceptable price and the vertical axis to unit cost. Both are expressed in terms of percentages compared to the priority competitor:

- The *productivity* dimension enables a brand or firm to position itself in terms of cost advantage or disadvantage compared to its priority competitor. A positioning in the upper part of the axis reveals a cost disadvantage and a cost advantage on the lower part.
- The *market power* dimension describes the position of the brand by reference to its buyers' maximum acceptable price compared to that of its priority competitor. A positioning to the right indicates a high brand strength and the capacity to charge a premium price. A positioning to the left suggests, on the other hand, that the brand has a weak market power and that it has to adopt a price lower than its priority competitors to be accepted by the market.

In Figure 10.1, the bisecting line separates the favourable and unfavourable positions. Four different competitive positioning can be identified:

1. The positioning in the *upper-left quadrant* is disastrous since the brand accumulates handicaps. The brand has a cost disadvantage over its priority competitor and has no market power to offset this cost handicap through a price premium. Sooner or later, a divestment or retreat strategy will have to be adopted.
2. The *lower-right quadrant* is the ideal situation where the brand would have the best of both worlds: low cost due to high productivity and high market-acceptable price due to high market power. Situations rarely observed in the real world, these two positions imply two different corporate cultures.

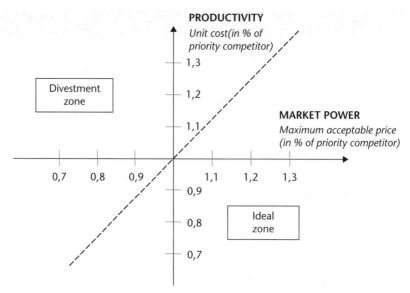

Figure 10.1   Competitive advantage analysis
Source: Lambin (2000/2007).

3. The *lower-left quadrant* depicts the positioning of a brand having a cost advantage but a weak market power compared to its direct competitor. The strategy to adopt here is to target price-sensitive market segments with a modest operational marketing budget or to sub-contract operational marketing, for instance, to a large retail chain.
4. The *upper-right quadrant* describes a situation frequently observed in highly industrialized countries: the firm has a cost handicap but has a market power sufficiently strong to offset the cost handicap through a higher market-acceptable price. The strategy here is to search for higher added value and/or higher quality activities that will justify a price premium in the eyes of the buyer.

The purpose of measuring business competitiveness is to allow the firm to find its own position on these axes and deduce its strategic priority objectives for each of the products of its portfolio.

To find its position along the *market power axis*, the firm will use information provided by brand image studies which help measure the brand's perceived value and estimate price elasticity. As for the *productivity axis*, the experience law can be used when applicable or else the firm can use information provided by the marketing intelligence unit which has, among other things, the task of monitoring competition. For many market metrics, the question is not how satisfied the customer is, but how this compares with how satisfied the competitors' customers are. For indicators of competitive superiority refer to Ambler (2000).

Competitive advantage based on core competencies

A more general way to look at the type of competitive advantage refers to the *core competency concept* developed by Prahalad and Hamel (1990). A core competence is a special skill or technology that creates unique customer value (see Exhibit 10.2). A company's specialized capabilities are largely embodied in the collective knowledge of its people and the organized procedures that shape the way employees interact. These core competencies can be viewed as the roots of a firm's competitive advantage.

When appropriately applied, core competencies can create sustainable sources of competitive advantage over time that are implementable in other seemingly unrelated fields of business. To be sustainable, a core competency should:

- provide significant and appreciable *value to customers* relative to competitor offerings;
- be *difficult for competitors to imitate* or procure in the market, thereby creating competitive barriers to entry; and
- enable a company to access a *wide variety of seemingly unrelated markets* by combining skills and technologies across traditional business units.

Exhibit 10.2   Four examples of core competencies

- 3M's competency was founded originally on sticky tape. Over time it has built from this unique bundle of skills in substrates, coatings, adhesives and various ways of combining them. These core competencies have allowed it to enter and excel in businesses as diverse as "Post-it" notes, magnetic tape, photographic film, pressure-sensitive tapes and coated abrasives.
- Casio's core competencies are in miniaturization, micro-processor design, material science and ultra-thin precision casings, the same skills it applies in its miniature card calculators, pocket TVs, musical instruments and digital watches.

- Canon, the number one in photography, thanks to its ability to combine and integrate optical and micro-electronic technologies and high-precision mechanics, was able to move from photography to video, low-price photocopiers, colour photocopiers, ink jet printers, laser printers and fax.
- Bic's core competence is the distribution of moulded plastic disposable mass consumer products (pens, lighters, razors).

Source: Authors.

Table 10.1   Sources of operational competitive advantage

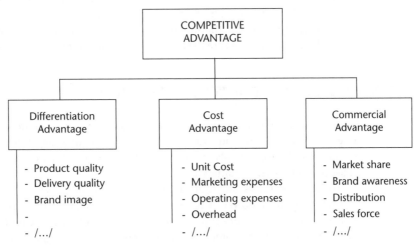

Source: Best R. (2003).

Identifying and developing core competencies involves isolating key abilities within the organization and then honing them into a definition of the organization's key strengths (Rigby, 1997). Successful diversification strategies are often based on core competencies.

Operational versus strategic competitive advantage

The search for a sustainable competitive advantage is at the core of the strategy formulation process and is one of the main responsibilities of strategic marketing. A company can outperform rivals only if it can establish a difference that it can preserve. In this perspective a distinction can be made here between operational and strategic competitive advantages (Porter, 1996). Gaining an operational competitive advantage in a given reference market means performing *similar activities better than rivals perform them (Table 10.1)*.

- Being better by offering a higher quality or a same quality at a lower price
- Being better by offering a product that reduces customers' costs
- Being better by offering lower cost and better quality at the same time
- Being faster in meeting customers' products or services
- Being closer to the customer and providing assistance in use

Constant improvements in operational effectiveness are necessary to achieve superior profitability, but it is not usually sufficient. Every department within the firm has this responsibility. Staying ahead of rivals on the basis of operational effectiveness becomes harder every day because of the rapid diffusion of best practices. Competitors can quickly imitate management techniques, new technologies, input improvements and superior ways to meet customers' needs.

In contrast, gaining a strategic competitive advantage is about being different. It means (a) deliberately choosing a *different set of activities from rivals* or (b) performing *similar activities but in a different way*, to deliver a unique mix of values. Ikea, the global furniture retailer based in Sweden, has chosen to perform activities differently from rivals. Same is the case for Ryan-Air in the airline market.

In the search for a competitive advantage, it is important to make a clear distinction between these two types of competitive advantage, because a strategic positioning is likely to be more sustainable in the long term than an operational competitive advantage. To understand how competitors will respond to the firm's marketing action, Coyne and Horn (2009) suggest to evaluate the situation in their terms and propose a set of questions to get ideas of what competitors are likely to do (Schuiling and Kapferer, 2004).

10.3   FORCES DRIVING INDUSTRY COMPETITION

The notion of extended rivalry, due to Porter (1980), is based on the idea that a firm's ability to exploit a competitive advantage in its reference market depends not only on the direct competition it faces, but also on the role played by rival forces, such as potential entrants, substitute products, customers and suppliers.

The first two forces constitute a direct threat; the other two an indirect threat, because of their bargaining power. It is the combined interplay of these five competitive forces, described in Porter's figure 1980, figure 2), which determines the profit potential of a product market. Clearly, the dominant forces determining the competitive climate vary from one market to another. Using Porter's analysis, we will examine the role of these four external competitive forces successively. The analysis of rivalry between direct competitors will be left for later in this chapter.

Threat of new entrants

Potential competitors, likely to enter a market, constitute a threat that the firm must limit and protect itself against, by creating barriers to entry. Potential entrants can be identified as follows:

- Firms outside the product market which could easily surmount the barriers to entry.
- Firms for which entry would represent a clear synergy.
- Firms for which entry is the logical conclusion of their strategy.
- Clients or suppliers who can proceed to backward or forward integration (Porter, 1980, p. 55).

The importance of the threat depends on the *barriers to entry* and on the strength of reaction that the potential entrant can expect. Possible barriers to entry are as follows:

- *Economies of scale*. These force the entrant to come in at large scale or else risk having to bear cost disadvantage.
- *Legal protection* obtained through patents, as we have seen in the case of the conflict between Kodak and Polaroid.
- *Product differentiation* and brand image, leading to a high degree of loyalty among existing customers who show little sensitivity to newcomers.
- *Capital requirements*, which can be considerable, not only for production facilities, but also for things like inventories, customer credit, advertising expenses, start-up losses and so on.
- *Switching costs*, that is, one-time real or psychological costs that the buyer must bear to switch from an established supplier's product to that of a new entrant.
- *Access to distribution channels*: distributors might be reluctant to give shelf space to a new product; sometimes the new entrant is forced to create an entirely new distribution channel.
- *Experience effects* and the cost advantage held by the incumbent, which can be very substantial, especially in highly labour-intensive industries.

Box 10.2   Implementation problem: how to spot potential competitors?

- Actively monitor notable market activities beyond your direct competitors.
- Take note of interesting mergers, acquisitions or alliances that may suggest threats or new business growth opportunities for your own company.
- Identify and track alliances and collaborations offering new products and services that change or shake up the industry.
- Ponder corporate alliances or mergers that are unexpected, surprising or combine firms from different industries.

- Look for pattern in alliances, mergers or acquisitions that combines apparently diverse product lines to create other value-added competences of offerings.
- Watch for newly emerging companies with proprietary new technologies, whose products or services may have broad applications.
- Form a cross-functional monitoring team or task force to search and evaluate alliances, mergers and acquisitions.

Source: Fox (2001).

Other factors which may influence the entrant's degree of determination are the expectation of sharp reactions from existing firms and of the dissuasive nature of the retaliations they may organize. The following factors will in particular influence the degree of deterrence in the response:

- A history and reputation of aggressiveness *vis-à-vis* new entrants.
- Degree of commitment of established firms in the product market.
- Availability of substantial resources to fight back.
- Possibility of retaliation in the entrant's home market.

Put together, sustainable entry barriers and the ability to respond are the elements that determine the entry-deterring price.

Threats of substitute products

Substitute products are products that can perform the same function for the same customer groups, but are based on different technologies. Substitute products go hand in hand with the definition of a market which is the "set of all technologies for a given function and a given customer group". Such products are a permanent threat because a substitution is always possible. The threat can be intensified, for instance, as a result of a technological change that modifies the substitute's quality/price as compared to the reference product market.

> The price decline in the microcomputer market has contributed to stimulate the development of electronic communication at the expense of traditional typographic equipment. Desktop publishing is taking over and many documents are now printed in house and not subcontracted to outside printing companies.

Prices of substitute products impose a ceiling on the price firms in the product market can charge. The more attractive the price–performance alternative offered by substitutes, the stronger the limit on the industry's ability to raise prices (Porter, 1980, p. 25).

> This phenomenon is observable, for instance, in the market of primary energy sources. The successive increases of oil prices have stimulated the development of alternative energy resources like solar and nuclear energy.

Clearly, substitute products that deserve particular attention are those that are subject to trends improving their price–performance trade-off with the industry's product. Moreover, in such a comparison, special attention needs to be given to switching costs (real or psychological), which can be very high and as far as the customer is concerned can offset the impact of the price differential.

Identifying substitute products is not always straightforward. The aim is to search systematically for products that meet the same generic need or perform the same function. This can sometimes lead to industries far removed from the main industry.

> For example, in the home-interior decoration market, the alternative technologies are: paint, wallpaper, textile, panels of wood, and so on. In the goods transportation market, the alternative technologies are: air, road, rail and water.

It would be insufficient simply to look at the common practices in the major customer groups, because of the information risks appearing too late. Therefore it is necessary to have a permanent monitoring system of major technological developments in order to be able to adopt a proactive rather than a reactive behaviour. In this perspective, the concept of *solution market* is useful because it induces the firm to define upfront its reference market in terms of the alternative technologies likely to perform the same core service to the buyer.

Bargaining power of customers

Customers have a bargaining power *vis-à-vis* their suppliers. They can influence an activity's potential profitability by forcing the firm to cut prices, demanding more extensive services, better credit facilities or even by playing one competitor against another. The degree of influence depends on a number of conditions (Porter, 1980, pp. 24–7):

- The customer group is concentrated and purchases *large volumes* relative to seller sales; this is so for large distributors, and, in France, for large shopping centres.
- The products that customers purchase from the industry represent a significant fraction of their *own costs*, which drives them to bargain hard.
- The products purchased are standard or *undifferentiated*. Customers are sure that they can always find alternative suppliers.
- The customers' *switching costs*, or costs of changing suppliers, are few.
- Customers pose a *credible threat of backward integration*, and are therefore dangerous potential entrants.
- The customers have *full information* about demand, actual market prices and even supplier costs.

These conditions apply equally to consumer goods as well as industrial goods; they also apply to retailers as against wholesalers and to wholesalers as against manufacturers. Such a situation, where buyers' bargaining power is very high, is seen in Belgium and France in the food sector, where large-scale distribution is highly concentrated and even terms to manufacturers can be dictated.

These considerations underline the fact that the choice of buyer groups to target is a crucial strategic decision. A firm can improve its competitive position by a *customer selection policy*, whereby it has a well-balanced portfolio of customers and thus avoids any kind of dependence on the buyer group.

Bargaining power of suppliers

Suppliers can exert bargaining power because they can raise the prices of their deliveries, reduce product quality or limit quantities sold to a particular customer. Powerful suppliers can thereby squeeze profitability out of an industry unable to recover cost increases in its own prices.

> For instance, the increase in the price of basic steel products, imposed in Europe between 1980 and 1982 by the Davignon plan, contributed to profit erosion in the downstream steel transformation sector. Intense competition prevented firms in this sector from raising their prices.

The conditions making suppliers powerful are similar to those making customers powerful (Porter, 1980):

- The supplier is in a monopoly position.
- The supplier group is dominated by a few companies and is more concentrated than the industry it sells to.

- It is not facing other substitute products for sale to the industry.
- The firm is not an important customer of the supplier.
- The supplier's product is an important input to the buyer's business.
- The supplier group has differentiated its products or has built up switching costs to lock the buyers in.
- The supplier group poses a credible threat of forward integration.

The four factors of external competition, together with rivalry among existing firms within the same product market, determine a firm's potential profitability and market power.

By way of illustration, the results of a competitive structure analysis in the private insurance brokerage market are presented in Figure 10.3.

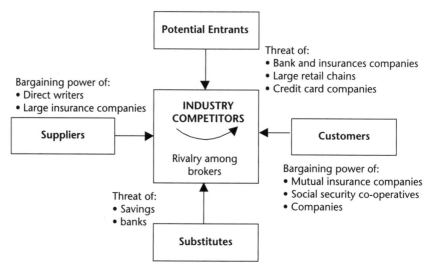

Figure 10.2 Competition analysis: the private insurance brokers' market
Source: MDA Consulting Group, Brussels.

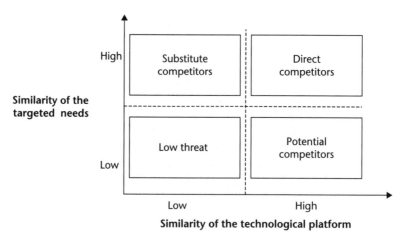

Figure 10.3 Competitors' identification matrix
Source: Adapted from Bergen and Peteraf (2002).

Competitors' identification

The five forces model is helpful for scanning the global competitive landscape of the reference market, but does not permit identification of the most dangerous competitors. There may be a temptation for management to pay attention only to competitors who display a product or technology overlap, because these competitors are salient. Note that the reference market definition in terms of solution sought and the macro-segmentation approach should help avoiding this myopic approach of competition definition. The diagram presented in Figure 10.4 can help management to maximize their awareness of competitive threats and to classify the types of competition they face or will face in a near future.

In Figure 10.4, the vertical axis measures the degree (low–high) to which a given competitor overlaps with the focal firm in terms of customers needs served. This is consistent with the solution market definition and recognizes that competition may include firms that do not share the same technological platform (e.g., paint versus wall paper for home-interior decoration).

The horizontal axis refers – also at two levels – to resource similarity as the extent to which a given competitor possesses strategic resources and capabilities comparable to those of the focal firm. We can therefore identify four types of competitors.

- The *direct competitors*, that is, the firms that score high in terms of both market needs and technological platform.
- The *potential competitors* scoring high in terms of technological platform but that not presently serve the same market needs.
- The *substitute competitors* that serve the same market needs than the focal firm but with different types of resources and/or technologies.
- The *sleeping competitors* that constitute presently a low threat, having different market targets and technologies.

This framework can be useful not only for increasing awareness of the various dimensions of the competitive landscape, but it can be used to track potential competitors movements' over time.

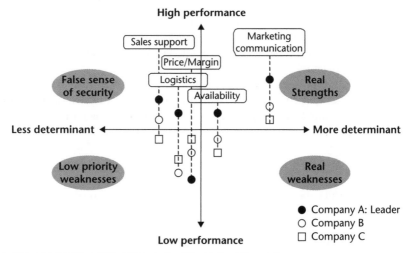

Figure 10.4 Impact of a successful differentiation strategy: the office equipment market
Source: Lambin (2007).

10.4   COMPETITIVE ADVANTAGE BASED ON MARKET POWER

The intensity and form of the competitive struggle between direct rivals in a product market vary according to the nature of the actual competitive structure. This defines the degree of interdependence between rivals and the extent of *market power* held by each competitor. To analyse a particular market situation, it is convenient to refer to the various competitive structures proposed by economists, for which numerous theoretical and empirical studies exist. Four competitive structures are generally distinguished: pure (or perfect) competition, oligopoly, monopolistic (or imperfect) competition and monopoly. We will examine each of these alternatives successively and describe the expected competitive behaviour in each case.

Pure or perfect competition

Perfect competition is characterized by the existence in the market of a large number of sellers facing a large number of buyers. Neither of the two groups is powerful enough to influence prices. Products have clearly defined technical characteristics, are perfect substitutes and sell at the market price, which is strictly determined by the *interplay between supply and demand*. In this kind of market, sellers have no market power whatsoever, and their behaviour is not affected by their respective actions. Key features are therefore the following:

- Large number of sellers and buyers.
- Undifferentiated and perfectly substitutable products.
- Complete absence of market power for each player.

This kind of situation can be seen in industrial markets for unbranded products, and in the *commodity markets*, such as soft commodities and the minerals and metals market. These are normally organized markets (terminal markets) such as the London Metal Exchange (LME) or the various commodity futures exchanges. In a perfectly competitive market, the interplay between supply and demand is the determining factor. As far as the firm is concerned, price is given (the dependent variable) and the quantity supplied is the action variable of interest.

To improve performance, the firm's only possible courses of action are either to modify its deliveries to the market or to change its production capacity upward or downward, depending on the market price level. In the short term, it is essential for the firm to keep an eye on competitors' production levels and on new entrants in order to anticipate price movements.

In the long term, it is clearly in the firm's interest *to release itself from the anonymity of perfect competition* by differentiating its products to reduce substitutability, or by creating switching costs to the buyers in order to create some form of loyalty. One way of achieving this, for example, is to exercise strict quality control accompanied by a branding policy.

A number of countries exporting food products follow this kind of strategy to maintain their product's price and demand levels: Colombian coffee, Spanish oranges, Cape fruits and Chiquita bananas are attempts at this type of differentiation. Table 10.2 shows the price differentials observed for branded and non-branded vegetables.

Another way is to develop, downstream in the industrial chain, higher added value activities incorporating the commodity, with the objectives of stabilizing the level of demand

Table 10.2 Price differentials: branded products versus store brands

Sun Maid Raisins	$4.47/lb	Store Brand raisins	$3.06/lb
Campbell's Children & Stars	$1.69/lb	Store Brand Chicken & Stars	$0.89/lb
Heinz Ketchup	$1.="/lb	Store brand Ketchup	$0.84/lb
Welch's Grape Juice	1.85/qt	Store Brand Grape Juice	$1.30/qt

Source: Example quoted by Stanton and Herbst (2005, p. 10).

and gaining protection from wild price fluctuations. It is for instance, the strategy followed by the steel industry which diversifies its activity by entering downstream in sectors of transformation of primary steel products such as steel shingles of steel storage equipment.

How to escape from the anonymity of price competition?

This question is relevant for all the basic products labelled *"commodities"*, that is, standard products sought by customers for their core function at the lowest possible price. Such is the case for most agricultural products (wheat, corn, coffee, cocoa, sugar and so on), non-ferrous products (copper, tin, aluminium, cobalt and so on), chemical and petrochemical products, but also for products like fruit, concentrated fruit juice, textiles and so on. For the majority of these commodities, organized markets, or bourses, like the LME or the London Commodity Market, exist where it is the interplay of supply and demand that determines *the market price*, which is then used as a reference price by the buyers and imposed on the seller.

From the commodity firm's point of view, two steps are required to escape from this competitive stalemate: (a) a systematic search for differentiation opportunities and (b) a fine market segmentation to undercover segments of customers having more demanding purchase criteria.

A commodity is always a bundle of attributes

In approaching a commodity market, it is essential to analyse customers' needs in terms of a *"solution sought"* and not only in terms of quantity to be sold. As explained above, to the customer a product is always a package of benefits or a bundle of attributes comprising, of course, the core service or function, but also peripheral services, necessary or added, which accompany the core service provided by the commodity. In a pure competition market, only the core service is identical from one rival to the other and cannot therefore justify a price premium. But the seller can still differentiate from competition through the other services or attributes of the bundle, such as services, guarantee, assistance in use, technical support and so on, and that, not only at the purchase phase, but also at each phase of the cycle *"acquisition–use–maintenance–destruction–recycling"* of the commodity.

The problem is to discover what are the sensitive services to which the buyer is likely to respond and at what phase of the cycle. Hence the importance of a fine market segmentation.

Box 10.3 Implementation problem: how to escape from the anonymity of price competition

- A commodity is always a bundle of characteristics or attributes.
- Differentiation opportunities always exist.
- A commodity market is never completely homogeneous.

- Three types of segments always exist: price-conscious customers, service customers and commitment-focused customers.

As shown by Hill, McGrawth and Dayal (1998), differentiation opportunities always exist, even in commodity markets, either through value creation or through delivery mode.

Segmentation of a commodity market

In commodity markets, it is common practice to segment customers by product and consuming industry and not by reference to their purchasing behaviour. In reality, no market is completely homogeneous in terms of customers' needs or expectations and, the objective of market behavioural segmentation is to uncover customer(s) group(s) having different purchase criteria, more specific or more demanding, and who would be ready to pay a price higher than the reference market price to obtain exactly what they need.

According to Hill, McGrath and Dayal (1998), three types of customers always exist, even in commodity markets – the incorrigibles, the potentials and the gold standard customers:

- *The incorrigibles*, also called the price-sensitive buyers, are the pure price buyers who treat suppliers as the enemy and focus exclusively on current delivered price. They are primarily concerned with the cost, as the product usually represents a major portion of their total product cost or because their needs are fairly standard. They will switch suppliers for even the slightest price differential. Unfortunately, they constitute half of the market or more. They are not attractive customers but are so prevalent that no supplier can seriously think about refusing them.
- *The potentials*, or the service customers, also place a high emphasis on pure price, but are occasionally willing to entertain the notion of selective relationships involving certain products or services. Customers in this segment, representing 30–45 per cent of the market, have some degree of interest in partnering in certain circumstances for reducing delivery costs, to avoid supply interruptions or for specific industrial applications. Once it is possible to move the dialogue beyond delivery price, the potential for differentiation exists.
- *The gold standard customers,* also called the commitment-focused customers, value long-standing relationships through which superior product applications can be developed and employed in their own products and processes. They will pay a premium price for offerings that deliver true value in terms of process enhancement, cost reduction or benefits to end-user. They typically represent a small portion of the total market, anywhere from 5 to 25 per cent.

Hill, McGrath and Dayal (1998) reports that one study in steel strapping found that 8 per cent of the customers fit into this last category, while another piece of research carried out by BAH found that segment ranging as high as 22 per cent in some chemical markets.

> While most wheat buyers require wheat to meet only two or three specifications, demanding buyers such as the Japanese may have a list of 20 requirements. Using its computerised capacity to monitor the precise content of the wheat in all 1500 of Australia's silos, the Australian Wheat Board track down the hard-to-find wheat the Japanese demand. Across all their customers, the Board earn a high price realisation of $2 a ton, a significant advantage in a low margin business. (Hill, McGrath and Dayal, 1998, p. 29)

This example, the steel industry, reveals differentiation opportunities for the seller who can propose offerings having superior value to the buyer. An interesting observation made in this steel survey reported by McKinsey (Schorsch, 1994) is that each industry segment contains price, service and commitment buyers. Performance requirements simply do not correlate with industry segments (car customers, pipe and tube makers, construction and so on).

Oligopoly

Oligopoly is a situation where the number of competitors is low or a few firms are dominant. As a result rival firms are highly interdependent. In markets concentrated in this way, each firm knows well the forces at work and the actions of one firm are felt by the others, who are inclined to react. Therefore, the outcome of a strategic action depends largely on whether or not competing firms react.

The more undifferentiated the products of existing firms, the greater the dependence between them will be; in this case we talk about *undifferentiated oligopoly*, as opposed to *differentiated oligopoly*, where goods have significant distinctive qualities of value to the buyers. Oligopolistic situations tend to prevail in product markets having reached the maturity phase of their life cycle, where primary demand is stagnant and non-expansible. As holds the "rule of three" (Sheth and Sisodia, 2002) in this type of markets there is only room for three full generalists along several specialists.

The mechanisms of a price war

In undifferentiated oligopoly, products are perceived as "commodities" and buyers' choices are mainly based on price and the service rendered. These conditions are therefore ripe for intense price competition, unless a dominant firm can impose a discipline and force a leading price. This situation is one of *price leadership*, in which the dominant firm's price is the reference price used by all competitors. On the other hand, if price competition does develop, it generally leads to reduced profitability for everyone, especially if primary demand is non-expansible. A *price war* then gets under way, as follows:

- A price cut initiated by one firm creates an important market share movement due to buyers attracted by the reduced price.
- The firm's market share increases. Other firms feel this immediately, given that their own shares drop. They begin to adopt the same price cut to overturn the movement.
- Price equality between rivals is restored, but at a lower level, which is less profitable for all.
- Since primary demand is non-expansible, the price cut has not contributed to increasing the market size.

Lack of co-operation or discipline causes everyone's situation to deteriorate. In a non-expansible market, competition becomes a *zero-sum game*. Firms seeking to increase sales can only achieve it at the expense of direct competitors. As a result, competition is more aggressive than when there is growth, where each firm has the possibility of increasing its sales by simply growing at the same pace as primary demand, which is keeping its market share constant.

Alternative competitive behaviours

In a stagnant oligopolistic market, explicit consideration of competitors' behaviour is an essential aspect of strategy development. *Competitive behaviour* refers to the attitude adopted by a firm in its decision-making process, with regard to its competitors' actions and reactions. The attitudes observed in practice can be classified into five typical categories:

- *Independent behaviour* is observed when competitors' actions and/or reactions are not taken into account, either implicitly or explicitly, in the firm's decisions. This attitude is observed in particular with regard to operational decisions, and is sometimes seen even in the case of strategic choices, in firms with a dominant market position.

- *Co-operative behaviour* corresponds to a confident or complacent attitude which seeks, tacitly or explicitly, understanding or collusion rather than systematic confrontation. Tacit agreement is frequently seen between medium-sized firms; explicit or cartel agreement, on the other hand, takes place more between large firms in oligopolistic markets which are not subject to competition regulations or which are controlled very little in this respect. Anti-trust officials in the United States and the Competition Commission in the EU are actively pursuing cartel agreements and can impose severe fines and prison sentences (see Exhibit 10.3).

- *Follower behaviour* is based on an explicit consideration of competitors' actions; it consists of adapting one's own decisions to the observed decisions of competitors, without, however, anticipating their subsequent reactions. If all existing competitors adopt this kind of behaviour, a succession of mutual adaptations is observed, until stability is achieved.

- *Leader behaviour* is a more sophisticated behaviour. It consists of anticipating competitors' reactions to the firm's own decisions, assuming they have the previous type of behaviour; here, the firm is assumed to know its rivals' reaction functions and to incorporate it when elaborating its strategy. As strategic marketing develops, it is seen ever more frequently in oligopolistic markets, where competition laws are strictly enforced.

- *Aggressive or warfare behaviour* also consists in anticipating competitors' reactions to the firm's decisions. But in this case, rivals' behaviour is assumed to be such that they always adopt the strategy most harmful to their adversaries. This type of behaviour is mainly observed in oligopolistic markets where primary demand is stagnant and any one firm's gains must be at the expense of the others. This kind of situation is analysed in game theory as a "zero-sum" game, with optimal strategy being the one with the lowest risk of loss.

The most frequent behaviour in undifferentiated oligopoly is of the follower or leader kind. It is, however, not rare to observe aggressive behaviour of the kind described in game theory, especially as regards price decisions, with the risk of leading to price wars which are generally harmful to all.

Exhibit 10.3   Anti-trust laws in action

Two top European companies have been fined a record $725 million in the United States for their part in a nine-year conspiracy to control the market of vitamins. A former executive was jailed for four months and fined $100,000 for his role in the cartel. The cartel lasted almost a decade and involved a highly sophisticated and elaborate conspiracy to control everything about the sale of these products. The companies acted as if they were working for the same business, referred by executives as Vitamins Inc. Executives met once a year for a summit to fix their annual budget, setting prices, carving geographic markets and setting volumes of sales. The summit was followed by monitoring meetings, quarterly reviews and frequent correspondence. The European Commission was also investigating whether pharmaceutical companies had been involved in a vitamin price fixing cartel.

Source: The Financial Times, 21 May 1999.

Marketing warfare

In industrialized economies, oligopolistic situations are frequent. In many industrial sectors, firms face each other with weakly differentiated products, in stagnant and saturated markets, where one firm's gains are necessarily another's losses. A key factor in success is thwarting competitors' actions. This kind of competitive climate obviously breeds the adoption of *marketing warfare*, which puts the destruction of the adversary at the centre of preoccupations. Kotler and Singh (1981), Ries and Trout (1986), Durö and Sandström (1988) have taken the analogy with *military strategy* even further and proposed various typologies of competitive strategies directly inspired from von Clausewitz (1908). As put by Ries and Trout (1986, p. 7):

> The true nature of marketing is not serving the customer, it is outwitting, outflanking and outfighting your competitors.

This point of view is in conflict with the market-driven orientation which suggests that a balance should be maintained between customer and competitor orientations. What is the advantage, indeed, of beating competitors in products that the customer does not want?

The competitive reaction matrix

Firms compete with one another by emphasizing different elements of the marketing mix and by insisting differently on each component of the mix. The competitive reaction matrix presented in Table 10.3 is a useful instrument for analysing alternative action–reaction patterns among two competing companies (Lambin, 1976, pp. 22–7). The matrix might include two brands, the studied brand and its priority competitor, and three or four components of the marketing mix, such as price, media advertising, promotion or product quality.

> In Table 10.3, the horizontal rows designate the actions initiated by our brand A. The alternative actions might be to cut price, increase advertising or improve quality. The responses of brand B, the direct competitor, are represented by the vertical columns. The coefficients in the matrix are the reaction probabilities of brand B reacting to brand A's move.

On the diagonal we have the *direct reaction probabilities*, or the likelihood of brand B responding to a move of brand A with the same marketing instrument, that is, meeting a price cut with a price cut. Off diagonal, we have the *indirect reaction elasticity*, or the probabilities of brand B responding to brand A with another marketing instrument, for example, meeting a price cut with increased advertising. These reaction elasticities can be estimated by reference to past behaviour or by seeking management's judgement concerning the strengths and weaknesses of competition. Once the matrix is developed, management can review each potential marketing action in the light of probable competitor reactions. The entries of the matrix are probabilities, as in Table 10.3, their horizontal sum must be equal to one.

Table 10.3 Competitive reaction matrix

Brand A Actions	Competing Brand B's Reactions		
	Price (p)	Advertising (a)	Quality (x)
Price	Pp,p*	Pp,a	Pp,x
Advertising	Pa,p	Pa,a	Pa,x
Quality	Px,p	Px,a	Px,x

*The first subscript is for the brand initiating the move; the second for is for the rival's response.
Source: Lambin (1976, p. 24).

For example, if management considers that there is a 70 per cent chance that competition will meet our price cut, but only a 20 per cent chance that it will meet a quality increase, it might consider that a quality increase programme will help more to develop a unique marketing approach than the price cut, since it is less likely to be imitated.

The competitive matrix is useful in helping to develop a distinctive marketing approach to the market and to anticipate competitors' reactions. More columns can be added, representing other marketing instruments. Delayed responses can also be analysed. For an example of an application in the electric razor market, see Lambin, Naert and Bultez (1975).

Competitors' analysis and monitoring system

The attitude to be adopted towards competitors is central to any strategy. This attitude must be based on a refined analysis of competitors. Porter (1980, p. 47) describes the purpose of analysing competitors as follows:

> The objective of a competitor analysis is to develop a profile of the nature and success of the likely strategy changes each competitor might make, each competitor's probable response to the range of feasible strategic moves other firms could initiate, and each competitor's probable reaction to the array of industry changes and broader environmental shifts that might occur.

There are several broad areas of interest that constitute the structure to guide the collection and analysis of information about competitors. The relevant questions are the following:

- What are the competitors' major objectives?
- What is the current strategy being employed to achieve the objectives?
- What are the capabilities of rivals to implement their strategies?
- What are their likely future strategies?

Together, these areas of information collection and analysis (see also Box 10.4) comprise a fairly complete picture of the competitors' activities. Some companies have discovered the importance of competitor analysis. Some examples are:

- IBM has a commercial analysis department with thousands of branch office representatives responsible for reporting information about the competition.
- Texas Instruments has employees analyse government contracts won by competitors to discern their technological strengths.
- Citicorp has an executive with the title "manager of competitive intelligence".
- McDonald's distributes a Burger King and Wendy's Competitive Action Package to its store managers.

Box 10.4   Implementation problem: questions to be addressed in a competitor's monitoring system

- Who are the priority competitors?
- What are competitor's mains strengths and weaknesses?
- What type of competitive advantage do we have over priority competitors?
- What is the current strategy of priority competitors?
- How are priority competitors performing financially?
- What proactive and reactive competitive actions can be expected?

Strong competitive interdependence in a product market is not very attractive, because it limits the firm's freedom of action. To escape it, the firm can either try to differentiate itself from rivals or seek new product markets through creative market segmentation.

Imperfect or monopolistic competition

Monopolistic competition is halfway between competition and monopoly. There are many competitors whose market powers are evenly distributed. But their products are differentiated in the sense that, from the customer's point of view, they possess significantly distinct characteristics and are perceived as such by the whole product market. Differentiation may take different forms – for example, the taste of a drink, a particular technical characteristic, an innovative combination of features which provides the possibility of a variety of different uses, quality and extent of customer services, a lower cost of utilization, the distribution channel, power of brand image and so on. According to Chamberlin (1933, 1962, p. 56), a product is differentiated,

> if any significant basis exist for distinguishing the goods (or services) from one seller from those of another. Such a basis may be real or fancied, so long as it is of any importance whatsoever to buyers, and leads to a preference for one variety of the product over another?

Monopolistic competition is therefore founded on a *differentiation strategy* designed to generate on external competitive advantage.

Conditions for successful differentiation

For a *differentiation strategy* to be successful, a number of conditions need to be present:

- The differentiation should provide something that is *unique*, beyond simply offering a low price.
- The element of uniqueness must represent some *value to customers*.
- This value can either represent a *better performance* (higher satisfaction) or *reduced cost*.
- The value to buyers must be high enough for them to be prepared to pay a *price premium* to benefit from it.
- The element of differentiation must be *sustainable*; in other words, other rivals should not be able to imitate it immediately.
- The price premium paid by buyers must *exceed the cost supplement* borne by the firm to produce and maintain the element of differentiation.

Finally, in so far as the element of differentiation is not very apparent and is unknown by the market, the firm must produce *signals* to make it known.

Benefits of successful differentiation

The effect of differentiation is to give the firm some degree of *market power*, because it generates preferences, customer loyalty and lower price sensitivity. The result is a sort of "mini-monopoly". The customer's bargaining power is thus partially neutralized.

Differentiation also protects the firm from rival attacks, given that as a result of the element of differentiation, substitution between products is reduced. The monopolistic firm is relatively independent in its actions *vis-à-vis* its rivals.

> Differentiation partially insulates sellers from ruinous cutthroat price competition. Tag Heuer, for example, the Swiss seller of upscale sports watches, does not tremble when Timex cuts

prices on sport watches; neither does Nike when faced with a price reduction in no-name, sell-them-out-of-bins sneakers. Differentiation exerts control over prices by reducing the direct substitutability of once-similar products. The true beauty of differentiation is that it allows consumers to elect to pay higher prices. (Schnaars, 1998, p. 35)

Finally, it also allows the firm to defend itself better against suppliers and substitute products. *This is the typical competitive situation that strategic marketing seeks to create.*

The importance/performance matrix presented in Figure 10.5 provides a good illustration of a successful differentiation strategy. The matrix is based on a survey conducted among the customers of three competing brands (brands A, B and C). Brand A is the leader with the highest market share and is perceived by customers as performing better than its competitors on four criteria out of five, despite the fact that brand A is the most expensive.

Exhibit 10.4　The search for differentiation ideas

A differentiation strategy gives the firm the opportunity to claim its difference with its direct competitors. This strategy makes it possible to increase market share or to keep it unchanged at the same or at a higher price,. This strategy is feasible only if some distance exists on one or several important product attributes compared to competition. Chetochine (1997, p. 141) suggests four differentiation dimensions likely to create that distance vis-à-vis direct rivals.

A product or service can be different because it has one or several of the following innovative features: reformulating, simplifying, accelerating or improving.

■ *Reformulating:* a product or service based on another technology or on another way to proceed, even if it produces similar results at the same price (phone banking).

■ *Simplifying:* a product that saves efforts, steps or energy (the software Windows).

■ *Accelerating:* a product that generates time savings compared to traditional products (the self-scanning system in supermarkets).

■ *Improving:* a product providing to the user better service or a better performance (Pentium in microcomputers).

A product can distance itself from rivals on several dimensions. Phone banking, for example, is at the same time a new procedure, simplifying and accelerating, but not necessarily better in terms of service quality.

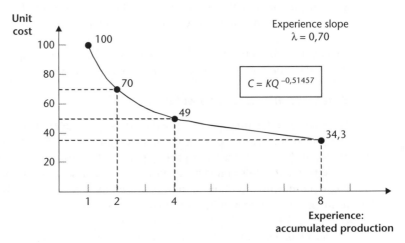

Figure 10.5　Example of an experience curve

In monopolistic competition, the firm offers a differentiated product and thus holds an external competitive advantage. This "market power" places it in a protected position, and allows the firm to earn profits above the market average. Its strategic aim is therefore to exploit this preferential demand, while keeping an eye on the value and duration of the element of differentiation.

Monopoly

This type of competitive structure is a limiting case, as for perfect competition. A single producer facing a large number of buyers dominates the market. Its product is therefore, for a limited period of time, without any direct competitor in its category. This kind of situation is observed in the introductory stage of a product's life cycle, namely, in emerging industries characterized by high-technology innovations.

If monopoly exists, the *innovative firm* has a market power that in principle is substantial. In reality, new entrants, who are attracted by the possibility of growth and profits, rapidly threaten this power. The *foreseeable duration of monopoly* then becomes an essential factor. It will depend on the innovation's power and the existence of sustainable barriers to entry. A monopoly situation is always temporary, due to the rapid diffusion of technological innovations. We saw in the previous chapter the strategic options and the risks that characterize innovation monopoly. A monopolist is also subject to competition from substitute products.

The logic of state or government monopolies is different from that of private firms. It is no longer the logic of profit, but that of public good and public service. Fulfilling these objectives in public services is hard because there is no incentive to adopt a market orientation. On the contrary, the public or state organization favours the adoption of a self-centred or bureaucratic orientation. This is one of the reasons in favour of the policy of deregulation adopted in many European countries. This problem is dealt with in the field of social marketing, or marketing of non-profit organizations, which has developed quite substantially over the last few years.

Dynamics of competition

Concluding the analysis of competitive forces, it is clear that market power and profit potential can vary widely from one market situation to another. We can thus put two limiting cases aside: one is the case where profit potential is almost zero; in the other case, it is very high. In the first case, which is the case of *perfect competition*, the following situation will be observed:

- Entry into the product market is free.
- Existing firms have no bargaining power as against their clients and suppliers.
- Competition is unrestrained because of the large number of rival firms.
- Products are all similar and there are many substitutes.

The other limiting case, which is close to the case of *monopoly*, is where profit potential is extremely high:

- There are powerful barriers that block entry to new competitors.
- The firm has either no competitors or a few weak competitors.
- Customers cannot turn to substitute products.
- Customers do not have enough bargaining power to make prices go down.
- Suppliers do not have enough bargaining power to make increased costs acceptable.

This is the ideal situation for the firm that will have a very strong *market power*. Market reality is obviously somewhere in between these two extreme cases. It is the interplay of competitive forces that favours one or other of these situations.

10.5　COMPETITIVE ADVANTAGE BASED ON COST DOMINATION

Gaining market power through successful product differentiation is one way to gain a competitive advantage. Another way is to achieve cost domination *vis-à-vis* competition through better productivity and cost controls. Cost reductions can be achieved in many ways:

> Scale economies – experience effects – lower cost of inputs – more efficient use of the production capacity – more efficient manufacturing technology – better product design – more efficient organization.

In many industries, where the value added to the product accounts for a large percentage of the total cost, it has been observed that there is an opportunity to lower costs as a firm gains experience in producing a product.

The observation that there is an *"experience effect"* was made by Wright (1936) and the Boston Consulting Group (1968) towards the end of the 1960s. They verified the existence of such an effect for more than 2,000 different products, and deduced a law known as the *experience law* (see Figure 10.6).

This law, which has had great influence on the strategies adopted by some firms, translates and formalizes at the firm level what economists study at the aggregate level: improvements in productivity. We will first present the theoretical foundations of the experience law, and then discuss its strategic implications.

The experience law defined

The strategic importance of the experience law stems from the fact that it makes it possible not only to forecast one's own costs, but also to forecast competitors' costs. The law of experience stipulates that:

> the unit cost of value added to a standard product, measured in constant currency, declines by a constant percentage each time the accumulated production doubles.

A certain number of points in this definition deserve further comments:

- The word "experience" has a very precise meaning: it designates the *cumulative number of units produced* and not the number of years since the firm began making the product.

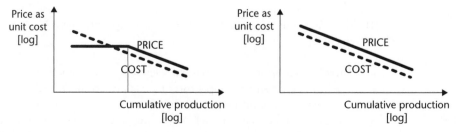

Figure 10.6　Price penetration strategies

- Thus the *growth of production per period* must not be confused with the growth of experience. Experience grows even if production stagnates or declines.

- The experience law is a *statistical law* and not a natural one; it is an observation, which is statistically verified in some situations, but not always. Costs do not spontaneously go down; they go down if someone pushes them down through productivity improvements.

- Costs must be measured in *constant monetary units*, that is, they must be adjusted for inflation. Inflation can hide the experience effect.

- The experience effect is always stronger during the *launch and growth stages* of a new product's development cycle; later improvements are proportionally weaker and weaker as the product market reaches maturity.

- The experience law applies only to *value-added costs*, which are costs over which the firm has some control, such as costs of transformation, assembly, distribution and service. Recall that value added is equal to selling price minus input costs: the cost of value added is given by unit cost minus input costs.

In practice, total unit cost is often used as the basis of observation of experience effects, especially because it is more easily accessible than value added cost. The error introduced in this way is not too high when the cost of value added represents a large proportion of the total unit cost.

Causes of experience effects

Several factors contribute to drive unit costs down the experience curve. They are the improvements adopted by management in the production process as a result of learning from accumulated output. Abell and Hammond (1979) have identified six sources of experience effects:

- *Labour Efficiency*. As workers repeat a particular task, they become more dexterous and learn improvements and short cuts that increase their efficiency.

- *Work Specialization and Methods Improvements*. Specialization increases worker proficiency at a given task.

- *New Production Processes*. Process innovations and improvements can be an important source of cost reductions, such as the introduction of robotics or of computer-assisted systems.

- *Better Performance from Production Equipment*. When first designed, a piece of production equipment may have a conservatively rated output. Experience may reveal innovative ways of increasing its output.

- *Changes in the Resource Mix*. As experience accumulates, a producer can often incorporate different or less expensive resources in the operation. For instance, less skilled workers can replace skilled workers, or automation can replace labour.

- *Product Redesign*. Once the firm has a clear understanding of the performance requirements, a product can be redesigned to incorporate less costly materials and resources.

These factors are all under the control of the firm. They are part of the general policy of the firm of productivity improvements aiming at making an equivalent product for less cost or at making a better product for the same cost or a combination of the two. Thus experience *per se* does not generate cost reductions, but rather provides *opportunities for cost reductions*. It is up to management to exploit these opportunities.

Exhibit 10.5   The mathematics of experience curves

The mathematical expression for the experience curve is as follows:

$$C_p = C_b \cdot \left(\frac{Q_p}{Q_b}\right)^{-\epsilon}$$

C_p = projected unit cost (p)
C_b = base unit cost (b)
Q_p = projected experience (cumulated volume)
Q_b = base *experience (cumulated volume)*
ϵ = constant: unit cost elasticity

Thus, we have,

$$\text{Projected cost} = \text{Base cost} \cdot \left(\frac{\text{Projected experience}}{\text{Base experience}}\right)^{-\epsilon}$$

The cost elasticity (ϵ) can be estimated as follows:

$$\frac{C_p}{C_b} = \left(\frac{Q_p}{Q_b}\right)^{-\epsilon}$$

and hence:

$$\epsilon = -\frac{\log C_p - \log C_b}{\log Q_p - \log Q_b}$$

In practice, it is convenient to refer to a doubling of experience. When the ratio of projected experience to base experience is equal to 2, we obtain,

$$\frac{C_p}{C_b} = 2^{-\epsilon}$$

where, $2^{-\epsilon}$ is defined as Lambda (λ), the slope of the experience curve.

Source: Lambin (2000/2007).

Formulation of the experience law

The general expression of the experience curve is presented in Exhibit 10.5.

> In Figure 10.6 we can see that the cost of the first unit is €100 and that of the second is €70. When the cumulative quantity has doubled from 1 to 2, unit cost has decreased by 30 per cent; the cost of the fourth unit will therefore be €49, the cost of the eighth unit €34.3, of the sixteenth €24 and so on. In this example, the rate of cost decline is 30 per cent per doubling, and the experience slope is 70 per cent. This corresponds to a cost elasticity of –0.515.

Often, the co-ordinates of an experience curve are expressed on a logarithmic scale, so as to represent it as a straight line. The larger the slope of the curve, the steeper the straight line. Experience slopes observed in practice lie between 0.70 (high degree of experience effect) and 1.00 (zero experience effect). The Boston Consulting Group observes that most experience curves have slopes between 70 and 80 per cent.

For a given firm, the impact of experience effects depends not only on its experience slope, but also on the speed at which experience accumulates. The possibility of reducing costs will be higher in sectors that have fast-growing markets; similarly, for a given firm, the potential for cost reduction is high if its market share increases sharply, irrespective of whether or not the reference market is expanding.

Strategic implications of the experience law

The experience law helps us understand how a competitive advantage can exist based on a disparity in unit costs between rival firms operating in the same market, and using the same means of production. The strategic implications of the experience law can be summarized as follows:

- The firm with the largest cumulated production will have the *lowest* costs, *if the experience effect is properly exploited.*
- The aggressive firm will try to drive down as *rapidly as possible* its experience curve, so as to build a cost advantage over its direct competitors.
- The goal is to grow faster than priority competitors, which implies *increased relative market share.*
- This growth objective is best achieved *right at the start*, when gains in experience are most significant.
- The most effective way of gaining market share is to adopt a *price penetration* strategy, whereby the firm fixes price at a level which anticipates future cost reductions.
- This strategy will give the firm *above-normal profit* performance.

Thus, in an experience-based strategy, building market share and penetration pricing are the key success factors for achieving a competitive advantage based on cost domination. Figure 10.7 illustrates the mechanism of a price penetration policy.

The firm anticipates the movement of its unit cost in terms of cumulative production. It sets itself a target to reach, which implies a faster sales growth than in the reference market, and hence an increase in its relative market share. The selling price, when launching the product, is determined with respect to this anticipated volume. Once the level of experience has been reached, future cost decreases will be reflected in the price to maintain the advantage over priority competitors. The pricing strategy illustrated in Figure 10.7 is more frequently observed because it is less risky: the price is reduced in parallel with the cost decline.

Assessing competitive costs disparities

If cumulative production does lead to the expected cost reduction, and if the dominant firm manages to protect the benefit of the experience it acquires, the experience effect creates

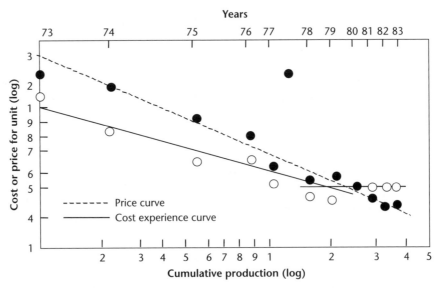

Figure 10.7   The experience curve as an early warning system
Source: Adapted from Sallenave (1985).

an entry barrier to new entrants and a cost advantage for the leader. Firms with low market shares will inevitably have higher costs, and if they fix their prices at the same level as the dominant competitor they have to suffer heavy losses. Furthermore, the firm with the highest market share also enjoys larger cash flows. It can reinvest in new equipment or new processes and thus reinforce its leadership.

To illustrate, let us examine the data in Table 10.4. A comparison is made of movements in unit costs as a function of experience, for experience slopes equal to 70 per cent, 80 per cent and 90 per cent, respectively.

Let us consider the case of two firms, A and B, using the same technology and having the same initial conditions; they both have an experience slope of 70 per cent. Firm A is at its first doubling of cumulative production, while firm B is at its fourth. Their costs are 70 and 24, respectively. One can imagine that it might be quite hard for firm A to close this gap, given that it needs to increase its market share quite considerably to achieve cost parity.

Now let us assume that the two firms A and B have the same experience; they are both at their fourth doubling. However, firm A has better exploited cost reduction opportunities and is on an experience curve of 70 per cent, whereas firm B's experience curve has a slope of only 90 per cent; their unit costs are 24 against 66. Here too, it would be difficult to close the gap. Experience effects can therefore create large disparities in costs of firms which are of equal size, but have failed to incorporate this potential equally in productivity improvements.

Experience curves as an early warning system

As mentioned above, the main usefulness of the experience curve is to assess the dynamics of cost competition between two or more firms operating in the same reference market and to alert management as to the necessity of making timely strategic changes. The short case presented in Figure 10.7 illustrates this last point.

The chart shows the cost and experience curves of a polyester fibre manufacturer. Prices and costs are expressed in constant dollars per kilogram. Prices declined on a 75 per cent experience curve while the slope of the cost curve was only 86 per cent. In this example, management of the plant could have predicted years before it was too late that the cost and price curves were converging rapidly.

In 1980, the plant made no profit. Its management immediately embarked on a cost reduction programme, but at the same time demand slowed down. The plant was unable to operate at capacity level, which would have made the cost reduction programme effective. Unit costs remained unchanged. The plant closed down in 1983.

Table 10.4   Evolution of unit cost as a function of experience effects

Cumulative production (× 1,000)	Number of doubling	Slope of the experience curve		
		70 per cent	80 per cent	90 per cent
1	–	100	100	100
2	1	70	80	90
4	2	49	64	81
8	3	34	51	73
16	4	24	41	66
32	5	17	33	59
64	6	12	26	48

Had management read the early warning given by the experience curve analysis, it would have reacted early enough to decide between several possible remedial actions:

- Increase the capacity of the plant to accumulate faster and drive the unit cost down.
- Retool and/or improve the production process to operate on a 75 per cent cost slope that is a slope compatible with the price slope.
- Specialize in special purpose fibres and sell them at a higher price than the normal price for regular polyester fibre.
- Sell the plant while it was profitable or convert it to another production line.

Thus, the experience curves can be used to anticipate future developments and *to simulate contemplated strategies*.

This type of simulation exercise can be very instructive, as the following example shows.

> Consider a firm with 6 per cent of a market that is growing at an 8 per cent real growth rate and whose leader has 24 per cent share. To catch up with the leader's share, our firm would have to grow at a 26 per cent growth rate in nine years, if the leader held its share by growing at the 8 per cent industry rate. That means expanding at over three times the industry rate for nine years, and that sales and capacity have to expand by 640 per cent. (Abell and Hammond, 1979, p. 118)

This is typically a "mission impossible". Before embarking on an experience-based strategy, it is essential to calculate the time and the investment required to achieve the objective. Some companies, such as Texas Instruments, use experience curve simulations systematically before pricing a new product.

Limits of the experience law

The experience law is not universally applicable; it holds mainly in sectors where large scale brings economic advantage and in which the process of learning is important (Abernathy and Wayne, 1974). To be more specific, situations in which the experience law is of little relevance are the following:

- Learning potential is low or the part of value added cost in the total cost is not very significant.
- One competitor has access to a special source of supplies, thus having a cost advantage, which bears no relation to its relative market share.
- Technology changes rapidly and neutralizes the experience-based cost advantage.
- The market is not price-sensitive.
- There is large potential for product differentiation.

Thus, if a firm is dominated by a competitor having a major cost advantage, two basic strategies can be adopted to circumvent the experience advantage:

- A *differentiation strategy* offering distinctive features valued by the buyer, who is ready to pay a premium price that would offset the cost handicap.
- A *technological innovation strategy* that would place the firm on a new and steeper experience curve, thereby neutralizing the cost advantage of the current market leader.

The experience curve gives the firm an *operational competitive advantage*. As already mentioned, this type of advantage is not always sustainable in the long term because of the rapid diffusion of best practices in a given sector, which enables competitors to easily imitate and neutralize the cost advantage.

10.6   THE INTERNATIONAL COMPETITIVE ADVANTAGE

International trade theory has traditionally placed the emphasis on country comparative advantages. The focus was on a country's natural endowments, its labour force and its currency's values as main sources of competitiveness. Recently, economists have turned their attention to the question how countries, governments and even private industry can alter the conditions within a country to create or reinforce the competitiveness of its firms. The leader in this area of research is Michael Porter (1990).

Industries globalize because shifts in technology, buyer needs, and government policy or country infrastructure create major differences in competitive position among firms from different nations or make the advantage of global strategy more significant (Porter, 1990, p. 63).

According to Porter four broad attributes contribute to shape the environment in which local firms compete. These attributes promote or impede the creation of competitive advantage:

1. *Factor Conditions.* The nation's position in factors of production such as skilled labour or infrastructure necessary to compete in a given industry. Porter notes that although factor conditions are very important, more so is the ability of a nation to continually create, upgrade and deploy its factors and not only the initial endowment.
2. *Demand Conditions.* The nature of home demand for the industry's product or service. The quality of home demand is more important than the quantity of home demand in determining competitive advantage. By quality, Porter means a highly competitive and demanding local market.
3. *Related and Supporting Industries.* The presence or absence in the nation of supplier industries and related industries that are internationally competitive. A firm that is operating within a mass of related firms and industries gains and maintains advantages through close working relationships, proximity to suppliers and timeliness of product and information flows.
4. *Firm Strategy, Structure and Rivalry.* The conditions in the nation governing how companies are created, organized and managed and the nature of domestic rivalry. Porter notes that no one operational strategy is universally appropriate. It depends on the fit and flexibility of what works for that industry in that country at that time.

In the analysis of home demand composition, Porter identifies three home demand characteristics particularly significant in achieving a national competitive advantage:

■   *Large Share of Home Demand.* A nation's firms are likely to gain competitive advantage in global segments that represent a large share of home demand but account for a less significant share in other nations. These relatively large segments receive the greatest and the earliest attention by the nation's firms, but tend to be perceived as less attractive by foreign competitors. The nation's firms may gain advantages in reaping economies of scale.

A good example is Airbus Industries' entry into commercial airliners. Airbus identified a segment of the European market that had been ignored by Boeing: a relatively large capacity plane for short hauls. Such a need was quite significant in Europe with its numerous capital cities within short flying distances and served by few airlines, in sharp contrast with the US situation.

■ *Sophisticated and Demanding Buyers.* A nation's firms gain competitive advantage if domestic buyers are, or are among, the world's most sophisticated and demanding buyers for the product or service. Such buyers provide a window into the most advanced buyer needs. Demanding buyers pressure local firms to meet high standards in terms of product quality and services.

Japanese pay great attention to writing instruments, because nearly all documents have until recently been hand-written in Japan due to the impracticality of typewriters in reproducing Japanese characters. Penmanship is an important indication of education and culture. Japanese firms have been the innovators and have become world leaders in pens. (Porter, 1990, p. 91)

■ *Anticipatory Buyer Needs.* A nation's firms gain advantages if the needs of home buyers anticipate those of other nations. This means that home demand provides an early warning indicator of buyer needs that will become widespread.

Scandinavian concern for social welfare and for the environment tends today to be ahead of that in the United States. Swedish and Danish firms have achieved success in a variety of industries where the heightened environmental concern anticipates foreign needs, such as in water pollution control equipment. (Porter, 1990, p. 92)

The composition of domestic demand is at the root of national advantage. The effect of demand conditions on competitive advantage also depends on other factors presented above. Without strong domestic rivalry, for example, rapid home market growth or a large home market may induce complacency rather than stimulate investment. Without the presence of appropriate supporting industries, firms may lack the ability to respond to demanding home buyers.

Chapter Summary

Competitive advantage refers to a product superiority held by the firm over its direct competitor. Competitive advantages can be classified in two main categories: external advantages based on market power due to superior value to the buyer and internal advantages based on productivity generating a cost advantage. A firm's ability to exploit a competitive advantage depends on the strength, not only of direct competition, but also of other rival forces, such as potential entrants, substitute products, customers and suppliers. The intensity of direct competition varies according to the extent of market power held by each competitor. In an oligopoly, the degree of interdependence among rivals is high and explicit consideration of competitors' behaviour is an essential aspect of strategy development. In a monopolistic situation, products are differentiated in a way which represents a value to the buyer, either by reducing their cost or by improving their performance. The effect of product differentiation is to give the firm some degree of market power, customer loyalty and weaker price sensitivity. This is the typical competitive situation that strategic marketing seeks to create for the firm. Another way to gain a competitive advantage is cost domination through better productivity and cost controls. In many industries, there is an opportunity to lower costs as experience increases in producing a product. The strategic importance of the experience law stems from the fact that it is possible not only to forecast one's own costs, but also to forecast competitors' costs. Porter has identified four determinants of international competitive advantage which can be used by governments or management to create a favourable context in which a nation's firms compete.

BIBLIOGRAPHY

Abell, D.E. and Hammond, J.S. (1979), *Strategic Market Planning*, Englewood Cliffs, NJ, Prentice-Hall.

Abernathy, W. and Wayne, K. (1974), Limit of the Learning Curve, *Harvard Business Review*, 52, 5, pp. 109–19.

Ambler, T. (2000), Marketing Metrics, *Business Strategy Review*, 11, 2, pp. 59–66.

Begley, T.M. and Boyd, D.P. (2003), The Need for a Corporate Global Mind-Set, *MIT Sloan Management Review*, 44, 2, pp. 25–32.

Bergen, M. and Peteraf, M.A. (2002), Competitor Identification and Competitor Analysis: A Broad-Based Managerial Approach, *Managerial and Decision Economics*, 23, 4/5, pp. 157–69.

Best, R.J. (2003), *Market-Based Management,* Englewood Cliffs, NJ, Prentice-Hall.

Boston Consulting Group (1968), *Perspectives on Experience*, Boston.

Chamberlin, E.H. (1933/1962), *The Theory of Monopolistic Competition*, Cambridge, MA, Harvard University Press.

Chetochine, G. (1997), *Stratégies d'entreprise face à la tourmente des prix*, Rueil Malmaison, Editions Liaisons.

Coyne, K.P. and Horn, J. (2009), Predicting Your Competitor's Reaction, *Harvard Business Review*, April, pp. 90–7.

Durö, R. and Sandström, B. (1988), *Le marketing de combat*, Paris, Les Editions d'Organisation.

Fox, K.A. (2001), Invisible Competition: Some Lessons Learned, *Journal of Business Strategy*, 22, 4, pp. 36–8.

Hill, S.I., McGrath, J. and Dayal, S. (1998), How to Brand Sand?, *Strategy and Business*, 11, Second Quarter, pp. 22–34.

Kotler, P. and Singh, R. (1981), Marketing Warfare in the 1980s, *Journal of Business Strategy*, 1, 3, pp. 30–41.

Lambin, J.J. (1976*), Advertising, Competition and Market Conduct in Oligopoly over Time*, Amsterdam, North-Holland and Elsevier.

Lambin J.J. (2007), *Market-Driven Management: Strategic and Operational Marketing*, London, Palgrave Macmillan, Second edition.

Lambin, J.J. (2000/2007*), Market-Driven Management: Strategic and Operational Marketing*, London, Palgrave Macmillan.

Lambin, J.J., Naert, P.A. and Bultez, A. (1975), Optimal Marketing Behavior in Oligopoly, *European Economic Review*, 6, 2, pp. 105–28.

Porter, M.E. (1980*), Competitive Strategy*, New York, The Free Press.

Porter, M.E. (1990), *The Competitive Advantage of Nations*, London, Macmillan.

Porter, M.E. (1996), What is Strategy?, *Harvard Business Review*, 74,6, pp. 61–78.

Prahalad, C.K. and Hamel, G. (1990), The Core Competence of the Corporation, *Harvard Business Review*, 68, 3, pp. 79–91.

Ries, A. and Trout, J. (1986*), Marketing Warfare*, New York, McGraw-Hill.

Rigby, D.K. (1997), *Management Tools and Techniques: An Executive Guide*, Boston, MA, Bain.

Sallenave, J.P. (1985), The Use and Abuse of Experience Curves, *Long Range Planning*, 18, 1, pp. 64–72.

Schnaars, S.P. (1998), *Marketing Strategy, Customers & Competition*, New York, The Free Press, 2nd edition.

Schorsch, L.L. (1994), You Can Market Steel, *The McKinsey Quarterly*, 1, pp. 111–20.

Schuiling, I. (2002), La force des marques locales et ses déterminants spécifiques par rapport au marques internationales. Applications dans le marché alimentaire., PhD Thesis, Université Catholique de Louvain.

Schuiling, I. and Kapferer, J.N. (2004), Real Differences between Local and International Brands: Strategic Implications for International Marketers, *Journal of International of Marketing*, 12, 4, pp. 97–112.

Sheth, J. and Sisodia, R. (2002), The Rule of Three in Europe, *European Business Forum*, 10, Summer, pp. 53–7.

Stanton, J. L. and Herbst, K.C. (2005), Commodities Must Begin to Act Like Branded Companies, *Journal of Marketing Management*, 21, 1/2, pp. 7–18.

Von Clausewitz, C. (1908), *On Wars*, London, Routledge & Kegan.

Wright, T.P. (1936), Factors Affecting the Cost of Airplanes, *Journal of Aeronautical Sciences*, 3, pp. 16–24.

 WEB SITE COMPANION FOR CHAPTER 10

Visit the Market-driven Management accompanying website at www.palgrave.com/business/lambin3 to find:

Note on Market Share Movements Analysis

CHAPTER ELEVEN

MARKET TARGETING AND POSITIONING DECISIONS

Having completed the market segmentation and the "attractiveness/competitiveness" analyses of the different product markets and segments, the next task is to decide what type of market coverage and what positioning strategies to adopt within each targeted segment. Several market coverage strategies can be considered. Once the market coverage decisions are made, the choice of the positioning strategy will provide the unifying concept for the development of the marketing programme. This is one of the most important steps of the strategic marketing phase because it is the way the firm will identify how to best differentiate its brand versus all competitive brands. Several difficult questions have to be addressed. Do segments mesh with company's long-run objectives? Will segments move the company towards its goals? Does company possess skills and resources to succeed in the target segment? Can the firm develop some superior advantage over competition?

Learning Objectives

When you have read this chapter, you should know and understand:

- The market targeting options to be considered
- The objectives and tools of strategic positioning
- The conditions for a successful differentiation strategy
- The usefulness of the value chain in the search for differentiation
- The different approaches in international market targeting

11.1 REFERENCE MARKET COVERAGE STRATEGIES

The firm can consider different market coverage strategies. There are described in Figure 11.1, where the two extremes are the "mass marketing" strategy and a "mass customization" strategy. Several intermediate options exist, however.

Focused strategy

The market boundaries are defined narrowly in terms of functions, technology and customer groups. This is the strategy of the *specialist* seeking a high market share in a narrow niche. The firm is concentrating its resources on the needs of a single segment or on a few

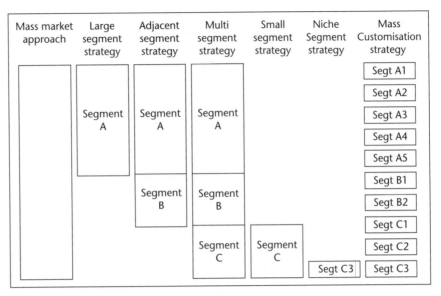

Figure 11.1 Alternative market coverage strategies

segments, adopting a specialist strategy. The specialization can be based on a function (functional specialist) or on a particular customer group (customer specialist):

- *Functional specialist.* The firm serves a single or narrow set of functions but covers a broad range of customers. The market boundaries are defined narrowly by function, but broadly by customer group. Firms manufacturing intermediate components fall into this category.
- *Customer specialist.* The market boundaries are defined broadly by function but narrowly by customer group. The focus is on the needs of a particular group of customers. Companies specializing in hospital or hotels equipment belong to this category.

Through focused marketing, the company can expect to reap the benefits of specialization and of improved efficiency in the use of the firm's resources. The feasibility of a focused strategy depends on the size of the segment and on the strength of the competitive advantage gained through specialization.

Full market coverage

Function and customer group defines the market boundaries broadly. The firm covers the whole market. A steel company is a good example of this kind of market. Two options are open to the firm adopting a full market coverage strategy: undifferentiated or differentiated marketing strategy.

- By adopting an *undifferentiated marketing strategy or a mass marketing strategy*, the firm ignores market segment differences and decides to approach the entire market as a whole and not take advantage of segmentation analysis. It focuses on what is common in the needs of customers rather than on what is different. The rationale of this middle of the road or standardization strategy is cost savings, not only in manufacturing, but also in inventory, distribution and advertising. In affluent societies, this strategy is more and more difficult to defend, as it is rarely possible for a product or a brand to please everyone.

■ In a *differentiated marketing strategy or a mass customization strategy*, the firm also adopts a full market coverage strategy but this time with tailor-made programmes for each segment. This was the slogan of General Motors, claiming "to have a car for every 'purse, purpose and personality'". This strategy enables the firm to operate in several segments with a customized pricing, distribution and communication strategy. Selling prices will be set on the basis of each segment's price sensitivity. This strategy generally implies higher costs, since the firm is losing the benefits of economies of scale. On the other hand, the firm can expect to hold a strong market share position within each segment.

Differentiated marketing does not necessarily imply full market coverage. The risk may be to over-segment the market, with the danger of cannibalism among the brands of the same company.

Mixed strategy

The firm is diversifying its activities in terms of functions and/or customer groups. This is one of the objectives of portfolio analysis, to ensure that the firm's portfolio is well balanced in terms of profit and growth potentials and well diversified in terms of risks.

The choice of any one of these market coverage strategies (see Figure 11.1) will be determined (a) by the number of identifiable and potentially profitable segments in the reference market and (b) by the resources of the firm. If a company has limited resources, a focused marketing strategy is probably the only option. In most cases, market coverage strategies are defined in only two dimensions: needs–functions and customer groups, because in general firms master only one technology, even if substitute technologies exist.

For example (see Figure 11.2), fruit jam is in direct competition with melted cheese and chocolate pasta. Because the manufacturing requirements are so different, none of the firms operating in the sector of fruit transformation also has industrial operations in these adjacent sectors.

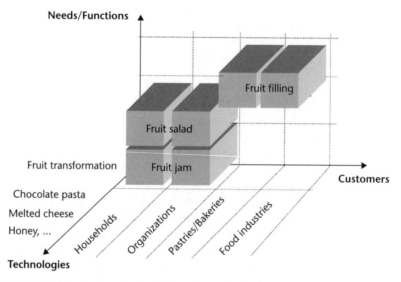

Figure 11.2 Example of limited market coverage in the fruit transformation market
Source: Lambin (2007).

Hyper-segmentation versus counter-segmentation

A segmentation strategy can result in two extreme policies:

- A *hyper-segmentation policy*, which develops made-to-order products tailored to individual needs, offering many options and a variety of secondary functions along with the core function and this at a high cost.
- A *counter-segmentation policy*, offering a basic product with no frills or extras, few options and at much lower cost.

This is the *standardization–adaptation* dilemma which is faced by companies having to define a global or transnational strategy.

In the design of a segmentation strategy, two logics are often in conflict: the market-driven or the supply-driven logic:

- The *market-driven logic* calls for maximum adaptation to the diversity of needs and leads to the development of products customized by reference to client individual preferences.
- The *supply-driven or manufacturing logic* tries to improve productivity as much as possible through product maximum standardization.

It is clear that increasing the number of formats, designs, sizes and colours of the same product in order to meet the diversity of needs can be counter-productive and undermine the productivity of the manufacturing process by reducing the potential gains due to economies of scale.

> During periods of affluence of the last decade, companies operating in B2C markets tended to follow hyper-segmentation strategies by refining their segmentation strategies. The result was a proliferation of brands, an increase of production and marketing costs and eventually of retail prices.

The behaviour of the new consumers gradually led them to become more aware of the "price/satisfaction" ratio in their purchasing decision process.

> More and more consumers behave like smart buyers and make trade-offs between price and product benefits. The success of generic brands and of private labels in Western economies is an example of this evolution.

In several sectors, and particularly in the FMCG sector, there is a trend towards a return to *voluntary simplicity* that is towards less sophisticated products, providing the core function without frills, but sold at much lower prices thanks to their high level of standardization. This evolution explains the success of low-cost distributors like *Lidl* and *Aldi*. Thus, we have here a segmentation strategy based on the "price/satisfaction" ratio, a segment too often neglected by manufacturers and very well covered today by large retailers.

Selection of priority segments

The segment targeting decision is compatible with broad market coverage and with the selection of one or several segments, where the firm will invest by priority. A golden rule is to target by priority customer group(s) for whom the product value is the highest and not – as it is tempting to do – the customer group(s) having the highest value for the firm (see Figure 11.3).

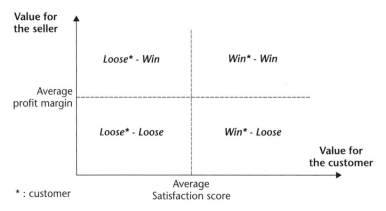

Figure 11.3 Identification of the priority segment(s)
Source: Lambin (2000/2007).

	Intellectuel Mode *(think)*	**Affective Mode** *(feel)*
High Involvement	*Learning* *(learn – feel – do)*	*Affective* *(feel – learn – do)*
Low Involvement	*Routine* *(do – learn – feel)*	*Hedonism* *(do – feel – learn)*

Figure 11.4 The involvement grid
Source: Adapted from Vaughn (1986).

To illustrate this point in Figure 11.4, the customers' value is measured by his or her satisfaction score and the firm's value by the gross profit margin generated by the product. Each indicator is represented at two levels, low and high. Four different targets can be identified. The ideal target is of course in the upper right quadrant which is a win–win situation and the least interesting is the lower left quadrant. The firm having a product orientation will be inclined to privilege the upper left quadrant since this target is more profitable for the firm. On the contrary, the customer-oriented firm will concentrate its marketing efforts on the two right targets, while trying to improve the profitability of the lower right offering.

11.2   THE STRATEGIC POSITIONING DECISION

Once the market coverage decisions are made, the next step is to decide on the positioning strategy to adopt within each targeted segment(s). Selection of the positioning strategy provides the unifying concept for the development of the marketing programme. This is one of the most critical steps in the implementation of strategic marketing, because the firm has to decide how to best differentiate its brand from competing brands.

Positioning defined

The word "positioning" has been popularized by Ries and Trout (1981). They considered that positioning was the process of *positioning the product on the consumers' mind*. Our definition is slightly different. We define positioning,

> as the decision of the company to choose the benefit(s) that the brand has to put forward to gain a distinctive place in the market.

The positioning can be summed up in four key questions

- A brand for what? This refers to the brand promise and the customer benefit.
- A brand for whom? This refers to the target segment.
- A brand for when? This refers to the use or consumption situation.
- A brand against whom? This question refers to the direct competitor.

Positioning strategy is the operational way to implement a differentiation strategy based (a) on the internal analysis of the firm's strength and weaknesses, (b) on the competitive context and (c) on the type of distinctive and unique benefit the brand can provide to the customer.

The objective of the company will be then to communicate clearly this differentiation element to potential customers so that it is clearly registered in their minds. The perception of the brand in the mind of consumers is called brand image. The positioning will be the basis of the operational marketing programme which should be consistent with the chosen brand positioning.

Conditions for positioning development

When selecting a positioning basis, a certain number of conditions must be carefully met:

- To have a good understanding of the *present positioning* of the brand or firm in the customers' minds. This knowledge can be acquired through brand image studies.
- To know the present positioning of *competing brands*, in particular those brands in direct competition.
- To select one positioning and to identify the most relevant and credible *arguments* which justify the chosen positioning.
- To evaluate the size and the potential profitability of the market involved by such a positioning.
- To verify whether the contemplated positioning is really specific and distinctive, while being suspicious of false market niches invented by advertising people or discovered through an invalidated qualitative study.
- To verify whether the brand has the required *personality potential* to achieve the positioning in the minds of customers.
- To verify whether the contemplated positioning justifies a price premium.
- To assess the *vulnerability* of the positioning. Do we have the resources required to occupy and defend this position? Do we have an alternative solution in case of failure?
- To ensure *consistency* in the positioning with the different marketing mix instruments: pricing, distribution, packaging, services and so on.

Thus, not all brand or product differences are meaningful to customers. The claim of differentiation should be "unique", "important" to the customer, "sustainable", "communicable" and "affordable".

Once the positioning strategy is adopted and clearly defined, it is much simpler for operational marketing people to translate this positioning in terms of an effective and consistent marketing programme.

Ways to position the brand versus competition

There are different ways to position the brand against competition. One can identify three types of differentiation strategies: product differentiation, price differentiation and image differentiation.

- *Product differentiation:* The most classical way of positioning a brand is to leverage the product benefits. Product characteristics such as performance, durability, reliability, design, novelty and so on can be used to base a differentiation strategy. *Bang and Olufsen* is positioned on a superior design; *Duracell* on superior durability; *Miele* on superior reliability.
- *Price differentiation:* Some companies can use price as a way to be different versus competition. There might be a different pricing strategy: the highest price in its category (*Gucci* in perfume, *Cartier* in jewellery); the best value for money (*Ikea* in the furniture industry; *Nivea* in the cosmetic sector), the lowest price in the category (*Ryanair* in the airline sector and *Aldi* in the food retail market).
- *Image differentiation.* In many sectors, brands cannot be differentiated on the basis of tangible characteristics. A certain image will differentiate a brand versus competition. In the perfume sector, each brand wants to own a certain image territory. This is similar in the cigarette (*Marlboro*) or alcohol (*Absolute Vodka*) sectors.

Credibility of the chosen positioning

Some companies are adopting a multiple benefit positioning strategy. It is the case, for instance, of the all-in-one product *Aquafresh*, the toothpaste brand launched by GlaxoSmithKline offering three benefits: anti-cavity protection, better breath and whiter teeth. The challenge is to convince people that the brand delivers all three benefits.

As the number of claims increases, the risk of a credibility gap also increases. As indicated by Kotler and Keller (2006), four major positioning errors should be avoided.

- *Underpositioning.* Potential customers have only a vague idea of the brand's distinctive claim. They do not see anything special about it.
- *Overpositioning.* Customers have a too narrow image of the brand, because it is perceived as too specialized or not affordable.
- *Confused positioning.* Customers are confused because the firm make too many claims or change its positioning too often.
- *Doubtful positioning.* Potential customers may find it hard to believe the brand claims in view of the past history of the brand, its price or its manufacturer.

This last error is probably the most frequent one observed, as illustrated by the Bata Company case in India (see Exhibit 11.1)

11.3   POSITIONING RESPONSE BEHAVIOUR

One can identify different ways in which potential customers or customers respond to perceived information and producer stimuli. Here, "response" means all mental or physical activity caused by a stimulus. A response is not necessarily manifested in external actions, but may be simply mental.

Exhibit 11.1   The Bata Company in India, an example of doubtful positioning

In the early 1990s, Bata decided to embrace the high-end segments of the Indian shoe market as a part of its target market. It launched quite a few brands for this segment with higher price tags. The move landed Bata in trouble. This segment was not meant for Bata. In the first place, this segment was not for a company like Bata. Second, the segment did not gel with Bata's distinctive competence. The segment constituted a mere 5 to 10 per cent of the footwear market in India. It could not provide the volumes that Bata was used to at the mass-market end and high volume was essential for Bata to have a healthy bottom line. Worse still, the adoption of the segment misdirected Bata's entire strategy. The top end of the market suddenly became the main focus of the company and it forgot its bread and butter shoes that had given the company its identity. And small regional players started nibbling away at Bata mainstay.

Actually Bata was squeezed at both ends. At the lower end, smaller competitors attacked Bata's mass range of canvas shoes and school shoes slots, which the company had practically vacated on its own by ignoring them completely. At the high end, niche players, who were better prepared, were challenging Bata. From a market share of around 15 percent in the mid-1980s, Bata found its share down to 10 percent of the footwear market in the mid-1990s.

After learning the lessons the hard way, Bata did an about-turn from its adventure with the high-end segment and returned to the mass segment. The new strategy was to get back to the original customers at the low end and keep that part of the market as its core focus. The company, of course, did not totally give up the new segment it had got to in the early 1990s. Brands like Hush Puppies, for instance, continued to be sold by Bata, but in a selective way and through select stores only.

Source: Chawla (2003).

Economic theory is only interested in the act of purchase per se and not in the overall behavioural process which leads to purchase. From the economist's point of view, as we saw earlier, preferences are revealed by behaviour and consumers' response is the same as the demand expressed by the market in terms of quantities sold. In reality, market demand defined in this way is an "ex-post" or historical observation, often of little practical value to the decision-maker. Market analysts hope to retrace and understand the process followed by the buyer so as to intervene in that process in a better informed manner and to be able to measure the effectiveness of marketing actions. Therefore, response behaviour is a much broader notion to the marketer than it is to the economist.

The "learn–feel–do" hierarchy

The various response levels of the buyer can be classified into three categories: cognitive response, which relates to retained information and knowledge, affective response, which concerns attitude and the evaluation system and behavioural (or conative) response, which describes action: not only the act of purchasing, but also after-purchase behaviour. Table 11.1 describes the main measures currently used for each response level.

It has been postulated by practitioners in communication that these three response levels follow a sequence and that the individual, like the organization, reaches the three stages successively and in this order: cognitive (learn) – affective (feel) – behavioural (do). We then have a learning process which is observed in practice when the buyer is heavily involved by his or her purchase decision, for example, when the perceived risk (Bauer, 1960) or the brand sensitivity (Kapferer and Laurent, 1983) is high.

The learning response model was originally developed to measure advertising effectiveness (Lavidge and Steiner, 1961) and later extended to include the process of adoption of new products (Rogers, 1962). Palda (1966) has shown that this model is not always applicable

Table 11.1   Key measures of market response

• **Cognitive response**
Saliency – Awareness – Recall– Recognition – Knowledge – Perceived Similarity.
• **Affective response**
Consideration Set – Importance – Determinance – Performance – Attitude – Preference – Intention to Buy.
• **Behavioural response**
Fact-finding behaviour – Trial purchase – Repeat purchase – Brand repertoire – Share of category requirement (exclusivity) – Brand loyalty – Satisfaction/dissatisfaction.

Source: Lambin (2007).

and that uncertainty remains as to the causal links and direction existing between the intervening variables. Moreover, the learning process hypothesis implies a well-thought-out buying process, observed only when the buyer is heavily involved in his or her purchase decision. Psycho-sociologists have also shown that other sequences exist and are observed, for example, when there is minimal involvement (Krugman, 1965), or when there is cognitive dissonance (Festinger, 1957).

Although the learning process hypothesis is not generally applicable, the "learn–feel–do" model remains valuable in structuring the information collected on response behaviours, particularly when complemented with the concepts of "perceived risk" and of "buyer involvement", discussed in this chapter.

The Foote, Cone and Belding (FCB) involvement grid

The various paths of the response process may be viewed from a more general framework, which includes the degree of involvement and the perception of reality mode. Brain specialization theory proposes that anatomical separation of the cerebral hemispheres of the brain leads to specialized perception of reality – the left side of the brain (or the intellectual mode) and the right side (or the affective or sensory mode):

- The left side, or intellectual mode, is relatively more capable of handling logic, factual information, language and analysis that is the cognitive "thinking" function.
- The right side, or affective mode, which engages in synthesis, is more intuitive, visual and responsive to the non-verbal, which is the "feeling" function.

In order to provide a conceptual framework which integrates the "learn–feel–do" hierarchy with the consumer involvement and the brain specialization theory, Vaughn (1986) presented a grid in which purchase decision processes can be classified along two basic dimensions: "high–low" involvement and "think–feel" perception of reality. Crossing the degree of involvement with the mode of reality perception leads to the matrix in Figure 11.5 in which we can see four different paths of the response process:

- *Quadrant (1)* corresponds to a buying situation where product involvement is high and the way we perceive reality is essentially intellectual. This situation implies a large need for information due to the importance of the product and mental issues related to it. Quadrant (1) illustrates the learning process described earlier, where the sequence followed was "learn–feel–do".

Major purchases with high prices and significant objective and functional characteristics such as cars, electrical household goods and houses follow this process. Industrial goods also fall in this category. These factors suggest a need for informative advertising.

- *Quadrant (2)* describes buying situations where product involvement is also high. Specific information is, however, less important than an attitude or an *emotional arousal*, since the product or brand choice reveals the buyer's system of values and personality and relates to the buyer's self-esteem. The sequence here is "feel–learn–do".

In this category we find all products that have important social and/or emotional value, like perfumes, clothes, jewellery and motorcycles. These factors suggest a need for emotional advertising.

- *Quadrant (3)* describes product decisions which involve minimal thought and a tendency to form buying habits for convenience. As long as the product fulfils the expected core service, we find low product involvement and routine behaviour. Brand loyalty will be largely a function of habit. The hierarchy model is a "do–learn–feel" pattern.

Most food and staple package goods belong in this category, which is somewhat like a commodity limbo. As products reach maturity, they are likely to descend into this quadrant. These factors suggest a need for advertising, which creates and maintains habits and stimulates a reminder of the product.

- *Quadrant (4)* illustrates a situation where low product involvement coexists with the sensory mode. Products in this category cater to personal tastes involving imagery and quick satisfaction. The sequence is "do–feel–learn".

In this category, we find products like beer, chocolates, cigarettes, jams and fast food restaurants. For these product categories, there is a need for advertising, which emphasizes personal satisfaction. For an illustration of this matrix, see Ratchford (1987, p. 30).

An interesting observation emerging from consumer involvement analyses (see Kapferer and Laurent, 1983) is the large number of "low risk–low involvement" product decisions. This fact constitutes a challenge for the firm and suggests that marketing and communication strategies must be adapted to deal with this situation where consumers just do not care very much about a large number of purchase decisions they make.

Attribute-based perceptual maps

The problem of *redundancy* remains as a final question about the relevance of attributes. Two attributes are said to be redundant when there is no difference in their significance.

> For example, in a study of heavy trucks market in Belgium, two criteria of "loading capacity" and "engine capacity" were spontaneously evoked as important attributes. The two criteria are being used interchangeably, neither existing without the other.

If two determinant attributes are retained, but they both indicate the same characteristic, this situation is equivalent to selecting only one attribute. The analyst should establish a list of determinant but non-redundant attributes.

Brand image studies measure customers' perceptions and help in discovering market expectations. The perceptual map of Figure 11.5 illustrates this point. This map is based on the rating scores of 12 attributes obtained from a sample of regular users of skin-care and make-up brands. A PCA of these scores identified two macro-attributes, which summarize 83 per cent of the total variance.

> The first axis is total quality as perceived by the respondents and includes the following micro-attributes: "technical quality", "extent of product line", "quality of packaging", "information",

"attractive promotions". These attributes are mentally opposed to "attractive prices". The second axis is strongly correlated with the attributes 'Medicare products", "laboratory tests" and opposed to "luxury design". This axis reflects the para-medical nature of these products.

In the map of Figure 11.5, we can see that the brands Rubinstein, Lauder and Lancôme are well positioned along the total quality dimension, but poorly placed on the paramedical dimension. In contrast, the brands Biotherm and Clarins are perceived as paramedical brands while not having a high-quality image. It is interesting to observe that the upper right quadrant is unoccupied, a positioning probably difficult to defend.

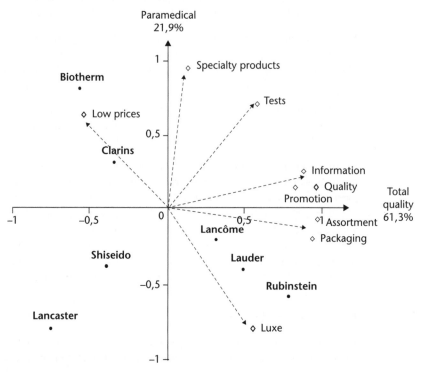

Figure 11.5   Attribute-based perceptual map: the skin-care and make-up market
Source: Van Ballenberghe (1993).

Exhibit 11.2   Principal components analysis

The method used for this purpose is factorial analysis, for example, *Principal Components Analysis (PCA)*. This method is a statistical technique which organizes and summarizes a set of data (the *N* determinant attributes in this case) into a reduced set of factors called the principal components or "macro-characteristics", which are independent of each other and which contrast best the objects under study (see Hair et al., 1992). The output of a PCA is an attribute-based perceptual map. Each brand is positioned along the two or three retained components, which can be interpreted by the correlation observed between these principal components and each attribute. The interpretation of a perceptual map resulting from a PCA is as follows: Two brands are close on the perceptual map if they are evaluated in the same way according to all retained attributes. Two attributes are close if they lead to the evaluation of brands in the same manner.

Strategies for changing a positioning

Knowledge of the way consumers perceives competing products in a segment is important in determining the strategy to be adopted to modify an unfavourable positioning. Six different strategies may be considered (Boyd, Ray and Strong, 1972):

- *Modifying the product*. If the brand is not up to market expectations of a particular characteristic, the product can be modified by reinforcing the given characteristic.
- *Modifying attribute weights*. Convince the market that more importance ought to be attached to a particular characteristic that the brand exhibits well.
- *Modifying beliefs about a brand*. The market may be badly informed and underestimate some real distinctive qualities of the brand. This entails perceptual repositioning.
- *Modifying beliefs about competing brands*. This strategy is to be used if the market overestimates some characteristics of competitors. It implies the possibility of using comparative advertising.
- *Attracting attention to neglected attributes*. This strategy usually involves the creation of a new benefit not yet considered by the target segment.
- *Modifying the required attribute level*. It is possible that the market expects a quality level, which is not always necessary, at least as far as some applications are concerned. The firm can try to convince the segment that the quality offered for that particular dimension is adequate.

The major advantage of multi-attribute models over a simple overall attitude measure is in gaining an understanding of the attitudinal structure of the segment under study, in order to identify the most appropriate strategies of positioning and communication.

11.4   THE VALUE CHAIN IN DIFFERENTIATION ANALYSIS

In the search for source uniqueness on which to base a differentiation strategy, two pitfalls should be avoided:

identify elements of uniqueness which customers value but that the firm is incapable of supplying;

identify elements of uniqueness which the firm is able to supply but which is not valued by customers.

For this purpose the value chain model (Porter, 1980) provides a particularly useful framework. See Figure 2 in Porter (1980).

Every firm is a collection of activities that are performed to design, produce, market, deliver and support its products. These activities can be divided into two broad types, *primary* activities and *support* activities. A value chain is constructed for a particular firm on the basis of the importance and of the separateness of different activities and also on the basis of their capacity for creating differentiation.

The search for differentiation

By way of illustration, representative sources of differentiation for *primary activities* could be:

- *purchasing*: quality and reliability of components and materials;

- *operations*: fast manufacturing, defect-free manufacturing, ability to produce to customer specifications and so on;
- *warehousing and distribution*: fast delivery, efficient order processing, sufficient inventories to meet unexpected orders and so on;
- *sales and marketing*: high advertising level and quality, high sales force coverage and quality, extensive credit to buyers and so on; and
- *customer service*: in-use assistance, training for customers, fast and reliable repairs and so on.

Similarly, for *support activities*, potential sources of differentiation are:

- *human resources*: superior training of personnel, commitment to customer service, stable workforce policies and so on;
- *R&D:* unique product features, fast new product development, design for reliability and so on; and
- *infrastructure*: corporate reputation, responsiveness to customers needs and so on.

The objective is to identify the *drivers of uniqueness* in each activity, that is the variables and the actions through which the firm can achieve uniqueness in relation to competitors' offerings and provide value to the buyer. The merit of the value chain model is to suggest that the search for a sustainable competitive advantage is the role of every function within the organization and not only of the marketing function.

It is interesting in this respect to make reference to the work of Simon (1996), already quoted in this book, who has analysed the strategies adopted by a sample of 122 firms (a majority of German firms) which are (a) world or European leaders in their reference market, (b) of small or medium size and (c) unfamiliar to the general public. Simon' research results show that the type of competitive advantage held by those *Hidden Champions* is largely based on product superiority and on technology innovation.

Measuring market power

The degree of *market power* is measured by the firm's ability to dictate a price above that of its priority competitors. One measure of this sensitivity is the price elasticity of the firms for the differentiated product's demand. The lower this demand elasticity, the less volatile or sensitive will market share be to a price increase.

> If brand A has price elasticity equal to –1.5 and brand B an elasticity of –3.0; the same price increase of 5 per cent will lower demand for A by 7.5 per cent and demand for B by 15 per cent.

Therefore, a firm or brand with market power has a less elastic demand than an undifferentiated product. As a result, the firm is in a position to make the group of customers who are sensitive to the element of differentiation *accept a higher price*.

The brand strength refers to the buyers' degree of attachment or loyalty to a brand or a company. Probably the best test of brand loyalty would be to know what a customer would do if he (or she) does not find the preferred brand in the visited store. Will he or she switch to another brand or visit another store to find the preferred brand? To measure brand power, one can identify at least five indicators of a brand's strength:

1. *Lower price sensitivity*. A strong brand displays a stronger resistance to a price increase than its competitors.

2. *Acceptable price premiums.* A brand is strong if people are prepared to pay more for it. Conversely, a weak brand has to propose a price lower than the price charged by its competitors.
3. *Exclusivity rate.* The more loyal customer is the one for whom the brand represents a higher share of category requirement.
4. *Dynamic loyalty rate.* An alternative to share of category requirement is to look at patterns of purchasing over time, and uses this to estimate the probability of a consumer buying the brand on the next purchase occasion.
5. *Positive attitudinal measures.* Indicators like familiarity, esteem, perceived quality, purchase intentions (brand loyalty) and so on are also good indicators of a brand's strength.

11.5 TARGETING INTERNATIONAL MARKET SEGMENTS

Global market segmentation can be defined as the process of identifying specific segments, whether they are country groups or individual buyer groups, of potential customers with homogeneous attributes who are likely to exhibit similar buying behaviour. There are three different approaches for global segmentation: (a) identifying clusters of countries that demand similar products; (b) identifying segments present in many or most countries; and (c) targeting different segments in different countries with the same product (Takeuchi and Porter, 1986, pp. 138–50).

Targeting country clusters

Traditionally, the world market has been segmented on geographic variables, that is, by *grouping countries* that are similar in terms of climate, language, religion, economic development, distribution channel and so on. Products rarely require modification or tailoring for every single country, except for such things as labelling and the language used in the manuals and catalogues.

> On the European scene, natural clusters of countries would be, for example, the Nordic countries (Denmark, Norway, Sweden and maybe Finland); the Germanic countries (Germany, Austria, part of Switzerland), the Iberian countries, and so on. With this country segmentation strategy, products and communication would be adapted for each group of countries.

Within the European community, an argument in favour of this country approach lies in the very high diversity of the different countries, as evidenced by the comparison of their socio-demographic profiles. See the social portrait of Europe published by the European Commission (EC) (Eurostat, 1991, 1996).

However, this approach presents three potential limitations: (a) it is based on country variables and not on consumer behavioural patterns, (b) it assumes total homogeneity within the country segment, and (c) it overlooks the existence of homogeneous consumer segments that might exist across national boundaries. With the growth of regionalism within Europe, the second assumption becomes more and more a limiting factor. In fact, with the elimination of country borders more European firms are defining their geographic market zones by reference to regions and not to countries.

Selling to universal segments across countries

Several trends are influencing consumption behaviour on a global scale and many consumer products are becoming more widely accepted globally, such as consumer electronics, automobiles, fashion, home appliances, food products, beverages and services. Many of these products respond to needs and wants that cut across national boundaries.

Thus, even if product needs overall vary among countries, there may be a segment of the market with identical needs in every country. The challenge facing international firms is to identify these "universal" segments and reach them with marketing programmes that meet the common needs of these potential buyers. These universal segments are most likely to be high-end consumers, sport professionals, executives of multinational companies or, in general, sophisticated users, because these groups tend to be the most mobile and therefore the most likely to be exposed to extensive international contacts and experiences.

> A growing market segment on a global scale is composed of consumers aspiring to an "élite lifestyle". This élite, in Tokyo, New York, Paris, London, Hong Kong, Rio de Janeiro and so on, is the target of brands that fit the image of exclusivity like Mercedes, Gucci, Hermès, American Express, Gold Card, Chivas, Godiva and so on.

Such high-end brands can be targeted internationally to this universal segment in exactly the same way they are currently positioned in their respective home market. The size of universal segments can be small in each country. What is attractive is the cumulative volume. For example, *Godiva* pralines are present in more than 20 different countries all over the world, sometimes with modest market shares. It is, nevertheless, the world's leading chocolate maker.

Targeting diverse segments across countries

Even if product needs vary among countries, the same product can sometimes be sold in each country but in different segments, by adopting different market positioning based on non-product variables such as distributive networks, advertising and pricing.

> The positioning adopted for the Canon AE-1 provides a good example of this international segmentation approach. The AE-1 was targeted towards young replacement buyers in Japan,

---

Exhibit 11.3   The case of Black & Decker

The case of Black & Decker provides a good illustration of this strategy. Black & Decker are established in 50 countries and manufacture in 25 plants, 16 of which are outside the United States. It has a very high level of brand awareness worldwide, sometimes in the 80–90 per cent range. For Black & Decker the potential economies of scale and cost savings of globalization were considerable. The challenges to be overcome were the following:

Different countries have different safety and industry standards that make complete standardization impossible.

European and American consumers have very different responses to product design and even to colours.

Consumers use the products in different ways in different countries. For example, Europeans are more power-oriented in their electric tools than Americans.

upscale first-time buyers of 35-mm single-lens reflex cameras in the USA, and older and more technologically sophisticated replacement buyers in Germany. Three different marketing programmes were developed for Japan, the USA and Europe (Takeuchi and Porter, 1986, p. 139).

This approach requires important adaptations of communication and selling strategies, which contribute to increasing costs, or at least to preventing cost decreases as a consequence of standardization.

Of the three segmentation approaches, universal segmentation is the most innovative and also most likely to give the firm a significant competitive advantage, because product and communication can be standardized and transferred among countries. This gives the brand a reputation and coherence in image and positioning which is internationally reinforced. The diverse segmentation approach has the merit of taking into consideration differences in consumer behaviour among countries and of introducing adaptations to accommodate these differences. On the other hand, because of these country-to-country adaptations, the brand image in each country will probably be different.

The case of universal segments

The global approach in segmenting world markets looks for similarities between markets. The traditional international approach is multi-domestic, which tends to ignore similarities. The global approach actively seeks homogeneity in product, image, marketing and advertising message, while the multi-domestic approach maintains unnecessary differences from market to market. The goal, however, is not to have a uniform product line worldwide. Rather, the goal is to have a product line that is as standardized as possible, while recognizing that allowances for some local conditions are both necessary and desirable.

Trade-off between standardization and customization

In the great majority of market situations, some degree of adaptation will be necessary. The essence of international segmentation can be summarized as follows: *think of global similarities and adapt to local differences*. This perspective should help management to determine similarities across national boundaries while assessing within-country differences. Three types of product policy can be considered:

- *Universal Product:* the physical product sold in each country is identical except for labelling and for the language used in the manuals.
- *Modified Product:* the core product is the same, but some modifications are adopted, such as voltage, colour, size or accessories, to accommodate government regulations or to reflect local differences in taste, buying habits, climate and so on.
- *Country-Tailored Product:* the physical product is substantially tailored to each country or group of countries.

The financial and cost implications of these alternative product policies are, of course, particularly important.

Table 11.2 Strategies of international segmentation

Global marketing strategies	Expectations of segments				
	Homogeneous		Similar		Different
	Same culture	Different culture	Same culture	Different culture	
1. *Unchanged product and*	1	–	–	–	–
operational marketing	–	2	2	2	–
2. *Unchanged product and*	–	–	–	3	3
adapted operational marketing	–	–	–	–	4
3. *Adapted product and*					
operational marketing					
4. *New product and specific*					
operational marketing					

Source: Adapted from Blanche (1987).

Establishing a world brand

Every product does not have the same global potential, and some products may be easier than others to develop as world brands (see Table 11.2). Several brands are on the market that are recognized as world brands: *Coca-Cola, Marlboro, Kodak, Honda, Mercedes, Heineken, Swatch, Canon, Gucci, British Airways, Perrier, Black & Decker, Hertz, Benetton, McDonald's, Godiva* and many others. It is worth noting that the popularity of these brands is independent of the attitude towards their country of origin.

In reality, the global potential of a product is closely linked to the universality of the benefit sought. To the extent that a product is a proven success in meeting the needs of a particular group of buyers in a given country, it is logical to expect a similar success with the same group of people in another country, provided of course the product is adapted to local consuming habits or regulations. In other words, as suggested by Quelch and Hoff (1986), the driving factor in moving towards global marketing should be "the efficient worldwide use of good marketing ideas rather than scale economies from standardization".

The closer the product is to the *high-tech/high-touch poles*, the more universal it is. These two product categories have in common the fact of (a) being high-involvement products and of (b) sharing a common language (Domzal and Unger, 1987, p. 28):

■ *High-tech products* appeal to highly specialized buyers who share a common technical language and symbols. This is the case among computer users, tennis players and musicians, who all understand the technical aspects of the products. This is true for heavy machinery, computer hardware and financial services, but also for personal computers, video equipment, skiing equipment and so on. The mere existence of a common "shop talk" facilitates communication and increases the chance of success as global brands.

■ *High-touch products* are more image-oriented than features-oriented products, but they respond to universal themes or needs, such as romance, wealth, heroism, pla, and so on. Many products like perfume, fashion, jewellery and watches are sold on these themes.

For these two product categories, customers all over the world are using and understanding the same language and the same symbols. Worldwide brand standardization appears most feasible when products approach either end of the high-tech/high-touch spectrum (Domzal and Unger, 1987, p. 27).

Chapter Summary

The firm can consider different market coverage strategies. There are described in Figure 11.1, where the two extremes are the "mass marketing" strategy and a "mass customization" strategy. Several intermediate options exist, however. Selection of the positioning strategy provides the unifying concept for the development of the marketing programme. This is one of the most critical steps in the implementation of strategic marketing, because the firm has to decide how to best differentiate its brand from competing brands. There are different ways to position the brand against competition. One can identify three types of differentiation strategies: product differentiation, price differentiation and image differentiation. The effect of differentiation is to give the firm some degree of *market power*, because it generates preferences, customer loyalty and lower price sensitivity. In the search for a differentiation strategy, the value chain model (Porter, 1980) provides a particularly useful framework. There are three different approaches for global segmentation: (a) identifying clusters of countries that demand similar products; (b) identifying segments present in many or most countries; and (c) targeting different segments in different countries with the same product.

BIBLIOGRAPHY

Bauer, R.A. (1960), Consumer Behaviour as Risk Taking, in *Proceedings Fall Conference of the American Marketing Association*, Hancock, A.S. (ed.), Chicago, IL, pp. 389–98.

Blanche, B. (1987), Le marketing global: paradoxe, fantasme ou objectif pour demain?, *Revue Française du Marketing*, 115, p. 114.

Boyd, H.W., Ray, M.L. and Strong, E.C. (1972), An Attitudinal Framework for Advertising Strategy, *Journal of Marketing*, 36, 2, pp. 27–33.

Chawla, A. (2003), BATA, *Wrong Target*, in *Marketing Management, Workshop of Educational Institutes*, Bhopal, June.

Domzal, T. and Unger, L.S. (1987), Emerging Positioning Strategies in Global Marketing, *The Journal of Consumer Marketing*, 4, 4, pp. 23–50.

Eurostat (1991/1996), A Social Portrait of Europe, Brussels, European Commission.

Festinger, L. (1957), *A Theory of Cognitive Dissonance*, New York, Harper and Row.

Hair, J.F., Anderson, R.E., Tatham, R.L. and Black, W.C. (1992), *Multivariate Data Analysis*, New York, Maxwell Macmillan.

Kapferer, J.N. and Laurent, G. (1983), *La sensibilité aux marques*, Paris, Fondation Jours de France.

Kotler, P. and Keller, K.L. (2006), *Marketing Management*, Upper Saddle River, NJ, Prentice-Hall, 12th edition.

Krugman, H.E. (1965), The Impact of Television Advertising: Learning without Involvement, *Public Opinion Quarterly*, 29, 3, pp. 349–55.

Lambin J.J. (2007), *Market-Driven Management: Strategic and Operational Marketing*, London, Palgrave Macmillan, Second edition.

Lambin, J.J. (2000/2007*)*, *Market-Driven Management: Strategic and Operational Marketing*, London, Palgrave Macmillan.

Lavidge, R.J. and Steiner, G.A. (1961), A Model for Predictions Measurement of Advertising Effectiveness, *Journal of Marketing*, 25, 6, pp. 59–62.

Palda, K.S. (1966), The Hypothesis of a Hierarchy of Effects, *Journal of Marketing Research*, 3, 1, pp. 13–24.

Porter, M.E. (1980), *Competitive Strategy*, New York, The Free Press.

Quelch, J. and Hoff, E.G. (1986), Customizing Global Marketing, *Harvard Business Review*, 64, 3, pp. 59–68.

Ratchford, B.T. (1987), New Insights about the FCB Grid, *Journal of Advertising* Research, 27, 4, pp. 24–38.

Ries, A. and Trout, J. (1981), *Positioning: The Battle for Your Mind*, New York, McGraw-Hill.

Rogers, E.M. (1962), *Diffusion of Innovations*, New York, The Free Press.

Simon, H. (1996), *Hidden Champions*, Boston, MA, Harvard Business School Press.

Takeuchi, H. and Porter, M.E. (1986), *Three Roles of International Marketing in Global Industries*, in *Competition in Global Industries,* Porter, M.E. (ed.), Boston, MA, Harvard Business School Press.

Van Ballenberghe, A. (1993), Le comportement des consommateurs en période de promotion: analyse des perceptions des marques, Unpublished Working paper, Louvain-la-Neuve, Louvain School of Management, Belgium.

Vaughn, R. (1986), How Advertising Works: A Planning Model Revisited, *Journal of Advertising Research*, 26, 1, pp. 57–65.

CHAPTER TWELVE

FORMULATING A MARKETING STRATEGY

The objective of this chapter is to examine how a market-driven firm can select the appropriate competitive strategy to achieve an above-average profit performance in the different business units included in its product portfolio. Two sets of factors determine the performance of a particular business unit: first, the overall attractiveness of the reference market where it operates, and second, the strength of its competitive position relative to direct competition. The reference market's attractiveness is largely determined by forces outside the firm's control, while the business unit's competitiveness can be shaped by the firm's strategic choices. Product portfolio analysis relates attractiveness and competitiveness indicators to help guide strategic thinking by suggesting specific marketing strategies to achieve a balanced mix of products that will ensure growth and profit performance in the long run. In this chapter, we shall first define the conceptual bases of portfolio analysis and then describe the types of mission or objectives the firm should assign to each of its business units given their differentiated positions along the attractiveness–competitiveness dimensions. Finally, we shall discuss the strategic alternatives open to the firm in the field of international development.

Learning Objectives

When you have read this chapter, you should be able to:

- Conduct a product portfolio analysis, using the Boston Consulting Group's (BCG) growth–share matrix, the multi-factor portfolio matrix or the SWOT analysis
- Discuss the merits and limitations of these two product portfolio analysis methods
- Understand the different views of strategy
- Describe the objectives and risks associated with the choice of a specific generic strategy
- Define the different strategic options a firm can contemplate in designing a development or growth strategy
- Describe the different competitive strategies a firm can consider vis-à-vis its rivals and their conditions of application
- Discuss the objectives and the various forms of international development.

12.1 PRODUCT PORTFOLIO ANALYSES

The purpose of a product portfolio analysis is to help a multi-business firm decide how to allocate scarce resources among the product markets they compete in. In the general case, the procedure consists in cross-classifying each activity with respect to two independent dimensions: the attractiveness of the reference market where the firm operates, and the firm's capacity to take advantage of opportunities within the market. Various portfolio models have been developed, using matrix representations where different indicators are used to measure attractiveness and competitiveness. Here we shall concentrate on the two most representative methods: the BCG method called the "growth–share" matrix (Henderson, 1970; Boston Consulting Group, 1972) and the "multi-factor portfolio" matrix attributed to General Electric and McKinsey (Hussey, 1978; Abell and Hammond, 1979). Although the two methods have the same objectives, their implicit assumptions are different and the two approaches will likely yield different insights (Wind, Mahajan and Swire, 1983).

The BCG growth–share matrix

The BCG matrix is built around two criteria: the reference market's growth rate (corrected for inflation), acting as an indicator of attractiveness, and market share relative to the firm's largest competitor, measuring competitiveness. As shown in Figure 12.1, we have a double-entry table where a cut-off level on each axis creates a grid with four quadrants:

- Along the *market growth* axis, the cut-off point distinguishing high-growth from low-growth markets corresponds to the growth rate of the GNP in real terms, or to the (weighted) average of the predicted growth rates of the different markets in which the products compete. In practice, high-growth markets are often defined as those growing by more than 10 per cent per year. Markets growing by less than 10 per cent are deemed low growth.
- Similarly, on the *relative market share* axis the dividing line is usually put at 1 or 1.5. Beyond this level, relative market share is high; below, it is low.

Thus the matrix relies on the concept of relative market share to leading competitor, which calculates the ratio of unit sales for one firm to unit sales for the largest share firm.

> If company A, for example, has a 10 per cent share of the market and the largest share belongs to company B, with 20 per cent, then company A has a relative market share of 0.5 (10 per cent/20 per cent). It has a low market share since the ratio is less than one. Similarly, company B has a relative market share of 2 (20 per cent/10 per cent). It has a high share of the market.

The use of relative market share is based on the assumption that market share is positively correlated with experience and therefore with profitability. Therefore the competitive implications of holding a 20 per cent market share are quite different if the largest competitor is holding 40 per cent or only 5 per cent.

We thus obtain four different quadrants, each of which defines four fundamentally different competitive situations in terms of cash flow requirements and which need to be dealt with by specific objectives and marketing strategies.

Basic assumptions of the growth–share matrix

There are two basic assumptions underlying the BCG analysis: one concerns the existence of experience effects and the other the product life cycle (PLC) model. These two assumptions can be summarized as follows:

- Higher relative market share implies cost advantage over direct competitors because of experience effects; where the *experience curve concept* applies, the largest competitor will

Product Portfolio	Brand Sales (in million of €)	Number of Competing firms	Sales of 3 firm's largest competitors (in millions of €)			Market growth
Brand A	0.5	8	0.7	0.7	0.5*	15%
Brand B	1.6	22	1.6*	1.6	1.0	18%
Brand C	1.8	14	1.8*	1.2	1.0	7%
Brand D	3.2	5	3.2*	0.8	0.7	4%
Brand E	0.5	10	2.5	1.8	1.7	4%

The BCG growth-share matrix

Total brand sales (in millions): 0.5 + 1.6 + 1.8 + 3.2 + 0.5 = 7.6 €
Brand shares in total company sales:
A = 6.6% B = 21.0% C = 23.7% D = 42.1% E = 6.6%
Brand relative market share (firm's to largest competitor)
A = 0.5 / 0.7 = 0.71
B = 1.6 / 1.6 = 1.0
C = 1.8 / 1.2 = 1.5
D = 3.2 / 0.8 = 4.0
E = 0.5 / 2.5 = 0.2

Average market growth rate
(15% + 18% + 7% + 4% + 4%) / 5 = 9.6% (or 10%)

The BCG growth-share matrix

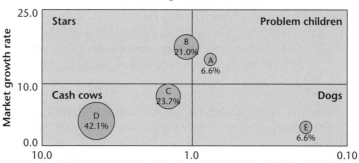

Figure 12.1   The BCG growth–share matrix
Source: Lambin (2000/2007).

be the most profitable at the prevailing price level. Conversely, lower relative market share implies cost disadvantages. The implication of this first assumption is that the expected cash flow from products with high relative market share will be higher than those with smaller market shares.

■ Being in a fast *growing market* implies greater need for cash to finance growth, added production capacity, advertising expenditures, and so on. Conversely, cash can be generated by a product operating in a mature market. Thus, the *PLC model* is employed because it highlights the desirability of a balanced mix of products situated in the different phases of the PLC.

The implication of this second assumption is that the cash needs for products in rapidly growing markets are expected to be greater than they are for those in slower growing ones. As discussed above, these assumptions are not always true. On this topic, see Abell and Hammond (1979, pp. 192–3).

Defining the type of business

Keeping in mind these two key assumptions, we can identify four groups of product markets having different characteristics in terms of their cash flow needs and/or contributions:

- *Low growth/high share or cash cow products*: These products usually generate more cash than is required to sustain their market position. As such, they are a source of funds for the firm to support diversification efforts and growth in other markets. The priority strategy is to "harvest".
- *Low growth/low share, dogs or lame ducks products:* Dogs have a low market share in a low-growth market, the least desirable market position. They generally have a cost disadvantage and few opportunities to grow, since the war is over in the market. Maintaining these products generally turns into a financial drain without any hope of improvement. The priority strategy here is to "divest" or in any case to adopt a low profile and to live modestly.
- *High growth/low share or problem children products*: In this category we find products with low relative market shares in a fast growing market. Despite their handicap vis-à-vis the leader, these products still have a chance of gaining market share, since the market has not yet settled down. However, supporting these products implies large financial means to finance share building strategies and to offset low profit margins. If the support is not given, these products will become dogs as market growth slows down. Thus, the alternatives here are to build market share or to divest.
- *High growth/high share or stars products*: Here we have the market leaders in a rapidly growing market. These activities also require a lot of cash to finance growth; but because of their leading position they generate significant amounts of profits to reinvest in order to maintain their market position. As the market matures, they will progressively take over as cash cows.

Every activity can be placed in a matrix similar to Figure 12.1. The significance of an activity can be represented by a circle of size proportional to sales volume, sales revenue or profit contribution. This analysis should be made in a dynamic way, that is by tracking the progression or movements of each business unit over a period of time, as illustrated in Figure 12.2.

Diagnosing the product portfolio

In this approach, it is important to properly define the reference market in which the activity is competing. Relative market share compares the strength of a firm relative to its competitors. If the market is defined too narrowly the firm appears as the segment leader; if it is too wide, the firm appears too weak. The following points arise from the analysis:

- The position in the matrix indicates the *credible strategy* for each product: maintain leadership for stars; abandon or have a low profile for dogs; selective investment and growth for problem children; maximum profitability for cash cows.
- The position in the matrix helps evaluate *cash requirements and profitability potential*. Profits are usually a function of competitiveness; cash requirements generally depend on the phase of the product's life cycle, that is, on the reference market's degree of development.

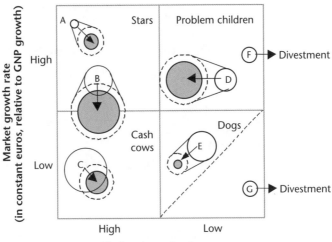

Figure 12.2   Dynamic analysis of the product portfolio
Source: Day (1977). Reproduced with permission.

- Allocation of the firm's total sales revenue or profit contribution according to each quadrant allows *balancing of the product portfolio*. The ideal situation is to have products that generate cash and products in their introductory or growing stage that will ensure the firm's long-term viability. The needs of the second category will be financed by the first.

Based on this type of diagnostic, the firm can envisage various strategies either to maintain or to restore the balance of its product portfolio. To be more specific, it allows the firm:

- to develop *portfolio scenarios* for future years on the basis of projected growth rates and tentative decisions regarding the market share strategies for the various activities, assuming different competitive reaction strategies;
- to analyse the potential of the existing product portfolio, and to put a figure on the *total cash flow* it can expect from each activity, every year, until the end of its planning horizon;
- to analyse the *strategic gap*, that is the observed difference between expected performance and desired performance; and
- To identify the *means to be employed* to fill this gap, either by improving existing products' performance, or by abandoning products that absorb too much cash without any realistic hope of improvement, or finally by introducing new products that will rebalance the portfolio structure.

Too many ageing products indicate a danger of decline, even if current results appear very positive. Too many new products can lead to financial problems, even if activities are quite healthy, and this type of situation inevitably risks loss of independence.

Figure 12.3 describes two successful and two unsuccessful trajectories that can be observed for new or existing business units:

- The *"innovator trajectory"*, which uses the cash generated by the cash cows to invest in R&D and to enter the market with a product new to the world that will take over from existing stars.

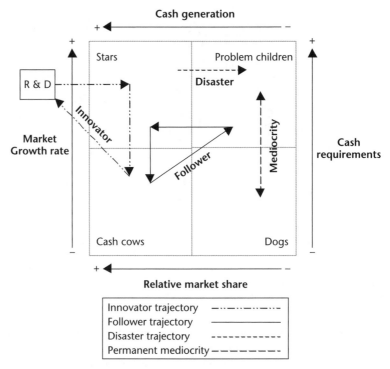

Figure 12.3 Portfolio scenarios alternatives
Source: Adapted from Day (1977). Reproduced with permission.

- The *"follower trajectory"*, which uses the cash generated by the cash cows to enter as a problem child in a new market, dominated by a leader, with an aggressive market share build-up strategy.
- The *"disaster trajectory"*, whereby a star product evolves to the problem children quadrant as a consequence of insufficient investment in market share maintenance.
- The *"permanent mediocrity trajectory"*, which involves a problem child product evolving to the dogs' quadrant as a consequence of the failure to build market share for the product.

Let us remember that this type of diagnostic is valid only if the underlying assumptions mentioned earlier hold true. But, as already mentioned, the links between relative market share and profitability on the one hand and growth rate and financial requirements on the other are not always observed (see Abell and Hammond, 1979, pp. 192–3).

Limitations of the growth–share matrix

The most important merit of the BCG method is undoubtedly that it provides an appealing and elegant theoretical development which establishes a clear link between strategic positioning and financial performance. It is true that the initial assumptions are restrictive. But if they are true, they allow accurate analysis and valuable recommendations. General managers can thus concentrate on the major strategic problems and analyse the implications of alternative business strategies. Furthermore, the method is based on *objective indicators* of attractiveness and competitiveness, thus reducing the risk of subjectivity. Finally, it should also be added that the matrix provides a *visual, vivid and easy aid to comprehend synthesis* of the firm's activities, thus facilitating communication.

There are, however, a number of *limitations and difficulties* which need to be emphasized because they reduce the generality of the approach:

- The implicit hypothesis about the relation between relative market share and cash flows means that this technique can only be used when there is an experience effect, that is in *volume industries*. Thus the experience effect might be observed in only some product markets and not in all the product markets which are in the firm's portfolio (Figure 12.4).
- The method is based on the notion of *"internal" competitive advantage only* and does not take into account any *"external" competitive advantage* enjoyed by the firm or the brand as a result of a successful differentiation strategy. Thus, a so-called dog could very well generate cash despite its cost disadvantage if the market accepts the paying of a premium price for the product, given its distinctive qualities.
- Despite its simple appearance, some *measurement problems* can arise. Should the definitions of the product market be broad or narrow? What share of what market? How do we determine market growth rate? Wind, Mahajan and Swire (1983) have shown that the analysis is very sensitive to the measures used. For a discussion of these questions, see Day (1977, pp. 35–7).
- The recommendations of a portfolio analysis remain very vague and at most constitute *orientations* to be clarified. To say that in a given product market a strategy of "harvest" or "low profile" should be adopted is not very explicit. In any case, it is insufficient for an effective determination of policies regarding prices, distribution, communication and so on. The main purpose of a portfolio analysis is to help guide, but not substitute for, strategic thinking.

These limitations are serious and restrict the scope of the growth–share matrix significantly, which is not equally useful in all corporate situations. Other methods based on less restrictive assumptions have been developed.

The multi-factor portfolio matrix

The BCG matrix is based on two single indicators. But there are many situations where factors other than market growth and share determine the attractiveness of a market and the strength of a competitive position.

Clearly, a market's attractiveness can also depend on factors such as market accessibility, size, existing distribution network, structure of competition, favourable legislation and so on.

> The market for portable computers is in principle highly attractive if we judge it by its high growth rate. There are, however, many other factors, such as rapid change in demand, expected price changes, products' fast rate of obsolescence, intensity of competition and so on, which make this a risky and therefore relatively less attractive market.

Similarly, a firm's competitive advantage may be the result of strong brand image or commercial organization, technological leadership, distinctive product qualities and so on, even if its market share is low relative to the major competitor.

> When, in 1982, IBM introduced its personal computer, its competitiveness was very low according to the BCG matrix, since its market share was zero. Yet many analysts perceived IBM's competitive potential as very high because of its reputation in the computer market, its important technological know-how, its available resources and its will to succeed.

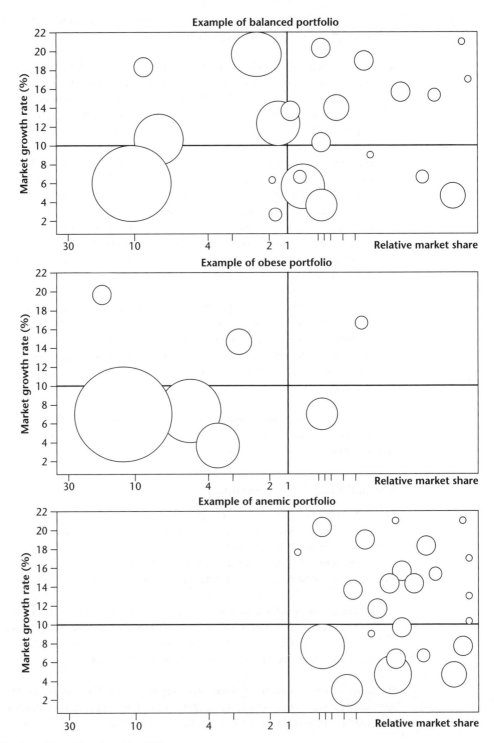

Figure 12.4 Comparison of three brands' portfolios
Source: Lambin (2000–2007).

It is clear that several factors need to be taken into account to measure correctly the market's attractiveness and the firm's competitiveness potential. Instead of using a single indicator per dimension, multiple indicators can be used to assess attractiveness and competitiveness and to construct a composite index for each dimension. For an extensive list of possible factors, see Abell and Hammond (1979, p. 214). Thus, the BCG matrix described in the preceding section may be viewed as a special case of a more general theory relating market attractiveness and business competitiveness.

Development of a multi-factor portfolio grid

To illustrate, Table 12.1 presents a battery of indicators selected to measure the *attractiveness* of five product markets from the textile industry, as well as a series of indicators evaluating the competitiveness of the company Tissex, which operates in these five product markets.

Since each situation is different, the relevant list of factors has to be identified and a multi-factor portfolio grid is necessarily company-specific. The selection of the relevant factors is a delicate task and should involve several people from the strategic marketing group and from other departments as well. Precise definition of each indicator must be given and the nature of the relationship should be clearly determined. Once the grid is developed, each product market is evaluated against each indicator:

- A scale of 5 points is used, with "low", "average" and "high" as reference points for scores equal to 1, 3 and 5, respectively.
- As far as indicators of competitiveness are concerned, ratings are not attributed "in abstract", but relative to the most dangerous competitor in each product market or segment.
- If some indicators appear to be more important than others, weighting can be introduced, but the weights must remain the same for every activity considered.

Table 12.1 Multi-factor portfolio grid

Indicators of attractiveness	Weight (100)	Evaluation scale		
		Weak 1 2	Moderate 3 4	Strong 5
Market accessibility		Outside Europe and USA	Europe and USA	Europe
Market growth rate	_____	≤5%	5–10%	≥10%
Length of the life cycle		≤2 years	2–5 years	≥5 years
Gross profit potential		≤15%	15–25%	≥25%
Strength of competition		Structured oligopoly	Unstructured competition	Weak competition
Potential for differentiation		Very weak	Moderate	Strong
Concentration of customers		Very dispersed	Moderately dispersed	Concentrated
Relative market share		≤1/3 leader	≥1/3 leader	Leader
Unit cost		> direct competitors	= direct competitors	< direct competitors
Distinctive qualities		"Me too" product	Moderately differentiated	"Unique selling proposition"
Technological know-how		Weak control	Moderate control	Strong control
Sales organization		Independent distributors	Selective distribution	Direct sales
Image		Very weak	Fuzzy	Strong

Source: Lambin (2000/2007).

■ The ratings should reflect, as much as possible, future or expected values of the indicators and not so much their present values.

■ A summary score can then be calculated for each product market's global attractiveness and the firm's potential competitiveness.

Contrary to the BCG approach, subjective evaluations enter into these measures of attractiveness and competitiveness. But the process may nevertheless gain in interpersonal objectivity, to the extent that many judges operate independently. Their evaluations are then compared in order to reconcile or to explain observed differences and disagreements. This process of reconciliation is always useful in itself.

Interpretation of the multi-factor grid

We then obtain a two-dimensional classification grid similar to the BCG matrix. It is current practice to sub-divide each dimension into three levels (low, average, high), thus obtaining nine squares, each corresponding to a specific strategic position.

Each zone corresponds to a specific positioning. The firm's different activities can be represented by circles with an area proportional to their share in the total sales revenue or profit contribution. The four most clearly defined positionings are those corresponding to the four corners of the matrix in Figure 12.5:

■ In quadrant C, both the product market's attractiveness and the firm's competitive potential are high; the strategic orientation to follow is *offensive growth*. The characteristics are similar to those of "stars" in the BCG matrix.

■ In quadrant A, both attractiveness and competitiveness are low; strategic orientation is *maintenance without investment* or *divestment*. We have the case of "dogs" as in Figure 12.1.

■ Quadrant B depicts an intermediate situation: competitive advantage is low, but the reference market's attraction is high. This is typically the case of "problem children". The strategy to follow is *selective growth*.

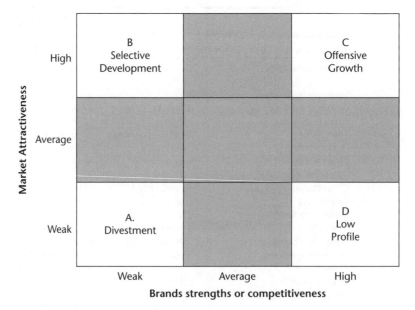

Figure 12.5 Multi-factor portfolio grid
Source: Adapted from Abell and Hammond (1979).

- In quadrant D, we have the opposite situation. Competitive advantage is high but market attractiveness is low. A skimming and maintenance strategy without major new investment is called for. This is the equivalent of the "cash cows" positioning in the BCG matrix.

The other intermediate zones correspond to strategic positions which are less clearly defined and often hard to interpret. The fuzzy value of the summary scores can reflect either very high marks on some indicators and very low marks on others, or simply an average evaluation on all the criteria. The latter case is often observed in practice and reflects imprecise information or simply lack of it.

Choice of future strategy

We thus have a visual representation of the firm's growth potential. By extrapolating each activity's expected growth under the assumption of "no change" strategy, the firm is in a position to assess its future position. Alternative strategic options can also be explored, such as:

- *Investing to hold* aims at maintaining the current position and keeping up with expected changes in the market.
- *Investing to penetrate* aims at improving the business position by moving the business unit to the right of the grid.
- *Investing to rebuild* aims at restoring a position which has been lost. This revitalization strategy will be more difficult to implement if the market attractiveness is already medium or low.
- *Low investment* aims at harvesting the business, which is the business position is exchanged for cash, for example, by selling the activity at the highest possible price.
- *Divestment* aims at leaving markets or segments of low attractiveness or segments where the firm has not the capacity to acquire or to sustain a competitive advantage.

Figure 12.6 shows an example of multi-factor portfolio analysis. It represents the portfolio of a firm from the food industry. Note that product markets' attractiveness is very average and the firm's competitiveness is evaluated as low for almost all the products considered. The future of this firm is clearly very bleak.

Evaluation of the multi-factor portfolio grid

The *multi-factor portfolio model* leads to the same kind of analyses as the BCG matrix, with one major difference: the link between competitive and financial performance (that is cash flow) is lost. However, since this model is not based on any particular assumption, it does overcome many of the shortcomings of the BCG method and it is more widely applicable. Furthermore, it is much more flexible because the indicators used are company-specific.

The use of these types of matrix suffers nevertheless from certain *limitations*:

- Measurement problems are more delicate and *risk of subjectivity* is much higher here. This shows up not only in the choice of indicators and their possible weighting, but especially when it comes to marking the criteria. The risk of subjectivity is greater for indicators of competitiveness, where there is necessarily self-evaluation.
- When the number of indicators and the number of activities to evaluate are high, the *procedure becomes heavy* and demanding, especially when information is scarce or imprecise.

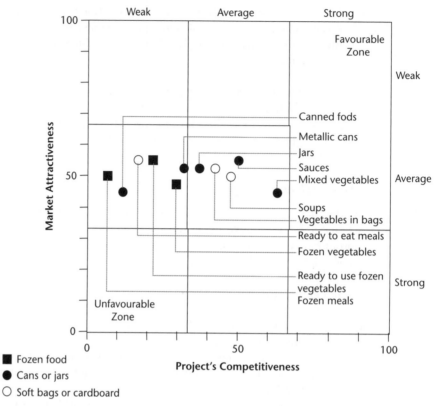

Figure 12.6 Example of a multi-factor portfolio
Source: MDA Consulting Group, Brussels.

- The *results are sensitive* to the ratings and to the weighting systems adopted. Manipulation of weights can produce a desired position in the matrix. It is therefore important to test the sensitivity of results to the use of alternative weighting systems.
- As for the BCG matrix, *recommendations remain very general* and need to be clarified. Furthermore, the link with financial performance is less clearly established.

The two approaches will very likely yield different insights. But as the main purpose of a product portfolio analysis is to help guide, but not substitute for, strategic thinking, the process of reconciliation will be useful. Thus it is desirable to employ both approaches and compare results (Day 1977, p. 38).

The SWOT analysis

A widely used framework for organizing the bits and pieces of information gained from the company internal information system and from the macro-marketing environment is a SWOT analysis, an acronym for Strengths, Weaknesses, Opportunities and Threats. Developed at Harvard by Andrews (1971, 1980, 1987), it is in fact a multi-factor analysis similar to the two preceding methods with these two differences:

- The analysis is purely qualitative and is not based on objective measures or hard data.
- It gives a different definition of the two concepts of market attractiveness (external factors) and company competitiveness (internal factors).

SWOT analysis is a simple, straightforward model that provides direction and serves as a catalyst for the development of a viable marketing plan. It fulfils this role by structuring the *assessment of the fit* between what an organization can (strengths) and cannot (weaknesses) presently do, and the environmental conditions working for (opportunities) and against (threats) the firm. Alternative strategies for the firm are developed through an appraisal of the opportunities and threats it faces in various markets, and an evaluation of its strengths and weaknesses. If done correctly a firm can highlight its strengths and minimize its weaknesses to pursue opportunities and avoid threats.

The issues that can be considered in a SWOT analysis are numerous and will vary depending on the particular firm and industry being analysed. A list of potential issues is proposed in Box 12.1.

The SWOT analysis is more qualitative and general than the BCG or the multi-factor portfolio methods. In addition to its apparent simplicity, its merit is to provide a more comprehensive view of the firm's strategic potential. In that sense, the SWOT analysis method can be more pro-active than the traditional product portfolio methods.

Box 12.1   Implementation problem: which potential issues to consider in a SWOT analysis?

Potential internal strengths

- Abundant financial resources
- Any distinctive core competence
- Well-known as the market leader
- Economies of scale
- Proprietary technology
- Patented process
- Lower costs
- Good market image
- Superior management talent
- Better marketing skills
- Outstanding product quality
- Partnership with other firms
- Good distribution skills
- Committed employees

Potential external opportunities

- Rapid market growth
- Rival firms are complacent
- Changing customer needs and tastes
- Opening of foreign markets
- Mishap of a rival firm
- New uses for product discovered
- Economic boom
- Deregulation
- New technology
- Demographic shifts
- Other firms seek alliances
- High brand switching
- Sales decline for a substitute
- New distribution method

Potential internal weaknesses

- Lack of strategic direction
- Weak spending on R&D
- Very narrow product line
- Limited distribution
- Higher costs
- Out-of-date products
- Internal operating problems
- Weak market image
- Poor marketing skills
- Limited management skills
- Under-trained employees

Potential external threats

- Entry of foreign competitors
- Introduction of new substitutes
- PLC in decline
- Changing customers needs/tastes
- Rival firms adopt new strategies
- Increased regulation
- Recession
- New technology
- Demographic shifts
- Foreign trade barriers
- Poor performance of ally firms

Source: Ferrell, Hartline, Lucas and Luck (1999, p. 62).

Portfolio models in practice

As evidenced by the multi-year international survey sponsored by the consultancy firm Bain & Company about management tools and techniques (Bain and Company, 2005), it appears (see Table 12.2) that strategic planning and portfolio analyses are ranked among the most popular managerial tools used by companies.

A portfolio analysis leads to different strategic recommendations according to the positioning of activities in the portfolio. As we saw, such recommendations are mainly general guidelines, such as invest, maintain, harvest, abandon, and so on, which require clarification and need to be put in a more explicit operational perspective.

Benefits of product portfolio analyses

Portfolio analysis is the outcome of the whole *strategic marketing process* described in the last four chapters of this book. A portfolio analysis rests on the following principles, irrespective of the method used:

- An accurate division of the firm's activities into product markets or segments.
- Measures of competitiveness and attractiveness allowing evaluation and comparison of different activities' strategic values.
- Links between strategic position and economic and financial performance, mainly in the BCG method.

Matrix representations help to synthesize the results of this strategic thinking exercise and to visualize them in a clear and expressive manner. Contrary to appearances, they are not simple to elaborate. They require complete and reliable information about the way

Table 12.2 Top ten tools usage over time and satisfaction

1993	2000	2006	2008	Satisfaction 2008
Mission statements (88%)	Strategic planning (76%)	Strategic planning (88%)	Benchmarking (76%)	3.82
Customer satisfaction (86%)	Mission statements (70%)	Crm (84%)	Strategic planning (67%)	4.01*
Tqm (72%)	Benchmarking (69%)	Customer segmentation (82%)	Mission statements (65%)	3.91*
Competitor profiling (71%)	Outsourcing (69%)	Benchmarking (81%)	Crm (63%)	3.83
Benchmarking (70%)	Customer satisfaction (60%)	Mission statements (79%)	Outsourcing (63%)	3.79
Pay-for-performance (70%)	Growth strategies (55%)	Core competencies (79%)	Balanced scorecard (53%)	3.83
Reengineering (67%)	Strategic alliances (53%)	Outsourcing (77%)	Customer segmentation (53%)	3.95*
Strategic alliances (62%)	Pay-for-performance (52%)	Business process reengineering (69%)	Business process reengineering (50%)	3.85
Cycle time reduction (55%)	Customer segmentation (51%)	Scenario and contingency planning (69%)	Core competencies (48%)	3.82
Self-directed teams (55%)	Core competencies (48%)	Knowledge management (69%)	Merger & acquisitions (46%)	3.83

*significantly above the overall mean. Scale: 1 to 5.
Source: Rigby, D.K. (2010).

markets function, about the firm's and its rivals' strengths and weaknesses. More specifically, this analysis implies:

- Considerable effort to *segment the reference market*. This is particularly important, because the validity of the recommendations is conditioned by the initial choice of segmentation.
- Systematic and careful collection of *detailed information*, which does not normally exist as such and needs to be reconstituted by cross-checking and probing; quality of results also depends on the reliability of this information.

This kind of analysis cannot be improved and it relies particularly on top management's complete support. Such a tool is obviously not a panacea, but it has the merit of emphasizing some important aspects of management:

- It moderates *excessively short-term* vision by insisting on keeping a balance between immediately profitable activities and those that prepare the future.
- It encourages the firm to keep both market *attractiveness and competitive potential* in mind.
- It establishes *priorities* in allocation of human as well as financial resources.
- It suggests differentiated development strategies per type of activity on a more data-oriented basis.
- It creates a *common language* throughout the organization and fixes clear objectives to reinforce motivation and facilitate control.

The main weakness of methods of portfolio analysis is that they can give an image of the present, or indeed of the recent past, and devote too little time to assessing future changes and strategic options for dealing with these changes. There is also a risk of too mechanistic an application of these methods. As already underlined, different methods could lead to very different classifications. The tools described here must be viewed more as guides to informed reasoning than as prescriptive tools.

These matrices can also be used in a dynamic perspective, for instance in comparing the present market positions held within each product market with the targeted positions for the next period. The matrix presented in Figure 12.6 is useful in this respect because it permits us to analyse the changing competitive positions of each business unit over time (Hussey, 1978).

12.2 THE CHOICE OF A GENERIC STRATEGY

The first step in elaborating a development strategy is to clarify the nature of the *sustainable competitive advantage* which will serve as the basis for later strategic actions and tactics. We saw in the previous chapter that competitive advantage can be described by reference to two aspects: *productivity* (cost advantage) and *market power* (advantage in terms of maximum acceptable price). The question is to know which of these two aspects should be given priority, given the firm's characteristics, its strengths and weaknesses and those of its rivals. In other words, which advantage is "sustainable" in a given product market? This question can be examined from two perspectives: within the framework of existing markets and of future markets.

Two ways to approach strategy

What is strategy? Two different views of strategy can be adopted, which are more complementary than opposed. The first view of strategy, promoted by Porter (1985, 1996), is mostly relevant when the objective is to target existing or articulated needs in existing markets, while the second, promoted by Hamel and Prahalad (1994), is more oriented towards latent needs and future markets.

Competing for existing markets

A first view consists in selecting a market or a product market where the firm wants to be active and in which the firm will try to differentiate itself *vis-à-vis* direct competition, *either by performing different activities from rivals or by performing similar activities in different ways* (Porter, 1996). Identifying a strategic sustainable competitive advantage then requires an analysis of the competitive structure, and, more specifically, answers to the following questions:

- What are the *key success factors* in a given product market or segment?
- What are the firms' *strengths and weaknesses* with regard to these factors?
- What are the strengths and weaknesses of the firms' *direct rival(s)* with regards to the same key success factors?

This systematic search for a sustainable competitive advantage is at the core of a differentiation strategy.

Competing for future markets

A second view of strategy is more proactive. The goal here is…*to build the best possible assumption base about the future (through foresight) and thereby develop the prescience needed to proactively shape industry evolution* (Hamel and Prahalad, 1994, p. 73). Industry foresight helps managers answer three critical questions:

- First, what new types of customer benefit should we seek to provide in five, ten or fifteen years?
- Second, what new competencies will we need to build or acquire to offer these benefits to customers?
- Third, how will we need to reconfigure the customer interface over the next few years?

This view of strategy is more proactive, since the objective here is to identify, understand and influence forces shaping the future of industry. As illustrated by Hamel and Prahalad, the Apple company has such a point of view (Exhibit 12.1). More than a differentiation strategy of being better, faster, simpler, cheaper and so on, the objective here is more fundamental and is to regenerate the core strategy of the firm and to reinvent the industry.

Kim and Mauborgne (1997) have proposed five recommendations in what they call a *value strategy* development:

- Challenge the inevitableness of industry conditions.
- Competition is not the benchmark.
- Focus on what most customers' value.
- Ask what we would do if we were starting anew.
- Think in terms of the total solution buyers seek.

To adopt *value or discontinuous innovation strategy*, it is necessary to create solutions to problems customers do not even know they have (Exhibit 12.2). Discovering new solutions

---

Exhibit 12.1   The strategy of Apple

Apple decided to reinvent the industry by exploring new sectors moving from computers to music with the invention of the i-pad and i-Tunes in 2003, the introduction of the i-Phone in 2007 and the i-pad in 2010. Every time, Apple has succeeded to revolutionize the way the consumer is satisfied. The brand has never been the first but has tried to do things better and differently than what was been done previously.

Apple entered the mobile phone sector in 2007,and decided to challenge the market leader Nokia by targeting

a small part of the market (smart phones only) and position themselves as innovative, fashionable and easy to use. In Q2 2010, Apple succeeded to generate more than 50% of the profit of the total mobile phone industry with only 5% of market share.

Source: Authors.

Exhibit 12.2   The value strategy of Ryanair

Ryanair, the UK airline company created in 1985, decided to compete in Europe by following a value strategy. They became European market leader, with 70 millions of travellers in 2010. The concept was to offer the lowest price for travelling, following a "no-frills strategy". This was a new way of looking at the industry in Europe at that

time. They focused on what a specific consumer segment wanted most: lowest prices for airlines tickets. The tickets are offered at very low prices and every extras have to be paid (food, luggage etc).

Source: Authors.

---

means going beyond the old ones by challenging the fundamental rules of business and redrawing the boundaries to create new markets and industries.

Generic strategies in existing markets

Generic strategies will be different according to the type of competitive advantage sought, that is whether they are based on productivity and therefore cost advantage, or whether they rest on an element of differentiation and are therefore based on a price premium. Porter (1980, p. 35) suggests there exist four generic competitive strategies to outperforming other firms in an industry: overall cost leadership, differentiation, focused differentiation or cost focus.

Overall cost leadership

This first generic strategy is based on *productivity* and is generally related to the existence of an experience effect. This strategy implies close scrutiny of overhead costs, of productivity investments intended to enhance the value of experience effects and of product design costs, and on cost minimization in service, selling, advertising and so on. Low cost relative to competitors is the major preoccupation of the entire strategy.

Having a cost advantage constitutes an effective protection against the five competitive forces:

- Relative to its *direct competitors*, the firm is in a better position to resist a possible price war and still make a profit at its rivals' minimum price level.

- Powerful *buyers* can only drive down prices to the level of the most efficient competitor.
- Low cost provides a defence against powerful *suppliers* by providing more flexibility to cope with input cost increases.
- A low-cost position provides substantial *entry barriers* in terms of scale economies or cost advantage.
- A low-cost position usually places the firm in a favourable position *vis-à-vis substitutes* relative to competitors in the industry (Porter, 1980, p. 36).

Thus, cost leadership protects the firm against all five competitive forces, because the least efficient firms are the first to feel the effects of the competitive struggle.

Differentiation

The objective here is to give distinctive qualities to the product that are significant to the buyer and which create something that is perceived as being unique. What the firm tends to do is to create a situation of monopolistic competition in which it holds some *market power* because of the distinctive element (Chamberlin, 1933).

We saw before that differentiation can take many forms: design or brand image, technology, features, customer service, dealer network and so on. Differentiation, like cost domination, protects the firm from the five competitive forces, but in a very different way:

- Relative to its *direct rivals*, differentiation provides the firm with insulation against competitive rivalry because of brand loyalty and resulting lower price sensitivity. It also increases margins, which avoids the need for a low-cost position.
- The resulting customer loyalty, and the need for a competitor to overcome uniqueness, provides *entry barriers*.
- Higher profitability increases the firm's ability to resist cost increases imposed by powerful *suppliers*.
- Finally, the firm that has differentiated itself to achieve customer loyalty should be better positioned *vis-à-vis substitutes* than its competitors (Porter, 1980, p. 37).

Successful differentiation enables the firm to realize higher profits than its rivals because of the higher price the market is willing to accept and despite the fact that costs are generally higher. This type of strategy is not always compatible with high market share, since most buyers are not necessarily prepared to pay a higher price, even though they recognize product superiority.

Differentiation strategies generally imply large investments in operational marketing, particularly in advertising expenditures to inform the market about the product's distinctive qualities.

Focus

A third generic strategy is focusing on the needs of a particular segment, group of buyers or geographic market, without claiming to address the whole market. The objective is to take a restricted target and to serve its narrow strategic target more effectively than competitors who are serving the whole market. It implies either differentiation or cost domination, or both, but only *vis-à-vis* the particular target.

For example, a paint manufacturer can decide to address professional painters only, excluding the public at large, car manufacturers and the naval industry.

In the car industry, Mercedes addresses only the high end of the market, but it covers that segment more effectively than other car manufacturers having a full line of models.

The focus strategy always implies some limitations on the overall market share achievable. A focus strategy can give the firm a large share of the market in the targeted segment, but it may be low relative to the whole market.

Risks associated with generic strategies

The choice of one strategy over another is not a neutral decision, in the sense they involve differing types of risks and also different priority preoccupations in the organization. Exhibit 12.3 summarizes the risks inherent in each generic strategy.

The implementation of these strategies implies different resources and different know-how:

- A cost domination strategy assumes sustained investment, a high degree of technological competence, close control of manufacturing and distribution costs and standardized products to facilitate production.
- A differentiation strategy assumes significant marketing know-how as well as technological advance. The ability to analyse and anticipate trends in market needs plays a fundamental role here. Interfunctional co-ordination between R&D, production and marketing is vital.
- Finally, a *concentration* strategy also assumes the previous characteristics *vis-à-vis* the targeted segment.

Exhibit 12.3　Risks associated with generic strategies

Risks of overall cost leadership

- Technological changes that nullify past investments or learning.
- Low-cost learning by industry newcomers or followers, through imitation or through their ability to invest in state-of-the-art facilities.
- Inability to see required product or marketing change because of the attention placed on costs.
- Inflation in costs that narrows the firms' ability to maintain enough of a price differential to offset competitors' brand images or other approaches to differentiation.

Risks of differentiation

- The cost differential between low-cost competitors and the differentiated firm becomes too great for differentiation to hold brand loyalty. Buyers sacrifice some of the features, services or image possessed by the differentiated firm for large costs savings.

- Buyers' needs for the differentiating factor fall. This can occur as buyers become more sophisticated.
- Imitations narrows perceived differentiation, a common occurrence as industries mature.

Risks of focus

- The cost differential between broad range competitors and the focused firm widens to eliminate the cost advantages of serving a narrow target or to offset the differentiation achieved by focus.
- The differences in desired products or services between the strategic target and the market as a whole narrows.
- Competitors find sub-markets within the strategic target and out-focus the focused.

Source: Adapted from Porter (1980, pp. 45–46).

12.3   ASSESSING GROWTH OPPORTUNITIES

There are growth objectives in most strategies considered by firms, whether they are of sales growth, market share, profits or size. Growth is a factor that influences firm vitality, stimulates initiatives and increases motivation of personnel and management. Independent of this element of dynamism, growth is necessary in order to survive assaults from competitors, thanks to the economies of scale and experience effects it generates.

A firm can envisage growth objectives at three different levels:

- A growth objective within the reference market it operates; we shall refer to this as *intensive growth*.
- A growth objective within the industrial chain, lateral expansion of its generic activity, backwards or forwards; this is *integrative growth*.
- A growth objective based on opportunities outside its normal field of activity; this is *growth by diversification*.

To each of these growth objectives correspond a number of possible strategies. It is interesting to examine them briefly.

Intensive growth

A strategy of *intensive growth* is called for when a firm has not yet fully exploited the opportunities offered by its products within its "natural" reference market. Various strategies may be envisaged: market penetration, market and product development strategies.

Market penetration strategies

A market penetration strategy, also called *organic growth*, consists of trying to increase or maintain sales of current products in existing markets. Several options are open.

1. *Primary demand development*: to increase size of total market by expanding – primary demand, for example:

   - Broadening the customer base by converting non-users into users (see Exhibit 12.4).
   - Increasing the frequency of purchase among present users.
   - increasing the average quantity purchased per use occasion.
   - identifying and promoting new uses.

Note that this strategy can benefit all competitors since it influences primary demand more than selective demand.

2. *Market share increase strategy*: to increase sales by attracting buyers from rival brands, through significant spending on marketing mix variables. For example:

   - improved product or service offering
   - positioning the brands
   - aggressive pricing
   - significant reinforcement of the distribution and service network
   - major promotional efforts.

Exhibit 12.4   Proximus stimulates mobile phone consumption

The Belgian mobile phone operator Proximus is the market leader in Belgium. The company dominates the market with the largest market share. The objective is to stimulate mobile phone use. The strategy is twofold: (a) reach non-users and convert them targeting the older population segment and (b) increase the usage rate of existing users. To achieve this second objective, the company organize promotions that stimulate consumption, by offering free SMS, free minutes or lower rates at certain moment of the week or the week-end. This motivates people to use more and when the promotion is over, they continue to do so.

Source: Authors.

This more aggressive strategy will be mainly observed in market situations where primary demand is non-expansible, having reached the maturity phase of the product life cycle.

3. *Market acquisition*: to increase market share substantially by acquisition or joint venture. For example:

   ■ acquisition of competitor to obtain its market share
   ■ joint venture to achieve control of a significant market share.

4. *Market position defence*: to defend current market position (that is customer relationships, network, share, image and so on) by adjusting the marketing mix. For example:

   ■ product or service minor modifications or repositioning
   ■ defensive pricing
   ■ sales and distribution network reinforcement
   ■ stepped-up or redirected promotional activities.

5. *Market rationalization*: to modify significantly the markets served to reduce costs and/or increase marketing effectiveness. For example:

   ■ concentration on most profitable segments
   ■ use of the most effective distributors
   ■ limiting individual customers served via minimum volume requirements
   ■ selective abandonment of market segments.

6. *Market organization*: to influence, using legally accepted practices, the level of competition within one's industry to enhance economic viability. For example:

   ■ establishment of industry-wide competitive rules or guidelines, usually under government supervision
   ■ creation of joint marketing research organizations to improve information systems.
   ■ agreement on capacity stabilization or reduction.

These last three strategies are more defensive, aiming at maintaining the level of market penetration.

Market development strategies

A *market development strategy* refers to a firm's attempt to increase the sales of its present products by tapping new or future markets. This objective can be achieved using four alternative approaches:

1. *Unarticulated or latent needs among served customers*: to propose solutions to customers' needs not yet perceived or expressed. The objective here is to lead customers with new products (like digital photography), to educate them and to create a new market through a proactive marketing strategy.
2. *New market segments*: to reach new (un served) groups of customers within the same geographic market. For example:

    ■   Introducing an industrial product to the consumer market or vice versa.
    ■   Selling the product to another customer age group (sweets to adults)
    ■   Selling the product to another industrial sector.

3. *New distribution channels*: to distribute the product through another channel of distribution, complementary to the current ones. For example:

    ■   Adopting a direct marketing system for specific groups of customers
    ■   Distributing the products through vending machines
    ■   Developing a franchise system parallel to the existing network.

4. *Geographic expansion towards other parts of the country or to other countries*. For example:

    ■   Shipping existing products to foreign markets relying on local agents or on an independent worldwide trading company.
    ■   Creating an exclusive network of distributors to handle foreign business.
    ■   Acquiring a foreign company in the same sector.

Market development strategies rely mainly on the distribution and marketing know-how of the firm.

Product development strategies

A *product development* strategy consists of increasing sales by developing improved or new products aimed at current markets. Several different possibilities exist:

1. *Discontinuous innovations*: to launch a new product or service that represents a major change in the benefits offered to customers and in the behaviour necessary for them to use the product. Customers must in some way discontinue their past patterns to fit the new product into their lives (mobile telephone and self-banking are good examples).
2. *Features addition strategy*: to add functions or features to existing products in order to expand the market. For example:

    ■   Increasing the versatility of a product by adding functions
    ■   Adding an emotional or social value to a utilitarian product
    ■   Improving the safety or convenience of the product.

3. *Product line extensions strategy*: to increase the breadth of the product line by introducing new varieties to increase or maintain market share. For example:
    ■   Launching different packages of different sizes
    ■   Launching different product categories under the same umbrella brand name
    ■   Increasing the number of flavours, scents, colours or composition
    ■   Offering the same product in different forms or shapes.

The strategy of line extension can lead to product proliferation and the question of cannibalization and synergistic effects should be addressed explicitly.

Exhibit 12.5   IKEA geographic expansion

IKEA, the leader in the worldwide furniture market, has followed an aggressive market expansion strategy to fuel its growth. Their objective is to offer their products to the highest number of people in the world. They decided to expand internationally to not rely only on European markets that could stabilize. They expanded successfully in the United States in 1985, in Eastern European countries in the 1990s and in China in 1995. They are now present in more than 38 countries.

Source: Authors.

---

4. *Product line rejuvenation strategy*: to restore the overall competitiveness of obsolete or inadequate products by replacing them with technologically or functionally superior products. For example:

    ■   Developing a new generation of more powerful products
    ■   Launching environmentally friendly new models of existing products
    ■   Improving the aesthetic aspects of the product.

5. *Product quality improvement strategy*: to improve the way a product performs its functions as a package of benefits. For example:

    ■   Determining the package of benefits sought by each customer group
    ■   Establishing quality standards on each dimension of the package of benefits
    ■   Establishing a programme of total quality control.

6. *Product line acquisition*: to complete, improve or broaden the range of products through external means. For example:

    ■   Acquisition of a company with a complementary product line
    ■   Contracting for the supply of a complementary product line to be sold under the company's name
    ■   Joint venture for the development and production of a new product.

7. *Product line rationalization*: to modify the product line to reduce production or distribution costs. For example:

    ■   Product line and packaging standardization
    ■   Selective abandonment of unprofitable or marginal products
    ■   Minor product redesign.

The lever used in product development strategies is essentially R&D. These strategies are generally more costly and risky than market development strategies.

Integrative growth

An integrative growth strategy is justified when a firm can improve profitability by controlling different activities of strategic importance within the industrial chain. It describes a variety of make-or-buy arrangements firms use to obtain a ready supply of strategic raw materials and a ready market for their outputs. Examples include ensuring stability of supplies, controlling a distribution network, or having access to information in a downstream activity to secure captive markets. There is a distinction between backward integration, forward integration and horizontal integration.

Backward integration

A *backward integration* strategy is driven by the concern to maintain or to protect a strategically important source of supplies, be it raw or semi-processed materials, components or services. In some cases, backward integration is necessary because suppliers do not have the resources or technological know-how to make components or materials which are indispensable to the firm.

Another objective may be to have access to a key technology which might be essential to the success of the activity. For example, many computer manufacturers have integrated backwards in the design and production of semiconductors in order to control this fundamental activity.

Forward integration

The basic motivation for a *forward integration* strategy is to control outlets without which the firm will choke. For a firm producing consumer goods, this involves controlling distribution through franchises or exclusive contracts, or even by creating its own chain stores, such as Yves Rocher or Bata. In industrial markets, the aim is mainly to ensure the development of downstream industries of transformation and incorporation that constitute natural outlets. This is how some basic industries actively participate in creating intermediary transformation activity.

In some cases, forward integration is done simply to have a better understanding of the needs of buyers of manufactured products. The firm creates in this case a subsidiary playing the role of a pilot unit: to understand problems of users in order to meet their needs more effectively. The adoption of *solution-to-a-problem* strategy generally implies some form of forward integration. The new development strategy adopted by Xerox provides a good example of a forward integration strategy.

Horizontal integration

A *horizontal integration* strategy has a totally different perspective. The objective is to reinforce competitive position by absorbing or controlling some competitors. There can be various arguments for this: neutralizing a dangerous rival, reaching the critical volume so as to benefit from scale effects, benefiting from the complementarity of product lines and having access to distribution networks or to restricted market segments.

Growth by diversification

A strategy of *growth by diversification* is justified if the firm's industrial chain presents little or no prospect of growth or profitability. This may happen either because competitors occupy a powerful position, or because the reference market is in decline. Diversification implies entry into new product markets. This kind of growth strategy is as such more risky, since

---

Exhibit 12.6   Virgin diversification strategy

Virgin, the European Company created by Richard Branson, has pursued a strong diversification strategy since its creation in many sectors outside its core business. They have moved from music production, to travel, to drinks or games. They have indeed created Virgin Records, Virgin Radio, Virgin video games, Virgin holidays, Virgin Airlines, Virgin Hotels, Virgin Cola etc. It is one of the few European company that has succeeded to diversify in so many different business sectors.

Source: International Herald Tribune, 18 June 1999.

the jump into the unknown is more significant. It is usual to establish a distinction between concentric diversification and pure diversification.

Concentric diversification

In a *concentric diversification* strategy, the firm goes out of its industrial and commercial network and tries to add new activities, which are related to its current activities technologically and/or commercially. The objective is therefore to benefit from synergy effects due to complimentarily of activities, and thus to expand the firm's reference market.

A concentric diversification strategy usually has the objectives of attracting new groups of buyers and expanding the reference market of the firm.

Pure diversification

In a pure diversification strategy, the firm enters into new activities which are unrelated to its traditional activities, either technologically or commercially. The aim is to turn towards entirely new fields so as to rejuvenate the product portfolio. At the end of 1978, for example, Volkswagen bought Triumph-Adler, which specializes in informatics and office equipment, for this very reason.

Diversification strategies are undoubtedly the most risky and complex strategies, because they lead the firm into unknown territory. To be successful, diversification requires important human as well as financial resources. Drucker (1981, p. 16) considers that a successful diversification requires a common core or unity represented by common markets, technology or production processes. He states that without such a unity core, diversification never works; financial ties alone are insufficient. Other organizational management specialists believe in the importance of a *corporate culture* or a *management style* which characterizes every organization and which may be effective in some fields and not others.

The rationale of diversification

Calori and Harvatopoulos (1988) study the rationales of diversification in the French industry. They identify two dimensions. The first relates to the *nature of the strategic objective*: diversification may be defensive (replacing a loss-making activity) or offensive (conquering new positions). The second dimension involves the *expected outcomes* of diversification: management may expect great economic value (growth, profitability) or first and foremost great coherence and complementarity with their current activities (exploitation of know-how).

Cross-classifying these two dimensions gives rise to four logics of diversification, as shown in Table 12.3.

- *Expansion*, whereby the firm tries to reinforce its activity (offensive aim) while taking full advantage of its know-how (coherence). This kind of diversification strategy has been followed by Salomon, for example, world leader in ski bindings, which has gone into the market for ski boots, then the market for cross-country skiing and more recently into manufacturing golf clubs and ski poles.
- *Relay*, which seeks to replace a declining activity (defensive objective), while using high quality staff (coherence). Framatome followed this strategy at the end of the 1970s, when the market for nuclear plants started to shrink.
- *Deployment* is an offensive strategy seeking high economic value. This was the case for Taittinger diversifying into the deluxe hotel business.

Table 12.3 The rationales of diversification

Type of objective	Expected outcome	
	Coherence	Economic value
Offensive	Expansion	Deployment
Defensive	(Salomon)	(Taittinger)
	Relay	Redeployment
	(Framatome)	(Lafarge)

Source: Calori and Harvatopoulos (1988).

■   *Redeployment* which is defensive in nature but seeks a new channel for growth. This strategy was followed by Lafarge which merged with Coppée and entered into biotechnology when faced with decline in the building industry.

Two more particular logics must be added to these basic ones: diversification driven by image improvement (*the logic of image*), and diversification driven by the will to watch the growth of a new promising technology (*the logic of window*).

Diversification strategy based on core competencies

A particular form of diversification is based on the resources or the competencies that a firm considers as fundamental and intrinsically part of its core business. These core *competencies* can be used in different domains of activities as long as the objective of coherence is met.

> As a general rule, any successful diversification strategy is more or less based on synergies coming from the main activity of the firm. The provisional assessment of core competencies, talents or knowledge synergies between the present and the contemplated domain of activity constitutes a critical challenge in the design of a diversification strategy. The main risk is the over-evaluation of competencies' synergy between the two fields of activity.

It is important that management define the logic of diversification from the outset and as clearly as possible. Upon this logic, will depend the criteria for assessing and selecting potential activities. The alternative growth strategies reviewed in this chapter are summarized in Exhibit 12.7.

The impact of disruptive technological innovations

On the technology front, and in parallel with globalization, one observes a convergence of markets triggered by disruptive technological innovations, which upset traditional market boundaries and change the traditional definition of an industry.

> Digitalization for example eliminates boundaries between printing, photography, television and image processing systems. Convergence is also observed in information technology, telecommunication, banking and insurance, office automation, etc.

By disruptive innovations, we mean a new way of playing the competitive game that is *both different and in conflict with the traditional way* adopted by established leaders (Charitou and Markidès, 2003). Examples include Internet banking, direct insurance, low-cost airlines, home book retailing. As a result, established leaders in a variety of industries were asking the same question: Should we respond to these disruptive innovations, with the risk of damaging our core business?

Convergence leads companies to define their reference market in terms of generic needs instead of technologies and products, since technologies are fast changing whilst generic needs are stable. As a result, many firms tend to view themselves as a service firm, where the

---

Exhibit 12.7   Alternative growth strategies

1. Intensive growth: to grow within the reference market

1.1. Penetration strategy: increase sales of existing products in existing markets:

- Primary demand development.
- Market share increase.
- Market acquisition.
- Market position defence.
- Market rationalization.
- Market organization.

1.2. Market development strategy: increase sales of existing products in new markets:

- Target new market segments.
- Adopt new distribution channels.
- Penetrate new geographic markets.

1.3. Product development strategy: increase sales in existing markets with new or modified products:

- Features addition strategy.
- Product line extensions strategy.

- Product line rejuvenation strategy.
- Product quality improvement strategy.
- Product line acquisition.
- Product line rationalization.
- New product development strategy.

2. Integrative growth: to grow within the industrial chain

2.1. Backward integration.
2.2. Forward integration.
2.3. Horizontal integration.

3. Growth by diversification: to grow outside the industrial chain

3.1. Concentric diversification.
3.2. Pure diversification.

Source: Lambin (2000/2007).

---

physical product is secondary but where the company mission is to propose to the client a *solution-to-a-problem* and not simply a product.

It is the case, for instance, of the company Automatic Systems, initially a manufacturer of metallic gates and doors, now selling "access control systems"; of Nestlé, who, in addition to selling the Nescafé brand, is selling the Nespresso system; of IBM, who is selling "computerised solutions to managerial problems"; of Microsoft, selling the Office system; of Starbucks, who organises the distribution of its products in a franchised network of coffee shops, etc.

The fast development of technology also has a strong impact on innovation strategies. A distinction is often made between a *market-pull innovation*, that is, one that directly meets observed articulated needs, and a *technology or company-push innovation*, that is, one that results from research, creativity and technological opportunities and target latent needs.

- In the first case of *market-pull innovation*, needs are expressed and articulated. The objective is to find wants and to fill them. Primary demand is latent and the task is to develop and stimulate this latent demand through operational marketing. This is *response strategic marketing*, the traditional role of strategic marketing, which still prevails in developing and growing economies.
- In the second situation of *company-push innovations*, the products or services proposed are often ahead of expressed market needs. With so-called *discontinuous or disruptive innovations*, the market boundaries are not well defined, needs are not articulated, the competitive environment is blurred and often the innovation upsets existing market

practices and habits. Thus the key question is to know whether there is a need in the market for the company-push innovation (Exhibit 12.8).

In highly industrialized countries, it is the second situation – leading to proactive *strategic marketing* – which tends to prevail and to generate most growth opportunities. The role of operational marketing is more complex and risky here, since primary demand must be created.

The characteristics of high-technology industries have implications for the new product development process, namely speed and flexibility in product development, close cooperation with customers and systematic monitoring of the technological environment. Thus, in high-technology markets, strategic marketing has a crucial role to play, particularly in organizing *cross-functional structure*, namely the "R&D-Production-Marketing" interface to disseminate the market orientation culture throughout the entire organization.

12.4   CHOOSING A COMPETITIVE STRATEGY

An important element of a growth strategy is taking explicit account of competitors' positions and behaviour. Measuring business competitiveness helps to evaluate the importance of the firm's competitive advantage compared with its most dangerous rivals, and to identify their competitive behaviour. The next task is to set out a strategy based on a realistic assessment of the forces at work, and to determine the means to achieve defined objectives.

Kotler establishes a distinction between four types of competitive strategy; his typology is based on the level of market share held and comprises four different strategies: market leader, market challenger, market follower and market nicher (Kotler, 2006, p. 319).

Exhibit 12.8   How the Internet killed the phone business

The term "disruptive technology" is popular, but is widely misused. It refers not simply to a clever new technology, but to one that undermines an existing technology – and which therefore makes life very difficult for many businesses which depend on the existing way of doing things. /.../. This week has been a coming out party of sorts for another disruptive technology, "voice over Internet protocol" (VOIP), which promises to be even more disruptive, and of even greater benefit to consumers, than personal computers. VOIP's proponent is Skype, a small firm whose software allows people to make free calls to other Skype users over the Internet, and very cheap calls to traditional telephones – all of which spell trouble for incumbent telecom operators. On 12 September 2005, eBay, the leading online auction-house, announced that it was buying Skype for $2.6 billion, plus an additional $1.6 billion if Skype hits certain performance targets in

coming years. /.../ The fuss over Skype in recent weeks has highlighted the significance of VOIP, and the enormous threat it poses to incumbent telecom operators. For the rise of Skype means nothing less than the death of the traditional telephone business, established over a century ago. /.../ "We believe that you should not have to pay for making phone calls in future, just as you don't pay to send e-mail," says Skype co-founder, Niklas Zennstrom. /.../ As is always the case with a disruptive technology, the incumbents it threatens are dividing into those who are trying to block the new technology in the hope that it will simply go away, and those who are moving to embrace it even though it undermines their existing businesses.

Source: The Economist (2005).

Market leader strategies

In a product market, the market leader is the firm that holds a dominant position and is acknowledged as such by its rivals. The leader is often an orientation point for competitors, a reference that rival firms try to attack, to imitate or to avoid. The best-known market leaders are IBM, Procter & Gamble, Benetton, Nestlé, L'Oréal and so on. A market leader can envisage different strategies.

Primary demand development

The market leader is usually the firm that contributes most to the growth of the reference market. The most natural strategy that flows from the leader's responsibility is to *expand total demand* by looking for new users, new uses and more usage of its products. Acting in this way, the market leader contributes to expanding the total market size which, in the end, is beneficial to all competitors. This type of strategy is normally observed in the first stages of the product's life cycle, when total demand is expansible and tension between rivals is low due to high potential for growth of total demand.

Defensive strategies

A second strategy open to a firm with large market share is a *defensive strategy*: protecting market share by countering the actions of the most dangerous rivals. This kind of strategy is often adopted by the innovating firm which finds itself attacked by imitating firms once the market has been opened. This was the case for IBM in the mainframe computer market, for Danone in the fresh products market, for Coca-Cola in the soft drink market and so on. Many defensive strategies can be adopted:

- Innovation and technological advance which discourages competitors.
- Market consolidation through intensive distribution and a full line policy to cover all market segments.
- Direct confrontation that is direct showdown through price wars or advertising campaigns.

We have seen this type of strategy between firms such as Hertz and Avis, Coca-Cola and Pepsi Cola, and between Kodak and Polaroid.

Aggressive strategies

A third possibility available to a dominant firm is an *offensive strategy*. The objective here is to reap the benefits of experience effects to the maximum and thus improve profitability. This strategy is based on the assumption that market share and profitability are related. In the previous chapter, we saw that this relationship was mainly observed in volume industries, where competitive advantage is cost-based. Its existence has also been empirically established by works of PIMS (Buzzell, Gale and Sultan, 1975) and confirmed by Galbraith and Schendel (1983). Although increasing market share is beneficial to a firm, there exists a limit beyond which the cost of any further increase becomes prohibitive. Furthermore, an excessively dominant position also has the inconvenience that it attracts the attention of public authorities who are in charge of maintaining balanced competitive market conditions. This, for instance, is the task of the Competition Commission within the EU, and of anti-trust laws in the United States. Dominant firms are also more vulnerable to attacks by consumer organizations, which tend to choose the most visible targets, such as Nestlé in Switzerland and Fiat and Montedison in Italy.

De-marketing strategy

A strategy open to a dominant firm: *reduce its market share* to avoid accusations of monopoly or quasi-monopoly. Various possibilities exist. First, it can use *de-marketing* to reduce the demand level in some segments by price increases, or reduce services as well as advertising and promotion campaigns. Another strategy is *diversification* towards product markets different from those where the firm has a dominant position. Finally, and in a very different perspective, a last strategy could be a *communication or public relations strategy* with the objective to promote the social role of the firm *vis-à-vis* its different publics.

> For example, mass food distributors having a dominant position in some markets, like to enhance their role in the fight against inflation through their pricing policy and namely through the launching on a large scale of "no frills-low price" private labels which are 30 to 40 per cent less expensive than national brands.

In some cases, anti-trust laws may force companies to downsize.

Market challenger strategies

A firm that does not dominate a product market can choose either to attack the market leader and be its challenger, or to become a follower by falling into line with the leader's decisions. Market challenger strategies are therefore aggressive strategies with a declared objective of taking the leader's position.

The challenger faces two key questions: (a) the choice of the battleground from which to attack the market leader and (b) evaluation of the latter's a reactive and defensive ability. In the *choice of the battleground*, the challenger has two possibilities: frontal attack or lateral attack. A *frontal attack* consists of opposing the competitor directly by using its own weapons, and without trying to use its weak points. To be successful, a frontal attack demands a balance of power heavily in favour of the attacker. In military strategy, this balance is normally put at 3 to 1.

> For example, when in 1981 IBM attacked the microcomputer market with its PC, its marketing tools, advertising in particular, were very clearly superior to those of Apple, Commodore and Tandy, which dominated the market. Two years later IBM had become the leader.

Lateral attacks aim to confront the leader over one or another strategic dimension for which it is weak or ill prepared. A lateral attack may, for example, address a region or a distribution network where the leader is not well represented, or a market segment where his or her product is not well adapted. A classic market challenger strategy is to launch a price attack on the leader: offer the same product at a much lower price. Many Japanese firms adopt this strategy in electronics or cars (Kotler *and Singh,* 1981).

This strategy becomes even more effective when the leader holds a large market share. If the latter were to take up the lower price, it would have to bear large costs, whereas the challenger, especially if it is small, loses only over a low volume.

Lateral or indirect attacks can take various forms. There is direct analogy with military strategy and one can define strategies of outflanking, encircling, guerrilla tactics, mobile defence and so on. See Kotler and Singh (1981) and Ries and Trout (1986) on this topic.

Before starting an offensive move, it is essential to assess correctly a dominant firm's *ability to react and defend*. Porter (1980, p. 68) suggests using the three following criteria:

- *Vulnerability:* to what strategic moves and governmental, macro-economic or industry events would the competitor be most vulnerable?
- *Provocation:* what moves or events are such that they will provoke retaliation from competitors, even though retaliation may be costly and lead to marginal financial performance?
- *Effectiveness of retaliation:* what moves or events is the competitor impeded from reacting to quickly and/or effectively given its goals, strategy, existing capabilities and assumptions?

The ideal is to adopt a strategy against which the competitor cannot react because of its current situation or priority objectives.

As was underlined earlier, in saturated or stagnant markets the aggressiveness of the competitive struggle tends to intensify as the main objective becomes how to counter rivals' actions. The risk of a strategy based only on *marketing warfare* is that too much energy is devoted to driving rivals away at the risk of losing sight of the objective of satisfying buyers' needs. A firm which is focusing entirely on its rivals tends to adopt a reactive behaviour which is more dependent on rivals' actions than the developments in market needs. A proper balance between the two orientations is therefore essential (Oxenfeld and Moore, 1978).

Market follower strategies

As we saw before, a follower is a competitor with modest market share who adopts an adaptive behaviour by falling into line with competitors' decisions. Instead of attacking the leader, these firms pursue a policy of "peaceful coexistence" by adopting the same attitude as the market leader. This type of behaviour is mainly observed in oligopolistic markets where differentiation possibilities are minimal and cross-price elasticities are very high, so that it is in no one's interest to start a competitive war that risks being harmful to all.

Adoption of a follower's behaviour does not permit the firm to have no competitive strategy, quite the contrary. The fact that the firm holds a modest market share reinforces the importance of having clearly defined strategic objectives which are adapted to its size and its strategic ambition. Hamermesch, Anderson and Harris (1978) analyse strategies of small firms and show that these firms can overcome the size handicap and achieve performance sometimes superior to dominant rivals. In other words, not all firms with low market share in low-growth markets are necessarily "dogs" or "lame ducks".

Hamermesch, Anderson and Harris (1978, pp. 98–100) have uncovered four main features in the strategies implemented by companies with high performance and low market share:

- *Creative market segmentation:* To be successful, a low market share company must compete in a limited number of segments where its own strengths will be most highly valued and where large competitors will be most unlikely to compete.
- *Efficient use of R&D:* Small firms cannot compete with large companies in fundamental research; R&D should be concentrated mainly on process improvements aimed at lowering costs.
- *Think small:* Successful low market share companies are content to remain small. Most of them emphasize profits rather than sales growth or market share, and specialization rather than diversification.

■ *Ubiquitous chief executive*: The final characteristic of these companies is the pervasive influence of the chief executive.

A market follower strategy therefore does not imply passivity on the part of the chief executive of the firm, rather the concern to have a growth strategy which will not entail reprisals from the market leader.

Market niche strategies

A nicher is interested in one or few market segments, but not in the whole market. The objective is to be a large fish in a small pond rather than being a small fish in a large pond. This competitive strategy is one of the generic strategies we discussed earlier, namely focus. The key to a focus strategy is specialization in a niche. For a niche to be profitable and sustainable, five characteristics are necessary (Kotler, 2006, p. 395):

■ Sufficient profit potential.
■ Growth potential.
■ Unattractive to rivals.
■ Market corresponding to the firm's distinctive competence.
■ Sustainable entry barrier.

A firm seeking a niche must face the problem of finding the feature or criterion upon which to build its specialization. This criterion may relate to a technical aspect of the product, to a particular distinctive quality or to any element of the marketing mix.

From that point of view, it is interesting to refer once more to Simon (1996a, 1996b) who has analysed the strategies adopted by a sample of 122 firms (a majority of German firms) which are (a) world or European leaders in their reference market, (b) of small or medium size and (c) unfamiliar to the general public. The nine main lessons are summarized in Exhibit 12.9.

12.5 INTERNATIONAL DEVELOPMENT STRATEGIES

We emphasized in the second chapter that internationalization of the economy means that a growing number of firms operate in markets where competition is global. As a result, international development strategies concern all firms, irrespective of whether they actively participate in foreign markets or not. We will examine here the stages of international development as well as the strategic reasoning of a firm that pursues an international marketing development strategy.

Steps in the internationalization of markets

The period now referred to as the "Golden Sixties" corresponds to the beginning of the internationalization of markets, a process that has continued up to the 1990s. At the European level, internationalization took the form of the creation of the Common Market; at the world level it took the form of GATT (General Agreement on Tariffs and Trade) and the resulting progressive liberalization of trade, the end of the Cold War and the expansion of East–West trade. All these factors contributed to the widening markets, and, in general, to the intensification of competition and the reappraisal of established competitive positions.

Exhibit 12.9   The nine lessons from the hidden champions

1. Set clear and ambitious goal. Ideally a company should strive to be the best and to become the leader in its market.

2. Define the market narrowly and in so doing include both customer needs and technology. Don't accept given market definition but consider the market definition itself part of strategy; Stay focused and concentrated. Avoid distractions.

3. Combine a narrow market focus with a global orientation, involving world-wide sales and marketing. Deal as directly as possible with customers around the globe.

4. Be close to customers in both performance and interaction. Make sure that all functions have direct customer contacts. Adopt a value-driven strategy. Pay close attention to the most demanding customers.

5. Strive for continuous innovation in both product and process. Innovation should be both technology- and customer-driven. Pay equal attention to internal resources and competencies and external opportunities.

6. Create clear-cut competitive advantage in both product and service. Defend the company' competitive position ferociously.

7. Rely on your own strengths. Keep core competencies in the company, but outsource non-core activities. Consider co-operation as a last resort rather than a first choice.

8. Try always to have more work than heads. Select employees rigorously in the first phase, and then retain them for the long term. Communicate directly to motivate people and use employee creativity to its full potential.

9. Practise leadership that is both authoritarian in the fundamental and participative in the details. Pay utmost attention to the selection of leaders. Observing their unity of person and purpose, energy and perseverance, and the ability to inspire others.

Source: Adapted from Simon (1996a, 1996b).

To the various stages of international development there often correspond specific forms of organization at the international level, which reflect different views of international marketing. Keegan (1989/2004) suggests the following typology:

- *Domestic organization:* The firm is focused on its domestic market, and exporting is viewed as an opportunistic activity. This type of organization is frequently in the "passive marketing" stage as described above.

- *International organization:* Internationalization takes place more actively, but at this stage the firm's orientation is still focused on the home market, which is considered as the primary area of opportunity. The *ethnocentric* company, unconsciously, if not explicitly and consciously, operates on the assumption that home country methods, approaches, people, practices and values are superior to those found elsewhere in the world. Attention is mostly centred on similarities with the home country market. The product strategy at this stage is a "market extension" strategy that is products that have been designed for the home country market are "extended" into markets around the world.

- *Multi-domestic organization:*. After a certain period of time, the company discovers that the difference in markets demands adaptation of its marketing in order to succeed. The focus of the firm is now multinational (as opposed to home country) and its orientation is *polycentric*. The polycentric orientation is based on the assumption that markets around the world are so different and unique that the only way to succeed is to adapt to the unique and different aspect of each national market. The product strategy is adaptation, which is to change or adapt products to meet local differences and practices. Each country is managed as if it were an independent entity.

■ *Global or transnational organization:* A global market is one that can be reached with the same basic appeal and message and with the same basic product. Both the product and the advertising and promotion may require adaptation to local customs and practices. The *geocentric* (or *regiocentric*) orientation of the global corporation is based on the assumption that markets around the world are both similar and different, and that it is possible to develop a global strategy that recognizes similarities, which transcend national differences while adapting to local differences as well. This last stage is, at the moment, taking shape in the world and in particular in the European economy. It implies important changes in the logic of strategic marketing.

In the European and in the world economies, this internationalization process took place during the years 1960–2000. This process also required a reinforcement of the analytical capabilities of the firm to successfully enter foreign markets.

Objectives of international development

International development is no longer limited to large enterprises. Many small firms are forced to become international in order to grow, or simply to survive. Objectives in an international development strategy may be varied:

■ To enlarge the *potential market*, thus being able to produce more and achieve better results thanks to economies of scale. For many activities, the critical volume is at such a level that it demands a large potential market.
■ To extend the product's *life cycle* by entering markets which are not at the same development stage and still have expandable total demand, whereas in the domestic market of the exporting firm demand has reached the maturity phase.
■ To diversify *commercial risk* by addressing buyers in different economic environments and enjoying more favourable competitive conditions.
■ To control *competition* through diversification of positions on the one hand and surveillance of competitors' activities in other markets on the other.
■ To reduce *costs of supplies and production* by exploiting different countries' comparative advantages.
■ To exploit *excess production capacity* by exporting goods at low (marginal cost) prices.
■ To achieve *geographic diversification* by entering new markets with existing products.
■ To *follow key customers* abroad to supply or to service them in their foreign locations.

The phenomenon of globalization of markets must also be added to these basic objectives: take advantage of the progressive liberalization of world trade.

Forms of international development

A firm's internationalization does not happen overnight, but results from a process that can be subdivided into six levels of growing internationalization (Leroy, Richard and Sallenave, 1978):

1. *Exporting* is the most frequent form. Often, the first attempts to export result from a necessity to clear surplus production. Later, exports can become a regular activity, but

one which is reconstituted every year without there being any kind of medium- or long-term commitment to foreign countries. Relations are purely commercial.

2. The second stage is the *contractual stage*. Here the firm seeks more long-term agreements so as to stabilize its outlets, especially if its production capacity has been adjusted in terms of the potential to export. It will then sign long-term contracts, either with an importer or with a franchised distributor, or with a licensed manufacturer if it is an industrial firm.

3. In order to control the foreign partner or to finance its expansion, the firm may directly invest its own capital; this is the *participatory stage* which leads to commercial companies or co-ownership production.

4. After a few years, involvement can become absolute, with the firm owning 100 per cent of the capital of the foreign subsidiary; this stage is *direct investment* in a subsidiary with controlled management.

5. Gradually, the foreign subsidiary looks for ways of autonomous development, using local finance, national managers and its own programme of R&D which is distinct from the parent company. This is the *autonomous subsidiary stage*. If the parent company has many subsidiaries of this kind, this subsidiary becomes a multinational company. It would probably be more appropriate to use the term "multidomestic", because it emphasizes the point that each of these companies is more concerned about its own internal market, and the group's various companies coexist independently of each other.

6. The final stage of development is the one which is taking shape at the moment. It is the stage of the *global enterprise* that addresses the international market as if it were a single market. This kind of firm bases itself on interdependence of markets, and the latter are therefore no longer administered autonomously.

Chapter Summary

Product portfolio analyses are designed to help guide a multi-product firm's strategic thinking by evaluating each activity with reference to indicators of attractiveness and of competitiveness. The growth–share matrix has the merit of simplicity and objectivity, but its underlying assumptions are restrictive and limit its scope of application. The multi-factor matrix is more widely applicable and more flexible because the indicators used are company-specific, but the risk of subjectivity is higher and the procedure is more demanding in terms of available information. In elaborating a development strategy, the firm should clarify the nature of the sustainable competitive advantage which will serve as the basis for later strategic actions and tactics. Two views of strategy exist, one which is more relevant in existing markets, and the other being better adapted for strategy development in future markets. Three generic options can be adopted in existing markets: overall cost leadership, differentiation or focus. The choice of one generic strategy is not neutral, but implies different resources, know-how and risks. In assessing growth opportunities, growth objectives can be considered at different levels: within the reference market (intensive growth), within the supply chain (integrative growth) or outside the current field of activity (diversification). For each of these three development strategies, several options are open which should be systematically explored in a strategic thinking exercise. A development strategy should explicitly take into account competitors' positions and behaviour on the basis of a realistic assessment of the forces at work. One can distinguish four types of competitive strategies: market leader, market challenger, market follower or market nicher. As a consequence of the globalization of the world economy, international development is no longer limited to large enterprises and is motivated by a variety of strategic objectives. A firm's internationalization does not happen overnight but results from a process which can be subdivided into different stages of international involvement and also in various organizational forms.

BIBLIOGRAPHY

Abell, D.E. and Hammond, J.S. (1979), Strategic Market Planning, Englewood Cliffs, NJ, Prentice Hall.

Andrews, K.R. (1971/1980/1987), *The Concept of Corporate Strategy*, Homewood, IL, R.D. Irwin.

Boston Consulting Group (1972), *Perspectives on Experience*, Boston, MA, The Boston Consulting Group.

Buzzell, R.D., Gale, B.T. and Sultan, G.M. (1975), Market Share, a Key to Profitability, *Harvard Business Review*, 53, 1, pp. 97–106.

Calori, R. and Harvatopoulos, Y. (1988), Diversification: les règles de conduite, *Harvard-L'Expansion*, 48, Spring, pp. 48–510.

Chamberlin, E.H. (1933), *The Theory of Monopolistic Competition*, Cambridge, MA, Harvard University Press.

Charitou, D. and Markidès, C. (2003), Responses to Disruptive Strategic Innovation, *MIT Sloan Management Review*, 54, 2, pp. 55–63.

Damon, D. (2006), HP invades Kodak's Kingdom, *International Herald Tribune*, February 24.

Day, G.S. (1977), Diagnosing the Product Portfolio, *Journal of Marketing*, 41, 2, pp. 29–38.

Drucker, P.F. (1981) The Five Rules of Successful Acquisition, *The Wall Street Journal*, 15, October, p. 16.

Galbraith, C. and Schendel, D. (1983), An Empirical Analysis of Strategy Types, *Strategic Management Journal*, 4, 2, pp. 153–73.

Hamel, G. and Prahalad, C.K. (1994), *Competing For the Future*, Boston, MA, Harvard Business School Press.

Hamermesch, R.G., Anderson, M.J. and Harris, J.E. (1978), Strategies for Low Market Share Businesses, *Harvard Business Review*, 56, 3, pp. 95–102.

Henderson, B.B. (1970), *The Product Portfolio*, Boston, MA, The Boston Consulting Group.

Hussey, D.E. (1978), Portfolio Analysis: Practical Experience with the Directional Policy Matrix, *Long Range Planning*, 11, 4, pp. 2–8.

Keegan, W.J. (1989/2004), Global Marketing Management, Englewood Cliffs, NJ, Prentice-Hall, 4th Edition.

Kim, W.C. and Mauborgne, R. (1997), Value Innovation: The Strategic Logic of High Growth, *Harvard Business Review*, 75, 1, pp. 102–12.

Kotler, P. (2006), *Marketing Management*, Englewood Cliffs, NJ, Prentice-Hall, 12th edition.

Kotler, P. and Singh, R. (1981), Marketing Warfare in the 1980s, *Journal of Business Strategy*, 1, 3, pp. 30–41.

Lambin, J.J. (2000/2007), *Market-Driven Management: Strategic and Operational Marketing*, London, Palgrave Macmillan, Second edition.

Lambin, J.J. (2000/2007*), Market-driven Management: Strategic and Operational Marketing*, London, Palgrave Macmillan.

Leroy, G., Richard, G. and Sallenave, J.P. (1978*), La conquête des marchés extérieurs,* Paris, Les Editions d'Organisation.

Oxenfeld, A.R. and Moore, W.L. (1978), Customer or Competitor: Which Guide Lines for Marketing? *Management Review*, 67, 8, pp. 43–8.

Porter, M.E. (1980), *Competitive Strategy*, New York, The Free Press.

Porter, M.E. (1985), *Competitive Advantage*, New York, The Free Press.

Porter, M.E. (1996), What is Strategy?, *Harvard Business Review*, 74, 6, pp. 61–710.

Ries, A. and Trout, J. (1986), *Warfare Marketing*, New York, McGraw-Hill.

Rigby, D.K. (2010), *Management Tools 2011 An Executive Guide*, Bain and Company.

Simon, H. (1996a), *Hidden Champions*, Boston, MA, Harvard Business School Press.

Simon, H. (1996b), You don't Have to be German to be a "Hidden Champion", *Business Strategy Review*, 7, 2, pp. 1–13.

Stratégor (1997), *Stratégie, structure, décision, i*dentité, Paris, InterEditions, 3rd edition.

Strom, S. (1999), Sony, in a Giant Overhaul, Sets Sights on Networking, *International Herald Tribune*, March 9.

The Economist (2005), How the internet killed the phone business, September 17, p.11.

Wind, Y., Mahajan, V. and Swire, D.S. (1983), An Empirical Comparison of Standardized Portfolio Models, *Journal of Marketing*, 47, 2, pp. 89–99.

PART FOUR

IMPLEMENTING OPERATIONAL MARKETING

CHAPTER THIRTEEN

NEW PRODUCT DECISIONS

The objective of this chapter is to analyse the concepts and procedures that allow a firm to implement new product development strategies. Redeployment, diversification and innovation are at the heart of all development strategies. In a constantly changing environment, a company must continuously re-evaluate the structure of its portfolio of activities, meaning the decisions to abandon products, modify existing ones or launch new products. These decisions are of the utmost importance to the survival of the company and involve not only the marketing department, but all the other functional areas as well. In this chapter, we shall examine the ways of establishing a dialogue between the various functional areas that play a role in the development of a new product. We do this in such a way as to minimize the risks in the strategy during the innovation process.

Learning Objectives

When you have read this chapter, you should be able to know and understand:

- The components of innovation
- The distinction between market-pull and technology-push innovation
- The organizational procedures of the new product development process
- The methods of idea generation
- The methods of idea screening
- The analysis of the customer's adoption process
- The concept of portfolio of projects

13.1 THE STRATEGIC ROLE OF INNOVATIONS

New product decisions are complex and risky decisions, but they are of vital importance for the development and survival of the firm. The acceleration of technological change has reinforced this importance. In 1995, the share of sales derived from new or improved products commercialized within the previous five years was 45 per cent on average (Page, 1993). This percentage is even higher for high-tech products and tends to increase with time:

> 1976–1981: 33 per cent
> 1981–1986: 40 per cent
> 1986–1990: 42 per cent
> 1990–1995: 45 per cent

New products also have a decisive impact on corporate profits. A study made by the Product Development and Management Association (PDMA), indicated that

on average 23.2% of 1990 profits came from internally developed new products introduced during the previous five years. Furthermore, this percentage is expected to increase to 45.6% for new products introduced during the 1990–1994 period. (Page, 1993, p. 285)

The data presented in Table 13.1 are interesting to assess the share of turnover generated by innovations. Examining first the bottom line, we observe that in the EU15, 10 per cent of companies can be considered to be "highly innovative", with over half of their turnover generated by new or renewed products or services and that 20 per cent are "non-innovator" companies with 0 per cent coming from innovations. Country by country comparison shows that this proportion differs considerably between EU member states. Portugal, the

Table 13.1   Innovation in Europe: percentage of turnover coming from new products or services introduced during 2002–2004

	Sample size	0%	1–5%	6–10%	11–20%	21–50%	51% or more
Deutschland	286	14%	25%	17%	16%	16%	11%
Denmark	185	15%	17%	24%	16%	22%	6%
Ireland	95	19%	14%	19%	17%	19%	12%
Italy	294	21%	22%	22%	16%	13%	7%
Sweden	172	21%	24%	21%	13%	10%	11%
Portugal	87	22%	14%	15%	17%	17%	15%
Austria	172	22%	23%	21%	14%	11%	9%
Finland	90	23%	34%	17%	10%	12%	5%
UK	282	23%	13%	20%	14%	16%	14%
Spain	287	23%	15%	11%	19%	19%	13%
Nederland	198	23%	34%	19%	12%	9%	3%
Luxemburg	92	24%	32%	16%	18%	8%	2%
France	286	27%	26%	17%	12%	11%	7%
Ellas	94	32%	21%	15%	12%	13%	8%
Belgium	188	34%	20%	20%	11%	8%	7%
EU 15	**2849**	**20%**	**22%**	**18%**	**15%**	**14%**	**10%**

Source: Flash Eurobarometer 144 (2004).

Exhibit 13.1   Components of an innovation: two examples

- **The disengageable T-bar and downhill skiing**

  - The *need:* to avoid the long and tiresome process of climbing back up snow-covered slopes.
  - The *concept:* traction by a disengageable cable with a seat.
  - The *technology:* mechanics.

- The problem of aeronautic vibrations

  - The *need:* to eliminate the vibrations that affect electronic equipment in an aeroplane.
  - The *concept:* a sort of mesh covering.
  - The *technology:* a resilient steel weave.

  Source: Example quoted by Barreyre (1980).

United Kingdom and Spain have the highest proportion of highly innovative companies. Belgium, Greece and France the highest proportion of non-innovative companies. Prahalad and Mashelkar (2010) have analysed the way to manage innovation supported by limited resources. An interesting analysis presented in more detail in Chapter 21 shows also the link between product innovations, advertising and stock returns (Srinivasan, Pauwels, Silva-Risso and Hanssens, 2009).

Components of an innovation

According to Barreyre (1980), an innovation may be sub-divided into three elements (see Exhibit 13.1):

- A *need* to be satisfied or a function to be fulfilled.
- The *concept* of an object or entity to satisfy the need.
- The *inputs* consisting of a body of existing knowledge as well as materials and available technology, which allow the concept to become operational.

> If we consider the need for music listening, the vinyl technology (long playing records) was replaced successively by the tape (minicassette), the laser (compact disc) and by the digital technology (iPod). Both the concept and the technology were innovative.

The degree of risk associated with an innovation will thus depend on two factors: (a) the degree of originality and complexity of the concept, which will determine the receptivity of the market and transfer costs for the user (*market risk*); (b) the degree of technological innovation pertaining to the concept, which will determine the technical feasibility of the innovation (*technology risk*).

Added to these two intrinsic risks is the degree of familiarity that the firm itself has with the market and the technology (*strategy risk*).

A true innovation is a product; a service, a concept which brings a new solution to consumers' problems, either by providing a better solution than the existing ones proposed by competition or by offering a new or an additional function.

Market-pull versus technology-push innovations

A distinction can be made between a *market-pull innovation*, that is, one that directly answers observed needs, or a *technology-push* innovation, that is, one that results from R&D efforts and meets latent needs. This distinction is important because these innovations imply different marketing strategies: *response strategic marketing* for innovation coming from the market (*Is it doable?*) and *supply-driven or proactive strategic marketing* for technology-led innovations (*Is there a need?*).

Technology-push innovations are often disruptive innovations, fulfilling needs not explicitly articulated by potential customers, and anticipating market demand to be created by operational marketing. For these reasons, these innovations are generally more risky. Having a strong market orientation very early in the development process is vital.

> R&D isn't worth anything alone; it has to be coupled with the market. The innovative firms are not necessarily the ones that produce the best technological output, but the ones that know what is marketable.

Thus, while a proactive innovation strategy must include R&D, it must also have a strong market orientation that is critical to the successful development of new products. So there is no opposition between market-pull and technology-push strategies; *both have to be market-driven.*

13.2 ORGANIZATION OF THE NEW PRODUCT DEVELOPMENT PROCESS

The data presented in the previous section illustrate the *high risk* involved in launching a new activity. This risk may be reduced, however, by implementing a systematic evaluation and development procedure for new products. The key success factors (KSF) are those that are controllable by the company. The purpose of this section is to examine the procedures and organizational methods that reduce the risk of failure throughout the innovation process. The objective is to organize a *systematic and continuous dialogue* between the relevant functions within an organization, which is R&D, marketing, operations and finance. In a market-driven company, developing a new product is a *cross-functional effort*, which involves the entire organization.

If it is true that top management has the final say in decisions concerning new product launches, it remains the case that an organizational structure with specific responsibilities is essential in managing and co-ordinating the entire innovation process. Different organizational structures are possible. Large companies have created *new product management* functions or *new product departments*, as Nestlé, Colgate Palmolive, Johnson & Johnson and General Foods have done.

Cross-functional organizational structures

A more flexible solution, which is available to all companies regardless of their size, is the *new products committee* or *venture team* in charge of a specific project.

- *New products committee* is a permanent group of persons, which meets periodically, say, once a month. It comprises individuals from different functions (i.e., R&D, operations, marketing, finance and human resources). Ideally, it is presided over by the managing director, whose responsibility is to organize and manage the development process of a new product from its conception to its launching.
- *Self-organizing project teams or "*venture teams*"* are groups formed for the development of a specific project (task force). This group is composed of people from various departments, from which they are temporarily separated, either completely or partially. This allows better concentration on the creation of a new activity.

The Page study (1993) is instructive on the evolution observed on the organizational structures used for new product development. The respondents were asked to indicate which of six forms of new product organization structure best described the ones used by their firm. The multi-disciplinary team was by far the most widely used organization with a score of 76 per cent of the sample businesses while the new product department had a score of only 30 per cent (Page, 1993, p. 277). Ernst, Hoyer and Rübsaamen (2010) highlighted the importance of co-operation between sales, marketing and R&D to succeed in the new product development phase.

No matter which organizational structure is adopted, the most important thing is a *structure open to the ideas of new activities.* The objective is to institutionalize preoccupation with new products within the company and to do so in a way that is flexible and favours an entrepreneurial approach to problems. Two processes are currently adopted by innovative companies, the sequential or the parallel development process.

Sequential development process

The *sequential development process*, evidenced by the Booz, Allen and Hamilton's study (1982), is where the project moves step by step from one phase to the next: concept development and testing, feasibility analysis, prototype development, market test and production. The whole process is described in Figure 13.1.

The merits of the sequential approach have already been discussed. But although it contributes to reducing the new product failure rate, it also has some shortcomings:

- First, the sequential process in itself leaves little room for integration since each functional specialist passes the project to the next one.
- The move to the next phase is done only after all the requirements of the preceding phase are satisfied. A bottleneck in one phase can slow or even block the entire process.
- Moreover, this product planning process is slow and requires long lead times. It avoids errors, but at large cost in terms of time.
- Changes in the market, entry of new competitors and risk of copying often result in a product arriving too late in the market.

Thus long lead times can very well increase rather than reduce the risk of failure. This will be particularly important for high-technology products, where speed is a KSF.

Speed as a strategy

The basic philosophy of the sequential development process is to go slowly, to avoid product failure and postpone heavy spending until it is clear that the product concept under study will be a winner. Schnaars (1998, pp. 168–70) mentions nine reasons to support the view that speed is a source of competitive advantage:

1. *Competitive advantage is not sustainable.* A truly sustainable competitive advantage has proved to be an elusive goal for companies. Speed as strategy sidesteps this problem by replacing it with quick response.
2. *Avoiding the need to predict the future.* Firms end up preparing a future that never comes. Moving quickly with markets, rather than trying to guess in which direction they will move, substitutes flexibility for forecasting.
3. *The law of large numbers.* A key benefit of speeding many new products to market without a great deal of formal market research is that the market decides which product will be successful and which will fail.
4. *Profits from new products.* Firms without a steady flow of new products ultimately face decline. The evidence shows that profit comes mainly from new products.
5. *Shorter PLCs.* Long-term growth has been replaced by a series of short-lived fads. That means that firms must get to the market before the peak of popularity passes.
6. *More competition in growth markets.* In the past, profits were supposed to be highest in the growth stage of the PLC. Today, most growth markets are crowded with competitors and are intensely competitive.
7. *Rampant copying.* Competitors routinely steal new product ideas in test markets. Today extensive testing is all but impossible. It would invite too many copycats.

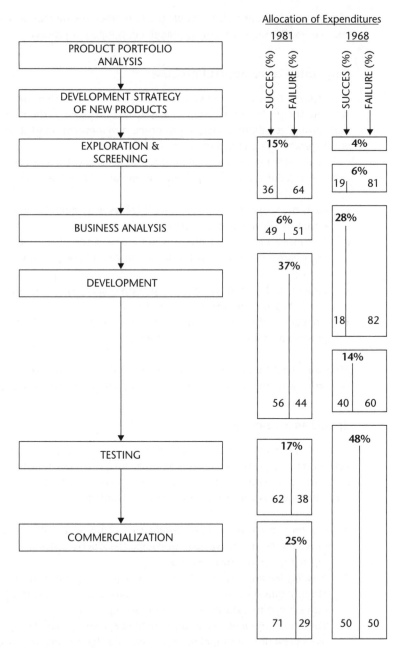

Figure 13.1 The new product development process
Source: Adapted from Booz, Allen and Hamilton (1982).

8. *Gaining shelf space early*. A growing number of new products must compete for limited retail shelf space. That means that firms must get to the market quickly or risk being closed out of the best distribution outlets.
9. *Fostering a sense of creativity and experimentation*. A fast-moving strategy promotes a culture of doing and trying rather than a culture of bureaucrats and paperwork.

The parallel development process tries to take the best of the two worlds by combining systematic analysis with speed (Stalk, 1988).

Parallel development process

The *parallel development process* advocated by Takeuchi and Nonaka (1986) speeds the process by relying on self-organizing project teams whose members work together from start to finish. Under this organizational scheme, the process development process emerges from the constant interaction of a multi-disciplinary team. Rather than moving in defined, highly structured stages, the process is born out of the team members' interplay. One of the potential benefits of the parallel development process is the *overlapping of the tasks* assumed by the different departments.

> While design engineers are still designing the product, production people can intervene to make sure that the design is compatible with production scale economies and marketing people can work on the positioning platform to communicate to the market.

The parallel development process is described in Figure 13.2. The merits of this organizational structure are important:

- The system facilitates better cross-functional co-ordination since each function is associated in the entire development process.
- Several activities can be organized simultaneously, which accelerates the process because the amount of recycle and rework – going back and doing it again – is greatly reduced.
- Each activity is better controlled since it directly determines the subsequent activities.
- Substantial timesaving are made due to the more intensive work and to the improved spontaneous co-ordination.

This type of organizational structure, because it stresses multi-functional activities, promotes improved teamwork. To go further on this topic see Larson and Gobeli (1988).

13.3   NEW PRODUCT IDEA GENERATION

Naturally, the development process for innovation begins with researching new product ideas, which are in line with the chosen development strategy. Some companies adopt an empirical approach to this problem, relying on a spontaneous stream of ideas originating from external and internal sources. However, the mortality rate of these ideas is very high; therefore, it is essential to feed on new ideas regularly. Generally, ideas, especially good ones,

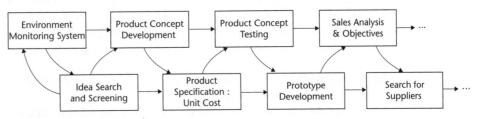

Figure 13.2   Parallel development of new products
Source: Lambin (2007).

do not happen by themselves; organization and stimulation are needed to generate them. A company may use different methods for collecting ideas. These methods try to anticipate the change in needs and not simply respond to the demands expressed by the market. This is a "proactive" versus a "reactive" approach. A creative idea is nothing but an unexpected combination of two or more concepts. *Creativity* can therefore be defined as

> the intellectual exercise of linking information in an unpredictable way so as to produce a new arrangement.

Idea generation methods can be grouped into two broad categories: (a) functional analysis methods which analyse products in order to identify possible improvements, and (b) methods which interview directly or indirectly customers to detect unsatisfied needs or ill-resolved problems with the existing products.

Methods of functional analysis

The rationale behind functional analysis methods is that a product's users can provide useful information on how the product could be modified and improved.

- *Problem/opportunity analysis* starts with the customer. It is linked to the study of user behaviour in order to identify the kinds of problems a user may encounter during use of the product. Every problem or difficulty brought up could give rise to a new idea for improvement or modification. This modification is frequently used in industrial market studies with a panel of user clients.
- *The attribute listing method* has the same objectives as problem analysis, but instead of examining how the customer uses the product, it examines the characteristics of the product itself. The method consists of establishing a list of the principal characteristics and then recombining them in such a way as to create some improvement. Osborn (1963) defined a list of questions intended to stimulate ideas for new products.

  Can the product be used in any new way? What else is like the product and what can be learned from this comparison? How can the product be changed in meaning, function, structure, and use pattern? What can be added to the product? To make it stronger, longer, thicker, and so on? What to delete? What to subtract, how to make it smaller, condensed, lower, shorter, lighter, and so on? (Osborn, 1963, pp. 286–7).

- *Morphological analysis* consists of identifying the most important structural dimensions of a product and then examining the relationship between these dimensions in order to discover new and interesting combinations.

  Suppose we are studying a cleaning product. The six key structural dimensions are as follows: product support (brush, rag, sponge, and so on), ingredients (alcohol, ammonia, disinfectant, and so on), things to be cleaned (glass, carpet, sinks, walls, cars, and so on), substance to be got rid of (grease, dust, blood, paint, and so on), product texture (cream, powder, salt, liquid, and so on), and packaging (box, bottle, aerosol, bag, and so on).

Paired combinations of these dimensions are evaluated and considered in terms of their potential value as new products.

A last method for idea generation must be added, one that is old but very effective: *the suggestion box*. This can prove to be very helpful if certain rules are followed. Two rules are particularly important: follow up promptly on the proposed ideas and provide a complete recognition system to motivate employees.

There are other and varied methods for idea generation. Systematic analysis of competitive products through *reverse engineering* is also widely used. The most important objective for a firm is to keep a permanent portfolio of new product ideas, which is sizeable enough to allow the firm to face the competition in an environment where innovation is omnipresent.

Creativity groups and brainstorming

Methods which are likely to stimulate creativity can be grouped into two categories: unstructured and structured methods. *Unstructured methods* are essentially based on imagination and intuition. These methods are usually implemented in the form of *creativity groups*, relying on the hypothesis that a group of individuals is usually more creative than a person working alone. This assumption is based on the synergy effect or the interaction between group members.

Brainstorming is probably the most popular method, mostly because it is easy to organize. The only goal of a brainstorming session is to produce as many ideas as possible. Six to ten participants with diverse backgrounds and experience, from both within and outside the company, are gathered together and are given the objective of generating the greatest possible number of ideas on a particular theme in a spontaneous manner. The major rules governing a brainstorming session, according to Osborn (1963, p. 156), are the following:

- No evaluation of any kind is permitted, since criticism and judgement may cause people to defend their ideas rather than generate new and creative ones.
- Participants should be encouraged to think of the wildest ideas possible.
- Encourage a large number of ideas.
- Encourage participants to build upon or modify the ideas of others, as combinations or modifications of previously suggested ideas often lead to new ideas that are superior to those that sparked them.

This type of exercise is usually very effective; it is not out of the ordinary for a group to generate more than 100 ideas during a brainstorming session. Another somewhat more structured method is synectics (Gordon, 1965).

Synectics is another creativity method also developed by Gordon, which tackles the problem indirectly. The assumption is that habits prevent the development of a really new vision of a too familiar problem (see Exhibit 13.2).

> For a professional whose reflexes and perceptions of the environment have been moulded by a growing market and confirmed by success, it is very difficult to see the opportunity of doing the same thing differently. The acquired professionalism hides the perception of new way of operating. The adoption of a discontinuous strategy requires new reflexes and a distance from traditional activities. (Bijon, 1984, p. 104)

To become creative, it is sometimes necessary to take some distant view and to make a "creative detour", before coming back to the problem under study. Once the problem is formulated in different, but related contexts, one is led to discover analogies and to propose more relevant and creative ideas.

Exhibit 13.2   Selected examples of prediction errors

1895: Lord Kelvin, President of the Royal Society (UK):

It is impossible to design flying machines heavier than air.
1899: Charles Duell, Director of the Patent Office (USA):

Everything has already been invented.

1905: Grover Cleveland, President of United States:

Reasonable women will never ask for the right of vote.

1920: Robert Millikan, Nobel Prize for Physics:

Man will never be able to exploit atomic power.

1947: Thomas J. Watson Sr., President of IBM Corp.:

I believe that there is a total market for approximately five computers.

1977: Ken Olsen, CEO Digital Equipment Corp.:

Why people would like to have a computer at home?

Source: Quoted by de Brabandère (1998, pp. 99–107).

New product generation from customer ideas

The idea generation methods presented so far are usually *manufacturer-active*, that is, the manufacturer plays the active role. In industrial markets, von Hippel (1978) has shown that often a customer request for a new product can generate a new product idea, at least in situations where the industrial customer is overtly aware of his new product need.

In the B2C sector, the role of the consumer is essentially that of a respondent, "speaking only when spoken to". It is the role of the manufacturer to obtain information on articulated or latent needs for new products and to develop a responsive product idea. In the B2B sector, it is often the role of the *would-be customer* to develop the idea for a new product and to select a supplier capable of making the product. We have here a *customer-active paradigm*.

Any statement of need made by a professional customer contains information about what a responsive solution should be. Consider the following statement of need of manufacturing firm X:

> (a) ... we need higher profits in our semi-conductor plant; (b) ... which we can get by raising output ... (c) ... which we can best do by getting rid of the bottleneck in process step ... (d) ... which can best be done by designing and installing new equipment ... (e) ... which has the following functional specifications ... (f) ... and should be built according to these blueprints. (von Hippel 1978, p. 41)

This need statement already contains the key elements of the solution to a problem sought by the would-be customer. The firm needs only to instruct its R&D and manufacturing people to manufacture the product according to the customer specifications spontaneously provided. This example underlines the importance of a systematic dialogue with customers to generate new product ideas.

In the field of industrial goods, there are also several markets in which *everyone knows* what the customer wants, but progress in technology is required before the desired product can be realized.

> In the computer, plastics and semi-conductor industries, every one knows that the customer wants more calculation per second and per dollar in the computer business; every one knows that the customer wants plastics which degrade less quickly in sunlight; and everyone knows that the semi-conductor customer wants more memory capacity on a single chip of silicon.

In these sectors, a customer request is not required to trigger a new product, only an advance in technology.

Idea generation methods are numerous and varied. Cooper (1993, p. 133) proposes a list of 25 different methods. What is important for the firm is to have permanently a *portfolio of new product ideas* sufficiently diversified to enable the firm to meet the challenge of competition in an environment where innovation is permanent and a KSF for survival and development.

13.4 NEW PRODUCT IDEA SCREENING

The objective of the second stage in the development process is to screen the ideas generated in order to eliminate the ones that are incompatible with the company's resources or objectives or simply unattractive to the firm. The purpose is to spot and drop unfeasible ideas as soon as possible. This is therefore an *evaluation phase*, which presupposes the existence of criteria for choice. The goal of this screening is not to do an in-depth analysis, but rather to make a quick, inexpensive, internal evaluation about which projects merit further study and which should be abandoned. Therefore this is not yet a feasibility study, but simply a preliminary evaluation.

Typically, the new product committee is in the best position to do the screening. A single and effective method is the *evaluation grid*, which has the following basic principles:

- An exhaustive inventory of all the KSF in each functional area: marketing, finance, operations and R&D.
- Each factor or group of factors is weighted to reflect its *relative importance*.
- Each new product idea is scored against each KSF by the *judges* of the new product committee.
- A desirability or *performance index* is calculated.

This procedure ensures that all the important factors have been systematically and equally considered and that the objectives and constraints of the company have been attended to.

When computing the performance index, it is preferable to adopt a *conjunctive method* and not a simple weighted average procedure (compensatory approach). The conjunctive method does not result in a global score, but aids in identifying ideas which are or are not compatible with the company's objectives or resources. The conjunctive approach presupposes that a maximum and minimum level of performance for each project has been specified. Only those ideas which satisfy each specified threshold are retained.

Several standard evaluation grids exist in the marketing literature, the best known being that of O'Meara (1961) and of Steele (1988). Such checklists provide a useful guideline for ideas evaluation. Ideally, an evaluation grid should be tailor-made and be adapted to the company's own needs. It is up to the new product committee to establish an appropriate structure, which reflects the corporate objectives and the unique situational factors of the firm. Figure 13.3 shows an evaluation grid used in a consumer goods company to evaluate the marketing feasibility of new product ideas. Similar grids have been developed for the other functions: R&D, operations and finance.

Cooper (1993, p. 335) has also developed a diagnostic and screening grid. The questionnaire comprises 30 questions to be answered by several judges who evaluate the project on each criterion on a 10-point scale and who express their degree of confidence on their own evaluation, also on a 10-point scale. The profile of the project is then evaluated and

New product idea: ————————   Score: —

	SCORES				Not relevant
	Very good	*Good*	*Weak*	*Very weak*	
1. Market trend	Emerging	Growing	Stable	Declining	
2. Product life	10 years plus	5–10 years	3–5 years	2–3 years	
3. Spread of diffusion	Very fast	Fast	Slow	Very slow	
4. Market size (volume)	>10 000 T	5000–10 000 T	1000–5 000 T	1000 T	
5. Market size (value)	1 billion	0.5–1billion	100–500 M	> 100 million	
6. Buyer's needs	Not met	Poorly met	Well met	Very well met	
7. Receptivity of distribution	Enthusiastic	Positive	Reserved	Reluctant	
8. Advertising support required	Weak support	Moderate support	Important support	Strong support	
9. Market accessibility	Very easy	Easy	Difficult	Very difficult	

INDICATORS OF COMPETITIVENESS	SCORES				Not relevant
	Very good	*Good*	*Weak*	*Very weak*	
1. Product's appeal	Very high	High	Moderate	Weak	
2. Distinctive qualities	Exclusivity	Major distinctive quality	Weak distinctive quality	'me too' product	
3. Strength of competition	Very weak	Weak	High	Very high	
4. Duration of exclusivity	> 3 years	1–3 years	–1 year	–6 months	
5. Compatibility with current products	Very good	Good	Weak	Very weak	
6. Level of price	Lower price	Slightly lower	Equal price	Higher price	
7. Compatibility with existing distribution network	Fully compatible	Easily compatible	Compatible but difficult	New network	
8. Capacity of the sales force	Very good	Good	Weak	Very weak	
9. Level of product quality	Clearly superior	Superior	Same	Inferior	

Figure 13.3   Example of a new product screening grid
Source: Lambin (2000/2007).

compared with the observed profiles of hundreds of projects, which belong to the *NewProd* data bank. The simulation model provides a probability of success and also analyses the strong and the weak points of the project.

13.5   NEW PRODUCT CONCEPT DEVELOPMENT

At this phase of the development process, we move from "product ideas" to "*product concepts*". The ideas having survived to the screening phase are now defined in more elaborated terms.

Product concept definition

A *product concept* can thus be defined as:

> a written description of the physical and perceptual characteristics of the product and of the "package of benefits" (the promise) it represents for an identified target group(s) of potential customers.

This is more than a simple technological description of the product, since the product's benefits to the potential user are emphasized. The product concept definition highlights the notion of a product as a package of benefits. In defining the concept, a company is forced to be explicit in its strategic options and market objective. A clear and precise definition of the product concept is important in many respects:

- The concept definition describes the *positioning sought* for the product and therefore defines the means required to achieve the expected positioning.
- The product concept is a kind of *specification manual for R&D*, whose job it is to examine the technical feasibility of the concept.
- The description of the product's promise serves as a *briefing* for the advertising agency that is in charge of communicating the new product's identity and claims to the marketplace.

Thus, the product concept defines the *reference product market or segment* in which the future product should be positioned. Four questions come to mind:

1. Which attributes or product characteristics do potential customers react favourably to?
2. How are competitive branded products perceived with regard to these attributes?
3. What niche could the new product occupy, considering the expectations of the target segment and the positions held by competition?
4. What is the most effective operational marketing programme that will achieve the desired positioning?

The answers to these questions presuppose the existence of a fine-tuned market segmentation analysis, which is able to quantify the size of the potential market.

Designing a green product concept

Sensitivity towards the environment is today a must for business success and the accountable firm should assess the environmental implication of a new product not only at the concept development phase, but also at each phase of the PLC "from *cradle to grave*". Numerous opportunities exist for refining existing products or developing new ones that meet environmental imperatives and satisfy customers' expectations. These opportunities must be considered in a proactive way very early in development process. Ideas for action are presented in Exhibit 13.3.

While adopting the green product concept, the firm has to be careful and must *prove its environmental credentials in scientific terms* and by reference to the entire life cycle of the

---

Exhibit 13.3   The green product concept: ideas for action

- Source reduce and packaging
- Eliminate or lightweight packaging
- Concentrate products
- Use bulk packaging or large sizes
- Develop multi-purpose products
- Use recycled content
- Conserve natural resources, habitats and endangered species
- Make products more energy efficient
- Maximize consumer and environmental safety

- Make products more durable
- Make products and packaging reusable or refillable
- Design products for remanufacturing, recycling and repair
- Take products back for recycling
- Make products and packaging safe to landfill or incinerate
- Make products compostable

Source: Ottman (1993).

product. This is not always easy, because *"green" is relative* and also because large uncertainties remain on the ecological impact of products and raw materials.

Testing the new product concept

Concept testing represents the first investment (other than managerial time) a firm has to make in the development process. It consists of submitting a description of the new product concept to an appropriate group of target users to measure the degree of acceptance.

The product concept description may be done in one of two ways: neutral, that is, with no "sel"', or by a mock advertisement, which presents the concept as if it were an existing branded product. The former is easier to do and avoids the pitfalls of the inevitable and uncontrollable creative element inherent in an advertisement. The advantage of the advertisement, however, is that it more accurately reproduces the buying atmosphere of a future branded product and is therefore more realistic. The following descriptions illustrate "neutral" and "advertising" forms of concept testing, respectively, for a new dessert topping.

- Here is a new dessert topping made of fruit and packaged in a spray can. It comes in four flavours: strawberry, cherry, apricot and redcurrant. It can be used in cakes, puddings and frozen desserts.

  Here is a new delicious fruit topping for desserts conveniently packaged in a spray can. These new toppings will enhance the desserts you serve your family. Your choice among four flavours: strawberry, cherry, apricot and redcurrant will certainly embellish all your desserts including cakes, puddings, frozen desserts and more.

Twenty to fifty people with varying socio-demographic profiles are gathered to assess the degree of concept acceptance. They are shown slides or videos on the new concept and asked to react to it with questions similar to those presented in Box 13.1.

Obviously, the seven key questions in Box 13.1 are the one dealing with intentions to buy (question 5). A score of positive intentions (i.e., "would definitely buy" and "would probably buy" responses grouped together) that adds up to less than 60 per cent is generally considered insufficient, at least in the field of consumer goods.

Predictive value of buying intentions

Results from concept testing should be interpreted with care, especially when the concept is very new. Consumers are asked to express their interest in a product, which they have never seen or used. They are therefore often unable to judge whether or not they would like the new product. Numerous products which received mediocre scores during the

---

Box 13.1   Implementation problem: how to test a new product concept?

1. Are the benefits clear to you and believable?
2. Do you see this product as solving a problem or filling a need for you?
3. Do other products currently meet this need and satisfy you?
4. Is the price reasonable in relation to the value?
5. Would you (definitely, probably, probably not, definitely not) buy the product?
6. Who would use this product, and how often would it be used?
7. To what extent is the product concept compatible with a green environment?

concept-testing phase actually turned out to be brilliant successes. Inversely, expensive failures were avoided using concept testing.

Measuring intentions to buy is not always the best indication of the respondents' degree of conviction regarding a new product's ability to solve problems or to satisfy unmet needs. Yet, this is clearly a KSF. In a test situation, respondents may express a willingness to purchase a new product out of simple curiosity or concern for keeping up with the latest innovation, or a need for variety. In light of this, scores for intention tend to overestimate the true rate of acceptance.

In order to deal with this problem, Tauber (1973) suggests using concept-testing results based on measurements of perceived needs as well as of purchase interest. In an experiment on eight new product concepts, Tauber observed that virtually all the respondents who claimed that a product solved a problem or filled an unmet need had a positive intention to purchase the new product, while a considerable number of respondents who expressed purchase interest did not believe the product solved a problem or filled an unmet need. This observation suggests that overstatement of purchase intent may be simply those with curiosity to try but with little expectation of adopting. Thus, basing new product decisions on purchase intent data could be misleading in predicting the true rate of product adoption for regular use.

A more reliable way to estimate the adoption rate of a new product for regular use would be to base the decision on the percentage of people giving an affirmative answer to both questions, that is, *they do intend to buy and they are convinced that the new product solves a problem or fills an unmet need*. In most cases, the ranking of product concepts is significantly different from the ranking observed for the positive purchase intention.

The use of conjoint analysis

More elaborate approaches to concept testing may be used, including the *conjoint analysis*, which has been successfully used over the last few years (Green and Srinivasan, 1978). The distinctive value of conjoint analysis is to allow the impact of the product concept's key characteristics on product preferences, information which is not revealed by an overall reaction to the concept. The basic principles of this method were described in Chapter 7 and an example was presented in Chapter 8.

In concept testing, conjoint analysis helps in answering the following questions:

- What is the *partial utility or value* that a target group attaches to different characteristics of the product concept?
- What is the *relative importance* of each product characteristic?
- What kind of *trade-offs* are potential buyers ready to make between two or more product characteristics?
- What will be the *share of preferences* with regard to different product concepts, each representing a different bundle of characteristics?

The collected data are simple rankings of preference for the various concept combinations. Each concept constitutes a different assortment of characteristics. These preference data are submitted to one of the conjoint analysis algorithms and the output is partial utilities for each component of the product concept and for each individual respondent.

Conjoint analysis results provide the market analyst with four useful results:

- The identification of the *best concept*, that is, the combination of concept components with the highest utilities, among all possible combinations.

- Information on what will be *the utility or disutility of any change* in the concept characteristics. This enables a selection of the most attractive trade-offs among concept components.
- Information on the *relative importance* of each component.
- Possibility of constructing *segments* based on the similarity of the respondents' reactions to the tested concepts.

On the basis of these results, alternative scenarios can be developed and the expected share of preferences estimated in each case.

The problems raised by concept testing are usually less subtle in B2B *markets*, since industrial clients' needs are generally more clearly specified. Moreover, the respondent is a professional, and trade-off analysis is a more natural way of thinking. Conjoint analysis has many applications within industrial markets.

Example of a concept test

To illustrate the contribution of conjoint analysis, let us examine the following example. The product studied is a hairspray, targeted at the Belgian market and defined in terms of the following five characteristics:

- *Design*: two designs are considered: the existing one and a new one.
- *Product's claim*: "styling spray", "extra strong hair spray" or "fixing spray".
- *Price*: three price levels are considered; 2, 3 and 4 euros.
- *Product range*: the product may be offered singly or included in a range comprising a gel, a mousse and a styling cream.
- *Brand*: the brand may be A, B or C.

These variables give a total of 108 possible combinations for new product concept (2×3×3×2×3). Using a fractional factorial design we can reduce the number of concepts to be tested to 18. All pertinent information on each of the characteristics is retained, but information on interactions of orders greater than 2 are lost. In order to estimate partial utilities, regression analysis is conducted, using binary variables (0, 1) to describe the presence or absence of the product characteristics at each level. Figure 13.4 shows the average utility curves obtained from the sample examined.

The results show that consumers are very sensitive to the brand name and that they noticeably prefer brand B to the other brands. They also show the price elasticity to be –0.81. The new design is also clearly preferred over the old one. With regard to the product's claim, there appears to be very little sensitivity on the part of the respondents, who probably understand the claim poorly (Rochet, 1987).These results are useful to develop alternative launching scenarios and to obtain estimates of the likely rate of adoption of the new product concept.

13.6 BUSINESS ANALYSIS AND MARKETING PROGRAMMING

Once the product concept has been developed and accepted by top management, it is up to the marketing department to quantify the market opportunity and to develop alternative marketing programmes. This implies sales forecasting and market penetration objectives under different marketing budgets. The economic viability of the new product within the chosen time horizon must be assessed and the risk of the new venture evaluated.

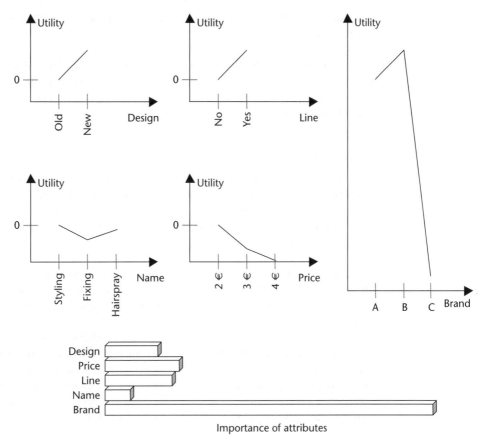

Figure 13.4 Example of conjoint analysis: hairspray products
Source: Adapted from Rochet (1987).

Estimating sales volume

Estimating the sales projection for the first three years is the first problem to examine, which will condition the rest of the analysis. Given estimates of total potential sales in the target segment, what will be the expected sales volume or market share of the new product under different assumptions regarding the size of the marketing efforts? Different methods to approach this question can be used – subjective methods, feasibility studies and methods based on a test market:

■ *Subjective methods* rely on the marketing information system of the firm, but also on experience, judgment and on information accumulated more or less informally within the firm. This accumulated knowledge is based on sales history of similar products, on information from distributors, on the sales force, on comparison with competing products and so on.

■ *Feasibility studies* aim to gather the missing information in the field by directly interviewing potential customers, distributors, retailers and so on. Purchasing intention scores are collected and used to estimate sales volume.

■ *Market tests* allow for observation of customer behaviour in the real world. Trial and repeat purchase rates can be estimated and used for early projection of sales. Alternatives to market tests are in-home use tests, mini-test panels, laboratory experiments and regional introduction.

These three groups of methods are not exclusive and may be used jointly where uncertainty and the degree of newness for the company are high. Regardless of the approach adopted, the marketing department needs to set a sales revenue objective and to estimate whether sales will be high enough to generate an acceptable profit.

Typical sales patterns

The new product sales pattern over time will differ according to whether it is a one-time purchase product, a durable good or a frequently purchased product.

For *one-time purchased products*, the expected sales curve increases steadily, peaks and then decreases progressively as the number of potential buyers diminishes. Thus, in this case, the occupation rate of the market is the key variable.

- For *durable goods*, total demand can be sub-divided into two parts: first equipment and replacement demand. First equipment demand is time dependent and determined by income variables, while replacement demand is determined by the product's obsolescence, be it technical, economic or style.
- Purchases of *frequently purchased products* can be divided into two categories: first-time and repeat purchases. The number of first-time purchasers initially increases and then diminishes as the majority of potential buyers have tried the product. Repeat purchases will occur if the product meets the requirements of a group of buyers, who eventually will become loyal customers, and the total sales curve will eventually reach a plateau. In this product category, repeat purchases are the best indicator of market satisfaction.

The typical sales patterns for trial, repeat and total sales of a frequently purchased product are presented in Figure 13.5.

Panel data projection methods

In the case of frequently purchased products, the Parfitt and Collins theorem (1968) can be used to decompose market share and to generate *market share projections*. These measures are

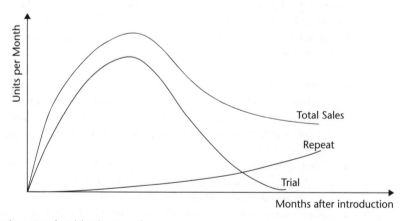

Figure 13.5 Typical sales pattern for trial and repeat sales

normally obtained from a consumer's panel. Market share can be divided into three distinct components:

1. The *penetration rate* of a brand is defined as the cumulative trial, that is, the percentage of buyers having made a trial purchase at time *t*; this rate first increases after launching and then tends to stabilize fairly rapidly as the stock of potential first-time buyers diminishes.
2. Those buyers having tried the product express the *repeat purchasing rate* as the proportion of total purchases in the product field. After a certain number of purchases, the repeat purchase rate will level off to some equilibrium state.
3. The *intensity rate*, or buying level index, compares the rate of quantities purchased of the studied brand to the average quantities purchased within the product category. A distinction can be made here between heavy, light or average buyers (by volume) in the product field.

The *expected market share* is estimated by multiplying these three values.

> Suppose that the estimated rate for trial purchase is 34 per cent and that the repeat purchase rate is around 25 per cent. If the average quantities purchased are the same for the brand and the product category, the expected market share will be:
>
> 34 per cent × 25 per cent × 1.00 = 8.5 per cent.

In cases of segmented markets, the expected market shares are calculated for each group. For example, the buying level index may vary according to the type of buyer. It may reach 1.20 for heavy buyers and 0.80 for light buyers. The expected market share in each of these cases will be around 10.2 and 6.8 per cent, respectively.

This kind of market share projection can be quickly formulated after the first few months of launching a new product. This method also allows for measurement of the impact that advertising and promotional activities have on market share. For more on this topic, see Parfitt and Collins' seminal article (1968).

No method can estimate future sales with certainty. Therefore, it is useful to give a range of estimations, with minimum and maximum sales, in order to assess the extent of risk implied by the new product launch.

13.7 THE CUSTOMER ADOPTION PROCESS

The design of a new product-launching plan, to be effective, must be based on a good understanding of the adoption process of the innovation followed by the target group of customers. In the general case, the adoption process can be described as a sequence of steps (see Table 13.2) followed by the prospect, from the stage of innovation discovery to its possible adoption or rejection.

This adoption process described by Rogers (1962) and by Robertson (1971) is very similar to the learning process and also to the Lavidge and Steiner (1961) model which is commonly used in the analysis of advertising effectiveness. As shown in Table 13.2, this adoption process can be sub-divided into six phases:

1. *Knowledge:* the potential customer knows of the branded product's existence; informative advertising and word-of-mouth communication play an important role at this stage.

Table 13.2   The adoption process of an innovation

Stages of the process	Hierarchy of effects (Lavidge and Steiner, 1961)	Adoption process (Robertson, 1971)
Cognitive level	Awareness ↓ Knowledge ↓	Knowledge ↓ Comprehension
Affective level	Liking ↓ Preference ↓	Attitude ↓ Conviction ↓
Behavioural level	Conviction ↓ Purchase ↓ Loyalty/Forgetting	Trial ↓ Adoption

Sources: Adapted from Lavidge and Steiner (1961); Robertson (1971).

2. *Comprehension:* it is based on knowledge and represents the customer's conception of what the branded product is and what functions it can perform.

3. *Attitude:* attitude is thought of as the predisposition of the individual to evaluate an object of his or her environment in a favourable or unfavourable manner. Concept advertising, distributors and prescribers are the main sources of influence.

4. *Conviction:* the individual develops a favourable attitude, is convinced of the product's superiority and that purchase is the appropriate course of action.

5. *Trial:* the individual uses the branded product on a limited scale, stimulated by a promotion or by sampling.

6. *Adoption:* the customer accepts the branded product and continues to purchase and/or use it. The adoption process is now complete and it is the intrinsic product quality that will determine the level of satisfaction.

In the design of a launching plan, it is therefore important to select the types of marketing instrument better adapted to each stage and to monitor the progress made by the target group along the adoption process.

Duration of the diffusion process

The speed of diffusion will be a function of the type of innovation. Five characteristics have been found to affect diffusion speed (Rogers, 1962, 1995, p. 208):

- *Relative advantage:* the degree of improvement that the innovation represents over existing alternatives (fax machines' superiority over telex).
- *Complexity:* the inherent difficulty associated with the new idea or product. High levels of complexity can make it more expensive for a customer in terms of learning costs (personal computers).
- *Compatibility:* how well the innovation fits with the existing practices of potential adopters. If customers have to modify their prior use patterns, changeover or adoption costs exist and the speed of diffusion will be slower. Conversely, if the product is fully compatible with prior use, the adoption can be very rapid (fluoridated toothpaste versus the electric toothbrush).
- *Communicability:* the ease with which the essence of the innovation can be conveyed to potential adopters. Some benefits have a high degree of visibility and some products

lend themselves well to usage demonstration like cars, telephones, VCRs and so on. Conversely, innovations with long-term benefits (like health protection) are more difficult to promote and therefore are susceptible to diffuse more slowly.

■ *Trialability:* the innovation's capability of being tried out in a smaller scale prior to purchase, thereby reducing the adoption costs.

Other factors can also determine the speed of diffusion like the degree of uncertainty of the innovation itself, particularly in the case of discontinuous innovations (Frambach, 1995). Three sources of uncertainty may exist:

■ Uncertainty concerning the reality of the benefits claimed, particularly when those benefits are expected in the long term.
■ Uncertainty concerning the adoption costs (resistance to change) associated with the implementation of the innovation in the customer's life or organization.
■ Uncertainty concerning the pace of innovation itself and the length of its PLC.

The analysis of these factors prior to the launching of the innovation is useful to evaluate correctly the duration of the introductory phase and also to design the most appropriate communication programme.

Categories of adopters

■ Rogers (1962, p. 5) defines the diffusion process as *the manner in which new ideas, products or practices spread through a culture*, or (in marketing terms) through a target market. Rogers proposed classifying adopters by reference to the timing of adoption into five types, ranked from those who first adopt the innovation to those who come last to the adoption phase.

The basic assumption is that the numbers of people falling into each category will approximate a normal distribution.

■ *Innovators* (2.5 per cent): the very early purchasers of the innovation; they are independent, venturesome and willing to try new ideas at some risk. They represent a very small proportion of the market.
■ *Early adopters* (13.5 per cent): a larger group composed of opinion leaders in their social group. They adopt new ideas early, but with prudence.
■ *Early majority* (34 per cent): they adopt new ideas before the average person but they need information and they are not leaders.
■ *Late majority* (34 per cent): they are sceptical; they adopt an innovation only after a majority of people has tried it. They follow the majority rule.
■ *Laggards* (16 per cent): they are tradition bound; they are suspicious and resistant to changes.

This categorization approximately follows a normal distribution, its cumulative distribution taking the form of an *S-shaped diffusion* curve.

13.8 PRICING NEW PRODUCTS

The more a new product is distinct and brings an innovative solution to the satisfaction of a need, the more sensitive it is to price. This price is a fundamental choice upon which depends the commercial and financial success of the operation. Once the firm has analysed costs, demand and competition, it must then choose between two very contradictory strategies: (a) a high initial price strategy to skim the high end of the market and (b) a strategy of low price from the beginning in order to achieve fast and powerful market penetration.

Skimming pricing strategy

This strategy consists of selling the new product at a high price and thus limiting oneself to the upper end of the demand curve. This would ensure significant financial returns soon after the launch. Many considerations support this strategy; furthermore, a number of conditions need to be met for this strategy to prove successful (Dean, 1950):

- When there are reasons to believe that the new *PLC* will be short, or when competition is expected to copy and to market a similar product in the near future, a skimming price strategy may be recommended because a low price strategy would make the innovation unprofitable.
- When a product is so innovative that the market is expected to mature slowly and the buyer has no elements on which to compare it with other products, *demand is inelastic*. It is tempting to exploit this situation by setting a high price and then readjusting it progressively as the market matures.
- Launching a new product at a high price is one way of *segmenting the market*. The segments have different price elasticities. The launching price skims the customers who are insensitive to price. Later price cuts then allow the firm to reach successively more elastic segments. This is a form of time-discriminatory pricing.
- When demand is hard to evaluate, it is *risky to anticipate* what kind of demand growth or cost reduction can result from a low price. This is particularly true when the manufacturing process is not yet stabilized and costs are likely to be underestimated.

To be effective, the introduction of a new product requires heavy expenditure on advertising and promotion. When the firm does not have the *financial means* necessary for a successful introduction, charging high prices is one way of generating the resources.

Price skimming strategy is definitely a cautious strategy, which is more financial than commercial. Its main advantage is that it leaves the door open for a progressive price adjustment, depending on how the market and competition develop. From a commercial point of view, it is always easier to cut a price than to increase it. The importance of the strategy lies mainly in its financial aspect: the fact that some capital, which can be used for alternative activity, is freed early on.

Penetration price strategy

Penetration strategy, on the other hand, consists of setting low prices in order to capture a larger share of the market right from the start. It assumes the adoption of an intensive distribution system, the use of mass advertising to develop market receptivity and especially an adequate production capacity from the beginning. In this case the outlook is more commercial than financial. The following general conditions must prevail to justify its use:

- Demand must be *price-elastic* over the entire demand curve; there are no upper segments to be given priority and the only strategy is to address the whole market at a price low enough to satisfy the greatest number.

- It is possible to achieve *lower unit costs* by increasing volumes significantly, either because of economies of scale or because of potential experience effects.
- Soon after its introduction, the new product is threatened by *strong competition*. This threat of new entrants is a powerful reason for adopting low prices. The penetration strategy is used here to discourage competitors from entering the market. Low prices act as very efficient barriers to entry.
- The top range of the market is *already satisfied*; in this case, penetration policy is the only valid policy to develop the market.
- Potential buyers can easily integrate the new product in their consumption or production; the *transfer costs* of adopting the product other than its price are relatively low and, therefore, a mass market can be developed rapidly.

A penetration price strategy is therefore more risky than a skimming price strategy. If the firm plans to make the new product profitable over a long period, it may face the situation that new entrants might later use new production techniques, which will give them a cost advantage over the innovating firm.

13.9 ASSESSING THE FINANCIAL RISK

The launch of a new product is a strategic decision process which concerns every function within the firm and not only the marketing function. The success of this process largely depends on a sound co-ordination of each function involved. Moreover, the time factor is important and may modify the profitability of the new product. To ensure a good co-ordination, the firm must have at its disposal analytical tools to monitor the development process step by step and to assess its conformance with the profitability and timing objectives.

For each product launch, it is important to determine as precisely as possible when the elimination of risk is supposed to occur. There are three levels of risk, identified in Figure 13.6:

1. The *simple break-even point*, the moment where the new activity leaves the zone of losses and enters into the zone of profits.
2. The *equilibrium break-even point*, when the present value of total receipts covers the present value of total expenses. The company has recouped its capital layout.
3. The *capital acquisition point*, the point where the new activity generates a financial surplus allowing for reinvestments to prolong the economic life of the activity or for supporting the development of other businesses within the firm.

Ideally, the capital acquisition point should be reached before the maturity phase of the product's life cycle in order to allow the company timely redeployment, which is before competitive pressure begins to erode profit margins. These three criteria will eventually determine the economic viability of the project. To be operational these criteria must be viewed in a dynamic perspective.

How do we proceed to select priority projects when financial resources are limited, opportunities too many and the risks very different from one project to the other?

There is a vast literature in the field of capital budgeting on this topic, but the methods proposed are strictly financial, quantitatively oriented and do not consider qualitative criteria, which are often very important to assess the attractiveness of a particular project. Moreover, they required precise financial data, which often are not available at the evaluation phase of a project.

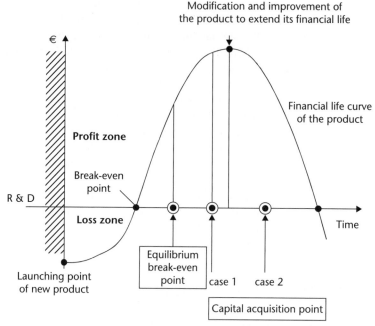

Figure 13.6 Assessing the financial risk of a new product
Source: Adapted from Daudé (1980).

A crude but useful financial indicator is the *payback period index* (in years) which answers the question *when shall I get all my money back?* This index is calculated as follows:

$$Payback = \frac{Development\ and\ commercial\ costs}{(Annual\ sales(\$/year)) \cdot (Profit\ margin\ as\ a\%\ of\ sales)}$$

This criterion is simple, easily understood and is based on data usually available at the evaluation phase. The reciprocal of this index gives a very crude estimate of the return as a percentage. Alternative and more rigorous methods are net present value (NPV) or discounted cash flow (DCF) as well as internal rate of return (IRR).

It is often useful to add explicitly a risk factor and qualitative indicators similar to those used in the screening grid (see Figure 13.1). We would then have a new project evaluation matrix similar to that presented in Figure 13.7. In this matrix the projects are evaluated along two dimensions:

- The first horizontal dimension measures *the value to the firm* of each project, using a multi-attribute composite index based on quantitative and qualitative indicators reflecting the value of the project to the firm.
- A second vertical dimension measuring *the probability of technological and/or commercial success of each project* as evaluated by management after the investigation or development phase.

We thus have a two-dimensional grid composed of four quadrants, where each project is represented by a bubble denoting the size of the resources to be devoted to each project:

- In the *upper right quadrant* are *the Pearls*, that is, projects having a high value to the firm and a high probability of success.

- In the lower right quadrant are *the Buds*, very desirable projects for the firm but still having a low probability of success.
- In the upper left quadrant are *the Bread and Butter* projects, with a good probability of success (and a low risk) but of ordinary or low value to the firm.
- In the lower right quadrant are *the Lost Causes*, the bad projects, a low commercial pay-off and a low probability of success.

This project portfolio grid is used during the annual budgeting exercise to identify the priority projects. Decision rules might be:

- allocate resources by priority to the development and the launching of Pearls projects;
- invest in some Buds projects to reinforce their competitiveness by gathering additional market information or by redesigning the product concept;
- cut back on Bread and Butter projects which often absorb too much time and resources; and
- delete from the portfolio the Lost Causes projects.

This type of portfolio analysis is also useful to help the firm to allocate R&D efforts towards new projects.

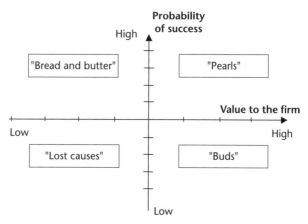

Figure 13.7 Portfolio analysis of new product concepts
Source: Adapted from Cooper (1993).

Chapter Summary

The new product development process consists of three phases: (a) idea phase (idea generation and screening), (b) concept phase (concept development, concept testing, business analysis) and (c) launching phase. In market-driven companies this process tends to be more a parallel than a sequential development process in order to ensure better inter-functional co-ordination. The concept development phase is crucial for incorporating the market orientation upfront and also for adopting a thorough approach to product greening. In the business analysis, the economic viability of the new product must be assessed in a dynamic perspective under alternative marketing programmes and the risk of the new venture evaluated. The market-oriented firm tries to have a permanently balanced portfolio of projects, a useful tool for identifying priority projects.

BIBLIOGRAPHY

Barreyre, P.Y. (1980), Typologie des innovations, *Revue Française de gestion*, January–February, pp. 9–15.

Bijon, C. (1984), La stratégie de rupture, *Harvard-L'expansion*, Autumn, pp. 98–104.

Booz, E., Allen, J. and Hamilton, C. (1982*), New Product Management for the 1980s*, New York.

Cooper, R.G. (1993), *Winning at New Products*, Reading, MA, Addison-Wesley, 2nd edition.

Daudé, B. (1980), Analyse de la maîtrise des risques, *Revue Française de Gestion,* January–February, pp. 38–48.

De Brabandère, L. (1998), *Le management des idées*, Paris, Dunod.

Dean, J. (1950), Pricing Policies for New Products, *Harvard Business Review,* 28, 6, pp. 28–36.

Ernst, H., Hoyer, W.D. and Rübsaamen, C. (2010), Sales, Marketing, and Research-and-Development Cooperation across New Product Development Stages: Implications for Success, *Journal of Marketing,* 74, pp. 80–92.

Flash Eurobarometer 144 (2004), *Innobarometer: A survey organised in 2003 by the Directorate General Enterprise,* Brussels, European Commission.

Frambach, R.T. (1995), *Diffusion of Innovations in Business-to-Business Markets,* in *Product Development,* Bruce, M. and Biemans, W.G. (eds), New York, John Wiley & Sons.

Gordon, J.J. (1965), Stimulation des facultés créatrices dans les groupes de recherche synectique, Paris, Hommes et Techniques.

Green, P.E. and Srinivasan, V. (1978), Conjoint Analysis in Consumer Research: Issues and Outlook, *Journal of Consumer Research,* 5, 2, pp. 103–23.

Lambin, J.J. (2000/2007), *Market-Driven Management, Strategic and Operational Marketing,* London, Palgrave Macmillan, First and second editions.

Lambin, J.J. (2000/2007*), Market-Driven Management: Strategic and Operational Marketing,* London, Palgrave Macmillan.

Larson, E.W. and Gobeli, D.H. (1988), Organizing for Product Development Projects, *Journal of Product Innovation Management,* 5, 3, pp. 180–90.

Lavidge, R.J. and Steiner, G.A. (1961), A Model of Predictive Measurement of Advertising Effectiveness, *Journal of Marketing,* 25, October, pp. 59–62.

O'Meara, J.T. (1961), Selecting Profitable Products, *Harvard Business Review,* 39, 1, pp. 110–18.

Osborn, A.F. (1963), *Applied Imagination,* New York, Charles Scribner's Sons, 3rd edition.

Ottman, J.A. (1993), *Green Marketing,* Lincolnwood, IL, NTC Business Books.

Page, A.L. (1993), Assessing New Product Development Practices and Performance: Establishing Crucial Norms, *Journal of Product Innovation* Management, 10, 4, pp. 273–90.

Parfitt, J.M. and Collins, J.K. (1968), Use of Consumer Panels for Brand Share Prediction, *Journal of Marketing Research,* 5, 2, pp. 131–45.

Prahalad, C.K. and Mashelkar, R.A. (2010), Innovation's Holy Grail, *Harvard Business Review,* July–August, pp. 132–41.

Robertson, T.S. (1971), *Innovative Behavior and Communication,* New York, Holt, Rinehart and Winston.

Rochet, L. (1987), *Diagnostic stratégique du potentiel d'extension d'une marque de laque,* Louvain-la-Neuve, Institut d'Administration et de Gestion.

Rogers, E.M. (1962/1995), Diffusion of Innovations, New York, The Free Press, 4th edition.

Schnaars, S.P. (1998), *Marketing Strategy: Customers and Competition,* New York, The Free Press, 2nd edition.

Srinivasan, S., Pauwels, K., Silva-Risso, J. and Hanssens, D.M. (2009), Product Innovations, Advertising, and Stock Returns, *Journal of Marketing,* 73, pp. 24–43.

Stalk, G. (1988), Time – The Next Source of Competitive Advantage, *Harvard Business Review,* 66, 4, pp. 41–51.

Steele, L.W. (1988), Selecting R&D Programs and Objectives, *Research & Technology Management*, March-April, pp. 17–36.

Takeuchi, H. and Nonaka, I. (1986), The New Product Development Game, *Harvard Business Review*, 64, 1, pp. 137–46.

Tauber, E.M. (1973), Reduce New Product Failures: Measure Needs as well as Purchase Interest, *Journal of Marketing*, 37, 3, pp. 61–70.

Von Hippel, E. (1978), Successful Industrial Products from Customer Ideas, *Journal of Marketing*, 42, 1, pp. 39–49.

CHAPTER FOURTEEN

BRAND MANAGEMENT

Brand management has become an important topic for both academics and marketers. The objective of this chapter is first to describe the reasons for the growing importance of brands for customers and for firms. We will define what the concept of brand covers and examine the brand functions from the manufacturer's and the customers' point of view. Three key concepts will be reviewed: brand identity, brand image and brand equity. In the second part of this chapter, we will focus on brand strategies. We will first identify how to create a brand, going from the brand identity creation to the selection of name and logo. We will also examine what are the key strategies available to develop a branding strategy covering, in particular, brand extension strategies and brand internationalization. We will end this chapter with a review of brand portfolio management and of the tools to evaluate brand value.

Learning Objectives

When you have read this chapter, you should be able to understand:

- The growing importance of brands for consumers and companies
- The functions of brands for both the customer and the manufacturer
- The concepts of brand identity, brand image and brand equity
- The advantages and risks of brand extension and of co-branding
- The usefulness of brand portfolio management
- The methods of brand evaluation

14.1 STRATEGIC ROLE OF BRANDING

Brands have been considered as key strategic assets since many years in the FMCG industry. Companies such as P&G, Unilever, L'Oréal or Nestlé have strategically were among the first to focus on brand management. After an intensive phase of mergers and acquisitions, a very limited number of FMCG multinationals own now the majority of well-known brands in the world. Services companies have also developed strong brands in banking (UBS, HSBC), airlines (British Airways, Singapore Airlines), express mail (DHL, Federal Express), credit cards (Visa, Master Card) or Internet (Yahoo, Google, Amazon).

Even B2B companies have started to successfully use branding strategies. A case in point is the Intel brand, which was created before the end of patent expiration, a very successful example of "component branding". The Intel brand is now ranked among the top five brands worldwide in terms of value. Other examples of successful component brands are

Goretex and Lycra. B2B companies such as Arcelor or Total are also deploying branding strategies to improve the perception of their corporate image by end-users. Last but not least, the development of private labels in the food sector has been a great success in Europe over the past few years.

What is a brand?

According to the definition given by the American Marketing Association,

> a brand is a name, term, sign, symbol, or design or a combination of them intended to identify the goods and services of one seller or group of sellers and to differentiate them from those of competition.

A branded product is formed by a set of tangible and intangible attributes, the core service plus peripheral services, necessary or added and by a set of mental associations. By mental associations, we mean intangible benefits such as personality, emotional or symbolic attributes that are recorded in the customers' minds and which form what Kapferer (2004/2008) calls the brand identity.

> The strength of a brand like Mercedes cannot be understood by referring only to its tangible benefits of quality and solidity. It covers also elements such brand personality (serious, sober, cold), country of origin (German) or emotional benefit (social achievement).

Some brands are differentiated mainly by reference to tangible benefits: Volvo (safety), Mr Proper (grease removal), Bang and Olufsen (design), while other brands base their differences more on intangible benefits (Lancôme, Chanel or Gucci). All strong brands are, however, recorded in the mind of consumers as *a set of strong rational and emotional associations*. In this chapter, we place more emphasis on the role and importance of those mental associations or intangibles attributes.

Brands are now present everywhere. They exist because they generate trust. This trust is based on a close relationship that brands have built over the years with consumers. We find brands mainly in product categories where perceived risks are high. The higher is the perceived risk in a product category, the more significant will be the role of a brand to minimize perceived risks. There are many types of risks, not only functional risks – such as performance or safety – but also social or psychological risks.

In view of the importance of brands for the customers, for the firms and for the financial markets, brands have to be managed carefully, developed and even nurtured to ensure their long-term development and, therefore, the firm's long-term performance. P&G was the first company to create the concept of "brand management" as early as the 1930s. It consisted of having one manager responsible of developing a brand as a mini CEO. Since then, most firms having strong brands have adopted the brand management system.

Importance of brands

By the end of the 1980s, companies realized that acquisitions of brands were becoming more important than the acquisitions of plants, workers or other tangible assets. Brands started to be viewed as a real asset that was providing a strong competitive advantage for firms owning them. They were not only strong barriers to entry for competition, but also a source of increased profit performance. They were generating steady revenues thanks to the high rate of customer loyalty. For the financial markets, this was the best guarantee of increased value for shareholders. This explained the wave of mergers and acquisitions that started mid-1980s and that were exclusively driven by the motivation of acquiring strong brands. It was key for multinational companies to acquire powerful brands, possibly international brands, to become a global leader. Many brands were purchased at very high prices. Perrier, for example, was bought by Nestlé for €2.4 billions. The trend is still the same as indicated by the recent purchase of Rolls Royce by BMW.

In 2003, BMW acquired the Rolls Royce name for more than £40 millions. Interestingly, BMW could only acquire the right to use the name and exploit the famous "spirit of ecstasy" logo but could not buy the plants and the know-how of Rolls Royce skilled workers. They felt that the brand was so strong that they had no problem investing another £65 millions to build a plant and hire new workers.

Coca-Cola has also been trying during several years to buy the well-known French Orangina soft drink brand that was finally purchased by its rival Cadbury Schweppes. They were ready to pay more that €800 million. This also explained the recent acquisition of Gillette by P&G in 2005 to add two global brands – Gillette and Duracell – to their existing brand portfolio.

Some brands are still very attractive potential purchase for some companies:

The well-known European cosmetic leader Nivéa (Beiersdorf from Germany) is viewed as such a valuable asset that two multinational companies (P&G and L'Oréal) have been fighting for some years to acquire this company, so far without success.

Brands are also important for consumers. Today it is difficult to find product categories where products are not branded. Brands are everywhere, not only for fashion, clothes or perfumes but also in services, Hi-Fi or the Internet, despite some negative reactions raised against the pre-eminence of brands in the lives of consumers. The Internet has certainly upended how consumers engage with brands. For a review of brands in the digital age, see Edelman (2010) and Barwise and Meehan (2010). See also the article from *The Economist* (2011) untitled "Why consumers balk at companies' efforts to rebrand themselves".

14.2 THE BRANDED PRODUCT AS A BUNDLE OF ATTRIBUTES

A brand is perceived by a potential customer as a bundle of attributes and of mental associations which, taken together, will form the distinctive elements of the brand's identity. The composition of the bundle, the relative importance and the perceived presence of the attributes will contribute to influence potential customers' purchasing decision.

The different elements of the conceptual brand model are presented in Table 14.1. The integration of these elements leads to a measure of the brand perceived value for a specific potential client, which can be interpreted as an indicator of his or her brand purchase probability.

Objective characteristics

They are the antecedents of the tangible and intangible attributes, that is, the technical characteristics generating the attributes or the benefits sought. They constitute the technical profile of the brand. In general, several characteristics are required to produce the benefit

Table 14.1   Modelling the branded product as a bundle of attributes

Objective characteristics	Tangible and intangible attributes	Evaluation of attributes		Partial utilities	Total utility
		Importance	Performance		
C1	A1	W1	X1	u 1	U
C2	A2	W2	X2	u 2	
...	....	....	....	...	
Cn	An	Wn	Xn	u n	
Reality	Bundle of attributes	Priorities	Perceptions	Values	
Technical description	Qualitative research	Proportion scale	Interval scale	Integration Model	

Source: Lambin (1989).

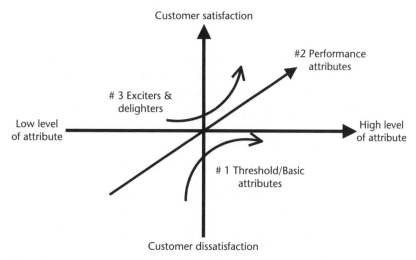

Figure 14.1   The Kano diagram
Source: Walden (1993).

sought. Potential customers rarely give much attention to the objectives characteristics, being more interested by the benefits generated, except when those characteristics reinforce the prestige or the credibility of the brand.

Attributes

By "attribute", one designates the advantage or the benefit sought by the customer and which is used as a selection criterion. Customers generally consider several attributes in evaluating a brand. These attributes can be functional and tangible (power, comfort…), but also intangible (trust, reliability…). The global evaluation of the brand requires a process integrating the specific evaluations made on each attribute.

An attribute is a variable likely to have different values or levels (discreet or continuous) measuring the degree of presence of the attribute in the focal brand. Each brand constitutes a specific bundle of attributes, given that the attributes are present at different levels in each bundle.

Attributes can be classified by focusing on their impact on customer's satisfaction. Using the Kano diagram presented in Figure 14.1, one can distinguish three types of attributes:

- *Basic attributes* are the "must have" factors that a product must deliver to be acceptable by customers. Customers barely notice them, but poor delivery leads to complaints (a TV set in a hotel room). These basic attributes are also called threshold factors (see curve # 1 in Figure 14.1) because at higher levels they provide diminishing returns in terms of customer satisfaction (i.e., increasing the number of ashtrays in a car).

- *Performance attributes* keep adding to customer satisfaction when more of them are provided. Continuing improvements in fuel economy fall in this category. Similarly, in the microprocessor industry more calculation per second, in the plastic industry less degradation in sunlight and so on. As far as the customer is concerned there is no saturation effect. These attributes provide ample opportunities for valuable differentiation. Typically, customers shop around to get the best deal on performance attributes.
- *Excitements attributes* are unexpected and highly appreciated benefits. If not delivered, they do not increase dissatisfaction; but if delivered, they inspire a more than proportional increase in satisfaction (see curve # 3 in Figure 14.1). They are the "nice-to-have" attributes.

If these excitements attributes are tangible they tend to be short-lived because they are rapidly matched by competition, thereby destroying the excitement effect. If they are mental associations generated by the prestige of the brand or by its positioning, they are part of the brand identity. These mental associations are particularly important in B2C markets.

Importance of attributes

The attributes considered do not have the same importance for the potential customer. The attribute's importance for a particular individual reveals his or her value system and the priorities given to each benefit sought, given the potential customer will have to make trade-offs or compromise between the different benefits.

Every reasonable individual wishes to obtain the most for the least: the best service, the best performance but also the lowest possible price, fast delivery and so on. Given that these expectations are generally incompatible, potential customers are induced to search for compromises and to decide what are finally the most important benefits.

Knowing what are the priorities for different segments of the market enables the firm to design different brand concepts targeting specific segment(s) and to respect the diversity of customers needs.

Market research studies have demonstrated that individuals (at least when confronted with articulated needs), and of course organizations, are perfectly able to conceptualize and communicate their preferences in a survey.

Performance: the attribute's perceived degree of presence

A particular attribute can be perceived as very important for an individual but not perceived by this individual as very present in a particular brand. The importance scores must therefore be complemented by scores revealing the perceived degree of presence in each attribute.

Consumers have preconceived ideas and perceptions regarding brand performance attributes. These perceptions are based on past experience, word-of-mouth communication, objective information or simply advertising. These perceptions, which do not necessarily correspond to the reality of the brand, are nevertheless components of the brand image and therefore a reality for the firm. These perceptions can be measured by qualitative and quantitative market research.

To identify a brand, consumers use not only the brand name but also other observable characteristics like the packaging, the design, the logo, the colours and so on. Those external characteristics are part of the brand equity since they are used by potential customers to assess the presence of performance and excitement attributes and to classify brands according to the type of promise they represent.

The value of a particular attribute

The value of a specific attribute is determined by the conjunction of two factors: its importance score and its perceived degree of presence score. This value is called the attribute partial utility, that is, the subjective values associated at each attribute level. The total utility of brand for a specific individual is given by the sum (or the product) of all partial utilities. This supposes the use of an integration model. The most frequently used model is the compensatory and additive model (Fishbein reference):

- compensatory, because a weak score on a particular attribute can be compensated by a high score on another attribute; and
- additive, because it is assumed that mentally individuals evaluate the total utility by simply making the sum of the partial utilities. This implies the lack of interaction among attributes.

Other integration models can be used. In particular non-compensatory models that should be used when consumers tend to privilege some attributes over others, like safety for instance (disjunctive model), or when minimal values are expected on the degree of presence of some attributes (conjunctive model).

The total utility measured reveals the attitude of a particular individual vis-à-vis a brand and is therefore a good leading indicator of his or her purchase probability. This information is of great value for designing a branding strategy. Several options can be considered:

- adding important performance or excitement attributes currently not present in the brand;
- augmenting the degree of presence of key attributes;
- communicating better about the key attributes present in the brand, but ignored by the market.

14.3   FUNCTIONS OF THE BRAND

The brand plays an important role in a market economy, not only for the customer but for the producer as well. We will examine separately the brand functions in the B2C and in the B2B markets.

Functions of the brand for the customer in B2C markets

Five distinct functions of direct use to the customer can be identified, and four brand functions of strategic importance to the firm:

1. *A land marking function.* A brand name is perceived by the potential buyer as a message proposing a specific package of attributes both tangible and intangible, and the buyer uses this information to guide his (or her) choice given the needs or the consumption situation confronted. In this sense, the brand is a *signal* to potential buyers who can identify, at a low personal cost, the set of existing solutions to their problems.

By structuring supply, this brand's land marking function contributes to the market transparency, a service particularly useful in industrialized economies where brands proliferate.

2. *A decision simplification function*. The brand is a simple and practical way to memorize the brand characteristics and to put a name to a specific assortment of benefits. Easy to memorize and to recognize, the brand makes possible a *routine purchase behaviour*, thereby reducing the time spent shopping, a task more and more perceived as a bore by buyers attracted by more stimulating activities. Similarly, the advertiser having promoted a promise to the market can simply re-advertise the brand name or simply its logo. Thus, all the importance of the brand's logo, colour, sign from a semiotic perspective.

3. *A guarantee function*. A brand is a signature which identifies the producer and creates a long-term responsibility, since the brand owner commits himself or herself to give a specific and constant level of quality. A brand represents a pact between brand owner and consumer. The more a brand is known, the more this pact is binding, since the producer cannot afford to deceive his or her customer base and to undermine the brand's accumulated capital of goodwill. The fiction of "generic products" without brand names, popular a few years ago, has triggered strong negative reactions from the consumerists who rightly want that the product's origin be clearly identified.

4. *A personalization function*. The diversity of taste and preferences is central in a market economy. To meet this diversity, firms market-differentiated products, not only on tangible attributes, but on the intangibles as well, such as emotion, aesthetics, social image and so on. Brands give consumers the opportunity to claim their difference, to demonstrate their originality, to express their personality through their brand choices. Viewed in this perspective, the brand is a social communication tool giving to consumers the possibility to privilege certain attributes in their choices, thereby communicating their value system.

5. *A pleasure-giving function*. In affluent societies, consumers' primary or basic needs are largely met, and the needs for novelty, change, surprise, and stimulation become vital necessities. The need to try varied experiences, to live different life styles, the possibility to try new products and to have new sources of satisfaction form an important subject matter in this type of societies. Brands like Swatch, Club Med, McDonald, Cartier, Coca-Cola contribute to the fulfilment of those needs through their branding policies.

On the Internet the land marking function of the brand is particularly important.

Functions of the brand for the producer in B2C markets

To the above five functions mainly useful to the customer, other brand's roles must be added which are critical for the firm's long-term and competitive strategy:

1. *A positioning tool*. It is the same land marking function described above but viewed from the brand owner's side. A brand gives to the firm the opportunity to position its offering vis-à-vis competition, to express its difference and to claim its distinctive characteristics. This positioning function is very important for advertising communication, particularly in markets where comparative advertising is authorized. Viewed in this perspective, the brand is a competitive weapon which contributes to increase market transparency. Is it necessary to repeat that this process of competitive emulation remains the best protection for consumers against abuse of power?

2. *A communication function.* The brand is of strategic importance to manufacturers because it enables the firm to communicate directly with end-consumers regardless of the actions of the middlemen. This communication link is vital to the survival of many of the world's leading grocery companies. Without brands, such manufacturers would be at the mercy of large retail chains whose influence and power over the last ten years have grown dramatically.

3. *A protection function.* Property rights (trade marks, patent, copyrights,) protect the brand name against imitations or counterfeiting. The firm can take action for infringement of patent or trademarks in order to establish its intellectual property rights. A brand owner can register the brand in several product categories according to an international classification. He or she thereby has a clear legal title, which enables him or her to oppose any fraudulent imitation, forgery or counterfeit. A centralization procedure (convention of Madrid) facilitates the registration at the international level, but it is only in 1993 that the concept of European Community brand was been established along with common rules of property rights (de Maricourt, 1997, p. 693). This manufacturers brands' protection function is particularly important today in view of the "copycat" own label strategy adopted by some large retail chains in France and in the United Kingdom (see Kapferer, 1991), and also by manufacturers based in Latin America or in Asia.

4. *A capitalization function.* The brand, and in particular the brand image, serves to capture not only the past advertising investments put into it, but also the capital of satisfaction generated by the brand. Many brands are more than a 100 years old (see Exhibit 14.1). To the firm, they constitute a valuable asset, an intangible capital, resulting from several years of past advertising investments. Brands therefore introduce stability into businesses; they allow planning and investment in a long-term perspective.

5. *A loyalty function.* The existence of the brand permits to create a relationship with customers as they will be willing to repurchase the same brand. Having a group of loyal customers is vital for the long-term development of the brand.

6. *A barrier to entry function.* As a result of the previous functions, brands create a real *barrier to entry* for competitors. Not only do they benefit from a group of loyal customers, but they also enjoy a high awareness and strong image. It would be extremely costly for any new competitors to invest in order to reach similar awareness and image levels. These entry barriers are in fact financial and linked to the economies of scale that strong brands can benefit from. Brands such as Coca-Cola and Pepsi Cola have created real entry barriers. It is nearly impossible for any brand to launch a Cola drink and compete with them. It would cost fortunes to reach same levels of awareness and it might even be impossible, whatever the investments, to build such strong images.

Exhibit 14.1   The history of selected brands

The need to associate a new product with a brand name has first implied the use of the company name or his founder's name. Cinzano is one of the oldest names in the business. As far back as 1757, Carlo Stefano Cinzano and Giovanni Giacomo Cinzano were distilling the beverage that bears their name in a factory near Turin. Among the brands born during the last century, some of them are still alive and well: Nestlé (the milky flour from Henri Nestlé, 1867), Maggi (soups from Jules Maggi, 1883), Levi's (from Levi Strauss & Co, 1856), the biscuits of Mr. Lefèvre and Miss Utile (1856) that subsequently became the brand Lu and the aperitif anise from Pernod (1850). Today, the brand is a part of our daily environment.

Source: Adapted from de Maricourt (1997, p. 687).

The functions of the brand in B2B markets

Globally the functions performed by the B2B brands are similar to the ones described for the B2C brands with the exception of the pleasure-giving function. As shown by Malaval (2001) differences exist, however, as the result of two characteristics specific to B2B brands, such as brand purchasibility and brand visibility. B2B brands sold to the industrial firm are neither always visible nor purchasable by the end-user:

■ The brand *purchasibility* can be defined as the possibility for the general public to buy or not to buy the industrial good as a separate product and not only as an incorporated part in the finished product. The individual consumer, for example, cannot purchase an Intel microprocessor or an air-bag cushion. Other industrial goods, however, like spare parts or office equipment, can be purchased by visiting specialized distributors. Depending on the situation, the role of the brand will be different and sometimes confined to the sole customer incorporating firm.

■ The brand *visibility* by the general public is determined by the possibility for the consumer to know the B2B brand, either through direct physical contact with the brand or through communication. Different levels of visibility exist: at the purchasing time, during utilization, during disassembling or without any visibility. Depending on the situation, the B2B functions and communication mode and target will have to be adapted accordingly.

For the direct customer two functions of the B2B brands are particularly relevant. The first is linked to the safety and guarantee functions and the second to the role of the supplier's brands for the incorporating customer.

The traceability function

A brand has a land marking function, a signal, a signature and a guarantee providing to the customer a double safety: first, a certainty regarding the product sourcing and authenticity and, second, the certainty that, in case of product deficiency, recourse can be had from the supplier.

The function of traceability refers to the possibility to track the incorporated product and to identify the components of the finished product. In case of quality problems, the customer-manufacturing firm has the possibility to reassure itself – and also to reassure its own customers – that the responsibility of the upstream supplier is engaged and will be easily demonstrated, in order to obtain repair or compensation. Thus, traceability is the response provided by the supplier to the customer's expectation of guarantee for itself and its own customers. For the decision centre and for the purchaser, the supplier's brand contributes to reduce the perceived risk, in particular when the brand is strong and well known in the market.

The facilitation functions

Beyond the traditional functions of a brand, B2B firms have specific expectations regarding their suppliers. Malaval (1998, 2001) has analysed the expectations and fears of a large sample of industrial firms.

The positive expectations can be regrouped into four categories presented here in an order of decreasing importance:

1. Performance facilitation in the *production* process, that is, the capacity of the supplier's brand to improve the manufacturing process of the client, through better quality control or through better maintenance.

2. Performance facilitation in *innovation*, that is, the capacity of the supplier's brand to improve the design of the customer's end-product.
3. Performance facilitation in *operational marketing*, that is, the capacity of the supplier's brand to give a commercial argument or distinctive profile thanks to the reputation of the supplier's brand.
4. Performance facilitation in the *decision-making process*, that is, the capacity to facilitate the acceptance of change and of new materials and to obtain rapidly a consensus within the firm's decision centre.

The most important expectation is on the technical partnership. Purchasers are in general more sensitive to the performance facilitation in the decision process, while marketing people have greater expectations regarding the commercial impact of the component brand.

Fears vis-à-vis strong suppliers' brands

Malaval (2001) has also studied the main perceived risks associated with the adoption of strong suppliers' brands. By decreasing order of importance, the main fears are the following:

1. The risk of a *too high price* justified by the communication investments made on the brand.
2. The *risk of dependence* vis-à-vis the supplier's brand, that is, the difficulty of changing of suppliers given the technical choices made and given the possible impact of the supplier's brand on the end-customer.
3. The risk of *too strong influence* and impact of the brand's supplier on the internal organization of the firm.
4. The risk of *arrogance* from the staff of the supplier's brand reflecting an unfavourable balance of power.

Logically, it is the risk of excessive price that is perceived as the most important.

The challenge of invisible suppliers' brands

The specific functions of the suppliers' brands described so far are mainly instrumental vis-à-vis direct customers, that is, the professional purchasers, and not so much vis-à-vis end-customers, the general public at large. Since a large number of suppliers' brands cannot be purchased and are not visible by the general public, these brands are generally unknown with some exceptions like Gore Tex, Lycra, Rhodyl or Tetra Pak.

During the past few years, one has observed a growing number of B2B firms adopting communication strategies targeting the general market, and not only specialized professionals. This evolution can be explained by the following considerations:

- The willingness of the B2B firms to differentiate their offerings, too often perceived as commodities or as raw materials with no added value.
- The necessity to explain the "how" and the "why" of sophisticated products, in particular, in the high-tech sectors.
- The concern to communicate the identity of the supplier in order to increase its awareness and reputation among professionals and the general public.
- The objective of leapfrogging direct customers by inciting end-customers to demand the supplier's brand in the finished product, thereby reducing the pressure on prices.

Exhibit 14.2   Examples of strong B2B brands

Construction industry

Acova, Grohe, Isover, Lafarge, Legrand, Somfy, Technal, Villeroy & Boch

Packaging industry

Ato, BSN, Combibloc, Elopak, Mead Emballages, PLM, Saint Gobain Emballages, Tetra Pak

Automotive equipment industry

Bertand Faure, Bosch, Michelin, Sommer Allibert, Valeo

Textile industry

DMC, Dorlastan, Gore-Tex, Lycra, Rhovyl, Tactel, Tergal, Woolmark

Source: Malaval (1998).

- The concern to certify a product during and after utilization, based on the guarantee and given the commitments taken regarding the after-sales services.
- The objective to meet the expectations of end-consumers who, better informed and more professional, want more detailed information and a guarantee.

Successful examples of such communication strategies are given by suppliers' brands like Intel and Gore-Tex, among many others (see Exhibit 14.2).The discussion would not be complete without mentioning the fast development of private labels in FMCG markets. This point will be covered in more detail in the next chapter.

14.4   KEY BRAND MANAGEMENT CONCEPTS

Branding is not only about image or about communication. Strong brands are not artificial build-up. They are based on outstanding product or service and strive to remain at the top. If physical product concepts follow a certain life cycle and die one day, if well managed, a brand can live forever.

> The CEO of P&G cites as an example the brand Tide, launched in 1947 and still in a growth phase in 1976. In reality, the product was modified 55 times in its 29 year existence to adapt to market changes including consumption habits, characteristics of washing machines, new fabrics, etc. (Day, 1981, p. 61). This brand is still alive and well in 2011.

Brand positioning

Having segmented the reference market, the firm decides to cover by priority one or several segments and to "position" its offering (brand) in a way which is both consistent with potential customers' expectations and different from competitors' offerings. It consists in giving a "raison d'être" to a product.

The firm at the very start of the brand development process makes the positioning decision. It is based on an in-depth analysis of the market, consumers and competitors that can be summed by the four following questions:

- A brand for what? This refers to the brand promise and the customer benefit.
- A brand for whom? This refers to the target segment.

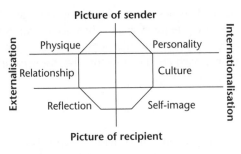

Figure 14.2   The brand identity prism
Source: Kapferer (2004, p. 107). Reproduced with permission.

■ A brand for when? This refers to the use or consumption situation.

■ A brand against whom? This question refers to the direct competitor.

It is the platform of the brand success. In the FMCG sector, when competition was less intense, it was common to base brand positioning on the brand's Unique Selling Proposition (USP) than on the uniqueness or the exclusive benefit offered by this brand in the market. It is not always easy to find today a sustainable USP in the light of the high number of "me-too" brands existing in the market. Moreover, traditional USP brand positioning tends to focus only on the brand's tangible attributes but do not give enough information on the brand personality or country of origin. (Some authors translate USP as Unique Selling Personality.) This is also why the concept of brand identity was created end-1980s (Kapferer, 1991) (see Figure 14.2).

Brand identity

Brand identity is close to the concept of brand positioning but it is more complete, because it communicates other elements about the brand that are strategically important for its development.

> How to distinguish between Coca-Cola and Pepsi-Cola, between Hertz and Avis, between Google and Yahoo? The positioning of these brands is largely similar but their personalities can be very different.

Kapferer (1991, 2004) has developed the "brand identity prism" that defines the brand identity in terms of six facets:

1. *Physique:* The brand's tangible attributes.
2. *Personality:* The brand has also a certain personality that can be described and measured by human's personality traits.
3. *Culture:* Set of values that the brand is built on, influenced by country of origin image.
4. *Relationship:* Style of the relationship created with consumers.
5. *Reflection:* They way consumers using the brand would like to be seen.
6. *Self-image:* The image that people have of themselves when using the brand.

For example, the identity of the sport car Porsche in France (Variot, 1985) can be described as follows:

1. *Physical:* Performance.
2. *Personality:* Perfectionist.
3. *Relationship:* Personal rather than family oriented.
4. *Cultural:* German technology.
5. *Reflection:* Winners' car.
6. *Self-image:* Surpassing oneself.

The brand identity concept is used in designing advertising messages. This advertising approach is very demanding because it requires great coherence of expression. The reason is that form, style and tone are more important than substance in constructing the image. Good examples of this creative approach are the different advertising campaigns launched by Perrier in Western Europe (see Table 14.2).

Brand image

Brand positioning and brand identity are manufacturer's concepts. They have been created by the seller and should not be confused with the brand image. The brand image is the perception of the brand identity in the minds of consumers. Large differences can exist between the brand identity and the brand image. The brand or corporate image can be defined in the following terms.

> The set of mental representations, both cognitive and affective, a person or a group of person holds vis-à-vis a brand or a company.

A good understanding of the brand image and of its perceived strengths and weaknesses is an indispensable pre-requisite to any strategy and communication platform definition. In this respect, it is useful to make a distinction between three levels of brand image analysis:

1. The *perceived image* or how the people see and perceive the brand: an *outside-in perspective*, based on field interviews within the reference market or segment.
2. The *actual image* or the reality of the brand, an *inside-in perspective* based on the brand' strengths and weaknesses identified by the firm through an internal audit.
3. The *desired image* (its identity) or the way brand management wishes the brand to be perceived by the target segment as a result of a positioning or brand identity decision.

Clearly, important differences can exist between these three levels of image measurement and reconciliation may be necessary.

- A gap may exist between the actual image and the perceived image, in a positive or negative sense.
- If the gap is in favour of the brand, communication has an important role to play in the reconciliation process; in the opposite case, the brand concept must be revised.

Table 14.2 The identity of Levi's brands of jeans

Attributes and benefits	Associations
– Product-related attributes	– Blue denim, shrink-to-fit cotton fabric, button-fly, two horse patch, and small red pocket tag.
– User imagery	– Western, American, blue collar, hard working, traditional, strong, rugged, and masculine.
– Usage imagery	– Appropriate for outdoor work and casual social situations.
– Brand personality	– Honest, classic, contemporary, approachable, independent, and universal.
– Experiential benefits	– Feeling of self-confidence and self-assurance
– Symbolic benefits	– Comfortable fitting and relaxing to wear.
– Functional benefits	– High quality, long lasting and durable.

Source: Adapted from Keller (1998).

■ A gap may also occur between the desired image and the reality of the brand, that is, its know-how, its quality or its communication; it is the credibility of the positioning strategy which is at stake here.

This last problem is particularly acute in service firms where the contact personnel directly contribute to the perceived image of the firm. Internal marketing has an important role to play here.

To measure the perceived image, the analysis will be based on the three levels of market response using successively indicators of the cognitive, affective and behavioural response.

Brand equity concept

The last few years have seen brand equity become one of the hottest topics in business among professionals and academic researchers (Aaker, 1991, 1996; Kapferer, 1991), although the economists have adopted the concept since many years (Nerlove and Arrow, 1962). Two definitions are currently used.

> Broadly stated, brand equity refers to the "capital of goodwill" accumulated by a brand and resulting from past marketing activities (Nerlove and Arrow, 1962)

Alternatively,

> A consumer perceives a brand's equity as the "value added" to the functional product or service by associating it with the brand name (Aaker, 1991)

In both definitions the concept refers to the brand's strength which can vary largely among brands and which is determined by its awareness, personality, perceived quality, leadership or stock value.

The idea was to find a concept summarizing the strength of a brand. The brand equity concept was created because traditional data such as market share or volume sold were not satisfactory to reflect the value of a brand, and because they did not take into account the associations that existed in the consumer's mind.

The concept has two faces. On the one hand, it gives a financial definition of the brand equity to evaluate the brand's "financial" value (*financial brand equity*). It is especially important for financial analysts and companies to evaluate this strategic company asset. On the other hand, it covers the value of the brand from the customer's viewpoint, the *customer-based brand equity*, as a set of associations made by the customers and generating the brand strength.

Exhibit 14.3   Price advantages of the strongest brands

To gauge how important brands are to customers during the purchase process, McKinsey (1996) examined 27 case studies, based on over 5,000 customer interviews in the United States, Europe and Asia. On average, prices of the strongest brands (in terms of the brand's importance behind the decision to buy) were 19 per cent higher than those of the weakest brands. Relative to second-tier brands, the leading brands commanded an average price premium of 5 per cent.

Source: Court et al. (1996, p. 178).

Figure 14.3 Brand equity sequence

Feldwick (1996) suggests to referring to three, distinct but complementary, meanings:

1. The set of perceptions, associations or beliefs, both cognitive and affective, the cus-
    tomer has about a brand, which is traditionally called the *brand image*.
2. The strength of customers' *attachment to a brand* revealed, namely, by the price pre-
    mium customers are ready to pay.
3. The total value of a brand as a *separable asset*, when it is sold or included in a balance
    sheet.

These three different meanings are linked and the causal chain would be (1) brand attributes,
(2) brand strength and (3) brand value (see Figure 14.3). The attributes of the brand influence what we can call the strength of the brand that leads to the financial value of the brand
on the market.

A study by Rego, Billett and Morgan (2009) shows how consumer-based brand equity has
an impact on the firm's risk. Other authors have evaluated what is the financial return impact
of building brands (Krasnikov, Mishra and Orozco, 2009; Mizik and Jacobson, 2009).

14.5   BUILDING A SUCCESSFUL BRAND

The branding decision is at the interface of strategic and operational marketing. Branding
is about de-commoditizing products. Brand development can be viewed as an iceberg. The
visible part of the iceberg shows the brand name, its advertising and its logo. But the brand
can only be successful if the foundations of the brand are well built. In the hidden part of
the iceberg, one must have effective R&D, reliable manufacturing and logistics, appropriate
selection of a target segment and a creative brand positioning/identity decision. These elements are essential to brand success (see Figure 14.4).

Brand architecture

Brand architecture is the way in which the brands within a company's portfolio are related
to, and differentiated from, one another. The architecture should specify brand roles and
the nature of relationships between brands. Following Aaker and Joachimsthaller (2000), we
identify four generic brand naming strategies:

1. *A branded house strategy.* Companies like Nivéa, Virgin, Sony, Adidas and Mercedes-Benz
    choose to use a single name (a company name or a master brand) across all the activities
    and this name is how all their stakeholders know them. The advantage is to minimize
    communication and support costs as all products carry the same name and benefit from
    the master brand's awareness and image, which is used as an umbrella brand. A single
    brand communicated across products and over time is much easier to recall. A func-
    tional descriptor accompanies the master brand to describe the offering (GE Capital,
    Nivéa Deodorant, Virgin Music and so on). The risk of this strategy is the brand diluting
    effect if the products are too different or not performing equally. Also, it doesn't allow
    too different identities when targeting different product markets.

Table 14.3   Evaluation of selective European brands

Brands	Countries	Value ($ b)	Brands	Countries	Value ($ b)
Nokia (8)	Finland	29.50	Allianz (67)	Germany	4.90
Mercedes (12)	Germany	25.18	Santander (68)	Spain	4.85
BMW (15)	Germany	22.32	Hermès (69)	France	4.78
Louis Vuitton (16)	France	21.86	Porsche (72)	Germany	4.40
H&M (21)	Sweden	16.14	Barclays (74)	United Kingdom	4.22
SAP (26)	Germany	12.76	Cartier (77)	France	4.05
Nescafé (27)	Switzerland	12.75	Moët & Chandon (79)	France	4.02
Ikéa (28)	Sweden	12.49	Crédit Suisse (80)	Switzerland	4.01
HSBC (32)	United Kingdom	11.56	Shell (81)	Netherlands	4.00
Philips (42)	Netherlands	8.70	UBS (86)	Switzerland	3.81
Gucci (44)	Italy	8.35	Nivéa (87)	Germany	3.73
L'Oréal (45)	France	7.98	Smirnoff (89)	United Kingdom	3.62
Zara (48)	Spain	7.47	Ferrari (91)	Italy	3.56
Siemens (49)	Germany	7.32	Johnnie Walker (92)	United Kingdom	3.56
BMW (53)	Germany	6.89	Heineken (93)	Netherlands	3.52
Axa (56)	France	6.69	Zurich (94)	Switzerland	3.50
Nestlé (57)	Switzerland	6.55	Armani (95)	Italy	3.44
Danone (58)	France	6.36	Lancôme (96)	France	3.40
Adidas (62)	Germany	5.50	Burberry (100)	United Kingdom	3.11
Audi (63)	Germany	5.46			

Source: Interbrand (2010).

2. *House of brands strategy*. At the other extreme, companies like Unilever and P&G have focused on individual sub-brands. Unilever used to operate with 1,400 brands with little connections to each other and still operates today with 400 brands. It gives the possibility to the firm to cover the same market with different brands or to target specific segments. Each brand is independent and there is no link to the company. If there is a problem of quality with one particular brand, it will not affect other products or the company reputation. Another advantage is to avoid a brand association that would be incompatible with an offering. For example, Volkswagen would adversely affect the images of Porsche and of Audi if the brands were linked. It is, however, a costly strategy because each brand has to be supported individually.

3. *The endorsed brand strategy*. The brands are still independent but they are endorsed by the corporate brand or by the company name. Examples of *strong endorsements* are Kit-Kat by Nestlé, Polo by Ralph Lauren or Lycra by DuPont. Another type of endorsement is a *linked name*, like Nesttea, Nescafé and Nesquick from the Nestlé company or like the HP Jet series: Laserjet, DeskJet, OfficeJet, Inkjet. A linked name provides the benefit of a separate name without having to establish a second name from scratch. A weaker endorsement type is the *token endorsement* taking the form of a logo or of a seal of guarantee. It is a way to support brands not yet well established by providing reassurance and credibility. Finally, in a *shadow endorsement* the brand is not connected visibly to the endorser but many consumers know about the link. Two examples are Lexus from Toyota and Dockers from Levi Strauss. Endorsements reduce marketing support costs.

4. *Sub-brands*. Sub-brands are brands connected to a master (or umbrella brand) brand that augment or modify the associations of the master brand, for example, Sony Walkman. A common role of a sub-brand is to extend a master brand into a new segment. It is more than a functional descriptor; it has a co-driver role, like Gillette Sensor, for instance, or Porsche Carrera.

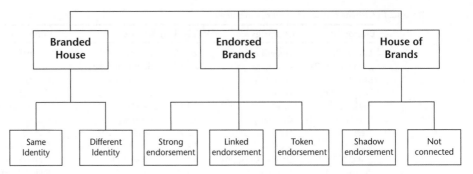

Figure 14.4   The brand architecture
Source: Adapted from Aaker and Joachimsthaller (2000).

Brand name and logo selection

Finding the right name is important because it will help communicate the benefits of the brand and its personality. This name has to fit with the brand identity. If the brand is supposed to have a dynamic or fun personality, the brand name has to be selected accordingly.

Certain criteria have to be taken into account in the name selection. The name should be simple and easy to memorize to facilitate brand recall and recognition in the consumers' minds. It has to be international to meet the challenge of globalization. The brand name should not be too descriptive or too generic to avoid the risk of being easily copied by competition, especially by private labels.

> It is only recently that pharmaceutical companies have realized that they did not sell products but brands and that they should not necessarily name their products by reference to the generic molecule name. Strong brands like Viagra and Prozac have succeeded to create their own personality.

The logo is the flag of the brand. Certain brands are so strong that they are recognized by their logo only. Good examples are Nike, Mercedes, Ferrari, Lacoste. Some symbolic persons or animals can also serve as identifier of the brand such as the Bibendum of Michelin, Mr Proper, the horse of Ferrari, the elephant of Côte d'Or. Firms are inclined to giving more importance to their brand symbols as a way to cultivate the brand cultural identity.

Characteristics of successful brands

Peter Doyle has identified five major characteristics of successful brands that can be summarized as follows (Doyle, 1994, 2003):

- *A quality product*. Satisfactory experience in use is the major determinant of brand success. Quality or sustained quality is the number one requirement. If the brand quality deteriorates, customers will switch to competing brands and the brand positioning will be undermined.
- *Being the first in the market*. The innovator is not necessarily successful but being the first facilitates market penetration. It is easier to take a position in the customers' mind when the brand has no competitors and comes with an innovative proposal.
- *Unique positioning*. If the brand is not the innovator, it must have a unique positioning concept that will differentiate the brand from competing brands: The case of Swatch in the traditional watch market is good example.

- *Strong communication programme.* To be successful the brand requires strong advertising, selling and promotional support to communicate the brand' proposition and to create the brand identity.
- *Time and consistency.* Building a successful brand takes time and requires investment to maintain, to rejuvenate and/or to reposition the brand in a changing environment.

Keller (2000) in a similar study has identified ten traits of successful brands:

1. The brand excels at delivering the benefits customers truly desire.

2. The brand stays relevant.

3. The pricing strategy is based on consumers' perceptions of value.

4. The brand is properly positioned.

5. The brand is consistent.

6. The brand portfolio and hierarchy make sense.

7. The brand makes use of and co-ordinates a full repertoire of marketing activities to build equity.

8. The brand's manager understands what the brand means to consumers.

9. The brand is given proper support and that support is sustained over the long run.

10. The company monitors sources of brand equity.

Brand life cycles

The typical brand life cycle profile is described in Figure 14.5. Caron (1996) studied the historical evolution of more than 1,000 brands and identified five phases in the typical brand life cycle (see Exhibit 14.4). The profile of the cycle is very similar to the one observed by Hinkle (1966) in the US food and cosmetic sectors (see Figure 14.5).

It is clear that the life cycle of a brand is essentially determined by factors under the control of the company: the marketing strategy adopted and the amount of effort dedicated to it.

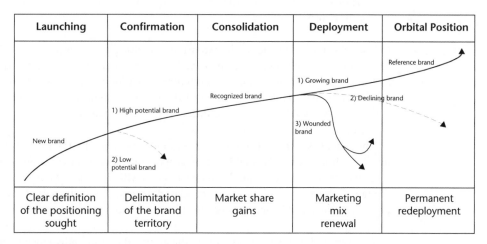

Figure 14.5 Typical brand life cycle
Source: Adapted from Caron (1996).

Exhibit 14.4   The brand life cycle

Caron (1996) reports that Carré Noir has studied the strategy of a sample of 1,000 brands and has observed that the typical brand life cycle consists of a total of five phases. In about 85 per cent of the studied cases the BLC was limited to two or four.

1. *Launching.* More than 1 million brands are registered every year in the world, of which 61,583 were registered in France in 1995. During this phase, marketing efforts are concentrated on the new brand for establishing its identity.
2. *Confirmation.* Once the fashion effect is gone, sales of the low-potential brands fall and these brands are delisted from the distributors' purchasing centres. The surviving brands delimit their brand territory.
3. *Consolidation.* The recognized brands have to reaffirm their national and/or international strategic ambition, claim their difference, improve their distribution rate and so on. The objective is to "hold" and to increase their market share.
4. *Deployment.* Thanks to a constant renewal of their marketing mix to meet the market changes, the expanding brands redeploy and win a new breed of consumers. Some do not find rejuvenating ideas to reinvent themselves and decline. Others have accidents.
5. *Orbital position.* The brand is fully in charge. Rich from its accumulated experience and consolidated by its success, reputation and status among its customer base, the brand has reached the high orbit. To keep that position, the brand will have to continuously create its own style and language that will be assimilated by its customers.

Even in this final phase, the brand remains threatened. The five phases' difficult trajectory of development (see Figure 14.5) looks like a real combat track.

Source: Adapted from Caron (1996).

Brand extension and stretching strategies

In targeting different customer segments, the firm can use the same or different brand names.

- A *brand extension strategy* means using a brand name successfully established for one segment to enter another one within the same market. For example, the brand name of the facial cream Nivéa has been used by Beiersdorf to cover other needs in the cosmetic market.
- A *brand stretching strategy* means transferring the successful brand name to quite different markets. This is the strategy adopted by Canon to move from cameras to copiers, printers and so on.

Companies have used the brand extension/stretching strategies frequently in the last few years. The idea is to benefit directly from the awareness and image of a strong existing brand by using the same brand name for launching new products in different categories. It is the idea of umbrella branding, discussed in the previous section. Initially, only luxury goods companies extended their name to different product categories; however, this is now common in many different business sectors.

The rapid development of brand extension is explained by the high cost of introducing new brands in the markets and also of supporting them by advertising. The key question is to evaluate how far the brand can be stretched without risks. The risks are, first, to dilute the brand image of the mother brand; second, to reduce the chances of success of the new product if the brand image does not fit the new brand concept.

For example Levi's, which has built a brilliant brand in jeans, attempted to market a range of high quality formal suits to middle-class males under the Levi's name. The brand extension failed because the new target market did not see the informal, denim association of the Levi's name as adding value in this sector. (Doyle, 1994, p. 176)

The decision between brand extension and individual brand names should be guided by the similarity of the competitive advantage and of the target market segment, as illustrated in Figure 14.6.

- If the brands appeal to the same target segment and have the same competitive advantage, then a pure brand extension strategy is safe and consistent. This would be the case of Nivéa in the cosmetic market.
- If the competitive advantage is the same but the target markets are different, the brand can be extended but qualified to give a signal to the target segment. For example, both the Mercedes-200 and -500 base their competitive advantage on quality but the more expensive Mercedes-500 targets the prestige-conscious segment.
- If the company has different competitive advantages but targets the same segment it could use both company and brand names.
- Finally, if both the target and the competitive advantages are different, using unique brand names is the more appropriate strategy (Doyle, 1994, 2003).

Co-branding strategies

Co-branding consists of making an alliance between two brands to launch a new product or promotion. It can constitute a way to grow the business. The value of co-branding can be to benefit from the awareness of both brands and to broaden the consumer target by benefiting from the consumers of the other brand. In some cases, co-branding also permits more rapid access into new markets via the network of the co-brand. When two leading brands are partners, it can reinforce the brand loyalty because both brands are very trusted brands. Co-branding also allows one to leverage the technological advantage or other know-how of one of the partners. It also reduces the cost of development of the new initiative as costs are shared between both firms.

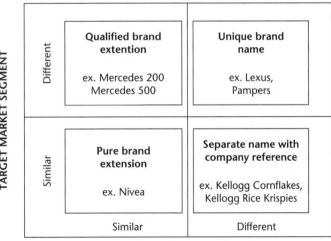

Figure 14.6 Brand extension strategies
Source: Adapted from Doyle (1994, 2003).

Exhibit 14.5   Example: Co-branding Philips–Nivéa

Philips is a strong proponent of co-branding to improve its brand image to end-consumers. It has made several partnerships these last few years with Beiersdorf (Nivéa), Douwe Egberts (Senseo), P&G and Inbev. Concerning the co-branding with Nivéa, they decided to create Philipshave Cool Skin together. This was a new electric shaver with Nivéa dispensing. This co-branding made sense as both brands were leaders in their respective markets. Many advantages were identified in this partnership: possibility to attract new users and to enter new channels of distribution that they had no access to so far; reinforcement of their respective brand image and combined advertising support; shared development launch costs of this new initiative.

Source: Industry.

Co-branding also has its limits. Long lead times are often needed to develop and finalize such deals. There is the risk that the new product will cannibalize one of the existing products (Yolka). It is also important to ensure that both brands are equally strong so that each brand benefits from the deal. It does not make sense for a strong brand to get associated with a less-known brand. The partners also need to take into account the difficulty in evaluating the benefits that will need to be shared by both partners after the launch. There are two types of co-branding:

- *Strategic co-branding* represents long-term associations and relatively large investments from both partners (Swatch and Mercedes (Smart), Douwe Egberts and Philips (Senseo), Nestlé and Krups (Nespresso).
- *Tactical co-branding* represents short-term alliances that usually cover promotional deals. They imply relatively low investments from both partners. It focuses more on communications activities than product initiatives (P&G and Fisher Price).

Nestlé and Coca-Cola created together the "Beverage Partners Worldwide" firm to market drinks based on teas. It would exploit the know-how of Nestlé in that type of product and the commercial network of Coca-Cola.

In Chapter 19, which is devoted to communication, we will see how building brand communities has become a key competitive advantage for brands in the Internet age. It is interesting to review Fournier and Lee (2009) on this topic as well as Schau, Muniz and Arnould (2009), who show how brand communities create value for the firm.

14.6   INTERNATIONAL BRANDING STRATEGIES

In the current context of globalization, firms have concentrated their efforts in developing international brands. As a result, international brand portfolios have been restructured and many successful local brands have been eliminated.

Unilever, for example, is at the end of the process of eliminating 1200 brands from its brand portfolio to concentrate on just 400 brands. P&G has kept 300, after selling many local brands. L'Oréal has built its success on 16 worldwide brands. Nestlé has been giving priority to their six strategic worldwide brands including Nescafe and Buitoni, and Mars has been investing since many years mainly in global brand names.

Strong local brands have essentially been eliminated from multinational brand portfolios, not because they do not represent strong brand franchises locally, but rather because their relative sales volumes do not permit economies of scale.

> In Europe, at the end of the 1990s, Procter and Gamble were seriously thinking about eliminating the leading detergent in Italy - known as Dash – despite the fact that the brand was a national institution and extremely profitable in Italy. The company's motivation at the time was that the Dash brand was creating cost complexities, where Ariel was the European leader.

Advantages of international and global brands

It is clear that international and global brands present many important advantages to the firm. They generate strong economies of scale. It is well known that a globalized brand can generate significant cost reductions in all areas of the business system, including R&D, manufacturing and logistics. The move to a single global brand name also provides substantial economies in packaging and communication costs. Another advantage is the development of a unique brand image across countries. The speed to market for new product initiatives that international brands offer is also very important for international companies. They can now launch new product initiatives in the fast moving goods industry on a regional or global scale within 12 to 18 months. Another advantage is the possibility of supporting any global brand with very large budgets in the communication area. This is especially important today in the context of very high advertising and media costs. Research has shown that being global has an impact on consumer perception. It gives a sense of excellence and a set of obligations (Holt, Quelch and Taylor, 2004).

Advantages of local brands

Local brands also present some interesting advantages that are not often highlighted. Local brands represent many years of marketing investment. They are well known in their markets, and often create strong relationships with local consumers over the years. In Europe, there are still many more local than international brands, even if the trend is for the proportion of local brands to diminish. Whilst industries such as the car industry, computers and high-tech businesses are well-known for their strong international brands, many sectors are still characterized by having many local brands.

> In the oil industry in Germany, British Petroleum (BP) acquired the local leader Aral and decided, in view of its strong brand equity, to keep the local brand name. In France, the leading whisky brands are not the well-known J&B or Johnny Walker but the local Label 5, Clan Campbell and William Peel. In the Czech Republic, Danone did not succeed in imposing its "Lu" brand on that market, and has had to use the local brand franchise "Opavia" to develop its business. In Belgium, the leader in the mineral water market is the local leader Spa, with shares well ahead of the international leader Evian. (Schuiling and Kapferer, 2004)

The advantages of local brands are the following:

- *Local brands offer a better response to local needs.* A local brand can be designed to respond to the specific needs of the local market. The local brand product has the flexibility to be developed so that it genuinely provides an answer to a particular need of local consumers. Such local branding can not only provide a unique product, but also select its positioning and generate an advertising campaign that reflects local insights.

■ *Local brands can be also more flexible on pricing.* They can offer the price that is in line with the strength of the brand. Such flexibility can lead to increased profits when prices can be fixed at a higher level.

■ *A local brand can also be used to respond to local or international competition, or even fight against retailer brands.* A local brand can be repositioned and the marketing mix adapted accordingly. In contrast, the marketing strategy for an international brand has to follow a pre-defined regional or global marketing strategy.

Local brands offer also the possibility of better balancing a portfolio of brands and therefore better balancing the risk on a worldwide basis. An international portfolio that mostly comprises international and global brands can be very powerful, but also presents risks. A problem arising with one of these mega brands in one particular country can have a negative impact on a worldwide basis

Impact on international positioning strategies

Too often the globalization versus customization debate is presented in terms of an "all or nothing" question. In reality, intermediate solutions exist and the real question is to know how to reconcile the two approaches. We support the view that branding and positioning are two independent decisions, which can occur in varying combinations as shown in Table 14.4.

Brand and position globally

In *Strategy #1,* brand names and positioning are globalized. This situation will tend to prevail in a global environment where the global forces are strong and the local forces weak.

> Classical examples of this strategy are Marlboro, Coca-Cola, Gillette Sensor, Sony Walkman, McDonald, Levi, Gucci, Pampers, etc.

These genuinely global brands deliver the same benefits (tangible and intangible) to consumers who value them in all countries: Coke for the convenience and the appeal of American young imagery; Sony for the attraction of "music on the move"; Hermes for fashion and romance. These benefits can be hard-to-copy innovations like Pampers or Apple, or emotional benefits as in the case of Louis Vuitton or Cartier.

> An especially strong kind of positioning to be exploited globally involves national stereotypes: German quality in cars, for example, or French style and romance in perfume, or English conservatism in men's tailoring, or American youth and fun in fast food.

P&G seems to have adopted this policy regarding brand names since 70 per cent of its turnover is made by brands sold all over the world, such as Oil of Olaz, Ariel, Pampers, Clearasil

Table 14.4 Alternative international branding and positioning strategies

Brand name	International positioning	
	Global	Local
Same brand name	Strategy #1 Brand and position globally	Strategy #2 Brand globally and position locally
Different brand names	Strategy #3 Brand locally and harmonize position	Strategy #4 Brand and position locally

Source: Adapted from Sandler and Shani (1992).

and Vicks. One exception is the P&G shampoo Wash & Go which has been launched in 60 different countries, but under 6 different brand names. The concept "two in one" is the same in each market, however. Slight variations in the advertising expressions also exist. This last example illustrates the fact that a complete globalization will probably never be possible.

Brand globally but adopt a local positioning

Strategy #2 globalizes brand names but localizes the strategic positioning. This situation will probably prevail in transnational environments where both global and local forces are strong.

> Examples of this strategy are given, namely, by Bacardi and Volvo truck and also to a lesser degree by P&G with the shampoo Wash & Go. These firms use the same brand name worldwide but the positioning themes and/or expressions are adjusted in each country.

In instances where brand standardization tends to be high, localized advertising gives the firm the possibility to take into account local culture and sensitivity and to position the brand in the local market.

Brand locally and harmonize positioning globally

Strategy #3 harmonizes the brand positioning but keeps local brand names. This is a strategy adopted by European firms, like Unilever and Kraft, having developed their portfolio of brands through acquisitions. Unilever management, for example, seems to believe (Fraser, 1990) that as long as core brand values can be harmonized, the name does not really matter. Unilever tends to draw the line in its harmonizing policy at changing names.

> Unless the original name is meaningless, it would be very dangerous to drop it. Names that have been built up over years and years are an essential part of brand's franchise or equity. (Fraser, 1990)

This is the justification of the approach taken with a Unilever fabric softener called Cajoline in France, Coccolino in Italy, Kuschelweich in Germany, Mimosin in Spain and Snuggle in the United States. Although the name is different in every country, it suggests cuddly softness everywhere. And the product benefits are always presented by a talking teddy bear, a universally understood symbol of softness. Far from being a disadvantage, the different names actually bring the brand closer to the hearts of local consumers.

> The "same positioning–different name" approach has also been used for the fish fingers of Unilever. The well-known salty sea captain has appeared in commercials throughout Europe even though he is variously known as Birds Eye, Findus or Iglo. All he has to do is change his cap and speak a different language in each country, which leads to significant cost savings in the production of television commercials.

Kraft General Food also manages to combine centralized European marketing with local brand sensitivity. It does not, for example, market a multinational ground coffee brand, but it does own over a dozen such brands in various European countries where it is the uncontested number one.

> Because of the way the company grew, mainly via acquisitions, we control many local brands. There was a tentative effort by Klaus Jacobs (the former proprietor of Jacobs Suchard which was

bought by General Foods) to internationalize them. But it has been abandoned. Discouraged by the costs of such an alignment, management also recognized the gigantic waste that killing off the local brands, rich in capital and heritage, would represent. (Subramanian, 1993)

This attitude is very different from the one adopted by Mars. Has Mars carried things too far by investing major sums in the name changes of successful brands: Raider to Twix, Marathon to Snickers, Kal-Kan to Whiskas? Too much centralization leads naturally to excessive standardization.

In Europe, the dominant concept seems to be "brand locally and harmonize positioning globally", taken as a way to manage European diversity. For the Americans, on the contrary, the natural concept seems to be "brand and position globally".

Brand and position locally

Strategy #4 will be adopted in environments where the local forces are strong and the global forces weak. In general, it is considered that this situation prevails in the food sector where tastes, flavours, colours are important factors.

This strategy of complete decentralization seems more and more difficult to maintain for an international firm, because *speed and scale* are and will be more and more crucial success factors in the newly integrated European market.

> We were at trouble competing well with companies like P&G because we needed speed and scale – and we didn't have that when we had to go through 16 or 17 countries, explains Alfred Jung, one of Lever's first Euromanagers. (Dalgic, 1992)

At Unilever, two types of difference can exist: (a) same product but different brand names or (b) same brand name but different products.

> Iced sparkling tea is sold under the brand name Liptonic in France, Lipton Ice Tea in Belgium and Lipton Ice in the United Kingdom. On the other hand, under the same brand name Lipton Ice Tea, the drink is sparkling in France and non-sparkling in France. Similarly, Calvé is a salty mayonnaise in Belgium and a sweet one in Holland.

It is clear that with the development of cross-border purchases, this diversity of brand names and content is very confusing for the consumer and that some degree of standardization is required. In the European context, the word *harmonization* of branding policies rather than "standardization" is probably more appropriate.

Brand portfolio management

It is not only necessary to create and manage a brand; it is also essential for the company to manage successfully a *portfolio of brands*. Many companies own many brands and the relationships between these brands have to be managed in a logical way in the brand portfolio. Acquisitions often leave companies with far more brands than they can profitably handle. Taking a stricter look at marketing resources forces companies to look more critically at their brand portfolio composition. There are a number of issues to address:

- How do brands relate to the corporate brand?
- What do the brands derive from the parent brand? And what do they give back?
- What role does each brand have in the portfolio?
- Are the different brands and sub-brands sufficiently differentiated?

- Does the customer understand the differentiation?
- Is the whole architecture of the brand portfolio greater than the sum of its parts?

This is a complex matter and currently a very hot topic for marketers. In order to manage a brand portfolio properly, it is essential to follow the following steps:

Each brand should have a clear role to play within the portfolio

For example, in Europe Ariel is targeted to the demanding housewives that are looking for a superior cleaning performance, Bonux is targeted to housewives looking for a value for money proposition, Dreft is targeted to housewives who want to treat their garments carefully and Vizir is targeted to housewives searching for simplicity and rapidity. Each brand is positioned on a distinctive benefit.

Each brand should be ensured to receive the right level of resources from the company (financial, sales, R&D)

For example, L'Oreal has made clear decisions in the way they manage their innovations and give priority to their brands. They first release the best innovations through the premium brands in the selective distribution channel such as Lancôme and then through the L'Oréal brand in supermarkets at a later stage.

The firm should clearly know which brand to build, which brand to eliminate, which brand to extend or even to acquire

For this, the firm must know which segments of the market the firm wants to cover by priority. A manager having portfolio responsibilities can only do this at the highest level of the organization. The ideal brand portfolio will have the following characteristics:

- Fits the company future vision and destination.
- Prioritizes markets and key segments.
- Efficiently covers those priority segments.

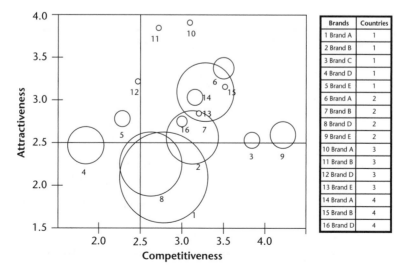

Figure 14.7 A multi-factor brand portfolio
Source: Industry.

- Ruthlessly prunes out those that do not fit.
- Fills gaps through new or extended brands and acquisitions.

To achieve these objectives the techniques of portfolio analyses are useful and in particular the multi-factor portfolio matrix. An example of a brand portfolio in the food sector is presented in Figure 14.7.

Examples of indicators of market attractiveness and of competitiveness (brand's strengths) are presented in Table 14.5 with a set of scores for each indicator proposed by Davidson (1997). This type of quantified analysis is a useful graphic device for comparing the competitive positions of brands on common criteria and for guiding strategic investment priorities. Answers to the following questions can be obtained:

- On what basis should brands be invested in for future growth?
- Which should be maintained as local players, which should enter the global arena? And, if they should, how?

Table 14.5 Example of brand portfolio score sheet

Market attractiveness		Brand's strengths	
Score sheet	Maximum score	Score sheet	Maximum score
– Market size	8	– Brand profitability	12
– Market growth rate	15	– Relative consumer value	15
– Profitability	20	– Relative brand share	9
– Pricing trends	10	– Market sector position	7
– Competitive intensity	10	– Sales level and trend	7
– Failure risk	6	– Differentiation	12
– Opportunity to differentiate	10	– Distribution strength	7
		– Innovation record	6
– Segmentation	9	– Extendibility	10
– Retail structure	12	– Awareness and loyalty	7
		– Investment support (adv. and R&D)	8
Total	**100**	**Total**	**100**

Source: Davidson (1997).

Table 14.6 Examples of brand proliferation

Colgate-Palmolive	Crest
Colgate	Crest
Colgate 2 in 1	Crest Dual Action Whitening
Colgate Baking Soda and Peroxide	Crest Multi-care
Colgate Fresh Confidence	Crest Neat Squeeze
Colgate Max fresh	Crest Sensitive
Colgate Sensitive	Crest Tartar Protection
Colgate Simply White	Crest Vivid White
Colgate Sparkling White	Crest Whitening
Colgate Total Whitening	Crest Whitening Expression
Colgate Cavity Protection	Crest Extra Whitening
Colgate Tartar Control	Crest Rejuvenating Effects
Colgate Total	Crest Cavity Protection
Colgate Children's	Crest Kids
(2 in 1 Kids, Colgate Barbie, Blue's Clues, Fairly Odd Parents)	

Source: Industry.

- What can be extended?
- What should be sold off or killed?

Portfolio analysis also a firm to avoid major mistakes in portfolio management, the major mistake being to allow each brand to be managed in isolation because what is right for an individual brand may be wrong for the portfolio. Here are the major mistakes:

- Too many brands in too many segments; there may be too many brands in relation to consumer needs, retailer space and company ability to promote.
- Duplication and overlap.
- Gaps in priority market segments.
- Inefficiencies in operation and the supply chain.
- Diffused and therefore ineffective resource allocation.

The use of a family tree can also be useful (Aaker 2004) to evaluate the portfolio structure.

For more information regarding the impact of good brand portfolio strategy and firm performance, see Morgan and Rego (2009) who have analysed 72 firms in consumer markets over 10 years.

Chapter Summary

A brand is perceived by a potential customer as a bundle of attributes and of mental associations which, taken together, will form the distinctive elements of the brand identity. The composition of the bundle, the relative importance and the perceived presence of the attributes will contribute to influence potential customers' purchasing decision. Brands are now present everywhere. They exist because they generate trust. This trust is based on a close relationship that brands have built over the years with consumers. The brand plays an important role in a market economy, not only for the customer, but for the producer as well. In this chapter, the brand functions in the B2C and in the B2B markets are examined. Having decided to cover by priority one or several segments, the firm has to "position" its offering (brand) in a way which is both consistent with potential customers' expectations and different from competitors' offerings. It consists in giving a "raison d'être" to a product. Kapferer (1991/2004) has developed the "brand identity prism" that defines the brand identity in terms of six facets. Brand positioning and brand identity are manufacturer's concepts. They have been created by the seller and should not be confused with the brand image. The brand image is the perception of the brand identity in the minds of consumers. In both definitions, the concept refers to the brand's strength which can vary largely among brands and which is determined by its awareness, personality, perceived quality, leadership or stock value. The brand equity concept was created to summarize the strengths of a brand because traditional data such as market share or volume sold were not satisfactory to reflect the value of a brand, and because they do not take into account the association that exists in the consumers' mind. Brand architecture is the way in which the brands within a company's portfolio are related to, and differentiated from, one another. The architecture should specify brand roles and the nature of relationships between brands. Companies have used the brand extension/stretching strategies frequently in the last few years. The idea is to benefit directly from the awareness and image of a strong existing brand by using the same brand name for launching new products in different categories. It is clear that international and global brands present many important advantages to the firm. They permit the generation of strong economies of scale. It is well-known that a globalized brand can generate significant cost reductions in all areas of the business system, including R&D, manufacturing and logistics.

BIBLIOGRAPHY

Aaker, D.A. (1991), *Managing Brand Equity*, New York, The Free Press.

Aaker, D.A. (1996), *Managing Strong Brands*, New York, The Free Press.

Aaker, D.A. (2004), *Brand Portfolio Strategy*, New York, The Free Press.

Aaker, D.A. and Joachimsthaller, E. (2000), *Brand Leadership*, New York, The Free Press.

Barwise, P. and Meehan, S. (2010), The One Thing You Must Get Right When Building a Brand, *Harvard Business Review*, December, pp. 80–4.

Caron, G. (1996), Le devenir des marques, *Futuribles*, Févier, pp. 27–42.

Court, D., Freeling, A., Leiter, M. and Parsons, A.J. (1996), Uncovering the Value of Brands, *The McKinsey Quarterly*, 4, pp. 176–8.

Dalgic, T. (1992), Euromarketing: Charting the Map for Globalization, *International Marketing Review*, 9, 5, pp. 31–42.

Davidson, H. (1997), *Even More Offensive Marketing*, London, Penguin Books.

Day, G.S. (1981), Product Life Cycle's Analysis and Applications, *Journal of Marketing*, 45, 4, pp. 60–7.

de Maricourt, R. (1997), *Marketing Européen: Stratégies et Actions*, Paris, Publi-Union.

Doyle, P. (1994/2003), *Marketing Management and Strategy*, New York, Prentice-Hall, 1st and 2nd editions.

Edelman, D.C. (2010), Branding in the Digital Age: You're Spending Your Money in All the Wrong Places, *Harvard Business Review*, December, pp. 62–9.

Feldwick, P. (1996), What Is Brand Equity Anyway, and How Do You Measure It?, *Journal of Market Research Society*, 38, 2, pp. 85–104.

Fournier, S. and Lee, L. (2009), Getting Brand Communities Right, *Harvard Business Review*, April, pp. 105–11.

Fraser, I. (1990), Now only the Name's not the Same, *Eurobusiness*, April, pp. 22–5.

Hinkle, J. (1966), *Life Cycles*, New York, Nielsen Cy.

Holt, D.B., Quelch, J.A. and Taylor, E.L. (2004), How Global Brands Compete, *Harvard Business Review*, September, pp. 103–11.

Interbrand (2010), *Best Global Brands 2010*, www.interbrand.com.

Kapferer, J.N. (1991), *Les Marques Capital de l'entreprise*, Paris, Editions d'Organisation.

Kapferer, J.N. (2004/2008), *The New Strategic Brand Management*, London, Kogan Page.

Keller, K.L. (1998), *Strategic Brand Management*, Upper Saddle River, NJ, Prentice-Hall, 1st and 2nd editions.

Keller, K.L. (2000), The Brand Report Card, *Harvard Business Review*, 78, 1, pp. 147–57.

Krasnikov, A., Mishra, S. and Orozco, D. (2009), Evaluating the Financial Impact of Branding Using Trademarks: A Framework and Empirical Evidence, *Journal of Marketing*, 73, pp. 154–66.

Lambin, J.J. (1989), La marque et le comportement de choix de l'acheteur, in *La marque*, Kapferer, J.N. and Thoenig, J.C. (eds), Paris, Ediscience international.

Malaval, P.H. (1998/2001), *Strategy and Management of Industrial Brands, Business to Business, Products & Services*, Kluwer Academic Publishers.

Mizik, N. and Jacobson, R. (2009), Valuing Branded Businesses, *Journal of Marketing*, 73, pp. 137–53.

Morgan, N.A. and Rego, L.L. (2009), Brand Portfolio Strategy and Firm Performance, *Journal of Marketing*, 73, pp. 59–74.

Nerlove, M. and Arrow, K. (1962), Optimal Advertising Policy under Dynamic Conditions, *Economica*, 29, pp. 131–45.

Rego, L.L., Billett, M.T. and Morgan, N.A. (2009), Consumer-Based Brand Equity and Firm Risk, *Journal of Marketing*, 73, pp. 47–60.

Sandler, D.M. and Shani, D. (1992), Brand Globally but Advertise Locally, an Empirical Investigation, *International Marketing Review*, 9, 4, pp. 18–31.

Schau, H.J., Muniz Jr., A.M. and Arnould, E.J. (2009), How Brand Community Practices Create Value, *Journal of Marketing*, 73, pp. 30–51.

Schuiling, I. and Kapferer, J.N. (2004), Real Differences between Local and International Brands: Strategic Implications for International Marketers, *Journal of International Marketing*, 12, 4, pp. 97–112.

Subramanian, D. (1993), In Search of Eurobrands, *Media & Marketing*, pp. 22–3.

The Economist (2011), Why consumers balk at companies'efforts to rebrand themselves? December 15.

Variot, J.F. (1985), *L'identité de marque*, Paris, Institut de recherches et d'études publicitaires, Journées d'études de l'IREP, Juin.

Walden, D. (1993), Kano's Methods for Understanding Customer-defined Quality: Introduction to Kano's Methods, *Center for Quality Management Journal*, 2, 4.

CHAPTER FIFTEEN

DISTRIBUTION CHANNEL DECISIONS

In most markets, the physical and psychological distance between producers and end-users is such that intermediaries are necessary to ensure an efficient matching between segments of demand and supply. Distributors and facilitating agencies are required because manufacturers are unable to assume by themselves, at a reasonable cost, all the tasks and activities implied by a free and competitive exchange process. The use of intermediaries means a loss of manufacturer control of certain distributive functions, since the firm sub-contracts activities that could, in principle, be assumed by marketing management. Thus, from the firm's point of view, channel decisions are critical ones, which involve developing a channel structure that fits the firm's strategy and the needs of the target segment. The design of a channel structure is a major strategic decision, neither frequently made nor easily changed. In this chapter, we shall first examine the channel design decisions from the manufacturer's point of view (see Figure 15.1) and then analyse the type of positioning strategies available to retailers in consumer markets.

Learning Objectives

When you have read this chapter, you should be able to:

- Understand the role and the functions performed by distribution channels in a market economy
- Understand why companies use distribution channels and the tasks performed by the different actors in these channels
- Identify the main configurations of a distribution channel and analyse the distribution cost structure of each possible channel
- Explain the different market coverage and communication strategies open to the manufacturer
- Understand the emerging role of private labels in B2C markets
- Describe the alternative entry strategies in foreign markets open to the international firm

15.1 THE ECONOMIC ROLE OF DISTRIBUTION CHANNELS

A distribution channel is the structure formed by the interdependent partners participating in the process of making goods or services available for consumption or use by consumers or industrial users. These partners are the producers, intermediaries and end-users. Distribution channels are *organized* structures performing the tasks necessary to facilitate

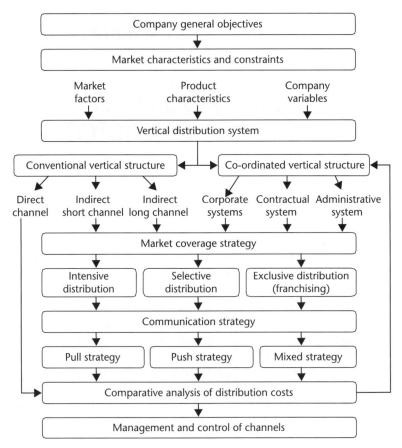

Figure 15.1   Overview of distribution channel decisions
Source: Lambin (2000/2007).

exchange transactions. Their role in a market economy is to bridge the gap between manufacturers and end-users by making goods available where and when they are needed and
under the appropriate terms of trade. The functions of a distribution channels are to create
time, space and state utilities that constitute the added value of distribution.

The tasks of distribution

Channels of distribution provide many functions. These occur for the benefit of the producer
or consumer or both. For producers, distribution channels perform seven different functions:

1. *Transporting:* to make the goods available in places close to consumers or industrial
   users.
2. *Breaking of bulk:* to make the goods available in quantity or volume adapted to consumers' purchasing habits.
3. *Storing:* to make the goods available at the time of consumption, thereby reducing the
   manufacturer's need to store its own products in company-owned warehouses.
4. *Sorting:* to constitute a selection of goods for use in association with each other and
   adapted to the buyer's use.
5. *Contacting:* to establish personalized relationships with customers who are numerous
   and remote.

6. *Informing:* to collect and disseminate information about market needs and about products and terms of trade.
7. *Promoting:* to promote the products through advertising and promotions organized at the point of sales.

In addition to these basic functions, intermediaries also provide services such as financial credit, guarantees, delivery, repairs, maintenance, atmosphere and so on. The main economic role of distribution channels is *to overcome the existing disparities* between demand and supply.

The distribution flows

These functions give rise to distribution flows between partners in the exchange process. Some of these flows are forward flows (ownership, physical and promotion), others are backward flows (ordering and payment) and still others move in both directions (information). The five main flows are the following:

1. *Ownership flow:* the actual transfer of legal ownership from one organization to another.
2. *Physical flow:* the successive movements of the physical product from the producer to the end-user.
3. *Ordering flow:* the orders placed by intermediaries in the channel and forwarded to the manufacturer.
4. *Payment flow:* successive buyers paying their bills through financial institutions to sellers.
5. *Information flow:* the dissemination of information to the market and/or to the producer at the initiative of the producer and/or the intermediaries.

The key question in designing a channel of distribution is not whether these functions and flows need to be performed, but rather who is to perform them. These functions and the management of these distribution flows can be shifted between channel's partners. The problem is to decide who could perform these economic functions most efficiently: the producer, the intermediary or the consumer.

Rationale for marketing channels

The distribution functions cannot be eliminated, but rather simply assumed by other more efficient channel members. Innovations in distribution channels largely reflect the discovery of more efficient ways to manage these economic functions or flows. Various sources of efficiency enable intermediaries to perform distribution functions at a lower cost than either the customer or the manufacturer could by himself or herself. This is particularly true for consumer goods, which are distributed to a large number of geographically dispersed customers.

Contractual efficiency

The complexity of the exchange process increases as the number of partners increases. As shown in Figure 15.2, the number of contacts required to maintain mutual interactions between all partners in the exchange process is much higher in a decentralized exchange system than in a centralized one. Figure 15.2 shows that, given three manufacturers and five retailers who buy goods from each other, the number of contacts required amounts to 15. If the manufacturer sells to these retailers through one wholesaler, the number of necessary

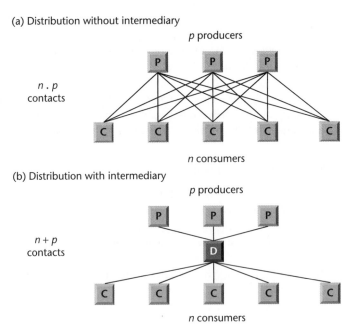

Figure 15.2 Contractual efficiency of distribution

contacts is reduced to eight. Thus, a centralized system employing intermediaries is more efficient than a decentralized system of exchange, by reducing the number of transactions required for matching segments of demand and supply.

Economies of scale

By grouping the products of several manufacturers, intermediaries can perform one or more distribution tasks more efficiently than manufacturers. For example, a wholesaler's sales representative can spread costs over several manufacturers and perform the selling function at a lower cost per manufacturer than if each firm paid its own company sales representative.

Reduction of functional discrepancies

By purchasing large volumes of goods from manufacturers, storing them and breaking them down into the volume customers prefer to purchase, wholesalers and retailers enable manufacturers and their customers to operate at a more efficient scale. Rather than having to make small production runs to fill the orders of individual customers, manufacturers can achieve economies of scale. Similarly, their customers can buy small quantities without having their capital tied up in large inventories.

If a particular organization is responsible for two separate functions (for instance, manufacturing and distribution) that have different optimum levels of operations, there is a risk for one of the two functions, or even for each of them, to operate at a sub-optimum level. Costs go up and prices have to be higher. When some functions are sub-contracted to middlemen the producer's costs and prices are lower.

Better assortment

At the manufacturer's level, the assortment of goods produced is largely dictated by technological considerations, whereas the assortment of goods consumers usually desire is dictated by the use situation. Typically, consumers desire a *limited quantity of a wide variety of goods*. The role of intermediaries is to create wide assortments and to make it possible for consumers to acquire a large variety of products from a single source with one transaction. This reduces the time and effort that consumers must expend in finding the goods they need. The same economy of effort also exists on the manufacturer's side. For example, a manufacturer of a limited line of hardware items could open its own retail outlets only if it were willing to accumulate a large variety of items generally sold at this type of outlet. In general, hardware wholesalers can perform this assortment function more efficiently than individual manufacturers.

Better services

The intermediary is close to the end-users and therefore can have a better understanding of their needs and desires and adapt the assortment to local situations.

The superior efficiency of intermediaries in a market system is not absolute however. A particular middleman will survive in the channel structure as long as the other channel partners in the exchange process consider that there is no other more efficient way to perform the function. Thus, the issue of who should perform various distribution tasks is one of relative efficiency.

15.2   CHANNEL DESIGN ALTERNATIVES

The design of a channel structure implies decisions regarding the responsibilities to be assumed by the different participants in the exchange process. From the manufacturer's point of view, the first decision is whether or not to sub-contract certain distribution tasks and, if so, to what extent to sub-contract and under which trade conditions.

Types of intermediary

There are four broad categories of intermediary that a firm might include in the distributive network of its product: wholesalers, retailers, agents and facilitating agencies.

Wholesalers

These intermediaries sell primarily to other resellers, such as retailers or institutional or industrial customers, rather than to individual consumers. They take title of the goods they store and can provide quick delivery when the goods are ordered because they are usually located closer to customers than manufacturers. The case of wholesalers in the pharmaceutical industry described in Exhibit 15.1 is illustrative in this respect.

They purchase in large lots from manufacturers and resell in smaller lots to retailers. Wholesalers generally bring together an assortment of goods, usually of related items, by dealing with several sources of supply. In the food industry, full-service wholesalers have been confronted with the competition of mass retail distributors who have assumed by themselves the wholesaling function. Wholesalers have reacted by creating *voluntary chains* that consist of a wholesaler-sponsored group of independent retailers engaged in bulk buying and in common merchandising.

There are two types of wholesalers: Cash-and-carry ones operate stores, similar to warehouses, where they sell food and drink, mostly to traditional retailers and small Hotel-Restaurant-Café (HORECA). Customers select and take away their purchases themselves. Delivery wholesalers, by contrast, deliver goods from their warehouses direct to their

---

Exhibit 15.1   Wholesalers in the pharmaceutical industry

- How 350 pharmaceutical laboratories and 250 suppliers of para-pharmaceutical products can respond as rapidly as possible to the needs of 22,000 French pharmacies, knowing that 12 million health products are sold every day?

- To do the job specialty wholesalers have netted the French territory with warehouses to meet this demand. As a result, today these wholesalers distribute 81 per cent of health products. The remaining

19 per cent are delivered directly to hospitals (12 per cent) or to pharmacies (7 per cent).

- Twice a day, pharmacists place their orders through tele-transmission, to be served early afternoon before the end of schools' closing hour, or the following morning before the store's opening hour. The staff has less than two hours to handle the orders.

Source: Le Monde, 16 March 1993.

---

customers, mostly mid-sized large service operators. Delivery wholesalers are particularly numerous; generally small, local family businesses, they supply 50 to 60 per cent of the market in all countries. Cash-and-carry outlets serve 10 to 20 per cent of it and other intermediaries, such as retail hypermarkets and a few food manufacturers, supply the rest. Wholesalers play an important role in European markets.

Retailers

Retailers sell goods and services directly to consumers for their personal, non-business use. Retailers take the ownership of the goods they carry, and their compensation is the margin between what they pay for the goods and the price they charge their customers. There are several schemes for classifying retailers. A traditional classification makes a distinction between three types of independent retailers: food retailers, specialty retailers and artisan retailers (bakers and butchers).

They can also be classified according to the level of service they provide (self-service versus full-service retailing) or according to their method of operation (low margin/high turnover or high margin/low turnover). Low margin/high turnover retailers compete primarily on a price basis, while high margin/low turnover retailers focus on unique assortment, specialty goods, services and prestigious store image. The number of independent retailers has drastically decreased in most European countries, mainly due to the competition of mass merchandisers.

Integrated distribution

Since the beginning of the century, profound changes have taken place in the distribution sector and it is useful to briefly summarize this evolution:

- The first revolution goes back to 1852 with the establishment of the first *department store* in Paris. The innovating principles were broad assortment, low mark-ups and rapid turnover, marking and displaying the prices, free entry without pressure or obligation to purchase. The best-known department stores today are Harrods in London, Galeries Lafayettes in Paris, Macy's in New York, La Renascente in Milan and so on.

- The next generation of stores was the *specialty-stores chain* located in suburban shopping centres closer to consumers. A store concept based on a limited assortment and economies of scale due to large purchased quantities.

- The next generation was the *popular store*, which sells goods at low prices by accepting lower margins, working on higher volume and providing minimum service (typically Prisunic in France and Belgium).
- The fourth revolution is the *supermarket* revolution; a store concept based on self-service operations and designed to serve the consumer's total needs for food, laundry and household maintenance products. The one-stop shopping concept, supermarkets have moved towards larger stores, the superstore or the *hypermarché* as Carrefour in France.

The supermarket concept has been extremely successful in Europe, in particular in the FMCG sector. Six managerial rules characterized this selling formula:

1. A broad assortment and wide variety of popular merchandise to facilitate multiple-item purchases and fast stock rotation.
2. A low purchase price thanks to the high volume purchased and strong bargaining power vis-à-vis suppliers.
3. Low margins and low sales prices.
4. Dynamic promotional activities in order to stimulate store traffic.
5. Economies of scale on physical distribution (in transportation, handling and packaging).
6. Long credit terms (typically 90 days) for products usually sold within 15 days in order to generate substantial financial by-products.

Exhibit 15.2   Forms of co-operation between resellers

Retailer co-operatives

Groups of independent retailers forming their own co-operative chain organization. Typically, they agree to concentrate their purchases by forming their own wholesale operations. In many cases, they also engage in joint advertising, promotion and merchandising programmes.

Wholesales-sponsored voluntary chains

Wholesalers organize voluntary chains by getting independent retailers to sign contracts in which they agree to standardize their selling practices and to purchase a certain proportion of their inventories from the wholesaler. This gives the wholesaler greater buying power in its dealings with manufacturers. Some voluntary chains also have a common brand store.

Franchise systems

Franchising is a form of co-operation between distinct enterprises in which a supplier (franchisor) grants a dealer (franchisee) the right to sell products for some type of consideration, such as some percentage of total sales. The franchisor helps to furnish equipment, buildings, management know-how and marketing assistance.

The franchisee must agree to operate according to the rules of the franchisor.

Rack jobbing

Rack jobbers perform purchasing and stocking function for retailers. Impulse products that have short life cycles (such as toys, books, records) may be supplied by rack jobbers to avoid the inconvenience to retailers of having to deal with unfamiliar products. They physically maintain the goods by refilling shelves, fixing displays and maintaining inventory records. Retailers only have to furnish space. Thus limited-service wholesalers usually operates on a consignment basis. The retailer is remunerated by some percentage of sales.

Cash and carry wholesalers

Cash and carry wholesalers are limited-service wholesalers that sell to customers who will pay cash and furnish transportation or pay extra to have products delivered. The middlemen usually handle a limited line of products such as groceries, construction materials, electrical supplies or office supplies.

Source: Authors.

This selling formula has given a substantial competitive advantage to integrated distributors over independent retailers. The situation is changing today as new expectations emerge among consumers and as independent distributors propose new store concepts.

The new food discounters

The fifth revolution in mass merchandising is currently taking place with a new breed of retailers called the *hard discounters*, led mainly in Western Europe by the German distributors Aldi and Lidl. It is a retailing system characterized by the permanent and generalized adoption of low prices, thanks to a systematic cost control and limited service policies.

The main features of discount retailing, sometimes called *minimum marketing*, as observed in a typical Aldi store, are the following:

- a limited store size included between 3,000 and 7,000 square feet in the United Kingdom, the average size in France being 662 square metres (*LSA*, 1998);
- a small product range, approximately 600 lines, with a single offer per product category, mainly set out in full boxes on pallets;
- approximately 70 per cent of the range is own brand or at least a brand name with a "packed exclusively for Aldi" qualification;
- prices aim to be 20–25 per cent lower than average major multiples;
- limited number (four or five) of multi-functional sales attendants;
- prices are memorized by checkout operators and there is no ePoS;
- only cash payments, credit cards are not accepted;
- plastic bags are charged for and the stores are often renovated warehouses or cinemas.

According to a survey published by the *LSA* (1998), hard discounting is in good shape in France with more than 2,000 units in 1998 and a growing market share of 6 to 7 per cent, with the German retail giants Lidl and Aldi leading, followed by Leader Price and ED Le Marché Discount. The growth of hard discounters is also significant in the United Kingdom, with Aldi and Rewe (Penny) from Germany and Netto from Denmark. The two UK discount chains, Kwik Save and Lo Cost, dominate the discounting market.

Agents

These are functional intermediaries who do not take title of the goods with which they deal but who negotiate sales or purchases for clients or principals. They are compensated in the form of a commission on sales or purchases. They are independent business persons or freelance salespeople who represent client organizations. Common types of agent include import or export agents, traders, brokers and manufacturers' representatives. Manufacturers' representatives usually work for several firms and carry non-competitive, complementary goods in an exclusive territory or foreign country.

Facilitating agencies

Facilitating agencies are business firms that assist in the performance of distribution tasks other than buying, selling and transferring title. From the firm's standpoint, they are subcontractors carrying out certain distribution tasks because of their specialization or special expertise. Common types of facilitating agencies are transportation agencies, storage agencies, advertising agencies, market research firms, financial agencies, insurance companies and so on. These agencies are involved in a marketing channel on an as-needed basis and they are compensated by commissions or fees paid for their services.

Many different types of institutions participate in a distribution channel. The channel structure will be determined by the manner in which the different distribution tasks have been allocated among the channel participants.

Cybermediaries

With the development of e-commerce, new types of intermediaries emerge performing key functions that make exchanges easier, cut the costs of carrying out the sales transaction and improve the responsiveness to customers' needs. These functions are the following:

- *Aggregation*. The aggregated demand of buyers by a single intermediary or the aggregation of several suppliers by a distributor are alternatives to the situation where each buyer must find a direct source of good and each producer must sell products directly to individual customers. This aggregation process cuts transaction costs and favours economies of scale.
- *Trust*. Intermediaries can also provide a guarantee and protect buyers (or sellers) against opportunistic or manipulative actions. This function is particularly important in the anonymous world of e-commerce, where mechanisms assuring confidence in the retailer, confidentiality and security are not yet fully established.
- *Facilitation*. Transferring information to a decentralized market can be costly because each participant must seek out and exchange information with other economic players. A broker can speed up this process. Intermediaries can also speed up exchanges by offering associated services, such as managing financial and administrative arrangements.
- *Matching*. Intermediaries have several ways to find buyers and vice versa. They can be database administrators, focusing efforts on customer about suppliers' preferences and sending selective information.

As e-commerce continues to develop, these new intermediary functions will grow more important and sophisticated (Jallat and Capek, 2001).

Configurations of a distribution channel

Distribution channels can be characterized by the number of intermediary levels that separate the manufacturer from the end-user. Figure 15.3 shows the different channel designs commonly used to distribute industrial or consumer goods. A distinction can be made between direct and indirect distribution systems:

- In a *direct distribution system*, the manufacturer sells directly to the end-user and there is no intermediary in the channel. This structure is also called a direct marketing system.
- In an *indirect distribution system*, one or several intermediaries participate and bring the product closer to the final buyer. An indirect system is said to be "short" or "long" depending on the number of intermediary levels.

In the field of consumer goods, distribution channels tend to be long and involve several intermediaries, typically wholesalers and retailers. In industrial markets, channels are generally shorter, particularly when buyers are large and well identified. From the producer's point of view, the longer the channel, the more difficult the problem of control.

In most market situations, companies use *multiple channels* to reach their target segments, either to create emulation among distributors or to reach separate target segments having

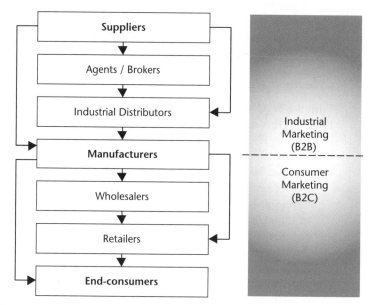

Figure 15.3   Structure of a conventional vertical marketing system
Source: Lambin (2000/2007).

different purchasing habits. For example, many industrial companies use distributors to sell and service small accounts and their own sales force to handle large accounts.

Types of competition among distributors

In a distributive network several types of competition may exist among distributors (Palamountain, 1955):

- *Horizontal competition*. The same type of intermediaries at the same channel level competing with each other.
- *Intertype competition*. Different types of intermediaries at the same channel level competing with each other (self-service versus full-service).
- *Vertical competition*. Channel members at different levels in the channel competing with each other, such as retailers integrating the wholesaling function or vice versa.
- *Channel system competition*. Complete channel systems competing with each other as units. For instance, the competition between indirect distribution through wholesalers and retailers and direct marketing through direct mail.

Distribution has experienced large changes over the last 30 years, which have contributed to reinforcing the competitive struggle among intermediaries. The growth of vertical marketing systems illustrates this evolution. For more details on distribution network redesign and marketing competitiveness, see Shang, Yildirim, Tadikamalla, Mittal and Brown (2009).

15.3   FACTORS AFFECTING THE CHANNEL STRUCTURE

The selection of a particular channel design is largely determined by a set of constraints related to market and buyer behaviour factors and to product and company characteristics. These factors and their implications for the channel configuration are described in Table 15.1.

Table 15.1 Factors affecting channel structure

Influencing factors	Channel structure			
	Direct	Indirect short	Indirect long	Comments
Market factors				
Large number of buyers		**	***	
High geographical dispersion		**	***	
Purchases in large quantity	***			
Buying highly seasonal		**	***	
Product characteristics				
Perishable products	***			
Complex products	***			
Newness of the product	***	**		
Heavy and bulky products	***			
Standardized products		**	***	
Low unit value		**	***	
Company variables				
Large financial capacity	***	**		
Complete assortment	***	**		
High control sought	***	**		

Source: Authors.

The number of potential buyers determines the *size of the market*. A very general heuristic rule about market size relative to channel structure is if the market is large, intermediaries are more likely to be needed. Conversely, if the market is small, a firm is more likely to avoid the use of intermediaries and to assume most of the distribution tasks. Also, the more *geographically dispersed* the market, the more difficult and expensive distribution is. The more geographically dispersed the market, the more likely it is that intermediaries will be used because of the high costs involved in providing adequate services to many dispersed customers.

Patterns of buying behaviour also influence the channel structure. If customers typically buy in very *small quantities* and if demand is highly *seasonal* a long distribution channel involving several intermediaries will be more appropriate.

Product variables

Characteristics of the product also determine the channel structure. Channels should be as short as possible for highly *perishable products*. Heavy and *bulky products* have very high handling and shipping costs and the firm should try to minimize these by shipping the goods only in truckload quantities to a limited number of places; the channel structure should also be short.

Short structures are also desirable for *complex and technical products* requiring extensive after-sales service and assistance in use. Similarly, for *innovative products* requiring aggressive promotion in the introductory stage of the PLC, a shorter channel will facilitate the development and control of promotion activities aiming at creating product acceptance by the market. Long channel structures will be more adequate, on the other hand, when products are highly standardized and when they have *low unit value*. In this latter case, many other products handled by the intermediaries can share the costs of distribution.

For example, it would be difficult to imagine the sales of packages of crisps by the Smiths Company to the consumer. Only by spreading the costs of distribution over the wide variety of products handled by wholesale and retail intermediaries is it possible to buy a packet of crisps at retail for €1.20.

A manufacturer's channel choice is also influenced by the *extent of its product line*. The manufacturer with only one item may have to use wholesaling intermediaries, whereas it could go directly to retailers if it made several products that could be combined on a large scale. A retailer ordinarily cannot buy a truckload of washing machines alone, but it might buy a truckload of mixed appliances.

Company variables

The key variables here are the size and the financial capability of the producer. Large firms in general have large financial resources and therefore the capacity to assume several distribution tasks directly, thereby reducing their dependence on intermediaries. Several distribution activities, such as transportation and storage, imply fixed costs. Large companies are better able to bear these costs. On the other hand, the use of intermediaries implies a cost, which is proportional to the volume of activity, since their compensation takes the form of commissions on actual sales revenue. Therefore, small firms will be inclined to have extensive recourse to intermediaries. In some cases, the entire output is sold under the retailer's brand. The disadvantage of this arrangement is that the producer is completely at the mercy of its one large retailer.

Other considerations are also important. For example, the lack of marketing expertise necessary to perform the distribution tasks may force the firm to use the services of intermediaries. This happens frequently when the firm is penetrating new or foreign markets. Also, high-technology companies built upon the engineering abilities of management often rely heavily on distributors to do the marketing job. A manufacturer may establish as short a channel as possible simply because it wants to *control the distribution* of its product, even though the cost of a more direct channel is higher.

15.4 VERTICAL MARKETING SYSTEMS

If the adopted channel structure is indirect, some degree of *co-operation* and co-ordination must be achieved among the participants in the channel (see Exhibit 15.2). Two forms of vertical organization can exist: conventional vertical structures and co-ordinated vertical structures, called vertical marketing systems:

- In a *conventional vertical structure*, each level of the channel behaves independently as a separate business entity seeking to maximize its own profit, even if it is at the expense of the overall performance of the distribution channel. This is the traditional way in which a distribution network works, where no channel member has control over the others.
- In a *co-ordinated vertical structure*, the participants in the exchange process behave like partners and co-ordinate their activities in order to increase their bargaining power and to achieve operating economies and maximum market impact. In this type of vertical organization, a channel member takes the initiative of co-ordination, be it the manufacturer, the wholesaler or the retailer.

Several forms of vertical marketing system have emerged. A distinction is usually made between corporate, contractual and administered vertical marketing systems.

Corporate vertical marketing systems

In corporate vertically integrated marketing systems a particular firm achieves co-ordination and control through corporate ownership. The firm owning and operating the other units of the channel may be a manufacturer, wholesaler or retailer. Firms such as Bata in shoes and Rodier in clothing own their own retail outlets. However, it is not always the manufacturer that controls the channel system through forward integration. Backward integration occurs when a retailer or a wholesaler assumes ownership of institutions that normally precede them in the channel. Sears in the United States, for example, and Marks & Spencer in the United Kingdom have ownership interest in several manufacturing firms that are important suppliers of their private brands.

Contractual vertical marketing systems

In a contractual vertical marketing system, independent firms operating at different levels of the channel co-ordinate their activities through legal contracts that spell out the rights and duties of each partner. The three basic types of contractual system are retail co-operatives, wholesale-sponsored voluntary chains and franchise systems. Franchise systems have expanded the most in recent years. Their organization is discussed in more detail in the next section.

Administered vertical marketing systems

In this third system, firms participating in the channel co-ordinate their activities through the informal guidance or influence of one of the channel members (and not through ownership or contractual agreements). The leading firm, usually the manufacturer, bases its influence on the brand or company reputation or managerial expertise. Companies like L'Oréal in cosmetics and P&G in detergents are examples of firms having successfully achieved this form of co-operation.

Vertical marketing systems have become the dominant mode of distribution in the field of consumer marketing over the last 20 years. They can be viewed as a new form of competition, *channel system competition*, setting complete channels against other complete channels, as opposed to traditional vertical competition, opposing channel members at different levels of the same channel, that is, retailers versus wholesalers, manufacturer versus wholesaler, and so on. Vertical marketing systems help eliminate the sources of conflict that exist in conventional vertical structures, and increase the market impact of their activities.

15.5   MARKET COVERAGE STRATEGIES

If the decision made by the producer is to use intermediaries to organize the distribution of its products, the firm must then decide on the number of intermediaries to use at each channel level to achieve the market penetration objective. Three basic market coverage strategies are possible:

- Hollywood distributes its chewing gums wherever possible: in food stores, tobacconists, drug stores, through vending machines and so on.
- Pierre Cardin distributes his dresses and women's suits in carefully selected clothing stores and tries to be present in the most elegant shops.
- VAG (Volkswagen Audi Group) distributes its cars through exclusive dealerships; each dealer has an exclusive territory and no other dealer is authorized to carry the VAG makes.

Hollywood is adopting an *intensive* distribution strategy, Cardin a *selective* strategy and VAG an *exclusive* strategy. The best strategy for a given product depends on the nature of the product itself, on the objective being pursued and on the competitive situation.

Consumer goods classifications

In the field of consumer goods, the choice of a particular market coverage strategy is largely determined by the shopping habits associated with the consumers of the distributed product. Consumer goods fall into four sub-groups: convenience goods, shopping goods, specialty goods and unsought goods. The purchasing behaviour associated with these products varies primarily in the amount and type of effort consumers exert in buying these products.

Convenience goods

Convenience products are purchased with as little effort as possible, frequently and in small quantities. We have here a routine buying behaviour. Convenience goods can be further sub-divided into staple goods, impulse goods and emergency goods:

- *Staple goods* are purchased on a regular basis and include most food items. Brand loyalty facilitates routine purchase and the goods must be pre-sold, namely, through repetitive advertising.
- *Impulse goods* are purchased without any planning (crisps, magazines, sweets and so on). These goods must be available in many places; the packaging and the in-store displays in supermarkets are important in the sale of these products.
- *Emergency goods* are those needed to fill an unexpected and urgent need. These goods are purchased immediately as the need emerges and therefore they must be available in many outlets.

For these three product categories, the firm has practically no alternative. These products require intensive market coverage. If the brand is not found at the point of sale, consumers will buy another brand and the sales occasion will be lost.

Shopping goods

Shopping goods are high-perceived-risk products. For these products, consumers are willing to spend time and effort to shop around and to compare product alternatives on criteria such as quality, price, style, features and so on. Examples include major appliances, furniture and clothing, that is, expensive and infrequently bought products. Prospective buyers visit several stores before making a decision and sales personnel have an important role to play by providing information and advice.

For shopping goods, maximal market coverage is not required and a selective distribution system will be more appropriate, more especially as the co-operation of the retailer is necessary.

Specialty goods

Specialty goods are products with unique characteristics and sufficiently important to consumers that they make a special effort to discover them. Examples would include specific brands, fancy goods, exotic foods, deluxe clothing, sophisticated photographic equipment and so on. For these products, prospective buyers do not proceed to comparisons; they search for the outlet carrying the wanted product. Brand loyalty or the distinctive features of the product are the determining factors. For specialty goods, retailers are especially important; thus the firms of such goods will tend to limit their distribution to obtain strong support from the retailers. A selective or exclusive distribution system is the best option for the producer.

Unsought goods

Unsought goods are products that consumers do not know about or know about but do not consider buying. Examples are heat pumps, smoke detectors, encyclopaedias and life insurance. Substantial selling efforts are required for those products. The co-operation of the intermediaries is indispensable, or the firm must adopt a direct marketing system.

Other factors must be taken into consideration in the choice of a market coverage strategy. As a general rule, selective and exclusive distribution systems imply a higher level of co-operation among distributors, a reduction of distribution costs for the supplier and a better control over sales operations. On the other hand, in both cases, there is a voluntary limitation of the product retail availability. Thus potential buyers will have to actively search for the product. The firm must therefore maintain a good balance between the benefits and the demerits of each distribution system.

Intensive distribution

In an intensive distribution system, the firm seeks the maximum possible number of retailers to distribute its product, the largest number of storage points to ensure maximum market coverage and the highest brand exposure. This strategy is appropriate for convenience goods, common raw materials and low-involvement services. The advantages of intensive distribution are to maximize product availability and to generate a large market share due to the brand's broad exposure to potential buyers. There are, however, significant disadvantages or risks associated with this strategy:

- The sales revenue generated by the different retailers varies greatly, while the contact cost is the same for each intermediary. If the firm receives many small orders from an intensive network of small retailers, *distribution* costs (order processing and shipping) can become extremely high and undermine the overall profitability.
- When the product has an intensive distribution in multiple and very diversified sales points, it becomes difficult for the firm to control its marketing strategy: discount pricing, poor customer service and lack of co-operation from retailers are practices difficult to prevent.
- Intensive distribution is hard to reconcile with a *brand image* building strategy and with a specific product positioning strategy due to the lack of control of the distributive network.

For these reasons, market-driven companies are induced to adopt a more selective distributive system once the brand awareness objectives have been achieved.

Selective distribution

In a selective distribution system, the producer uses fewer distributors than the total number of available distributors in a specific geographic area. It is an appropriate strategy for shopping goods that customers buy infrequently and compare for differences in price and product features.

A selective distribution may also be the result of the refusal from distributors to carry the product in their assortment. To have a selective distribution, the firm must decide the criteria upon which to select its intermediaries. Several criteria are commonly used:

The *size of the distributor*, measured by its sales revenue, is the most popular criterion. In the majority of markets, a small number of distributors achieve a significant share of total sales revenue. In the food sector, for instance, the concentration ratio is very high in Switzerland, the United Kingdom and Belgium, where the first five distributors in the food sectors account for 82, 53 and 52 per cent, respectively, of the total turnover (Nielsen, 2009). In these conditions, it is obviously unprofitable to contact all distributors.

- The *quality of the service* provided is also an important criterion. Intermediaries are paid to perform a certain number of well-defined functions and some dealers or retailers are more efficient than others.
- The *technical competence* of the dealer and the availability of up-to-date facilities, mainly for complex products where after-sales service is important, is a third important criterion.

In adopting a selective distribution system, the firm voluntarily agrees to limit the availability of its product in order to reduce its distribution costs and to gain better co-operation from the intermediaries. This co-operation can take various forms:

- Participating in the advertising and promotion budget.
- Accepting new products or unsought products requiring more selling effort.
- Maintaining a minimum level of inventory.
- Transferring information to the producer.
- Providing better services to customers.

The *main risk* of a selective distribution system is to have insufficient market coverage. The producer must verify whether the market knows the distributors handling the brand or the product. If not, the reduced availability of the product could generate significant losses of sales opportunities. It may happen that the firm has in fact no alternative and is forced to maintain a certain degree of selectivity in its distributive network. For example:

- A retailer will accept a new product, which is not yet a proven success, only if it receives an exclusive right to carry the product in its territory.
- If the assortment is large because the consumer must be able to choose among several product forms (design, colour, size), selectivity will be necessary; otherwise the expected sales revenue will be too low to motivate the retailer.
- If the after-sales service implies long and costly training of the dealers, selectivity will be necessary to reduce the costs.

If the firm decides to adopt a selective distribution system, it is important to realize that this decision implies the adoption of a "short" indirect distribution channel. It is very unlikely indeed that wholesalers will agree to voluntarily limit their field of operation simply to meet the strategic objectives of the producer.

Exclusive distribution and franchise systems

In an exclusive distribution system, the manufacturer relies on only one retailer or dealer to distribute its product in a given geographic territory. In turn, the exclusive dealer agrees not to sell any competing brand within the same product category.

Exclusive distribution is useful when a company wants to differentiate its product on the basis of high quality, prestige or excellent customer service. The close co-operation with exclusive dealers facilitates the implementation of the producer's customer service programmes. The advantages and disadvantages of exclusive distribution are the same as in selective distribution, but amplified. A particular form of exclusive distribution is franchising.

Franchising is a contractual, vertically integrated marketing system which refers to a comprehensive method of distributing goods and services. It involves a continuous and contractual relationship in which a *franchiser* provides a licensed privilege to do business and assistance in organizing, training, merchandising, management and other areas in return for a specific consideration from the *franchisee*. Thus, the franchisee agrees to pay an initial fee, plus royalties calculated on the sales revenue, for the right to use a well-known trademarked product or service and to receive continual assistance and services from the franchiser. In fact, the franchisee is buying a proven success from the franchiser.

Types of franchise systems

The franchiser may occupy any position within the channel; therefore there are four basic types of franchise system:

1. The *manufacturer–retailer franchise* is exemplified by franchised automobile dealers and franchised service stations. Singer in the United States, Pingouin and Yves Rocher in France are good examples.
2. The *manufacturer–wholesaler* franchise is exemplified by soft drink companies like Coca-Cola and 7-Up who sell the soft drink syrups they manufacture to franchised wholesalers who, in turn, carbonate, bottle, sell and distribute to retailers.
3. The *wholesaler–retailer* franchise is exemplified by Rexall Drug Stores, by Christianssens in toys and Unic and Disco in food.
4. The *service sponsor–retailer* franchise is exemplified by Avis, Hertz, McDonald's, Midas and Holiday Inn.

The faster growing franchises include business and professional services, fast food, restaurants, car and truck rentals, and home and cleaning maintenance.

Characteristics of a good franchise

A good franchise must be above all a *transferable proven success*, which can be replicated in another territory or environment. According to Sallenave (1979, p. 11), a good franchise must:

- be related to the distribution of a *high-quality* product or service,
- meet a *universal need* or want which is not country- or region-specific,
- be a *proven success* in franchiser-owned and -operated pilot units which serve as models for the other franchisees,
- ensure the full transfer of *know-how* and provide the training of the franchisee in the methods of doing business and modes of operation,
- offer to the franchisees *initial and continuing service* to gain immediate market acceptance and improve modes of operation,
- have a regular *reporting* and *information system* which permits effective monitoring of the performance and collection of market information,
- specify initial franchise *fees* and the royalty fees based on the gross value of a franchisee's sales volume (generally 5 per cent),

- involve the franchisee in the *management* and development of the franchise system,
- specify *legal provisions* for termination, cancellation and renewal of the franchise agreement, as well as for the repurchase of the franchise.

Franchise systems constitute a viable alternative to completely integrated corporate vertical marketing systems. In a franchise system, *funds are provided by the franchisees*, who invest in the stores and in the facilities. From the franchiser's point of view, the establishment of franchised dealers is an ideal means to achieve rapid national or international distribution for its products or services without committing large funds and while keeping the control of the system through contractual agreements.

> John Y. Brown, President of Kentucky Fried Chicken Corporation, has stated that it would have required $450 million for his firm to have established its first 2,700 stores if they would have been company-owned. This sum was simply not available to his firm during the initial stages of its proposed expansion. The use of capital made available from franchisees, however, made the proposed expansion possible. (McGuire, 1971, p. 7)

Thus a franchise system is *an integrated marketing system controlled by the franchiser but financed by the franchisees*. A successful franchise is a partnership in which the mutual interests of both franchiser and franchisees are closely interdependent.

Benefits to the franchiser

The motivations of the franchiser for creating and developing a franchise system are the following:

- To acquire funds without diluting control of the marketing system.
- To keep high flexibility in the use of the capital collected for developing the system.
- To avoid the fixed overhead expenses associated with distribution through company-owned branch units or stores.
- To co-operate with independent business people, the franchisees, who are more likely to work hard at developing their markets than salaried employees.
- To co-operate with local business people well accepted and integrated in the local community or in the foreign country.
- To develop new sources of income based on existing know-how and marketing expertise.
- To achieve faster sales development thanks to the snowball effect generated by the franchising of a successful idea.
- To benefit from economies of scale with the development of the franchise system.

Franchisers provide both initial and continuous services to their franchisees (McGuire, 1971). *Initial services* include market survey and site selection, facility design and layout, lease negotiation advice, financing advice, operating manuals, management training programmes and franchisee employee training. *Continuous services* include field supervision, merchandising and promotional materials, management and employee retraining, quality inspection, national advertising, centralized purchasing, market data and guidance, auditing and record keeping, management reports and group insurance plans.

The franchise system is present in almost all business fields, and total franchise system sales have grown dramatically during the last decade.

Benefits to franchisees

From the perspective of the potential franchisee, the most important appeal is to benefit from the franchiser's reputation of quality and corporate image. Franchising has several other strong appeals that explain the success of this distribution arrangement:

- Franchising enables an individual to enter a business that would be prohibitively expensive if the individual tried to go it alone.
- The amount of uncertainty is reduced, since the business idea has been successfully tested.
- The extensive services provided by the franchiser, both initial and continuous, reduce the risks of the operation.
- Franchising offers better purchasing power, access to better sites and the support of national advertising.
- The introduction of new products and the constant rejuvenation of the product portfolio are made possible.
- Managerial assistance in marketing and finance is provided.
- The opportunity is provided for individuals to operate as independent business people within a large organization.

Franchising is a very flexible organization and many variants exist. *Three basic rules* must be met to have a successful arrangement:

- The will to work as partners.
- The right to mutual control.
- The value of the business idea.

This last condition is crucial. Franchising will work only if the business idea is a proven success. It is not a solution for a firm to declare itself a franchiser if there is no proven success.

15.6   COMMUNICATION STRATEGIES IN THE CHANNEL

Gaining support and co-operation from independent intermediaries is a key success factor for the implementation of the firm's marketing objectives. To obtain this co-operation, the firm can adopt two very distinct communication strategies: a *push* strategy or a *pull* strategy. A third alternative is a combination of the two.

Push strategies

In a push communication strategy, the bulk of the marketing effort is devoted to incentives directed to wholesalers and retailers to induce them to co-operate with the firm, to carry the brands in their range, to keep a minimum level of inventory, to display the products and to give them enough visibility on their shelf spaces. The objective is to win *voluntary co-operation* by offering attractive terms of trade, that, is larger margins, quantity discounts, local or in-store advertising, promotional allowances, in-store sampling and so on. Personal selling and personal communication are the key marketing instruments here. The role of the sales representatives and of the merchandisers will be particularly important. Table 15.2 lists a variety of incentives the firm can use to increase the motivation of channel members.

Table 15.2   Incentives for motivating channel members

Functional performance	Examples of channel incentives
• *Increased purchases or carry large inventories*	Large margins, exclusive territories, buy-in promotions, quantity discounts, buy-back allowances, free goods, shelf-stocking programmes.
• *Increased personal selling effort*	Sales training, instructional materials, incentive programmes for channel members' salespeople.

• *Increased local promotional effort*
  – Local advertising
  – Increased display space
  – In-store promotions
	Co-operative advertising, advertising allowance, print, radio, TV ads for use by local retailers.
	Promotion allowances tied to shelf space.
	Display racks and signs, in-store demonstrations, in-store sampling.

• *Improved customer service*	Service training programmes, instructional materials, high margins on replacement parts, liberal labour cost allowances for warranty service.

Source: Adapted from Boyd and Walker (1990).

A programme of incentives is indispensable to get the support of intermediaries. The larger their negotiation power, the more difficult it will be for the firm to obtain the support of distributors. In markets where distribution is highly concentrated, it is the intermediary who specifies the conditions for carrying the brand. The risk of an exclusive push strategy is the absence of countervailing power and the dependence of the firm on the intermediary who controls access to the market.

The only alternative for the firm is the adoption of a direct marketing system which completely bypasses intermediaries. This is a costly operation, however, since all distribution tasks must then be assumed by the firm. Recent developments in communication technologies present new opportunities, however.

Pull strategies

When adopting a pull strategy, the manufacturer focuses its communication efforts on the end-user, bypassing intermediaries and trying to build company demand directly among potential customers in the target segment. The communication objective is to create strong customer demand and brand loyalty among consumers in order to pull the brand through the distribution channel, forcing the intermediaries to carry the brand to meet consumers' demand.

To achieve these objectives, the manufacturer will spend the largest proportion of its communication budget on media advertising, consumer promotions and direct marketing efforts aimed at winning end-customer preferences. If this branding policy is successful, the manufacturer has the power to influence channel participants and to induce them to carry the brand, since a substantial sales volume will be achieved. The strategic objective is to neutralize the bargaining power of the intermediary who could block access to the market.

> Procter & Gamble generally adopts a pull strategy in its new product launching strategies. However, the consumer advertising campaign starts only when the new brand has achieved almost 100 per cent distribution at retail. It goes without saying that such a result can be achieved only because P&G's sales reps are in position to demonstrate to retailers the advertising that will be organized to support the new product market introduction. Thus, retailers are willing to co-operate with the company.

Pull strategies imply in general large financial resources to cover the costs of brand image advertising campaigns. These costs are fixed overhead expenses, while the costs of a push strategy are proportional to volume and therefore easier to bear, particularly for a small firm.

In fact, a pull strategy must be viewed as a *long-term investment*. The goal of the firm is to create a capital of goodwill, brand *equity*, around the company name or around the brand. A strong brand image is an asset for the firm and is the best argument for obtaining support and co-operation from intermediaries.

In practice, these two communication strategies are used in combination, and it is hard to imagine a market situation where no incentives would be used to motivate intermediaries. With the development of marketing expertise and the increased cost of personal selling, the trend among market-driven companies is to reinforce branding policies and pull communication strategies. As the average cost of a call to a customer made by a salesperson keeps on increasing, the selectivity of mass media tends to improve and therefore to lower the unit cost of a contact through advertising.

15.7   DISTRIBUTION COST ANALYSIS

The distribution cost is measured by the difference between the unit sales price paid by the end-user and the unit cost paid to the producer by the first buyer. Thus, the distribution margin measures the *added value* brought by the distribution channel. If several intermediaries participate in the distribution process, the distribution margin is equal to the sum of the different distributors' margins. The margin of a particular distributor is equal to the difference between its selling price and its purchase cost. The two definitions coincide when there is only one intermediary in the channel.

Trade margins

A trade margin is often expressed as a percentage. This is sometimes confusing, since the margin percentage can be computed on the basis of purchase cost (C) or on the basis of selling price (P). The trade margin (D) is then referred to as a "mark-up" or as a "discount". The conversion rules are presented in Table 15.3.

Suppose a retailer purchases an item for £10 and sells it at a price of £20, that is, at a £10 margin. What is the retailer's margin percentage? As a percentage of the selling price, it is

£10/£20 × 100 = 50 per cent

As a percentage of cost, it is

£10/£10 × 100 = 100 per cent

Trade margins are usually determined on the basis of selling price, but practices do vary between firms and industries.

Trade margins are based on a distributor's place in the channel and represent payment for performing certain distribution tasks. In some cases, several margins are quoted to distributors, as illustrated in Table 15.4. The manufacturer's problem of suggesting a list price, that is, the final suggested price of the product, is more complex, as the number of intermediaries between the producer and the final consumer increases.

List price versus invoice and pocket prices

Distribution margins are generally only a part of the total trade margin, and managers who oversee pricing often focus on invoices prices, which are readily available, but the real story

Table 15.3 Definitions of trade margins

- **Distributor margin**

    Distributor margin = sales price – purchase cost

    $$D = P - C$$

- **Distributor margin in per cent**

Discount	Mark-up

    $$D\star = \frac{P - C}{P} \qquad D^0 = \frac{P - C}{C}$$

- **Transformation rules**

    $$D\star = \frac{D^0}{1 + D^0} \qquad D^0 = \frac{D\star}{1 - D\star}$$

- **Examples of "discount" versus "mark-up"**

Discount	Mark-up
50%	100%
33%	50%
30%	42.86%
25%	33.33%
20%	25%

- **Retail price determination**

    If the purchase cost is €90 and the discount 25%,
    then retail price will be €90 /(1–25%) = €90/75% = €120

    Since a 25% discount is the equivalent of a 33.33% mark-up,
    we also have
    €90 × (1+33.33%) = €90 × 1.3333 = €120

- **Purchase cost determination**

    If the retail price is €120 and the discount 25%, the purchase
    cost is,
    €120 × (1 – 25%) = €120 × 75% = €90.

    Since a 25% discount is the equivalent of a 33.33% mark-up,
    we also have,
    €120 / (1+33.33%) = €120 / 1.3333 = €90.

Source: Lambin (2000/2007).

Table 15.4   Developing a price structure

- Trade margins are based on a distributor's place in the channel and represent payment for performing certain distribution tasks.
- Prices are usually quoted to distributors as a series of numbers depending on the number of functions performed.
- In the case of large retail chains, we would have the following quotation:
  30, 10, 5, and 2/10, net 30

The first three numbers represent successive discounts from the list price:

- 30 per cent: as functional discount for the position the retailer occupies in the channel;
- 10 per cent: as compensation for performing the storage function, usually performed by the wholesaler;
- 5 per cent: as an allowance for the retailer's efforts to promote the product through local advertising;
- 2/10: as cash discount, 2 per cent, as reward for payment of an invoice within 10 days.
- Net 30: the length of the credit period; if the payment is not made within 10 days, the entire invoice must be paid in full within 30 days.

Source: Adapted from Monroe (1979, p. 169).

goes much further. A distinction must be made among *list price, invoice price, pocket price and pocket margin*:

- The *list price* is the standard price published in the firm's tariff or price list.
- The *invoice price* is the list price after deduction of *on-invoice leakages* that should be considered in addition to the standard distributor discount, like special distributor discount, end-customer discount and on-invoice promotion.
- The *pocket price* is the invoice price after deduction of *off-invoice leakages* like cash discount for prompt payment, the cost of carrying accounts receivables, co-operative advertising allowances, rebates based on distributor total annual volume, off-invoice promotional programmes and freight expenses.

In a case reported by McKinsey (Marn, Roegner and Zawada, 2003), the *invoice price* and the *pocket price* were, respectively, at 67.2 per cent and 50.9 per cent of the list price, including a 16.3 per cent in revenue reductions that didn't appear on invoices.

For companies offering customized products, unique solution packages or unique forms of logistical or technical support, the cost of these services should be subtracted from the pocket price to identify the *pocket margin*, the true measure of profitability. In another case, also reported by McKinsey, the costs of customer-specific services averaged 17 per cent of the list price, leaving a pocket margin of 28 per cent, to be compared with the standard gross margin of 45 per cent.

Comparison of distribution costs

The distribution margin compensates the distribution functions and tasks assumed by the intermediaries in the channel. If some of these distribution tasks are assumed directly by the producer, it will have to support the organization and the costs implied. By way of illustration, Table 15.5 shows a cost comparison of two indirect distribution channels: a "long" indirect channel involving two intermediaries, wholesalers and retailers and a "short" indirect channel involving only retailers, the wholesaling function being assumed by the manufacturer.

Table 15.5 Distribution cost analysis of two distribution channels

Distribution tasks	Indirect long channel		Indirect short channel	
	Cost	Comments	Cost	Comments
Transport	Covered by the wholesaler margin	M → W: In charge of M, More expensive W → R: In charge of R, Cheaper	–	M → warehouses: In charge of M, Cheaper Warehouses → R: In charge of R, More expensive
Assortment	16% of the manufacturer' sales revenue (SR)	In charge of W and R, better assortment	–	In charge of R: risk of incomplete assortment
Storage		Warehouses: in charge of W	€750,000	7 warehouse (Fewer)
		Stocks: in charge of W	2.5% of SR.	4 rotations/year (Rate 10%)
		Clients: in charge of W	1.25% of SR.	Payment at 45 days (rate 10%)
Contacts		In charge of W Risk of inertia	€500,000	25 salespeople at €20,000 More dynamic (Push strategy)
Information	2.5% of Sales revenue	Push strategy on W and R	1.5% of SR.	Pull strategy
Sales administration	€30,000	Mainly in charge of W, small team	€200,000	Mainly in charge of M; large team
Total cost	€30,000 + 18.5% of SR.	Cost proportional to the level of activity	€1,450,000 + 5.25% of SR.	Largest part of cost is fixed

Source: Lambin (2000/2007).

In the *indirect long channel*, most of the physical distribution tasks (storage and transportation) are taken on by wholesalers and the distribution costs are largely proportional to the rate of activity and covered by the wholesalers' distributors' margin. The manufacturer has to maintain a minimum sales administration unit and the overhead costs are minimized. In this type of conventional vertical marketing organization, however, the producer is dependent on the goodwill of the distributors and has only limited control on the sales organization. To offset this handicap, the producer can create its own sales force (merchandisers) to stimulate sales at the retailers' level and also to use mass media advertising to create brand awareness and brand preference among end-users through a "pull communication" strategy.

Examining now the cost structure of the *indirect short channel*, one observes that overheads or fixed costs represent the largest share of total distribution costs. It means that the manufacturer has to support the costs of the physical distribution functions and organize a network of warehouses plus a much more extensive sales administration unit. The financial costs involved in inventory management and the customers' accounts receivable, as well as the selling function, are also completely assumed by the producer.

By adopting a selective distribution strategy, the firm has to contact 2,500 retailers at least once a month. One sales representative can perform on average 4.8 calls per day during 250 working days per year. The required sales force is therefore 25 sales representatives to achieve the market coverage objective.

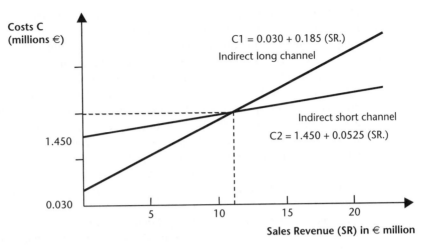

Figure 15.4 Comparing the cost structures of two distribution channels

Thus, adopting an indirect short distribution channel implies a major financial risk for the producer. The benefits of this strategy, however, are better control of the commercial organization and a closer contact with the end-users. The two cost equations are compared in Figure 15.4.

In general, the sales revenue expectations are not the same for each distribution channel. The profitability rate of each channel will be determined as follows:

$$R = \frac{\text{Sales revenue - Distribution costs}}{\text{Distribution costs}}$$

Where R is an estimate of the expected rate of return when all the costs are taken into account for each channel. This quantitative indicator must of course be interpreted with care and with due consideration of the more "qualitative" factors discussed above.

15.8 IMPACT OF INTERNET ON CHANNELS' DECISIONS

Internet technology is improving the efficiency of markets, creating market environment close to the situation of pure (or perfect) competition, where the tools of strategic marketing (differentiation, innovation and loyalty) are to some extent neutralized. In this new context, as suggested by Drucker (2000), the firm controlling the delivery to the market has a major competitive advantage. In traditional business structures, selling is seen and organized as a servant to production. In e-business, instead of selling what it makes, *the virtual company will sell what it can deliver, no matter who makes the products*. The contact with the market and the *savoir-faire* in terms of physical distribution and logistics become the core competence.

The temptation of disintermediation

A strategic issue raised by Internet is the reconfiguration of the distributive network. A commonly held view is that Internet will enable companies to deal directly with the end-customer, leapfrogging existing distribution networks and thereby reducing transaction costs. Why remunerate middlemen, the thinking goes, if one can communicate directly with the customer through an electronic link, giving him or her the possibility to place an order directly at a lower cost? This is called *disintermediation*.

Once the potential of Internet applications is identified, and before considering disintermediation, it is useful to verify whether each online application "complements" or "replaces" off-line operations. Online applications do not systematically replace traditional activities. In many cases, the best solution is a combination of the two, thereby promoting complementarities (the click-and-brick concept). A mistake would be to do online only what is done manually off-line, simply to generate cost reductions.

In reality, the challenge is far greater. Taken separately, the cost of the direct contact is indeed lower, but managers need to view the *total cost of the transaction*. In many situations, the reduced cost of the person-to-person relationship can be offset by substantially increased logistics costs. The issue is not one of sidelining distributors, rather of redistributing the tasks and functions among the existing actors in the chain. This redistribution (or re-allocation) of tasks is particularly relevant for product information, advice to customers, after-sales services, physical delivery, product and service bundling and product demonstrations or trials.

Going online and offline simultaneously?

Offering the same products to the same customers under the same brand simultaneously online and offline is likely to generate major channel conflicts. As suggested by Van Camp (2001), these conflicts can be internal or external. *Internal conflicts* are those between two or more of the channels to market the company employs; external conflicts involve third parties.

When a firm wants to add an online channel to its on-land existing distributive network, four types of internal conflicts are to be expected.

- *Cross-channel cannibalization*. The creation of a new sales channel will trigger a redistribution of total sales volume across channels, which translates into cannibalization of existing channels in favour of the new one. The key question is to know whether the new online channel has a complementary or a substitute effect on company sales.
- *Underutilization of real estate*. Most retail channels comprise physical assets of some sort, for example, stores, branch offices or call centres. Optimization of the number, size and utilization of these assets is important, as they represent a large part of a company's total cost. If substantial volume is moved to the online channel, the balance will be upset with a negative impact on the overall cost base.
- *Price disparities between channels*. Online price levels tend to be substantially lower than in other channels, because Internet-based companies enjoy a much lower cost base and accept lower margins than traditional players. To be competitive online, these sites will have to match their Internet-based competitors. But does that mean they have to lower prices in other channels accordingly? Large price differences may upset customers who feel they pay too much offline.
- *Channel de-synchronization*. The two types of channels have very different practices and the natural tendency is to manage them independently. The problem is that customers

do not differentiate between channels for the same brand. They simply select the most convenient channel, expecting a certain degree of integration between online and offline channels.

In addition to these internal conflicts, *external conflicts* can also arise when independent third parties are associated in the distributive network. Direct online sales by the manufacturer have always risked antagonizing the retailers they depend upon to sell their products.

- *Alienating traditional retailers by going direct to the market.* Traditional channels partners are of course upset to see manufacturers go direct to market to establish a direct contact with their end-customers. As the online channels takes volume away from traditional channels, they may withdraw support for the company's products and turn to competitors.
- *Losing channel control.* Manufacturers try to control their channels by setting regional sales quota and by providing strict guidelines on product presentation and promotion. However, it is difficult to maintain the same control over the online channels of their downstream channel partners. As more and more retailers create their own click-and-brick businesses, manufacturers may find it increasingly difficult to prevent their products from being offered online.
- *Moving value upstream.* Value-added activities such as customization and information about product models and performance, which were once performed downstream, may nowadays be done by the manufacturer itself. The provision of services and of information by manufacturers reduces the role and the value added by retailers, whose roles are limited to the physical tasks of distribution which are also the most costly.

Several options exist to reconcile online and offline channels, which thus minimize potential conflicts.

- To place on the company's website little more than a banner presenting the company and a catalogue of products without price list. The distributors then perceive the site as a promotional support.
- Charge on the website the same price as the market price but add delivery costs, which makes the traditional distributor's offering attractive.
- Sell on the website but return a commission to the distributors located in the geographic zone where the product is sold.
- Adopt the same pricing strategy as the distributors, which is an aggressive strategy, creating direct competition vis-à-vis its own distributor network.

To meet this challenge of selling online by manufacturers, the owner of Shopatron Company (www.shopatron.com) has developed a website that allows manufacturers to sell online without annoying retailers (Birchall, 2008). His business takes customer orders and places them on Confident order exchange (Coex), an Internet-based online exchange, where orders are taken up by a local retailer for delivery or the goods are held in a store to be picked up. Shopatron has now more than 400 brand manufacturers on its Coex system, which offers a solution to channel conflicts. Manufacturers pay a single set-up charge, followed by a low monthly fee. Retailers can join for free, but pay a percentage of each sales and credit card processing cost to Shopatron. As consumer demand for in-store pick-up increases, this system provides a win–win solution.

Thus, the issue raised by the Internet on distribution channel management is more a question of re-allocation of the distribution tasks among the different actors. It would be possible for a firm, for example, to deal directly with the end-customer where the provision of up-to-date information is at stake, while leaving to intermediaries those tasks requiring physical proximity.

Securing e-commerce

The majority of surveyed consumers still express reservations about online purchasing. Three main reservations are regularly mentioned: (a) low confidence in electronic payments security, (b) uncertainties about the delivery of the goods, and (c) protection of private life. Web companies have a vested interest in the success of the online channels and therefore have to maintain and develop customer confidence in online services by addressing these problems.

E-commerce encourages *payment transactions* which do not require physical funds, but involve only data transfer through credit or debit cards. Credit cards are the dominant form of payment, but the importance of popular debit cards, like Bancontact/Mister Cash, is growing. This allows merchants and consumers to pay and receive payment immediately, due to the electronic nature of this medium. Credit and debit cards are fast and easy but they do have a significant disadvantage. They do not require a signature to authorize a transaction, and this can lead to higher fraud rates. All a thief needs is a valid credit card number, name and expiration date. Security is an extremely important issue in e-commerce and thus merchants must take steps to ensure the security of their transactions. One way e-marketers are addressing transaction security is through the use of encryption algorithms (to know more about transaction security, read Strauss, El-Ansary, and Frost (2006, p. 78–81)). This is also the role of e-market facilitators. Single factor identification, such as a username–password combination, is recognized as not strong enough to defend merchants or their customers. E-market facilitators like Entrust (www.entrust.com), Ogone (https://secure.ogone.com), or Saferpay (www.saferpay.com) have developed Internet platforms for processing electronic payments in total security, using multi-factor authentication. For sellers, using these services may be expensive and require a sufficient sales volume to be justified.

The organization of a *convenient system for delivering* or collecting the goods purchased is a second important issue in e-commerce. The US case of Shopatron described in the previous paragraph is a good illustration of the type of solution provided by an e-market facilitator. In Europe, Kiala (www.kiala.com) is the leading service provider having set up a network of collection points enabling customers to pick up, pay for and return their purchased goods quickly where and when it suits them better. The Kiala points network consists of nearby stores – grocery stores, dry-cleaners, newspaper shops, gasoline service stations and so on – which offer easy access, wide opening hours even during the weekend, quality service, no queue and secured storage space. As a result, customers can optimize their time by picking up their goods at a place of their own choice. The network is supported by an up-to-date communication technology which allows customers to track and trace their parcels on the Kiala's Internet site and to be notified of their arrival or of their delay.

In China, the postal system is unreliable and credit card use is low, China still being a cash-driven economy. Innovation is a necessity. Dangdang (www.dangdang.com) is an online retailer aspiring to be the Amazon.com of China. For organizing delivery, Dangdang has a ready fleet of couriers on bicycles who zip around China's major cities, delivering packages and collecting cash.

Private life protection is the third concern raised by many consumers. The individualization of online communication creates the need for personalized data to customize the offering. Therefore, any scrap of information that attracts a potential customer has commercial value. This explains the importance of personal data banks and the highly sensitive issue of privacy and of private life protection on the Internet. A recent analysis of online consumer data (Story, 2008) has shown that large Web companies – Yahoo, Google, Microsoft or AOL – are learning more than ever before about the gritty details of what people search for and do on the Internet, gathering clues about typical user preferences several hundred times a month. These companies use that data to predict what content people will most likely respond to. They can charge steep prices for carefully tailored ads because of their high response rates. These Web companies also noted that they have consumer protection policies, for example, letting users choose not to be targets of some advertising, letting users edit the search histories that are linked to their user names or voluntarily obscuring people's computer identification addresses. Microsoft says it does not link any of its visitor's behaviour to their user names, even if those people are registered.

Keeping private life off the Internet is also everybody's direct responsibility. Curtis (2007) (www.ezinearticles.com) proposes ten privacy protection tips based on a combination of technology and common sense.

The geographic market coverage

Adopting Internet technology does not necessarily imply that companies should suddenly start operating on a global stage. If Internet facilitates communication, international physical delivery and logistics still require specific competence and significant financial resources. Thus, decisions concerning market coverage should be taken only after considering the physical (delivery) and psychological (communication) implications.

The spectacular development of the New Information and Communication Technologies (NICTs) and the resulting globalization of the world market can give the illusion that distance does not matter anymore. In reality, distance is a multi-dimensional concept and a distinction must be made between the four dimensions of distance (Ghemawat, 2001): geographic (physical remoteness), administrative (preferential trading agreements), economic (wealth differences), and cultural (linguistic ties). The NICTs have eliminated only one component of geographic distance: the communication link.

As a result, an increasing number of companies are succeeding overseas without massive foreign investment by adopting a global business model called *netchising* (Morrison, Bouquet and Beck, 2004). This new business model relies on the Internet for procurement, sales and maintaining customer relationships, and non-equity partnership arrangements to provide direct customer interfaces and local adaptation and delivery of products and services. *Netchising* offers potentially huge benefits over traditional exporting or foreign direct investment approaches to globalization.

Chapter Summary

Distribution channels are organized structures performing the tasks necessary to facilitate exchange transactions. The functions of distribution channels are to create time, space and state utilities which constitute the added value of distribution. Distributors (wholesalers, retailers, agents, brokers) are required because manufacturers are unable to assume by themselves, at a reasonable cost, all the tasks implied by a free and competitive exchange process. Distribution channels can be characterized by the number of intermediary levels that separate the supplier from the end-user. The selection of a particular channel design is determined by factors related to market, buyer behaviour and company characteristics. When the channel structure is indirect, some degree of co-operation and co-ordination must be achieved among the participants in the vertical marketing system. Regarding the number of intermediaries necessary, three market coverage strategies are possible: intensive, selective or exclusive distribution. Exclusive distribution through franchising is a popular system present in almost all business fields. The distribution margins, or trade margins, compensate the distribution functions and tasks assumed by the intermediaries in the channel.

BIBLIOGRAPHY

Birchall, J. (2008), How to Cut in the Middleman?, *Financial Times*, March 12.

Boyd, H.W. and Walker, O.C. Jr. (1990), *Marketing Management: A Strategic Approach*, Homewood, IL, R.D. Irwin.

Curtis, T. (2007), Keeping Your Private Life off the Internet – Top 10 Privacy Protection Tips, *Ezine Articles*, October.

Drucker, P. (2000), Can e-Commerce Deliver? The World in 2000, *The Economist*, 122.

Ghemawat, P. (2001), Distance Still Matters: The Hard Reality of Global Expansion, *Harvard Business Review*, 79, 8, pp. 137–47.

Jallat, F. and Capek, M.J. (2001), Disintermediation in Question: New economy, New Networks, New Middlemen, *Business Horizons*, 44, 2, pp. 55–60.

Jupiter Research (2005), *European Online Retail Forecast 2005 to 2010*.

Lambin J.J. (2000/2007), *Market-Driven Management, Strategic and Operational Marketing*, London, Palgrave Macmillan, First and second Editions.

LSA (1998), Le hard discount en pleine forme, 1571, February 12, pp. 28–31.

Marn, M.V., Roegner, E.V. and Zawada, C.C. (2003), The Power of Pricing, *The McKinsey Quarterly*, 1, pp. 27–39.

McGuire, E.P. (1971), *Franchised Distribution*, New York, The Conference Board, Report 523.

Monroe, K.B. (1979), *Pricing: Making Profitable Decisions*, New York, McGraw-Hill.

Morrison, A, Bouquet, C. and Beck, J. (2004), Netchising: The Next Global Wave?, *Long Range Planning*, 37, pp. 11–27.

Nielsen A.C. (2006/2009), *Consumer insights into globalization*, A.C. Nielsen Worldwide.

Palamountain, J.C. (1955), *The Politics of Distribution*, Cambridge, MA, Harvard University Press.

Sallenave, J.P. (1979), *Expansion de votre commerce par le franchisage*, Montréal, Gouvernement du Québec, Ministère du Commerce et du Tourisme.

Story, L. (2008), Internet Firms Keeping ever-closer Tabs on You, *International Herald Tribune*, 11 March.

Strauss, J., El-Ansary, A., and Frost, R. (2006), *E-Marketing*, New Jersey, Pearson Prentice-Hall, 4th edition.

Van Camp, F. (2001), *Online and Onland? Channels Conflicts and How to Avoid them*, Rotterdam Arthur D. Little, E-Business Center.

Shang, J., Yildirim, T.P., Tadikamalla, P., Mittal, V. and Brown, L. (2009), Distribution Network Redesign for Marketing Competitiveness, *Journal of Marketing*, 73, pp. 146–63.

WEB SITE COMPANION FOR CHAPTER 15

Visit the Market-driven Management accompanying website at www.palgrave.com/business/lambin3 to find:

Note on Direct Marketing
Note on Entry Strategies in Foreign Markets

CHAPTER SIXTEEN

THE BATTLE OF THE BRANDS IN B2C MARKETS

A significant change in the last few decades, in Europe and in the United States as well, is the growing power of the retailers. From passive intermediaries in the channel, retailers are now active marketers developing new store concepts and own-labels brands designed for well-targeted segments. They are now directly competing with manufacturers' brands; they have the power to dictate terms to their suppliers and to push their brands off the shelves if they are not leaders in their product category.

Learning Objectives

When you have read this chapter, you should be able to:

- Understand the emerging role of private labels in B2C markets
- Describe the alternative entry strategies in foreign markets open to the international firm
- Understand the strategic options for brand manufacturers

Several factors explain this shift of power from manufacturers to retailers:

1. The high *concentration rate* of retailers, specifically in the FMCG sector: in 12 European countries, the top three retailers account for 50 per cent of the market.
2. The adoption by retailers of sophisticated *store brand policies* targeted to segments often neglected by manufacturers (the low end of the market) and the growth of private labels, with market share as high as 42 per cent in Switzerland, 30 per cent in Great Britain and higher than 15 per cent in six other European countries.
3. Several retailers are adopting rapid internationalization strategies, like Wal-Mart in Germany and the United Kingdom, Carrefour-Promodès in Latin America and Japan, Delhaize in Eastern Europe, the United States and Asia, Ikea in the world and most recently in Russia and Malaysia, the Dutch Ahold, the German Aldi, the British Tesco and so on.
4. The emergence of a new breed of retailers, the *hard discounters*, who in warehouse stores, charge very low prices on their own private brands while excluding suppliers' brands from their shelves (Kearney A.T., 2011).

The result has been to deeply transform consumer markets and to modify the balance of power between manufacturers and retailers. Today powerful brands like Coca-Cola and Nestlé need large retailers more than retailers need them, even if the development of e-commerce creates new opportunities for manufacturers who could strike back and bypass traditional intermediaries.

Vertical competition reduces the market power of large international brands, facilitates adaptation to local needs and stimulates price competition, as evidenced by the success of private labels.

In consumer markets, retailers are today irreplaceable actors actively and constructively participating in the globalization process. In these markets, being consumer-driven is not enough. The firm must become *distributor-driven* to avoid the risk of being de-listed and should design retailer-driven *B2B* marketing programmes based on in-depth understanding of their generic needs, such as a desired store image, efficient order fulfilment, protection from undue competition and so on.

Significant changes have occurred during the 1990s in the way retailers, and in particular large retailers, perceive their roles in the exchange process. Traditionally, retailers have limited their role to intermediaries, acting rather passively between the producer and the consumer by simply performing the physical tasks of distribution and by making the goods available to consumers in the condition, place and time required by them. From this rather passive role, intermediaries are increasingly adopting an innovative and active role, thereby modifying the balance of power between manufacturers and retailers.

This evolution has coincided with significant socio-cultural changes in affluent economies, which have induced retailers to redefine their roles as economic agents and to adopt a more market-driven perspective. From a traditional "shop" or "in-house" orientation, retailers are now discovering strategic marketing and are moving away from a business philosophy where the marketing function is confined to the physical distribution tasks and to the purchasing function.

16.1 MAJOR CHANGES IN THE RETAILING SECTOR

In many West European countries, retailing has become a mature industry, and several indicators confirm this observation:

- Keeping pace with the growth of the economy, the retailing industry has experienced *zero or minimal growth* for several years, particularly in the food sector. The share of large retail chains has reached a plateau and is even declining in some markets.
- The *proliferation of retailers* has created over-capacity, and today a retailer must compete against a crowd of competitors, not only in the food sector, but also in sectors like clothing, household appliances and even in the newest product categories like home computers.
- *Competition* is intensive and based almost exclusively on price for all the branded products. In most product categories, consumers can buy exactly the same product or brand at a discount store at bargain prices as they could at a department store at its full price.
- In several European countries, *a high level of concentration* is observed among large distributors. A good review of the evolution of retailing in Europe is available in Colla (2004). Favaro, Romberger and Meer (2009) also provide a good review on how the evolution of retailing is in a recession.

All these characteristics – maturity, over-capacity, concentration and price competition – are typical of commodity markets, suggest that the retailing industry has become *commoditized*.

This conclusion must be qualified, however, by country and by product category. Several factors explain this evolution:

- During the 1960s, *manufacturers' brand names* became prominent in a broadening range of product categories, and more and more retailers began featuring these brands. Thus, the presence of the brand in the retailer's assortment became the determining choice criterion in choosing a particular store. In the process, retailers abdicated much of their stores' marketing and positioning responsibilities to the manufacturers.
- This situation has stimulated the development of *discount stores*, who sell well-known brands exclusively on bargain pricing with minimum services.
- The proliferation of slightly differentiated brands and the adoption of *intensive distribution strategies* by manufacturers have also contributed to reducing store differentiation, with most stores carrying the same assortments of brands.
- Retailers once had the major responsibility for *after-sales service*, and choosing a retailer was important when one bought products like appliances and consumer electronics. Now consumers can get after-sales service for most products independently of the retailer, and this type of store differentiation is also waning.
- The lack of customer services at retail to improve productivity has generated an important *self-production of services* by consumers which contributes to increase the "total price" of mass distribution (de Maricourt, 1988).
- Finally, the tremendous growth in *bank credit cards* also contributes to undermine store loyalty. Consumers no longer choose a store because they have established credit there: bankcards entitle customers to buy items almost anywhere they please.

These factors have all contributed to reducing store differentiation and loyalty, to killing the concept of *shopping for enjoyment* and to modifying consumer's buying behaviour, particularly for working housewives attracted by other more rewarding and stimulating activities.

16.2   CHANGES IN CONSUMERS' RETAIL BUYING BEHAVIOUR

Retail consumers today behave differently, not only because of the social and demographic changes described above, but also because they are more educated and professional in their purchase decisions. One of the biggest changes is the rise of the *smart shopper*. Being a smart shopper implies several capabilities:

- Being informed about the products one wants to buy and being able to compare and choose independently of brand, advertising, store and sales person's recommendations. It means finding the best value for money.
- Being able to separate the product features and the benefits and services provided by a store to augment the product value. Smart shoppers distinguish between what is inherent in the product and can therefore be obtained anywhere they buy it, and what a specific store adds to the purchase. They routinely compare stores as well as brands on this basis.
- Being able to recognize that brands have become increasingly similar. They will not necessarily choose a well-known brand over a less-well-known one simply because it is familiar or because of its image. The product must also be viewed as offering superior value.

In addition, for many consumers, and for a broadening range of goods, shopping is no longer viewed as fun or recreational, but rather as a tedious task to be performed as economically and efficiently as possible. In their search for value, an expanding group of consumers seek not only good merchandise but savings of time and effort as well.

16.3   DIFFERENTIATION STRATEGIES OF THE RETAILER

Confronted with these changes, the retailer has to review his or her traditional strategic positioning by redefining the *store concept* and by adopting a positioning which provides unique value to consumers. The adoption of a store differentiation strategy becomes a necessity in a marketplace where retailing has become commoditized. Thus the concepts of strategic marketing developed for product marketing can be directly applied to retail marketing.

The multi-attribute concept of a store

From the consumer standpoint, the store concept can be viewed as a package of benefits and the multi-attribute product concept is useful here to help design the store concept. Six different characteristics or attributes can be identified in a store, which constitute as many action variables for the retailer:

- *Location.* This defines the territorial coverage or trading area within which to develop business relations. The alternatives are downtown location, community, suburban or regional shopping centres.
- *Assortment.* The number of product lines that will be sold, which implies decisions on the product assortment breadth (narrow or wide) and product assortment depth (shallow or deep) for each product line.
- *Pricing.* The general level of prices (high or low gross margins) and the use of loss leaders, discount pricing and price promotions.
- *Services.* The extent of the service mix. A distinction can be made between pre-purchase services (telephone orders, shopping hours, fitting rooms and so on), post-purchase services (delivery, alterations, wrapping and so on) and ancillary services (credit, restaurants, baby sitting, travel agencies and so on); see de Maricourt (1988).
- *Time.* The time required for a shopping trip. Proximity is the key factor, but also opening and closing hours, accessibility, ease of selection, fast completion of transaction and queuing time at checkout counters.
- *Atmosphere.* The layout of the store, but also the light, the space, the musical ambience, the look and the interior decoration and so on.

These store attributes are used by consumers when they compare retail stores. It is up to the retailer to define a store concept based on some innovative combination of these attributes and which constitutes a package of benefits differentiated from the competition.

Store positioning strategies

The positioning strategies to be adopted by the retailer vary with sectors. Retail outlets can be classified according to two dimensions, that is, the level of the gross margin (high or

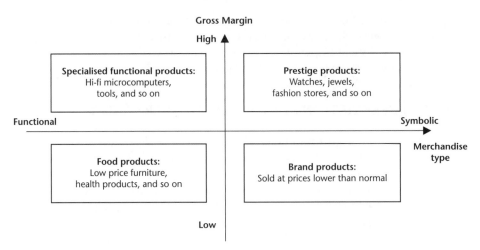

Figure 16.1   Retail positioning strategies
Source: Adapted from Wortzel (1987).

low), and the type of benefit sought by the consumer, that is, symbolic or functional. We thus have a two-dimensional map as shown in Figure 16.1, which describes four distinct positioning strategies:

- Among the functional products sold with a high gross margin (upper left quadrant), we have the *specialty stores* with selected or specialized assortments in food or in audio-visuals, computers, tools and so on.
- Among the functional products with low margins are the "everyday" food products sold in *supermarkets and superstores*, low-price furniture (Ikea), do-it-yourself centres, cheap audio-visual goods and so on.
- The symbolic products with high margins are sold through *prestige specialty stores*, like fashion stores (Benetton, Rodier), jewellery, watches and so on.
- Symbolic products sold at low prices, these are distributed through *discount stores* selling national brands at prices lower than those prevailing in conventional stores.

Three basic store positioning strategies can be adopted by the retailer: product differentiation, service and personality augmentation and price leadership:

1. A *product differentiation strategy* is based on offering products that are intrinsically different, for example, different brands or different styles from those in the same product category offered by other stores.
2. In a *service and personality augmentation strategy*, a retailer offers products that are intrinsically similar to those offered by competitors, but adds specific services and personality to differentiate the store.
3. A *price leadership strategy* means offering the same products as the competition at lower prices.

Several alternative positioning strategies can be contemplated by the retailer who has under his or her control several action variables. Thus, a strategic marketing plan can be elaborated and implemented through an action programme consistent with the chosen objectives to gain a sustainable competitive advantage over competition.

16.4   PRIVATE LABEL DEVELOPMENT

Large retailers have successfully implemented differentiation strategies based on private brand development during the last decade.

This development coincides with the growth of the market power held by large retailers due namely to three groups of factors:

1. The creation of powerful *purchasing centres at the European level*, which has contributed to a substantial increase in the bargaining power of large retailers.
2. The development of *centralized warehousing and delivery systems* which has created a physical barrier between the supplier and the local supermarket.
3. The generalization of *electronic point of sales* (ePoS), a computerized system for recording sales at retail checkouts which provides the retailer with instant information on each product sold at the retail outlet.

As a result of these technological changes, one observes a shift in the balance of power between suppliers and retailers.

This increased market power has induced retailers to develop their own branding policies in order to improve their profitability. This private label strategy goes back more than 20 years in Western Europe, but it has been gaining a new dimension recently. Several types of private labels exist in the European market:

■   *Store brand names.* The proposition here is to provide the same performance as national brands, but at more moderate prices. Typical examples are Delhaize, St. Michael from Marks & Spencer and Casino. The brand name is that of the chain and is used as a way of furthering the store's image.
■   *Generic brands.* The products are unsophisticated, presented in a simple package at lowest prices and without a brand name. Typically, the white products from GB in Belgium come in this category.
■   *Invented brand names.* The retailer presents them as regular brands but they are distributed exclusively in the stores of the chain. Many retail chains sell invented brands such as Beaumont at Monoprix, O'Lacy at Asko and Saint Goustain and Chabrior at Intermarché.
■   *First price.* Their role is to stave off the invasion of the hard discounters, namely, Aldi. The name of the store is not mentioned.

It is worth noting that the development of private labels has been stimulated by the growth of the "first price" brands and by the dynamism of hard discounters like Aldi and Lidl (Germany and Denmark) and Kwik-Save (UK) which operate through warehouse retail stores.

This offensive of private labels has been fruitful and, as a consequence, national brands' loyalty is decreasing and suppliers are forced to reduce their price differentials.

It, however, seems that in France and in the United Kingdom, private labels are stagnating at the current level reached. In a survey carried out in France by LSA (1997), only 24 per cent of the consumers interviewed were in favour of an extension of the range of private brands in their usual store and 70 per cent were opposed, a result similar to that observed in

1995. For a comparison between European and US discounters, see Steenkamp and Kumar (2009).

16.5   STRATEGIC OBJECTIVES OF DISTRIBUTORS

Retailers' marketing strategies tend to become more sophisticated. They do not simply imitate existing products but develop new product concepts targeted at well-defined market segments and which are then produced by international manufacturers specializing in private labels. For retailers, three objectives can be pursued with private labels:

- To reduce the power of manufacturers by reducing their volume and their brand franchise and to eliminate small competitors.
- To enhance category margins since private labels can deliver 5–10 margin points more than national brands.
- To provide a differentiated product to build the retailer's image.

This last objective is now gaining in importance among the most sophisticated and dynamic retailers (see Figure 16.2).

- *Same quality, cheaper.* It is the most common strategy adopted for store brands: to propose a level of quality similar to that offered by the leading national brand but at a price 15 to 20 per cent lower.
- *Lower quality, cheaper.* This strategy is based on the invented brand names and on the generic brands: to propose a lower level of quality in simplified packages at a price 30 to 40 per cent lower than the prices charged by national brands.
- *Better quality, same price.* To propose a level of quality higher than national brands at the same price. Sainsbury in the United Kingdom for a certain number of product categories, using invented brand names exclusively found in Sainsbury stores, adopts this positioning strategy.

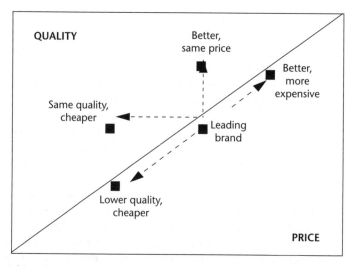

Figure 16.2   Price quality ratios for private labels
Source: Lambin (2000/2007).

- *Better quality, higher price.* A less frequent strategy, adopted by distributors targeting the high end of the market with homemade or handicraft products.

As a result of these aggressive price label strategies, there is general pressure on prices. In large supermarket chains, three types of brands are observed within the same product category:

- *National brands* and preferably the brand leader in the product category (the A brands) and which are supported by heavy advertising and promotional activities.
- *Own labels, store or umbrella brands* (the B brands) created by the retailer to improve profitability and to build the store image.
- *First prices* (the C brands) which are used as price fighters to stop the *hard discounters* by offering an alternative to customers.

In this competitive struggle, the weakest manufacturers' brands are the first to be eliminated from the supermarkets.

16.6   STRATEGIC OPTIONS FOR MANUFACTURERS' BRANDS

Confronted with the growing power of large supermarket retailers, what are the defence strategies for consumer brand manufacturers? Four basic strategic options exist:

- *Pull strategy.* To promote an innovative (unique) product or well-differentiated brand through creative segmentation and media advertising targeted at the end-consumer, in order to induce the distributor to list the brand in his or her assortment.
- *Direct marketing.* To bypass the retailers by adopting a *non-store marketing* strategy where purchases are made from the home and delivered to the home.
- *Sub-contracting marketing.* To concentrate on R&D and manufacturing and to leave the marketing function to a well-diversified group of retailers.
- *Trade marketing.* To view distributors as intermediate customers and to design a retailer-driven marketing programme.

In what follows, we shall review the strategic options available to a national brand through a pull strategy and through trade marketing.

Alternative options in a pull strategy

From the manufacturer's point of view, the ideal situation is to have a well-differentiated brand, strongly supported by advertising and demanded by consumers. In this situation of manufacturer's domination, the distributor is captive and is forced to list the brand in his or her assortment. Such a situation is not likely to prevail indefinitely, however, and even big-name manufacturers can be threatened by private labels as illustrated by the success story of Classic Cola of Sainsbury against the mighty Coca-Cola.

> Classic Cola, a private label made by the Cott Corporation for J. Sainsbury in the United Kingdom, was launched at a price 28 per cent lower than Coca-Cola. Today the private label accounts for 65 per cent of total cola sales through Sainsbury and for 15 per cent of the UK cola market.

Once confronted with the private label challenge, how should national brands react? Hoch (1996) suggests four basic strategic moves that a national brand can make to improve its competitive position. These options are meant to be neither mutually exclusive nor exhaustive (see Figure 16.3):

1. *Wait and do nothing.* In markets characterized by high volatility and fluctuation, it may be imprudent for a national manufacturer to react quickly and aggressively.
2. *Increase distance from private labels.* Distancing moves could be to "provide more for money" or "new and improved" products. It does necessarily imply line extensions, which too often tend to dilute rather than enhance the core brand.
3. *Reduce the price gap.* Empirical evidence shows that small price gaps increased unit sales of national brands relative to the private label. Because consumers appear more willing to trade up quality rather down, price changes by national brands affect private labels more than corresponding changes by private labels affect national brand sales.
4. *Formulate a "me too" strategy.* Two options are possible here. To introduce a "value flanker" by offering a lower-priced, possibly lower-quality item to crowd out the private label. The risk here is to cannibalize sales currently accruing to the premium national brand. In another strategy, the national brand can elect to manufacture private labels directly for the retailer.

Regarding this last strategy, Quelch and Harding (1996, p. 103) suggest that private label manufacturing opportunities often appear profitable to manufacturers, because they are evaluated on an incremental marginal cost basis. If private label manufacturing were evaluated on a full cost rather than on an incremental basis, it would in many cases appear much less profitable. Every company considering producing private label goods should answer three questions: (a) what is the true contribution from private label products? (b) what fixed

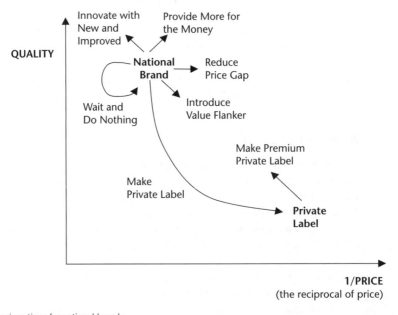

Figure 16.3 Strategic options for national brands
Source: Hoch (1996). Reproduced with permission. (c) 1996 from MIT Sloan Management Review/Massachusetts Institute of Technology. All rights reserved. Distributed by Tribune Media Services

costs are attributable to private label production? (c) how much will the private label goods cannibalize the company's national brands?

Trade marketing

Trade marketing is simply the application of the marketing concept to distributors who are no longer viewed as "intermediaries" in the channel but as partners or customers in their own right. The marketing process targeted to resellers or distributors can be sub-divided into four phases:

- Segmentation of the reseller population, or the identification of groups of distributors having the same expectations from suppliers.
- Selection of one or several segment(s) to be targeted by priority.
- Analysis of their needs, that is, understand factors that shape resellers' decisions, their functioning mode, their objectives and expectations.
- Design of an adapted marketing programme.

Efficient order fulfilment is one domain of application of trade marketing where the benefits for the two parties are directly observable. In this partnership approach, the goal is to maximize the profits for the entire supply chain. This requires (a) that the supplier is linked with store-shelf inventory data, which is updated immediately customers buy products from the store, (b) production based on real-time store sales forecast,

---

Exhibit 16.1   EDI and EWR: two important tools of trade marketing

EDI: electronic data interchange

This system of data interchange between suppliers and resellers is becoming more and more popular in the United States and in Europe. Its principle is simple: to establish a direct connection which hooks together computers of the commercial partners via telephone lines to swap information. Once established, this connection facilitates and accelerates communication within the chain and generates substantial cost savings. One of the benefits of EDI is the time reduction for order taking. If order taking for 500 stores generally requires 12 hours, 10 minutes are sufficient with EDI. This operation is followed up by a control which takes two hours for validating the orders. EDI also contributes to the reduction of the execution costs of an order, from its initiation to its transmission: it is €0.46 with EDI against €2.59 with a magnetic support and €8.23 for a paper document. EDI creates a new management mode: the one of real-time commerce.

EWR: efficient warehouse response

EWR can be defined as a logistic partnership proposing an exchange of information through EDI. This communication between manufacturers and resellers is mainly concerned with inventory flows, the objective being to achieve productivity gains at each level of the logistic chain. These cost savings are then shared between the channel partners. The main benefits expected are:

- Produce and sell as much as possible in real time
- Reduce the number of stock outs
- Gain a better understanding of stocks movements and of demand to reduce real inventory
- Rationalize the flow of merchandise to generate economies of scale

The most important field of application of EWR is the optimization of the flow of goods; the other domains are organization of sales promotions and new product development.

Source: Adapted from Vandaele (1998).

(c) relocation by the supplier of warehouse facilities closer to the stores. These actions together minimize the inventory costs throughout the system, and the supplier is able to pass on the savings to resellers, and through them, to consumers. Both consumers and resellers get better value in terms of lower prices and merchandise availability due to reduced stock outs.

In order to manage this B2B relationship with resellers, suppliers will have to develop an in-depth understanding of their logistic problems, their desired store image and the perceived importance of a particular product category for the chain store's positioning. The most fundamental change is the shift from an adversarial practice to one of partnership. A good understanding of the objectives and constraints of the intermediate customer is a pre-requisite for the development of a successful relationship marketing strategy. To go further on the subject of trade marketing see Vandaele (1998), Corstjens and Corstjens (1996) and Buzzell and Ortmeyer (1995).

Chapter Summary

Distributors are increasingly adopting an innovative and active role, thereby modifying the balance of power between manufacturers and retailers. Maturity, over-capacity, concentration and price competition are typical characteristics suggesting that the retailing industry has become *commoditized*. Retail consumers today behave differently, not only because of the social and demographic changes described above, but also because they are more educated and professional in their purchase decisions. From the consumer standpoint, the store concept can be viewed as a package of benefits and the multi-attribute product concept is useful here to help design a store concept. Retail outlets can be classified according to two dimensions: the level of the gross margin (high or low) and the type of benefit sought by the consumer, that is, symbolic or functional. Retailers' marketing strategies tend to become more sophisticated. They do not simply imitate existing products but develop new product concepts targeted at well-defined market segments which are then produced by international manufacturers specializing in private labels. Four basic strategic options exist for the brand manufacturer: a pull strategy, direct marketing, sub-contracting operational marketing and trade marketing.

BIBLIOGRAPHY

Buzzell, R.D. and Ortmeyer, G. (1995), Channel Partnerships Streamline Distribution, *Sloan Management Review*, 36, 3, pp. 85–9.

Colla, E. (2004), The Outlook for European Grocery Retailing: Competition and Format development, *International Review of Retail Distribution and Consumer Research*, 14, 1, pp. 47–69.

Corstjens, J. and Corstjens, M. (1996), *Store Wars*, New York, John Wiley.

de Maricourt, R. (1988), Vers une nouvelle révolution de la distribution: de l'hypermarché à l'hyperservice, *Revue Française du Marketing*, 118.

Favaro, K., Romberger, T. and Meer, D. (2009), Five rules for retailing in a recession, *Harvard Business Review*, April, pp. 64–72.

Hoch, S.J. (1996), How Should National Brands Think about Private Labels? *Sloan Management Review*, 37, 2, pp. 89–102.

Kearney, A.T. (2011), *A.T. Kearnyt, 2011 Global Retail Development Index*, HYPERLINK "http://www.atkearney.com" www.atkearney.com

Lambin, J.J. (2008), *Changing Market Relationships in the Internet Age*, Louvain-la-neuve, Presses Universitaires de Louvain.

Lambin J.J. (2000/2007), *Market-Driven Management, Strategic and Operational Marketing*, London, Palgrave Macmillan, First and second editions.

Libre Service Actualités (LSA) (1996), L'Europe des achats: le nouveau pactole, 1481, 29, pp. 26–30.

LSA (1997), Marque de distributeurs: les clients les perçoivent mal, 1540, 22, pp. 30–4.

Quelch, J.A. and Harding, D. (1996), Brand versus Private Labels: Fighting to Win, *Harvard Business Review*, 74, 1, pp. 99–109.

Steenkamp, J.-B. E.M. and Kumar, N. (2009), Don't be Undersold!, *Harvard Business Review,* December, pp. 90–5.

Vandaele, M. (1998), *Commerce et industrie: le nouveau partenariat*, Paris, Librairie Vuibert.

Wortzel, L.H. (1987), Retailing Strategies for Today's Mature Market-place, *Journal of Business Strategy*, 7, 4, pp. 45–56.

CHAPTER SEVENTEEN

PRICING DECISIONS

Each product has a price, but each firm is not necessarily in a position to determine the price at which it sells its product. But when the firm has developed strategic marketing and thus has gained some degree of market power, setting the price is a key decision, which conditions the success of its strategy to a large extent. From the firm's point of view, the question of price has two aspects: the price is an instrument to stimulate demand, much like advertising, for example, and at the same time price is a determinant factor of the firm's long-term profitability. Therefore the choice of a pricing strategy must respect two types of coherence: an *internal coherence* that is setting a product price respecting constraints of costs and profitability and an *external coherence* that is setting the price level keeping in mind the market's purchasing power and the price of competing goods. After describing the strategic role of price in marketing, we will analyse pricing decisions that emphasize costs, competition and demand successively. Figure 17.1 describes the general problem of price setting in a competitive environment.

Learning Objectives

When you have read this chapter, you should be able to:

- Understand the buyer's perception of price and its significance for the firm
- Analyse the cost and profit implications of different pricing alternatives
- List and explain the factors affecting the customer's price sensitivity
- Describe and compare different methods of pricing in a market-oriented perspective
- Discuss the impact of the competitive structure on the firm's pricing strategy
- Describe the way to approach the problem of setting the price for a set of related products
- Explain the pricing issues facing a firm operating in foreign markets

---

17.1 THE CUSTOMER'S PERCEPTION OF PRICE

Price is the *monetary expression of value* and as such occupies a central role in competitive exchange. From the customer's point of view, the price he or she is willing to pay measures the intensity of the need and the quantity and nature of satisfaction that is expected. From the seller's point of view, the price at which he or she is willing to sell measures the value of inputs incorporated in the product, to which the seller adds the profit that is hoped to be achieved. Purchasing behaviour can be seen as a system of exchange in which searching for satisfaction and monetary sacrifices compensate each other.

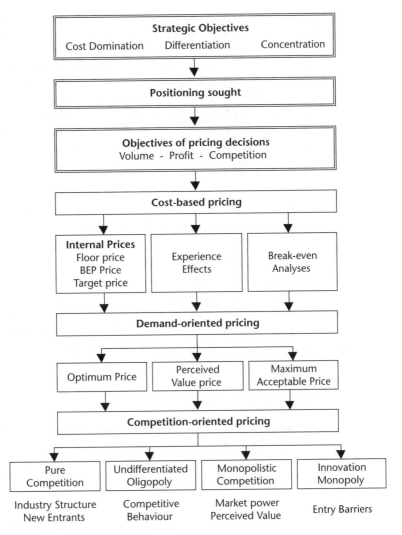

Figure 17.1 Pricing decisions: an overview

Market definition of price

Formally, monetary price can be defined as a ratio indicating the amount of money necessary for acquiring a given quantity of a good or service:

$$\text{Price} = \frac{\text{Amount of money provided by the customer}}{\text{Quantity of goods provided by the seller}}$$

In fact, the notion of price is wider and goes beyond the simple coincidence of purely objective and quantitative factors. The amount of money paid measures incompletely the sacrifices made, and, in the same way, the quantity of good obtained measures actual satisfaction imperfectly.

The price as a measure of value

As far as the customer is concerned, a product is a bundle of *benefits* and the services that are derived from the product are many, not only the product's core service, but also the other peripheral services – both objective and perceptual – that characterize the product or the brand. Therefore the price must reflect the value of all such satisfaction to the buyer.

> Let us compare two watches having the same objective technical quality. Brand A is a prestigious one, with an elegant design, sold exclusively by watchmakers; it carries a five-year guarantee and is advertised using sport and theatre personalities. Brand B is little known, soberly designed, sold in department stores with a 6-month guarantee and advertised as being reliable. Although these two watches provide the same core or functional service (time measurement), we can see that they are two distinct products and their value as perceived by potential buyers will be very different.

Therefore, from the customer's point of view, price must be conceived as the compensation for all services rendered and set according to the total value or total utility perceived by the buyer, hence the importance of a well-defined positioning before setting the selling price.

The total cost of acquiring a product

Just as the obtained quantity of goods measures actual satisfaction imperfectly, the amount of money paid measures the importance of actual sacrifice imperfectly. In fact, the price is the money received by the seller as result of a transaction. It does not reflect all the costs supported by he customer. These costs borne by the customer not only cover the price paid, but also the *terms of exchange, that is,* all the concrete practical procedures that lead to transfer of ownership, such as conditions of payment, delivery terms and times, after-sales service and so on. In some cases, the buyer may have to bear important costs to compare prices, transact and negotiate. This can happen if, for example, the buyer is located in isolated regions. Similarly, the customer may face high *transfer costs*, if he or she changes suppliers after having set the product specifications in relation to a given supplier. The main sources of transfer costs are as follows:

- Costs of modifying products so as to fit a new supplier's product.
- Changes in habits of consuming or using the product.
- Expenditures on training and reorientation of users.
- Investments to acquire new equipment necessary for the use of the new products.
- Psychological costs related to change.

All these costs may be higher for some clients than for others. When transfer costs exist, the real cost to the buyer is much higher than the product's monetary price.

Therefore, from the customer's point of view, the notion of price goes well beyond that of monetary price. It involves *all the benefits provided by the product and all the monetary and non-monetary costs borne by the customer*. Hence measures of price sensitivity must take into account all these benefits and costs as well as the product's nominal price. Viewed from the customer's perspective, the price can be redefined as follows:

$$\text{Price} = \frac{\text{Total cost (monetary and non-monetary) supported by the customer}}{\text{Total benefits (tangible and intangible) provided by the product}}$$

To illustrate the complexity of price viewed in the customer perspective, one can identify eight different ways of changing the above price ratio (Monroe, 1979):

- Change the quantity of money given up by the buyer.
- Change the quantity of goods and services provided by the seller.

- Change the quality of goods or services provided.
- Change the premiums or discounts to be applied for quantity variations.
- Change the time and place of transfer of ownership.
- Change the place and time of payment.
- Change the acceptable forms of payment
- Change the name or the brand of the product.

Importance of pricing decisions

The following points highlight the importance of pricing strategies in the current macro-marketing environment:

- The chosen price directly influences *demand level* and determines the level of activity. A price set too high or too low can endanger the product's development. Therefore, measuring price sensitivity is of crucial importance.
- The selling price directly determines the *profitability of the operation*, not only by the profit margin allowed, but also through quantities sold by fixing the conditions under which fixed costs can be recovered over the appropriate time horizon. Thus, a small price difference may have a major impact on profitability.
- The price set by the firm influences the product or the brand's general perception and contributes to the *brand's positioning* within potential buyers' evoked set. Customers perceive the price as a signal, especially in consumer goods markets. The price quoted invariably creates a notion of quality, and therefore is a component of the brand image.
- More than any other marketing variables, the price is a direct mean for *comparison between competing products or brands*. The slightest change in price is quickly perceived by the market, and because of its visibility it can suddenly overturn the balance of forces. The price is a forced point of contact between competitors.
- Pricing strategy must be compatible with the *other components of operational marketing*. The price must allow for financing of promotional and advertising strategy. Product packaging must reinforce high quality and high price positioning; pricing strategy must respect distribution strategy and allow the granting of necessary distribution margins to ensure that the market coverage objectives can be achieved.

Recent developments in the economic and competitive environment have played their part in increasing the importance and complexity of pricing strategies significantly:

- Acceleration of technological progress and *shortening of product life cycles* means that a new activity must be made to pay over a much shorter time span than previously. Given that correction is so much more difficult, a mistake in setting the initial price is that much more serious.
- *Proliferation of brands* or products that are weakly differentiated, the regular appearance of new products and the range of products all reinforce the importance of correct price positioning; yet small differences can sometimes modify the market's perception of a brand quite significantly.
- *Legal constraints*, as well as regulatory and social constraints, such as price controls, setting maximum margins, authorization for price increases and so on limit the firm's autonomy in determining prices.
- *Reduced purchasing power* in most Western economies makes buyers more aware of price differences, and this increased price sensitivity reinforces the role of price as an instrument of stimulating sales and market share.

Given the importance and complexity of these decisions, pricing strategies are often elaborated by the firm's general management.

Alternative pricing objectives

All firms aim to make their activities profitable and to generate the greatest possible economic surplus. This broad objective can in practice take different forms and it is in the firm's interest to clarify from the outset its strategic priorities in setting prices. Generally speaking, possible objectives can be classified in three categories, according to whether they are centred on profits, volumes or competition.

Profit-oriented objectives

Profit-oriented objectives are either profit maximization or achievement of a sufficient return on invested capital. *Profit maximization* is the model put forward by economists. In practice, it is difficult to apply this model. Not only does it assume precise knowledge of cost and demand functions for each product; it also assumes a stability that is seldom enjoyed by environmental and competitive factors. The objective of *target return on investment* (ROI) is widespread. In practice it takes the form of calculating a target price, or a sufficient price; that is, a price, which, for a given level of activity, ensures a fair return on invested capital. This approach, often adopted by large enterprises, has the merit of simplicity, but is incorrect, because it ignores the fact that it is the price level that ultimately determines the demand level.

Volume-oriented objectives

Volume-oriented objectives aim to maximize current revenue or market share, or simply to ensure sufficient sales growth. Maximizing market share implies adopting a *penetration price* that is a relatively low price, which is lower than competitors' prices, in order to increase volume and consequently market share as fast as possible. Once a dominant position is reached, the objective changes to one of sufficient or "satisfactory" rate of return. This is a strategy often used by firms having accumulated a high production volume and who expect reduced costs due to learning effects. A totally different strategy is that of *skimming pricing*. The goal here is to achieve high sales revenue, given that some buyers or market segments are prepared to pay a high price because of the product's distinctive (real or perceived) qualities. The objective here is to achieve the highest possible turnover with a high price rather than high volume.

Competition-oriented objectives

Competition-oriented objectives aim either for price stability or to be in line with competitors. In a number of industries dominated by a leading firm, the objective is to establish a stable relationship between prices of various competing products and to avoid wide fluctuations in prices that would undermine customers' confidence. The objective of keeping in line with other firms reveals that the firm is aware of its inability to exercise any influence on the market, especially when there is one dominant firm and products are standardized, as in undifferentiated oligopolies. In this case, the firm prefers to concentrate its efforts on competing on features other than price. Forms of non-price competition will often prevail in this type of market.

To elaborate a pricing strategy, three groups of factors must be taken into consideration: costs, demand and competition. We will now examine successively each of these factors and their implications for price determination.

17.2 COST-BASED PRICING PROCEDURES

Starting with cost analysis is certainly the most natural way to approach the pricing problem, and it is also the one most familiar to firms. Given that the manufacturer has undergone costs in order to produce and commercialize a product, it is natural that its main preoccupation would be to determine various price levels compatible with constraints such as covering direct and fixed costs and generating a fair profit. Figure 17.2 shows a typical cost structure in which the definitions of the main cost concepts are given.

Cost-based price concepts

Prices which are based on costs and make no explicit reference to market factors are called *cost-based prices*. Cost analysis identifies four types of cost-based prices, each responding to specific cost and profit requirements.

The "floor price"

The *floor price*, or the minimum price, corresponds to direct variable costs (C), also known as "out-of-pocket costs". It is the price that only covers the product's replacement value, and therefore implies zero gross profit margins.

$$\text{Floor price} = \text{Direct variable cost}$$

This price concept is useful for negotiating exceptional orders or for second market discounting, when the firm has unused capacity and has the possibility to sell in a new market such that there will be a negligible loss of sales in its main market. Floor prices, also called *marginal price*, are the absolute minimum selling price the firm should accept. Any price

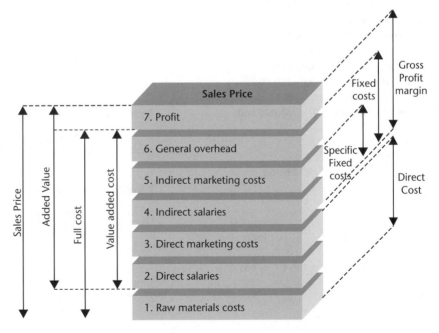

Figure 17.2   The elements of price
Source: Adapted from Monroe (1979).

above the floor price can allow a firm to use its production capacity to a maximum and still generate extra funds to cover overheads or improve profits. Exceptional orders, generics for large retail chain and foreign markets provide opportunities for this form of discriminatory pricing strategy.

The "break-even price"

The *break-even price* (BEP) corresponds to the price where fixed and direct costs are recovered, given the sales volume assumed. It ensures that both the product's replacement value and fixed costs (*F*) are recovered.

$$\text{BEP} = C + F / E(Q)$$

where $E(Q)$ denotes expected sales volume. The BEP corresponds to the full cost concept, where the level of activity is used as a criterion for allocating the fixed costs.

BEPs are usually calculated for different volume levels, as shown in the example of Exhibit 17.1. This defines a range of minimum prices. Note that the BEP depends on the volume of activity and only coincides with the full cost at that level.

The "target price"

The *target price*, or sufficient price, includes, apart from direct and fixed costs, a profit constraint, which is normally determined by reference to a "normal" rate of return (*r*) on

---

Exhibit 17.1   Example of cost-based price determination

Basic data:

Production capacity:	180,000 units
Capital invested (*K*):	€24,000,000
Expected rate of return (*r*):	10%
Direct cost (*C*):	€105/unit
Fixed cost (*F*):	€9,000,000/year
Expected sales = $E(Q) = Q_2 = 120,000$ units	
Pessimistic estimate = $Q_1 = 90,000$ units	
Optimistic estimate = $Q_3 = 150,000$ units	

Floor prix (P_L):

$$P_L = C = €105/\text{unit}$$

BEP (P_t):

$$P = C + \frac{F}{E(Q)} = 105 + \frac{9,000,000}{E(Q)}$$

$P_{t_1} = 205\ €\ P_{t_2} = 180\ €\ P_{t_3} = 165\ €$

Target price (P_c):

$$P = C + \frac{F}{E(Q)} + \frac{r \cdot K}{E(Q)}$$

$$P = 105 + \frac{9,000,000}{E(Q)} + \frac{(0,10) \times (24,000,000)}{E(Q)}$$

$P_{c_1} = 231.7\ €\ P_{c_2} = 200\ €\ P_{c_3} = 181\ €$

Contemplated sale price (P_V):

$$P_V = 195\ €/\text{unit}$$

Break-even in volume:

$$Q_n = \frac{F}{P - C} = \frac{9,000,000}{195 - 105} = 100,000\ \text{units}$$

Break-even in sales revenue:

$$SR_n = \frac{F}{\dfrac{P - C}{P}} = \frac{9,000,000}{0,46} = 19,565,217\ \text{euros}$$

Source: Lambin (2000/2007).

invested capital (K). This cost-based price is also calculated with reference to an assumed level of activity.

$$\text{Target price} = C + \frac{F}{E(Q)} + \frac{r \cdot K}{E(Q)}$$

where K denotes invested capital and r the rate of return considered as sufficient or normal. Like the BEP, the target price depends on the activity volume being considered.

The "mark-up price"

The *mark-up price* is set by adding a standard mark-up to the BEP. Assuming that the firm wants to earn a 20 per cent mark-up on sales, the mark-up price is given by

$$\text{Target price} = \frac{\text{BEP}}{(1 - \text{desired margin})}$$

This pricing method, popular for its simplicity, ignores demand and competition. It will work only if the expected sales level is achieved.

The risk of circular logic

Target and mark-up prices are used widely, because of their simplicity and the apparent security arising from the illusory certainty of a margin, since mark-up and target pricing procedures promise to ensure a given return on cost. Their most important shortcoming is the lack of any relationship between price and volume. In fact, they implicitly contain a built-in circular logic: volume determines costs, which determine price, which in turn determines the level of demand.

Indeed, there is no guarantee that the adopted target price or mark-up will generate the activity volume on the basis of which it was calculated. Table 17.1 shows what happens to the target price if the firm's sales volume is below the assumed level.

In the example, the expected activity level is 120,000 units and the corresponding target price is £2,000. If demand is only 90,000 units, to maintain the desired profitability level the price would have to be increased and the product sold at £2,317.

Is raising price the appropriate response in the face of declining demand? Similarly, if the firm's sales exceed expectations, fixed costs are spread over a larger volume and the target price declines. Should management respond to excess demand by cutting prices?

This pricing behaviour runs counter to economic logic and leads to inappropriate recommendations. The firm that sets price from the sole perspective of its own internal needs generally forgoes the profit it seeks. If all firms within a given industry adopt the same mark-up or target rate of return, prices tend to be similar and price competition is minimized. In practice, cost-based prices are used only as a convenient starting point, because, in general, firms have more reliable information about costs than about demand factors.

Usefulness of cost-based pricing

Cost-orientated prices constitute a starting point for setting a market price. They cannot be the only basis for determining prices because these pricing procedures ignore demand, the

---

Box 17.1   Implementation problem: how much pocket money are we making on this product?

Managers who oversee pricing often focus on invoices prices, which are readily available, but the real story goes much further. A distinction must be made among *list price, invoice price, pocket price and pocket margin*.

From the standard list price, there are several "on-invoice" and "off-invoice" leakages that should be considered. In a case reported by McKinsey (Marn, Roegner and Zawada, 2003), the *on-invoice leakages* included standard distributor discount, special distributor discount, end-customer discount and on-invoice promotion. *Off-invoice leakages* included cash discount for prompt payment, the cost of carrying accounts receivables, cooperative advertising allowances, rebates based on distributor's total annual volume, off-invoice promotional programs and freight expenses. In the end, the

invoice price and the pocket price were, respectively, at 67.2 per cent and 50.9 per cent of the list price, including a 16.3 per cent in revenue reductions that didn't appear on invoices.

For companies offering customized products, unique solutions packages or unique forms of logistical or technical support, the cost of these services should be subtracted from the pocket price to identify the *pocket margin*, the true measure of profitability. In another case also reported by McKinsey, the costs of customer-specific services averaged 17 per cent of the list price, leaving a pocket margin of 28 per cent, to be compared with the standard gross margin of 45 per cent.

Source: Marn, Roegner and Zawada (2003).

---

product's perceived value and competition. However, they do have a real *usefulness*, because they provide answers to the following types of questions:

- What are the sales volume or sales revenue required to cover all costs?
- How does the target price or the mark-up price compare with prices of direct competition?
- To what level of market share does the level of sales at the break-even point correspond?
- What is the expected sales increase required to cover a fixed cost increase, such as an advertising campaign, assuming constant price?
- If prices go down, what is the minimum volume increase required to offset the price decrease?
- If prices go up, what is the permissible volume decrease to offset the price increase?
- What is the implied price elasticity necessary to enhance or maintain profitability?
- What is the rate of return on invested capital for different price levels?

Cost analysis is a first necessary step, which helps to identify the problem by focusing attention on the financial implications of various pricing strategies. Armed with this information, the firm is better placed to approach the more qualitative aspects of the problem, namely, market sensitivity to prices and competitive reactions.

Initiating price cuts

Initiating a *price cut* with a view to stimulate demand is relevant only when total demand for the product can grow. Otherwise, if the firm reduces its price and if all the competitors react immediately and follow suit, the profits of each will drop and their respective market shares will remain exactly as before in a market that remains the same size, although average price has decreased. There are, however, some situations, which might be favourable to a price cut in a non-expansible market, without entailing rapid reactions from competitors:

- When competitors' costs are higher and they cannot lower their prices without endangering profitability; not following the price cut implies a loss of market share unless factors of differentiation neutralize the price difference.

- Smaller firms can use a price cut more easily. This represents a lighter investment for them as opposed to larger enterprises, which hold a higher market share, because the cost of promoting a product via price is proportional to sales volume. Larger competitors may indeed prefer to maintain their prices and react on a different front, for example, by increasing advertising, which represents a fixed cost.

A firm may therefore choose not to follow a price cut, particularly when its product's perceived value is above that of its immediate competitors. It will then be protected from the effects of a price cut by differentiation factors, such as brand image, range of services or customer relations. Changing suppliers implies transfer costs, which are not always compensated by the price difference. In industrial markets, for example, it is frequently observed that customers accept price differentials of up to 10 per cent without much difficulty if relationships with the usual supplier are well established.

Determining the cost of a price cut

It is important to realize that the *cost of a price cut* is often very high, especially for a firm with a high proportion of variable costs. The data in Table 17.1 define the necessary increases in sales revenue and in volume required to retain the same gross margin (25 per cent in this case) at different levels of price cut.

In this particular case, where the gross margin of 25 per cent before the price cut is to be held, the number of units sold must more than double to compensate for a price cut of 15 per cent. One can imagine that the necessary increase in sales can rapidly be above the impact that can reasonably be expected from a price cut.

Furthermore, it can be shown that a price cut is less favourable to a firm with high variable costs, because the necessary increase in sales to keep the same margin will be higher, the higher the proportion of variable costs (Monroe, 1979, p. 73). In general, for a price decrease, the necessary volume increase to maintain the same level of profitability is given by

$$\text{Volume increase (\%)} = (\frac{x}{M^\star - x}) \times 100$$

where x is the percentage price decrease expressed as a decimal and $M^\star$ is the gross profit margin as a percentage of selling price before the price cut.

To illustrate, if a price cut of 9 per cent is envisaged and the gross profit margin is 30 per cent, the required sales volume increase is

$$\text{Volume increase (\%)} = (\frac{0.09}{0.30 - 0.09}) \times 100 = 42.86\%$$

Table 17.1 Minimum volume and sales revenue increase required for offsetting a price decrease

Price decrease (per cent)	Percentage minimum sales revenue increase required	Percentage minimum volume increase required
5	18	25
10	50	66
15	112	150
20	300	400

Source: Assuming a gross profit margin of 25 per cent.

If the gross profit margin were to decrease to 25 per cent or 20 per cent the same price cut of 9 per cent would require sales increases of 56.25 per cent and 81.82 per cent, respectively. For the derivation of the break-even formula, see Nagle and Holden (1987, pp. 44–6).

Therefore, the firm having the lowest variable costs will be induced to initiate a significant price cut, in the knowledge that other firms could not follow suit.

Computing implied price elasticity

It is also possible to derive implied *price elasticity* from these figures. This is the price elasticity that should prevail within the targeted group of buyers before profits could be increased.

In the previous example, the price cut of 9 per cent ought to give rise to a 42.86 per cent increase in sales volume in order to retain the gross profit margin at 30 per cent. Therefore, the implied price elasticity is

$$\varepsilon = \frac{+\,42.86\%}{-\,9\%} = -4.76$$

A price elasticity of –4.8 per cent is very high and assumes a very price-sensitive demand. If it is considered that the product market's demand is less elastic, and if profit is the only choice criterion, then the price cut is not economically justified.

The risk of a *price war* is always present in an oligopolistic market, which explains why firms are reluctant to initiate price cuts. There are, however, situations where a price cut can improve the competitive position of the firm. Reducing the profit margin with price cuts may be compensated for by market share gains, which in the long run mean higher profitability because of cost reductions due to experience effects. Another reason for a price war might be to eliminate a potentially dangerous competitor.

Experience curve pricing

In sectors where the cost of value added represents a large proportion of total unit cost, substantial cost reductions can be obtained as accumulated production increases. If consumers in this market are price-sensitive, a good strategy for the firm having the largest experience is to price aggressively, even below current cost, as illustrated in Figure 17.3(a).

This strategy presents several advantages. First, competing firms will have to leave the market and the leading company will be confronted with fewer rivals. Second, the firm can benefit from the sales of the other firms and gain experience more rapidly. Also, because of the lower prevailing market price, new buyers will be encouraged to enter the market.

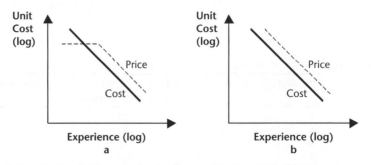

Figure 17.3   Experience curve pricing strategies (logarithmic axes)

However, pricing below cost cannot be maintained for extended periods of time. A less aggressive pricing strategy is the one depicted in Figure 17.3(b) where a parallel is maintained between cost and price reductions.

Initiating price increases

Initiating a *price increase* is also a difficult decision. The firm initiating the increase must be certain that competitors are willing to follow suit. Generally speaking, this willingness depends on the prevailing market conditions at the time, and in particular when production capacity is fully used and demand is growing. As in the case of a price cut, before starting any initiative, it is in the firm's interest to evaluate its margin for manoeuvre.

If price is increased, the permissible volume decrease, that is, leaving the previous level of profit unchanged, is determined as follows:

$$\text{Permissible volume decrease (\%)} = \frac{x}{M^* + x} \times 100$$

where x is the percentage price increase expressed as a decimal. If a 9 per cent price increase is contemplated and if the gross profit margin is 30 per cent, the percentage sales volume decrease is

$$\text{Volume decrease (\%)} = \frac{x}{M^* + x} \times 100 = 23.08\%$$

and the implied price elasticity is –2.56. For the price increase to enhance profit, market demand must have a price elasticity below the implied price elasticity of –2.6.

17.3 DEMAND-ORIENTED PRICING PROCEDURES

Pricing based exclusively on the firm's own financial needs is inappropriate. In a market economy, it is the buyer who ultimately decides which products will sell. Consequently, in a market-driven organization an effective pricing procedure *starts with the price the market is most likely to accept*, which in turn determines the target cost. As illustrated in Figure 17.4, it is the market-acceptable price that constitutes the constraint for R&D, engineering and purchasing. Thus, price determination in a demand-oriented procedure puts customer sensitivity as the starting point.

The price elasticity concept

An important concept in demand analysis is the *notion of elasticity*. Elasticity directly measures customers' price sensitivity and ideally allows the calculation of quantities demanded at various price levels. Recall the definition of price elasticity: it is the percentage change in a product's unit sales resulting from a 1 per cent change in its price.

$$\varepsilon = \frac{\% \text{ of variation of unit sales}}{\% \text{ of variation of price}}$$

Price elasticity is negative, since a price increase generally produces a decline in sales while a price cut generally produces an increase in sales. As an illustration, Table 17.2 compares the impact of price elasticity on quantities and on sales revenue for an elastic (–3.7) and an inelastic (–0.19) demand.

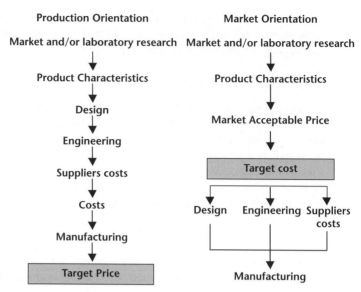

Figure 17.4   Price determination in a market-oriented perspective
Source: Lambin (2007).

Table 17.2   Impact of price elasticity on quantity and on sales revenue

	Elastic demand curve: $\varepsilon=-3.7$			Inelastic demand curve: $\varepsilon=-0.19$	
Price	Quantity (in 1,000)	Sales revenue (in 1,000 $)	Price	Quantity (in 1,000)	Sales revenue (in 1,000 $)
12,000	80	960,000	8.00	300	2,400
9,000	400	3,600,000	6.00	320	1,920
7,000	1,200	8,400,000	4.00	340	1,360

We will first examine the main factors affecting price sensitivity, and then describe various approaches that can be adopted to measure it.

Factors affecting price sensitivity

Every buyer is sensitive to prices, but this sensitivity can vary tremendously from one situation to another, according to the importance of the satisfaction provided by the product, or conversely depending on the sacrifices, other than price, imposed by obtaining the product. Nagle and Holden (1994) have identified nine factors affecting buyers' price sensitivity:

1. *Unique-value effect:* buyers are less price-sensitive when the product is unique.
2. *Substitute awareness effect:* buyers are less price-sensitive when they are less aware of substitutes.
3. *Difficult comparison effect:* buyers are less price-sensitive when they cannot easily compare the quality of substitutes.
4. *Total expenditure effect:* buyers are less price-sensitive the lower the expenditure is to a ratio of their income.
5. *End benefit effect:* buyers are less price-sensitive the lower the expenditure is compared with the total cost of the end-product.
6. *Shared cost effect:* buyers are less price-sensitive when part of the cost is borne by another party.

7. *Sunk investment effect:* buyers are less price-sensitive when the product is used in conjunction with assets previously bought.

8. *Price-quality effect:* buyers are less price-sensitive when the product is assumed to have more quality, prestige or exclusiveness.

9. *Inventory effect:* buyers are less price-sensitive when they cannot store the product.

The questions to examine for assessing customers' price sensitivity are presented in Box 17.2.

Note that these determinants of price sensitivity apply equally to the decision of buying a particular product category (primary demand price sensitivity) and that of buying a particular brand within a product category (interbrand price sensitivity). In the first case, the question would, for example, be to choose between a laptop computer and a hi-fi; in the second case, the alternatives would be, for example, to buy an Asus or an HP laptop computer. The price level of the alternatives affects both kinds of decision.

Box 17.2   Implementation problem: how to identify factors affecting price sensitivity?

1. The unique value effect
- Does the product have any (tangible or intangible) attributes that differentiate it from competing products?
- How much do buyers value those unique, differentiating attributes?

2. The substitute awareness effect
- What alternatives do buyers have (considering both competing brands and competing products)?
- Are buyers aware of alternative suppliers or substitute products?

3. The difficult comparison effect
- How difficult is it for buyers to compare the offers of different suppliers? Can the attributes of a product be determined by observation, or must the product be purchased and consumed to learn what it offers?
- Is the product highly complex, requiring a costly specialist to evaluate its differentiating attributes?
- Are the prices of different suppliers easily comparable, or are they stated for different sizes and combinations that make comparisons difficult?

4. The total expenditure effect
- How significant are buyers' expenditures of the product in cash terms and (for a consumer product) as a portion of their incomes?

5. The end benefit effect
- What benefits do buyers seek from the product?

- How price-sensitive are buyers to the cost of the end benefit?
- What portion of the benefit does the product's price account for?

6. The shared cost effect
- Do the buyers pay the full cost of the product?
- If not, what portion of the cost do they pay?

7. The sunk investment effect
- Must buyers of the product make complementary expenditures in anticipation of its continued use?
- For how long are buyers locked in by those expenditures?

8. The price-quality effect
- Is a prestige image an important attribute for the product?
- Is the product enhanced in value when its price excludes some consumers?
- Is the product of unknown quality, and are there few reliable cues for ascertaining quality before purchase? If so, how great would the loss to buyers be of low quality relative to the price of the product?

9. The inventory effect
- Do buyers hold inventories of the product?
- Do they expect the current price to be temporary?

Source: Adapted from Nagle and Holden (1994).

Price sensitivity of the B2B customer

In B2B markets, customers' needs are generally well defined and the functions performed by products clearly specified. In these conditions, it is sometimes easier to determine the importance of price to the B2B customer. Porter (1980, pp. 115–18) observed that customers who are *not price-sensitive* tend to have the following behavioural characteristics or motivations:

- The cost of the product is a small part of the customer's product cost and/or purchasing budget.
- The penalty for product failure is high relative to its cost.
- Effectiveness of the product (or service) can yield major savings or improvement in performance.
- The customer competes with a high-quality strategy to which the purchased product is perceived to contribute.
- The customer seeks a custom-designed or differentiated variety.
- The customer is very profitable and/or can readily pass on the cost of inputs.
- The customer is poorly informed about the product and/or does not purchase from well-defined specifications.
- The motivation of the actual decision-maker is not narrowly defined as minimizing the cost of inputs.

Industrial market research studies can help in identifying these behavioural characteristics or requirements. These are useful to know in order to direct pricing policy.

Optimum price based on elasticity

The economic and marketing literature contains many econometric studies on measuring price elasticity, as shown in Table 17.3. For a summary of elasticity studies, see Hanssens, Parsons and Schultz (1990). Tellis (1988) found a mean price elasticity of –2.5. Broadbent (1980) reported an average price elasticity of –1.6 for major British brands. Lambin, covering a sample of 137 brands, reported an average price elasticity of –1.74 (Lambin, 1976, 1988). Bijmolt, Van Heerde and Pieters (2005) observed an overall mean price elasticity of –2.62.

Economic theory shows that the less elastic (in absolute terms) the demand for a product, the higher the optimal price, that is, the price that maximizes profit; if we know the elasticity, the optimal price can be calculated as follows:

$$P_{opt} = C \times \frac{\varepsilon}{\varepsilon + 1}$$

Or, in words,

$$\text{Optimal Price} = \text{Unit direct cost} \times \text{cost mark-up}$$

Where

$$\text{Cost mark-up} = \frac{\text{price elasticity}}{\text{price elasticity} + 1}$$

Thus, the optimal price is obtained by multiplying the unit variable cost (or marginal cost) by a percentage, which depends on the price elasticity and is independent of cost. The derivation of this optimization rule is presented in Lambin (1998, p. 301).

Table 17.3 Optimal cost mark-up as a function of price elasticity

Price Elasticity $\varepsilon_{q,p}$	Optimal cost mark-up $\varepsilon_{q,p/\varepsilon_{q,p}+1}$	Price elasticity $\varepsilon_{q,p}$	Optimal cost mark-up $\varepsilon_{q,p/\varepsilon_{q,p}+1)}$
–1.0	–	2.4	1.71
–1.2	6.00	2.6	1.00
–1.4	3.50	...	...
–1.6	2.67	**3.0**	**1.50**
–1.8	2.22	4.0	1.33
–2.0	**2.00**	5.0	1.25
–2.2	1.83	...	...
...	...	15.0	1.07

Box 17.3   Implementation problem: how to calculate the optimal price elasticity between –1.7 and –2.0

By way of illustration, if $\varepsilon = -2{,}1$ and $C = €105$, the optimal price is equal to

$$P_{opt} = (105) \cdot \left(\frac{-2.1}{(-2.1)+1} \right) = (105) \cdot (1.9) = 205 \text{ euros}$$

The optimal mark-up here is equal to 1.9.

Table 17.3 shows that the optimal mark-up is higher when price elasticity is lower in absolute value, that is, closer to unity, and gives some comparisons of mark-up coefficients for a range of elasticity.

One observes that, when price elasticity is high, which is the case in highly competitive markets of undifferentiated products, mark-up is close to unity; the firm's market power is weak and the price accepted by the market is close to unit costs. Conversely, the closer elasticity is to unity, the higher is the price acceptable by the market.

Optimization rules proposed by economic theory, initially developed in the monopoly case (Dorfman and Steiner, 1954), have been extended to the oligopoly case (Lambin, Naert and Bultez, 1975) and also to the dynamic case when market response is distributed over time (Nerlove and Arrow, 1962; Jacquemin, 1973).

Methods of price sensitivity measurement

Several methods exist to estimate customers' price sensitivity. These methods can be grouped into four main categories:

1. *The expert judgement* method consists in asking market experts to provide three estimates or points of the price response curve, successively the lowest realistic, the highest realistic prices and the associated sales volume, plus the expected sales at the medium price.
2. *Customer surveys, directs or indirect*. The most popular is the indirect method through conjoint analysis.
3. *Price experimentations, field or laboratory experiments*. We are here in the domain of causal research.
4. *Econometric studies* based on time series data or on panel data. As underlined above, the availability of scanner data greatly facilitates this type of analysis, particularly in the food sector.

Each of these methods has its own advantages and disadvantages.

Usefulness of elasticity measures

Knowledge of the order of magnitude of an elasticity is on the whole useful in many ways:

- Elasticity provides information about the direction in which prices should change in order to stimulate demand and increase turnover.
- Comparing elasticity of competing brands identifies those that can withstand a price increase better, thus revealing their market power.
- Comparing elasticity of products in the same category helps to adjust prices within the category.
- Cross-elasticity help to predict demand shifts from one brand to another.

To illustrate, Table 17.4 shows estimated price elasticity in the car market and in the market for air transport in the United States. Although the estimates have insufficient precision for the exact calculation of prices, the results are, nevertheless, very enlightening as far as pricing policy orientation for each product category is concerned.

Limitations of price elasticity measures

Despite the relevance of these works, there have been very few practical applications of this highly quantitative approach to the problem of pricing, except maybe in some large enterprises. The reason is that the notion of elasticity presents a number of conceptual and operational difficulties, which reduce its practical usefulness:

- Elasticity measures a relationship based on buying behaviour and is therefore only observable *after the fact*; its predictive value depends on the stability of the conditions that gave rise to the observation; it cannot, for example, be used to determine the price of new products.
- In many situations, the problem is not so much to know how to adapt prices to present market sensitivities, but to know how to change and *act upon this sensitivity* in the direction sought by the firm. From this viewpoint, it is more interesting to know the product's perceived value by the targeted group of buyers.
- Elasticity measures the impact of price on quantity bought, but does not measure the effect of price on the propensity to try the product, on repeat purchases, exclusivity rate and so on. But these are all important notions for understanding consumers' response mechanisms with respect to prices. Therefore, *other measures*, which are less aggregate, need to be developed for marketing management.

Table 17.4 Price elasticity estimates: two examples from the US market

Demand for automobiles		Demand for air transport	
Sub-compact	−0.83	First class	−0.75
Compact	−1.20	Economy	−1.40
Intermediate	−1.30	Discount	−2.10
Full-size	−1.54		
Luxury	−2.07		

Source: Automobile data from Carlson (1978); air transport data from Oum and Gillen (1981).

Furthermore, in practice it is often very hard to get sufficiently stable and reliable estimates of price elasticity, which could be used to calculate an optimal selling price. A summary of econometric work on marketing variables elasticity is presented in Table 17.5.

In a recent meta-analysis of price elasticity based on 81 publications and 1,860 price elasticity estimates, the overall mean price elasticity was –2.62 (median = –2.22, standard deviation =2.21). The frequency distribution of the observed price elasticities is strongly peaked; 50 per cent of the observations are between –3 and –1, and 80 per cent between –4 and 0 (Bijmolt, Van Heerde and Pieters, 2005). This average price elasticity of –2.62 is substantially larger in magnitude than the average price elasticities reported in Table 17.5.

Value pricing

Value pricing is a customer-based pricing procedure, which is an outgrowth of the *multi-attribute product concept*. From the customer's viewpoint, a product is the bundle of benefits that is received when using the product. Therefore, the customer-oriented company should set its price according to customers' perceptions of product benefits and costs. To determine the price, the marketer needs to understand the customers' perceptions of benefits as well as their perceptions of the costs other than price. Customers balance the benefits of a purchase against its costs. When the product under consideration has the best relationship of benefit to cost, the customer is inclined to buy the product. This customer-based pricing procedure can be implemented in different ways.

Table 17.5 Comparing average elasticity of marketing variables

Published sources	Number of observations	Average value of estimated elasticity			
		Advertising	Price	Quality	Distribution
Lambin (1976, 1988)	127	0,081	–1,735	0,521	1,395
Leone and Schultz (1980)	25	0,003–0,230	–	–	–
Assmus, Farley and Lehmann (1984)	22	0,221 (0,264)	–	–	–
Hagerty, Carman and Russel (1988)	203	0,003 (0,105)	–0,985 (1,969)	0,344 (0,528)	0,304 (0,255)
Neslin and Shoemaker (1983)	25	–	–1,800	–	–
Tellis (1988)	220	–	–1,760	–	–

Box 17.4   Implementation problem: how to evaluate customer-perceived value of my product?

- If I bought this desktop computer at this store, I feel I would be getting my money' worth.
- If I acquired this desktop computer at this store, I think I would be getting good value for the money I spend.
- The desktop would be a worthwhile acquisition because it is reasonably priced.

- Buying this desktop computer from this store makes me feel good.
- I would get a lot of pleasure knowing that I got this desktop at this price from this store.
- Taking advantage of this price give me a sense of joy.

Source: Xia and Monroe (2004).

The product's perceived value

The basic idea behind this method is the same: it is the product or the brand's perceived value which should determine the price level. By analysing and measuring the buyers' perception and its determinants using the compositional method, a score of total perceived value can be derived and used to set the price. The notion of perceived value is a direct extension of the multi-attribute attitude model.

By way of illustration, let us examine the data of Table 17.6 and the scores given by a sample of potential buyers to brand A and to its direct competitor brand B, over six tangible and intangible attributes. In the example presented, respondents have first evaluated on a 10-point scale the importance of each attribute and then on a 10-point scale also the performance of each brand on each attribute.

The total perceived value of each brand is obtained by multiplying the scores given to each attribute by their respective degree of importance and by summing the weighted scores. The totals obtained are then expressed in index form by reference to the direct competitor. One obtains, respectively,

$$\text{brand A}=1.24 \text{ and brand B} = 0.81$$

Thus, one observes that brand A has higher perceived value than brand B, its direct competitor, because brand A performs better on the most important attributes (A6, A2 and A3). If these results can be considered as representative of the target segment perceptions, and assuming that the other marketing factors are equal, the maximum acceptable price (MAP) for brand A could be determined by reference to the average perceived value (here 7.95), with brand A's MAP 10.7 per cent higher and brand B's price 11 per cent lower.

> If the average market price is equal to €5,000, brand A could charge a maximum price as high as €5,535 while brand B, to be accepted by the market, should charge a price as low as €4,450.

If brand A charges a price lower than its MAP, it will have an operational competitive advantage over brand B (better at the same price), which sooner or later will translate into a market share gain. This pricing procedure, based on a compositional approach, is particularly useful when price sensitivity is strongly influenced by qualitative attributes like brand image effect.

Table 17.6 Perceived value analysis: an example

Attributes other than price (1)	Importance of attributes (2)	Absolute performance (scale from 1 to 10)		Relative performance
		Brand A (3)	Direct Competitor (4)	Brand A (5 = 3÷4)
Tangibles				
A1	10	8,1	7,2	1,13
A2	20	9,0	7,3	1,23
A3	20	9,2	6,5	1,42
A4	15	8,0	8,0	1,00
Intangibles				
A5	10	8,0	8,0	1,00
A6	25	9,4	6,4	1,47
Total	100	–	–	–
Absolute performance	–	8,8	7,1	–
Relative performance	–	1,24	0,81	–

The maximum acceptable price

This second pricing procedure is particularly useful for setting the price of industrial products, whose core benefit to the buyer is a cost reduction. To evaluate what the customer is prepared to pay, the procedure followed is to identify and evaluate the different satisfactions or services provided by the product as well as all the costs (other than price) it implies. Thus the procedure is the following:

- Understand the total use of the product from the buyer's point of view.
- Analyse the benefits generated by the product.
- Analyse the costs implied by the acquisition and the use of the product.
- Make cost–benefit trade-offs and determine the MAP.

The highest price that the customer will be willing to pay for the product is given by

benefits – costs other than price = MAP

The benefits to consider can be functional (the core service), operational, financial or personal. Similarly, the implied costs other than prices are just as diverse: acquisition costs, installation, risk of failure, habit modification and so on.

If the target market is segmented, this analysis should be done for different groups of customers with non-identical behaviour. Comparing the MAP with competitors' prices helps evaluate the firm's margin for manoeuvre.

Box 17.5   Implementation problem: how to calculate MAP

- Product description
  - A chemical compound to be used in conjunction with the regular water-softening chemicals.

- Uses of the product
  - To disperse the water-softening compounds, thus lengthening their economic life.
  - To reduce rust formation in the boiler system.

- Benefits of the product
  - Core benefit: Reduce the amount of softening chemicals by 35 per cent.
  - Prevent rust formation.
  - Reduction in time and effort required for regenerating the softeners.

- Costs other than price
  - Installation of a dispenser and of a storage tank in the plant.
  - Service of the installation and technical assistance.
  - Risk of breakdown.
  - Lack of reference of the supplier.

  - Custom modification.

- Costs–benefits trade-off analysis
  - Average use: 40,000 gallons of softening per year.
  - Cost per gallon: 50 cents.
  - Average cost saving: 14,000 gallons (35 per cent), or €7,000.
  - Volume of Aqua-Pur – ratio: 1/7, or 3,715 gallons (26,000/7).
  - Cost of installation: €450, or €90 per year over five years.
  - Cost of maintenance: €320 per year.
  - Total maximum acceptable cost: €7,000 – (€90+€320) = €6,590.
  - Maximum acceptable unit price: €6,590/3,715 gallons = €1.77 per gallon.
  - Price of direct competitor: €1.36.

Source: Lambin (2000/2007).

Contributions of conjoint analysis

The same kind of result can be obtained with a *decompositional approach*, or the conjoint analysis method. To illustrate, we refer to a conjoint analysis based on a sample of 200 individuals and made in the blended cigarettes market, in order to compare the price sensitivity of four leading brands: Marlboro, Barclay, Camel and Gauloises Blondes (see Lambin 1998, pp. 150–2). Let us examine here the results obtained for two respondents (no. 17 and no. 86, respectively). The utilities are expressed here in terms of preference ranks lost when the price increases from its lowest level (F57) to a higher one. For respondent no. 17, the following utilities were obtained:

$$(F62; U = -2.5), (F67; U = -3.5) \text{ and } (F72; U = -5.0)$$

We thus have three observations and using ordinary least squares (OLS) average price elasticity was calculated as $\varepsilon = -3.59$ ($R^2 = 0.958$). For respondent no. 86, we obtained the following pairs of values:

$$(F62: U = -0.25), (F67: U = -1.25), (F72: U = 1.50)$$

The calculated elasticity here is $\varepsilon = -1.11$ ($R^2 = 0.914$).

Box 17.6   Implementation problem: how to create economic value for both the customer and the seller?

An example of value pricing taken from the telecommunication switch market is presented in the figure below. The customer's current telecommunication switch had a total cost of purchase of €1,000. The purchase price was only €300, but an additional €200 was spent for installation and start-up, as well as €500 in usage and other post-purchase costs. The business's new product offered customers a solution that could cut the start-up costs in half and reduce the usage cost by €100. At which price to sell the product? The customer MAP is €500, corresponding with the competitor's price. But the product has to be priced in a way that creates economic value for both customers and the seller. By setting its price at €375 (€75 more than the existing product) the seller created a solution that added €125 per switch to the customer's bottom line, while keeping a competitive advantage over its direct rival.

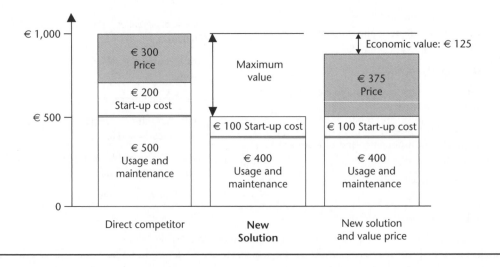

Note that the difference in price sensitivity between the two respondents is quite high. Now suppose that we have similar information for a representative sample of 200 buyers. Average price elasticity could be estimated for the whole sample as well as for sub-groups of buyers of high or low price sensitivity.

This kind of elasticity coefficient measures price sensitivity in terms of utility rather than in terms of quantity. Although more vague, it is, nevertheless, useful for comparison of different buyers' relative price sensitivities and to determine the best price level.

Flexible pricing strategies

Firms do not have a single price, but a variety of prices adapted to different market situations. Flexible pricing strategies occur in market situations where the same product is sold to different customers at different prices. Flexible pricing strategies arise primarily because of customers' heterogeneity, showing different price sensitivities, but also because of cost differences or promotional objectives. Price flexibility can be achieved in different ways: by region, period, product form or from one segment to another. We shall examine four different ways of achieving price flexibility. In the economic literature, the term *price discrimination* has been used to designate pricing variations not justified by cost differences.

Second market discounting

This situation occurs when a firm has excess production capacity and has the opportunity to sell in a new market such that there will be a negligible increase in fixed or variable costs and no loss of sales in its first market. The minimum acceptable selling price the firm should accept is the floor price that is the unit direct cost. Opportunities for this pricing strategy exist in foreign trade, private label brands or special demographic groups, like students, children or senior citizens. The essential requirement for this strategy is that customers of the lower price market cannot resell the product in the higher price market because of the high transaction costs implied.

Periodic discounting

The pricing problem is different here. How to price a product confronted with different price sensitivities among potential buyers at the beginning and at the end of the seasonal period? Some buyers want to buy only at the beginning of the period and are not very price-sensitive, while others want to buy the product at any time, but are price-sensitive. To exploit the consumers' heterogeneity of demand, the firm will sell at the high price at the beginning of the period and systematically discount the product at the end of the period. This is the principle often involved in the temporal markdowns and periodic discounting of off-season fashion goods, off-season travel fares, matinee tickets and happy hour drinks.

An essential principle underlying this strategy of periodic discounting is the manner of discounting, which is predictable over time and generally known to consumers, who will, therefore, behave accordingly (Tellis, 1986, p. 150).

Random discounting

Which pricing strategy should be adopted in a market where the same product is sold at a low price by some firms and at a high price by others, knowing that some buyers are ready to spend time searching for the low price while others are not ready to do so? In this case, we have heterogeneity of demand with respect to perceived search costs among consumers. The objective of the firm is twofold here: (a) to sell at a high price to the maximum number of "uninformed" consumers and at the same time (b) to prevent "informed" consumers from buying at the low price of the competition.

The recommended strategy here is *random discounting*, which involves maintaining a high price and discounting the product periodically "at random". The manner of discounting is crucial: it should be indiscernible or random so those uninformed buyers will buy randomly, usually at the high price and the "informed" will look around or wait until they can buy at the low price (Tellis, 1986, p. 150).

Promotional prices

Companies are often led to temporarily reduce their prices in order to stimulate sales. Promotional prices can take various forms: loss leader pricing as frequently adopted by department stores or supermarkets, special events pricing, low interest financing as often proposed by car dealers, cash rebates, warranties and service contracts and so on. Every promotion is in fact a *disguised price reduction* having the merit of being temporary and therefore enabling the seller to go back easily to the initial price.

During the last decades, promotions of all kinds have proliferated with, as the main result, a loss of credibility of the pricing policies adopted by manufacturers and resellers as well. To regain this credibility, two pricing policies are today of current application by resellers in the food sector namely: either *every day fair pricing* or *every day low pricing* (EDLP), that is slightly reduced price available on a permanent basis. This last pricing policy is the one adopted by the supermarket chain Colruyt in Belgium, which has developed a very sophisticated system of price monitoring and commits itself to the lowest price charged in the market.

One form of promotional pricing regaining popularity among manufacturers is cash rebates, which can be used to stimulate sales without actually cutting prices. Cash rebates are coupons offered to encourage purchase and which have to be mailed back to the manufacturer after the purchase. The rebate may be as high as €75 for a Nikon camera or €50 for an image scanner. By comparison with a price cut, this promotional practice has a certain number of advantages for the manufacturer:

- The basic price is not modified and therefore the promotion has no negative effect on the brand image.
- Manufacturers can offer price cuts directly to customers, independently of the retailer who could keep the same price on the shelf and pocket the difference.
- Rebates can be rolled out and shut off quickly, leaving manufacturers to fine-tune inventories or respond quickly to competitors without actually cutting the price.
- Cash rebates are inexpensive to the extent that many customers never bother to redeem them, allowing manufacturers to offer phantom discounts.
- Because customers fill out forms with names and addresses and other data, rebates also set off a gusher of information about customers useful in direct marketing.

According to a study published by the *Wall Street Journal* (1998), only 5 to 10 per cent of customers redeem cash rebates. For more details about price promotion, see Tsiros and Hardesty (2010).

Price administration

Price administration deals with price adjustments for sales made under different conditions, in different quantities, to different types of intermediary in different geographic locations, with different conditions of payment and so on. These price adjustments or discounts are designed to reward customers whose buying behaviour contributes to cost reductions for the firm. This is the case for quantity discounts, cash payment discounts, seasonal discounts, functional discounts and so on. For more on this topic, see Monroe (1979, chapter 11). Price undercutting can, however, damage brand equity and erode profit margins (Bertini and Wathieu, 2010).

Pricing of services and 'yield management'

Differential pricing is of common application in the service sector, and more particularly in sectors with limited and fixed production capacity, like hotels, airlines, media and so on who have to yield income from perishable assets (see Exhibit 17.2). These sectors have in common the following characteristics:

- the proposed service cannot be stocked;
- the service can be booked in advance;
- the production capacity is fixed and its increase would be very costly; and
- the market can be segmented on the basis of price and service flexibility criteria.

In the airline market, typically the market can be sub-divided into two distinct segments:

- business travellers who are not price-sensitive, very sensitive to schedule flexibility and to comfort; they make their reservations at short notice; and
- vacationers who are very price-sensitive, organize their holidays several weeks or months ahead and are ready to accept restrictions reducing their flexibility like advance booking, penalty for change, minimal comfort and so on.

Using this heterogeneity of demand, airline companies sell their regular tickets at a high price and give high discounts to travellers purchasing their ticket well before their departure date. The problem for these companies is to allocate the production capacity in a dynamic way among different price categories in order to optimize sales revenue.

Exhibit 17.2   Yield management: basic principles

For the majority of seasonal products, the initial launching price is high and then progressively marks down to move the stock. Markdown will continue until the last product is sold. A similar system can be used by services to reach optimal capacity but it will not optimize revenues. Yield management works just the opposite. The lowest-discount items are sold first and the highest priced sold last.

If all the seats on a 200-seat aircraft were priced at a discount fare of €125, the plane would fill quickly with leisure travellers. However, many individuals would be willing to pay more than €125 for a seat. These individuals tend to be business travellers who may not know their schedule until a day or two prior to departure or want more comfort than is offered in the coach section. In fact, these individuals may be willing to pay €300, €400 or more for the seat. Based on historical data and analysis of when passengers made reservations, yield management will build a price schedule and reserve some of the seats for business travellers who are less price-sensitive. They will price these seats at €350. Working backward, the airline may price the next 30 at €275 and so on; and the last 60 at €125. To get the €125 price, the airline may have restrictions such as at least 30-day advance reservations, no refunds or exchange without a penalty and a Saturday night stayfree. Instead of the €25,000 sales revenue earned at the €125 price, €40,500 would be generated. When sales lag behind the schedule, the price is lowered to fill the seats that were allocated. As soon as all seats are sold at one price range, the price is increased to the next level. This increase in price will slow demand.

Source: Adapted from Kurtz and Clow (1998, pp. 254–55).

By combining low tariffs and rigid schedules, airline companies can charge a sufficiently low price to attract vacationers without making price concessions to non-price-sensitive travellers. This pricing method initially developed by American Airlines is now in application in numerous service sectors (Smith, Leimkuhler and Darrow, 1992; Mohammed, 2011).

Customizing prices in online markets

Online commerce greatly facilitates one-to-one relationships and therefore should also facilitate price customization, that is, the charging of different prices to end-customers on the basis of what they are willing to pay. In the real world, implementation is difficult and Reinartz (2001) has identified five conditions to be held, regardless of whether the context is online or offline:

1. Customers must be heterogeneous in their willingness to pay. Some are prepared to pay a high price, others will only be willing to buy at the lower price available.
2. The market must be *segmentable* (see Table 17.7). The Web has significantly improved a firm's ability to segment a market in terms of willingness to pay by tracking individual purchase through the Internet.
3. Limited arbitrage. A person having purchased a product at lower price should not be able to resell it for a profit to customers having a higher willingness to pay.
4. The costs of segmenting must not exceed the revenue due to customization. Internet technology has contributed to reduce these costs substantially.
5. Notions of perceived fairness must not be violated. Perceived fairness is when the buyer feels that both parties in a transaction have gained.

This last condition is crucial. Nobody likes to learn that the very same product has been sold under the same trade terms but at a lower price.

In September 2000, Amazon.com charged consumers different prices for exactly the same DVD with price differentials as high as €15. The knowledge that Amazon sells at different

Table 17.7   Flexibility in the prices of services

Single price	Personalized price	Price implying customer participation	Price change over time
1. A flat rate for an unlimited usage (amusement parks, ski pass)	3. A reduced price linked to a status (student or senior rates)	5. Price reduction for self-service (cafeteria, self-banking, ...)	8. Price reduction in low season (low traffic)
2. A single price for a well-defined need (postal rate, subway ticket, ...)	4. A reduced price linked to a specific characteristic (handicapped, birthday, ...)	6. Price reduction for customer participation in the "servuction" process	9. Price reduction for early or late booking. (*yield management*)
		7. Price reduction for participation in the selling process.	10. Price reduction for early reservation (*yield management*)
			11. High price for fast service (express or rush service)

Source: Adapted from Durrande-Moreau (2002).

prices provoked resentment and a feeling that the company is profiteering at the consumer's expenses.

Price customization is a very challenging strategy and should be adopted with care even if, from a technological point of view, such an implementation is indeed possible.

17.4 COMPETITION-ORIENTED PRICING PROCEDURES

As far as competition is concerned, two kinds of factors greatly influence the firm's autonomy in its pricing strategy – the sector's *competitive structure*, characterized by the number of competing firms, and the importance of *the product's perceived value*:

- *Competitive structures*. Clearly, when the firm is a monopoly, autonomy is great in setting its price; it tends to diminish as the number of competitors increases; we have monopoly and perfect competition at the extremes, and differentiated oligopoly and monopolistic situations as the intermediate positions.
- The *product's perceived value* results from the firm's efforts to differentiate in order to achieve an external competitive advantage; where an element of differentiation exists and is perceived by the buyer as of value, the buyer is usually prepared to pay a price above that of competing products. In this case, the firm has some degree of autonomy over prices.

Table 17.8 presents these two factors, each at two levels of intensity (low or high). We can thus identify four distinct situations, in each of which the question of price determination takes on a different form.

Reality is, of course, more complex and there is a continuum of situations. Nevertheless, it is helpful to place a product in one of these quadrants to understand the problem of price determination:

- When the number of competitors is low and the product's perceived value is high, we are in structures close to *monopoly or differentiated oligopoly*. Price is a tool for the firm, which has a margin for manoeuvre varying with the buyer's perceived value of the differentiating attribute.
- At the other extreme, where there are many competitors and products are perceived as a commodity, we are close to the *perfect competition* structure where prices are largely determined by the interplay of supply and demand. The firm has practically no autonomy in its pricing strategy.
- The lower-left quadrant, with a low number of competitors and low perceived value, corresponds to an *undifferentiated oligopolistic* structure in which interdependence between competitors is often high, thus limiting their autonomy. Here prices will tend to be aligned with those of the market leader.

Table 17.8 Competitive environments of pricing decisions

Perceived value of the product	Number of competitors	
	Low	High
High	Monopoly or differentiated oligopoly	Monopolistic competition
Weak	Undifferentiated oligopoly	Pure or perfect competition

■ Finally, in the upper-right quadrant we have highly differentiated products offered by a large number of competitors; this corresponds to *imperfect or monopolistic competition* where there is some degree of autonomy, this being limited by the intensity of competition.

These market structures are very different and they can be observed at various stages of a product market's life cycle.

Anticipating competitors' behaviour

In many market situations, competitors' interdependence is high and there is a "market price" which serves as reference to all. This is usually the case when there is *undifferentiated oligopoly*, where total demand is no longer expanding and the offerings of existing competitors are hardly differentiated. This type of competitive structure tends to prevail during the maturity stage of a product's life cycle.

In these markets, the firm can align itself with competitors' prices or those of the industry leader. It can fix its price at a higher level, thus taking the risk of losing some market share. Alternatively, it can fix its price below the market level, thus seeking a competitive advantage that it cannot find from other sources, but also taking the risk of launching a price war. The problem therefore is to determine *relative price*. The outcome of these strategies largely depends on the reactions of competitors.

The objective of analysing competition in pricing strategies is *to evaluate competitors' capabilities to act and react*. In particular, one needs to estimate the reaction elasticity of the most dangerous competitor(s) if prices were to go up or down.

The direction and intensity of competitors' reactions vary when prices move upwards or downwards. The firm faces a *kinked demand curve*. Elasticity is different on either side of the market price because of different competitive reactions. Some conditions are more favourable to price decreases and some to price increases. These are the conditions that need to be identified.

The risk of a price war is always present in oligopolistic markets and this why firms are reluctant to start reducing prices. In few cases, however, a price war can help companies to improve their competitive positions. The Boston Consulting Group contributions on the experience curve have shown that reduced profit margins due to price reductions can be offset by market share gains which in the long term generate improved profitability thanks to cost reductions. Another objective of a price war can be the elimination a potentially dangerous competitor.

Pricing in an inflationary economy

During inflation, all costs tend to go up, and to maintain profits at an acceptable level, price increases are very often a necessity. The general objective is that price should be increased to such a level that the profits before and after inflation are approximately equal. Decline in sales revenue caused by the price increase should be explicitly taken into account and the market reaction evaluated.

It should be noted that it is not always necessary for a company to increase prices to offset inflationary effects. Non-price measures can be taken as well to reduce the impact of inflationary pressures, namely, by improving productivity to offset the rise in costs. Also, price increases well above inflationary pressures can be justified to the market if the brand has a competitive advantage over competing brands.

Price leadership

Price leadership strategy prevails in oligopolistic markets. One member of the industry, because of its size or command over the market, emerges as the leader of the industry. The leading company then makes pricing moves, which are duly acknowledged by other members of the reference market.

Initiating a price increase is typically the role of the *industry leader*. The presence of a leader helps to regulate the market and avoid too many price changes. Oligopolistic markets, in which the number of competitors is relatively low, favour the presence of a market leader who adopts an anticipative behaviour and periodically determines prices. Other firms then recognize the leader's role and become followers by accepting prices. The leadership strategy is designed to stave off price wars and "predatory" competition, which tends to force down prices and hurts all competing firms. There are different types of leadership:

1. *Leadership of the dominant firm*, that is, the firm with the highest market share. The dominant firm establishes a price and the other producers sell their products at this price. The leader must be powerful and undisputed and must accept maintaining a high price.
2. *Barometric leadership* which consists of initiating desirable price cuts or price increases, taking into account changes in production costs or demand growth. In this case the leader must have access to an effective information system providing him or her with reliable information on supply and demand, competition and technological change.
3. *Leadership by common accord*, where one firm is tacitly recognized as leader, without there being a formal understanding or accord. The latter would in fact be illegal. Such a leader could be the most visible firm in the sector, for example, the firm that leads in technology. It should also have a sensitivity to the price and profit needs of the rest of the industry.

According to Corey (1976, p. 177), the effective exercise of leadership depends on several factors:

- The leader must have a superior market information system for understanding what is going on in the market and reacting in a timely way.
- It should have a clear sense of strategy.
- It should have a broad concern for the health of the industry.
- The price leader should use long-term measures to assess managerial performance.
- It should want to lead and to act responsibly.
- It will tend to behave in a way that preserves short-run market share stability.

On the whole, the presence of a leader acts as a *market stabilizer* and reduces the risk of a price war.

17.5   IMPACT OF INTERNET ON PRICING DECISIONS

One of the most dramatic changes expected of online shopping was the ability of consumers to compare prices for comparable products. Consequently, it was expected that people who use the Internet pay lower prices for the goods they buy; lower here means prices less than they would pay for the same goods at a traditional physical store. Research results provide support for this expectation but also identify circumstances in which Web users end up paying higher prices. Instead of a new age of perfectly competitive markets, research has found more price variations than expected, despite the availability of price comparison websites.

Price comparison sites

One of the most important differences from physical markets is the ease with which online consumers and rival retailers can access comparative information about competing products characteristics and prices. There are sites like Kelkoo (www.kelkoo.com), PriceScan (www.pricescan.com) or Priceline (www.priceline.com) or Expedia for airlines (www.expedia.fr) that search the Net for the lowest possible price for goods and services.

Kelkoo.com, for instance, is the largest price comparison site in Europe. Kelkoo claims to have over 4 million visits per month from consumers within the United Kingdom alone, and price listings by over 4,000 retailers, including more than 40 of the 50 largest Internet retailers. Consumers now regularly check online prices and compare them with those in their local stores. As warned by Koch (2003), the price list users receive from the site reflects which firms have paid for the right to appear in favourable placement in the list. Thus, e-consumers can be misguided. Rather than helping them find the lowest price, the price comparison site may be helping them find its biggest advertiser.

In reality, price comparison sites give firms a means to monitor each others pricing policy, thereby exchanging pricing information and promoting price matching, an illegal behaviour in the physical market, but which can occur in the global electronic market with little effort. At price comparison sites like Kelkoo, the number of firms selling a given product changes almost daily and an online retailer needs to monitor this number and must be prepared to adapt its price in real time to respond to changes in the competitive structure of the market.

Price discovery mechanisms on the Internet

In any e-market, there are four main transaction mechanisms.

- *Standard price offerings*, that is, predetermined prices for a given product or service. This is similar to the typical catalogue pricing system used in B2C markets.
- *Auction*, a method in which one organization or an individual bids against others to buy goods from a supplier.
- *Reverse auction*, also called request for quote (RFQ), is a method of procurement in which an organization sets a price it is willing to pay and suppliers then bid to fulfil it. This method is used when buyers search for a product that does not exist yet or when they search for a better price for an existing product.
- *Exchanges*. Exchanges tend to be Internet-based spot market for commodity products. Exchanges match "bid offers" with "ask offers" on e-market rules and inform the parties involved in the potential match.

Thus electronic markets allow new price discovery mechanisms. An example is airlines' last-minute auction for unsold seats to the highest bidder.

Are Internet prices lower?

Several studies indicate that a large majority of Net buyers rate "lower prices" as the reason for buying online followed by "convenience" as a second reason. The most comprehensive evidence available is provided by Harris and Abate (2000) and indicates that most Internet prices are lower than those charged by brick-and-mortar stores. Even after taking shipping costs into account, Internet prices were 38 per cent lower for apparel items; 28 per cent lower for prescription drugs, alcohol, and cigarettes; 4 per cent lower for home electronics and groceries; 4 per cent higher for hardware and 9 per cent higher for toys. Overall, reports Lehman Brothers, the Net prices of 93 different items were 13 per cent lower than brick-and-mortar prices, shipping included. Similar observations are made on e-marketplaces, where sellers are feeling price pressure when existing customers move online.

Thus, the good news is that many consumers often do pay less when they shop on the Internet. The bad news is that there are situations in which buyers and sellers have different (asymmetric) information, which can result in higher prices.

Pricing flexibility online

Flexible pricing strategy has already been a popular strategy for many established companies and perhaps the best example is the airline industry which charges different prices for different people based on their travel patterns, what is called dynamic pricing or "contextual pricing" (Ozer, 2002).

Net sellers using CRM software are collecting extensive information about e-consumers and can use this information to test their price sensitivity. The Internet gives companies better information about customers' price sensitivity. It also gives them the flexibility to adjust prices instantly as circumstances change. Here are two examples.

- *Measuring customers' tolerance to higher prices.* All products have a pricing indifference band: a range of prices within which price changes have little impact on consumers' willingness to make a purchase. *McKinsey (*see Baker, Lin, Marn and Zawada, 2001) *estimates* that price indifference bands can range from 17 per cent for branded consumer health and beauty products to as little as 0.2 per cent for some financial products. A product location within this band can dramatically affect a company's profit. Measurements of consumer tolerance for different prices levels are difficult, expensive and time-consuming in the offline market, but cheap and instantaneous on the Internet. For example, an Internet seller wants to test the sales impact of 3 per cent price increase, it might quote the higher price to every 50th visitor to its site, observe the results and try another experiment the next day and this very easily and at a zero cost. The seller could then segment prospective customers to tailor prices accordingly.
- *Adapting prices online.* Offline price changes take time and it may take several months to communicate changes to distributors, to print and send new price lists and to implement the changes. Online pricing allows companies to make instantaneous adjustments to list prices and to profit from even small fluctuations in market conditions. When capacity utilization is high, order lead times short or inventory levels low, prices can be raised temporarily. When demand sags, a company might try an auction, lower prices or targeted short-term promotions. Similarly, as products near the end of their life cycle, companies can test the consumers' willingness to continue to pay the established price or to delay price reductions for several weeks.

A successful flexible pricing strategy depends on how customers feel about it. As discussed below, perceived fairness should not be violated.

Online markets do present a number of novel features and characteristics that managers must be prepared to incorporate into their online business strategies. To go further on this topic, read the interesting article from Baye, Gatti, Kattuman and Morgan (2007).

Higher prices on the Internet?

Koch (2003) has identified several situations where Internet users end up paying higher prices.

- *Branding effects.* Differentiation and branding are the key tools used in the physical market to reduce consumers' price sensitivity. The same effect is observed on the Web. For the e-consumer, buying a well-known brand, even more expensive, reduces his or her risk. Net consumers generally prefer the familiar and, frequently, the familiar constitutes a heavily advertised company (like Microsoft) or highly popular portals (like Yahoo, Google, or MSN) or a brand also operating in the physical market. Analysis of consumer click-through behaviour reveals that most e-customers do very little cross-shopping, the majority purchasing their product (books, toys, music, electronic and so on) at the first website visited.
- *Auction frenzy.* In auctions, frequently successful bidders pay unrealistically high prices because caught up in the frenzy of competition and bid well over what they would offer in a brick-and-mortar environment. Most Net auctions exhibit asymmetric information in particular where experience goods are involved and their precise condition and quality are unknown to the bidder (Van Heck, 2002).
- *Tying and bundling.* Tying refers to the practice of binding the sales of one good to the sale of another, while bundling occurs when several items are packaged together and sold for a single price, yet can be purchased separately. If a firm ties or bundles products together, it will charge a higher price while the marginal cost of supplying information goods is very small. It boils down to forcing the e-customer to pay a higher price to obtain the product he or she really wants.
- *Data mining.* Popular portals like Google, Yahoo or MSN can keep track of where users go and what they do when they get there and then use the information to build a profile of their interests. If Yahoo knows you are interested in politics, it might arrange for you to have an attractive advertisement for a book about politics and convenience might dictate the purchase at the price offered rather than expanding an effort to search for a lower price.

A situation of "perfect price competition" is not necessarily prevailing in e-marketplaces. Sellers can design strategies to resist price pressure from customers by building new types of competitive advantage.

Price partitioning on the Internet

Online shopping also changes the price structures from what consumers are used to in the traditional shopping environment. Consumers are used to paying sales tax for their purchases. However, a shipping and handling fee is charged for online shopping. The shipping and handling fees thus become surcharges to the base price of the product.

Separating the total cost into a base price and one or more surcharges has been labelled *price partitioning*. Sellers are using different tactics to structure these surcharges to attract consumers. For example, they may list a low base price of the product but increase the shipping and handling fee so the store's product may look attractive in the price comparison sites. On the other hand, other sellers may include the surcharge in the base price and try to attract consumers by offering "free" shipping and handling. Xia and Monroe (2004) have examined empirically whether price partitioning on the Internet is effective. Overall, the results indicate that price partitioning can have a positive effect on consumers' price perceptions and on purchase intentions. This effect is due not only to a cost and benefit assessment by consumers, but also to the clarity that the partitioned prices offered. A partitioned price may enhance a store's perceived trustworthiness and perceived fairness.

Price customization online

Price customization is the charging of different prices to end-consumers based on a discriminatory variable, like weather, time of day, purchase quantity or a targeted segment or buyer's willingness to pay. Economists view the buyer's willingness to pay as the ultimate discriminatory variable because this approach maximizes firms' profit in economic terms.

The downside of customized pricing based on customers' willingness to pay is its implementation difficulty. Based on customer data generated by CRM software, we have seen that Internet technology through data mining facilitates breaking down the traditional barriers towards price customization.

In the real world, implementation is difficult and Reinartz (2001) has identified five conditions to be held, regardless of whether the context is online or offline.

1. Customers must be *heterogeneous* in their willingness to pay. Some are prepared to pay a high price, others will only be willing to buy at the lower price available.
2. The market must be *segmentable*. The Web has significantly improved a firm's ability to segment a market in terms of willingness to pay by tracking individual purchase through the Internet.
3. *Limited arbitrage*. A person having purchased a product at lower price should not be able to resell it for a profit to customers having a higher willingness to pay.
4. The *costs of segmenting* must not exceed the revenue due to customization. Internet technology has contributed substantially to reduce these costs.
5. Notions of *perceived fairness* must not be violated. Perceived fairness is when the buyer feels that both parties in a transaction have gained.

This last condition is crucial. Nobody likes to learn that the very same product has been sold under the same trade terms but at a lower price. In September 2000, Amazon charged different prices to consumers for exactly the same DVD with price differentials as high as €15. The knowledge that Amazon sells at different prices has provoked resentment and a feeling that the company is profiteering at the consumer's expense (Krugman, 2000).

Price customization is a very challenging strategy and should be adopted with care even if, from a technological point of view, such an implementation is indeed possible.

Chapter Summary

The choice of a pricing strategy must respect two types of coherence: an internal coherence that is, setting a price respecting constraints of costs and profitability, and an external coherence, that is, setting a price compatible with the buyer's price sensitivity and with the price of competing goods. Cost-based pricing (break-even, target and mark-up pricing) is the first and necessary step which helps to identify the financial implications of various pricing strategies. Pricing based exclusively on the firm's own financial needs is inappropriate, however, since in a market economy it is the buyer who ultimately decides which product will sell. In demand-oriented pricing, the notion of price elasticity is central although difficult to estimate empirically with sufficient precision. The factors affecting buyers' price sensitivity are useful to help estimate price elasticity in qualitative terms. Value pricing is a customer-based pricing procedure, which is an outgrowth of the multi-attribute product concept. Flexible pricing strategies (second market, periodic or random discounting) arise primarily because buyers' heterogeneity shows different price sensitivities. Two kinds of factors influence competition-oriented pricing: the competitive structure of the market and the product's perceived value. One objective of analysing competition in pricing is to evaluate competitors' capacity to act and react. Special issues in pricing are pricing new products (skimming versus penetration pricing), product line pricing (price bundling, premium pricing, image and complementary pricing) and international pricing (transfer price and export costs).

BIBLIOGRAPHY

Assmus, G., Farley, J.V. and Lehmann, D.R. (1984), How Advertising Affects Sales Meta-Analysis of Econometric Results, *Journal of Marketing Research*, 21, 1 , pp. 65–74.

Baker, W.L., Lin, E., Marn, M.V. and Zawada, C.C. (2001), Getting Prices Right on the Web, *McKinsey Quarterly*, 2, pp. 55–63.

Baye, M.R., Gatti, J.R.J., Kattuman, P. and Morgan, J. (2007), A Dashboard for Online Pricing, *California Management Review*, 50, 1, pp. 202–16.

Bijmolt, T.H.A., Van Heerde, H.J. and Pieters, R.G.M. (2005), New Empirical Generalizations on the Determinants of Price Elasticity, *Journal of Marketing Research*, 42, 2, pp. 141–56.

Blondé, D. (1964), *La gestion programmée*, Paris, Dunod.

Broadbent, S. (1980), Price and Advertising: Volume and Profits, *Admap*, 16, pp. 532–40.

Carlson, R.L. (1978), Seemingly Unrelated Regression and the Demand for Automobiles of Different Sizes: A Disaggregate Approach, *The Journal of Business*, 51, 2, pp. 243–62.

Corey, E.R. (1976), *Industrial Marketing: Cases and Concepts*, Englewood Cliffs, NJ, Prentice-Hall.

Dolan, R.J. and Simon, H. (1996), *Power Pricing*, New York, The Free Press.

Dorfman, R. and Steiner, P.O. (1954), Optimal Advertising and Optimal Quality, *American Economic Review*, 44, 5, pp. 826–33.

Durrande-Moreau, A. (2002), Service et tactiques de prix: quelles spécificités?, *Décisions Marketing*, 25, January–March.

Hagerty, M.R., Carman, J.M. and Russel, G.J. (1988), Estimating Elasticities with PIMS Data: Methodological Issues and Substantive Implications, *Journal of Marketing Research*, 25, 1, pp. 1–9.

Hanssens, D.M., Parsons, L.L. and Schultz, R.L. (1990), *Market Response Models: Econometric and Time Series Analysis*, Boston, MA, Kluwer.

Harris, E.S. and Abate, J.T. (2000), *United States: The Internet Price Index, Global Economic Monitor*, New York, Lehman Brothers.

Jacquemin, A. (1973), Optimal Control and Advertising Policy, *Metroeconomica,* 25, May, pp. 200–7.

Koch, J.V. (2003*)*, Are prices lower on the Internet? Not always, *Business horizons,* January–February, pp. 47–52.

Krugman, P. (2000), What Price Fairness? *New York Times*, October 4.

Kurtz, D.L. and Clow, K.E. (1998), *Services Marketing*, New York, John Wiley & Sons.

Lambin, J.J. (1976), *Advertising, Competition and Market Conduct in Oligopoly over Time*, Amsterdam, North-Holland.

Lambin, J.J. (1988), Synthèse des études récentes sur l'efficacité économique de la publicité, CESAM, unpublished working paper, Louvain-la-Neuve, Belgium.

Lambin, J.J. (1998), Le marketing stratégique, Paris, Ediscience international, 4th edition.

Lambin J.J. (2000/2007), *Market-Driven Management, Strategic and Operational Marketing*, London, Palgrave Macmillan, First and second editions.

Lambin, J.J., Naert, P.A. and Bultez, A. (1975), Optimal Marketing Behavior in Oligopoly, *European Economic Review*, 6, 2, pp. 105–28.

Leone R.P. and Schultz R. (1980), A Study in Marketing Generalizations, *Journal of Marketing*, 44, pp.10–18.

Marn, M.V., Roegner, E.V. and Zawada, C.C. (2003), The Power of Pricing, *McKinsey Quarterly*, 1, pp. 26–39.

Monroe, K.B. (1979), *Pricing: Making Profitable Decisions*, New York, McGraw-Hill.

Nagle, T.T. and Holden, R.K. (1987/1994), *The Strategy and Tactics of Pricing*, Englewood Cliffs, NJ, Prentice Hall, 2nd edition.

Nerlove, M. and Arrow, K.J. (1962), Optimal Advertising Policy under Dynamic Conditions, *Economica*, 29, pp. 129–42.

Neslin, S.A. and Shoemaker, R.W. (1983), Using a Natural Experiment to Estimate Price Elasticity, *Journal of Marketing*, 47, 1, pp. 44–57.

Oum, T.H. and Gillen, D.W. (1981), *Demand for Fare Classes and Pricing in Airline Markets*, Queen's University School of Business, Working Paper No. 80-12.

Oxenfeldt, A.R. (1966), Product Line Pricing, *Harvard Business Review*, 44, 4, pp. 137–44.

Ozer, M. (2002), The Role of Flexibility in Online Business, *Business Horizons*, January–February, pp. 61–8.

Porter, M.E. (1980), *Competitive Strategy*, New York, The Free Press.

Reinartz, W. (2001), Customising Prices Online, *European Business Forum*, 6, pp. 35–41.

Smith, B.C., Leimkuhler, J.F. and Darrow, R.M. (1992), Yield Management at American Airlines, *Interfaces*, 22, 1, pp. 8–31.

Tellis, G.J. (1986), Beyond the Many Faces of Price: An Integration of Pricing Strategies, *Journal of Marketing*, 50, 4, pp. 146–60.

Tellis, G.J. (1988), The Price Elasticity of Selective Demand: A Meta-Analysis of Econometric Models of Sales, *Journal of Marketing Research*, 25, 4, pp. 331–41.

Traylor, M.B. (1986), Cannibalism in Multibrand Firms, *The Journal of Consumer Marketing*, 3, 2, pp. 69–75.

Van Heck, E. (2002), How to Seize the Value of Online Auctions, *European Business Forum*, 3, 10, pp. 63–5.

Wall Street Journal (1998), Manufacturer's Boon: Few Consumers Redeem Rebates, February 11.

Xia, L. and Monroe, K.B. (2004), Price Partitioning on the Internet, *Journal of Interactive Marketing*, 18, 4, pp. 63–74.

Tsiros, M. and Hardesty, D.M. (2010), Ending a Price Promotion: Retracting It in One Step or Phasing It Out Gradually, *Journal of Marketing*, 74, pp. 49–64.

Bertini, M. and Wathieu, L. (2010), How to Stop Customers from Fiwating Price, *Harvard Business Review,* May, pp. 84–91.

Mohammed, R. (2011), Ditch the Discounts, *Harvard Business Review,* January–February, pp. 23–5.

WEB SITE COMPANION FOR CHAPTER 17

Visit the Market-driven Management accompanying website at www.palgrave.com/business/lambin3 to find:

Note on International Pricing

CHAPTER EIGHTEEN

MARKETING COMMUNICATION DECISIONS

We saw in Chapter 1 that market-driven management is an action-oriented process as well as a business philosophy. To be effectively implemented, the firm's strategic choices must be supported by dynamic action programmes, without which there is very little hope for commercial success. To sell, it is not enough to have a competitively priced product made available to target potential customers through a well-structured distribution network. It is also necessary to advertise the product's distinctive features to the target segment, and to stimulate the demand through selling and promotional activities. An effective marketing strategy requires the development of a communication programme having the two interrelated objectives of informing potential customers about products and services and persuading them to buy. Such a programme is based on various means of communication, the most important of which are personal selling, advertising, promotion, public relations and, last but not least, the Internet. The objective of this chapter is to examine the major decisions facing a firm when developing an integrated communication programme (see Figure 18.1).

Learning Objectives

When you have read this chapter, you should be able to know and/or understand:

- The concept of integrated marketing communication
- The nature of the different modes of marketing communication
- The steps in designing an effective communication programme
- The tasks and objectives of relationship selling
- The different objectives of advertising communication
- The roles and impact of sales promotions
- The objectives of public relations and of sponsoring

18.1 THE ROLE AND NATURE OF MARKETING COMMUNICATION

To ensure an efficient matching of segments of demand and supply, communication flows must be organized between the trading partners to facilitate the exchange process. It is therefore up to the producer to initiate and control these communication flows to create a brand or a corporate image consistent with the firm's strategic objectives.

Key changes in the field of marketing communication

Mass marketing communication has dominated the communication strategies of companies for the last 40 years. TV advertising was the main tool that was used to reach a large

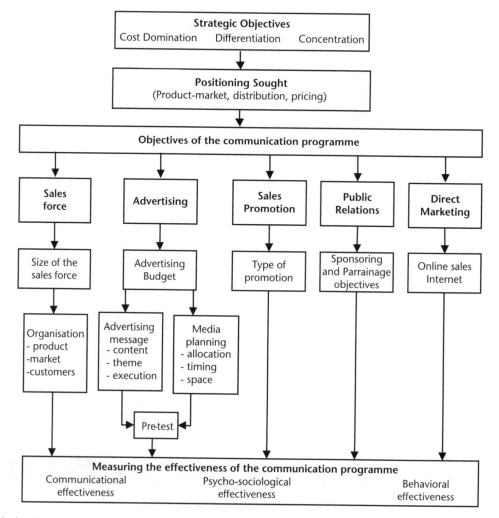

Figure 18.1   Overview of marketing communication decisions
Source: Lambin (2000/2007).

audience. The choice of media was therefore relatively easy for companies. Today, however, the media scene has totally changed. We face a fragmentation of media. New media tools such as the Internet, mobile phones, video games have been created and classical media tools are therefore much less effective than in the past.

The role of the consumer has also dramatically changed with regard to his or her relationship with the company. The consumer was relatively passive and was just receiving the information that the company was providing via advertising. He or she now has more power thanks to the information that can be gathered on the Internet. Moreover, the consumer is also requesting more attention from the company as individualized contacts can be developed via the Internet. We could even say that the consumer has become an actor as more and more he or she is giving his or her point of view on brands via blogs, social media or other interactive tools.

Finally, consumers are also facing a difficult choice as they are surrounded by a multitude of brands that are communicating many different messages. It is therefore critical for companies to find new ways to reach the consumers and to convince them to buy their brands. This is why new communications tools have to be identified to hook the attention of consumers.

As a result, the life of marketing managers has become much more complicated than in the past in view of this proliferation of new media. It is a real revolution in the way the brand has to communicate to the outside world and a challenge for marketing managers to integrate all these changes in a communication strategy.

The marketing communication mix

Marketing communication refers to all *the signals or messages* made by the firm to its various publics, that is, customers, distributors, suppliers, shareholders and public authorities, and also its own personnel. The five major communication tools, called the *communication mix*, are advertising, personal selling, promotion, public relations and direct marketing including online communication. Each of these communication tools has its own characteristics:

- *Advertising* is a unilateral and paid form of non-personal mass communication, designed to create a favourable attitude towards the advertised product and coming from a clearly identified sponsor.
- *Personal selling* has the objective of organizing a verbal dialogue with potential and current customers and to deliver a tailor-made message with the short-term objective of making a sale. Its role is also to gather information for the firm.
- *Promotion* includes all short-term incentives, generally organized on a temporary and/or local basis, designed to stimulate immediate purchase and to move sales forward more rapidly than would otherwise occur.
- *Public relations* involve a variety of actions aimed at establishing a positive corporate image and a climate of understanding and mutual trust between a firm and its various publics. Here, the communication objective is less to sell and more to gain moral support from public opinion for the firm's economic activities.
- *Direct marketing*. It regroups all the tools that the firm can use to have a direct contact with consumers through direct mail, catalogue selling, fairs and exhibitions, telemarketing and online communication.

Although these means of communication are very different, they are also highly complementary. The problem is therefore not whether advertising and promotion are necessary, but rather how to allocate the total communication budget to these various communication tools, given the product's characteristics and the chosen communication objectives.

Growing importance of online communication tools

With the development of the Internet, there are new many ways now to reach the firm's various public online. Online communication tools cover new communication tools such as:

- *Brand websites:* There are sites that give information about brands. It can be used to communicate with the target groups and to interact with it. Websites are also important to sustain or increase the loyalty of consumers.
- *Online advertising:* You have different forms of advertising. The most classical ones are banners. You can also find pop-ups that are banners and appear in a separate window. Interstitials are additional ads that appear temporarily when loading a new Web page.

- *E-mailing:* E-mails are used to send a promotional offer. Retention e-mails are sent with the purpose of strengthening the brand attitude. Examples are e-newsletters.
- *Blogs* are frequently updated personal Web journals that allow owners to publish ideas and information.
- *Online promotions* are promotions offered on the Web such as online contests and sweepstakes, e-sampling and e-couponing, advergames and online games.
- *Viral marketing:* It is a set of techniques that are used to spread news through the Net following a snowball effect in a very short period of time. The idea is to use "word of mouth" (word of mouse) on the Internet or on mobile to inform consumers.

News can be spread to millions of Internet users in a very short period of time. *Buzz* marketing is the same idea as viral marketing. It consists of spreading the news about a brand, a person, a product or an event on the Net. It is a kind of wild advertising that is spread by the consumers.

The concept of integrated marketing communication

In order to reach consumers effectively in the current media scene, integrated marketing communication has become a new and important way to develop communication strategies. It involves co-ordinating and integrating all communication tools of the company to achieve more consistency and effectiveness in the communication to consumers. The *American Association of Advertising Agencies* gives the following definition of integrated marketing communication:

> A concept of marketing communication planning that recognizes the added value of a comprehensive plan that evaluates the strategic roles of a variety of communication disciplines, e.g. general advertising, direct mail, sales promotion and public relations and combines these disciplines to provide clarity, consistency and maximum communication impact.

Traditionally, each communication tool, such as advertising, public relation, personal selling or promotion, was used in a relatively independent way and with specific objectives and this has contributed to weaken the effectiveness of the communication programme, as consumers were not receiving a coherent and consistent message. From a financial point of view, it is also clearly more efficient to communicate the same message everywhere.

To achieve this objective of integrated marketing communication, all the elements of the communication mix must be planned with the same message, a difficult task to implement as most of the time communication agencies have had a tendency to specialize in different fields and communication platforms and styles. Today, there are direct marketing agencies, public relation agencies, agencies specialized in Internet tools and so on.

Moreover, inside the company, different departments handle the different parts of the communication programme, for example, advertising is under the responsibility of one department, public relation of another and sales promotion of a third one. As a result there a tendency to change the structure of the organization in order to give the responsibility and the supervision of all communication tools of a single "communication manager". This is not necessarily easy to implement and this is why integrated marketing communication is slow to be adopted by companies. Today, some major agencies can offer integrated marketing communication services after having purchased several specialized agencies (De Pelsmacker, Geuens and Van den Bergh, 2010).

When talking about integrated marketing communication, we cover both offline communication tools such as advertising, public relation, sales promotion, direct marketing and online communication tools such as advertising on the Web, e-mails, blogs.

The choice of marketing communication tools

The choice of marketing communication tools will vary depending on different factors such as the target audience to be reached, the phase of the PLC, the objectives to be met and the types of products:

- *The target segment.* This is the most important criteria. If we are in business to cater to consumers, we need to see if the target segment is small or large. If it is large, advertising remains an important tool to reach consumers but it has to be complemented by new tools. If we are in B2B, the sales force remains an essential tool to reach companies.
- *The product life cycle.* The communication tools will be different following the phase of the PLC. If we are in the introduction phase, it will be important to use tools that generate awareness of the new brand such as advertising or buzz marketing. In the growing phase, trial will need to be generated with sales promotion, for example. In the maturity phase, loyalty needs to be created with loyalty type of sales promotion or trade promotion.
- *The objectives to be met.* As we have seen in the case of the PLC, the communication tools will vary in function of the communication objectives to be met: awareness, trial, loyalty.
- *The type of product.* If we need to give information about a complex product, it will be necessary to use a medium which allows to explain the benefits of the product such as TV advertising or print.

18.2   THE COMMUNICATION PROCESS

Any communication involves an *exchange of signals* between a sender and a receiver, and the use of a system of encoding and decoding which allows the creation and the interpretation of the message. Figure 18.2 describes the communication process in terms of nine elements.

1. *Sender:* the party sending the message to another party.
2. *Encoding:* the process of transforming the intended message into images, language, signs, symbols and so on.
3. *Message:* the information or the claim to be communicated to the receiver by the sender.
4. *Media:* the communication channel through which the message moves from the sender to the receiver.
5. *Decoding:* the process through which the receiver assigns meaning to the symbols transmitted.
6. *Receiver:* the target audience.
7. *Response:* the set of reactions that the receiver has after exposure to the message.
8. *Feedback:* the part of the target audience's response that the receiver communicates to the sender.
9. *Noise:* the distortions that occur during the communication process.

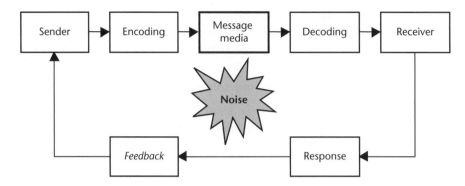

Figure 18.2   The communication process

Figure 18.2 describes the relationship between these nine factors and helps to determine the *conditions for effective communication*.

Three conditions can be identified:

- *Communication objectives*. Senders must know which audiences they want to reach and what type of response they want. This implies the choice of a target audience and the determination of specific communication objectives. These tasks are typically the responsibilities of strategic marketing people.
- *Message execution*. Communicators must be skilful in encoding messages and must be able to understand how the target audience tends to process messages. This involves designing advertisements and ensuring, through testing, that the target group processes them in the intended manner to produce the desired communication effect.
- *Media planning*. Two decisions are involved here. First, media selection, that is, "where" to reach the target audience most efficiently; second, media scheduling, that is, "how often" the target audience needs to be reached to produce the intended communication objective.

These last two tasks (message and media) are in general assumed by advertising agencies and/or by agencies specializing in media planning.

- *Communication effectiveness*. The advertiser must identify the audience's response to the message and verify to what extent the communication objectives have been achieved. This is again the task of marketing management.

Applying the concept of market orientation to advertising implies developing messages that relate to consumers' experience, namely, by adopting a language they can decode. These four conditions for efficient communication determine the various decisions to be taken in any marketing communication programme.

Relative importance of personal versus impersonal communication

The two most important tools of marketing communication are personal communication, assumed by the sales force, and impersonal communication, achieved through media advertising. The problem is to know when direct intervention by a sales representative is more effective than advertising. A comparison of the main features of each of these two means of communication is shown in Table 18.1 and in Figure 18.3.

This comparison suggests the following:

- Personal selling is by far the most efficient and powerful communication tool. But it costs almost a 100 times more to contact a prospect with a salesperson's visit than with an advertising message.
- Media advertising, however, has the advantage over personal selling in that it can reach a large number of people in a short period of time, while a sales representative can only visit a limited number of customers within a day.
- When a product is complex and difficult to use and is targeted to a limited number of people, a sales representative is clearly much more effective than an advertising message, which is necessarily too general and too simplistic.
- A salesperson acts directly and can obtain an immediate order from the customer, whereas advertising works through brand awareness and through attitude formation. These are often long-term effects.

Table 18.1   Comparing personal and impersonal communication

Elements of the communication process	Personal communication	Impersonal communication
Target	■ Very well-identified target	■ Average profile of the target
Message	■ Tailor-made message	■ Standard message
	■ Many arguments	■ Few arguments
	■ Weak control of form and content	■ Strong control of form and content
Media	■ Personalized and human contact	■ Impersonalized contact
	■ Few contacts	■ Several contacts
Receiver	■ Continued attention	■ Volatile attention
	■ Weak consequence of encoding error	■ Strong effect of encoding error
Response	■ Immediate behavioural response possible	■ Immediate behavioural response difficult

Source: Adapted from Darmon, Laroche and Petrov (1982, p. 398).

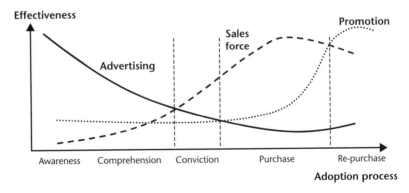

Figure 18.3   Marketing communication effectiveness at different stages of the adoption process
Source: Adapted from Kotler and Dubois (2000).

Table 18.2   Advertising expenditures in Europe

	Δ PUB 08/07	2008 M€	Δ PUB 09/08	2009 M€	Share 2009	Δ PUB – Δ PIB 09/08
France	1.4%	10,225	0.9%	10,320	4.6%	−2.4
Germany	1.7%	14,125	2.1%	14,419	6.5%	−1.2
Italy	2.8%	10,112	2.0%	10,319	4.6%	−0.5
Spain	−2.4%	7,393	0.0%	7,391	3.3%	−4.0
UK	1.5%	13,445	2.9%	13,839	6.2%	−1.0
TOTAL EU5	**1.2%**	**51,275**	**1.9%**	**52,253**	**23.5%**	**−1.5**
USA	1.5%	107,657	1.7%	109,478	49.2%	−2.6
Japan	0.7%	26,783	1.0%	27,059	12.2%	0.0
Total WW7	**1.3%**	**183,635**	**1.6%**	**186,607**	**83.9%**	**−1.8**
China	21.9%	12,983	15.0%	14,925	6.7%	1.5
Russia	28.1%	7,448	23.8%	9,218	4.1%	8.0
India	18.9%	4,588	18.7%	5,445	2.4%	8.1
Total RIC3	**23.2%**	**24,854**	**18.3%**	**29,398**	**13.2%**	**4.9**
South Korea	5.1%	5,949	7.4%	6,391	2.9%	0.1
Total WW11	**3.5%**	**214,439**	**3.7%**	**222,396**	**100.0%**	**−1.5**

Source: Adbarometer (2008).

Consequently, whenever the personal factor is not essential to communication, advertising is more economical in terms of both costs and of time. Recent developments in the field of advertising tend to reconcile the advantages of these two communication means, which is indeed the objective of interactive or response advertising.

It is therefore not surprising to observe that firms selling industrial goods devote a larger proportion of their communication budget to personal selling than firms operating in the field of consumer goods.

18.3   SELLING OR PERSONAL COMMUNICATION

Personal selling is the most effective means of communication at certain stages of the buying process, especially when preferences need to be developed and the decision to buy spurred on. Due to the developments in communication technology, the role of salespersons is now undergoing a major transformation. Their role in strategic marketing is on the increase and the more routine tasks are increasingly being assumed by cheaper impersonal means of communication.

Sales force tasks and objectives

The first step in developing a personal communication strategy is to define the role of the sales force in the overall marketing strategy. This can only be done by clearly defining the kind of relationship the firm wants to establish with its customers in each product market.

As illustrated in Figure 18.4, one can identify three types of activity that any sales force exercises:

- *Selling*, which implies prospecting and approaching potential buyers, negotiating sales conditions and closing sales.

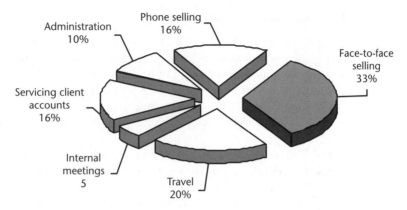

Figure 18.4 The tasks of the sales force
Source: O'Connell and Keenan (1990).

- *Servicing*, which implies delivery, technical assistance, after-sales service, merchandising and so on.
- *Information gathering*, which involves market research, business intelligence, monitoring of competitors' activities, needs analysis and so on.

Thus, the salesperson is not only the firm's commercial arm, but also an important element in its marketing information system.

In practice, the terms "salesperson" and "sales representative" can cover very different missions, depending on the emphasis placed on one or other of the three functions above. The following categories of salesperson can be identified:

- *The delivery person's* function is to ensure the physical delivery of the product.
- *The sales clerk's* role is to assist customers in their choice and to take orders. Sales clerks operate at the point of sale or stand behind the counter.
- *The travelling salesperson* visits the retailers or the distributors, takes their orders and performs non-selling activities such as checking inventory, handling retailers' complaints and so on.
- *The merchandiser's* role is not to sell but rather to organize promotional activities at the sales point and to arrange point-of-purchase displays.
- *The missionary delegate* is not permitted to take an order, but has a role to inform and educate potential users. This is typically the role played by the medical representatives in the pharmaceutical industry.
- *The sales engineer* has a technical competence and operates as a consultant *vis-à-vis* the customer, providing assistance and advice. It is the role played by IBM sales engineers.
- *The sales representative* is an independent salesperson selling durable goods like cars and vacuum cleaners, or services like insurance, where creative selling is very important.
- *The negotiator* is in charge of the financial engineering of vast industrial projects and is responsible for negotiations with government authorities and industrial partners.

Once the type of mission assigned to the salesperson is defined, the problem is to know how to organize commercial relations and which tasks to assign to the sales force, to the distribution network and to advertising.

The new role of the sales force

Generally speaking, the true role of a salesperson remains first and foremost tied to satisfying the need for two-way communication felt by well-informed customers who have demands about how the product can be adapted to their own needs. From the firm's viewpoint, the sales force's new effectiveness is mainly linked to their ability in collecting and transmitting information so as to increase the speed of adjustment to market changes. This is how a Japanese firm conceives the role of the sales force.

> Salesmen are irreplaceable canvassers of information; they must be trained: (a) to listen to the customer, much more than to know seductive sales speech of the kind: "the ten secrets of selling"; (b) to be humble when criticized, much more than display militant pride of the kind: "the products of firm X are the best"; (c) to be in solidarity with other salesmen and with his firm to facilitate cross-checking and return of information, much more than pursue the superficial solitude of the sales person who only tries to reach his quota in order to improve his own performance. (Xardel, 1982)

This evolution in the notion of the role of the sales force therefore tends to increase its direct participation in strategic marketing. In addition to operational marketing functions, the sales force now exercises various strategic functions. The typical *functions of the sales force* are:

- Winning acceptance for new products.
- Developing new customers.
- Maintaining customer loyalty.
- Providing technical service to facilitate sales.
- Communicating product information.
- Gathering information.

Several of these selling objectives, such as winning acceptance for new products, developing new customers and gathering information, are typically related to strategic marketing. The salesperson can therefore play an important role in strategic marketing, in so far as he or she participates in elaborating product policy through the information they supply regarding buyers' needs.

Opposition between transactional and relationship selling

As explained in Chapter 1 (see p. 10) commercial negotiation and selling techniques are often thought to be the same. These are, however, two completely different procedures.

> Selling is convincing someone – the customer – that a proposed product or service best answers his or her needs; "negotiating" is jointly analysing a situation where there is some common interest, even though diverging interests are apparent and each party has something to sell or conditions to impose, so as to come to a mutually satisfying agreement. (Guérin et al., 1979, quoted by Dupont, 1994, p. 247)

Selling techniques are indubitably efficient *to close the sale* and are often associated with various aggressive selling methods: hard sell or manipulative marketing. These techniques were popular in the 1960s in operational marketing when the *sales orientation* was predominant (see Chapter 1). They have been challenged over the past ten years, under the influence of all the changes in customer behaviour and in the competitive environment, as mentioned previously.

The differences between single transaction and relationship selling are many:

- Transaction selling focuses on a discrete, individual sale. The relationships end once the sale is consummated.
- Relationship selling is oriented towards a strong and *lasting relationship*. Maintaining and cultivating the customer base is the key objective, in order to create a mutually profitable relationship.
- Relationship selling presupposes the opportunity for *shared benefits*, while transaction marketing works on a model of contradictory needs: the buyer wants a good price; the seller wants a high profit.
- Single transaction sellers are sometimes part of the seedier side of marketing.

> New York City electronic retailers, for example, often run afoul of the authorities for advertising unrealistically low prices, then once the consumer is in the store, engaging in "bait-and-switch" and other less savoury sales tactics. They can get away with it because of the steady flow of tourists and the almost complete lack of repeat business. Their goal is not to build lasting relationships with customers but to make a continuous series of first-time purchases. Other merchants, with a greater incidence of repeat business, would not last long with such practices. (Schnaars, 1998, p. 190)

Relationship selling differs from transactional selling in other respects as well. While the latter focuses almost solely on price, the former shifts the *emphasis to non-economic benefits*, such as services, delivery time and the certainty of continued supply. Traditional selling techniques had to evolve towards relationship selling for three reasons:

1. In traditional selling (based on the systematic application of selling techniques), it is rarely understood that selling is above all an *act of communication*, a mutual discovery of questions and answers and not an unilateral act of manipulation.
2. If traditional selling techniques seem less efficient today and often come up against resistance and scepticism from well-informed prospects (partially due to consumerism), this is because the decision to buy depends more upon *complex mechanisms of social influence* and less upon elementary psychological mechanisms.
3. Traditional selling techniques do not consider the fact that the *practice of relationship selling*, that is, helping a customer find the solution to a problem, has become the core principle of a market-oriented strategy, where selling is *customer problem solving*, not merely selling available products.

As many markets reached maturity in highly industrialized economies, it became increasingly obvious that keeping existing customers happy was less costly than recruiting new customers, a difficult and risky strategy implying increased price competition. Progressively, in non-expansible markets, the objective of "customer retention" over customer attraction has gained acceptance.

This new paradigm implies that the objective becomes more to maximize customer share than market share. In practice, it means that once a customer is gained, to try to cover the largest share of his or her purchases within the product category. Instead of trying to close a transaction, it is preferable to build a long-lasting and mutually profitable relationship with the customer. The main differences between the two approaches are summarized in Table 18.3.

Table 18.3   The opposition between transactional and relationship selling

Criteria	Transactional selling	Relationship selling
Mission	Conquest	Loyalty building
Objective	Transactions, market share	Relationships, customer share
Organization	Brand (product) management	Customer management
Information	Market research	Dialogue, databases
Environment	Non-saturated markets	Saturated markets
Types of markets	B2C and B2B	B2B

Source: Adapted from Donaldson (1998).

This new selling orientation has several consequences for the marketing process:

- It creates a new culture where the relationship is more important than the transaction itself. Success is measured by reference to the number of lasting relationships generated.
- It creates a change in the analysis tools used. Personal data banks are key. All the information concerning the customer is recorded and everybody within the firm has free access to the bank.
- It creates a change in the selling and communication instruments used. The tools of direct marketing, *mailing, call centre* and so on, are the more popular instruments.
- A new managerial tool emerges CRM which, as *Market Driven Management*, is a new corporate philosophy requiring a deep reorganization of the firm's management, not only within the marketing department, but also within the other functions.
- CRM constitutes the natural continuation of the movement triggered by *Market Driven Management*, with a stronger emphasis on the relationship.

The practice of relationship or counselling selling – as opposed to the *impose–convince–suggest–please* system – is characterized by the importance given (a) to true and non-manipulative exploration of the customer's motivations and motives and (b) to the search for a long-lasting mutually satisfactory relationship between buyers and sellers. Relationship selling has shifted attention from "closing" a singular sale to creating the necessary conditions for a long-term relationship between the firm and its customers that in the long run breeds successful sales encounters.

> Relationship selling is customer-oriented, as opposed to traditional selling which is product-oriented. Selling is customer problem-solving, not merely selling available products. (Donaldson, 1998, p. 79)

In market-oriented firms, there is a tendency to change the vocabulary from sales force to *sales counsellors, professional representatives* or *sales consultants*.

In a company having chosen to develop a market-oriented strategy, commercial negotiation has received a mission, which is capital for the firm's survival: to build a sustainable relationship with customers. This means a relationship which is profitable for both parties. In relationship selling, *the profit centre is the customer* and not the product or the brand. Attracting new customers is viewed as an intermediate objective; maintaining the existing customer base is a major objective for a long-term mutually profitable relationship. In this context, the monitoring of the customer's portfolio composition and of the quality of the market share is of primary importance. Read Slymotsky and Shapiro (1993) on this subject.

Pitfalls of relationship selling

As pointed out by Schnaars (1998, p. 190), sometimes relationships are forced, namely, when the sellers engineer switching costs into their transactions that tie the customer in a way that denies the buyer a real choice and makes him a *captive customer*. Firms that rely on proprietary technologies and patented parts also force lasting relationships. Long-term contracts do the same. In each of these cases the seller may bolt given the opportunity to do so. There are other limitations to relationship marketing:

- The firm that builds a relationship usually charges a *premium price* and is therefore vulnerable to price competition from low-price sellers.
- Some customers may refuse to become dependent on a *single supplier*, a very sensitive issue in B2B markets.
- Customers may place their *easy-to-fill orders* to lower-price competitors and leave the more difficult or less profitable orders to the high-service firm.
- In other cases, there may be simply *no mutual benefit* for buyer and seller.

Relationship selling is particularly useful in B2B marketing where this supplier–customer link is especially close, lasting and important for both parties. This is also the philosophy underlying trade marketing, in the relationship binding manufacturers and distributors. In general, relationship selling is the irreplaceable complement to a strategy based on the *solution-to-a-problem approach* as described earlier.

Setting up a relationship selling process

Approaching customers in relationship selling is different from traditional selling because of the emphasis on pre-sales and post-sales activities. There are five different phases in relationship selling:

1. *Systematic search for information*. This means identifying prospects, potential customers who might need the product and who might buy it. This is a permanent activity.
2. *Selecting a target*. Here the purpose is to analyse the objective reasons why a prospect could become a prospective customer and have reasons for becoming a buyer. The real question is to find out to what extent our firm can be useful to this customer.
3. *Convincing good customers*. It is essential that the salesperson attract customers whose value and potential justify the time and effort which will be devoted to them. This is

Table 18.4 Typology of sales calls

- *Cold calling* – also called blind call.
- *Lead qualification* – determining if the firm or individual qualifies.
- *Lead development* – keeping the sales opportunity alive.
- *Proposal or closing* – going for the sale.
- *Up-sell and cross-sell* – finding other opportunities within the customer.
- *Relationship building* – creating more in-depth relationships with key people.
- *Routine servicing* – sometimes referred to "go see" call.
- *Problem resolution* – handling some type of problem.

Most B2B sales managers feel that between 8 and 10 calls are required to close a complex sale.

Source: Coe (2004).

the beginning of the selling phase itself, which includes the sales presentation, negotiation, answers to objections and the conclusion of the agreement.

4. *Building the relationship.* A relationship of trust must be built up and, once the relationship is established, the follow-up must be organized. The salesperson is the problem-solver, who sells, not a product, but the service (or the solution) provided by the product.

5. *Maintaining and reinforcing the relationship.* Maintaining a relationship is particularly based on personalized service achieved through better understanding of customers' needs. The objective is to maintain close contact with the customer and to build up customer loyalty. The firm can thus construct a barrier to competition, as changing suppliers would imply switching costs.

Relationship selling implies giving the role of advisor to the salesperson, as *a seller of solutions* (see Chapter 4). In a company which has opted for market orientation, a salesperson is a partner working towards the customer's long-term performance, even if he or she cannot see the possibility of an immediate sale. Relationship selling has developed substantially in the B2B context and is progressively gaining a foothold in B2C markets through the possibilities offered by direct and interactive marketing.

Organization of the sales force

A firm can organize its sales force in different ways. The organization can be by territory, by product, by customer or even a combination of these.

- *Territory-based organization.* This is the most common structure and also the simplest organization. The salesperson is the firm's exclusive representative for its full product line for all current and potential customers. This structure has several advantages: first, it defines clearly the sales representative's responsibilities; second, it motivates the salesperson, who has the full exclusivity on the territory; and finally, it minimizes costs and travel expenses. This structure is only appropriate when products are few in number or similar and when customers have the same kind of needs. A firm producing paints and varnishes, whose customers are wholesalers, retailers and industrial users (building painters, car bodies and so on), clearly cannot use the same salesperson to cultivate these different customer groups.
- *Product-based organization.* This second structure is preferable when products are very different, technically complex and require appropriate technical competence. In this case, the salesperson is more specialized and better equipped to meet clients' needs and also to counter rivals. The problem with this structure is that costs may increase manifold, since several salespersons from the same firm may visit the same customer. For example, Rank Xerox uses different salespersons for photocopying machines and for word-processing units.
- *Customer-based organization.* Organization by customer categories is adopted when clients' needs are very different and require specific abilities. Customers may be classified by industrial sector, by size or by their method of buying. We find here the same criteria as those of segmentation presented in Chapter 6.

The advantage of a customer-based structure is that each sales force is specialized and becomes very knowledgeable about specific customer needs. But if customers are dispersed geographically, this organization can be very costly. Most computer firms organize their sales force by customer groups: banks and insurance, industrial customers, retailers and so on.

Other more complex forms of organization combining pairs of criteria also exist. Salespersons can be specialized by product–territory, customer–territory or even by territory–customer–product. This normally happens in very large enterprises with many products and varied clients.

Deciding on the size of the sales force

Determining the number of salespeople is a problem logically similar to the advertising budget. In practice, however, it can be resolved more simply because market response is easier to measure. Different approaches are possible. The simplest no doubt is the one based on the salesperson's *work load*. The procedure is as follows:

The underlying philosophy in *the call-load ap*proach is that large customers should be serviced differently from medium-sized customers, and medium-sized customers differently from small customers.

- *The first step* is to have a *breakdown of customer by class, size, sector or geographic location*.
- *The next step* is to develop a theoretical *call frequency for each class*. Experience shows that as the customer grows larger, the number of sales calls does not grow in direct proportion to the increase in sales. Churchill *et al.* (1997) suggested that the relationship between customer size and sales calls can be clearly seen when these two factors are plotted on a semi-log paper, which reflects the presence of diminishing returns. For every customer class, multiplying the call frequency times the number of account in any class provides a specific call frequency.
- *In the third step*, the *number of calls* made by an average salesperson during one year must be determined.

The factors to consider here are number of working days after deducting holidays, weekends, vacations and so on; percentage of non-selling time devoted to sales meetings, sick leave, laboratory training and so on; number of calls made per day by salesperson and by territory; and variation in call capacity between urban and rural territories.

Box 18.1   Implementation problem: how to calculate the cost of a sales call

- **Number of calls per year**

Five weeks/year

- Two weeks for holiday
- Three weeks for vacation/time off/sick time
- Two weeks for meetings trade shows, etc.

45 selling weeks

Five days/week

- One day for calls/paper work

Four days/week selling time

Two to three face-to-face calls per day

= *360 to 540 calls per year*

- **Yearly cost of a salesperson**

$75K average compensation (salary, commission, bonus, etc.)

+ $15 k in benefits @ 20% salary

+$45K in travel costs $1K/week average

+$40K allocated for sales management cost @20% of $200K

= *$175 total cost of field person*

- **Cost per call**

$175/ 540 calls/year = $324 per call

$175/ 360 calls/year = $486 per call

Source: Coe (2004).

Given the number of visits that a salesperson can make in a given customer class, it is then possible to determine the size of the necessary sales force from the following expression:

$$FDV = \frac{(\text{Number of potential customers})\ (\text{Frequencies of visits})}{(\text{Avergae number of visits per salesmen})}$$

The calculation is repeated for each customer class. This approach is valid for current customers and must be extended to prospective customers as well. For other methods of setting the size of the sales force, see Semlow (1959) and Lambert (1968).

Other methods are based on direct or indirect measures of market response to an increase of the frequency of calls through the sales force. The method developed by Semlow is based on several indicators of buying power within each sales territory. A successful application of this method to the insurance sector is presented by Lambin (1965).

In B2B markets, direct sales measures of visit frequency are more easily obtainable. An econometric study conducted by Lambert (1968) in the hospitals market has contributed to improve in a significant way the overall allocation of selling efforts among sales territories.

18.4   SALES PROMOTION DECISIONS

Sales promotion includes all the incentive tools which, often locally and in a non-permanent way, are used by the firm to complement and reinforce advertising and the sales force action, and to stimulate quicker and/or larger purchase of a good or service. Sales promotion is part of the overall marketing strategy as suggested by the following definition:

> Sales promotion is a process combining a set of communication tools and techniques, implemented within the framework of the marketing plan designed by the firm, in order to induce among the target groups, in the short or in the long term, the adoption or the modification of a consuming or purchase behaviour. (Ingold, 1995, p. 25)

During the last decade, promotion has gained in importance and sales promotion expenditures have been increasing annually as a percentage of the total communication budget.

> According to the Havas study (1998), promotion expenditures in the UK amounted to 17,210 Mln GBP in 1997, against 15,917 Mln in 1996, or a 8.1 per cent increase. Direct marketing expenditures amounted to 2890 Mln GBP in 1997. In percent of total marketing communication expenditures, promotion amounted to 17.2 per cent and direct marketing to 18.8 per cent. (Havas, 1998, p. 26)

The share of promotion expenditures in the total marketing communication budget observed in each European country is shown in Table 18.5.

Several factors, both internal and external, have contributed to the rapid growth of sales promotion:

- Consumers, confronted with a decline of their purchasing power, are more price-sensitive and react positively to promotional activities.

Table 18.5 Objectives by types of promotions

Consumer promotions	Commercial promotions
Trial	Visit to new outlets
First purchase	Customer retention
Re-purchase	Visit frequency increase
Loyalty	First purchase
Retention	Purchase in new store facings
Reduced prices	Increase of the average basket
Increase of quantity purchased	
Increase of quantity consumed	
Purchase frequency increase	
Trial of a new variety	
Distributor promotions	**Network promotion**
List of new products	Increase of quantity sold
Stock	Gain in distribution presence
Facing increase	Introduction of new products
Point of purchase display	Increase in size or range
Participation to advertising	Reselling actions

Source: Ingold (1995, p. 63).

- Distributors, more concentrated and powerful, demand from manufacturers more promotions to help them build store traffic.
- Competition intensifies and competitors use consumer and trade promotions more frequently.
- Effectiveness of mass media advertising has declined because of rising costs, media clutter and similarity among competing brands.
- Companies confronted with a slowing down of sales are more concerned by short-term results.
- Any promotion is in fact a disguised price reduction, but which is limited in time and scope. This flexibility is highly praised by marketing people.

To these factors, one must also add the development of direct marketing, which by nature often has a promotional content.

Objectives of sales promotion

The objectives of sales promotion vary with the type of promotions; it is common practice to make a distinction according to the sender of the promotion (manufacturer or distributor) and according to the target (consumer, distributor, sales force). Following Ingold's classification (1995, p. 26), we will make a distinction between four types of promotions:

1. *Consumer promotions,* in this a direct, indirect or hypothetical benefit (samples, coupons, rebates, cash refund offer and so on) is proposed to consumers to stimulate the purchase of a product. Manufacturers generally offer consumer promotions through the distribution channel.
2. *Trade promotions* are proposed to retailers or wholesalers, generally taking the form of money allowances, to persuade them (a) to carry the brand, (b) to carry more units than the normal amount, (c) to promote the brand by featuring display or price reductions or (d) to push the products in their stores.

3. *Commercial promotions* are promotional activities organized by distributors and targeting their own customer base, generally using the financial support given by manufacturers.
4. *Sales force or network promotion*, where the objective is to stimulate all the partners involved in the selling activities (sales force, wholesalers, retailers) through individual incentives.

These distinctions are sometimes artificial to the extent where a specific promotion can take simultaneously one of these forms. The distinction remains useful, however, to define as clearly as possible the promotion objective. Examples of promotion objectives are presented in Table 18.5. For a more detailed description of these objectives, see Ingold (1995, pp. 63–70).

The different promotion tools

There are many different sales promotion tools which can be divided, as proposed by *LSA* (1982), into four main groups:

1. *Price reductions*. Essentially this is selling something for less money; several methods exist.
2. *Selling with premiums or gifts*. Small items are given to buyers either at the time of purchase or afterwards.
3. *Samples and trials*. Free distribution, trials or tasting allow consumers to test the product.
4. *Games and contests*. These games give buyers a chance to win a big prize.

There are many ways of using these sales promotion tools as shown in Table 18.6.

New sales promotion tools have appeared over the last few years based upon information obtained from bar codes, via, for instance, customer loyalty cards and coupons (see Exhibit 18.1). Electronic coupons are immediately distributed to customers targeted through their purchases electronically recorded when they pay.

> The system developed by Catalina Marketing is based on reading bar codes by an intelligent scanner and thus avoids giving out coupons to customers who would not be interested in the product. The scanner instructs the computer to print out a coupon for Fanta for someone who had just bought Orangina. Or a customer who had just bought baby products receives a coupon for Pampers.

This has just been brought before the courts in France by Orangina as unfair competition. A decision has not yet been made (*LSA*, 1997). It is the misappropriation of clientele which is at stake here.

> In other words, Orangina would accept that customers buying Coca-Cola get a coupon for Fanta (which belongs to the same group) or that those buying Mars get a Coca-Cola coupon (complementary product) but not a coupon from a competitor for the same product category.

The issue at stake is important: do distributors have the right to orient customers to any products they choose? May a distributor dispose of his or her clientele as he or she wishes?

Table 18.6 Description of promotion tools

1. Premiums	2. Games and contests	3. Price reductions	4. Trials and samples
With-pack premium: an extra product accompanies the product inside (in-pack) or on pack (outside).	*Contests:* possibility of winning a big prize in a contest based on consumer's observation, knowledge or suggestion.	*Coupons:* certificates entitling the bearer to a stated saving on the purchase of a specific product.	*Free sample:* offer on a limited base of a free amount of product or service.
Recipe: recipe files offered with purchased product.	*Sweepstakes:* diverse forms of games based on chance with a lottery draw.	*Special offer:* a reduced price for a limited period of time.	*Gifts:* merchandise offered as an incentive to purchase a product, to visit a store, etc.
Differed premium: an advantage, which is offered at a later date.	*Winner per store (or patronage award):* a lottery where a client may win even without purchasing.	*Extra-pack:* 3 products for the price of 2, 4 products for the price of 3, etc.	*Free trials:* invite prospective buyers to try the product without cost and without obligation to buy.
Sample: a sample is included.		*Banded pack:* two related products banded together.	*Demonstrations:* point of purchases (POP) displays and commercial presentations, sometimes with trials or tastiness.
Package: a reusable container, which can be used after consuming the product.		*Cash refund:* provide a price reduction after the purchase with proof of full payment.	
Premium (gifts): merchandise offered at a relatively low cost or free.		*Buy back:* the manufacturer buys back obsolete model of the brand.	
Self-liquidating premium: item sold below its normal retail price at no cost for the brand.			

Source: Adapted from LSA (1982).

Exhibit 18.1   Catalina electronic couponing

Catalina printers are installed in over 12,000 outlets, mainly in the United States, Great Britain, Japan and France. Over 700 French stores give out coupons called Eco-bo (Géant, Hyper U, Casino, Champion, Super U, Cora, Match and Intermarché). More than 400 brands are in the system and over 185 million coupons have been distributed. Over 15 million coupons have been returned by customers, which means a response rate of 8 to 10 per cent, compared to 2.4 per cent for coupons in mailboxes.

Source: LSA (1997, p. 19).

This explosion of sales promotion tools and actions has of course a negative side in that they present a high cost both for the manufacturer and for the distributor. At the same time the positive effect of promotions is assailed by competitors who counterattack a successful sales promotion action with a "reaction" sales promotion. While such an escalation of promotions benefits the consumer, it ends up by providing never-ending promotions, weakening their effect and provoking speculation and a state of expectancy from consumers. This explains the *Every Day Low Price* strategy that P&G launched with Wal-Mart in the United States where P&G promises to deliver its products without sales promotion but at the lowest possible cost.

Impact of promotions on sales

The effects of sales promotion are complex and go beyond just affecting sales even if that is the main objective. We can distinguish between effects on consumers and effects on distributors. Along with such immediate effects there are long-term consequences which can sometimes be negative for a brand. A distinction must be made between the impact on consumers and on distributors.

Impact of promotions on consumers

These effects are many and varied, as illustrated in Figure 18.5. They can be felt before, during and after the promotion action itself:

- *Internal transfer effect*. Loyal buyers take advantage of an offer but would have bought the brand in any case.
- *Anticipation effect*. Sales go down just before a promotion comes into effect because consumers wait for the promotion to buy. This is particularly true when the periodicity for sales promotions is regular.
- *Decay effect*. Sales go down after a special promotion because consumers have stocked up on the product.

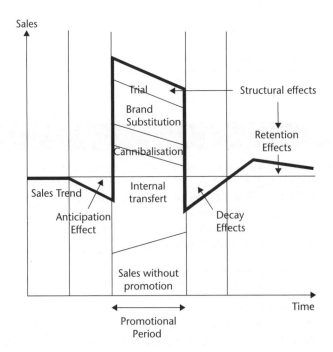

Figure 18.5   Impact of promotions on sales
Source: Ingold (1995). Reproduced with permission.

- *Cannibalization effect.* There are purchasing transfers among different sizes and varieties within a range of products during sales promotions.
- *Brand switching effect.* This is what was intended. Additional sales through a switch from some other brand to the brand under promotion.
- *Trial effect.* Whatever the tool, it induces consumers to use the product. This is especially important for new products.
- *Retention effect.* Here we have the positive effects that survive the period of promotion and can keep the product at a superior level of sales after the promotion.

These promotion effects vary according to the phase of the PLC reached by the reference market. During the introduction and growth phases, sales promotion has an accelerator effect in the development of primary demand, by inducing consumers to try out the product. In contrast, during the maturity phase of the PLC, the benefits obtained through promotion are made at the expense of competition, and this can trigger a chain reaction of sales promotion.

Impact of promotions on distributors

Sales promotions organized at the point of sales always have an impact on distributor behaviour. Three major effects can be identified:

- *Postponement effect.* Distributors know, and demand to know, the operational marketing programme of their suppliers and tend to defer purchases in order to stock up for sales promotions.
- *Overstocking effect.* When ordering at times of sales promotions, distributors tend to order as a function of their storage space, which decreases post-promotion orders.
- *Deviant ordering.* Some distributors only order when the products are on promotions and refuse to purchase the product at full price. This is the attitude adopted systematically by hard discounters who can then charge very competitive prices.

Promotions have an important role to play in creating traffic flow in the store and in stimulating shelf rotation. As mentioned earlier, sales promotions also add to logistic and administrative costs for distributors. This means that it is important to check that the proposed promotions are compatible with distributors operating mode.

Negative side effects of promotions

Overly frequent sales promotions can produce a certain number of negative side effects on buying behaviour and brand image. There are four types of negative effects:

- *Escalation of promotions.* As already mentioned, because of the very success of a first sales promotion, promotion after promotion may be launched. This is desirable neither for the manufacturer nor for the distributor.
- *Brand confusion.* If there are too many promotions the brand image is weakened and promotions can conflict with the brand positioning strategy.
- *Speculation.* If a growing number of purchases are made during sales promotions, consumers may change their buying behaviour by postponing their purchases. This of course is counterproductive, as the purpose of promotions is to increase sales in normal periods. The anticipation effect is then prevalent. It is, however, important to

distinguish between consumers who wait for sales promotion periods and the very particular group that waits for sales promotion actions.

■ *Difficulty in price comparison*. The multiplication of sales promotions increases the difficulty of evaluating a "fair price" and of comparing prices. This can reduce a consumer's sensitivity to prices.

Several authors, one of whom is Froloff (1992), can be consulted on the sensitivity of consumers to sales promotions.

Profitability of sales promotions

Measuring the effectiveness and profitability of sales promotions can often be done by direct observation when detailed sales figures are available, as is usually the case for consumer goods. The development of new measuring techniques based on scanning panels, mentioned earlier in Chapter 5, has revolutionized this. The Nielsen Company, in particular, has developed several tools, among which are Sabine and Scanpro, for directly measuring the impact of sales promotions. The Accuris group in Belgium has developed a measuring system helping companies optimize expenditures in sales promotions.

Pan-European promotions

With the globalization of markets, and particularly of the European economy, marketers are striving for a consistent and international message. Apart from the economies of scale to be gained, a consistent pan-European promotion message can help strengthen a brand. But setting up an effective pan-European promotion to run in 12 languages across a dozen countries sounds like the ultimate marketing nightmare. For companies having global brands – like Kodak, Mars, Swatch, British Airways, American Express and so on – the tools at their disposal for promoting them through retail channels around Europe are far from harmonious. Table 18.7 summarizes some of the tactics allowed in a few key European markets.

The European Commission is working to find agreement between member states on all forms of cross-border communications. They have even formed an expert group to advise and recommend on the issues. What is likely to emerge is a system of *mutual recognition* in which companies can carry out sales promotion activities in the target country as long as they are legal in the company's country of origin. The fact that on-pack, in-pack, vouchers and prize giveaways can be run in many European countries simultaneously will mean economies of scale in managing such campaigns. It also means that brand owners can print the same message – granted a multi-language one – on all European products rather than distinguishing which will be on some and not on others, as is required today. The issue of local adaptation will remain, however.

Table 18.7   Cross-border conflicts of European sales promotions

Tactic	Germany	France	UK	Netherlands	Belgium
Onpack price reductions	Yes	Yes	Yes	Yes	Yes
In-pack gifts	??	??	Yes	??	??
Extra product	??	Yes	Yes	??	??
Money-off vouchers	No	Yes	Yes	Yes	Yes
Free prize contest	No	Yes	Yes	No	No
Yes: legally allowed; ??: under review; No: not legally allowed.					

Source: Stewart-Allen (1999).

A sales promotion is trying to prompt changes in consumer behaviour, not attitudes, and people's behaviour differs from one market to another. You are never going to succeed if you try to homogenise the mechanics of a pan-European promotion. Even if the laws regarding sales promotion were the same in different countries, you probably wouldn't want to do it. (Kiernan, 1992)

For example, recently Pepsi ran an on-pack promotion across nine countries that offered exclusive Spice Girls prizes, with a menu of different tactics available in each of the countries where the promotion ran to ensure that the campaign was tailored to each market's needs and legal environment (Stewart-Allen, 1999, p. 10).

18.5   PUBLIC RELATIONS DECISIONS

In the first three styles of communication, the product or brand is at the heart of the advertising message. Institutional advertising does not talk about the product, but aims to create or reinforce a positive attitude towards the firm. The objective is therefore to create an image, but that of the firm is to describe the firm's profile and stress its personality in order to create a climate of confidence and understanding. The purpose is to *communicate differently* in a saturated advertising world and to fight against the fatigue of product advertising with a softer approach, by drawing attention to the firm itself, its merits, its values and talents. Clearly, the effectiveness of this kind of communication can only be evaluated in the long term and can essentially work on attitudes.

Objectives of public relations

Public relations group the communications tools developed by the firm to promote the corporate activities, goals and value and create a positive corporate image in the general public and more particularly among the key market actors, distributors, prescribers and institutional, financial and commercial partners. Public relations differ from other forms of marketing communication in three ways:

- *Objectives are different*. It is not a matter of selling but rather of gaining moral support from public opinion to pursue its economic activity.
- *Targets are more diversified*. The target is broader than just customers, covering all *market stakeholders* who, directly or indirectly, are active players in the market, including public opinion.
- *Tools are varied*. Along with the house journal and press releases, they include sponsoring and patronage. The objective is to use an intermediary (a journalist, an event) to convey the information with greater credibility.

In research conducted by des Thwaites, Anguilar-Manjarrez and Kidd (1998) in Canada to identify the objectives of sponsoring sport events, the objectives presented in Table 18.8 emerged.

The tools of public relations

There are many tools in public relations, which can be grouped under four headings:

- *Information on the company*, such as launching of new products, signing a major contract, R&D results, a merger or an acquisition and so on. Once the information is chosen, PR specialists organize press releases or a press conference.

- *Publications*, such as annual reports, house journals, catalogues and so on, which now are often directly available on CD-ROM or on the Internet.
- *Events or special occasions* or communication through events such as sport competitions, concerts, exhibitions sponsored by the company or through events specially organized by the company, such as open house days, factory visits, training sessions for dealers combined with leisure activities and so on.
- *Patronage*, where the company supports a particular cause of general interest, humanitarian, scientific or cultural.

The last two PR tools belong to what is called *institutional advertising* where the company tries to position itself in public opinion as a good corporate citizen. This type of communication can be very effective as illustrated by the data in Table 18.9 where the attitude scores of company's users and non-users of institutional advertising are presented (de Jaham, 1979).

Sponsoring and patronage

These are two specific ways of institutional advertising. The latter runs the risk of tiring the public, who can become irritated and view these campaigns as attempts at self-satisfaction. Hence new forms of communication have developed, based on the idea that "there is more splendour in being virtuous than taking credit for it" (Van Hecke, 1988).

Table 18.8   Sports sponsorship objectives

Objectives	Number	Mean	Std. Dev.
Community involvement	43	5.60	1.55
Enhance company image	44	5.32	1.39
Increase public awareness of the company	44	5.18	1.24
Corporate hospitality	41	4.88	1.40
Build business/trade relations and goodwill	40	4.82	1.55
Increase media attention	42	4.79	1.57
Reinforce market perception of product	41	4.56	1.90
Increase sales	40	4.55	1.69
Increase current product awareness	40	4.48	1.87
Identify product with a particular market segment	40	4.40	2.02
Enhance staff/employee's relations and motivation	41	4.37	1.88
Alter public perception of the company	41	4.07	1.77
Increase new product awareness	40	3.97	2.02
Alter market perception of product	39	3.90	1.90
Block competition	41	3.68	2.11
Personal objectives of senior managers	41	2.95	1.83
Counter adverse publicity	41	2.66	1.77
Mean scores based on a 7-point scale: 1 = not important; 7 = very important.			

Source: des Thwaites, Anguilar-Manjarrez and Kidd (1998, p. 41).

Table 18.9   Measuring the effectiveness of institutional advertising

Indicators of attitude	Types of advertisers	
	Non-users of institutional advertising (per cent)	Users of institutional advertising (per cent)
Awareness of company name and activities	82	93
Familiarity with company name and activities	63	77
Overall positive image of company	38	51

Source: de Jaham (1979).

A typical example of one of these media stunts is the financing by American Express of the restoration of Van Eyck's masterpiece *L'agneau mystique*, which considerably increased its prestige in a way that no other campaign could have done.

The objective is to increase awareness of the firm's brand and to improve its image by association with positive values. The event being supported, which often unfolds in an unpredictable manner, thus reinforcing the credibility of the message, must have a testimony value, in the sense that a link should exist between the sponsored event and the sponsoring organization, even if the link is indirect.

> Whether the firm is sponsoring an expedition in the Himalayas or a transatlantic race, it is emphasizing its adherence to moral values such as team spirit and courage. On the one hand it proves its open-mindedness and its harmonious integration in society, and on the other hand, with regard to internal communication, it increases support from its personnel and develops a favourable climate within the firm. (Van Hecke, 1988)

It should be noted that sponsorship is a commercial operation, implying a two-way relation of rights and obligations: on the one hand material or financial support for the sponsored event and on the other direct and methodical exploitation of the event by the firm. Thus sponsorship is distinct from patronage, in which generosity and lack of interest in profit are dominant.

It is clear that forms of advertising, pursued objectives and the means used to achieve them are very different. Before launching advertising, it is therefore important to have a clear view of the role that advertising is to play in the marketing programme.

Worldwide sponsorships expenditures

The figures of Table 18.10 and Figure 18.6 give an idea of the importance of sponsorship in the world as a marketing communication tool. There are several interesting observations that can be drawn from this table:

First of all, the table clearly shows that sponsorship is indeed a worldwide phenomenon in terms of the number of countries reporting substantial sponsorship activity.

A closer examination of these figures indicates that six countries (Germany, Italy, the United Kingdom, the United States, Japan and Australia) account for 70 per cent of total

---

Exhibit 18.2   Ambush marketing

In a survey conducted a month after the 1996 Olympics in Atlanta, consumers were asked to name the official sponsors of the Summer Games. For credit cards, 72 per cent named Visa while only 54 per cent named American Express. Those results were almost identical to a similar survey conducted after the 1994 Winter Olympics, in which 68 per cent named Visa and 52 per cent named American Express. One might conclude from these surveys that Visa does a better job than American Express in promoting its association with the Olympics Games – except Visa paid $40 million for the exclusive rights to be an official sponsor in the credit card category, while American Express was not an official sponsor of the Olympics Games. How did American Express achieve such a high level of recognition as an official sponsor without being one? It engaged in what is known as "ambush marketing", a strategy aimed at creating the false impression of being associated with an event to gain some of the benefits and recognition of official sponsors.

Source: Shani and Sandler (1999).

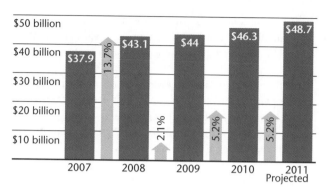

Figure 18.6 Total global sponsorship spending 2007–2011
Source: IEG Sponsorship Report (2011).

Table 18.10   Global sponsorship spending by region

	2009 spending	2010 spending	Increase from 2009	2011 spending (projected)	Increase from 2010 (projected)
Europe	$12.1 billion	$12.9 billion	5.8%	$13.6 billion	5.4%
Asla Pacific	$10 billion	$10.6 billion	5%	$11.1 billion	4.7%
Central/South America	$3.5 billion	$3.6 billion	3.8%	$3.7 billion	5.6%
All Other countries	$1.9 billion	$2 billion	5.1%	$2.1 billion	5.1%

Source: IEG Sponsorship Report (2011).

Table 18.11   North American sponsorship spending by property type

	2009 spending	2010 spending	Increase from 2009	2011 spending (projected)	Increase from 2010 (projected)
Sports	$11.28 billion	$11.66 billion	3.4%	$12.38 billion	6.1%
Entertainment Tours and Attractions	$1.64 billion	$1.75 billion	6.3%	$1.85 billion	5.9%
Causes	$1.51 billion	$1.62 billion	6.7%	$1.7 billion	5%
Arts	$820 million	$842 million	2.7%	$885 million	5.1%
Festivals, Fairs and Annual Events	$756 million	$782 million	3.4%	$820 million	4.9%
Associations and Membership Organizations	$496 million	$514 million	3.6%	$543 million	5.6%

Source: IEG Sponsorship Report (2011).

global expenditures, a fact which clearly associates large-scale sponsorship activity with mature consumer economies.

However, it is also important to note that even where sponsorship expenditure is minuscule in world terms, this medium still accounts for 5 or 6 per cent of advertising expenditures in the local domestic market, a share very close to that observed at world market level.

A special form of sponsorship, which is growing in popularity, is *cause-related marketing* which is gradually replacing philanthropy or charity. In this type of promotion, the firm commits itself to donate a part of the sales revenue generated to a cause or to a non-profit organization. The promotion organized by American Express to help finance the restoration of the Statue of Liberty in New York is an excellent example.

> There were three goals in the promotion: (1) increase the use of the Amex card by current holders; (2) encourage distributors to accept payment with the card; and (3) improve company image and profile. American Express promised to give 1 cent for every transaction in the US and 1 dollar for every new card issued during the last quarter of the year. The campaign was a success both for the sponsor and the cause. Close to 1.7 million dollars went to the renovation project and the rate of use of the Amex card increased by 2.8 per cent over the preceding year and was accepted more readily by distributors. (Meenaghan, 1998, p. 14)

Except for promotion activities directly linked to such a cause, it is difficult to measure the real impact of sponsoring and patronage activities (see Exhibit 18.2). Analysis of this kind of action for the Olympic Games shows that there are positive results for the companies involved. On this topic, see Stipp (1998).

Chapter Summary

Marketing communication refers to all the signals and messages made by the firm to its various publics. The four major communication tools, called the communication mix, are personal selling, advertising, sales promotion and public relations. The four tasks in designing a communication programme are communication objective, message execution, media planning and communication effectiveness. Due to developments in communication technology, the role of the sales force is undergoing a major transformation and relationship selling and commercial negotiation are tending to replace traditional selling techniques. This evolution gives salespeople an important new role to play in strategic marketing.

BIBLIOGRAPHY

Churchill, G.A., Ford, N.M. and Walker, O.C. (1997), *Sales Force Management*, Chicago, R.D. Irwin 5th edition.

Coe, J.M. (2004), The Integration of Direct Marketing and Field Sales to Form a New B2B Sales Coverage Model, *Journal of Interactive Marketing*, 18, 2, pp. 62–74.

Colombo, L. (2008), *EIAA Marketers' Internet Ad Barometer 2008*, European Interactive Advertising Association, November 29.

Darmon, R.Y., Laroche, M. and Petrov, J.V. (1982), *Le Marketing, Fondements et Applications*, Montreal, McGraw-Hill, 2nd edition.

Dartnell Corporation (1994), *28th Survey of Sales Force Compensation*, Chicago, IL, Dartnell Corporation.

De Jaham, M.R. (1979), Le défi de la publicité institutionnelle, *Revue Française du Marketing*, 77, pp. 33–41.

De Pelsmacker, P., Geuens, M. and Van den Bergh, J. (2010), *Marketing Communications, a European Perspective*, Prentice Hall, 4th edition.

des Thwaites, D., Anguilar-Manjarrez, R. and Kidd, C. (1998), Sports Sponsorship Development in Leading Canadian Companies: Issues and Trends, *International Journal of Advertising*, 17, 1, pp. 29–49.

Donaldson, B. (1998), *Sales Management: Theory and Practice*, London, Macmillan, 2nd edition.

Dupont, C. (1994), *La négociation: conduite, théorie et applications*, Paris, Editions Dalloz.

Froloff, L. (1992), La sensibilité du consommateur à la promotion des ventes: de la naissance à la maturité, *Recherche et Applications en Marketing*, 7, 3, pp. 69–88.

Havas (1998), *Europub; le marché publicitaire Européen*, Paris, Havas.

IEG Sponsorship report (2011), see http://www.sponsorship.com.

Ingold, P. (1995), *Promotion des ventes et action commerciale*, Paris, Vuibert.

Kiernan, P. (1992), The Euro Promo Comes of Age, *Marketing Week Sales Promotion,* 18 September.

Kotler, P. (1997), *Marketing Management*, Englewood Cliffs, NJ, Prentice Hall, 9th edition.

Kotler, P. and Dubois, B. (2000), *Marketing Management*, Paris, Public-Union.

Lambert, Z.V. (1968), *Setting the Size of the Sales Force*, Philadelphia, PA University Press.

Lambin, J.J. (1965), *La décision commerciale face à l'incertain,* Paris, Dunod.

Lambin, J.J. (2000/2007*), Market-Driven Management: Strategic and Operational Marketing*, London, Palgrave Macmillan.

Libre Service Actualité (LSA) (1982), Les techniques promotionnelles, 19 December, pp. 869–70.

LSA (1997), La justice veut moraliser le couponing électronique, 27 November, pp. 18–19.

Meenaghan, T. (1998), Current Developments and Future Directions in Sponsorship, *International Journal of Advertising*, 17, 1, pp. 3–28.

O'Connell, W.A. and Keenan, W. (1990), The Shape of Things to Come, *Sales & Marketing Management*, January, pp. 36–41.

Schnaars, S.P. (1998), *Marketing Strategy*, New York, The Free Press.

Semlow, W.J. (1969), How Many Salesmen Do You Need?, *Harvard Business Review*, 37, 3, pp. 126–32.

Shani, D. and Sandler, D. (1999), Counter-attack: Heading off Ambush Marketing, *Marketing News*, 18 January, p. 10.

Slymotsky, A. and Shapiro, B.P. (1993), Leveraging to Beat the Odds: The New Marketing Mind Set, *Harvard Business Review*, 71, 5, pp. 97–107.

Stewart-Allen, A.L. (1999), Cross-Border Conflicts of European Sales Promotions, *Marketing News*, 26 April.

Stipp, H. (1998), The Impact of Olympic Sponsorship on Corporate Image, *International Journal of Advertising*, 17, 1, pp. 75–87.

Van Hecke, T. (1988), Avis aux mécènes: la brique est porteuse, *La Libre Belgique*, 11 June.

Xardel, D. (1982), Vendeurs: nouveaux rôles, nouveaux comportements, *Harvard-l'Expansion*, 25, Summer, pp. 59–75.

CHAPTER NINETEEN

ADVERTISING OFFLINE AND ONLINE DECISIONS

Advertising is a means of communication by which a firm can deliver a message to potential buyers with whom it is not in direct contact. When a firm resorts to advertising, it is effectively following a *pull communication strategy*. Its main objective is to create brand image and brand equity, and to ensure co-operation from distributors. Just as the sales force is the best tool for a push strategy, advertising is the best means for a pull strategy. In Chapter 3, we described what advertising represents for the advertiser and its utility to the customer. Recall briefly that for the *firm*, the function of advertising is to produce knowledge for consumers and to generate interest among them in order to create demand for its product. For *consumers*, advertising allows them to learn about the distinctive characteristics claimed by the manufacturer. Advertising also helps them to save personal time, since the information reaches them directly without their having to collect it.

Learning Objectives

When you have read this chapter, you should be able to know and/or understand:

- The steps in designing an effective communication programme
- The different objectives of advertising communication
- The different advertising platforms
- The objectives and methods of media planning
- The methods of advertising budgeting
- The roles and impact of sales promotions
- The objectives of public relations and of sponsoring

19.1 THE VALUE OF ADVERTISING INFORMATION

The amount of information contained in advertising is an important societal issue and advertising's informational function lends some legitimacy to advertising in a market economy. The information categories or "cues" present in advertisements are listed in Table 19.1.

In a meta-analysis conducted by Abernathy and Franck (1996) across 118 data sets (for a total of 91,438 ads), the mean number of cues was 2.04. More than 84 per cent of the ads had at least one cue, 58 per cent had two or more cues and 33 per cent had three or more cues. The type of information most commonly presented is performance, which appeared in 43 per cent of the ads studied. Other common types of information are availability (37 per cent), components (33 per cent), price (25 per cent), quality (19 per cent) and special

Table 19.1   Advertising information content categories

1. *Price*: What does the product cost? What is the value retention capability?	8. *Nutrition*: Are specific data given concerning the nutritional content of the product or is a direct comparison made with other products?
2. *Quality*: What are the product's characteristics that distinguish it from competing products?	9. *Packaging*: What package is the product available in which makes it more desirable than alternatives?
3. *Performance*: What does the product do and how well it does do what it is designed to do in comparison to alternative purchases?	10. *Warranties*: What post-purchase assurances accompany the product?
4. *Components*: What is the product made of? What ingredients does it contain?	11. *Safety*: What safety features are available on a particular product compared to alternatives?
5. *Availability*: Where can the product be purchased? When will the product be available for purchase?	12. *Independent research*: Are results of research gathered by an independent research firm presented?
6. *Special offers*: What limited-time non-price deals are available with a particular purchase?	13. *Company research*: Are data gathered by a company to compare its product with a competitor's presented?
7. *Taste*: Is evidence presented that taste is perceived as superior by a sample of potential customers?	14. *New ideas*: Is a totally new concept introduced during the commercial? Are its advantages presented?

Source: Adapted from Resnik and Stern (1977).

offers (13 per cent). It is interesting to note that ads from developed and developing countries had relatively similar number of cues: on average, 2.08 and 1.92, respectively.

Given that advertising information is an information source dominated by the producer, it does not have the same value as other sources of information in the eyes of the consumer. It is indeed a sales appeal, which generates information designed to emphasize the positive aspects of the product. However, as far as the consumer is concerned, the utility of this type of information is twofold:

- on the one hand, the consumer can get to know the distinctive qualities claimed by the producer and to see whether what the product "promises" corresponds to what the consumer is seeking;
- on the other hand, it helps him save personal time, since the information reaches him or her without the consumer having to collect it.

Lepage (1982, p. 53) underlines the fact that the important point for the consumers is that the efficiency of the advertising message intended to reach them should be higher than it would have cost them to collect the same information by other means, for example, by displacing themselves. These two services performed by advertising have the effect of helping the consumer to perceive opportunities of choice and of new potential forms of satisfaction at a minimum cost (Kirzner, 1973).

19.2   ALTERNATIVE ADVERTISING OBJECTIVES

To determine the objectives of advertising communication, it is useful to refer back to the three levels of market response analysed in Chapter 11 (see Table 11.1).

- *Cognitive response*, which relates to awareness and to knowledge of the product characteristics. At this level, the advertiser can set objectives of information, recall, recognition or familiarity.

- *Affective response*, which relates to the overall evaluation of the brand in terms of feelings, favourable or unfavourable judgements and preferences. The objectives will be to influence attitude and to create purchase intention.
- *Behavioural response*, which refers to buying behaviour and to post-purchase behaviour, but also to all other forms of behavioural response observed as the result of a communication, such as visiting a showroom, requesting a catalogue, sending a reply coupon.

It is common practice to consider these three levels as a sequence, as potential buyers pass successively through the three stages: cognitive, affective and behavioural (Lavidge and Steiner, 1961). This sequence of reactions is known as the *learning model*. As noted in Chapter 11, this model needs to be adjusted in terms of the buyer's degree of involvement (see Figure 11.3, page 282). Although not generally applicable, the learning response model, nevertheless, remains a useful tool for defining the priority objectives of communication.

Keeping this hierarchy of objectives in mind, Rossiter and Percy (1997) have identified *five different communication effects* that can be caused, in whole or in part, by advertising. These effects reconstitute the process followed by the buyer when confronted with a purchasing decision; there can therefore be as many possible objectives for communication.

Development of primary demand

Existence of need is a prerequisite that determines the effectiveness of any act of communication. Every product satisfies a product category need. Perception of this need by potential buyers can be stimulated by advertising. Advertising thus helps develop total demand in the market. Three distinct situations can exist:

- The category need is *present and well perceived* by potential customers. In this case, generic advertising is not justified. This is the case for many low-involvement, frequently purchased products, where purchasing is done on a routine basis.
- The category need is *perceived but neglected or forgotten* and the role of generic advertising is to remind the prospective customer of a previously established need. This is the case for infrequently purchased or infrequently used products like pain remedies.
- The perception of the *category need is weak or not established* in the target group of potential users. In this case, generic advertising can sell the benefits of the product category. The typical example is the campaign in favour of the use of condoms to fight against the spread of AIDS. Selling category need is a communication objective for all new products, and in particular for new-to-the-world products.

In generic advertising campaigns, the advertising content places the emphasis on the core service of the product and/or on the product benefits (see Exhibit 19.1). This type of communication message will benefit not only the advertiser but also the competing firms.

Creating brand awareness

This is the first level of cognitive response. In Chapter 6, we defined brand awareness as the buyer's ability to identify a brand in sufficient detail to propose, choose or use a brand. Three kinds of advertising objective, based on awareness, can be identified:

- To create or maintain *brand recognition* so those buyers identify the brand at the point of sale and are induced to check the existence of a category need.

■ To create or maintain *brand recall* to induce buyers to select the brand once the category need has been experienced.

■ To emphasize *both brand recognition and brand recall*.

These communication objectives imply different advertising contents. For brand recognition, the advertising content will emphasize the visual elements (logo, colours and packaging), while for brand recall the advertising will seek to repeat the brand name in audio and visual media and in headlines and to associate the brand name with the core service.

Creating a favourable brand attitude

The objective is to create, improve, maintain and modify buyers' attitudes towards the brand. It is therefore affective response which intervenes here (see Exhibit 19.2). The following communication strategies are open to the advertiser:

■ To convince the target audience to give *more importance* to a particular product attribute on which the brand is well placed in comparison to rival brands.

■ To convince the target audience of the firm's *technological superiority* in the product category.

■ To *reinforce beliefs* and the conviction of the target audience on the presence of a determining attribute in the brand.

■ To *reposition the brand* by associating its use with another set of needs or purchase motivations.

Exhibit 19.1   Is advertising of prescription drugs different?

In the United States, since the Food and Drug Administration (FDA) relaxed its guidelines on television advertising in August 1997, spending on direct-to-consumer advertising has taken off. Spending in America on ads for prescription drugs, estimated at more than $1 billion in 1998, now exceeds that on beer advertising. A study published in 1998 by *Prevention* magazine and supported by the FDA found that 90 per cent of the 1,200 people questioned had seen a drug advertisement and a third had visited their doctors as a result. Remarkably, 80 per cent of doctors agreed to prescribe the drug.

In Europe, a 1992 ruling from the European Commission prohibits prescription-drug companies from selling their wares directly to Europe's consumers. This means they cannot advertise their products in the popular press or on television. They can pitch them to doctors and pharmacists only in medical journals and other professional publication. At the same time the European Commission and many European governments talk loftily of the need for "patient empowerment", greater public awareness and understanding about diseases and their therapies. Many advocates for patients' rights raise the following question: can patients simultaneously be asked to take more responsibility for their health and denied access to some of the information that may help them to do so?

It remains that it is right to treat advertising of prescription drugs differently from advertising of baked beans. Drugs have side effects and patients may ignore them more readily than their doctor would. Drug firms are also tempted to make misleading claims. In addition, in Europe, patients pay far less on the drugs bill than those in the United States. So advertising may encourage patients to put pressure on their doctors to dispense something that appears almost free to them, but raises the bill to the taxpayer.

However, consumer advertising is also a powerful way to stimulate public interest in health. It need not become a tough sell. Indeed in Europe, people still think of themselves as patients rather than health-care consumers. As a first step, it would be reasonable to insist that advertising gives information about diseases and alternative treatments rather than merely pushing a single product. If patients are to take more responsibility for their health, they do deserve reliable information on available treatments.

Source: Adapted from The Economist (1998, pp. 57–8).

- To *eliminate a negative attitude* by associating the brand with a set of positive values.
- To call attention to *neglected attributes* by consumers in their decision-making process.
- To alter the beliefs of the target audience about *competing brands*.

The last strategy can only be adopted in countries where comparative advertising is authorized, as in the United Kingdom. The European Commission has published a directive for comparative advertising in the EU.

It is important to identify clearly the implicit assumptions of a communication strategy based on brand attitude. They can be summarized as follows:

- The advertiser must emphasize the features or characteristics in which it has the strongest competitive advantage.
- It is useless to try to modify buyers' perceptions when the brand does not really have the claimed characteristic.
- The major criticism directed against advertising is the adoption of arguments or themes, which are totally unrelated to product attributes important to the buyer.

In other words, a *market-driven communication strategy* is based on the idea that advertising is mainly designed to help the buyer buy and not simply to praise the advertiser. This vision of a communication strategy falls well in line with the market orientation concept.

Stimulate brand purchase intention

Purchase intention is halfway between the affective and the behavioural response. Two kinds of situation may arise:

- The buyer is weakly or not at all involved in the purchasing decision and there is *no conscious, prior intention to buy* until the last minute at the point of purchase. This is the case for low-perceived-risk products and also for routinely purchased products. In this type of situation, to stimulate brand purchase intention is not an advertising objective.
- The buyer has a *conscious purchase intention* during advertising exposure. In the latter case, promotional advertising can play a role by using incentives (price reductions, special offers and so on) that precipitate the buying decision or encourage repurchase.

Recall that the intention to buy is only expressed when there is also a *state of shortage, that is, when the category need is felt*. Thus, the two states, need and intention, are closely associated. Yet intention to buy is not a frequently recurring event in the case of any particular consumer.

> Markets that are huge in their annual volume are made up of buying decisions made by very small numbers of people in a given period of time. For example, in a typical week in 1982, American retailers sold over $365 million worth of shoes. But during that week (as shown in our study that year) only six persons in 100 bought shoes for themselves or their children. Similarly, only 28 adults in 1,000 bought any kinds of women's slacks, jeans, or shorts in the course of a week, and only 21 bought a dress. Fourteen in 1,000 bought a small appliance; 18 in 1,000 bought furniture; 3 in 1,000 bought an article of luggage. (Bogart, 1986, p. 267)

Hence, many markets with very high turnovers, such as those mentioned in the examples above depend each week on the buying decisions of a small number of people. It is not surprising to find that advertising messages give rise to relatively few immediate purchase intentions, since in most cases the prerequisite, namely, the existence of a state of need, is not there.

Exhibit 19.2   Kodak focuses on teen-girl consumers

Eastman Kodak Co. has seen the future: it is female and barely adolescent. In an attempt to boost sales in what it regards as a lucrative demographic group, the US company is launching its first youth marketing campaign, one that targets so-called tween girls – generally defined as those 9 to 15 years old. Kodak's internal marketing presentations proclaim that this is an era of "girl power" in which females 13 to 15 are "hyper consumers" and the "key drivers" of today's trends and pop culture. Kodak says it will spend $75 million over 5 years to reach tweens through television, radio, print and Internet banner ads created by the ad agency Saatchi and Saatchi PLC./.../

A company study shows that tween girls are more likely than boys to own a camera, 75 to 49 per cent. An independent study used by Kodak shows that teen girls consider taking pictures as popular as dating. And pictures, they say, are more important possessions than their own pets. /.../ In its print ads, Kodak beckons to tween girls by saying that its disposable cameras "get guys to smile at you with the touch of a button" and that the camera "attracts a crowd like flies to the school cafeteria".

Source: The Wall Street Journal Europe (1999).

Purchase facilitation

This last objective of advertising communication deals with the *other marketing factors* (the four Ps), without which there can be no purchase: a product that keeps its promise, retail availability of the product, acceptable price and competence and availability of the sales force. When these conditions are not all met, advertising can sometimes help to reduce or minimize problems by, for example, defending the market price, or by working as a substitute to distribution through direct marketing.

Advertising objectives are numerous and very diversified and it is important to define them clearly before the organization of an advertising campaign. As already indicated above, it is up to strategic marketing people, generally brand managers, to propose the advertising communication objective.

19.3   THE DEVELOPMENT OF AN ADVERTISING CAMPAIGN

Advertising has been for decades the most important element of the communication mix. It is also the most visible one and companies spent a very large amount of money to support it. Advertising is still very important despite the proliferation of new communication tools. It is essential that the advertising development is managed in a very professional way. This requires the development of a good advertising strategy followed by a copy brief. It is also key to have the right testing tools to ensure advertising effectiveness.

The biggest advertisers in the world are first, P&G that spent more than $9 billion in 2009, followed by Unilever with $5.7 billion and L'Oréal with $4 billion. Table 19.2 shows that the big spenders are the very known FMCG companies that have to advertise their numerous brands as well as car owners such as General Motors, Toyota and Ford.

Steps in the development of an advertising campaign

In order to prepare a good advertising campaign, it is essential to follow different steps including the development of a clear copy strategy, also called the advertising strategy, and the development of a copy brief that will be given to the advertising agency. The copy strategy is based on the positioning of the brand and the copy brief is the document that is developed by the company to lead the development of the advertising with the advertising agency. It is the responsibility of the marketing manager to develop these elements.

Table 19.2 Worldwide media spending

Worldwide measured media spending	2009
P&G Co.	$9.73 billion
Unilever	$5.72 billion
L'Oreal	$4.04 billion
General Motors Co.	$3.67 billion
Toyota Motor Corp.	$3.20 billion
Coca-Cola Co	$2.67 billion
Johnson & Johnson	$2.60 billion
Ford Motor Co.	$2.45 billion
Reckitt Benckiser	$2.37 billion
Nestlé	$2.31 billion

Source: Adapted from Wentz and Johnson (2009).

Step 1 – Identification of the objectives

Specific objectives have to be identified for the advertising campaign. They are linked to the marketing objectives that have been selected for the brand. As explained above, the objectives can be to create awareness and a favourable brand attitude or to stimulate brand purchase intention. It will be important to use testing techniques to evaluate to what extent the advertising campaign objectives have been met.

Step 2 – Development of the copy/advertising strategy

The second step is that the copy/advertising strategy should be developed by the marketer. Sometimes, it is developed by the advertising agency when the marketing department of the company has not the appropriate resource people inside. The copy strategy is based on the positioning of the brand. It is the translation in communication words of the positioning of the brand. It is established for the long term. It should describe the content of the ad but not give indication on the message form.

Companies such as P&G develop the copy strategy following three phases:

- Consumer benefit (first paragraph). It explains the differentiation benefits of the brand versus competitors.
- Support or reason why (second paragraph). It gives the reason why the consumer has to believe that the benefit is offered.
- Style/brand character (third paragraph). It defines the brand as if it were a person.

Many brands don't necessarily have an objective support or reason, particularly in a market where the demonstration effect is less important. For example, products such as perfume or luxury brands don't need a support or "reason why". In order to be successful, a copy/advertising strategy should be specific and concrete. It should be based on consumer advantages, not in technical terms. It should be developed for the long term and not linked to a fashion.

Step 3 – Development of the copy brief

A copy brief should be developed by the marketing manager. This is a document that will be given to the creative person in the advertising agency who is in charge of developing the ad. It should give information concerning the target group, the advertising strategy but also on the context, the product, the competitive environment so that the creative person can understand the situation of the brand accurately. The copy brief should first:

- describe the project. It is important to explain the objectives to be met and the type of execution that is expected.

- include the copy strategy to remind the creative about the advertising strategy of the brand.
- give the competitive background. It is important to explain who the competitors are at that moment and what are their areas of strengths.
- identify the consumer insights. They are essential to understand how the consumers react in the product category. The identification of good consumer insights by the marketing team leads to the development of meaningful and effective advertising.
- define the objectives to be met and tested. It is necessary to have specific objectives and monitor the results by appropriate testing techniques.

Step 4 – The development of the creative idea

The creative person will need to translate the copy strategy into an interesting creative idea. This idea should be original, eye catching and memorable. The consumer insight that is provided in one of the sections of the copy brief can significantly help the creative to find a creative idea. These consumer insights are often revealed by qualitative research. It identifies what are the barriers to buy a certain brand or it gives a clear understanding on the way the consumers react before buying a brand.

Step 5 – Presentation and agreement on the board

The advertising agency will come back with various boards. It will be important to evaluate whether the boards are a good translation of the copy strategy and if the proposed creative idea has impact to convince consumers to buy the brand. It can take several months to get agreement on a board. The agency will have to come back several times to integrate the comments of the marketing team.

Step 6 – Production of the advertising

After the agreement of the marketing team on a board, the advertising agency can then prepare the shooting of the ad.

Exhibit 19.3   The Lovemark

The concept of Lovemark was created in 2005 by the Ken Roberts, CEO of the advertising agency Saatchi and Saatchi. The idea of this new concept is that in many markets, it has become more difficult to have significant differences between brands. If you offer a tangible benefit, you have the risk to be copied by other competitors.

Kevin Roberts recommends, in that context, to move from a transactional logic of a brand that is sold to a consumer to a relationship logic of a brand in which the brand has created a relationship with the consumers. In this case, if you have created a strong relationship with a brand, you can consider that you have created a Lovemark.

Nike, Apple, Virgin or Pampers are Lovemarks. If they disappear, no other brands can replace them satisfactorily.

As indicated in the Publicitor, the advantages of being a Lovemark are the following: (a) the level of implication is very high, the brand belongs to its consumers; 2) a lovemark has prestige beyond its market; (3) it increases the perceived value of the brand; (4) it survives crisis better; (5) it increases consumer loyalty (Le Publicitor).

For example, Proximus, the leading mobile operator in Belgium, wanted to develop a new service – Freestyle – targeted to young people that offers the possibility to spend a limited amount of money per month. The consumer insight that was discovered was that young people spend on mobile without limit and that they like to talk for hours with their friends. The creative idea was then, Take the time to say it. The advertising showed a young guy that had many problems but that didn't stop talking in a very "décallé" tone of voice.

19.4   PLATFORMS OF ADVERTISING COMMUNICATION

Since the advent of the early form of advertising, advertising communication objectives have diversified considerably, and different forms of advertising can be developed while using the same media. Two major classes of advertising can be identified: advertising with rational appeal and advertising with emotional appeal. Other ads can also exist using both rational and emotional appeal.

Advertising with rational appeal

These are advertising that are using rational arguments to convince consumers to buy the brand.

Ads for durable goods use more cues than ads for non-durable ads. Ads using a rational appeal are more effective when a product is new to the market. Ads for intangible products contain more information cues than ads for tangible products. The level of information varies also between different advertising media.

In ads with rational appeal, we can find ads with a demonstration, a problem solution, a testimonial, a slice of life, a comparison or an endorser:

- *Demonstration*. These are ads where a demonstration on how the product works is done. It is the example of the Gillette Fusion ad that shows how well the razor will work thanks to the three razor blades.
- *Problem/solution*. These are ads where a problem is first identified and then a solution is offered to solve the problem. This is the case of Antikal brand from P&G that shows first that there are a lot of limescale on the bath and then shows the effervescent action of the product that helps to remove the limescale with success.
- *Testimonial*. A well-known person will testify why he is using the product.
- *Slice of life*. It is a story based on a slice of life of persons.
- *Endorsers*. An expert is used to demonstrate the quality of the product. For example, a washing machine expert recommends the use of a certain washing powder. It is important that the endorser is perceived as credible in the product category. Celebrities can also be used as endorser. This is the case of George Clooney for Nespresso.

The use of celebrities in ads

Celebrities are often used in ads. It is an easy way to attract attention to the ad but it is important that the consumers do not only remember the celebrity and forget about the brand. The selected celebrity should be credible for the product category. There should be a fit between the brand and the celebrity in terms of brand image. The risk with a celebrity is also that the celebrity might have a problem, do something wrong. This would have a negative impact on the brand image.

The use of product placement

The placement of a "brand" in a film has become common practice. The idea is that consumers will be exposed to the brand in a more natural context. This might generate a positive feeling about the brand. The cost of product placement is also relatively low from 50 to 100,000 dollars. In the Bridget Jones diary film, Bridget Jones is using a Vodaphone mobile and is eating Ben & Jerry's ice cream. In the latest James Bond films, James Bond is not driving an Aston Martin but a BMW.

Advertising with emotional appeal

These are ads that try to provoke emotions rather than proposing the consumers to think. There are different forms of emotional appeal that can be developed in advertising as indicated by De Pelsmacker and Geuens (1996):

Humour can be used to provoke emotions. It is often used but the key question is to know whether this type of advertising is effective. Studies show that it attracts attention but it is not clear if it attracts attention to the brand itself. If you remember the joke and not the brand, you have not reached good effectiveness. Studies show that humour is more effective for low-involvement products than for high-involvement products. Humour seems also more effective for existing brands than for new and unfamiliar brands.

Warmth appeals are ads with positive feeling such as love, friendship, affection. Although there are mixed results about brand recall and recognition, warmth leads to a more positive affective response toward the brand.

Fear can be used to show the type of risk that the consumer would take when not buying the brand. You can have physical risk, social risk, financial risks or any other type of risk. Most studies show that threat appeals are capable of sensitizing people to threat and of changing their behaviour.

19.5   FORMS OF ADVERTISING COMMUNICATION

Since the advent of the early form of advertising, advertising communication objectives have diversified considerably, and different forms of advertising can be identified while using the same media.

Concept advertising

This is a media-advertising message with a mainly "attitudinal" communication objective: to influence the buyer's attitude towards the brand. Its role can be defined as follows,

> The creative efforts of many national advertisers are designed, not to induce immediate action, but to build favourable attitudes that will lead to eventual purchase. (Dhalla, 1978)

This definition implies that the effectiveness of this type of advertising can only be viewed from a long-term perspective. The notion of attitude holds a central position here. The objective is mainly to create an image based on communicating a concept.

Promotional advertising

This is a media-advertising message with a mainly "behavioural" communication objective: to influence the buyers' purchasing behaviour rather than their attitudes. The objective is to trigger the act of purchase. Its effectiveness is evaluated directly in terms of actual sales. This is the most aggressive type of communication, although it is not incompatible with image creation. However, its immediate purpose is to achieve short-term results.

Response advertising

This is a personalized message of an offer, having the objective of generating a "relationship" with the prospect by encouraging a response from the latter on the basis of which a commercial relation can be built.

This type of advertising tries to reconcile the characteristics of the two previous ones: building an image, but also encouraging a measurable response allowing an immediate appraisal of the effectiveness of the communication. This type of media advertising is expanding rapidly now, and is directly linked to interactive marketing;

Prerequisites of concept advertising

There are still too many firms that tend to assimilate advertising with marketing and to approach marketing by advertising. In fact, advertising is only a complement, which is sometimes, but not always, indispensable to a more fundamental process of strategic marketing. For advertising to be effective, a number of prerequisites should ideally prevail:

- Advertising is one element of the *marketing mix* and its role cannot be separated from the roles of the other marketing instruments. As a general rule, advertising will be effective only when the other marketing factors have been chosen: a differentiated and clearly positioned product sold at a competitive price through a well-adapted distribution network.
- Advertising is useful to the consumer mainly for complex products having *internal qualities* that cannot be discovered by inspection. For *experience goods* (such as food products or shampoos) and for *credence goods* (such as motor oil and medical services) consumers have lots to gain from truthful advertising.
- To be effective, advertising should promote a *distinctive characteristic* to clearly position the brand in the minds of consumers as being different from competing brands. The distinctive characteristic can be the promise of the brand, but also its personality, its look or its symbolic value.
- Advertising is particularly effective in markets or segments where *primary demand is expansible*. Its role is then to stimulate the need for the product category as a whole. In non-expansible markets, the main role of advertising is to stimulate selective demand and to create communication effects at the brand level.
- The size of the reference market must be large enough to absorb the cost of an advertising campaign, and the firm must have enough financial resources to reach the *threshold levels* of the advertising response function.

Thus, the advertising communication platform is the complement of a strategic marketing programme. The advertising positioning sought must be in line with the marketing positioning adopted and based on a sound strategic thinking, without which advertising cannot be effective.

19.6   MEDIA PLANNING

Having defined the target, message content and the expected response, the advertiser must choose the best combination of media support that will allow it to achieve the desired number of exposures to the target audience, within the limits imposed by the advertising budget. Exhibit 19.3 shows the definition of the most important concepts and terms used in the field of media planning.

Alternative media strategies

Different strategies of how to use the media can be envisaged (Chandon, 1976, p. 19–23). The choice will vary with the communication objectives, the message complexity or the competitive situation.

Reach versus frequency

The *first alternative* opposes the two objectives of "reach" and "frequency".

> Adopting an extensive campaign with a view to reaching the greatest number of people through maximum reach, or, on the contrary, adopting an intensive campaign to reach, as emphatically as possible, a restricted target through maximum frequency or repetition.

Generally, a high degree of reach is necessary when launching a new product or starting an ambitious programme of promotion. On the other hand, a high degree of frequency is required when the message is complex, the product frequently bought and the brand loyalty low. However, too much repetition is useless, as it may cause boredom or irritation. Krugman (1975, p. 98), for example, considers that three "perceived" exposures are often sufficient.

Continuity versus intermittence

The *second strategic option* is between "continuity" as opposed to "intermittence" in advertising:

> Seeking continuity of advertising efforts over time to overcome the forgetting rate, stimulate repeated purchases, oppose rivals' efforts, etc.; or, on the contrary, seeking intermittence (pulsing) so as to optimize consumer learning or reinforcement, or to "stretch budgets" to coincide with consumption patterns.

The problem is to decide how to schedule advertising. But there is no clear answer to the dilemma. It is important to take into account the nature of the product, its purchase frequency, seasonality in sales, rivals' strategies and the distribution of memory over time. The fact that the life of a message is a function of its communication quality renders the problem even more complicated.

Concentration versus diversification

Finally, the *third strategic choice* is between media "concentration" or media "diversification".

> Seeking diversification in various types of media so as to enjoy complementarity between them, obtain a better net reach, a better geographical allocation, etc., or, on the contrary, concentration on a single media, so as to dominate the medium best suited to the target, to personalize the campaign and the product and to benefit from economies of scale and discounts.

All depends on the adopted segmentation strategy. Diversification is desirable if the firm follows undifferentiated marketing; if, on the contrary, it follows a market nicher strategy, then it is probably more effective to concentrate on a single medium.

Criteria for Media Selection

Media selection is guided by quantitative and qualitative criteria that are listed below. Amongst *quantitative criteria*, the following are important:

- *Target audience* media habits, that is, the proportion of the target group that can be reached through the medium.

Exhibit 19.4   Definition of the parameters used in media planning

- *Target:* the specific group of prospects to be reached.
- *Circulation:* the number of physical units through which advertising is distributed.
- *Audience:* the number of people who are exposed to a particular vehicle.
- *Effective audience:* the number of people with the target's characteristics who are exposed to the vehicle.
- *Exposure:* the "opportunity to see" (OTS) or "opportunity to hear" (OTH) the message, which does not imply that the person actually sees or hears the advertisement.

- *Reach:* the number of different persons or households exposed to a particular medium vehicle at least once during a specified period of time.
- *Frequency:* the number of times within a specified period of time that a prospect is exposed to the message.
- *Gross rating point (GRP):* equal to reach multiplied by frequency and measures the total number of exposures (weight).
- *Impact:* the qualitative value of an exposure through a given medium.

- The *stability* of the reach over time, for instance, from one week to another or from one season to another.
- The possibility of having *frequent exposures* to the message.
- The medium *selectivity* in terms of socio-demographic or life style profiles.
- The *cost per thousand* persons reached, which is a function of the vehicle audience and of the medium cost.

These data are provided by the media themselves, by the media sales houses or by organizations responsible for the control of the media circulation or diffusion.

Qualitative criteria of media selection must complement the quantitative ones. The following can be noted in particular:

- *Audience attention* probability, which is, for instance, very high for cinemas and very low for outdoor advertising.
- The duration of the *message's life*, that is, the period during which the message can be perceived.
- The perceptual *environment* of the message.
- The *editorial quality* of the vehicle, that is, its prestige and credibility.
- The *technical quality* of the medium, for instance, the use of colour, the quality of sound or of images.
- The degree of *advertising saturation* of the vehicle and the presence of competitive advertising.

The final choice is summarized in a *media plan* describing budget allocation between the different media. Once one has chosen the media, the next decision is to select the *specific vehicles* to advertise in within the media. Although the choices are complex and numerous, a number of paid research services in media and vehicles selection provide data to help the decision-maker. The latter choice is now increasingly made using computer models of vehicle selection.

19.7   ADVERTISING BUDGET DECISIONS

Conceptually, advertising budget decisions can be analysed using marginal rules of economic theory. Expenditure on each method of communication is increased until any further increase reduces profits. Similarly, the allocation of total budget between different methods is such that each instrument is used to the level where all marginal revenues are equal. Economists have developed optimization rules based on elasticity (Dorfman and Steiner, 1954), also extended to situations of oligopoly (Lambin et al., 1975) as well as dynamic models to allow for lagged response to advertising (Palda, 1963; Jacquemin, 1973).

As for the selling price, this approach is rarely operational in practice because of all the problems of estimating response functions. It is therefore necessary to use other more general methods, and to only use marginal rules as guidelines. When available, the analysis of elasticity can be useful *a posteriori* to evaluate the effectiveness of advertising and of the sales force. In this section we will examine different methods of determining the advertising budget.

Cost-oriented advertising budgets

As for cost-oriented prices discussed in the previous chapter, cost-oriented budgets are calculated on the basis of cost considerations, without explicitly taking demand reactions into account. There are three types of cost-oriented budget: affordable, break-even and percentage of sales budgeting methods.

Affordable budget

The budget is directly linked to short-term financial possibilities of the company. Advertising will be appropriated after all other unavoidable investments and expenses have been allocated. As soon as things go badly, this budget can be eliminated, and if cash is abundant then it can be spent. The fiscal system also encourages this type of practice, since increased advertising expenditure reduces taxable profit. This is not a method as such, but rather a state of mind reflecting an absence of definite advertising objectives.

Break-even budget

The break-even budget method is based on the analysis of advertising's profitability threshold. The absolute increase in unit sales and in turnover necessary to recoup the incremental increase in advertising expenditures is simply obtained by dividing advertising expenditure (S) by the absolute gross profit margin or by the percentage of gross profit margin:

$$\text{Break-even volume} = S / P\text{–}C$$

and

$$\text{Break-even turnover} = S / (P\text{–}C/P)$$

For instance, if the gross profit margin is £60, or 30 per cent of the unit price, the absolute increase in unit sales to recoup a £1.5 million advertising budget will be

$$1,500,000/60 = 25,000 \text{ units}$$

and the break-even turnover

$$1,500,000/0.30 = £5,000,000$$

To determine the percentage increase of sales volume or turnover necessary to maintain the previous level of profit, one can use the following expression:

$$\text{Percentage sales increase} = \Delta Q/Q = 100 \times \Delta S/ (F+S+\text{Profit})$$

where ΔS is the proposed change in budget. The advertiser can determine by how much sales must increase to retain the same level of profit, and also calculate the implicit demand elasticity to advertising, by comparing expected sales levels "with advertising" to expected volume "without advertising".

Using this data, the advertiser can verify whether the proposed budget implies an unrealistic increase in market share given the state of the market, competitors' power and so on. The weakness of the method is that it is strictly an accounting exercise. But clearly some advertising objectives are not necessarily reflected in higher sales in the short run, even if they have been reached completely. Nevertheless, this type of analysis is useful because the advertiser is encouraged to view advertising as an investment rather than overhead costs.

Percentage of sales budget

The percentage of sales budget method is used frequently and treats advertising as a cost. In its simplest form the method is based on a fixed percentage of the previous year's sales. One advantage of this procedure is that expenditures are directly related to funds available. Another advantage is its relative simplicity.

Although this method is quite popular, it can easily be criticized from a logical point of view, because it inverts the direction of causality between advertising and sales. Relating advertising appropriation to *anticipate sales* makes more sense, because it recognizes that advertising precedes rather than follows sales. Nevertheless, this approach can lead to absurd situations: reducing the advertising budget when a downturn in sales is predicted, and increasing it when turnover is growing, with the risk of overshooting the saturation threshold.

In practice, however, it seems that this method is mainly used by managements with the objective of controlling total advertising expenditure at the consolidated level of turnover, in order to keep an eye on total marketing expenditures or to compare with competitors. More refined methods are used when deciding on advertising at the brand level.

Cost-oriented advertising budgets are only the first stage of the process of determining the advertising budget. They enable the firm to define the problem in terms of financial resources, production capacity and profitability. As for the determination of prices, these methods must be completed with an analysis of market attitudinal and behavioural responses.

Communication-oriented advertising budgets

This approach, also called the "task and objective" method, is the one most widely used. It emphasizes communication objectives and the means necessary to reach them. Two methods can be adopted: one based on "contact", defined in terms of reach and frequency, and one based on "perception".

Task and objective budgeting

The method starts either with an objective of reach and frequency for which a budget is calculated or with a budget constraint for which the best combination of reach and frequency is sought to maximize total exposure. By trying to maximize exposure, this approach places the emphasis on the first level of advertising effectiveness, that is, communication effectiveness, while clearly linking the communication objectives to costs.

As defined in Exhibit 19.3, the term "exposure" here has a very precise meaning, because it only refers to OTS or to OTH, which does not imply perception. Newspapers only sell OTS to advertisers: a certain number of readers (maybe) will have the paper in their hands, but this does not imply that they will see the advertisement, or that they will familiarize themselves with it or assimilate it. The method ensures the productivity of the budget by searching for the best way to spend the money in the media given the target audience and given an expected creative level of the campaign. This is why the task and objective method is widely used by advertising agency people. By way of illustration, let us consider the following example.

A company wants to reach women in the 25–49 age group. The socio-professional profile is determined by the following criteria: business, middle management, or owners of small-medium sized companies. The size of the target population is 3,332,000 women, or 16.7 per cent of women 15 years old and more. The vehicles are magazines selected for their affinity with the target. The budget is 650,000 francs.

The advertising agency has proposed the three media plans presented in Table 19.3. In the table are reported for each plan the number of ads per magazine, the reach, the frequency, the *GRP* and the budget. Logically plan 2 will be preferred because it has the highest GRP.

The value of this budgeting method is its attempt to search for the best possible allocation of the budget given the profile of the target group and the structure of the audience of each media or vehicle. Another advantage is its simplicity. The major drawback is its systematic overestimation of the number of people reached by the ad. The gap between the number of people "exposed" and the number of people having "perceived" the message may be very high.

Perceptual impact budgeting

Perceptual impact budget is based on psycho-sociological communication objectives. To achieve these objectives, conditions are defined in terms of the means used (media, reach, repetitions, perceptions and so on). Next, the cost of the various activities is calculated and

Table 19.3 Comparing three media plans

Media plans	Plan 1	Plan 2	Plan 3
Magazine 1	3(1+2)	4(1+3)	–
Magazine 2	2(2)	–	3(1+2)
Magazine 3	3(1+2)	4(1+3)	4(1+3)
Magazine 4	3(1+2)	4(1+3)	4(1+3)
Magazine 5	3(1+2)	4(1+3)	–
Magazine 6	3(1+2)	4(1+3)	4(1+3)
Budget (in FF)	660,500	652,120	650,130
Reach	67.07%	66.3%	65.4%
Frequency	3.7	4.1	3.7
Gross rating point	248.2	271.8	242.0

3(1+2)= 1 double page quadrichrome + 2 pages quadrichrome.
Source: Troadec (1984, p. 47).

the total determines the necessary budget. What is sought here is an impact on one of the three components of attitude (cognitive, affective or behavioural).

This is a much more fundamental approach, based on the learning process (Lavidge and Steiner, 1961) and the resulting hypothesis about the hierarchy of advertising effects (Colley, 1964). The difficulty with it is that the advertiser must be able to link the communication impact to the perceptual impact and the perceptual impact to the attitudinal impact and finally to the behavioural response. Typically, the budgeting problem is stated in the following terms:

> How many OTS or exposures to the message in a given medium are necessary to achieve, among 60 per cent of the potential buyers within the target group, the cognitive objective of "knowing product characteristics", the attitudinal objective "being convinced of product superiority" and the behavioural objective "intention to buy"?

In the task and objective budget example given above, all the women belonging to the target group were simply assumed to be exposed to the vehicle. This number should be corrected for two factors: first, the probability of reading which is in general specific to each magazine and, second, an estimate of the ad's perception probability. This perception probability will be determined by the creativity of the message, its relevance for the target group, its capacity to get attention and so on.

This method is much more demanding, but it has the advantage of requiring management and advertising people to spell out their assumptions about the relationships between money spent, exposure, perceptions, trial and repeat purchase.

Communication-oriented advertising budgets constitute the second stage of the process of determining the advertising budget. They are in fact an initial way of explicitly taking into account the market response. Because it is mainly based on intermediary objectives of communication, the advantage of the method is the emphasis it places on results directly attributable to advertising, and the fact that it allows the advertiser to control the advertising agency's effectiveness.

The limitations of these methods are that there is not necessarily any link between achieving the intermediate communicational objective and the final goal of improving sales. One cannot therefore view measures of communicational effectiveness as substitutes for direct measures linking advertising to sales or market share.

Sales-oriented advertising budgets

Determining a sales or market share-oriented advertising budget requires knowledge of the parameters of the response function. In some market situations, in particular where advertising is the most active marketing variable, it is possible to establish this relationship and then use it to analyse the effects of various levels of expenditure on market share and profits.

Various models of determination of advertising budget exist in the literature. The most operational among them are the model by Vidale and Wolfe (1957) and the model ADBUDG by Little (1970). Both models have some strong and some weak points that we shall consider briefly. The contribution of economic analysis will also be reviewed.

Budgeting to Maximize Profit

The advertising optimization rules are presented on page 516. These rules can be used to verify whether the current level of advertising spending is about right or whether the firm is over-advertising. As for the price optimization problem, these rules can be used as a guide for the budgeting decision.

The normative value of this type of economic analysis is reduced, not only because of the always present uncertainty about the true value of the response coefficients, but also because the advertiser faces multiple objectives other than profit maximization. Also, the advertising quality (copy and media) is taken at its average value, while large differences may exist from one campaign to another. For these reasons, the output of economic analysis should be used as a guideline for advertising budget decisions and be complemented by other approaches.

The Vidale and Wolfe Advertising Model

The *model developed by Vidale and Wolfe* expresses the following relationship between sales (in units or value) and advertising expenditure:

$$\frac{ds}{dt} = [(\beta) \cdot (A) \cdot \frac{S - s}{S}] - (1 - \lambda) \cdot (s)$$

where
ds/dt = rate of increase of sales at any time i
β = sales response constant when $q=0$
A = rate of advertising
s = company or brand sales
S = product category saturation level
λ = sales retention rate

In words, within a given period, the increase in sales (ds/dt) due to advertising is equal to

- The product of the sales response constant per dollar of advertising when sales are zero and of the rate of advertising during the period (response effect)...
- adjusted by the proportion of the untapped market potential (saturation effect)...
- reduced by the fraction of current sales that will decrease in the absence of advertising because of product obsolescence, competing advertising and so on. (depreciation effect).

This is an interesting model because it takes into account the main features of advertising response functions while explicitly setting out the key parameters to be estimated. By way of illustration, let us consider the following example.

> Sales of brand X are $ 40,000 and the saturation level is $100,000; the response constant is $4 and the brand is losing 10 per cent of its sales per period when advertising is stopped. By adopting a $10,000 advertising budget, the brand could expect a $20,000 sales increase.

$$ds/dt = 4 \, (10,000) \, (100,000 - 40,000/100,000) - 0.10(40,000) = 20,000$$

One can also state the problem in terms of the advertising budget required to achieve a given sales objective. Referring to Table 19.4, the equation has to be solved for A, the advertising budget.

The Vidale and Wolfe model does, however, have some weak points:

- The model does not allow explicit consideration of marketing variables other than advertising, such as price, distribution.

Table 19.4 Comparing two advertising budget models

---

* The Vidale and Wolfe model

$ds/dt = (ß) \cdot (A) \cdot (S–s/S)–(1–\lambda) \cdot (s)$

where
ds/dt = sales increase per period
$ß$ = sales response constant when $s = 0$
A = advertising expenditures
s = company or brand sales
S = saturation level of sales
λ = sales retention rate

*The ADBUDG model of Little

$$MS(t) = MS(min) + [MS(max) - MS(min)] \cdot \frac{Adv^\gamma}{\delta + Adv^\gamma}$$

where
$MS(t)$ = initial market share
$MS(min)$ = minimum market share with zero advertising
$MS(max)$ = maximum market share with saturation advertising
Adv = effective advertising (adjusted for media and copy effectiveness)
γ = advertising sensitivity coefficient
δ = constant

Source: Adapted from Vidale and Wolfe (1957) and Little (1970).

- The model does not integrate competitive advertising and is therefore implementable only in monopolistic situations.
- The model assumes that advertising merely obtains new customers and increased customer usage is neglected.
- The model does not explicitly consider possible variations in advertising quality, unless one could assume different sales constants per medium or per advertising theme.
- In some markets, it is difficult to estimate the absolute market potential.

Vidale and Wolfe's model has an interesting conceptual structure, but its range of application is limited.

The ADBUDG model of Little

The ADBUDG model, developed by Little (1970), can be applied to a market where primary demand is non-expansible and where advertising is a determinant factor in sales and market share development. The model establishes a relationship between market share and advertising and assumes that managers are able to provide answers to the following five questions:

- What is the current level of advertising expenditure for the brand?
- What would market share be if advertising were cut to zero?
- What would maximum market share be if advertising were increased a great deal, say to saturation (saturation advertising)?
- What would market share be if the current level of advertising were halved?
- What would market share be if the current level of advertising were increased half as much?

The market share level estimates in response to these five questions can be represented as five points on a market share response to advertising curve.

The ADBUDG model has the following mathematical expression:

$$MS(t) = MS(min) + \{MS(max) - MS(min)\} \cdot \frac{Adv^\epsilon}{\delta + Adv^\epsilon}$$

where

$MS(t)$ = initial market share

$MS(min)$ = minimum market share with zero advertising

$MS(max)$ = maximum market share with saturation advertising

Adv = effective advertising (adjusted for media and copy effectiveness)

γ = advertising sensitivity coefficient

δ = constant

the expected market share in any given period is then equal to:

- The *minimum market share* (min) expected at the end of the period if advertising is cut to zero (depreciation effect) ...
- plus a *fraction of the maximum market share change* due to advertising; this maximum change is equal to the difference between the maximum share expected with saturation advertising and the minimum share expected with zero advertising.
- The intensity of the response is determined by an *advertising intensity coefficient* characterized by two parameters: γ, which influences the shape of the response function and γ, which is a moderator factor. Both parameters are determined by input data.

Effective advertising is given by the following expression:

$$Adv(t) = \{medium\ efficiency(t)\}.\{copy\ effectiveness(t)\}.\{Adv.\ dollars\}$$

Both indices will be assumed to have a reference value of 1.0. These indices can be determined on the basis of copy testing and media exposure data.

This is an interesting model in many respects, and it has most of the features of advertising response functions. Furthermore, it can be easily estimated on microcomputers in interactive mode. Thus, users can test the model themselves without any help from outside experts. These are the model's strong points:

- The model parameters can be estimated either on the basis of management judgements using the five questions procedure outlined above or through econometric analysis of historical or experimental data.
- The dependent variable can be sales, market share or measures of cognitive response, like awareness.
- The advertising input data can be adjusted for advertising quality using indices of media efficiency and of copy effectiveness.

It is also possible to add marketing variables other than advertising, which makes the models more difficult to manipulate. The model used is then the BRANDAID model (Little, 1979).

The ADBUDG model was initially made essentially for interactive use relying on the *decision-maker's subjective judgements*. However, experience has shown that this approach is elusive because most decision-makers hold only a small fraction of the necessary information.

On the other hand, it forms a useful framework for integrating objective information coming from various sources and for simulating the implications of different advertising strategies on market share and profits (for a similar approach, see Lambin, 1972).

Table 19.5   European advertising spending by media

Advertising spending share in select Countries In Western Europe, by Media, 2009 (% of total)					
	France	**Germany**	**Italy**	**Spain**	**UK**
TV	31.2%	20.8%	53.7%	42.6%	25.5%
Magazines	19.9%	20.5%	13.2%	8.7%	10.7%
Internet	15.1%	14.8%	4.5%	10.5%	24.1%
Newspapers	14.8%	35.3%	17.4%	20.5%	28.7%
Outdoor	11.0%	4.5%	3.6%	7.9%	6.4%
Radio	7.2%	3.7%	7.0%	9.7%	3.5%
Cinema	0.8%	0.6%	0.6%	0.3%	1.2%

Note: numbers may not add up to 100% due to rounding.
Source: JPMorgan, "Advertising & Marketing Services - Advertising 101: A Primer with a Focus on Macro" as cited by Adweek, April 2,2009.

103259   www: **eMarketer**.com, 2009

19.8   EVOLUTION OF INTERNET SPENDING

The market share of online versus traditional media in Europe is a good indication of the increased importance of the Internet in total media spending. Table 19.5 shows that in 2009, the United Kingdom was the most advanced with 24.1 per cent of total spending on the Internet, followed by France with 15.1 per cent and Germany with 14.8 per cent. Countries in Southern Europe are less advanced, with 10.5 per cent in Spain and a low 4.5 per cent in Italy of total advertising spending on the Internet. It is interesting to note that in the United Kingdom, newspapers remain the most important medium, with spending at 28.7 per cent, but this is followed very closely by TV advertising at 25.5 per cent and Internet at 24.1 per cent, showing that Internet spending has reached almost the same level as the two traditional mediums of newspapers and TV.

It is clear from the data that in Europe, Internet has become the third most used medium. As indicated in the Table 19.6, the evolution over these last three years shows an increase in Internet spending of 5 per cent in 2010 versus 2009 and of 9 per cent in 2011 versus 2010. TV remains the most important advertising medium, with annual spending forecast at $33.213 millions in 2011 followed by newspapers at $30.324 millions and Internet at $17.767 millions.

19.9   BENEFITS OF INTERNET ADVERTISING

The most important benefit of Internet advertising is the availability of information. Consumers can learn about products as well as purchase them, at any hour. Companies that use the Internet can also save money because of reduced need for a sale force. Overall, Internet can help expand from a local market to both national and international marketplaces. And, in a way, it levels the playing field for big and small market players since, unlike traditional advertising media (press, radio and TV), entry into the Internet can be a lot less expensive. Other benefits of Internet advertising are:

- Advertising on the Internet is *measurable*. It is easy to monitor the number of hits and click that advertising receives.
- Online advertising creates the opportunity for *immediate interaction* with and feedback from consumers, while traditional media do not.

Table 19.6   Advertising expenditure in Western Europe by media, 2009–2011 (US $ million)

Media	2009	2010	2011
TV	32,352	32,344	33,213
Newspaper	30,803	30,140	30,324
Internet	15,618	16,333	17,767
Magazine	14,576	14,093	14,229
Radio	5,023	5,938	6,028

Source: Adapted from ZenithOptimedia (2009).

- The Web forte lies in its ability to provide *extensive product information* unlike traditional advertising media.
- It is possible to deliver messages over the Web to a very *narrowly defined target* group.
- Internet advertisements are not necessarily time-based. In the case of a website, it can be accessed *24 hours a day*.

More important are corporate websites where an entire site can be devoted to promote a company's brands. Such sites should not be necessarily sales-driven, but should focus on customer support and service, including product and supporting information to facilitate the buying process.

19.10   INTERNET: A CUSTOMER-DOMINATED MEDIUM

Differences versus television

As observed by Jakob Nielsen's Alertbox, Internet advertising is very different from television. It is mainly a *cognitive medium*, whereas TV is mainly an emotional medium. This makes TV more suited for the traditional type of advertising. Where TV is warm, the Web is cold. It is a user-driven experience, where the user is actively engaged in determining where to go next. The user is usually on the Web for a purpose and is not likely to be distracted from the goal by an advertisement, one of the main reasons the click-through rate is so low. The active user engagement makes the Web more cognitive, since the user has to think about what hypertext links to click and how to navigate. The user is not on the Web to get an experience but to get something done. The Web is not simply a customer-oriented medium; it is a *customer-dominate*d medium. The user owns the back button. There is no way of trapping users in an ad if they don't want it.

The challenge: personalized communication

The race to accumulate the most comprehensive database of individual information has become the new battleground for search engines as it will allow the industry to offer more personalized advertisements. These are the Holy Grail or the search industry, as such advertising would command high rates. Eric Schmidt, Google's chief executive, said gathering more personal data was a key way for Google to expand. "The goal is to enable Google users to be able to ask the question such as: 'What shall I do tomorrow and what job shall I take'" (Daniel and Palmer, 2007). In 2007, Facebook launched *Facebook* ads (www.facebook.com/advertising), a new system of advertising that helps businesses to spread information through the social graph and communicate with their customers based on their profile (location, age and interest) and their actions on the site. *Facebook* ads allow companies to target the exact people they want by three ways: building pages on Facebook; an ad system that facilitates the spread of brand messages virally through Facebook and an interface to gather insights into people's activity on Facebook. Brands and companies launching with Facebook Ads include, for example, Coca-Cola, Blockbuster, Sony Pictures, Herbal Essences and The New York Times Co.

19.11   ONLINE COMMUNICATION OBJECTIVES

The objectives that can be achieved via online communication tools are similar to the ones achieved via traditional tools. We see, however, in companies that few brand managers have yet a clear idea of which Internet tools should be used for which marketing objectives (De Pelsmacker, Geuens and Van den Bergh, 2010):

- Generating brand awareness. This can be best achieved via online advertising, viral marketing or online games.
- Creating or influencing brand image and attitude. Brand sites or online advertising are also good ways to influence the brand image.
- Generating trial. E-sampling, e-couponing, online contest are good tools to achieve this objective.
- Creating loyalty. Online loyalty promotions, brand websites, virtual communities can generate brand loyalty.

19.12   KEY ONLINE COMMUNICATION TOOLS

Online advertising

The types of Internet advertising

In the beginning of around 1997, advertising on the Internet meant *banner ads*, that is, small rectangular boxes containing text and perhaps a picture and placed on relevant websites.

A banner ad can have two different objectives: (a) branding effect to impress a company or a brand name in the consumers' mind or (b) an interaction effect that is trying to get the e-visitor to do something right now as he or she looks at the ad. The response expected is to click on the ad, or to call a free telephone number, or to go to the store, or to do some other active thing such as buying now, downloading something or signing up for something today.

At some point advertisers came to the conclusion that banner ads are not the most effective vehicle because banner ads are small and easily ignored and because the response rate to interactive ads is low. For most banner ads, the industry average seems to be between two and five clicks per 1,000 impressions of the ad. That is, if a banner ad appears on 1,000 Web pages, between two and five people will click on the ad to learn more. Those five clicks per 1,000 impressions does not have much value to most advertisers. The reason is because those five clicks will not all generate sales. Out of 100 clicks, perhaps one person *will actually come up with the desired response. So banner ads rates began to decline and* today the typical rate is 50 cents per 1,000 impressions.

Websites can charge a higher rate to get a targeted audience for the banner ad. For example, if you want to sell GPS, you can advertise on the *howstuffworks* article about GPS (www.howstuffworks.com), thereby obtaining a significant increase of "click-through" and response rate for the banner ad (Brain, 2007). Many other different advertising formats are on the Web today.

A *sidebar ad* is similar to a banner ad, but it is vertically oriented rather than horizontally. A side bar has more impact than a banner because it is two or three times larger than a banner and because the ad is with the viewer much longer. A typical sidebar ad has a click-through rate of 1 per cent (10 clicks per 1,000 impressions), or thee times that of a banner ad.

A *pop-up ad* is an ad that pops up in its own window when the e-visitor goes to a page. It obscures the Web page and it has to be moved out of the way. Pop-under ads are similar but place themselves under the content read and are less intrusive. These ads annoy many users because it takes time to eliminate them but they are much more effective than banner ads, with on average 30 clicks per 1,000 impressions

Interstitials are ads that appear temporarily when loading a new Web page. They can be static or dynamic. *Superstitials* are additional pop-up browser windows that are opened when a new Web page is opened.

Brand websites

Websites can be used first to deliver information about the brand to the audience, second to create personalized interaction with consumers and third to generate loyalty among these consumers.

It is essential to differentiate the websites versus competition as the key role of strategic marketing is to differentiate the firm's offerings from the competition's offerings. This objective of differentiation is more difficult online but also more important because of the lack of barriers to entry and the absence of protection of innovations. Strauss, El-Ansary, and Frost (2006, p. 221) propose six differentiations strategies unique to online businesses:

- *Site Environment/Atmospherics*. To create a user-friendly website that easily downloads, portrays accurate information, clearly shows the products and services offered and is easily navigated.
- *Making the intangibles tangible*. To make offerings more tangible by using 3-D images, product image enlargements, trial downloads or customer reviews.
- *Building trust*. To clearly define the company's private policy and make sure it is strictly enforced by using encrypted payment process for transaction.

- *Efficient and timely order processing.* To deliver what is promised to customers in a timely order, to meet the ease of ordering's motivation.
- *Pricing.* To offer price discounts as the main incentive, a strategy difficult to sustain, because pricing is easy to imitate.
- *Customer relationship management.* To forge long-term relationships with customers, customer tracking and personalization.
- Websites having a well-known and strong brand image have a competitive advantage and the "brand" can become synonymous with the product as the best online provider. For example, Amazon.com is recognized around the world as a leader on the Web in online book sales.

Viral marketing

Definition

Rayport (1996), from the Harvard Business School, coined the term *viral marketing* to describe the process of disseminating messages using pre-existing social networks, analogous to the spread of pathological and computer viruses. Viral marketing is then a marketing communication method that induces and encourages people to pass along voluntarily marketing messages promoting a brand or a company. Viral promotions may take the form of word of mouth or the form of video clips, images or text messages delivered through the Internet. The goal of marketers designing a viral communication campaign is to identify opinion leaders who will become "infected" by priority and who will go on in their social network to "infect" several other potential users. The total number of "infected users" will grow exponentially according to a logistic curve. Viral marketing is a legitimate communication method as long as it does not violate the basic principle that a person should know who is behind the campaign and when he or she is advertised to.

In viral marketing, the Internet user is really at the heart of the communication process as he or she participates in spreading the news. The receptor becomes the sender.

Buzz marketing is for certain specialists the same concept as viral marketing. For some others, buzz marketing refers more to the spread of news to opinion leaders only. There is not yet a consensus on these concepts.

Steps in the development of a viral campaign

It is essential to have a creative viral marketing campaign to motivate the Internet users to spread the news to their friends. The idea is to "contaminate" a clear target group. In order to develop a successful viral marketing campaign, it is important to:

- Identify clearly the target audience. Too often, the success of a viral marketing campaign is calculated based on the number of persons who have been reached. It is not the number of Internet users that have been reached that is important but the number of people in the target group that have been effectively reached.
- Be creative. It is important to generate the interest of the Internet user. He or she has to be surprised by the message to be tempted to open the ad or the message and send it to friends. Humour is often used to reach this objective.
- Respect the Internet users. Use addresses that are "opt in" in order not to create spam.

Viral campaigns can be created by companies to generate favourable word of mouth about their brands.

Bic has used a viral campaign to launch their new razor. Their objective was to reach men from 15 to 35 years old. They have sent their new razor first to a selected group of important (influent) bloggers with humoristic videos with the intention that the message would contaminate the target group. The concept was "shave the traders". The video was showing traders that were not willing to shave because of the crisis. The new Bic Comfort 3 advance was the solution.

Viral marketing can also be used by Internet users for the pleasure of informing people.

A video was showing the chemical reaction of a Mentos being plugged into a Coca-Cola Light. Within 3 weeks, 3 millions of Internet users saw the video.

Stealth marketing

Stealth marketing (also called buzz marketing) is an unethical form of viral marketing, consisting in artificially creating the impression of spontaneous word-of-mouth enthusiasm. It is a practice where people are paid to use or pitch products in public settings without disclosing the fact that they are being paid to do so. Stealth marketing can take several forms: paying celebrities or famous people money to *covertly* promote products; hiring actors to approach people in real-life situations to slip them a commercial message; embedding brands and logos in electronic games; embedding commercial messages in popular music and so on. As observed by Dunnewind (2004) from the *Seattle Times*, companies are increasingly targeting gregarious teens as underground spokespeople, paid in free products, discounts and cutting-edge cachet to market to friends, without disclosing that they are being compensated by a firm. Concerns about deception are heightened when minors are the target audience of stealth marketing, because children and teenagers tend to be more impressionable and easy to deceive.

Most marketing professionals agree that stealth marketing is absolutely wrong. The sponsoring company should be clearly identifiable, with zero tolerance for any tactics that could be considered covert, sneaky or deceptive. This view has been confirmed by the US Federal Trade Commission (2005), stating that "the failure to disclose (the sponsor) is fundamentally fraudulent and misleading and might violate federal prohibitions against unfair or deceptive acts and practices affecting commerce".

Online promotions

E-sampling	Internet offers new possibilities to reach consumers and can offer them samples at a lower cost. This is made possible because there is an opt-in feature that can be used and it is only the persons that are interested that will receive the sample.
E-coupons	They can be delivered via e-mails or via websites. The advantages of on-line coupons are that you can reach people that were not used to redeem coupons in newspapers, you lower your cost by not printing the coupons and by adapting the coupon to the profile of the users.
On-line contests, sweepstakes and games	These are the on-line versions of these traditional promotional tools.

Search engine optimization

It is important that your brand site is well positioned on the Web. Some companies are specialized in registering sites in top and niche search engines to improve their ranking on the engine.

E-mail marketing

It consists of using e-mails to reach the consumers directly. The advantages of e-mails are their low costs, their speed and their flexibility versus other traditional direct marketing techniques. Based on a study of Waring and Martinez (2002), e-mail marketing is more effective than other Web advertising techniques such as banners. Click-through rates of commercial e-mails vary between 2 per cent and 10 per cent.

Consumer-generated media

Consumer-generated media, also known as User-Generated Content (UGC), refers to various kinds of media content that are produced by end-users, as opposed to traditional media producers such as professional writers, publishers, journalists and licensed broadcasters. The term entered mainstream usage during 2005 after arising in Web publishing and new media content production circles. It reflects the expansion of media production through new technologies that are accessible and affordable to the general public. These include digital video, blogging, aggregators, and mobile phone photography. An online aggregator is an entity that collects and analyses information from different sources thereby defining a new landscape in information retrieval for goods and services on the Internet. Aggregators gather information from multiple sources with or without the permission or the knowledge of the underlying sources. By reducing the consumer's search cost and enabling transparent comparisons across different offerings, aggregators eliminate information asymmetry in the marketplace; for example, visit "howstuffworks.com" (www.howstuffworks.com) or Expedia (www.expedia.fr) for travelling. UGC is generally created outside of professional routines and practices. It often does not have an institutional or a commercial market context. UGC may be produced by non-professionals without the expectation of profit or remuneration. Motivating factors include connecting with peers, achieving a certain level of fame or prestige and the desire to express oneself.

19.13   THE EMERGENCE OF SOCIAL NETWORKS AND VIRTUAL COMMUNITIES

The development of social networks

The concept of social networks is not new. It was introduced in 1954 by the British anthropologist A. Barnes. It can be defined as a set of specific relations between a set of defined actors (Lazega and al, 2010). The newness is linked to the development of social networks on the Net with the introduction of Web 2.0. Over the years 2002 and 2003 we saw the emergence of the first social networks on the Net. The most popular ones today are MySpace, Facebook, Twitter, YouTube and LinkedIn.

We can also find many other ones such as Flickr, Digg, Friendster, Delicious, Gather, Xing, Viadeo and so on.

MySpace was launched in 2003. It initially targeted young people and artists. It was purchased by Rupert Murdoch for $580 millions in 2005. By late 2007, MySpace was the leading social network on the Net with about 100 millions users but it was overcome by Facebook mid-2009.

Facebook was created by Mark Zuckerberg in 2004. It was first launched for Harvard students. It was then expanded to all students in the United States and then rapidly to all potential users. It has become today the largest social network with more than 600 million Internet users. In Europe, there are more than 190 million users and 200 millions in the United States (Baudechon, 2011). Presence is established through a "profile". Users can communicate with other members of the site that they identify as "friends". They can also post pictures and exchange information on the "wall". They can also belong to common interest user groups as "fans". Companies can create special Facebook pages where they provide information about their brands.

Twitter was launched in 2006. It allows one to send small messages only, called "tweets" of maximum 140 characters, to other users. You can select "followers" with whom you will exchange information. Twitter covers an estimated 200 million users in 2011. Twitter is often described as the "SMS of Internet".

LinkedIn is a business-oriented social network site. It was founded in 2003 and is a professional network that had more than 100 million registered users in 2011.

Key facts on the use of social networks

Based on a study of eMarketer (2010), growth of the use of social networks in the United States and worldwide has been very rapid over the last three years with nearly two out of three Internet users (61 per cent) having a profile on a social network on a global basis. EMarketer estimates that by 2013, 67 per cent of US Internet users will be using social networking.

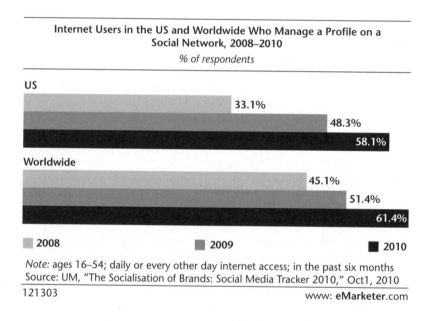

Internet Users in the US and Worldwide Who Manage a Profile on a Social Network, 2008–2010

% of respondents

US
- 2008: 33.1%
- 2009: 48.3%
- 2010: 58.1%

Worldwide
- 2008: 45.1%
- 2009: 51.4%
- 2010: 61.4%

■ 2008   ■ 2009   ■ 2010

Note: ages 16–54; daily or every other day internet access; in the past six months
Source: UM, "The Socialisation of Brands: Social Media Tracker 2010," Oct1, 2010
121303   www: **eMarketer**.com

In the United States, social networking reaches users from all generation and demographic groups. As indicated in the table below, the youngest age group is still the most represented, active and engaged with more than 88 per cent of users in 2010 between 18 and 24 years old. However, older age groups have increased their presence significantly over the past two years. For example, the 55–64 age group represents 48 per cent of presence on social media and is expected to reach up to 57 per cent by 2013.

In Europe, there is an estimated 100 millions users visiting monthly social networks, which represents 50 per cent of the Internet population in the five biggest European countries. EMarketer estimates that by 2015, 64 per cent of Internet users (142 million people) will be regular social network users, more than the double that in 2009. This increase is due to two factors: greater Internet access and increased usage among people aged 50 and older.

US Social Network User Penetration, by Age, 2009–2013

% of internet users in each group

	2009	2010	2011	2012	2013
0–11	12%	14%	15%	16%	17%
12–17	75%	78%	81%	84%	85%
18–24	83%	88%	90%	92%	93%
25–34	70%	77%	82%	84%	85%
35–44	52%	65%	72%	75%	77%
45–54	42%	53%	58%	63%	65%
55–64	35%	48%	52%	55%	57%
65+	20%	28%	31%	34%	36%
Total	**52%**	**60%**	**64%**	**66%**	**67%**

Note: internet users who use social networks via any device at least once per month
Source: eMarketer, Feb 2011

124530   www.**eMarketer**.com

Social Network Users and Penetration in the EU-5, 2009–2015

	2009	2010	2011	2012	2013	2014	2015
Social network users (millions)	68.2	86.2	100.1	112.1	123.1	133.1	141.9
–% change		30.5%	26.4%	16.2%	12.0%	9.9%	8.1%	6.6%
–% of internet users		36.9%	44.8%	50.1%	54.5%	58.2%	61.5%	64.4%
–% of population		21.6%	27.3%	31.6%	35.2%	38.6%	41.6%	44.2%

Note: CAGR (2009-2015)=13%; internet user who use social networks via any device at least once per month; includes France, Germany, Italy, Spain and the UK
Source: eMarketer, Jan 2011

124177   www.**eMarketer**.com

More time than never is spent on social networks. Internet users spend the highest proportion of their time on social networks (4.6 hours/week) surpassing time spent on e-mail (4.4 hours per week) (eMarketer, 2010).

Classification of social networks

We can classify social networks based on several criteria (Balagué and Fayon, 2010):

(1) *Personal or professional use:* Facebook is an example of a social network that is used for personal purpose while LinkedIn, Xing or Viadeo are professional social networks.
(2) *Generalist or specialist:* Facebook, Twitter, YouTube are more generalist social networks. Meetic.fr, Viadeo, Hairfflix for hair care specialists, Nurselinkup for nurses are more specialized on a certain theme or common subject. The latter are targeting niche users.
(3) *Centred on the community or on the user:* YouTube, Flickr are more centred on the community as the reason of being is the sharing of videos or photos. Facebook and Twitter are more centred on the individual.

Time Spent on Online Activities, by Type, Sep 2010		
% of internet users worldwide and hours per week		
	% doing activity dailay	**Hours per week spent on activity**
Email	72%	4.4
News	55%	2.7
Social	46%	4.6
Interest	46%	3.9
Knowledge	39%	3.1
Multimedia	37%	3.7
Gaming	27%	2.9
Browsing	24%	2.3
Admin	21%	1.7
Organize	19%	1.6
Shopping	12%	1.8

Note: n=48.804
Source: TNS, "Digital Life" Oct 10,2010

120762   www.**eMarketer**.com

Common characteristics

All social networks have their specificities but they have all the following characteristics:

- The network presents the identity of each member
- The address book constitutes the centre of the social network
- The relationship among individuals is linked to the agreement of both parties
- The profile can be public or private

A key difference however between Twitter and Facebook is that Twitter is asymmetric. You can "follow" somebody who does not follow you. Facebook is symmetric. When you become a friend of someone, he is automatically your friend (Baudechon 2011).

The use of social networks by companies

In view of the time spent by Internet users on social networks, it becomes necessary for companies to connect with potential consumers via these sites. Social networks are a reality that companies will have to integrate in their communication strategies. Some of the firms have learned about social networks in a defensive way because negative press on their brand was communicated via social networks and they had to learn how to manage this. Today, a defensive mode only is certainly not sufficient. It is necessary for companies to have a pro-active approach to social networks. For perspective, 80 per cent of US companies are using social networks for marketing purposes (Baudechon 2011).

The use of social networks represents a totally new way of communicating with consumers as companies could control in the past what was communicated on their brands. This is not the case anymore and it is also more complex to manage the brand's image. New techniques have to be learned and new strategies have to be put in place by companies to master the use of social networks. It is a great challenge and the ones that will do it properly faster will have a competitive advantage over others.

We will highlight what are the advantages of using social networks in a marketing strategy as well as the particularities of this media. We will also present the steps that have to be followed to have a good social network strategy.

Advantages of using social networks

The advantages are numerous but the way you have to use this medium is very different to classical media and is not necessarily easy. The first advantage is that the cost of using social networks is very low. It can be done at nearly no cost. This allows small companies to have the same chances than larger companies to compete on this medium. Second, it permits to target a limited audience of motivated potential users as users can select pages of firms for which they are "fans". Third, social networks have also viral power as news can be disseminated extremely fast on this media. Fourth, companies can communicate directly with users and interact with them and deliver fast and regular information on their brands. We can also highlight other advantages such as the ability to test ideas on new products, develop a virtual community of fans or identify ambassadors of the brand.

Difficulties of using social networks

The rules of communication are totally different on social media. It is first important to write in a language that is appropriate to social networks. It should not be too commercial. Second, it is necessary to update on a very regular basis the brand page and fuel it with new info. Third, firms must add value by creating pages that are useful for users, innovative and diverting. Fourth, companies should also be very transparent in the information communicated. Fifth, it is also essential not only to listen to consumers but also to provide answers to their requests.

Dr Pepper, for example, is well advanced in the use of social media. Dr Pepper has spent years to build their 8.5 millions fans. Careful tracking and testing is done to understand how to talk to their fans. They blast two messages daily to their fans and then listen to their fans' reactions. They can measure how many times a message is viewed, shared with other Facebook users and what fans' response says (Fowler 2011).

Criteria of success of social network management

The success of social network management is based on (1) the creation of a database integrating the content of the conversation of Internet users on the social networks; (2) the use of tools to analyse these conversations and (3) the ability to intervene on social networks in a subtle way.

In some companies, the function of "community manager" has been created. This person is responsible to manage the contacts with the consumers on the social networks on a constant basis. For example, the firm Eurostar in Belgium has appointed a person who is fully dedicated to the follow-up and management of what is happening on the different social networks.

Proactive and reactive use of social networks

As indicated previously, the use of social networks by firms has been done initially in a reactive way and should be done more and more in a proactive way:

Reactive way: Some companies had to react to negative information that was communicated on their brands.

Nestlé, for example, had a problem with its Kitkat chocolate bar. They had to face very negative comments from their fans on Facebook and Twitter about the fact that they were using palm oil to make their chocolate. Consumers considered that this was destroying Indonesia's forests and endangering orangutans. A video was even posted on the net showing a person eating a Kitkat and covered with the blood of orangutans. Nestlé was thinking to close their fan's page on Facebook in view of this very negative press and asked Google and YouTube to remove this video.

Proactive way: The most advanced companies in terms of digital media use social networks to communicate with their users. They are creating interaction with their users and are often delivering information concerning new products. Some are also proposing surveys to get the feedback of their consumers. This is a non-expensive way to contact users and enables also to target loyal users or "fans".

H&M, for example, has a brand page on Facebook and more than 6 million users. They ask the opinion of their users in terms of fashion or on the product range. They ask fans to participate in surveys or vote about the collection.

Some firms go even further in the use of social networks:

Lego, for example, has created their own social network, "My Lego Network", that regrouped more than 1 million members. They have developed the "Lego Ambassador" programme. The objective is to select individuals who will be integrated directly in the development of new products. Lego is selecting 40 ambassadors from 22 different countries. If one of these ambassadors identifies a good product idea, he or she can receive up to 1 per cent of the profit generated by the idea.

The power of consumers on social networks

In some occasions, the social network has an impact on the decisions taken in the marketing of the brand. It is the first time in history that consumers can have such a direct impact on the management of a brand. Some brands had to change some decisions on the brand because of negative reactions from consumers.

Gap, for example, in October 2010, informed the consumers via its page on Facebook that they would change its logo. Reactions from consumers via Facebook and Twitter were so negative and numerous that Gap decided to change strategy and return to the old logo.

This shows that consumers have much more power than in the past. This changes totally the rules of the games in the marketing area and obliges the marketers to review totally their interactions with consumers.

The professional use of Facebook

Facebook allows companies to create a page where the company can provide information on their brands. In order to develop a programme on Facebook effectively, the firm has to do the following (Balagué and Fayon, 2010).

- Creation of a page
- Development of the network
- Creation of potential groups in relation with the company page

- Participation in existing groups
- Creation of events on the firm's page or group
- Mail messages to fans
- Follow-up of competitors on Facebook
- Addition of links on the Facebook page towards other sites
- Creation of targeted advertising

It is interesting to note that the initial reason why people become fans of a page is linked to the ability to receive discounts and promotions (40 per cent) and to show the support to the company (39 per cent).

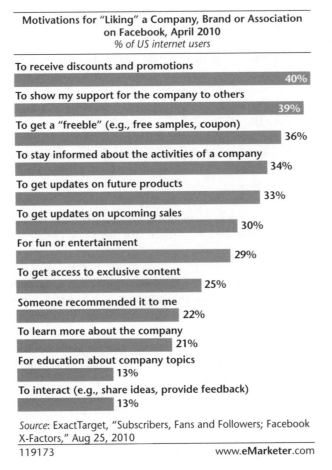

Motivations for "Liking" a Company, Brand or Association on Facebook, April 2010
% of US internet users

To receive discounts and promotions	40%
To show my support for the company to others	39%
To get a "freeble" (e.g., free samples, coupon)	36%
To stay informed about the activities of a company	34%
To get updates on future products	33%
To get updates on upcoming sales	30%
For fun or entertainment	29%
To get access to exclusive content	25%
Someone recommended it to me	22%
To learn more about the company	21%
For education about company topics	13%
To interact (e.g., share ideas, provide feedback)	13%

Source: ExactTarget, "Subscribers, Fans and Followers; Facebook X-Factors," Aug 25, 2010

119173   www.**eMarketer**.com

Concerning advertising on Facebook, there is the possibility to publish "flyers". It is then possible to target people by age, country, cities. It is also possible to organize polls quickly and at low cost. Tools such as Power Polls, My Poll, Polls or Lasonde can be used. "My questions" also allows one to ask a specific question to the community.

The professional use of Twitter

Twitter permits the creation of an account for a company. The interest of a company for Twitter is to rapidly communicate information on the company or the brand. Twitter has also a different audience from Facebook. It reaches an audience of bloggers with influence, journalists, early adopters, trend setters and so on (Baudechon 2011).

The tweets can be a source of interesting information. The Twitter Track application allows one to follow what is being said on the network.

In 2009, Twitter also introduced the function "Liste" which can regroup users by segmenting them by theme. To optimize the use of Twitter, it is important to build a broad network. The tool http://www.twiterio.fr/ permits one to find the most influential persons in the sector of activity of the company (Gossiaux, 2011).

It is also possible to make a search with search.twitter.com or supervise what is being said with "backtweets". It is also possible to post alerts on key words with "Twilert".

Evaluation of social networks effectiveness

Several measurement tools exist now to evaluate the effectiveness of a campaign on social networks:

- *Google analytics:* Free tool that give info on social networks movement
- *Omniture:* Proposes metrics on Facebook and Twitter and TweetMeme Analytics and so on.

The development of virtual communities

Social networks have led to the creation of virtual communities. A virtual community is a social network of individuals who interact through the Net in order to pursue mutual interests or goals.

From a marketing point of view, these virtual communities are very interesting as they represent a sort of segmentation on the Net that can enable the firm to reach a very specific audience.

The emergence of social networks has given the possibility to companies to create a virtual community about their brands.

In 2008, two brand lovers of Coca-Cola created a Coca-Cola page on Facebook. By April 2009, it had 3.3 millions fans, making it the second most popular profile on the social site. Today, they have up to 26 millions fans.

Companies are also using the Net to create their own virtual community of loyal users. They can communicate directly with their loyal users, give them a new product to test or reward their loyalty.

P&G has created their own social networks Tremor and Vocal Point attracting teenagers and housewives. They have attracted more than 250,000 US teenagers and several thousands of women. They consider that they "drive the business with consumer advocacy. P&G will give the possibility to the members of its social network to discover in priority the new products of the brand. It provides exclusive information on the brands and the company. It also engages the consumer to contribute to the development of the brand by a system of market research. The consumers are then "rewarded".

There are possible strategies with respect to virtual communities.

1) *You can penetrate an existing virtual community.* There are different techniques. Some are done with the agreement of the community. We talk about *permission marketing*. It can cover the sponsoring of an event of the community. Sometimes, some techniques consist in penetrating a community without agreement. We talk then about *undercover marketing.* Some representative of the brand can try to give comment in a forum, for example, to influence this community. This is not ethically acceptable and can backfire when this is identified.
2) *You can create a virtual community,* as mentioned above. From a brand point of view, it can be very attractive to create a community around a brand. It is, however, difficult to control a community. The most loyal consumers can become negative on the brand if there is a problem around the brand.

Chapter Summary

When a firm resorts to advertising, it is effectively following a pull communication strategy. Its main objective is to create a brand image and brand equity and to ensure co-operation from distributors. Advertising objectives can be defined by reference to the three levels of market response: cognitive, affective and behavioural. The share of sales promotion expenditure is growing in the total marketing communication budget as a result of the development of direct marketing. There are a large variety of promotion tools whose effects are complex and which can sometimes have a negative impact on the brand image. Public relations is a form of softer communication, which is gaining in popularity as one observes a decrease in the communication effectiveness of media advertising. Sponsorship and patronage are two special forms of institutional advertising, which are more frequently observed in industrialized economies.

BIBLIOGRAPHY

Abernathy, A.M. and Franck, G.R. (1996), The Information Content of Advertising: A Meta-analysis, *Journal of Advertising*, 25, 2, pp. 1–17.

Balagué and Fayon (2010), Facebook, Twitter et les autres, Pearson.

Baudechon Yves (2011), Training on Social Media, Media Lab.

Bogart, L. (1986), *Strategy in Advertising*, Lincolnwood Hill, NTC Business Book.

Brain, M. (2007), *How Web Advertising Works*, in (howstuffworks.com/web-advertising.htm).

Chandon, J.L. (1976), *L'état de l'art en matière de planification publicitaire*, unpublished paper, University of Nice.

Colley, R.H. (1961), *Defining Advertising Goals for Measured Advertising Results*, New York, Association of National Advertisers.

Daniel, C. and Palmer, M. (2007), Google's goal to organise your daily life, *The Financial Times*, May 23.

De Pelsmacker, P. and Geuens, M. (1996), *Marketing Communication*, London, Pearson Education.

De Pelsmacker, P., Geuens, M. and Van den Bergh, J. (2010), *Marketing Communications, A European Perspective*, Prentice Hall, 4th edition.

Dhalla, N.K. (1978), Assessing the Long Term Value of Advertising, *Harvard Business Review*, 56, 1, pp. 87–95.

Dorfman, P. and Steiner, P.O. (1954), Optimal Advertising and Optimal Quality, *American Economic Review*, 44, pp. 826–33.

Dunnewind, S. (2004), Teen Recruits Create Word-of-mouth "Buzz" to Hook Peers on Products, *The Seattle Times*, 23 November.

eMarketer (2009), Online Ad Spending in Western Europe, 1 October.

eMarketer (2010), The Socialisation of Brands: Social Media Tracker 2010, 1 October.

eMarketer (2010), US social network penetration, February 2011.

eMarketer (2010), Social Network users and Penetration in Europe, January 2011.

Fowler G.F. (2011), Are you talking to me?, *The Wall Street Journal*, 26 April.

Gossiaux, T. (2011), La gestion de la réputation d'une entreprise telle que Hamburg Mannheimer sur le net, Louvain School of management.

Jacquemin, A. (1973), Optimal Control and Advertising Policy, *Metroeconomica*, 25, May, pp. 200–7.

Kirzner, L.M. (1973), *Competition and Entrepreneurship*, Chicago, IL, Chicago University Press.

Krugman, H.E. (1975), The Impact of Television Advertising: Learning without Involvement, *Public Opinion Quarterly*, Autumn, pp. 349–56.

Lambin, J.J. (1972), A Computer On-Line Marketing Mix Model, *Journal of Marketing Research*, pp. 119–26.

Lambin, J.J., Naert, P.A. and Bultez, A. (1975), Optimal Advertising Behavior in Oligopoly, *European Economic Review*, 6, pp. 105–28.

Lavidge, R.J. and Steiner, G.A. (1961*)*, A Model of Predictive Measurement of Advertising Effectiveness, *Journal of Marketing*, 25, 6, pp. 59–62.

Lazega Emmanuel, Mounier Lise, Snijders Tom A.B., Tubaro Paola, 2010, Norms, status and the Dynamics of Advice Networks: A case study, *Social Networks*.

Lepage, H. (1982), *Vive le commerce*, Paris, Donod collection L'oeil économique.

Little, J.D.C. (1970), Models and Managers, The Concept of a Decision Calculus, *Management Science*, 16, pp. 466–85.

Little, J.D.C. (1979), Decision Support for Marketing Managers, *Journal of Marketing,* 43, pp. 9–26.

Palda, K.S. (1963), *The Measurement of Cumulative Advertising Effects*, Englewood Cliffs, NJ, Prentice Hall.

Rayport, J.F. (1996), The Virus of Marketing, *Fast Company*, December–January, pp. 68–9.

Resnik, A. and Stern, B.L. (1977), An Analysis of Information Content in Television Advertising, *Journal of Marketing,* 41, 1, pp. 50–3.

Rossiter, J.R. and Percy, L. (1997), *Advertising and Promotion Management*, New York, McGraw-Hill, 2nd edition.

Strauss, J., El-Ansary, A. and Frost, R. (2006), *E-Marketing,* New Jersey, Pearson Prentice-Hall, 4th edition.

The Economist (1998), Go on, It's Good for you, 8 August, pp. 57–8.

The Wall Street Journal Europe (1999), Kodak focuses on teen girl consumers, 19 June.

Troadec, L. and Troadec, A. (1984), *Exercices de marketing*, Paris, Les Editions d'Organisation.

Vidale, M.L. and Wolfe, H.B. (1957), An Operation Research Study of Sales Response to Advertising, *Operations Research*, June, pp. 370–81.

Waring, T. and Martinez A. (2002), Ethical Customer Relationships: A Comparative Analysis of US and French Organisations Using Permission-Based e-mail Marketing, *Journal of Database Marketing*, 10, 1, pp. 53–69.

Wentz, L. and Johnson, B. (2009), Top 100 Global Advertisers Heap Their Spending Abroad, *Advertising Age*, November 30.

ZenithOptimedia (2009), Advertising Expenditure Forecasts, December.

PART FIVE

IMPLEMENTATION OF MARKET-DRIVEN MANAGEMENT

CHAPTER TWENTY

MEASURING MARKETING PERFORMANCE

The objective of this chapter is to raise the issue of marketing accountability. A central problem in business today is that marketing lacks the kind of accountability and metrics common to the rest of the corporation. For a very long time, this imprecision has been tolerated and has been excused because marketing was supposed to be inherently "creative". Yet, as marketing consumes a larger and larger portion of the firm budget, it becomes more imperative to quantify marketing's direct contribution to the bottom line.

Learning objectives

When you have read this chapter, you should be able to know and/or to understand:

- The necessity to develop measures of marketing performance
- To understand the concept of brand equity
- To be able to select the appropriate measure of customer response
- To compute a marketing ROI
- To monitor the short and long terms effects of marketing outlays
- To understand the usefulness and limits of marketing models
- To estimate the impact of marketing on stock returns

20.1 THE CHALLENGE OF MARKETING MEASUREMENT

Marketing is traditionally one of the least measured functions of the firm, despite the fact that it represents a significant share of companies' budgets. This absence of marketing performance measurements is underscored by a study from the Chief Marketing Officer Council, representing 1,000 high-technology companies like Adobe, AT&T, Cisco, Dell, Microsoft, Sony and so on, with combined annual revenues of $450 billion.

> In a poll of 315 senior marketing executives, the CMO Council found that fewer than 20 percent of respondents have formal marketing performance measurement systems in place. In addition, 80 percent are dissatisfied with their ability to demonstrate their marketing programmes business impact and value. Nearly 90 percent of respondents believe measuring marketing performance is a key priority for their organisation. (CMO Council, 2004)

These results are especially significant given that technology companies tend to be among the heaviest spenders in marketing, with an average of more than 15 per cent of revenues being spent on marketing. This is several times the percentage spent on marketing by companies in many other major industries, including such marketing-driven industries as consumer packaged goods.

Why so many firms are unwilling or unable to measure their marketing performance? Different reasons are suggested by Palmer (2004).

- Marketing is not perceived as a strategic issue by board members having a weak MO.
- Imagination, creativity and/or sheer determination are perceived as more important success factors than objective measurements.
- Measuring marketing effectiveness is history; fighting for the next battle should take priority.
- Marketing effectiveness cannot be reliably measured and is a too long and too costly process.
- The environment changes too fast and results should be judged by the new realities and not those prevailing at the time of the action.

Cultural resistance to measurement and analytic thinking can be problematic, but in today's business environment these arguments are not accepted any more, in particular because the functions of measurement go beyond explaining what has happened in the past. Measurements also move the firm forward towards appropriate actions and improvements. One cannot manage that which is not measured (Eechambadi, 2005). In the United States, 70 per cent of marketers now say they use ROI calculations to guide long-term decisions on how they do business.

Development of appropriate marketing metrics

While manufacturing and service organizations can quantify their costs down to a fraction of a euro and project their ROIs, marketing remains a "dark science", in which charismatic marketing practitioners can generate desirable results but cannot tell you how they achieved them.

Marketing, however, has a long tradition of paying attention to measurement and the creation of metrics, as evidenced by the development of marketing research (Churchill and Iacobucci, 1992/2005). The problem is that most metrics used to assess the outcome of marketing activities are tactical and not directly relevant to the overall performance of the firm. Many companies do not even differentiate between necessary marketing expenditures (e.g., a catalogue) that are a cost of doing business, versus expenditures that are tactical with a short-term payoff (e.g., a promotion) versus expenditures that are investments in the future (e.g., a concept advertising campaign) with a longer-term payoff, such as building the brand's capital of goodwill.

Most marketers understand that while many marketing investments have some immediate payback, many require a bit of continuity to build their critical mass of contribution over time to achieve long-term objectives like building or maintaining brand equity or developing an emerging market. Unfortunately, accounting and finance people follow widely accepted accounting principles, requiring all marketing investments to be booked as expenses in the quarter in which they are incurred, even if the payoff is expected for a much later period.

The concept of brand equity

To refer to these lagged effects of marketing, the term brand equity as been popularized by Aaker in his 1991 bestseller book, but the concept is much older and is due to Nerlove and

Arrow (1960), who refer to the "'capital of goodwill' accumulated by a brand or a firm as a result of past advertising (marketing) efforts". In accounting terms, brand equity is viewed as "the intangible accumulated asset from past marketing efforts that has not yet been translated into profit". This concept of an asset is nothing new in the field of accounting: "receivables" in the balance sheet stands for money that will be paid and "inventory" stands for goods that will be sold. Similarly, brand equity refers to "...the latent benefit of past investments before the sales emerge" (Ambler, 2003, p. 51).

Other definitions of brand equity exist (Aaker, 1991; Srivastava and Shocker, 1991; Keller, 1998; Kapferer, 2004). The most compact one is due to Ambler (2003, p. 50): "What is in people's head about the brand." It is interesting to note that by "people" one refers not only to consumers but also to the other market stakeholders, like distributors, influencers, suppliers, shareholders, employees, a view very much in line with the MO concept described in this book.

The existence of lagged effect of advertising – and by extension of operational marketing – is an established scientific fact since more than 50 years now, as the result of the seminal work of Palda (1963) and of many others. Marketers invest financial resources at some point of time and do not expect – except for response advertising and promotions – to gain the reward in sales in the short term, but rather to create, grow or maintain the brand's capital of goodwill in people's mind that will eventually translate into sales and profit. The idea was to find a concept summarizing the strengths or "the health" of a brand. The brand equity concept was created because traditional data such as market share or volume sold were not satisfactory to reflect the value of a brand, since they do not take into account the mental associations that exist in the customers' mind. The concept has two faces. On the one hand, it gives a financial definition of the brand equity to evaluate the brand's "financial" value (*financial brand equity*). It is especially important for financial analysts and companies to evaluate this strategic company asset. On the other hand, it covers the value of the brand from the customer viewpoint: the *customer-based brand equity*, as a set of mental associations made by the customers and generating the brand's strengths.

Most CEOs today fully adhere to this idea, but they want more than an understanding of how marketing investments work; they want reliable measures of the impact on brand equity. In Table 20.1 are presented the marketing metrics most commonly used. These metrics are calculated differently in different sectors.

The tyranny of measurement

The difficulties of measuring performance vary with the type of marketing activities. According to the CMO Council's report, marketers say they are most capable of measuring

Table 20.1 Commonly used brand equity metrics

External marketing metrics			
Familiarity	Are potential customers familiar with the brand?	**Loyalty**	Are they loyal to the brand?
Penetration	Per cent of the segment having bought the brand	**Availability**	How easy is it to find the brand?
Perceived quality	How do they rate the brand?	**Relative price**	The price compared with competition
Satisfaction	How satisfied are they with the experience?	**Marketing ROI***	Return on the marketing investment

Source: Adapted from Ambler (2003), Davis (2007) and Lenskold (2003).

direct mail campaigns, website and Internet search engine presence, telemarketing and contact management programmes. They are least capable of measuring advertising and branding campaigns. A negative side effect of the measurement objective – known as the tyranny of measurement – is the *shortermism* it generates. As stated by Lapointe from *Marketing NPV* (2007), "this increasing emphasis on quantifiable results has created an environment in which marketers have been politically pressured to shift an increasing portion of their program portfolio into tactics that pay back NOW or not at all".

The advent of store scanners, which gives managers real-time sales data revealing the immediate effect of price promotions, has contributed to popularize the short-term perspective. In addition, this orientation is exacerbated by financial analysts and rating agencies who focus on quarterly figures to value firms and advise clients. As put by Lodish and Mela (2007), "If brands are built over years; why are they managed over quarters?"

How can the CMO choose between spending €1 million on a brand awareness advertising campaign or €1 million on a direct mail campaign? High brand awareness affects every other marketing campaign and sales activity. It improves the returns from direct mail, from response advertising and makes the sales team more effective: *But by how much?* Without clear measurable results, the impact is difficult to determine. That is why branding campaigns are considered more risky and therefore should have a higher return to account for these uncertainties. The temptation is to focus on marketing activities considered less risky and that can be measured well, while cutting back on longer-term investments in activities, not as measurable or measurable at a prohibitive cost, but that can build brand equity and augment shareholder value. This fact may explain the popularity of Internet advertising.

Acquiring Customer and Market data

Measuring marketing performance and productivity without data is of course a mission impossible. In addition to the traditional internal data recorded within the "order–shipping–billing" cycle, two types of external data are required: customer's response data and competitive intelligence data.

The customers' response data are those related to the levels of the customer engagement cycle described below. These data are called *external primary data,* because they have to be generated and/or collected by the firm through market surveys or market tests or purchased to syndicated scanner data companies such as ACNielsen (www2.acnielsen.com), *Research International* (www.research-int.com), *Taylor Nelson Sofres* (www.tnsglobal.com) or *Ipsos Mori* (www.ipsos-mori.com). The formation of a customer panel or even a user community can also provide a platform for data collection.

Competitive intelligence data are also required. Focusing exclusively on customers while ignoring competitor's performance can be misleading. An 80 per cent satisfaction level is great if the rate for competition is 70 per cent, but not so good if theirs is 90 per cent. Thus, what matters is *relative* customer satisfaction, *relative* perceived quality and *relative* price.

20.2   THE CUSTOMER RESPONSE CYCLE

Market-driven management needs a marketing measurement framework to analyse the way marketing activities and investments influence customers in different ways at different levels of relationship development. The conceptual framework is provided by the *response hierarchy model* developed by Howard and Sheth (1969), which retraces the purchasing process followed by the customer and proposes indicators of effectiveness for each level of the process.

In this model, the various response levels of the customer can be classified into three categories: (a) *cognitive response*, which relates to retained information and knowledge; (b) *affective response*, which concerns attitude and evaluation and (c) *behavioural response*, which refers to action, not only the act of purchasing, but also after-purchase behaviour. Table 20.2 describes the measures currently used by marketers for each response level.

It is generally agreed that these three response levels follow a sequence and that the individual, like the organization, reaches the three stages successively and in this order: cognitive (learn) – affective (feel) – behavioural (do). We then have a *learning process* which is observed in practice when the customer is heavily involved by his or her purchase decision, for example, when the perceived risk or the brand sensitivity is high in the customers' mind.

An operational definition of the "learn–feel–do" model is the *customer engagement cycle* (see Table 20.3) recognizing different levels of customer engagement which lend themselves to measurement. Four sets of metrics can be developed to track (a) the marketing activities, (b) the customer impact, (c) the market impact and (d) the financial impact of these actions, at each stage of the customer engagement cycle:

- *Marketing activities:* These metrics identify and quantify the particular actions undertaken to generate marketing results at each stage. Merely mapping out marketing activities, stage by stage, helps determining whether resource allocation is aligned with stated objectives.
- *Customer impact*: This second set of metrics looks at outcomes or effectiveness indicators. It measures operational results like customer awareness, customer attitude and preference, customer intention to buy and satisfaction and so on. This information is useful for determining which marketing tools or programmes are effective in moving customers to the next stage or for reallocating marketing investments.

Table 20.2 Key measures of customer response

- **Cognitive response**
Awareness – Saliency – Familiarity – Recall – Recognition – Knowledge – Perceived Similarity.
- **Affective response**
Attitude – Consideration – Affinity – Esteem – Relevance – Preference – Intention to Buy – Perceived value – Differentiation.
- **Behavioural response**
Fact-finding behaviour – Trial purchase – Repeat purchase – Share of category requirement (exclusivity) – Loyalty – Bonding – Satisfaction/dissatisfaction.

Source: Lambin (2000).

Table 20.3 Monitoring the customer engagement cycle

Metrics	Customer engagement cycle		
	Cognitive stage	**Affective stage**	**Behavioural stage**
Marketing activities	Brand awareness advertising campaign	Brand image advertising campaign	Direct mail or in store promotion
Customer impact	Awareness, recall, familiarity …	Esteem, affinity, consideration …	Repeat purchase, referrals …
Market impact	Improved competitiveness	Lower price sensitivity	Increased sales or market share
Financial impact	Reduced selling costs	Longer customer life cycle	Incremental revenue, better profitability

Source: Adapted from Eechambadi (2005).

- *Market impact:* This third set of indicators describes the resultant improvements in the brand or the firm's market position, such as sales and market share, lower price sensitivity, higher customer retention or stronger competitiveness. These improvements can be viewed as caused by the customer impact.
- *Financial impact:* This fourth set of metrics is designed to translate operational marketing metrics into financial outcomes, incremental revenue, increased customer profitability, lower sales or service cost, stronger customer lifetime value and so on.

The financial benefits from marketing activities can then be evaluated in several ways; ROI or on marketing expenditures (ROME), return on sales, return on assets, return on equity, net sales contributions. For a review of the methods used for measuring marketing productivity, see Powell (2002), Ambler (2003), Lenskold (2003) and in particular Davis (2007), who proposes 103 key marketing metrics.

Is measuring marketing ROI a realistic objective?

By marketing ROI, we mean *Return on Marketing Investments*. For too long, marketers have not been held accountable for showing how marketing expenditures add to shareholder value. In today's environment of financial austerity, Board members and Corporate Financial Officers (CFOs) are applying growing pressure on Corporate Marketing Officers (CMOs) to provide evidence that their marketing expenditure is worth it. And not only do marketers have to be accountable for their marketing expenditures, they also need to prove that they have the appropriate metrics and that measurement itself is feasible. In a growing number of companies, unless a given marketing investment can clearly be shown to generate sales, profits or leads, its value is questionable.

Computing marketing ROI

If marketing is to be a credible contributor to marketing success of the firm, it must speak the same financial language as the rest of the firm. And it must translate outcomes into economic metrics comprehensible outside the marketing department. Any marketing expenditure must be weighed against alternative non-marketing investments and measured against the potential for increasing profitability as a result of marketing in a given quarter versus not making the expenditure at all (Stewart, 2006).

The computation of the ROI formula is straightforward. The ROI is presented as a percentage and is calculated by dividing the return by the investment, where "return" is defined as the revenue generated by the marketing investment, less cost of goods sold, less investment. The ROI value will be a positive percentage, a negative percentage or zero. A positive ROI indicates that you have earned more than enough profits to cover your investment. If ROI is negative, you have lost money. Zero ROI is your income-based break-even point.

The *ROI threshold*, also called the hurdle rate, is the minimum ROI level for which a company will make investments. The ROI threshold is used to guide marketing managers in their decisions for which campaigns and which incremental investments should be pursued. It is the minimum ROI that management expects from any marketing investment. For example, if a company's threshold is 25 per cent, funding will be provided for any investment opportunity that exceeds that level and rejected for an investment project below that level. A company may choose multiple ROI thresholds based on the level of risk anticipated for the marketing investment. From a financial point of view, the ROI threshold should represent the company's cost of securing capital.

Computing the minimum return

In computing marketing ROI, the difficulty lies in obtaining reliable estimates of the revenue generated by the marketing investment. While some forms of operational marketing investments, like direct mail, promotion or response advertising, are intended to generate immediate sales and lend themselves to measurement with a reasonable degree of accuracy, a brand image campaign or a sponsorship can create emotional connections and brand preferences that last over a very long period of time and may have implications on brand equity and on how the stock market values the company. For marketing investments of this type, it is difficult to force investments decisions into a standard marketing ROI equation, since the incremental revenue will be impossible to identify for each investment.

The problem can be approached from another perspective. Using the ROI threshold or a target ROI, the minimum return that must be reached to recover the investment can be calculated and converted into a sales target. If the ROI target is 20 per cent, the return target formula is obtained by multiplying the investment by 1 plus the ROI target. For example, if the investment is €800,000, the minimum target return will be €960,000 (or €800,000 × 1.20). Alternatively, dividing the marketing investment by the gross profit margin (in value or in per cent) will determine the sales (volume or value) required to recover the marketing investment. Without this type of analysis, sales target may be set too low and investments decisions can be made that do not recover the investment. In this approach, the marketing teams responsible for creating the brand image campaign are induced to recognize that they are expected to generate incremental revenue.

Once the minimum target returns is determined, the CMO can convert this figure into sales objective to be achieved by the operational marketing campaigns having received the support of the brand image campaign or of the sponsorship. As explained by Lenskold (2003, p. 157) the CMO has three options – aggregate, allocate or ignore:

- *Aggregate:* Where a sponsorship or a brand image advertising campaign can be matched with operational marketing campaigns that generate sales through its support, the aggregated ROI is a strong measure.
- *Allocate:* For a general brand image campaign that supports a number of customer segments, products or markets, the target return can be allocated into the ROI calculations for the associated operational marketing campaigns. The allocation process is justified provided that the target audience, the products or services promoted the message and positioning and the timing of the campaigns are the same.
- *Ignore:* Where brand image advertising has such a broad impact and long-term benefits, it is best to ignore this type of investment for ROI measurement and assess its effectiveness using brand equity metrics.

The allocation process will provide insights into how operational marketing managers perceive the value of a sponsorship or brand image support. If the general consensus is that this type of general advertising is not providing a lift in sales, additional testing or analysis may be justified.

Measuring the long-term effect of marketing

Long-term effects of marketing are much harder to measure. A very large number of studies on the impact of marketing activities on brand performance are concentrated on activities having a short-term impact. A limited number of studies have analysed the longer-term impact of marketing instruments. As already underlined, one plausible reason many firms adopt a short-term emphasis on marketing activities is that they have a large short-term effect that lends itself to easy measurement.

Ataman, van Heerde and Mela (2006) propose another explanation, referring implicitly to a "principal–agent" problem (Alchian and Demsetz, 1972), where the interests of an agent (the brand manager) are not aligned with those of the principal (the shareholder). Brand managers have a brief tenure in which to be promoted, often spending a year before moving to another assignment. As such, long-term effects benefit their successor (or the shareholder), while short-term effects benefit them. Since there is little incentive to invest in long-term brand building, brand managers may choose to ignore the instruments that do lead to beneficial long-term effects, such as concept advertising, new product introductions or improved distribution that take months or years to manifest.

In a white paper published by the marketing research firm *eNumerys Global (2007)*, it is suggested to leverage consumer-based equity metrics to measure the long-term effects of marketing on sales, in addition to the short-term effects measured by the marketing mix models utilizing a three-stages approach depicted in Figure 20.1 (flow 3). This would provide a more complete measure of marketing ROI and bridge the gap that exists in how brands are measured and valued and the process of marketing budget allocation that eventually drives brand value.

In B2C markets, consumer tracking surveys regularly measure constructs like brand awareness and knowledge, brand interest and brand intention to buy. Similarly, more specific indicators of brand equity could be monitored over time. Here are four examples of indicators that could be introduced in a scale (Likert type) with value of (1) for strongly disagree and (7) for strongly agree.

I am ready to pay a higher price to buy brand A
If brand A is not available in my usual store, I am ready to visit anther store.
Brand A has element of uniqueness of value for me.
Brand A is superior over its direct competitors.

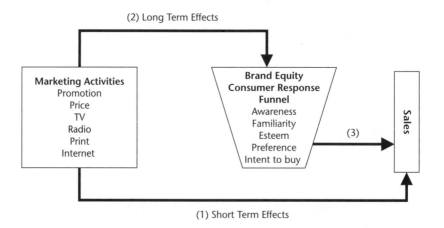

Figure 20.1 Measuring short- and long-term marketing effectiveness
Source: Adapted from eNumerys Global (2007).

In addition to the functional benefits of the brand, attitudinal and emotional indicators reflecting aspirational values of consumers are also included. Examples could be:

Brand A makes me feel confident of my look.
Brand A makes me feel like a great mom.

Monitoring the evolution of the functional and attitudinal indicators and relating their changes with the marketing activities undertaken to support the long-term value of the brand equity can be part of a more general evaluation system of the firm's strategic brand management.

20.3   USEFULNESS OF MARKETING MODELS

Marketing models measure the impact of marketing activities, competitive effects and market environment factors on sales or market share of a brand. Mathematical model building has for years remained confined in the domain of academia with the pioneering works of scholars like Bass and Buzzell (1961), Montgomery and Urban (1969), Little (1970 and 1979) who introduced the concept of decision support system (DSS), Lilien and Rangaswamy (1998) and many others. For a comprehensive review of the marketing models proposed in the academic and professional literature, see Lilien, Kotler, and Moorthy (1992) and Leeflang, Wittink, Wedel and Naert (2000). Building on these early works, many international marketing research companies have developed marketing mix models useful to set communication budgets or to re-engineer budget allocations among brands, regions or media, *Mindshare* (WPP), *Data2Decisions*, *eNumerys Global* being examples. For a review of the professional literature, see Dyson (2002) and Ruffle (2007).

This methodology is increasingly used in the consumer packaged goods industry given the proliferation and accessibility of high-frequency sales and marketing data on a weekly or monthly base. The technology has also improved. A brand manager today has the technological power on his or her desk to pull together all relevant sources of information, from hard sales data through consumer brand equity metrics and qualitative opinions about how the brand works. The pressure for greater marketing accountability already mentioned has also contributed to add impetus to this methodology.

Connecting brand equity metrics and sales

Brand equity metrics are currently collected by brand managers in the form of brand tracking surveys. The challenge is to uncover the connection between performance metrics such as awareness, preference, intention to buy, satisfaction to ROI. In other words, can one translate a percentage point of awareness generated by a brand advertising campaign to a financial value of "X" euros? The stand-alone financial value of one point of brand awareness is zero, except if this metric is integrated within the context of the customer engagement funnel and viewed as a first step of the customer response chain leading to sale and market share. To build market share, the objectives are successively (a) brand awareness among the target segment, (b) a favourable attitude and interest in the brand, (c) intention to buy, (d) convenient brand availability and (e) satisfaction. Each step along the customer engagement chain indicates how customer response influences market share.

Best (2004) has suggested that market share can be estimated from the combination of a set of hierarchical marketing metrics indicating how customers respond to the firm's marketing efforts. Using this model, the impact of a change of one marketing metric – for instance, awareness – on the market share index can be calculated and converted into incremental revenue and in profit contribution after subtraction of the advertising cost. The calculated market share index is simply an approximation of what market share should be. The model provides a mechanism to assess the market share change when a certain level of improvement is made in a key marketing metric. It also enables the firm to identify sources of lost market share opportunity. The inputs of the model are branding equity metrics regularly collected by brand managers.

Marketing mix modelling

Marketing mix models are typically estimated using historical hard sales and marketing data on a weekly or monthly base using multivariate regression methods. The typical output is a decomposition of sales into baseline and marketing incremental, including sales due to each specific marketing activity. As illustrated in Figure 20.1 (flow 1), these models measure the short-term effect in sales due to individual marketing activity and can provide estimates of the ROI of each marketing instrument. Once these relationships are established, the model can be used to simulate the sales impact of changing investments in the different marketing instrument, to reallocate the marketing budget and to generate sales forecast and run "what if" scenarios. As underlined by Dyson (2002), to be successful the modelling approach requires frequent interaction and communication between the modelling and marketing teams.

Weaver (2004) from *Data2Decisions Ltd* reports that significant financial benefits result from using software systems that calculate payback from advertising. Sales can increase by around 10 per cent simply by re-phasing media spend. On a wider scale, advertising effectiveness can be improved by 25 per cent to 50 per cent by using the results of ad spend assessments to re-engineer budget allocations.

Limitations of marketing mix models

Marketing mix models have two important limitations. First, since they are based on an analytical assessment of the past, they will provide unreliable forecast when applied in situations where important changes are under way, for instance, when the Internet is transforming decision processes. When consumer decision processes, media, distribution channels are stable, these models work well. Thus, a marketing model is not a cure-all and blind faith in its results can be deceptive. As lucidly explained by Wittink (2005): "Many marketing models are, at best, descriptive. In that case, the estimated effects may properly describe how consumers act under prior conditions. As long as researchers do not capture how consumers may change behaviour" as a function of change in market conditions, the models will fail to make correct predictions of marketplace outcomes." Some markets are easier to model than others. FMCG suit sales modelling analysis because they have short consumer purchase cycles. Also, sales are tracked accurately and in detail using weekly data from scanners. The automotive sector is much harder to model because of its much longer purchase cycle.

There is a second important limitation. Standard marketing mix models only account for the short-term sales effect due to marketing activities and ignore the impact of marketing on brand equity (see Figure 20.1, flow 2). Thus, calculating marketing ROI on the basis of the short-term effects only can be seriously misleading since the long-term effect of the different marketing instruments can be very different. For example, a brand image advertising campaign has generally a very modest positive short-term effect on sales but can have a much stronger long-term effect through its impact on brand equity metrics like awareness, esteem or preference. According to Lodish and Mela (2007, p. 108), the long-term effect of advertising can be 60 per cent greater than its short-term impact. On the contrary, promotions or temporary price cuts generally have a strong impact on short-term sales, but their total impact is smaller than their short-term effects, due to stockpiling and competitive retaliation. In addition, they do not contribute to reinforce brand equity. In fact, frequent promotional discounting may even lower brand equity by commoditizing the brand through increasing consumer focus on pricing.

Who should be in charge of measuring marketing performance?

To avoid the pitfall of *shortermism* mentioned above, CMOs need to sit down with CFOs to determine the appropriate marketing measures and who is best suited to monitor these measures. Delegge (2007) considers that the Finance Department should take the responsibility for determining, managing and monitoring financial and non-financial metrics. Ambler (2000, p. 65) proposes the following reasons for this transfer of responsibility:

- Marketers are widely seen as selective and/or manipulative in the way they present information. Independence would add credibility.
- Metrics are not high on marketers' priorities. Marketers are more interested in making runs than in scoring. Perhaps this is as it should be.
- Marketing information is widely dispersed in large organizations. Only part of it exists in the marketing department.

We do not agree with this very negative view of marketers even if we believe that the financial accountability of marketing should be improved. A partnership between the Finance and Marketing departments should facilitate cross-functional coordination and thereby reinforce marketing credibility.

20.4   MARKETING IMPACT OF STOCK MARKET VALUES

Among the stakeholders, investors are particularly important market players in the global market, and it is imperative that companies understand the needs of investors and their perception of the company. Calls for increased corporate transparency are becoming ever more frequent and detailed. Whereas investors may have been simply looking for a stable pattern of earnings growth and/or dividend distribution in the past, today they wish to project trends for the key drivers of future value creation such as new product development and innovative use of new business practices. On the other hand, the collapse of *Parmalat* in Italy, *Lernout & Hauspie* in Belgium, *Enron* in the United States and other financial scandals have created a crisis in investors' confidence. Companies need to find ways to restore their credibility and reconnect with their investor base.

Treating investors like customers

Companies need to start applying to investors the same kind of strategic discipline they typically apply to customers. This does not mean that corporate executives should let investors determine the business strategy any more than they should let customers determine product strategy. What it does mean is developing a detailed process for ensuring that a company' strategy is informed by the perspectives and requirements of the investors base, and then working over time to create alignment between strategy and shareholders (Hansell and Olsen, 2002).

As in any strategic marketing exercise, the first step is to systematically segment the market. Different classes of investors have different appetites for growth, profitability, cash flow generation and risk. Who are the target groups? Are they banks, analysts, fund managers, private investors, previous shareholders, customers, employees? What needs and expectations do these groups have? Should all groups or only selected groups be addressed? Having analysed investors' needs, Simon, Ebel and Hofer (2002) report the following observations:

- Expectations and requirements of each group vary significantly.
- Large companies should address all target groups.
- The quality of information collected by companies about their investors is generally poor.
- Systematic target thinking is rudimentary at best.

The output of this segmentation analysis should be a fact-based view of why each group of investors has chosen to put their money with the company.

Communicating with investors

Investor-oriented companies do not view communication with investors as an exercise in sales, nor do they rely exclusively on analysts to reflect the views of the capital market. Instead, they engage directly in a continuous dialogue with both current and potential investors. Investors often have information and perspectives that managers lack. They meet regularly with management teams across a wide range of companies. There is no law against asking investors good questions and listening carefully to their answers.

Investors are often overwhelmed by a plethora of expensive information that is of little interest to them such as annual reports filled with formal historical data. More transparent financial reporting down to the level of the strategic business unit is essential. Increasingly, investors aren't just looking at earnings per share; they are looking at how these earnings are generated, which includes the company strategy, growth plans, competitive advantage and so on. Once a company knows what shareholders really value, it can start building the internal system necessary to deliver the kind of performance those shareholders want and to predict and communicate results in a way that avoids negatives, surprises, and builds credibility over time (Thomas, Gietzman, and Shyla, 2002)

There are of course situations when the imperatives of a company's long-term strategy and the needs of current investors are in conflict. Once a company has developed an in-depth understanding of its investor base, it can identify such disconnects, analyse their causes and prepare to migrate to those investors that make the most sense given the company' strategy. Just as some customers are more profitable than others, some investors are more attractive than others. Cultivating these aligned investors will help the company migrate toward an owner base that supports the long-term strategy and will reduce unnecessary volatility as short-term investors move into and out of the stock (Hansell and Olsen, 2002).

Impact of marketing on stock returns

Marketing managers are under increasing pressure to measure and communicate the value created by their marketing actions to top management, to shareholders and to investors. In particular, there is pressure on marketing managers to demonstrate the contribution of advertising to financial performance in view of the weak evidence for the profit contribution of advertising spending.

Srinivasan, Pauwels, Silva-Risso and Hanssens (2009) have examined how product innovations and marketing investments for such product innovations lift stock returns by improving the outlook on future cash flows. Their econometric study focuses, in the United States, on the 1996–2002 automobile industry's "big six" (Chrysler, Ford, General Motors, Honda, Nissan and Toyota) considering 53 brands in six major product categories. The main research question was, Do firms' marketing actions drive stock returns? The results are summarized in Table 20.4.

Referring to the data of Table 20.4 the authors have calculated the stock return impact of (1) introducing a new product by itself providing improvements of different levels, (2) introducing a pioneering innovation, (3) increasing advertising support for a new product introduction or for a pioneering innovation by $1 million, (4) increasing promotional incentives for a new product innovation by $1,000, (5) increasing customer liking for a new product introduction, (6) increasing the perceived quality for a new product introduction. Table 20.4 reports the effect of the marketing variables on stock returns. Several interesting observations emerge.

- For new product introductions, the return impact is U-shaped with the innovation level with a preference for new market entries (0.98 per cent) over minor updates (0.55 per cent). Moderate innovations do not offer much more advantage over minor innovations
- The gain generated by a pioneering innovation is much higher with 4.28 per cent increase in return, approximately seven times higher than that of a minor update. Thus investors perceived pioneering innovation as information about the firm's future financial performance.
- An incremental outlay of $1 million in advertising support of an innovation generates up to 0.10 per cent in stock returns but up to 0.91 per cent gains for advertising support of a pioneering innovation. These results demonstrate that innovation effects are enhanced by advertising support because investors look beyond the advertising expense which reduces immediate profits. Indeed, advertising works best when the firm has something new to offer the consumer.
- The reverse is true for promotional incentives for new product introductions with a negative effect (–0.20 per cent) in terms of stock return impact. Although advertising support is interpreted as signal of strength, price promotions are viewed by investors as a signal that an innovation is weak or performing below expectations in terms of sales.
- Finally improvements in perceived quality scores by 100 points (or a 45 per cent improvement relative to sample average) results in a stock return impact of 2.10 per cent. Investors view the quality signal as providing useful information about the future term prospects of the firm. As commented by the authors, favourable perceptions of product quality and value by customers lead to differentiation and higher brand loyalty. With respect to the brand's customer liking the main effect is not significant.

Similar results have been observed in other studies. See, for example, Kumar and Shah (2009 and Krasnikov, Mishra and Orozco (2009). These results are important because they relate marketing performance to

Table 20.4   Impact of firms' actions on stock returns

Impact of firms' actions	Effect on stock returns
New to company innovations	
Level 1 (trimming)	0.55%
Level 2 (styling)	0.43%
Level 3 (design)	0.38%
Level 4 (new benefit)	0.34%
Level 5 (entry in new category)	0.98%
Pioneering innovations	4.28%
Ad support for new products	0.10%
Ad support for pioneering innovations	0.91%
Promotional support for new products	–0.20%
Improvement in customer liking	NS
Improvement in perceived quality	2.10%

Source: Adapted from Srinivasan, Pauwels, Silva-Risso and Hansssens (2009).

reliable financial metrics. By doing so, marketers demonstrate the impact of both strategic and operational marketing on driving the boardroom's primary agenda of increasing the overall value of the firm.

Chapter Summary

Marketing is traditionally one of the least measured functions of the firm, despite the fact that it represents a significant share of companies' budgets. Market-driven management needs a marketing measurement framework to analyse the way marketing activities and investments influence customers in different ways at different levels of relationship development. If marketing is to be a credible contributor to marketing success of the firm, it must speak the same financial language as the rest of the firm. And it must translate outcomes into economic metrics comprehensible outside the marketing department. Among the stakeholders, investors are particularly important market players in the global market, and it is imperative that companies understand the needs of investors and their perception of the company.

BIBLIOGRAPHY

Aaker, D.A. (1991*), Managing Brand Equity*, New York, The Free Press.

Alchian, A. and Demsetz, H. (1972), Production, Information Costs and Economic Organization, *American Economic Review*, 62, 5, pp. 777–95.

Ambler, T. (2000), Marketing Metrics, *Business Strategy Review*, 11, 2, pp. 59–66.

Ambler, T. (2003), *Marketing and the Bottom Line*, London, FT Prentice Hall, 2nd edition.

Ataman, B., van Heerde, H.J. and Mela, C.F. (2006), The Long Term Effect of Marketing Strategy on Brand Performance, Submitted to *Journal of Marketing Research*, Second Revision, July 2006.

Bass, F.M. and Buzzell, R.D. et al. (1961), *Mathematical Models and Methods in Marketing*, Homewood IL, R.D. Irwin Inc.

Best, R.J. (2004), *Market-Based Management*, Upper Saddle River, Prentice-Hall, 3rd edition.

Churchill, G.A. and Iacobucci, D. (1992/2005), *Marketing Research: Methodological Foundations*, South Western Thomson.

CMO Council (2004), *Measures and Metrics: The Marketing Performance Measurement Audit*, Palo Alto, CA, CMO Council, April.

Davis, J. (2007), *Measuring Marketing: 103 Key Metrics Every Marketer Needs*, Singapore, John Wiley and Sons Asia.

Davis, J. (2007), *Measuring Marketing: 103 Key Metrics Every Marketer Needs*, Singapore, John Wiley and Sons Asia.

Delegge, P. (2007), The Bottom line on Marketing Accountability, *Marketing Today*, 17 December.

Dyson, P. (2002), Setting the Communication Budget, *Admap*, 433, pp. 39–42.

Eechambadi, N. (2005), *High Performance Marketing: Bringing Methods to the Madness of Marketing*, Dearborn Trade Publishing.

eNumerys Global (2007), *An Analytical Approach to Balancing Marketing and Branding ROI*, a white paper, www.enumerys.com.

Hansell, G. and Olsen, E.E. (2002), *Treating Investors Like Customers, The Boston Consulting Group*.

Howard, J.A. and Sheth, J.N. (1969), *The Theory of Buyer Behavior*, New York, John Wiley and Sons.

Kapferer, J.N. (2004), *The New Strategic Brand Management*, London, Kogan Page.

Keller, K.L. (1998), *Strategic Brand Management*, Upper Saddle River, NJ, Prentice-Hall.

Krasnikov A., Mishra S. and Orozco D., (2009), Evaluating the Financial Impact of Branding Using Trademarks: A Framework and Empirical Evidence, *Journal of Marketing*, November.

Kumar V. and Shah D., (2009), Expanding the Role of Marketing: from Customer Equity to Market Capitalization, *Journal of Marketing*, November.

Lambin, J.J. (2000*), Market-Driven Management: Strategic and Operational Marketing*, London, Palgrave Macmillan.

Lapointe, P. (2007), Bridging the GAAP, *Marketing NPV*, 4, 1 ("http://www.marketingnpv.com" www.marketingnpv.com).

Leeflang, P.S.H., Wittink, D.R., Wedel, M., and Naert, P.A.V. (2000), *Building Models for Marketing Decisions*, International Series in Quantitative Marketing, Springer.

Lenskold, J.D. (2003), *Marketing ROI*, New York, McGraw-Hill.

Lenskold, J.D. (2003), *Marketing ROI*, New York, McGraw-Hill.

Lilien, G.L. and Rangaswamy, A. (1998), *Marketing Engineering*, Computer-Assisted Marketing Analysis and Planning, Reading, MA, Addison Wesley Longman.

Lilien, G.L., Kotler, P., and Moorthy, K.S. (1992), *Marketing Models*, Englewood Cliffs, NJ, Prentice Hall International.

Little, J.D.C. (1970), Models and Managers: The Concept of Decision Calculus, *Management Science*, 16, pp. 466–85.

Little, J.D.C. (1979), Decision Support for Marketing Managers, *Journal of Marketing*, 43, pp. 9–26.

Lodish, L.M. and Mela, C.F. (2007), If Brands are Built over Years, Why are They Managed over Quarters? *Harvard Business Review*, July–August, pp. 104–12.

Montgomery, D.B. and Urban, G.L. (1969), *Management Science in Marketing*, Englewood Cliffs, NJ, Prentice-Hall.

Nerlove, M. and Arrow, K. (1960), Optimal Advertising Policy under Dynamic Conditions, *Economica*, 29, pp. 131–45.

Palda, K.S. (1963), *The Measurement of Cumulative Advertising Effects*, Englewood Cliffs, NJ, Prentice-Hall.

Palmer, A. (2004), *Introduction to Marketing*, Oxford University Press.

Powell, G.R. (2002), *ROMI – Return on Marketing Investment*, Albuquerque, RPI Press.

Ruffle, A. (2007), ROI: A Passing Fad or an Enduring Trend? *Admap*, Supplement February.

Simon, H., Ebel, B., and Hofer, M.B. (2002), The Challenge of Investor Marketing, *European Business Forum*, 11, Autumn, pp. 67–9.

Srinivasan, S., Pauwels, K., Silva-Risso, J. and Hanssens, D.M. (2009), Product Innovations, Advertising and Stock Returns, *Journal of Marketing*, 73, pp. 24–43.

Srivastava, R.K. and Shocker, A.D. (1991), Brand Equity: A Perspective on Its Meaning and Measurement, Cambridge, MA, Marketing Science Institute, pp. 91–124.

Stewart, D.W. (2006), *Making Marketing Accountable*, Graziado Business Report, 9, 3.

Thomas, A., Gietzmann, M. and Shyla, A. (2002), Winning the Competition for Capital, *European Business Forum, 9*, Spring, pp. 80–3.

Weaver, K. (2004), Calculating the Payback from Advertising, *Financial Marketing*, August.

Wittink, D.R. (2005), Econometric Models for Marketing Decisions, *Journal of Marketing Research*, 42, February, pp. 1–3.

CHAPTER TWENTY ONE

THE STRATEGIC AND OPERATIONAL MARKETING PLAN

Sound strategic thinking about the future must be spelled out in a written document, which describes the ends and means required to implement the chosen development strategy. In the short term, the firm's success is directly dependent on the financial performance of its ongoing activities. In the longer run, however, its survival and growth imply the ability to anticipate market changes and to adapt the structure of its product portfolio accordingly. To be effective, this strategic and proactive thinking must be organized in a systematic and formal way. The role of strategic marketing planning is the design of a desired future and of effective ways of making things happen. Its role is also to communicate these choices to those responsible for their implementation. This planning task is of course particularly hard when great uncertainties prevail in the firm's environment. Anticipating the unexpected is also part of the strategic planning process. In this chapter, we shall build on the concepts and procedures described in previous chapters and examine the steps needed to make strategic marketing happen in the firm.

Learning Objectives

When you have read this chapter, you should be able to:

- Understand the usefulness of formal strategic planning
- Define the structure and content of a strategic plan
- Conduct an external and internal audit (SWOT analysis)
- Define operational objectives and action programmes
- Prepare a projected profit and loss statement
- Test the robustness of a strategic plan

21.1 OVERVIEW OF MARKETING PLANNING

The raison d'être of a strategic plan is to formulate the main strategic options taken by the firm, in a clear and concise way, in order to ensure its long-term development. These strategic options must be translated into decisions and action programmes. We shall briefly examine the overall structure of a plan and the benefits expected from strategic planning.

Overall structure of the strategic marketing plan

As shown in this book, the strategic marketing process can be summarized around six key questions. The answers provided to these questions constitute the backbone of the plan and also the objectives for the firm:

1. What business are we in and what is the firm's mission in the chosen reference market?
2. Within the defined reference market, what are the targeted product markets or segments and what is the positioning strategy likely to be adopted within each segment?
3. What are the key business attractiveness factors in each segment and what are the opportunities and threats presented by the environment?
4. Within each segment, what are the firm's distinctive qualities, strengths and weaknesses and competitive advantages?
5. Which development strategy and strategic ambition should be adopted for each activity in the firm's product portfolio?
6. How do these strategic options translate into operational marketing programmes defined in terms of product, distribution, pricing and communications decisions?

Once the answers to these questions are obtained as the result of a strategic marketing audit, the task remains to summarize the options taken, to define the means required to achieve the stated objectives, to design the specific action programmes and, last but not least, to prepare projected profit and loss statements for each activity and for the company as a whole.

In fact, a strategic marketing plan is nothing more than a financial plan, but with much more information on the origins and destinations of the financial flows. As illustrated by Figure 21.1, the strategic marketing plan has direct implications on all the other functions of the firm and vice versa:

- R&D: market needs must be met through new, improved or adapted products and services.

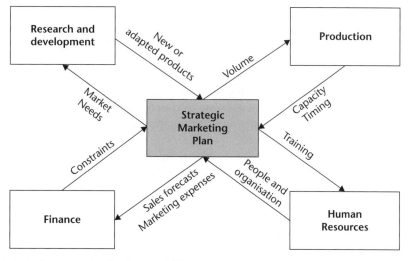

Figure 21.1   The strategic plan: a cross-functional responsibility
Source: Lambin (2000/2007).

- Finance: the marketing programme is subject to financial constraints and to availability of resources.
- Operations: sales objectives are subject to production capacity and to physical delivery constraints.
- Human Resources: the implementation of the plan implies the availability of qualified and well-trained personnel.

Thus strategic planning will result in a better integration of all the company's functions and contribute to maximization of efforts in reaching corporate goals. In a market-driven organization, the mission of strategic marketing is to identify prospects for growth and profit given the company resources and savoir faire. As already emphasized in this book, this role is much broader than the traditional domain of marketing management, and implies inter-functional co-ordination.

Importance of strategic planning

Every company, even those reluctant to engage in the idea of formal planning, has to formulate forecasts in a minimum of three areas:

- The calibration of the investment programme required to meet the level of market demand or to penetrate a new product market.
- The production programme organization needed, given the seasonality of sales and the periodicity of orders.
- The financial liquidity, based on income and expense forecasts, which is required to meet the financial liabilities.

These managerial problems are common to all companies and they imply that reliable sales forecasts should be handled properly.

In addition to this argument of necessity, other arguments in favour of formal strategic planning exist:

- The plan expresses the value system, philosophies and views of top management. This information gives people a sense of direction and a sense of how to behave.
- The plan presents the facts on "where the business has come from and where it stands". The situation analysis helps to understand the reasons for the strategic options taken by top management.
- The plan facilitates co-ordination among the different functions, maintains consistency in the objectives and facilitates trade-offs among conflicting goals.
- The plan is a monitoring instrument which provides the opportunity to review the progress made in implementing the plan and to redirect parts of the action programme that are off target.
- The plan minimizes the degree to which the company is taken by surprise to the extent that "best case–worst case" scenarios have been explored.
- The plan encourages a more rigorous management of scarce resources by using standards, budgets, schedules and so on, thereby reducing the risk of improvisation.

Most strategic plans are complemented by some form of contingency plan to be activated if certain events occur. Contingency plans are developed for factors which are key to the survival of the company.

Objections to formal planning

Although strategic planning is a widely adopted practice, a certain number of firms avoid using formal written strategic plans. Three types of objections to formal planning are usually given: the lack of relevant information, the futility of forecasting in a fast-changing environment and the rigidity of planning.

Lack of needed information

Ideally the planner would have at hand all the pertinent information required on industry and market trends, competitive intentions, market share, technological innovations and so forth. The most common complaint concerns lack of adequate information for the purpose of planning. On deeper investigation, however, it nearly always turns out to be a case of too much information rather than too little. The real problem is much more the lack of in-depth analysis.

The existence of a market information system is today a vital necessity to maintain the firm's competitiveness. Thus, market information and business intelligence systems must exist in any case, and this is a costly operation with or without formal planning.

Futility of forecasting

In a turbulent environment, what good are strategic plans which will be contradicted by future events? This attitude results from a misunderstanding as to the nature of forecasting, which is erroneously likened to a crystal ball. A forecast is a quantitative or qualitative estimate of what one expects, given a set of assumptions on the environment. A forecast is not an end in itself, but a forward thinking exercise, a tool used to increase the company's responsiveness and adaptability to the unexpected. This objective can be achieved even if the predicted outcome is not attained.

Bureaucratic rigidity

Formal planning would commit the firm to a given direction, whereas adaptability and flexible response are required in a fast-changing environment. This objection questions more the authoritarian planning style than planning itself. A plan should be designed to enhance creativity and quick reaction to changes. The mere fact of having analysed possible changes in the market in advance will help to revise programmes and objectives faster, whenever it is desirable to do so.

In practice, strategic planning is widely used, as evidenced by the Bain survey (2001) conducted every year.

21.2   CONTENT OF A STRATEGIC MARKETING PLAN

A strategic marketing plan typically sets out to answer the six key questions presented at the beginning of this chapter. In this section, we shall describe the basic elements of a strategic marketing plan and the type of information required on which to base recommendations.

The mission statement

Sometimes called a creed statement or a statement of business principles, a mission statement reveals the company's long-term vision in terms of what it wants to be and who it wants to serve. It defines the organization's value system and its economic and non-economic objectives. The mission statement is important from both an internal and external point of view:

- Inside the company, it serves as a focal point for individuals to identify with the organization's direction and to ensure unanimity of purpose within the firm, thereby facilitating the emergence of a corporate culture.
- From an external point of view, the mission statement contributes to the creation of corporate identity, that is, how the company wants to be perceived in the marketplace by its customers, competitors, employees, owners and shareholders, and by the general public.

A mission statement should include at least the four following components.

History of the company

Knowledge of the past history of the company, its origin and successive transformations is always useful to understand its present situation and the weight given to some economic or non-economic goals and objectives.

Materne-Confilux celebrated its 100th anniversary in 1987. This company has accumulated a broad experience in the field of purchase and transformation of fruits and has succeeded in maintaining a family managerial structure. This strong foothold in the fruit sector is a key factor to consider when exploring alternative diversification strategies.

In searching for a new purpose, a company must remain consistent with its past achievements and fields of competence.

Business definition

This is a key component in the mission statement. What customers buy and consider valuable is never the product, but rather its utility, that is, what a product or a service does for them (Drucker, 1973, p. 61). Thus, the market definition should be written in terms of the benefit provided to the buyer. The three relevant questions to examine here are:

- What business(es) are we in?
- What business(es) should we be in?
- What business(es) should we not be in?

These are not easy questions to answer, particularly when the environment is changing very quickly. Ideally, the mission statement should be stated in terms narrow enough to provide practical guidance, yet broad enough to stimulate imaginative thinking, such as openings for product line extensions, or for diversification into adjacent product areas. At the Grumman Corporation, the guidelines for the mission statement advise:

> We should be careful not to confine the market boundaries by our existing or traditional product participation. The market definition analysis is purposely meant to create an outward awareness of the total surrounding market and of its needs and trends that may offer opportunity for, or on the other hand challenges to, our current or contemplated position. (Hopkins, 1981, p. 119)

Every organization has a unique purpose and reason for being. This uniqueness should be reflected in the market definition. In a market-driven organization, the market definition will reflect the degree of customer orientation of the firm. By adopting a business definition formulated in terms of generic need or in terms of "solution to a problem", the firm empha-sizes its market orientation and limits the risk of market myopia.

Corporate goals and restraints

Goals set the direction for both long- and short-term development and therefore determine limitations and priorities to comply with. These general goals, usually defined at the corporate level, are constraints within which the strategic plan must be developed. They should be clearly defined in advance to avoid proposals that contradict objectives of general management or corporate shareholders.

These goals may be economic but also non-economic. Examples are a minimum rate of ROI, a growth objective, the conservation of the family ownership of the company, the refusal to enter particular fields of activity, a minimum level of employment and so on.

The description of available company resources (capacity, equipment, human resources, capital and so on) also forms part of the restraints and should be made explicit in order to avoid the adoption of a "mission impossible" given the resources needed. Codes of conduct and corporate ethics for dealing with others (customers, distributors, competitors, suppliers and so on) should also be formulated.

Basic strategic choices

Independent of the general goals imposed at the corporate level by general management, basic strategic options can be defined for each strategic business unit. For example, the extent of the strategic ambition and the role played by the firm in the target segment, that is, leader, follower, challenger or nicher, may be defined. The strategic ambition must of course be compatible with the available resources of the firm.

Reference could be made here also to the three basic positioning strategies suggested by Porter (1980): cost advantage, differentiation and focus. The type of competitive advantage sought should also be defined. At this stage of the strategic plan, only broad orientations are given. They will be redefined in quantitative terms in the action programmes developed for each business unit.

In a survey conducted in the United States by David (1989), out of a total of 181 responses received, 75 organizations provided a formal description of their mission statements. The main components included are summarized in Table 21.1.

External audit – market attractiveness analysis

This external audit – also called opportunities and threats analysis – is the first part of the situation analysis. An attractiveness analysis examines the major external factors that are

Table 21.1 What components are included in a mission statement?

• Customer	Who are the company's customers?
• Products and services	What are the firm's products or services?
• Location	Where does the firm compete?
• Technology	What is the firm's core technology?
• Concern for survival	What are the commitments to economic objectives?
• Philosophy	What are the basic beliefs, values, aspirations and philosophical priorities?
• Self-concept	What are the firm's major strengths and competitive advantages?
• Public image	What are the firm's public responsibilities and what image is desired?
• Concern for employees	What is the firm's attitude towards its employees?

Source: David (1989).
(A survey: N = 75)

factors which are out of the control of the firm, but that may have an impact on the marketing plan. The following areas should be reviewed:

- Market trends
- Buyer behaviour
- Distribution structure
- Competitive environment
- Macro-environmental trends
- International environment

These external factors may constitute opportunities or threats that the firm must try to anticipate and monitor through its marketing information system and through business intelligence. In what follows, we shall simply list the critical questions to address in each of these areas. The precise type of information required will of course differ by product category: consumer durable or non-durable goods, services or industrial goods.

Market trends analysis

The objective is to describe, segment by segment, the total demand's general trends within a three- to five-year horizon. The task is to position each product market in its life cycle and to quantify the market size. Both unit volume and monetary values should be identified.

Questionnaire 1: Reference market trends

- What is the size of the total market, in volume and in value?
- What are the trends: growth, stagnation, decline?
- What is the average per capita consumption?
- How far are we from the saturation level?
- What is the rate of equipment per household or per company?
- What is the average lifetime of the product?
- What is the share of replacement demand of total demand?
- What is the seasonal pattern of total sales?
- What are the main substitute products performing the same service?
- What are the major innovations in the sector?
- What are the costs per distribution channel?
- What is the structure of the distributive system?
- How will supply–demand relationships affect price levels?
- What is the level of total advertising intensity?
- What are the most popular advertising media?

This list is certainly incomplete. It simply illustrates the type of information required. If the product studied is an industrial good, several information items should pertain not only to the direct customers' demand, but also to the demand expressed further down the line in the industrial chain by the customers of the direct customers.

Customer behaviour analysis

The task here is to analyse customer behaviour in terms of purchasing, use and possession. In addition to a description of buyers' purchasing habits, it is also useful to know the buying process and to identify the influencing factors.

Questionnaire 2: Customer behaviour analysis

- Per segment, what is the customer's socio-demographic profile?
- What is the composition of the buying centre?
- Who is the buyer, the user, the payer?
- What is the decision process adopted by the customer?
- What is the level of involvement of the buyer, the user, the payer?
- What are the main motivations of the buying decision?
- What is the package of benefits sought by the buyer, the user, the payer?
- What are the different uses of the product?
- What changing customer demands and needs do we anticipate?
- What are the purchasing frequency and periodicity?
- To which marketing factors are customers most responsive?
- What is the rate of customer satisfaction or dissatisfaction?

These descriptive data must be complemented with measures of the cognitive and affective response (recall, attitudes, preferences, intentions and so on), as well as with brand or company image analyses.

Distribution structure analysis

This part of the external audit is probably more relevant in the field of consumer goods than in the sector of industrial goods, where direct distribution is common practice. The objective is to assess the future development of distribution channels and to understand the motivations and expectations of the company's trading partners.

Questionnaire 3: Structure and motivation of distribution

- What are industry sales by type of outlet?
- What are product type sales by type of outlet?
- What are product type sales by method of distribution?
- What is the concentration ratio of distribution?
- Is distribution intensive, selective or exclusive?
- What is the share of advertising assumed by distributors?
- What change does one observe in the assortments?
- What is the market share held by private brands?
- Which market segments do the different channels cover?
- What are the total distribution costs?
- What is the distribution margin for each channel of distribution?
- What kind of distributor support is currently provided?
- What is the potential of direct distribution?

The distributor, as a business partner, has strong negotiation powers vis-à-vis the firm. One of the roles of a distribution analysis is to assess the degree of autonomy or dependence of the firm in the distributive system.

Competitive environment analysis

The competitive structure of a market sets the framework within which the firm will operate. As put by Porter (1980), "The essence of strategy formulation is coping with competition." The basic attractiveness of a market segment is largely determined by the strength of competitors' capabilities. Assessment of what is driving competition is of vital importance to the firm.

Questionnaire 4: Competition Analysis

- What is the market's competitive structure?
- What is the market share held by the top three rivals?
- What type of competitive behaviour is dominant?
- What is the strength of competing brands' images?
- What is the nature of the competitive advantage of direct competitors?
- To what extent are these competitive advantages well protected?
- What are the competitors' major objectives?
- What is the current strategy being used to achieve the objectives?
- What are the strengths and weaknesses of competitors?
- What are their likely future strategies?
- Are there entry barriers in this market?
- Which are the main substitute products?
- What is the bargaining power of customers and suppliers?

The gathering of this type of information implies the development of a competitor intelligence system. For a more detailed framework of competitor analysis, see Porter (1980, chapter 3).

Macro-environmental trends

This section describes the macro-environmental trends – demographic, economic, political/legal and socio-cultural – that bear on the studied market's future development. These external factors can provide productive opportunities or severe limitations for the company's products.

Questionnaire 5a: Economic macro-environment

- What is the expected GNP rate of growth?
- What major economic changes could affect our business?
- What is the expected level of employment?
- What is the expected rate of inflation?
- Do these trends affect our business and how?

Questionnaire 5b: Technological environment

- What major changes are occurring in product technology?
- How can we adjust our activities to cope with these changes?
- What major generic substitutes might replace our product?
- Do we have the required R&D capabilities?
- Do we need to update our equipment and at what cost?

Questionnaire 5c: Socio-demographic and cultural macro-environment

- What are the major demographic trends that affect our business?
- What is the cultural climate within which our business operates?

- Are present and future life styles favourable to our business?
- Is society's attitude towards our business changing?
- Are there changes in society's values that could affect our business?

Questionnaire 5d: Political and legal macro-environment

- Are there any specific changes in the law that affects our company?
- Are there legal or political areas that affect our customers?
- Which regulations could affect our advertising or selling strategy?
- Is our industry subject to criticisms from consumer organizations?
- Are there political or legal trends that could be used to our advantage?

Questionnaire 5e: International environment

- To what extent are we dependent on imports for key components?
- What is the economic and political stability of the supplier country?
- What alternatives do we have should our imports be interrupted?
- What is the economic and political stability of the customer countries?
- What opportunities does the European single market represent?
- Are there emerging global segments in our business?
- Is our business affected by changing world trade patterns?

Questionnaire 5f: Ecological environment

- Are our products environmentally friendly?
- Do we use processes or raw materials that threaten the environment?
- Is green marketing a potential strategy for our company?
- Is our industry a potential target for environmentalists?
- How can we improve the ecological quality of our products?

Questionnaire 5g: Industry and corporate ethics

- Does our company or industry have a stated code of ethics?
- What is the ethical level of our industry?
- Are industry values in alignment with those expected by society?
- How could our industry improve its ethical practice?

This information, dealing with the macro-environment of the firm, is indispensable for exploring alternative scenarios of market development. Generally, at least two scenarios will be explored: a base scenario, but also one or several alternative scenarios based on vulnerability factors.

The sources of information are numerous and varied, but often very scattered. Professional organizations and local chambers of commerce have economic data available for their members to use in planning. In addition to national statistics and foreign trade institutes, international financial institutions like the Bank for International Settlements (BIS), the International Monetary Fund (IMF), the World Bank (WB), the Office for Economic Co-operation and Development (OECD), the United Nations (UN) and so on, are the major public sources, with periodic publications readily available. University research centres and large international consulting firms, like Business International, McKinsey, the Economist Intelligence Unit and so on, also publish newsletters, articles and monographs which are very useful for planning purposes.

Internal audit – company competitiveness analysis

The objective of the internal audit, also called the company strengths and weaknesses analysis, is to assess company resources and to identify the type of sustainable competitive advantage on which to base the development strategy. Strengths and weaknesses are internal factors, in contrast with opportunities and threats, which are external factors. Company strengths (or distinctive qualities) point to certain strategies the company might be successful in adopting, while company weaknesses point to certain things the company needs to correct. A competitiveness analysis should not be abstract. Reference to competition in general is too vague. Therefore, competition should be referred to in terms of the most dangerous competitors, called priority competitors.

To illustrate, distinctive qualities for a brand of laptop computer, as compared to those of the priority competitor, might be:

- Excellent brand awareness and an image of high quality.
- Dealers who are knowledgeable and well trained in selling.
- An excellent service network and customers who know they will get quick repair service.

The *weaknesses* of the same brand could be:

- The screen quality of the brand is not demonstrably better than the quality of competing machines, yet screen quality can make a big difference in brand choice.
- The brand is budgeting only 5 per cent of its sales revenue for advertising and promotion while major competitors are spending twice that level.
- The brand is priced higher relative to other brands without being supported by a real perceived difference in quality.

The strengths of the company or of the brand constitute potential *competitive advantages* on which to base the positioning and the communication strategy. The weaknesses determine the vulnerability of the brand and require remedial action. Some weaknesses may be structural that is linked to the size of the firm and therefore difficult to correct. Examples of structural weaknesses are:

- National market share leadership, if not accompanied by international distribution, creates home country vulnerability to the extent that the local company has little freedom for retaliation in the country of foreign competitors.
- If a single powerful distributor generates total sales volume, the company has weak bargaining power.
- A small or medium-sized company does not have the financial capability to use the most powerful media, like television advertising.

So a distinction must be made between the weaknesses that the company can correct and therefore which become priority issues that must be addressed in the plan, and the high-risk structural weaknesses which are beyond the control of the firm and which require a high degree of surveillance.

Competitiveness analysis is organized much like attractiveness analysis. The major difference comes from the fact that the company, and not the market, is the central subject of the analysis.

Company current marketing situation

Data on the served markets for each of the products of the company's portfolio, in volume and market shares for several years and by geographical areas, are presented, as well as data on the current marketing mix.

Questionnaire 6: Product portfolio analysis

- What is the rate of current sales per product, segment, distributive channel, region and country and so on, in volume and value?
- What is the current market share per product category, segment, distributive channel, region, country and so on?
- How does the quality of our products compare with that of competition?
- How strong is the company's product brand image?
- Does the firm have a complete product line?
- What is the structure of our portfolio of customers?
- How concentrated is our total turnover?
- What is the age profile of our product portfolio?
- What is the contribution margin per product, segment, channel and so on?
- What is the current level of nominal and relative prices?

This analysis is to be repeated for each product of the company's portfolio. Profit and loss statements for the last three years should be presented along with the current budget. A typical profit and loss statement is shown in Table 21.7.

Priority competitor analysis

Priority competitor(s) should be identified for each product market. For each of these competitors, the same data collected for the company products will be gathered and compared as shown in Table 21.2. Other information is required to assess the strength of priority competition.

Questionnaire 7: Priority competition analysis

- What is the relative market share?
- Does competition have a cost advantage?
- What is the relative price?
- What is the competitive behaviour of rivals?
- How strong is the image of competing products?
- On what basis are competing products differentiated?
- How large are their financial resources?
- What is their retaliation capacity in case of frontal attack?
- Which are their major sources of vulnerability?
- What type of aggressive actions could they take?
- What kind of retaliatory or protective actions could we adopt?
- What changes could modify the present balance of power?
- Is competition able to destroy our competitive advantage?

With the information provided by questionnaires 6 and 7, a product portfolio analysis can be conducted.

Table 21.2   Priority competitors analysis form (each factor must be evaluated on a 10-point scale)

Marketing variables	Our product	Competitor 1	Competitor 2	Competitor 3
Product				
Quality	——	——	——	——
Company price	——	——	——	——
Product line	——	——	——	——
Packaging	——	——	——	——
Evaluation on				
– Attribute 1	——	——	——	——
– Attribute 2	——	——	——	——
– Attribute 3	——	——	——	——
Distribution				
Dist. number	——	——	——	——
Dist. value	——	——	——	——
– channel 1	——	——	——	——
– channel 2	——	——	——	——
– channel 3	——	——	——	——
Facing	——	——	——	——
Margin	——	——	——	——
Discounts	——	——	——	——
Promotion	——	——	——	——
Sales force				
Size of sales force	——	——	——	——
Quality	——	——	——	——
Call frequency	——	——	——	——
Training	——	——	——	——
Advertising				
Size of budget	——	——	——	——
Media mix				
– medium 1	——	——	——	——
– medium 2	——	——	——	——
– medium 3	——	——	——	——
Advertising copy	——	——	——	——
Advertisement quality	——	——	——	——
Promotion				
Size of budget	——	——	——	——
Type of promotion				
– Consumer price	——	——	——	——
– Distribution margin	——	——	——	——
– Other promotions	——	——	——	——
Services				
Range of services	——	——	——	——
Delivery terms	——	——	——	——
After-sales service	——	——	——	——
R&D				
Size of budget	——	——	——	——
Staff	——	——	——	——
Performance in R&D	——	——	——	——
Marketing research				
Quality of MIS	——	——	——	——
Data banks	——	——	——	——
Performance	——	——	——	——

Distribution penetration analysis

Distributors, a company's partners in the marketing process, control the access to the end-users' market and play an important role in ensuring the success of the contemplated marketing programme. In addition, if they are powerful buyers they have a strong bargaining power vis-à-vis their suppliers. In fact, distributors must be viewed as intermediate customers just like end-user customers. The role of trade marketing is to analyse the needs and requirements of these intermediate customers in order to develop a mutually satisfactory exchange relationship.

Questionnaire 8: Distribution analysis

- How many distributors do we have in each channel?
- What is our penetration rate in number and value in each channel?
- What is the sales volume by type of distributor?
- What are the growth potentials of the different channels?
- What are the efficiency levels of the different distributors?
- Are the present trade terms motivating for distributors?
- What changes could modify relationships with our dealer network?
- Should the firm consider changing its distribution channels?
- What is the potential of direct marketing in our business?
- Are there new forms of distribution emerging in the market?

The objectives pursued by the firm and by its distributors are not exactly the same and conflicts can arise in the channels. Distributors are no longer passive intermediaries in most markets. The role of "trade marketing" is to ensure that the firm views distributors as partners and as intermediate customers.

Communication programme analysis

Mass media advertising, interactive advertising, personal selling, publicity, and so on are powerful competitive weapons if properly used, that is, when the target markets are well chosen and when the content of the communication programme is well in line with the product positioning, pricing and distribution strategies.

Questionnaire 9: Communication programme analysis

- What is the advertising intensity compared to direct competition?
- What is the advertising cost per thousand target buyers per medium?
- What is the communication effectiveness of media advertising?
- What are the consumers' opinions on the advertisement content?
- What is the number of reply coupons stimulated by direct advertising?
- How well are the advertising objectives defined?
- What are the sales or market share effectiveness of advertising?
- What is the impact of advertising on awareness, attitude and intentions?
- What is the average number of sales calls per sales representative per week?
- What is the number of new customers per period?
- What are the sales force costs as a percentage of total sales?

These questionnaires should be used as guidelines for periodically reviewing the company's marketing situation within the framework of a marketing audit.

Pricing policy analysis

Price is the only component of the marketing mix generating income, in contrast with the other marketing instruments. Price also has the highest visibility in the marketplace and can be easily compared with rivals.

Questionnaire 10: Pricing policy analysis

- What is the price elasticity of primary demand?
- What is the price elasticity of our own demand or market share?
- What are the market "maximum acceptable" prices of our brands?
- At what level are the perceived value prices of our brands?
- How do our prices compare with direct competitors' prices?
- Is price sensitivity very different from one segment to another?
- What is our policy in terms of price discounting?
- Are our prices stated in euros competitive in the European market?
- What type of price adjustment do we have to consider in the European market?

It is important to keep in mind that price is a determining factor in the brand positioning strategy and that it must be compatible with the other elements of the marketing mix.

21.3   OBJECTIVES AND PROGRAMMES

At this point, management knows the major issues and has to make some basic decisions about the objectives. Using the information provided by the strategic marketing audit and by the positioning statement, the firm's identified priority objectives must then be translated into operational action programmes.

Definition of objectives

Every firm has several objectives that can be grouped into two broad categories: marketing and non-marketing objectives:

- Non-marketing objectives have been described in the firm's mission statement. They describe the overall value system of the company and as such they apply for all market targets.
- Marketing objectives are of three types: sales, profit and customers. They should be defined for each product market or segment.

Sales objectives

It is a quantitative measure of the impact the firm "wants" to achieve in the future within a particular product market. It is not simply a forecast of what one "expects" may occur in the future. It is an active, not a passive, statement about the future. Sales objectives can be stated in currency, in volume or in market share. Examples of sales-oriented objectives are presented in Table 21.3.

Table 21.3   Examples of sales-oriented objectives

- Achieve total sales revenue of €2,150,000 by the end of 1992.
- Attain a 20 per cent market share of the management distance learning market.
- Reach a sales volume of 150,000 units per year.

- *Sales revenue objectives* are the most convenient way to express a sales objective because they are easily integrated in the accounting and financial system. Sales revenue may be misleading, however, if not adjusted for inflation and also for modifications in the sales mix if, for example, the share of high-priced products has changed from one period to another.

- *Unit sales* represent the best indicator provided there is no change in the volume definition. In the soft drink sector, for example, it is current practice to think in terms of case sales. What about cases of 12 or 18 bottles? Conversion to 'litre equivalent cases' must be made. In many markets a meaningful unit definition simply does not exist. For example, in life insurance the number of policies taken out is not a good indicator of sales performance.

- *Market share* is the best indicator of competitive performance. Also, in volume industries where experience effects occur, high market share implies a cost competitive advantage over direct competition.

Sales data are a key element in the projected income statement. They must be translated into financial terms.

Profit objectives

Marketing, as for all other functions within the firm, must be accountable for profits. The inclusion of formal profit objectives forces marketing people to estimate the cost implications of the stated sales objectives. Examples of profit objectives are presented in Table 21.4.

The definition of profit objectives implies a close inter-functional co-ordination within the firm. A statement of profitability cannot be made without a close look at the cost–volume relationship and capacity constraints. For new products, the investment in fixed costs and working capital, in addition to manufacturing and marketing costs, should be analysed before launching. Similarly, the marketing expenses involved in implementing the proposed marketing strategy must be carefully evaluated and their expected contribution to sales and/or market share development assessed.

Customer objectives

Customer objectives are deduced from the positioning statement. They describe the type of behaviour or attitude the firm would want customers to have towards its brands or services. Examples of customer objectives are presented in Table 21.5.

Table 21.4   Examples of profit objectives

- Produce net profits of €150,000 before tax by December 2007.
- Earn an average 15 per cent ROI during the next five years.
- Produce a dollar contribution of €350,000 at the end of the fiscal year.
- Produce net profits of €150,000 before tax by December 2007.

Table 21.5   Examples of customer objectives

- Create at least 60 per cent awareness for brand A within the 15–25 age group by the end of 2007.
- To increase by 20 per cent the repeat purchase rate of brand A within the 15–25 age group by the end of 2007.
- To position brand at the high end of the market in the minds of consumers belonging to the upper-income bracket.

These customer objectives are important because they provide directions to advertising people for the development of communication strategies and for supporting the positioning theme adopted.

Market share objectives

Market share is the best indicator of the brand's competitive performance based either on the product intrinsic superiority or on a more attractive price.

As suggested by Best (2004, p.74), an index of market share can be created from a combination of market share effects. The share development tree of Figure 21.2 traces a hierarchy of market share effects that leads to a particular level of indexed market penetration. Interestingly, it appears that the overall market share index is the interaction between effects. Should one perform poorly, the overall index will perform poorly. Each share effect is derived from a particular component of what is the "marketing mix". It includes,

$$\text{Market share} = \text{Communication} \times \text{Product} \times \text{Price} \times \text{Distribution} \times \text{Service}$$

Because there are many other factors that can affect actual market share, the market share index – 7.6 per cent in the example of Figure 21.2 – is simply an indicator of what market share should be, given certain expected levels of market performance. The market share development tree provides three important benefits:

- It helps in identifying important sources of lost market share opportunity.
- It provides a mechanism to assess the market share change when a certain level of improvements is directed in a key area of poor performance.
- It enables the brand manager to estimate what might be a reasonable market share potential given reasonable levels of performance in each area along the purchase path.

In the example of Figure 21.2, if a business could succeed in building its brand availability to customers intending to buy from 57 per cent to 70 percent, it could increase its overall market share index from 7.6 percent to 9.3 percent.

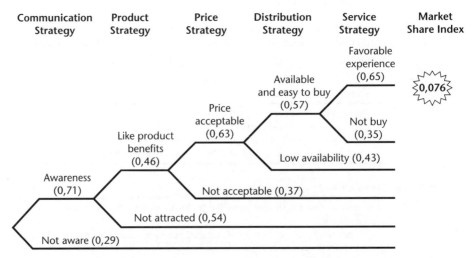

Figure 21.2 Marker share development tree
Source: Best (2004, p. 73).

This hierarchy of market share effects is based on a learning model that is observed mainly in markets where the degree of customers' involvement is high.

Integration of objectives

Kotler (1997/2005) suggests starting with the profit objectives and deducing the required sales and customer objectives:

> For example, if the company wants to earn €1,800,000 profit, and its target profit margin is 10 per cent on sales, then it must set a goal of €18 million in sales revenue. If the company set an average price of €260, it must sell 69,230 units. If it expects total industry sales to reach 2.3 million units, that is, a 3 per cent market share. To maintain this market share, the company will have to set certain goals for consumer awareness, distribution coverage, and so on.

Thus, the line of reasoning is the following:

- to define the expected net profit;
- to identify the turnover required to achieve this result;
- given the current average company price, to determine the required sales volume (in units);
- given the expected level of primary demand in the reference segment, to calculate the corresponding required market share;
- given this target market share, to determine the target objectives in terms of distribution and communication.

The corresponding marketing objectives should therefore be:

- to achieve a given turnover, which represents an increase over previous year of x per cent;
- This would imply a sales volume of x units, corresponding to a y per cent market share;
- to determine the level of brand awareness required to achieve this market share objective and also the required proportion of purchase intentions within the target segment;
- to determine the increase of distribution rate;
- to maintain the average company price.

This logical and apparently simple procedure is difficult to implement in the real world because it implies complete knowledge of the functional relationships between market share and price, market share and distribution, market share and awareness and so on. The merit of this approach is to identify clearly the required information for sound marketing planning.

Characteristics of good objectives

Sound marketing objectives should have the following characteristics. They must be (a) clear and concise, avoiding long statements and phrases; (b) presented in a written form to facilitate communication and to avoid altering objectives over time; (c) stated within a specific time period and (d) in measurable terms; (e) consistent with overall company objectives and purpose; (f) attainable but of sufficient challenge to stimulate effort; and (g) name specific results in key areas, such as sales, profits and consumer behaviour or attitudes (Stevens, 1982). In addition, individual responsibilities should be clearly defined as well as the calendar and the deadlines to be met.

21.4   SELECTION OF THE STRATEGIC PATH

To define an objective is one thing. To know how to reach that objective is another story, since the very same objective can be achieved in different ways.

A 10 per cent revenue increase can be obtained, for instance, by increasing the average selling price, or by expanding total demand through a price decrease, or by increasing market share without price change but through intensive advertising or promotional actions.

Clearly, these alternative actions are not substitutes and their efficiency will vary according to market and competitive situations. Thus, beyond the general directions given by the basic strategic options, it is necessary to specify the action programme segment by segment.

Alternative action programmes

A defence strategy

If the strategic option is *to defend current market* position with existing products in an existing segment, the alternative actions to consider in a market position defence strategy could be:

- Product or service modifications, for example, new features or packaging, or product repositioning through concept advertising.
- Sales, distribution and service network reinforcement.
- Stepped-up or redirected promotional activities.
- Defensive pricing through bundling or premium pricing.

A market penetration strategy

If the objective is *to increase the turnover by 10 percent* in a specific segment or product-market by adopting a market penetration strategy without modifying the composition of the product portfolio, the brand manager could adopt one the following alternative strategic paths:

- To target the non-users of the brand through promotional actions to induce a trial purchase.
- To stimulate irregular users to become regular users by proposing special deals at a reduced price.
- To increase consumption per usage occasion by offering larger packaging.

A market development strategy

If the objective were *to increase sales revenue* through a market development strategy without modifying the composition of the product portfolio, the strategic paths to consider would be the following:

- To extend the geographic distribution by creating a commercial network in a neighbouring country, where the per capita consumption of the product is much lower.

- To reinforce the distribution coverage by increasing the number of companies regularly visited by the sales force.
- To augment the number of facings in the supermarkets chains.

A brand extension strategy

If the objective is to complete, *improve or broaden the range of products*, the alternative of a product line extension strategy could be:

- Filling gaps in the existing product line.
- Introduction of new products to serve untapped segments in related business areas.
- Systematic brand proliferation to blanket the market.
- Acquisition of a company with a complementary product line.
- Contracting for the supply of a complementary product line to be sold under the company's name.
- Joint venture for the development and production of a new product line.

An international development strategy

If the objective is *international development* by shipping existing products to foreign markets, the alternatives could be:

- Use of an independent, worldwide trading company.
- Use of a network of export agents to handle all foreign business.
- Setting up of a network of distributors or import agents in target markets.
- Acquisition of a foreign company in the same industrial sector.
- A joint venture to enter a restricted foreign market.

These alternative strategy paths may have very different implications in terms of resources, both financial and human, and their feasibility must be carefully assessed.

The strategy statement

The strategy statement requires making basic choices among the strategy alternatives. It is a summary overview designed to state "how" the objectives for the business unit will be met. The strategy statement will govern not only marketing planning, but the manufacturing, financial and R&D functions. It is the mainstream guidance from which all subsequent planning functions flow. The strategy statement should address the following:

- Market segments selected and targeted.
- Positioning relative to direct competition.
- Product line requirements, mix, extensions and so on.
- Channels of distribution, direct, indirect and so on.
- Pricing and price structure.
- Personal selling.
- Advertising and promotion.
- After-sales, warranty, services and so on.
- Marketing research.

The strategy statement should not exceed two or three pages of text. At this point, general management should review and approve the objectives.

Criteria for selecting a strategic option

A certain number of simple rules, inspired by military strategy, should be followed in selecting a strategy:

- Feasibility: assess skills and resources constraints.
- Strength: always try to have a strength advantage.
- Concentration: avoid scattering of efforts.
- Synergy: ensure co-ordination and consistency in efforts.
- Adaptability: be ready to respond to the unexpected.
- Parsimony: avoid waste of scarce resources.

In the 2000s environment, forward thinking is a dynamic exercise which requires adaptability and flexibility.

21.5   DESIGN OF THE MARKETING PROGRAMME

Once the course of action is identified, a detailed description of the means required will be made for each component of the marketing mix. The strategy statement allows the product manager to prepare a supporting budget, which is basically a projected profit and loss statement.

The strategy statement gives a general direction that must then be translated into specific actions for each component of the marketing mix with a description of the resources available to implement those actions. These resources include human and financial resources; they are described in the action programme and in the budget.

The action programme includes a detailed description of the actions to be undertaken. In addition to financial considerations, the budget should also specify the timing of the action programmes and the responsibilities, that is, who is in charge of what. An example of budget structure is presented in Table 21.7 (see page 575).

The expected level of sales of a given brand is a function of the intensity and continuity of operational marketing efforts. The support given to each product of the firm's portfolio must be described with precision and summarized in financial terms in a projected profit and loss statement.

Negotiation of the marketing budget

Different budgeting modes can be adopted to design a strategic marketing plan. The ideal procedure should be as simple as possible and involve the whole organization and in particular the functions responsible for the plan implementation. The most popular budgeting process observed in a survey of 141 companies (Piercy, 1987, p.49), is the bottom-up/top-down process:

> Managers of the sub-units in marketing submit budget requests, which are co-coordinated by the chief marketing executive and presented to top management, who adjust the total budget size to conform with overall goals and strategies.

A good strategic marketing plan should be a written document: it takes the form of a contract. To be effective the plan should have the following characteristics:

- To be sufficiently standardized as to permit fast discussion and approval.
- To consider alternative solutions to be adopted if environmental conditions change or if corrective actions have to be taken.

- To be regularly re-examined or updated.
- To be viewed as a managerial aid, which implies being (a) strict on the applications of corporate goal and on long-term strategic options, and (b) flexible on short-term forecasts.

The planning horizon is in general a three-year moving horizon.

Usually, every month there is a comparison between current and expected results in order to monitor closely the implementation of the plan and to facilitate the adoption of fast remedial actions.

Alternative marketing programmes

In the design of the marketing programme, the product or brand manager has to decide on the level of each of the key marketing mix instruments, that is, price, advertising, visit frequency of the sales force to distributors, promotional activities to organize to support the brand in the distributive network and so on. Since these marketing instruments are partly substitutable, the brand manager can explore the sensitivity of the break-even volume to different combinations of the marketing mix variables. It is common practice to establish a base programme and then to analyse the implications of alternative scenarios. By way of illustration, let us consider the following (fictitious) case.

> The direct cost of a new product is £10 (C); the annual depreciation cost plus the share of general overhead (F) add up to £38,000. Executive opinion held that £16 is a price (P) on the low side while £24 is a price on the high side; and that £10,000 is a low budget for advertising (S) and personal selling (V), respectively, and £50,000 is a high budget. This yields eight strategy combinations.

The break-even volume can be estimated as a function of the elements of the marketing mix as follows:

$$Q_n = \frac{F+S+V}{P-C}$$

The break-even volume will vary with the product price and the marketing effort devoted to the new product,

$$Q_n = \frac{38000+S+V}{P-10}$$

In Figure 21.3, eight alternative marketing programmes are listed for this product along with the implied break-even volume. For example, in the case of Mix # 1, one has,

$$Q_1 = \frac{38,000+10,000+10,0000}{16-10} = 9,667 \text{ units}$$

Each mix is a polar case. They imply not only different break-even volumes, but also differences in the target market sensitivity to each element of the marketing mix.

- For example, Mix # 1 represents the common strategy of setting a low price and spending very little for promotion. This works well when the market is highly price-conscious, possesses good information about available brands and is not easily swayed by psychological appeals.

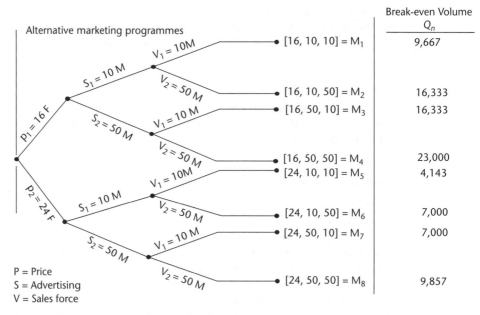

Figure 21.3   Minimum volume requirements as a function of marketing mix
Source: Adapted from an example presented by Kotler (1964, p. 44).

- Mix # 4 represents a strategy of low price and heavy promotions. The same low price policy as in Mix # 1 is supported by heavy promotion and advertising. Thus, we have here the maximum marketing pressure that should produce a high sales volume but also that requires a high sales volume to break even. In this launching strategy, the firm creates high barriers to entry.

- Mix # 5 consists of a high price and low promotion and is used typically in a seller's market where the firm wants to maximize short-run profits, since the break-even volume is very low (4,143 units). In this programme, it is implied that the market is not price-sensitive and that the reputation of the brand is sufficiently high and speaks for itself. This entry strategy does not create barriers of entry to competition attracted by the high market prices and by the absence of high communication costs.

- Mix # 8 consists of a high price supported by high communication; this strategy is often used in a market where customers are sensitive to psychological appeals and to quality. It is interesting to note that the break-even volume is approximately the same for Mix # 1 and Mix # 8. Yet, the high price, high promotion character of Mix # 8 promises greater losses or greater profits for deviations from the break-even volume.

The other mixes (# 2, 3, 6, 7) are variations on the same themes, with the additional feature that different assessments are made of the comparative effectiveness of advertising and personal selling. The alternatives presented here opposed a push versus a pull communication strategy. But it should be noted that while the division of a given budget between advertising and personal selling affects the actual sales volume, it does not affect the break-even volume.

Sales multiplier concept

In the field of FMCG, sales evolution beyond the first year is mainly determined by the repeat purchase rate. This rate is often difficult to estimate with precision. If the firm has information on the sales patterns of similar products, the product's penetration curve can be estimated on this basis. For example, the observation made by the firm could be the following:

> Brand sales in this type of product category have a short life cycle; they reach their maximum level after 12 months, stay on this plateau during the second year and then decay during the third year at a rate that varies with the size of marketing efforts.

If the average decay rate observed for similar products is 20 per cent, third-year sales would then be 80 per cent of second-year sales. The sales multiplier of first-year sales over three years would then be 2.80 (1+1+0.80). This number (2.80) is called the sales multiplier or "blow-up factor". With this information, it is possible to develop a projected profit and loss statement over three years.

Risk or sensitivity analysis

A projected profit and loss statement, such as presented in Table 21.6, is based on assumptions about the sales growth rate and the size of the marketing budget. Management knows that this information is imperfect and risk analysis consists in testing the sensitivity of these assumptions on expected sales and profit.

Given the absence of reliable information on the trial and repeat purchase rates of the product, first-year and subsequent years' sales cannot be determined with precision, and it is therefore useful to have a range of likely sales, and not only a point estimate, to assess the risk implications of the project. Suppose that the brand manager's opinion is summarized in the following terms:

> The product manager is satisfied with the sales estimate of 2 million cases for the first year, although admitting that it contains some uncertainty. When pressed, however, the product manager will admit that sales could be as low as 1 million cases in the first year, but points out that sales might also exceed the estimate by as much as 1 million cases. The operational definition of these extremes is that each has no more than 1 in 10 chance of occurring.

Using these estimates, one can derive a probability distribution for first-year sales and calculate the expected value of sales. The objective is to assess the risk of having a sales volume inferior to the break-even volume during the first year. The probability distribution is presented in Table 21.6.

The expected value of sales is 1,925,000 cases, which is very close to the deterministic estimation. There is, however, a 3 in 10 ten chance that the sales volume in the first year will fall below the break-even volume. This is a significant risk.

Risk can also be measured in financial terms by computing the value of perfect information or the cost of uncertainty. The expected Value under Perfect Information (VPI) is obtained by computing the expected value of the best conditional payoffs of Table 21.6.

$$E(VPI) = 0.10(0) + 0.20(0) + 0.25(0.938) + 0.25(4.635) + 0.10(8.331) + 0.10(11.028)$$

That is,

$$E(VPI) = €3.430 \text{ million}$$

Table 21.6   Expected value of sales and profit

Sales*		Probability	Expected Sales	Conditional Payoffs	Expected Profit
Classes	Mid-point				
0.5–1.0	0.75	0.10	0.075	−6.455	−0.646
1.0–1.5	1.25	0.20	0.250	−2.759	−0.552
1.5–2.0	1.75	0.25	0.438	+0.938	+0.235
2.0–2.5	2.25	0.25	0.562	+4.635	+1.159
2.5–3.0	2.75	0.10	0.275	+8.331	+0.833
3.0–3.5	3.25	0.10	0.325	+11.028	+1.203
Total	–	1.00	$E(q) = 1.925$	–	$E(\pi) = 2.232$

*In million cases or dollars.

Without perfect information, the optimal action is to go ahead, with an expected payoff of €2,232 million. Thus the expected gain from perfect information (or the uncertainty cost) is:

$$€3,430 \text{ million} – €2,232 \text{ million} = €1,198 \text{ million}$$

One observes that the uncertainty cost is high compared to the expected gain. Another way to assess the risk is simply to observe, referring to column 5 in Table 21.6, that there are 30 chances out of 100 to have a loss of at least €2,759,000 on this project. The cost of uncertainty measures in a way the opportunity cost of a decision taken under imperfect information. This amount also measures the value of additional information.

Calculation of the net marketing contribution

The net contribution is the direct measure of the adopted strategy's performance. The different elements of the Net Marketing Contribution (NMC) are presented in Figure 21.4. Each term of the equation lends itself to some strategic thinking in order to determine the best way to improve the overall profitability. Several questions can be raised:

- Do we have to enter this segment or if we are already in do we have to divest?
- Which primary demand development strategy to adopt?
- How to increase our market share in the target segment?
- How to improve the profitability per customer? To increase volume sold? To raise prices?
- How to decrease delivery and service costs to our customers?
- How to improve the effectiveness of our advertising, of our promotional activities of our sales force?

This last question is particularly sensitive: how to reduce fixed marketing expenses, for instance, in using intermediaries.

Gap analysis

In summarizing the objectives of each business unit, it is instructive to project the current performance trends to verify whether the projected performance is satisfactory. If gaps appear between the current and the desired performance, then strategic changes will need

Table 21.7 Projected profit and loss statements form

SEGMENT: _____ PRODUCT: _____ ZONE: _____

	Year −3 (200–)	Year −2 (200–)	Year −1 (200–)	Current year (200–) (200–) Budget estimated		Year +1 (200–)	Year+2 (200–)
• **Total market**							
– Volume (units)	———	———	———	———	———	———	———
– Dollar sales (€)	———	———	———	———	———	———	———
• **Company sales**							
– Volume (units)	———	———	———	———	———	———	———
– Marker share	———	———	———	———	———	———	———
– Sales Revenue (€)	———	———	———	———	———	———	———
• **Direct cost**	———	———	———	———	———	———	———
• **Gross profit margin**							
– Value	———	———	———	———	———	———	———
– Per cent of net turnover	———	———	———	———	———	———	———
• **Direct marketing costs**							
– Promotions	———	———	———	———	———	———	———
– Discounts	———	———	———	———	———	———	———
– Folders and mailing	———	———	———	———	———	———	———
– Misc.	———	———	———	———	———	———	———
– Total direct costs	———	———	———	———	———	———	———
• **Semi-fixed marketing costs**							
– Media advertising	———	———	———	———	———	———	———
– PoS	———	———	———	———	———	———	———
– Public relations	———	———	———	———	———	———	———
– Total semi-fixed costs	———	———	———	———	———	———	———
• **Fixed marketing costs**							
– Marketing department	———	———	———	———	———	———	———
– Sales force	———	———	———	———	———	———	———
– Market research	———	———	———	———	———	———	———
– Sampling	———	———	———	———	———	———	———
– Misc.	———	———	———	———	———	———	———
– Total fixed costs	———	———	———	———	———	———	———
• **Total costs**							
– in per cent of net turnover	———	———	———	———	———	———	———
• **Net contribution**							
– Value	———	———	———	———	———	———	———
– in per cent of net turnover	———	———	———	———	———	———	———
• **Net cumulative contribution**	———	———	———	———	———	———	———

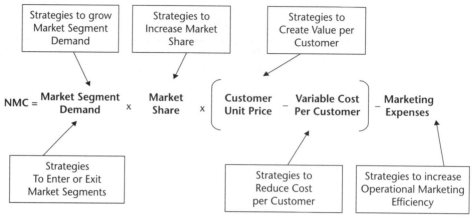

Figure 21.4   Computing the NMC
Source: Best (2004).

to be considered. The graph presented in Figure 21.5 illustrates the contribution of growth opportunities under two growth scenarios:

- An "all things being equal performance", where growth is achieved through a penetration strategy based on existing products and existing markets, assuming no change in the current strategy.
- A "desired performance", where growth is the outcome of the proposed marketing programme and of different growth opportunities.

As shown in Figure 21.5, the gap between these two performance levels can be sub-divided into two parts:

- An "operational gap', which reveals the improvement potential of existing businesses that could be achieved through a market and product rationalization strategy, that is, by reducing costs and/or improving marketing effectiveness, while keeping the structure of the product portfolio unchanged.
- A "strategic gap", which requires new growth opportunities, that is, new products, new markets, international development, diversification or integration.

These growth opportunities should be listed in order of priority and their potential financial contribution to the desired performance evaluated.

21.6   VULNERABILITY ANALYSIS AND CONTINGENCY PLANNING

The value of strategic planning is a continuing topic for debate. Not long ago, planning departments enjoyed a high status within the corporate organization. Today, most corporate planners downplay their formal planning roles. Experience with such largely unforeseen upheavals as the two oil crises of the 1970s, the stock market crash of 1987, the Gulf War, the East European revolutions and so on has revealed the shortcomings and the limitations of rigid planning procedures. Under fairly static conditions, planning works well, but when

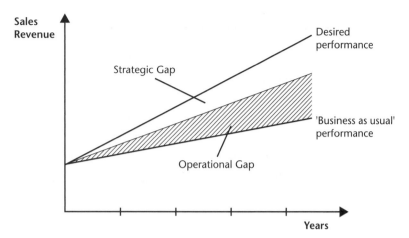

Figure 21.5   Gap analysis
Source: Thuillier (1987).

faced with uncertainties, turbulence, unanticipated market and competitive changes, general management becomes suspicious of the forecasts of revenue and profit performance that come from the business units.

Testing the robustness of a strategic plan

Just because a strategy must be developed and implemented under turbulent and uncertain conditions is no reason to abandon the discipline of structured planning. Planning is necessary for the functioning of the firm. To improve strategic planning performance, it is therefore important to test the robustness of the proposed strategy. Gilbreath (1987) suggests applying a "shake test" to the proposed strategy.

When structural or mechanical engineers wish to determine the reaction of a proposed design to mechanical vibrations, they either model it mathematically and calculate its response to input vibrations or, if feasible, build a prototype, put it on a special "shaking table" and actually witness the outcome. This is called a "shake test"... It is proposed that a similar exercise be applied to strategic plans – giving them the shake test before the unforgiving test our markets and competitors will surely apply (Gilbreath, 1987, p. 47).

Day (1986) proposed testing the robustness of a proposed strategy through the following seven "tough questions" to be examined by corporate management and operating managers:

- *Suitability*: is there a sustainable advantage given the potential threats to and opportunities for the business and in light of the capabilities of the firm?
- *Validity:* are the assumptions realistic? What is the quality of the information on which these assumptions rely?
- *Feasibility*: do we have the skills, resources and commitment?
- *Consistency*: does the strategy hang together? Are all elements of the strategy pointing in the same direction?
- *Vulnerability*: what are the risks and contingencies?

Table 21.8   Identifying vulnerability factors

Vulnerability factors	Stability factors
Reliance on fads	Single use
Technology dependence	Single distribution network
Heavy capital investment	Prescriptive identities
Building with products outside our control	Projection of lasting symbols
Multiple use of products	Technology transcendence
Multiple distribution network	Leasing, renting and joint ownership
Non-restrictive identities	Building with unchanging needs

Source: Adapted from Gilbreath (1987).

- *Adaptability*: can we retain our flexibility? How could the strategy be reversed in the future?
- *Financial desirability*: how much economic value is created? What is the attractiveness of the forecast performance relative to the probable risk?

Examples of vulnerability factors are presented in Table 21.8. Given the rapidity of environmental change, the test should be applied periodically to facilitate adaptability and revision. A good way to proceed is to apply this shake test with the assistance of outside persons to avoid the risk of myopia and wishful thinking.

Vulnerability analysis

The vulnerability of a strategic plan is determined by two factors: the strategic importance of risk and the degree of control the firm has over the risk factor. The risk factor is a combination of (a) the impact of extreme but plausible values on overall performance, and (b) the likelihood that these extreme values could occur during the planning period.

The vulnerability grid presented in Figure 21.6 can be used to position the different risk factors and to isolate those few that could cause the most damage. To each quadrant there corresponds a specific risk situation that requires appropriate action:

- In the *strategy quadrant*, that is, where both risk and degree of control are high, the risk factors are subject to company control, need to be understood very well and are the focus of major strategic actions and should be tightly monitored.
- In the *vulnerability quadrant*, the risks are high but the degree of control is weak. The factors positioned here are critical and must be continuously monitored. Contingency plans should be developed.
- In the *fine-tuning quadrant*, the risks are low but the degree of control high. These factors are controlled and managed by operational management.
- In the *non-strategy quadrant*, both risk and degree of control are low and the factors positioned here will be included in the base scenario.

The vulnerability quadrant deserves particular attention, since major and unanticipated crises could come from these risk factors. Alternative strategies should be developed for these risk factors.

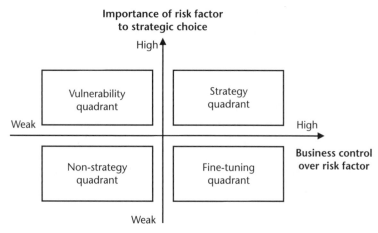

Figure 21.6   Vulnerability grid
Source: Day (1986).

Strategic surprise management

In spite of the best planning efforts, some issues or unexpected changes will slip by the environmental monitoring system and become "crises" or "strategic surprises" in Ansoff's terminology (1984). A crisis is characterized by four elements:

- The issue arrives suddenly, unanticipated.
- It poses novel problems in which the firm has little prior experience.
- Failure to respond implies either a major financial reversal or loss of a major opportunity.
- The response is urgent and cannot be handled promptly enough by the normal systems and procedures (Ansoff, 1984, p. 24).

The combination of these four elements creates major problems for the firm. A crisis or disaster can be any emergency that happens suddenly, that disrupts the routine of the organization and that demands immediate attention. Examples of crises are numerous.

> The "Nestlé kills babies" affair, the Tylenol incident, the Union Carbide disaster in Bhopal, the Société Générale of Belgium's takeover bid, the Pan Am Boeing 747 crash at Lockerbie, the Chernobyl and Three Mile Island nuclear accidents, the mad cow disease in the UK, the New York Madrid and London terrorist attacks and so on.

The suddenness and the prospect of a major loss create a danger of widespread panic, and "business as usual" managerial systems are inefficient to deal with a crisis. The firm needs to invest in a crisis recovery plan, because disaster recovery planning is more conducive to a rational perspective and more cost-effective if the process is begun before a crisis, rather than pulled together in the heat of battle (Phelps, 1986).

To develop a contingency planning system the following steps must be taken:

- To identify the sensitive factors and the zones of danger through a vulnerability analysis.
- To establish a monitoring system with warning signals based on early-warning indicators.

- To prepare a crisis recovery plan based on a previously identified alternative strategy.
- To adopt this procedure for the major risks.

According to Ansoff (1984) and Lagadec (1991), a crisis recovery plan should have the following characteristics:

- A emergency communication network which crosses normal organizational boundaries, filters the information and rapidly communicates with the entire organization.
- A repartition of top management responsibilities between three groups: one in charge of the organization's morale control and maintenance; one in charge of "business as usual" and one in charge of the response to the surprise.
- A strategic task force to deal with the surprise whose members crosses normal organizational lines.
- The task force and communication networks are pre-designed and trained under non-crisis conditions before they are put to the actual test.

This procedure will not eliminate the occurrence of completely unexpected events but will contribute to reduce the consequences of major risks that can be identified. As put by Augustine (1995, p. 151), "when preparing for crises, it is instructive to recall that Noah started building the ark before it began to rain". To go further on the topic of crisis management, see the excellent book by Lagadec (1991).

New roles of global strategic planning

Business International (1991) has conducted a survey with 18 of the world's leading global companies on three continents to gain insights into their approaches to global planning. The ten most frequently mentioned functions of corporate planners are the following:

- Compiling of information for top management.
- Competitor research.
- Forecasting.
- Consulting services.
- Creating a common language.
- Communicating corporate culture.
- Establishing and communicating corporate objectives.
- Group facilitation and team leadership.
- Guardianship of the planning system.
- Developing planning methods.

Most corporate planners downplay their formal planning roles and instead emphasize their functions as "facilitators", "communicators" or "consultants". They see their role less as representatives of corporate authority than as consultants charged with assisting the divisions in developing their own plan and strategies.

> ## Chapter Summary
>
> This chapter has provided a scheme for developing a formal strategic marketing plan. The role of strategic planning is to design a desired future for the company and to define effective ways of making things happen. The plan summarizes, in a formal way, the marketing strategy development phase. One of the key elements of the strategic plan is the mission statement which should reveal the company's long-term vision of what it wants to be and whom it wants to serve. The strategic plan is based on an external audit. The environment is ever-changing and complex and the firm must constantly scan and monitor the environment to identify the main threats and opportunities. The assessment of strengths and weaknesses is also an essential task in the strategic process. The objective is to evaluate company resources in order to identify a sustainable competitive advantage on which to base the development strategy. Using the information collected in the external and internal audits (SWOT analysis), the next task is to define priority objectives to be translated into operational action programmes and in a marketing budget. Testing the robustness of a strategic plan is useful to improve the strategic planning performance. Also, in the current turbulent environment, vulnerability and risk analysis is required to help the firm anticipate the unexpected through contingency planning and crisis management.

BIBLIOGRAPHY

Ansoff, H.I. (1984), *Implanting Strategic Management*, Englewood Cliffs, NJ, Prentice-Hall.

Augustine, N.R. (1995), Managing the Crisis You Tried to Prevent, *Harvard Business Review*, 73, 6, pp. 147–58.

Bain Survey (2001), Which Management Tools are Most Popular?, *European Business Forum*, 7, Fall.

Best, R.J. (2004), *Market-Based Management*, Upper Saddle River, NJ, Prentice-Hall, 3rd edition.

Business International (1991), The Changing Face of Corporate Planning in the 1990's, *Bimonthly Report*, 19 August.

David, F.R. (1989), How Companies Define Their Mission?, *Long Range Planning*, 22, 1, pp. 90–7.

Day, G.S. (1986), Tough Questions for Developing Strategies, *The Journal of Business Strategy*, 6, 3, pp. 67–75.

Drucker, P. (1973), Management, Tasks, Responsibilities, Practices, New York, Harper & Row.

Gilbreath, R.D. (1987), Planning for the Unexpected, *The Journal of Business Strategy*, 8, 2, pp. 44–9.

Hopkins, D.S. (1981), *The Marketing Plan*, New York, The Conference Board, Report No. 801.

Kotler, P. (1964), Marketing Mix for New Products, *Journal of Marketing Research*, 1, 1, pp. 43–9.

Kotler, P. (1997/2005), *Marketing Management*, Englewood Cliffs, NJ, Prentice-Hall International, 9th edition.

Lagadec, P. (1991*), La gestion des crises*, Paris, Ediscience International.

Lambin, J.J. (2000/2007*), Market-Driven Management: Strategic and Operational Marketing*, London, Palgrave Macmillan.

Phelps, N.L. (1986), Setting up a Crisis Recovery Plan, *The Journal of Business Strategy*, 6, 4, pp. 5–17.

Piercy, N.F. (1987), The Marketing Budgeting Process: Marketing Management Implications, *Journal of Marketing*, 51, 4, pp. 45–59.

Porter, M.E. (1980), Competitive Strategy, New York, The Free Press.

Stevens, R.E. (1982), *Strategic Marketing Plan Master Guide*, Englewood Cliffs, NJ, Prentice-Hall.

Thuillier, P. (1987), *De l'étude de marché au plan marketing*, Paris, Les Editions d'Organisation.

Index